GEORGE WHITEFIELD

A DEFINITIVE BIOGRAPHY

VOLUME II

BY

E. A. JOHNSTON

REVIVAL LITERATURE
PO BOX 505
SKYLAND, NC 28776
800-252-8896
www.revivallit.org

CONTENTS

PART TWO: THE LIONHEARTED EVANGELIST/THE GRAND ITINERANT

APPENDICES

Why did he marry? That is a question which cannot easily be answered, unless it be supposed that he wanted a matron for his Orphan House, in Georgia. Men like Whitefield and Wesley, almost always from home, ought to remain unmarried. Their wives, naturally enough, very often become Xantippes.

Luke Tyerman

CHAPTER 28

WHITEFIELD'S MARRIAGE

"Whitefield left Edinburgh on October 29, 1741, and rode on Earl Leven's horse, three hundred miles, to Abergavenny in Wales, for the purpose of marrying Mrs. James, a widow lady, who, up to this period of his history, is never even mentioned in any of Whitefield's letters. The marriage ceremony was performed at St. Martin's Chapel, near Caerphilly, in the parish of Eglws Ilan:—

GEORGE WHITEFIELD
And
ELIZABETH JAMES,
Married, November 14, 1741.

"Of Mrs. James's previous history, nothing has been published." [1]

So begins this odd chapter in George Whitefield's life. Very little is mentioned of Elizabeth James by any of Whitefield's biographers, most mention of her is made in passing. Gledstone merely comments:

"And she seems to have been as good a wife to him as perhaps any woman could have been. Home-life they could never know so long as he would preach all day, and write letters at night, and this practice he kept up until he died." [2]

Dr. Gillies, briefly and dryly, states:

"Mr. Whitefield having left Edinburgh in the latter end of October, 1741, set out for Abergavenny, in Wales, where, having some time ago formed a resolution to enter into the married state, he married one Mrs. James, a widow between thirty and forty years of age; of whom he says, 'She has been a housekeeper many years, once gay, but for three years last past a despised follower of the Lamb of God.' From Abergavenny he went to Bristol, where he preached twice a day with his usual success." [3]

Another biographer is more whimsical:

---

1   Tyerman, Vol. 1, p. 530.
2   Gledstone, p. 180.
3   Gillies, p. 83.

"This first visit to Scotland was suddenly broken for an interesting purpose. Was it that gift-horse that touched his imagination, I wonder? Anyway, Whitefield suddenly rode from Scotland to Wales to get married!

"We have no details of his courtship, and maybe there was none ... We need not accept too readily the suggestion that Whitefield's marriage was not a happy one. The general testimony of his references to the matter show that he, at least, found considerable satisfaction; whether Mrs. Whitefield was as happy and satisfied, it is hard to say. Women expected less of a husband in those days, and she was a woman of courage and resource ..."[4]

Another biographer compares the equally ill-fitted marriage of John Wesley and states:

"Both Whitefield and John Wesley married widows. It was not, however, to be expected from their antecedents, that they would settle down into quiet, stay-at-home, domestic characters, a result, no doubt, calculated on by their wives. Wesley's married life proved a very unhappy one; his partner was an extremely jealous woman, and resorted to means to satisfy and justify her suspicions, which at last ended in misery to herself, and put a stop to all social confidence between them. She left him several times, until at last he no longer sought for or desired her return, and they lived separate ever after. 'She put his letters,' says Southey, 'into the hands of his enemies; searched his pockets; and sometimes laid violent hands upon him, and tore his hair. She frequently left his house (her fortune he had settled upon her), till at last she seized on part of his journals and papers, which were never restored; and departed, leaving word that she never intended to return.' Wesley's notice of this in his diary is as follows:— 'I did not forsake her. I did not dismiss her. I will not recall her.' She never returned. Mrs. Wesley lived ten years after this last separation.

"Whitefield's motive in marrying, as his letters have shown, was for the sake of benefitting the poor orphans in Georgia. It must strangely have entered his head that his wife would contentedly stay at home alone whilst he was absent and at a distance, going from place to place. She was fond of rest and quiet; exertion of any kind soon became irksome; at first she went with him, but his journeys and voyages were soon too fatiguing for her; hence she ceased, after a few years, to be his travelling companion or fellow-labourer at the orphan house. Although, however, there was this absence of sympathy between them, they nevertheless lived happily together ..."[5]

We must ask ourselves the question, "how could Whitefield and Mrs. James live happily together when they were always apart?" Many of Whitefield's biographers try to defend his domestic happiness. Others are more forthright and frank. Cornelius Winter, who was one of Whitefield's traveling

4   Albert D. Belden, D.D., *George Whitefield: The Awakener*, (New York: MacMillan Company, 1953), pp. 126–127.
5   John Richard Andrews, *George Whitefield: A Light Rising in Obscurity* (Elibron Classics), pp. 139–140.

companions and aides during the last years of his life (as was Richard Smith) had some very frank comments about the unhappy union. Winter lived with the Whitefield's for about a year and a half in their home. He had this to say:

"He was not happy in his wife, but I fear some, who had not all the religion they professed, contributed to his infelicity. He did not intentionally make his wife unhappy. He always preserved great decency and decorum in his conduct towards her. Her death set his mind much at liberty. She certainly did not behave in all respects as she ought. She could be under no temptation from his conduct towards the sex, for he was a very pure man, a strict example of the chastity he inculcated upon others."[6]

A careful reading of his life will reveal that Whitefield was oblivious to the emotional needs of a wife and he knew little about romance. His idea of marriage was for a helpmeet in the work of serving his blessed Emmanuel. George Whitefield was married to Jesus Christ and no human wife could share that stage. Not one biographer of Whitefield has mentioned the possible difficulties of his step-daughter Nancy living with them. This third party may have resented Whitefield's absences and neglect of her mother and possibly contributed to the stressful union.

It is clear that Elizabeth James had been in love with Howell Harris. We learn of this love from the pen of Dallimore:

"He learned that Whitefield, who was then in America ... was praying for a woman who would make him a suitable wife. Thereupon Harris decided that Mrs. James could well fill this duel role. His thinking was that he himself was not worthy of so good a woman and that in making her available to Whitefield he would be performing the greatest possible kindness to each of them. He recognized that in thus giving her up he would suffer sorely, but he deemed the sacrifice worthwhile since it would allow him to devote himself solely to the Lord again.

"Therewith this 'resigning her to Bro Whit—' as he termed it, became Harris's fixed plan. Nevertheless, his love for her was not quenched and hers for him remained unchanged, and this was the situation when in March 1741 Whitefield returned from America.

"... Shortly after Whitefield arrived in England he received a letter from Harris warmly recommending Mrs. James as a governess for the orphans and as a wife for himself. After a little time, when his ministry took him to the west of England, he crossed into Wales and paid her a visit.

"Though the visit was short Whitefield manifestly recognized in her many of the qualities he wanted in a wife."[7]

6 William Jay, *Memoirs of the Life And Character of the Late Rev. Cornelius Winter* (New York: Samuel Whiting & Co., 1811, First American Edition), p. 62.
7 Dallimore, Vol. 2, pp. 104–105.

The problem was that Elizabeth James was *still madly in love with Howell Harris*. And unfortunately for her, he did not wish to marry her—or anyone else at that time. George Whitefield was a famous man and this fame must have played some part in her deciding to marry him and attempt to make him a dutiful wife and helpmeet. Little did she know that loneliness would be her best companion. He was always gone away preaching. When he was home he was either praying or writing letters or making journal entries. It appears that the marriage began well and with high hopes on each side. Though it has been said that the unlucky individual who fails to marry the person they truly love then has to settle for second best or less. Such was the case for Elizabeth James. And such was the case for George Whitefield, for at least he had *romantic affections* for the "other Elizabeth", Elizabeth Delamotte, who had refused his hand in marriage. So each party married for reasons other than love. And it was because of this that the marriage was not only ill-fitted for each but they were ill-fitted for one another.

There were glimpses of marital bliss at the birth of their son. But his sudden death turned that felicity into sorrow. Following the death of the baby, through the years of their eighteen year union, there were more sad occasions and personal sufferings in the form of miscarriages and still-birth that took their toll on the unhappy union. Whitefield's long absences from Elizabeth contributed to her unhappiness with him; and her inability to endure the harsh climate of Georgia as the hopeful headmistress of the Bethesda Orphan House was his biggest disappointment of her. So, as time grew on they grew apart. He makes little mention of her in his writings.

One biographer of Whitefield has some interesting insights into their union:

> "It is, indeed, almost a *misnomer,* to call Whitefield's conjugal life domestic. His engagements, like Wesley's, were incompatible with domestic happiness,— as that is understood by domestic men. Accordingly, their kind and degree of home enjoyment he neither expected nor proposed to himself. All that he wanted was a help meet, who could sympathize in his absorbing public enterprises, as well as in his personal joys and sorrows; and a home, where he might recruit after labour and exhaustion. And such a wife and a home he deserved, as well as needed. He mistook sadly, however, when he sought for such a wife in the ranks of widowhood, then. There were no *missionaries'* widows 'in these days.' A young female, of eminent piety and zeal, might have fallen in with his habits and plans, and even found her chief happiness in sustaining his mighty and manifold undertakings, like Paul's Phoebe: but a widow, who had been 'a housekeeper' (her own) 'many years,' and that in the retirement of Abergavenny, in Wales, could hardly be expected to unlearn the

domestic system of the country, nor to become a heroine for the world. Both Whitefield and Wesley forgot this obvious truth, and married widows.

> "How much Wesley smarted for this oversight, is as proverbial as it is painful. Mrs. Whitefield had none of Mrs. Wesley's faults. She had, however, no commanding virtues, running in grand parallel with any of the noble features of her husband's character; and thus, because she was not prominently a help to him, she seems to have been reckoned a hinderance ..."[8]

In the beginning we see that she respected him greatly and referred to him as "her master". In the end it is plain to see that George Whitefield is a man who should have never married. His long absences from her only contributed to his anxiety over her; he was an extremely sensitive man and the guilt he had from being constantly away from her merely divided them all the more. A marriage in many ways is like a garden; care and cultivation have to be constant or it will wither and die—such seems to be the sad case with the Whitefield marriage. Neglect ruined it. As a husband he was a great disappointment to her; as a wife she was a great disappointment to him. Sadly, his wife Elizabeth became to him another burden to carry (like the ongoing debts of the Orphan House in Savannah); is it no wonder that "her death set his mind much at liberty."

---

8   Philip, *Whitefield's Life and Times,* p. 253.

There is nothing in the appearance of this remarkable man which would lead you to suppose that a Felix would tremble before him. To have seen him when he first commenced, one would have thought him anything but enthusiastic and glowing: but, as he proceeded, his heart warmed with his subject, and his manner became impetuous, till, forgetful of everything around him, he seemed to kneel at the throne of Jehovah, and to beseech in agony for his fellow-beings. After he had finished his prayer, he knelt a long time in profound silence; and so powerfully had it affected the most heartless of his audience, that a stillness like that of the tomb, pervaded the whole house.

Eyewitness from The Rebels

CHAPTER 29

THE LIONHEARTED EVANGELIST

Luke Tyerman informs us that Whitefield took no honeymoon for, "within a week after his marriage, Whitefield again started out on his evangelistic ramblings, leaving his newly wedded wife behind him in Wales." Apparently Whitefield could not wait to further storm Satan's strongholds with his lionhearted field preaching.

In the spring of 1742 he launched an avalanche of preaching around London that was remarkable both in effort and results! Moorfields was again his stage as he began to nostalgically draw thousands to hear him again—he was back in full power and popularity from his disappointing return to London in 1741. We have the following scene:

"Whitefield had now spent nearly two months of wintry weather in the metropolis, and, of course, his ministry had been mainly confined to his wooden meeting-house, in the neighbourhood of Moorfields. At length, the sun was again shining, the birds were singing, and the breezes balmy. It was time for Whitefield to resume his 'field pulpit,' and to use the bright blue heavens as his sounding board. During the Easter holidays, commencing on Easter Monday, April 19, Whitefield preached six or seven sermons in his old open-air cathedral, Moorfields; and writing to a friend in Philadelphia, remarked, 'We have had a glorious Easter, or rather a *Pentecost.*' The scenes witnessed on these three memorable days—Monday, Tuesday, and Wednesday—are described by himself in two letters, written three weeks afterwards."[1]

Since, during this time in George Whitefield's life, he did not keep a journal, one must turn to the record of his existing letters to determine his activities. Thankfully, one finds in reading these letters of Whitefield written in 1742 that they have all the flair and color of his written journals! Whitefield comments in a letter dated April 6, 1742 how God was moving again in the metropolis, "I sleep and eat but little, and am constantly employed from

---

1   Tyerman, Vol. 1, p. 554.

morning till midnight ... my wife came up last Saturday ..." Mrs. Whitefield
is getting accustomed to her husband's harried schedule! We now turn to the
narrative which he had recorded in his correspondence during this time:

"London, April 22, 1742.

"... JESUS CHRIST is risen indeed. I have been preaching in Moorfields,
and our Saviour carries all before us. Nought can resist his conquering blood. it
would have delighted you, to have seen the poor sinners flock from the booths,
to see JESUS lifted up on the pole of the gospel. I have received many tickets
from young apprentices ... our society goes on wonderfully well. Every day we
hear of fresh conquests ...

"London, May 11, 1742.

"With this, I send you a few out of the many notes I have received from
persons, who were convicted, converted, or comforted in Moorfields, during
the late holidays. For many weeks, I found my heart much pressed to determine
to venture to preach there at this season, when, if ever, satan's children keep up
their annual rendezvous. I must inform you, that Moorfields is a large spacious
place, given, as I have been told, by one Madam Moore, on purpose for all sorts
of people to divert themselves in. For many years past, from one end to the
other, booths of all kinds have been erected, for mountebanks, players, puppet
shows, and such like. With a heart bleeding with compassion for so many
thousands led captive by the devil at his will, on Whit-Monday, at six o'clock in
the morning, attended by a large congregation of praying people, I ventured to
lift up a standard amongst them in the name of JESUS of Nazareth. Perhaps
there were about ten thousand in waiting, not for me, but for satan's instruments
to amuse them.—Glad was I to find, that I had for once as it were got the start of
the devil. I mounted my field pulpit, almost all flocked immediately around it. I
preached on these words, 'As Moses lifted up the serpent in the wilderness, so
shall the son of man be lifted up, &c.' They gazed, they listened, they wept; and
I believe that many felt themselves stung with deep conviction for their past sins.
All was hushed and solemn. Being thus encouraged, I ventured out again at
noon; but what a scene! The fields, the whole fields seemed, in a bad sense of the
word, all white, ready not for the Redeemer's, but Beelzebub's harvest. All his
agents were in full motion, drummers, trumpeters, merry andrews, masters of
puppet shows, exhibiters of wild beasts, players, &c. &c. all busy in entertaining
their respective auditories. I suppose there could not be less than twenty or
thirty thousand people. My pulpit was fixed on the opposite side, and
immediately, to their great mortification, they found the number of their
attendants sadly lessened. Judging that like saint Paul, I should now be called as it
were to fight with beasts at Ephesus, I preached from these words: "Great is
Diana of the Ephesians." You may easily guess, that there was some noise
among the craftsmen, and that I was honoured with having a few stones, dirt,
rotten eggs, and pieces of dead cats thrown at me, whilst engaged in calling them
from their favourite but lying vanities. My soul was indeed among lions; but far
the greatest part of my congregation, which was very large, seemed for a while

to be turned into lambs. This encouraged me to give notice, that I would preach again at six o'clock in the evening. I came, I saw, but what—thousands and thousands more than before if possible, still more deeply engaged in their unhappy diversions; but some thousands amongst them waiting as earnestly to hear the gospel. This satan could not brook. One of his choicest servants was exhibiting, trumpeting on a large stage; but as soon as the people saw me in my black robes and my pulpit, I think all to a man left him and ran to me. For a while I was enabled to lift up my voice like a trumpet, and many heard the joyful sound. GOD's people kept praying, and the enemy's agents made a kind of a roaring at some distance from our camp. At length they approached nearer, and the merry andrew, (attended by others, who complained that they had taken many pounds less that day on account of my preaching) got up upon a man's shoulders, and advancing near the pulpit attempted to slash me with a long heavy whip several times, but always with the violence of his motion tumbled down. Soon afterwards, they got a recruiting sergeant with his drum, &c. to pass through the congregation. I gave the word of command, and ordered that way might be made for the king's officer. The ranks opened, while all march'd quietly through, and then closed again. Finding those efforts to fail, a large body quite on the opposite side assembled together, and having got a large pole for their standard, advanced towards us with steady and formidable steps, till they came very near the skirts of our hearing, praying, and almost undaunted congregation. I saw, gave warning, and prayed to the captain of our salvation for present support and deliverance. He heard and answered; for just as they approached us with looks full of resentment, I know not by what accident, they quarrelled among themselves, threw down their staff and went their way, leaving however many of their company behind, who before we had done, I trust were brought over to join the besieged party. I think I continued in praying, preaching and singing, (for the noise was too great at times to preach) about three hours. We then retired to the tabernacle, with my pockets full of notes from persons brought under concern, and read them amidst the praises and spiritual acclamations of thousands, who joined with the holy angels in rejoicing that so many sinners were snatched, in such an unexpected, unlikely place and manner, out of the very jaws of the devil. This was the beginning of the tabernacle society.—Three hundred and fifty awakened souls were received in one day; but I must have done, believing you want to retire to join in mutual praise and thanksgiving to GOD and the Lamb."[2]

Such excitement was London in much want while Whitefield had been away on his journeys in America and Scotland. But now, he was back with full force and energy and his letters show how God was using him once more in the metropolis to the blessing of many!

The more Whitefield preached from Monday to Wednesday, the more persecution he received at the hands of Satan in the forms of his human dupes. For as George Whitefield became bolder in his proactive attacks on

---

2 *Works,* Vol. 1, Edward and Dilly, 1771, pp. 381–386.

the strongholds of Satan, so did the enemy of our souls become more angered and overt in displays of shame and chaos. The following account is as startling as it is interesting. Let us go now to his own words once again:

"London, May 15, 1742.

"Fresh matter of praise; bless ye the LORD, for he hath triumphed gloriously. The battle that was begun on Monday, was not quite over till Wednesday evening, though the scene of action was a little shifted. Being strongly invited, and a pulpit being prepared for me by an honest quaker, a coal merchant, I ventured on Tuesday evening to preach at Mary le bon fields, a place almost as much frequented by boxers, gamesters, and such like, as Moor-fields. A vast concourse was assembled together, and as soon as I got into the field pulpit, their countenance bespoke the enmity of their hearts against the preacher. I opened with these words—'I am not ashamed of the gospel of CHRIST, for it is the power of GOD unto salvation to every one that believeth.' I preached in great jeopardy; for the pulpit being high, and the supports not well fixed in the ground, it tottered every time I moved, and numbers of enemies strove to push my friends against the supporters, in order to throw me down. But the Redeemer stayed my soul on himself, therefore I was not much moved, unless with compassion for those to whom I was delivering my master's message, which I had reason to think, by the strong impressions that were made, was welcome to many. But satan did not like thus to be attacked in his strong-holds, and I narrowly escaped with my life: for as I was passing from the pulpit to the coach, I felt my wig and hat to be almost off. I turned about, and observed a sword just touching my temples. A young rake, as I afterwards found, was determined to stab me, but a gentleman, seeing the sword thrusting near me, stuck it up with his cane, and so the destined victim providentially escaped. Such an attempt excited abhorrence; the enraged multitude soon seized him, and had it not been for one of my friends, who received him into his house, he must have undergone a severe discipline. The next day, I renewed my attack in Moor-fields; but would you think it? after they found that pelting, noise, and threatnings would not do, one of the merry Andrews got up into a tree near the pulpit and shamefully exposed his nakedness before all the people. Such a beastly action quite abashed the serious part of my auditory; whilst hundreds of another stamp, instead of rising up to pull down the unhappy wretch, expressed their approbation by repeated laughs. I must own at first it gave me a shock; I thought satan had now almost outdone himself; but recovering my spirits, I appealed to all, since now they had such a spectacle before them, whether I had wronged human nature in saying, after pious Bishop Hall, 'that man, when left to himself, is half a devil and half a beast;' or as the great Mr. Law expressed himself, 'a motley mixture of the beast and devil.'—Silence and attention being thus gained, I concluded with a warm exhortation, and closed our festival enterprizes, in reading fresh notes that were put up, praising and blessing GOD amidst thousands at the tabernacle, for what he had done for precious souls, and on account of the deliverances he had wrought out for me and his people. I could enlarge; but being about to embark in the *Mary and Ann,* for Scotland, I must hasten to subscribe myself ...

P.S. I cannot help adding, that several little boys and girls who were fond of sitting round me on the pulpit, while I preached, and handing to me peoples notes, though they were often pelted with eggs, dirt, &c. thrown at me, never once gave way: but on the contrary, every time I was struck, turned up their little weeping eyes, and seemed to wish they could receive the blows for me. GOD makes them in their growing years great and living martyrs for him, who out of the mouth of babes and sucklings perfects praise!"[3]

Because of our lack of an existent diary or journal from Whitefield during this momentous time of God's using him so mightily in dangerous quarters, we have only the few scant accounts aforementioned by him in his letters. It was not uncommon for the Methodist ministers to be targets of violence during this time. Charles Square in Hoxton, was a favorite preaching place of the first Methodists. It was recorded in the *New Weekly Miscellany,* of the times, regarding the type of people who came to hear the preachers, we have the following description:

"... some are laughing, others swearing; some are selling gin, and others ballards. Some take the opportunity of vending the printed controversies between Mr. Whitefield and Mr. Wesley; others are in a maze to see religion brought into such contempt and ridicule by men in gowns ..."[4]

Whitfield continued his labors in the metropolis until the end of May with great success. As a matter of fact it is one of the most astonishing times of his career; it is a shame we have so little account of it. The following is from a newspaper of the time, the *Weekly History* detailing some of his activities before he sets sail for Scotland aboard the *Mary and Ann:*

"This evening, about six o'clock, the Rev. Mr. Whitefield purposes to preach at Charles Square, by Hoxton. To-morrow, about five p.m., at Kennington Common; and, on Tuesday next, about six p.m., at St. Mary le bone Fields. He preached, in Moorfields, every day in the holiday week; some days twice, and some thrice. The auditories were very large and attentive, and, for the most times, very quiet. Many souls have been wrought upon during the last week's preaching, and several of them of the most abandoned sort. The Society, in London, is in great order, and great grace is among its members. For some time past, there have been about twenty souls each week added to it. In about three weeks, Mr. Whitefield purposes setting out for Scotland, with an intent to visit Ireland also. He has been in London about two months, and has preached twice, and sometimes thrice, every day."[5]

---

3   Ibid, pp. 387–388.
4   Tyerman, Vol. 1, p. 558.
5   Ibid. p. 558.

Even Luke Tyerman is impressed with Whitefield's labors in London at this time for he writes with admiration and respect:

> "Seldom do the annals of the Christian Church present a more remarkable example of the power of the gospel truth. Here were assembled thousands, 'the devil's castaways,' as Whitefield would have called them,—the very scum of London's teeming population, many of them clad in rags, and almost all of them labelled with the marks of vice and wretchedness; and, yet, even in such a congregation, hundreds become penitent, and begin to call upon God for mercy. Even the wildest mob only need 'the truth as it is in Jesus' simply and faithfully proclaimed, for there is always in that glorious truth a something which meets the yearnings of the most degraded soul. Whitefield's Easter-tide services, in the midst of the Moorfield mobs, were not unworthy of the name he gave them—'a glorious Pentecost.'"[6]

George Whitefield set sail from London for Scotland aboard the *Mary and Ann,* he would arrive in Scotland on June 3rd, and for the next five months all of Scotland would be in ablaze for God!

---

6   Ibid. pp. 557–558.

He was given the nickname of a 'yill or Ale-minister' for, when he rose to speak, many of the audience left to quench their thirst in the public house … M'Culloch found himself at the threshold of his life's work as minister of Cambuslang. He could never have foreseen, nor could any have predicted, what were to be the fruits of this long-deferred task … an 'ardour of the soul' burned in an unprepossessing parish minister in the West of Scotland, and warmed others through him. That small flame kindled into a blaze, changed the course of the history of the Church of Scotland, and became one of the inspirations of the modern missionary movement.

Arthur Fawcett

CHAPTER 30

THE REVIVAL AT CAMBUSLANG

The revival that would sweep Scotland began well before George Whitefield entered it. True, he was one of the sparks that helped ignite it during his last preaching engagement in Scotland the previous year; however, God seemed pleased to use a small, unheard of parish minister in the faraway parish of Cambuslang to make the revival rage into a prairie fire. The minister's name was William M'Culloch. He was the true agent of the revival; by the time George Whitefield appeared on the scene (at the invitation of this humble man) the itinerant from England merely added gasoline to the flames! This revival at Cambuslang would become one of the most famous revivals in the history of the Church.

The previous visit to Scotland by Whitefield had converted many and caused much controversy among the members of the "Associate Presbytery" who, at first were kindly to him, then became his bitter enemies—though he kept a catholic and loving spirit toward them; especially toward the Erskine brothers. Whitefield was hurt by their destructive pamphlets printed against him, but he gave it up to God and kept no grudges against these good but misguided men. This second visit to Scotland, which lasted from June to October of 1742, was to be one of the most memorable time of his life. His previous preaching visit had borne fruit, much fruit, and fruit that had remained. We have the following observations from the pen of Tyerman:

"When Whitefield arrived in Edinburgh, a minister told him, that, though seven months had elapsed since his departure, scarcely one of his converts had 'fallen back, either among old or young.' This was a remarkable fact; but there was also another, equally deserving notice. As already shewn, up to the time of Whitefield's first visit to Scotland, the churches of that country, like those of England, were in the most deplorable condition. In many instances, ministers were unfaithful; in most instances, congregations were dead; and, as it respects the outside populace, it is not an extravagance to say, that, speaking generally, they were almost entirely regardless of religion, and were steeped in worldliness, frivolity, and vice. In the interval, however, between Whitefield's first and second visits, a most marvelous work of God had taken place. How far Whitefield's labours and influence, in 1741, had contributed to this, it, perhaps would be presumptuous to say."[1]

Upon examining the records of Whitefield's labors in Scotland during the year of 1741, it *would not* be presumptuous to say that although George Whitefield was not the singular instrument in this great movement of God throughout Scotland, he was a major influence on it. In this revival at Cambuslang, Scotland, God seemed pleased to use both a famous man, Whitefield, and a previously unheard of minister by the name of M'Culloch; who "was a man of genuine piety, and of considerable capacity; but had nothing particularly striking either in the manner or substance of his preaching". The revival at Cambuslang is one for the history books for all students of revival because it shows how the Almighty is pleased to use any instrument of his pleasing in sending forth His blessings. There could not been a man more plain than Rev. William M'Culloch. He was a highly intelligent man, skilled in mathematics, but unskilled in preaching. The first years of his ministry lean toward the mediocre. It wasn't until he became enthralled with how God was moving among His people in both New England, under Jonathan Edwards (with whom he began a correspondence) and in London and Glasgow under Whitefield (with whom he also began a correspondence) that he begins to be noteworthy.

Of his background we have the following:

"William M'Culloch was born in 1691 at Whithorn, in the countryside hallowed by the famous Candida Casa of St. Ninian; his father was the parish schoolmaster, who had once lived in Anwoth (where saintly Samuel Rutherford was minister) but in later years he moved to Wigtown. Of William M'Culloch's own childhood, we have only meagre information ... he received the rudiments of his education from his father, who perceiving his studious disposition, sent him to the Universities of Edinburgh and Glasgow."[2]

What makes this plain man stand out head and shoulders above everyone else in this great movement of God was his methodical habits of seeking God in Revival; he literally became a one-man movement to ensure his country parish would be benefactors of the winds blowing from heaven all around them. He, like Jacob, passionately grabbed hold of God and wrestled with him and would not let Him go until He blessed him! The most useful item

---

1   Rev. L. Tyerman, *The Life of the Rev. George Whitefield,* Vol 2, (London: Hodder and Stoughton, 1877), p. 1.
2   Arthur Fawcett, *The Cambuslang Revival* (London: Banner of Truth Trust, 1971), p. 34.

that can be personally and practically applied to any believer in the study of this historic revival is: God will use *anyone*. It is an encouragement just to study this plain saint's life! M'Culloch was no stranger to the "worthies" of his times for it was at Wigtown where the famous two martyrs, Margaret M'Lachland (age 63) and Margaret Wilson (age 18) were both drowned for their faith in 1685. The heart of Rev. M'Culloch was warmed by such accounts. And when he heard of the awakenings in England and New England his heart grew hotter! This is what Rev. William M'Culloch did to promote revival in his parish and to make his people knowledgeable about seeking God's blessings for themselves, he began sharing the accounts of the awakenings with his parish members and began to print the recent news in a periodical. He also drastically altered his subject of preaching to reflect searching sermons on Christ's righteousness and the need to be born again. All of this was accompanied with much fasting and prayer. All of this sacrifice was very acceptable to the Lord of Hosts for it wasn't long until He burned up the sacrifice with His Presence among the people of this little Scottish kirk. God had already been making preparations by raising up such unique men as Daniel Rowland, Griffith Jones, Howell Harris, Jonathan Edwards, John Wesley, and George Whitefield. These were *revival men*! We have the following observations from Fawcett:

"M'Culloch at Cambuslang was greatly moved by these reports from New England and made it his practice to take some of them into the pulpit during worship, and to read to his congregation the latest news from overseas. In the autumn of 1741, one of his congregation reflected: 'hearing a minister [M'Culloch] on a fast day, after sermon, read some papers relating to the success of the Gospel abroad; I was greatly affected at the thought that so many were getting good, and I was getting none.'

"Some few weeks later the Cambuslang minister took another step to arouse still greater interest. Whitefield had been at Glasgow in September 1741 for a few days. On 18 November 1741, the following advertisement was printed on the back of a pamphlet containing letters from Gilbert Tennent in America: 'Proposals that a paper be printed Weekly (Providence favouring and a sufficient Number of Subscriptions coming timeously in) and the several subscribers or some by their Order shall once a Week, call for this Paper at William Duncan's Shop in the Salt-Mercat of Glasgow, James McCoul's Shop in the Trongate or (Blank) Shop above the Cross; and pay a Half-penny at the Receipt of it and continue to do so for a Year, from the First of December 1741.' The appeal must have been successful, for in December 1741 there was issued the first number of the first religious periodical ever to be published in Scotland, and its editor was William M'Culloch. '*The Weekly History*: or An Account of the most Remarkable Particulars relating to the Present Progress of the Gospel. By the Encouragement of the Rev. Mr. Whitefield. Glasgow. Reprinted by W.

Duncan &c.' was thus begun. Each issue was of eight pages, and it was a compilation of reports, letters, poems and selections from devotional writers. At first, it was mainly a reprinting of matter from a London journal, the *Weekly History*, begun on 11 April 1741, but the revival which began at Cambuslang in February 1742 spread rapidly throughout the land, and soon provided more than enough material of purely Scottish interest. The paper ran for exactly fifty-two issues before M'Culloch discontinued it.

> "It was to an informed people that the Cambuslang revival came; they had been reading about stirring events elsewhere, and were prayerfully wishing that it might happen with them. And it did!"[3]

And should this pattern of pre-revival activity be copied by pastors today it may have the same results! One thing must be mentioned for the sake of revival history. This mighty revival was preceded by devastating droughts, famine, and hurricane. Storms were reported in 1739 of "unexampled violence" with extensive damage not only to Scotland but "to shipping and property throughout Europe. There was a great destructive hurricane in January 1740. A man sensitive to the movings and judgments of God, like M'Culloch, began to preach about these terrible events wrought by God upon man for sin. We see the following example of this:

> "So singular an event could not fail to impress M'Culloch, who, like most of his contemporaries, saw transcendental purpose in every unusual happening in the world of nature. One resident in Cambuslang, Andrew Faulds, a young man of twenty-one, recorded what happened: 'In all my Life, I never found any thing I read or heard come home with any Power to my Conscience or heart, till on a Fast day in the Parish, a little after the great Hurricane on the 13th of January (1740) … when hearing a Minister (26, i.e. M'Culloch) preach on that Text, Fire, hail, snow, vapour, stormy wind, obey his word, that Sentence he had in his Sermon, Will neither the Voice of God in the Tempests in the air, nor in the threatnings of devouring fire and everlasting Burnings awaken you? came home to me with a powerful Impression and made me see it as a Message sent from God to me.'

> "… After the catastrophic anger of the hurricane there came weary, famine-stricken months of dreadful hardship. During 1740 there was widespread distress throughout England, with hungry mobs attacking wagons taking grain to the ports. Cold and hunger reigned supreme.

> "… It has been estimated that at least 2,000 persons perished of hunger and cold during the great famine of 1739–1740, when the frost was so severe for peat mosses to be dug, and the inland waters were so frozen that wood and coals could not be carried … Little children searched among the miller's husks, hoping for some stray grains of corn, gnawing the stems of vegetables from the dunghill."[4]

---

3   Ibid. pp. 92–93.
4   Ibid. pp. 95–97.

It was no surprise then that the hearts of the people were ready to seek the Lord with much fasting and prayers. Back in the eighteenth century ministers did not fail to make the connection with natural calamities and the judgment of God upon Mankind. Today we miss out on many such great movements of God because we are too afraid to connect the two for want of being tarred and feathered. God has not changed—we have.

So, such were the conditions of the pre-revival: famine and drought both in the land and in the pulpit. Conditions could hardly get worse. Is it no wonder then when George Whitefield preached his way across Scotland in 1741 that the people were so hungry for the Word of God?

We have the following account from Philip:

"Whitefield went in the power of the Spirit from the Pentecost at Moorfields, to the Pentecost at Cambuslang, and Kilsyth, in Scotland. His return to the north was, however, wormwood and gall to some of the Associate Presbytery. Adam Gibb, especially, signalized himself on the very first Sabbath of Whitefield's labours in Edinburgh, by publishing a 'Warning against countenancing his ministrations.' This pamphlet is so strange, and now so rare, that I must preserve some specimens of it, as memorials of the provocation as well as opposition given to Whitefield by the seceders of that day.

"'. . . This man (Mr. George Whitefield) I have no scruple to look upon as one of the *false Christs*, of whom the church is forewarned, Matt. xxiv. 24 . . . I look upon him in his public ministrations to be one of the most fatal rocks whereon many are now splitting . . . the proper and designing author of his scheme, is not Mr. Whitefield, but Satan: and thus our contendings against Mr. W. must be proportioned, not to his design, but Satan's; while hereof he is an effectual though blinded tool . . . The complex scheme of Mr. W.,'s doctrine is diabolical, as proceeding through the diabolical influence, and applied to a diabolical use . . .'

"Thus caricatured and denounced, Whitefield came to Cambuslang; a parish four miles distant from Glasgow. He came by the special invitation of Mr. M'Cullock, the minister of the parish, to 'assist at the sacramental occasion, with several worthy ministers of the church of Scotland.' Gillies says, 'he preached no less than three times upon the very day of his arrival, to a vast body of people, although he had preached that same morning at Glasgow. The last of these exercises he began at nine at night, continuing until eleven, which he said he had observed such a commotion among the people as he had never seen in America. Mr. M'Culloch preached after him, till past one in the morning; and even then they could hardly persuade the people to depart. All night in the fields might be heard the voice of praise and prayer.'

"Whitefield said to a friend, before going to this sacramental service, 'I am persuaded I shall have more *power*—since dear Mr. Gibb hath printed such a bitter pamphlet.' He did not miscalculate. 'On Saturday,' he says, 'I preached to above twenty thousand people. In my prayer the power of God came down and was greatly felt.'"5

Such were the glorious scenes that the people of Cambuslang witnessed as Whitefield arrived. It is important to note we would not have this record substantiated had it not been for the faithful record keeping of two men: Rev. William M'Culloch (the parish minister at Cambuslang) and the Rev. James Robe (the parish minister at Kilsyth); these two men both interviewed the local people who had been affected and converted by the revival. Rev. M'Culloch also maintained a record of the different ministers who preached and their times and texts. We will look at that now for it is important to see *what texts of Scripture* were being preached during this remarkable movement of God. Here is M'Culloch's list:

"On Tuesday, the fast-day,—

1. Mr. Adams preached from Ps. cxix. 59: "I thought on my ways, and turned my feet unto thy testimonies.'

2. Mr. Robe from Isa. liii. 10: "He hath put him to grief; when thou shalt make his soul an offering for sin, he shall see his seed, he shall prolong his days, and the pleasure of the Lord shall prosper in his hands.'

"3. Mr. Henderson from Rom. viii. 33, 34: 'Who shall lay any thing to the charge of God's elect? It is God that justifieth: who is he that condemneth? It is Christ that died, yea, rather that is risen again, who is even at the right hand of God, who also maketh intercession for us.'

4. Mr. Currie from John iii. 29: 'He that hath the bride is the bridegroom; but the friend of the bridegroom, which standeth and heareth him, rejoiceth greatly because of the bridegroom's voice. This my joy, therefore, is fullfilled.'

On Friday evening,—

Mr. M'Culloch from Isa. liii. 11: 'He shall see of the travail of his soul, and shall be satisfied.'

On Saturday,—

1. Mr. Whitefield from John xiii. 8. 'If I wash thee not, thou hast no part with me.'

2. Mr. Webster from 1 Pet. ii. 7: 'Unto you, therefore, which believe, he is precious.'

3. Mr. Robe from his former text, Isa. liii. 10.

4. Mr. Bonar from the Song iii.3: 'Saw ye him whom my soul loveth?'

---

5   Philip, pp. 278–281.

On the Lord's day,—

1. Mr. M'Culloch preached the action sermon from 1 John iv. 10: 'Herein is love, not that we loved God, but that he loved us, and sent his Son to be the propitiation for our sins.'

2. The sermons at the tents during the table services are not given.

3. Mr. Whitefield exhorted in the evening after the other services were over, but without a text.

On Monday,—

1. Mr. Webster at seven o'clock a.m. from Luke xii. 32: 'Fear not, little flock; for it is your Father's good pleasure to give you the kingdom.

2. Mr Hamilton from 1 Thess. v. 17: 'Pray without ceasing.'

3. Mr. Whitefield from the parable of the marriage supper, Matt. xxii. 2–14.

4. Mr. M'Knight from Matt. xv. 28: 'O woman, great is thy faith: be it unto thee even as thou wilt.'

5. Dr. Gillies from Job xxii. 21: 'Acquaint now thyself with him, and be at peace; thereby good shall come unto thee.'"[6]

The above mentioned ministers were all faithful and respected men of their time. It is important again to remind ourselves that this great revival had commenced *before Whitefield had arrived in June*. In fact, a letter written from Rev. M'Culloch to Whitefield, dated, April 28th, 1742 attests to this fact. One can only imagine the heart of Whitefield warming as he read the following account:

"Rev. and very Dear Sir,—I have been so much employed daily for so long time in the Lord's work in this place, that I have not had leisure to write to you half so often as I inclined; but I cannot forget you one day, and would gladly hear more frequently from you, if your more important work will permit you now and then to employ a few minutes that way. It is matter of great joy to hear that our Immanuel is making such quick and amazing conquest in New England, and that his work still goes on and prospers with you. May he continue more and more to strengthen and furnish you for that great and extraordinary work to which he hath called you; and may he abundantly bless and promote your labours for the good of multitudes of souls, who may be as so many jewels in that crown of glory that our Lord will give you at his appearing! For my part, I cannot but often cry out, with wonder and astonishment, Whence is this to me, that the great God our Saviour should put so great and extraordinary a work into my hands—a work relating to the interests of his kingdom, and the bringing of souls to him—and that he should give any countenance at all, especially to the

---

6   D. MacFarlane, D.D., *Revivals of the Eighteenth Century* (Wheaton: Richard Owen Roberts Publishers, 1980), pp. 78–80.

worthless endeavours of such a poor sinful creature in this work? How well does it become me often to say and to sing, 'Not unto me, O Lord, not unto me, but unto thy name, O Lord, be all the glory, for thy mercy's sake, and for thy truth's sake!'

"Help us, dear brother, to praise him for his goodness, and for his works of mercy to perishing sinners, that are everywhere made to taste of his distinguishing goodness, and particularly in this place of late. To the praise of his own mercy and grace be it spoken, I believe that, in less than three months past, *about three hundred souls* have been awakened and convinced of their perishing condition without a Saviour, *more than two hundred of whom are, I believe, hopefully converted and brought home to God,* and have been at times filled with joy and peace in believing; and the rest are earnestly seeking for Jesus, and following on to know the Lord.

"We have had several glorious days of the Son of man since this work began. Last Lord's-day was a remarkable day of divine power amongst us. The Lord was with us of a truth. The arrows of conviction flew thick among my people, and though there were but a dozen persons that had been awakened that day, who came to my closet to talk with me at night after sermon, yet I am informed that a considerable number besides these were wounded in spirit, and either could not get into the house for the crowd, or went away wishing to conceal their distress as long as they could. Some have computed the number present hearing, the last two Lord's-days, at nine or ten thousand. Mr. Willison came from Dundee about three weeks ago, to see the Lord's work here, and he returned much pleased. I believe his sermons, while here, were blessed to many. Our dear brother, Mr. L——n, has been very assisting and encouraging to this work. We continue still to have a sermon here every day. I long much to see you here. Let me know by the first opportunity when you think to be with us. Cease not, dear brother, to pray for the continuance and spreading of this blessed work, and for your poor and unworthy, but affectionate brother in the Lord, Wm. M'Culloch."[7]

Whitefield did not linger long in London after receiving this wonderful news—for he was on the *Mary and Ann* the next month! He writes to a friend on board, dated May 26, 1742, "At present, my call is to Scotland." Whitefield arrived in Edinburgh on June 3rd. He then wrote a letter to Rev. M'Culloch immediately. We see the following:

"To the Reverend Mr. M'Culloch, at Cambuslang.

"Edinburgh, June 8, 1742.

"Reverend and very dear Brother,

I heartily rejoice at the awakening at Cambuslang, and elsewhere. I believe you will both see and hear of far greater things than these. I trust that not one

---

7   Ibid. pp. 58–60.

corner of poor Scotland will be left unwatered by the dew of GOD's heavenly blessing. The cloud is now only rising as big as a man's hand; yet a little while, and we shall hear a sound of an abundance of gospel rain. Our glorious Emmanuel has given us much of his divine presence since my arrival. O that it may accompany me to Cambuslang! GOD willing, I hope to be with you the beginning of next week; but cannot exactly tell the day. In the mean while, forget not to pray for, reverend and dear brother,

Yours most affectionately in CHRIST,

G.W."[8]

We are sure the heart of William M'Culloch thrilled at receiving Whitefield's reply! God was indeed moving about Scotland and it would be a refreshing gospel rain that would enter the history books. After preaching in Edinburgh Whitefield moved to Glasgow and preached there on the same day he would ride to Cambuslang. He would end up preaching four times in one day!

Much of the Presence of God was felt at the communion tables and it was here, at these outdoor ordinances that the people were so deeply moved; Whitefield was observed, while serving the Sacrament, to be enraptured with scenes of glory upon his countenance. The communion table were set up on the south side of the churchyard and it was here that thousands slowly passed to hand over their token and to receive communion. Two streams flowed together alongside a level green meadow, and it was "On this green … stood the communion tables at the great meetings in July and August, 1742, and the principal tent on these occasions is said to have stood on the stripe of ground separating the two streams."[9]

We now turn to the narrative provided for by Whitefield in his letters of this time of refreshing from the Lord. The first letter is dated July 7, 1742 and was written from Edinburgh.

"I arrived here last Saturday evening from the West, where I preached all the last week: as, twice on Monday at Paisley, six miles from Glasgow; on the Tuesday and Wednesday, three times each day, at Irvine, 16 miles from thence; on Thursday, twice at Mearns, fifteen miles from thence; on Friday, three times at Cambernauld; and on Saturday, twice at Falkirk, in my way to Edinburgh. In every place there was the greatest commotion among the people as was ever known. Their mourning in most of the places, was like the mourning for a first-born. The auditories were very large, and the work of GOD seems to be spreading more and more. Last sabbath-day I preached twice in the park, and once in the church, and twice every day since. A number of seats and shades, in the form of an amphitheatre, have been erected in the park, where the auditory

8   *Works,* Vol. 1, pp. 491–402.
9   Macfarlane, *Revivals of the Eighteenth Century,* p. 6.

sit in a beautiful order. I have received very agreeable news from my family abroad.—I purpose going to Cambuslang to-morrow, in order to assist at the communion; and shall preach at various places westward before I return here. I intend to embark for America as soon as possible after I leave Scotland. Thus you see, my dear brother, how I have been employed. O give thanks to our blessed Saviour, for his great unparalleled goodness to a most unworthy worm. Indeed I have seen and felt such things, as I never saw and felt before. I never was enabled to preach so powerfully as whilst I have been in the West ...

"To Mr. John Cennick.

My very dear Brother,   Glasgow, June 16, 1742

Last Lord's-day, I preached in the morning, in the park at Edinburgh, to a great multitude. Afterwards, I attended, and partook of the holy sacrament, and served four tables. In the afternoon, I preached in the churchyard, to a far greater number. Such a passover, I never saw before. On Monday, I preached again in Edinburgh. On Tuesday, twice at Kilsyth, to ten thousand; but such a commotion, I believe, you never saw. O what agonies and cries were there! Last night, God brought me hither. A friend met me without the town, and welcomed me in the name of twenty thousand. The streets were all alarmed. By three o'clock this morning, people were coming to hear the word of God. At seven, I preached to many, many thousands; and again this evening. Our Lord wounded them by scores. It is impossible to tell you what I see. The work flies from parish to parish. O what distressed souls have I beheld this day! *Publish this on the housetop; and exhort all to give thanks.*

(To this letter, Whitefield's wife added a postscript:)

"My husband *publicly declared here,* that, he was a *member of the Church of England,* and a curate thereof; and, yet, was permitted to *receive, and assist at the Lord's supper* in the churches at Edinburgh."[10]

Apparently Whitefield's wife returned to Wales for reasons unknown, for we see that in the next letter he is writing to her to inform her of the work still continuing.

"To Mrs. Whitefield.

My dear Love,   Edinburgh, July 7, 1742.

Since I wrote you last, I have seen such things as I never beheld before. Yesterday morning I preached at Glasgow to a very large congregation. At noon I came to Cambuslang, the place which GOD hath so much honoured. I preached at two, to a vast body of people, and at six in the evening, and again at nine at night. Such a commotion surely never was heard of, especially at eleven at night. It far out-did all that I ever saw in America. For about an hour and a half there was such weeping, so many falling into deep distress, and expressing it various ways, as is inexpressible. The people seem to be slain by scores. They are

---

10 *Works,* Vol. I, pp. 403–409.

carried off, and come into the house like soldiers wounded in, and carried off a field of battle. Their cries and agonies are exceedingly affecting. Mr. M'Culloch preached after I had ended, till past one in the morning, and then could scarce persuade them to depart. All night in the fields, might be heard the voice of prayer and praise. Some young ladies were found by a gentlewoman praising GOD at break of day. She went and joined with them. The LORD is indeed much with me. I have preached twice to-day already, and am to preach twice, perhaps three times more. The commotions increase. Tomorrow, and on sabbath-day, I shall preach at Calder; on Monday, here again; and on Tuesday at Kilsyth, and then, GOD willing, at Glasgow. I am persuaded the work will spread more and more. My kindest respects to all. Accept of the same from, my dear love,   Yours, &c.

G.W.

"To Mr. John Cennick. (Preaching in Whitefield's Tabernacle in London).

New-Kilpatrick,   July 15, 1742.

"… Last Thursday night, and Friday morning, there was such a shock in Edinburgh as I never felt before. O what a melting and weeping was there! I have heard blessed effects of it since. All glory be to GOD through CHRIST. On Friday night I came to Cambuslang, to assist at the blessed sacrament. On Saturday I preached to above twenty thousand people. In my prayer the power of GOD came down and was greatly felt. In my two sermons, there was yet more power. On sabbath day, scarce ever was such a sight seen in Scotland. There were undoubtedly upwards of twenty thousand people. Two tents were set up, and the holy sacrament was administered in the fields. When I began to serve a table, the power of GOD was felt by numbers; but the people crouded so upon me, that I was obliged to desist and go to preach at one of the tents, whilst the ministers served the rest of the tables. GOD was with them, and with his people. There was preaching all day by one or another, and in the evening, when the sacrament was over, at the request of the ministers I preached to the whole congregation. I preached about an hour and a half. Surely it was a time much to be remembered. On Monday morning, I preached again to near as many; but such an universal stir I never saw before. The motion fled as swift as lightning from one end of the auditory to another. You might have seen thousands bathed in tears. Some at the same time wringing their hands, others almost swooning, and others crying out, and mourning over a pierced Saviour. But I must not attempt to describe it. In the afternoon, the concern again was very great. Much prayer had been previously put up to the LORD. All night I different companies, you might have heard persons praying to, and praising GOD. The children of GOD came from all quarters. It was like the passover in Josiah's time. We are to have another in about two or three months, if the LORD will. One Mr. W——, a minister, who has great popular gifts, was as well as others much owned and helped at this time. On Tuesday morning I preached at Glasgow, (it was a most glorious time) and in the afternoon twice at Inchannon. The LORD gave a blow to many. Yesterday morning I preached there again, and here twice. Every time there was a great stir, especially at this place. A great company of awakened souls is within the compass of twenty miles, and the work seems to be spreading apace. I am exceedingly strengthened, O unmerited mercy! ..."[11]

One of the amazing things of this revival in Scotland in 1742 was that it was not localized it spread across the regions like a prairie fire. But amidst this wonderful blessing from heaven came much controversy and persecution from other ministers. We see some of what George Whitefield was facing in the form of opposition in the short excerpt from a letter dated, July, 21st:

"... The Messrs. Erskines and their adherents, would you think it, have appointed a publick fast to humble themselves, among other things, for my being received in Scotland, and for the delusion, as they term it, at Cambuslang, and other places; and all this, because I would not consent to preach only for them, till I had light into, and could take the solemn league and covenant.—But to what lengths may prejudice carry even good men?—From giving way to the first risings of bigotry and a party spirit, good LORD deliver us![12]

During this time of revival in Scotland Whitefield was in correspondence with the Orphan House in Georgia. Like Paul, he had the care of the churches! Here are some excerpts from two letters written from Cambuslang, and dated August 17, 1742; the first is addressed to Jonathan Barber, the lay chaplain at the Orphan House in Savannah. He writes:

"... I am just now about to publish a further account of the Orphan-house, and hope shortly to collect some more money towards its support. I am blessed with far greater success than ever, and satan roars louder. You will see by what I here send, how the archers of different classes shoot at me; but the LORD (for ever adored be his never-failing love) causes my bow to abide in strength, and enables me to triumph in every place. The comforts and success the LORD gives to me, is unspeakable. Last LORD's day, I believe there were here thirty thousand people, and above two thousand five hundred communicants. The work spreads, and I believe will yet spread. My bodily strength is daily renewed, and I mount on the wings of faith and love like an eagle. I can only cry Grace! Grace! My dear brother, I feel every day more and more, that I am a poor, very poor sinner. I often wonder why JESUS suffers me to live, much more to speak for him. But he will have mercy on whom he will have mercy. O free grace! Oh unparalleled love of an infinitely condescending GOD! Whilst I am musing, the fire kindles ...

11   Ibid. pp. 405, 409–410.
12   Ibid. p. 411.

"To Mr. Habersham, in Georgia.

""My very dear Friend and Brother,   Cambuslang, Aug. 17, 1742.

"... I have just now wrote to the trustees, and intend waiting upon them as soon as I come to London. I am persuaded the LORD will influence their hearts to do us justice. I am glad you wrote so properly to the General, and that GOD hath given you favour in his sight. 'When a man's ways please the LORD he makes his very enemies to be at peace with him.' I intend sending him and Mr. Jones a letter of thanks. I owe Mr. S—— only about ninety pounds, and about a hundred and fifty more in all, upon the Orphan-house account in England. I am just publishing a further account, which I am persuaded the LORD will bless. I would not have you to undertake any business you do not like. I think the LORD has fitted you for your present station. Professor Franck held it dangerous to change persons frequently, who were entrusted with the care of the orphans. I am of your opinion as to hiring servants.—It is impossible to tell you, my dear man, what I have seen, heard, and felt since I came last to Scotland. The glorious Emmanuel rides daily on in the chariot of his gospel, from conquering and to conquer. The congregations are just like that at Fogg-Manor.—I am opposed on all sides. Dear Mr. Erskine's people have lately kept a fast upon my account. The kirk presbyters also, now they see the Seceders splitting, notwithstanding I have been instrumental in GOD's hands, in some degree, in stopping the secession, begin to call some of their ministers to account for employing me: but who can stand before envy? In the midst of all, my dear Master keeps me leaning upon himself, and causes me to walk in the comforts of the Holy Ghost from morning to night ..."[13]

No matter how much George Whitefield wished to be with his friends at Bethesda in Georgia, it was not enough to tear him away from the scenes he was witness to while in Scotland. The work which he became a part of in June now had spread into more parishes by the fall. The revival was gripping the nation. Tyerman describes all of this activity with the following comment: "These were strange scenes. Much might be written respecting this remarkable work of God in Scotland; but want of space prevents enlargement." He goes on to recommend reading further accounts of it in "A Faithful Narrative of the Extraordinary Work of the Spirit of God, at Kilsyth, and other Congregations in the Neighbourhood." Written by the parish minister of Kilsyth, Rev. James Robe. We now turn to part of Rev. Robe's narrative:

"... about one in five came under faintings, tremblings, or other bodily distresses. The bodies of some of the awakened were seized with trembling, and fainting; in some of the women there were hysterics, and convulsive motions in others, arising from an apprehension and fear of the wrath of God ... Some,

13 Ibid. pp. 417–422.

who had been under deep apprehensions of Divine wrath, and had sunk under a
sense of their guilt, when the Lord opened their hearts to receive Him as offered
to them in the gospel, were surprised with joy and admiration. Some cried out
with a loud voice, shewing forth the praises of the Lord. Others broke forth into
loud weeping, from a sense of their vileness and unworthiness. Some had, for a
time, their bodies quite overcome, and were ready to faint, through the feeling
of such unexpected happiness. The countenances of others quite changed.
There was an observable serenity, a brightness, an openness, so that it was the
observation of some concerning them, that they had got new faces."[14]

To these "strange scenes" we also have George Whitefield's eyewitness
testimony taken from an extract of a sermon he preached in London in 1769.
Whitefield recalled about those glory days in Scotland:

"Once, when I was preaching in Scotland, I saw ten thousand people affected
in a moment, some with joy, others crying, 'I cannot believe,' others, 'God has
given me faith,' and some fainting in the arms of their friends. Seeing two
hardened creatures upon a tombstone, I cried out,'You rebels, come down,'
and down they fell directly, and exclaimed, before they went away, 'What shall
we do to be saved?'"[15]

It was these "strange scenes" that the men of the Associate Presbytery so
launched a vicious attack against, claiming it all was a work of the devil. Both
Rev. Robe and Rev. M'Culloch kept records of eyewitness testimonies to
defend this work of grace among the people of God. Even Luke Tyerman
was sympathetic to these strange occurrences, he comments about them:

"This is not the place to enter into any elaborate defence or condemnation of
such religious phenomena. They were not novel. Similar scenes had been
witnessed in Bristol, under Wesley's ministry, only three years before; and, at
this very time, and on a large scale, similar scenes were being witnessed, among
the Presbyterians of New England. Of course, they were denounced, especially
by the Erskines and their friends; but Mr. Robe, while not enamoured of them,
endeavoured to explain them, shewing that they were the natural results of deep
convictions and strong emotions; that exactly the same sort of thing had often
happened in the history of the Christian Church; and that the Bible itself
contained similar examples ..."[16]

It is important in this study of the great revival which began at Cambuslang,
Scotland to quote some first hand accounts of actual individuals who were
either "convicted" or "converted" by these outpourings of the Spirit of God
among the people. For it is by their personal descriptions of how they each
were affected is one of the most important aspects of the entire revival! We
go now to some extracts of actual "case studies" recorded faithfully by

---

14 Robe's Narrative, pp. 87, 159.
15 Gurney, *Whitefield's Eighteen Sermons,* 1771, p. 290.
16 Tyerman, Vol. 2, p. 8.

M'Culloch and Robe. First we will hear from a young woman, aged nineteen, by the name of Elizabeth Jackson. Here are her comments:

"In September 1741, I went to hear Mr. Whitefield in Glasgow. Some of his first sermons renewed my concern for a time; but those which he delivered on the Tuesday, just before leaving, melted my heart. Some weeks after that, I heard Mr. M'Culloch read some papers concerning the spread of the gospel in foreign parts, which moved me greatly, especially on observing how much good others were getting, while I was let alone. On hearing him afterwards preach from Ps. xxv. 11: 'For thy name's sake, O Lord, pardon mine iniquity, for it is great;' he observed that many asked and received not, because they asked not as the psalmist, earnestly; but as if they did not care whether they received it or not. This came home to me as if I were the very person meant. After that sin had become bitter to me, and also my undervaluing gospel mercies, I was led to see other evils both in my heart and life, and I now saw myself to be a hell-deserving sinner."[17]

The next individual was converted in the revival. He is George Tassie, a married man, age forty-one. Here is an extract from his account:

"... Hearing Mr. M'Culloch preach from these words: 'O Jerusalem, wash thine heart,' &c. (Jer. iv. 14), I did not very well understand what it was to have my heart washed; but afterwards I came to understand and experience it in my own case.

"On the Sabbath preceding the first sacrament at Cambuslang, Mr. M'Culloch preached from these words: 'But let a man examine himself,' &c. (I Cor. xi. 28), and took occasion to say, that many might get a token from a minister or elder without receiving any token from Christ; adding, that an unconverted soul could not derive any benefit from the Lord's supper. Some of the marks given I had no difficulty in finding, which gave me much peace and joy, believing, as I did, that the Lord made me welcome. Before going to the table I was in a very dead frame of mind; but when there, I could scarcely get another word said than, 'My Lord, and my God.' My heart clave to God as its portion for time and eternity, and I was at the same time much humbled because of my own unworthiness. Mr. Whitefield, on preaching from the text, 'Thy Maker is thy husband' (Isa. liv. 5), said, that he was come to woo a bride for his Master, the church's bridegroom; but that before any soul could be admitted into the marriage covenant with Christ, it behoved to become dead to the law and it own righteousness. I had great satisfaction in finding that I had become dead to both, and had betaken myself to Christ for righteousness and strength ...

And now, reflecting on the time that has passed since June 1742, I find that by grace I have been enabled to go on from day to day in the way of duty, endeavouring to live soberly, righteously, and godly. I find now that my chief end is to live and act for the glory of God, studying in all things conformity to his will."[18]

---

17 Macfarlane, *Revival Of The Eighteenth Century*, p. 124.
18 Ibid. pp. 138–139.

The next account is of a young teenager who fainted under conviction of sin while listening to the preaching of the revival. His name is Alexander Roger, age fifteen. In his words:

"Some time in the month of June 1742, I went to Cambuslang, to hear Mr. Whitefield preach. It was on a Thursday, and his text was, 'The harvest is past, the summer is ended, and we are not saved,' &c. (Jer. lxxx. 20–22). Among other things, he said, 'Many come out of curiosity to hear a poor child preach; and the same curiosity would induce them to go to the devil.' I thought myself described. I had come from no better motive; and I felt that without repentance I could not be saved. Again, addressing God, he said, 'O Lord, how many trample thy blood under their feet, and despise thee and thy gospel!' This led me to such a view of my sins, that I saw nothing but the wrath of God awaiting me, and hell ready to receive me. I was also deeply pierced with a sense of the evil of those sins which I could remember, as well as of the corruption and depravity of my nature and of my unbelief in not receiving but rejecting Christ, when offered to me in the gospel. My sense of guilt was such, that I would have thought it no injustice, on God's part, had he cast me immediately into hell. I even felt as if I were sinking into the bottomless pit, and that all around were ready to drag me down to it. My feelings of repentance were deep and sincere, and above all, on account of the dishonour which I had done to God.

"Under these awful feelings, I at last fainted away; and on recovering, I was enabled to return with a comrade to my father's house, which was about five miles distant. After reaching home, I attempted to pray, but I could not; my heart was hard as a stone. I had no peace at home, and therefore I returned to Cambuslang, and was in time to hear Mr. M'Culloch's first sermon that day. His text was, 'He hath filled the hungry with good things; and the rich he hath sent empty away.' (Luke i. 53.) When these words were first read, they came home to my mind with power. I thought much upon them; so much as to lose a considerable part of the sermon. My convictions of sin were so strong, that I was at last forced to cry, nevertheless that I did all I could to restrain myself. I continued in this state during all the time of that sermon, during the interval, and also during the second sermon.

"When it was over, I went alone to pray, pleading with God for grace to close with him on his own terms; and while so engaged, that saying of Scripture was powerfully borne in upon my mind, 'Fear thou not, for I am with thee: be not dismayed; for I am thy God: I will strengthen thee; yea, I will help thee; yea, I will uphold thee with the right hand of my righteousness.' (Isa. xli. 10.) I was now filled with joy and wonder at what God had done; and thus I was enabled, with all my heart, to believe on Christ—to receive and embrace him as offered in the gospel."[19]

As we examine these "case histories" from the awakening it is interesting to observe what the *texts of Scripture were* as the Spirit of God applied them to

---

19 Ibid. pp. 140–142.

the heart's of the hearers. It is also noteworthy to see that each individual comments that they each experienced a deep sense of sin and conviction in their hearts. They were "awakened" to their sinful condition under the faithful preaching of these ministers. The next account is given by a man called R. Shearer, age nineteen:

> "... When the awakening broke out at Cambuslang, I went thither and heard a sermon ... On a particular occasion, Mr. M'Culloch preached on these words, 'He that believeth on the Son hath everlasting life: and he that believeth not the Son shall not see life; but the wrath of God abideth on him.' (John iii. 36.) In speaking from this text, he said that the wrath of God rested on as many as believed not, wherever they went or whatever they did. This seemed to me very awful, and for a long time I felt as if this were my own case. On the 20th of June, when hearing Mr. Whitefield, the same words struck me as if the sword of divine justice was hanging over me, and even hell seemed less than my iniquities deserved. My feelings were such, that I was forced to cry out among the people on the brae. After sermon, I was assisted into the manse, thinking every moment that I was going to hell ..."[20]

The next individual effected by the revival was a man named Archibald Bell; he was married, thirty-eight years old and a tailor by trade. Here is his personal account:

> "... I went that same Sabbath to Cambuslang, counting on its proving a glorious day of the Son of man, as it proved.

> "Multitudes flocked thither, and so much did I feel, that I could, as I thought, have laid down my very life to help any of them to Christ. Mr. M'Culloch preached from these words, 'There are some of you that believe not.' (John vi. 64.) From this he showed, by many marks and characters, who they are that believe not. Every word of that sermon came with power to my heart, as if Jesus had said it, and to me alone. In this way I got a deeper sense of my unbelief, and was enabled to cast myself at his feet for mercy, closing with him on his own terms. My heart became sensibly warmed with love to Christ ..."[21]

The next account is of a man named James Tenant, unmarried and age twenty. He speaks of being "awakened". Here is an excerpt from his account of the revival:

> "But the first thing which really awakened me, was a lecture which I heard there towards the end of June, from Mr. Whitefield, on the conversion of the Philippian jailer. When he was speaking of the jailer's trembling, and falling down, and crying out, 'What shall I do to be saved? my conscience began to tell me that I was of all others lost and undone, unless the Lord should in pity deliver me. I fell into great terror, and trembled so much, that I had to be supported by those near. Still I had some glimmering of hope, believing Christ to be able and

20 Ibid. p. 152.
21 Ibid. p 165.

willing to save sinners, and so I began to pray. But not having had *particular* convictions of sin, I saw myself only in the general in a state of condemnation. I was taken to the manse to hear the exhortations usually addressed to the awakened; but as there was no minister present, I went to my quarters, and then to the fields, attempting to pray, and especially pleading for a more thorough sense of my sins and true condition ...

"On hearing Mr. Whitefield again, I was again seized with great fear and trembling, because of the wickedness of my heart and life, and was therefore unable to follow all he said. After this I followed him to Calder sacrament. Some advised me to go to the Lord's table, but the sense which I had of my own unworthiness prevented me. Still I attended all the days as a hearer, and learned from what I heard much of my own sinful condition. One night, when engaged in prayer with some others in a barn, I got a clear discovery of myself as still in an unconverted state; and so strong and piercing were my convictions that I was forced to cry out before all present ..."[22]

Our last observation of these personal accounts of the revival at Cambuslang come from a man named, Daniel M'Larty, unmarried and age twenty one. Here is his account:

"In the evening, when hearing Mr. Whitefield from Isa. liv. 5, 'Thy Maker is thine husband,' my joy was such, that I could scarcely refrain from crying out that I was ready to strike hands on the bargain; and on meeting a young man of my acquaintance after sermon, I threw my arms about him, exclaiming, that Mr. Whitefield had married my soul to Christ. I lay down on the brae, and was so filled with the love of Christ and disregard for the world, that I even wished to depart and be with Christ ... I never read my Bible, or ask a blessing to my food, or engage in prayer, or hear a sermon, or meditate on spiritual things, which I often do, without experiencing warm and lively feelings; and it is now June 1743 ..."[23]

Such were the rustling of the leaves of the mulberry trees by the Presence of the Lord during this blessed time in Scotland's history. But perhaps a even better picture of the scenes which occurred in Scotland at this time are best described by one who was used so mightily in the revival: so lastly we hear from Whitefield as he describes the incredible scenes of blessing to a friend in a letter from Cambuslang, dated August, 27, 1742.

"This day fortnight I came to this place, to assist at the sacramental occasion with several worthy ministers of the church of Scotland. Such a passover has not been heard of. The voice of prayer and praise was heard all night. It was supposed, that between 30 and 40,000 people were assembled, and 3000 communicated. There were three tents. The ministers were enlarged, and great grace was among the people. I preached once on Saturday, once on the Lord's

---

22 Ibid. p. 168–169.
23 Ibid. pp. 186–188.

Day morning, served five tables, and preached about ten at night to a great number in the Church-yard. Though it rained much, there was a great awakening. On Monday, at seven in the morning, the Reverend Mr. Webster preached, and there was a very great commotion, and also in the third sermon when I preached, a very great and serious concern was visible through the whole solemnity. The LORD's people went home much refreshed. On Thursday, I preached twice at Greenock; on Friday three times at Kilbride, and again on Saturday once, and twice at Stevenson; on Sunday four times at Irvine. On Monday once at Irvine, and three times at Kilmarnock; on Tuesday once at Kilmarnock, and four times at Stewarton; on Wednesday once at Stewarton, and twice at the Mearnes; and yesterday twice at this place. I never preached with so much apparent success before. At Greenock, Irvine, Kilbride, Kilmarnock, and Stewarton, the concern was great: at the three last very extraordinary. The works seems to spread more and more ...

'O for a passive, tender, truly broken, child-like heart! That we could watch in reality, and from moment to moment hear the cry of every Christian, with every call from GOD, whether by his providence or spirit. It is said, that GOD brought and kept Abraham at his feet. O that we were always there, waiting for divine direction! Blessed be his name, I am for the most part at the feet of JESUS, and indeed he graciously teaches me moment after moment ..."[24]

But as these wonderful accounts of the revival were distributed much opposition to the work increased. Bitter pamphlets were written against Whitefield at this time by men of the Associate Presbytery and these published to discredit the work that God was doing. Whitefield lamented to a friend, "One of the 'Associate Presbytery' has published the most virulent pamphlet I ever saw, ascribing all that has been done here, and even in New England, to the influence of the devil. O how prejudice will blind the eyes of even good men!" Also adding to the young evangelist's anxiety was trouble reported from Georgia. We see this from Tyerman:

"Whitefield had other troubles besides the bitter pamphlets that were published against him. The Spaniards had invaded Georgia. With forty sail of small galleys, and other craft, they had come into Cumberland Sound. With another fleet of thirty-six ships, they had entered Jekyl Sound. They had landed four thousand five hundred men, and marched, through the woods to Frederica. Half of their galleys also approached the same town, and twenty-eight sail attacked Fort William. Oglethorpe's military force was small, but proved victorious; and July 25, 1742, was appointed, by the General, 'as a day of public thanksgiving to Almighty God for His great deliverance in having put an end to the Spanish invasion.' Whitefield had heard of the invasion; but, as yet, he had not heard of the defeat. In a series of letters, written in July, his superintendent, Mr. Habersham, had informed him, that, finding the Orphan House in great

---

24 *Works*, Vol. 1, pp. 429–430.

danger of attack, they had removed all its inmates, eighty-five in number, to Mr. Jonathan Bryan's plantation, in South Carolina. They arrived at midnight on July 10; and, within six weeks afterwards, were safely back to Bethesda.

"... Besides the Spanish invasion, Whitefield had another trouble in Georgia. Mr Jonathan Barber, his lay-chaplain at the Orphan House, and Mr. Hunter, the house-surgeon, had been arrested at Savannah, and imprisoned above a week, for privately insulting the Savannah clergyman. These and other matters are mentioned in the following letters. At the time when they were written, Whitefield was in the midst of the marvellous revival scenes at Cambuslang.

"... The sacrament at Cambuslang was an event never to be forgotten. Thirteen ministers were present on Friday, Saturday, and Sunday; and, on Monday, twenty-four. 'All of them,' wrote the Rev. Mr. M'Culloch, the pastor of Cambuslang, 'appeared to be very much assisted in their work. Four of them preached on the fast-day; four on Saturday; on the Sabbath I cannot tell how many; and five on Monday. Mr. Whitefield's sermons, on Saturday and the two following days, were attended with much power, particularly on Sunday night, and on Monday; several crying out, and a great weeping being observable throughout his auditories. While he was serving some of the tables, he appeared to be so filled with the love of God, as to be in a kind of ecstasy, and he communicated with much of that blessed frame. The number present, on the Lord's-day, was so great, that, so far as I can hear, none ever saw the like since the revolution, in Scotland, or even anywhere else, at any sacrament occasion. This vast concourse of people came, not only from the city of Glasgow, but, from many places at a considerable distance. It was reckoned, that, there were two hundred communicants from Edinburgh, two hundred from Kilmarnock, a hundred from Irvine, and a hundred from Stewarton. Some, also, were from England and Ireland. A considerable number of Quakers were hearers. The tables were all served in the open air, beside the tent below the brae. Some estimated the number of persons present at fifty thousand; some at forty thousand; and the lowest estimate was upwards of thirty thousand. Not a few were awakened to a sense of sin; others had their bands loosed, and were brought into the liberty of the sons of God; and many of God's children were filled with joy and peace in believing.'

"Whitefield came back to Edinburgh early in September, and here he chiefly remained and laboured until his return to England at the end of October."[25]

This season of blessing had to come to an end. But before leaving Scotland Whitefield made three collections for the Orphans in Georgia. Of these times Whitefield told Howell Harris, "I and the people have been in the suburbs of heaven. Blessed be God! I live in heaven daily. O free grace!" Another remarkable event bears mentioning during this time—a reconciliation with John Wesley. Though they became friends once more

25 Tyerman, Vol. 2, pp 23–30.

(and remained so until George Whitefield died, twenty-eight years later) they no longer co-labored together. They each were called of God to their separate and individual ministries. It is an important piece of history to review the letter that Whitefield wrote to his old friend Wesley during this season of revival among people and friends:

"Edinburgh, October 11, 1742

"Reverend and Dear Sir,—About ten days ago, I sent you a packet, by my dear wife, which I hope you will have received ere this comes to hand. Yesterday morning, I had your kind letter, dated October 5.

"In answer to the first part of it, I say, 'Let old things pass away, and all things become new.' I can heartily say, 'Amen' to the latter part of it. 'Let the king live for ever, and controversy die.' It has died with me long ago.

"I shall not leave Scotland in less then three weeks. Before yours came, I had engaged to go through Newcastle, in my way to London [Charles Wesley was now at Newcastle, preaching with amazing pwer and success]. I rejoice to hear the Lord has blessed your dear brother's labours.

"I am enabled to preach twice daily, and find I walk in light and liberty continually. I thank you, dear sir, for praying for me, and thank our common Lord for putting it into your heart so to do. I have been upon my knees praying for you and yours. O that nothing but love, lowliness, and simplicity may be among us! The work is still increasing in Scotland. Dear friend, my soul is on fire. O let us not fall out in the way! Let us bear with one another in love. God be praised! For giving you such a mind. My kind love to all who love the Lord Jesus in sincerity. In much haste, and with great thanks for your last letter, I subscribe myself, reverend and very dear sir, your most affectionate, though younger, brother in the gospel of our glorious Emmanuel,

"George Whitefield."[26]

---

26 Ibid. pp. 34–35.

But the Lord said to him, "Go, for he is a chosen vessel of Mine to bear My name before Gentiles, kings, and the children of Israel. For I will show him how many things he must suffer for My name's sake."

Acts 9:15–16.

CHAPTER 31

LABORS AMIDST TRIALS

One of George Whitefield's greatest triumphs—his part in the revival at Cambuslang, Scotland—was balanced out by one of his largest personal tragedies—the death of his infant son. To better understand the personal pain that he (and his new wife) endured during this time one must be reminded that he, like Jesus, loved little children. His orphan-house-heart proved that he cared deeply for little ones. The death of his infant son was a shock to his soul from which he never quite recovered.

Whitefield had left the glorious blessings in Scotland, which had taken place from June through October of 1742, to return to London by November 6, 1742. Mrs. Whitefield was ill from the sea voyage, and he wrote to James Habersham at this time, "My wife lies now very weak. She was tossed for ten days in her voyage from Scotland: The ship was in imminent danger, but the LORD gave her much of his presence, and I trust she will be ready shortly for another voyage." Little did they know the personal turbulence they would soon be sharing. It would first arrive in the form of religious persecution. From his return to London in the fall of 1742, Whitefield soon encountered mob scenes much like the ones that had endangered the life of Howell Harris during Methodist persecution which had taken place in the town of Bala, Wales, in January of 1741. For it was there that Harris was brutally attacked by an angry mob. Sadly, the mob was comprised of local clergymen who attacked the Welsh evangelist in an effort to 'defend the Church'. Offering a free barrel of opened beer to anyone who would form the mob the scene soon grew ominous. We read:

> "The fury of the persecutors was such that one of them fell into a fit from the transport of his passion. Another was loud for hurling Harris from the top of a rock into the lake hard by. The women also were as fiendish as the men, for they besmeared him with mire, while their companions ... belaboured him with

their fists and clubs … inflicting such wounds that his path could be marked in the street by the crimson stains of his blood …"[1]

This violence soon spread to England. Both John and Charles Wesley encountered angry mob scenes and were attacked by Methodist-hating mobs; John Wesley was dragged through a town, "… a man catching me by the hair, pulled me back into the middle of the mob. They … carried me from one end of town to the other." It would not be long before Whitefield encountered mob scenes as well; this disturbance occurred in Hampton, England in July of 1743. Here is his account:

"On Thursday I came here, and expected to be attacked because I had heard, that the mob which had been so outragious towards you and others for so long time, had now threatened, that if ever I came there again, they would have a piece of my black gown to make aprons with. No sooner had I entered the town, but I saw and heard the signals, such as blowing of horns, and ringing of bells for gathering the mob. My soul was kept quite easy. I preached in a large grass plat from these words, 'And feeling the grace of GOD, he exhorted them with full purpose of heart to cleave unto the LORD;' and as it happened, I finished my sermon and pronounced the blessing, just as the ring-leader of the mob broke in upon us, which I soon perceived disappointed and grieved them very much. One of them, as I was coming down from the table, called me *coward*; but I told him, they should hear from me another way. I then went into the house, and preached upon the stair case to a large number of serious souls; but these real troublers of Israel soon came in to mock and mob us. But feeling what I never felt before, as you know I have very little natural courage, strength and power being given us from above, I leaped down stairs, and all ran away before me. However they continued making a noise about the house till midnight, abusing the poor people as they went home, and as we hear they broke one young lady's arm in two places. Brother A—— they threw a second time into the pool, in which operation he received a deep wound in his leg. John C——'s life, that second Bunyan, was much threatened.—Young W—— H—— they wheeled in a barrow to the pool's side, lamed his brother, and grievously hurt several others. Hearing two or three clergymen were in the town, one of whom was a justice of the peace, I went to them; but alas! I seemed unto them as one that mocked, and instead of redressing, they laid the cause of all the grievances at my door; but, by the help of my GOD, I shall still persist in preaching myself, and in encouraging those (as I know no law of GOD or man against it) who I believe are truly moved by the Holy Ghost. As I came out from the clergymen, two of the unhappy mobbers were particularly insolent, and huzza'd us out of town …"[2]

We see some daring on Whitefield's part! He will eventually take this mob to court and the trial of the Hampton rioters was ended in favor of

1   Hugh J. Hughes, *Life of Howell Harris* (London: 1892), p. 142.
2   *Works,* Vol. 2, pp. 35–36.

Whitefield. The threat of persecution did not dampen Whitefield's labors nor did the harsh weather. From his letters we see that in March of 1743, he preached wherever he could find a crowd, often beneath the sky. He noted:

"... On Tuesday a man was hung in chains at Hampton Common.—A more miserable spectacle I have not seen. I preached in the morning to a great auditory about a mile off the place of execution. I intended doing the same after the criminal was turned off; but the weather was very violent.—Thousands and thousands came and staid to hear; but, through misinformation, kept on top of the hill, while I preached at the bottom. After this I came to Gloucester, and preached in the evening in a barn: a night much to be remembered! ...

"... On Tuesday evening I preached at Gloucester with as convincing, soul-edifying power, as ever I felt in my life. The barn, though made more commodious, was and is generally quite crowded. On Friday morning I preached again; and afterwards went to Hampton; the snow falling and freezing on us all the way ..."3

But the thrust of his labors was to be focused on Wales, quite possibly because he was in South Wales with his wife and her relations. In Waterford, South Wales, he had the distinguished honor of presiding at the *very first* Association of the Welsh Calvinistic Methodists. We must follow this remarkable preaching schedule of Whitefield in Wales for during this tremendous time of labor we see he traveled in itinerancy of "... four hundred miles in three weeks, spent three days in attending two associations, preached about forty times, visited about thirteen towns, and passed through seven countries." We see that though he was married he "lived as though single".

We will now follow the narrative of Whitefield in Wales during this incredible month of April in 1743! The first record is dated April 7, 1743, and details his labors preceding the Wales visit.

He wrote:

"... I preached and took my leave of the Gloucester people with mutual and great concern, on Sunday evening last. It was past one in the morning, before I could lay my weary body down.—At five I rose again, sick for want of rest; but I was enabled to get on horseback and ride to Mr. F——'s, where I preached to a large congregation, who came there at seven in the morning, hoping to feel the power of a risen LORD. They were not disappointed of their hope. At ten I read prayers, and preached from these words,—'I am the resurrection and the life,' and afterwards was helped to administer the sacrament in Stonehouse church. Then I rode to Stroud, where I was enabled to preach to about twelve thousand, which uncommon freedom and power, in Mrs. G——'s field. Much

3   Ibid. pp. 9–10.

of the divine presence was there.—About six in the evening I preached to about the like number on Hampton Common; but scarce ever with a more pleasing convincing power. The order and solemnity wherewith the people broke up, was very instructive. After this I went to Hampton, and held a general love-feast with the united societies. My soul was kept close to JESUS; my bodily strength renewed; and I went to bed about midnight, very chearful and very happy. The next morning I went and preached near Dursley, to some thousands, with great convictions accompanying the word. About seven I reached Bristol, and preached with wonderful power to a full congregation at Smith's Hall; and afterwards spent the evening very agreeably with Mr. C—— of Bath, and some other dear friends. On Tuesday morning I preached again to a full congregation, and then set out for this place (Waterford South Wales) where we came about eight in the evening, and had sweet and profitable conversation with Mr. B—— and some others of the brethren. We sung an hymn, prayed, and parted in great harmony. On Wednesday about noon I opened the association with a close and solemn discourse upon walking with GOD. Indeed much of GOD was with us. The brethren and the people felt much of the divine presence. Afterwards we betook ourselves to business: several matters of great importance were dispatched. We broke up about seven, and met again about ten, and continued settling the affairs of the societies till about two in the morning. On Thursday we sat again till about four in the afternoon; then, after taking a little refreshment, and talking warmly of the things of GOD, I preached with great freedom upon the believer's rest, and then we went on with our business, and finished our association about midnight ...

"Lantrisant, in Wales April 10, 1743.

"Our blessed master still countenances my feeble labours. Yesterday I preached at Cardiff to a large congregation. The greatest scoffers sat quiet, and the children of GOD felt the divine presence. In the evening I went to Fulmon. Mrs. I—— received us kindly. GOD was pleased to speak for me in the society where I preached. This morning I preached again. It was a most remarkable time. I have been just now preaching with great power. Dear brother Harris is preaching in Welch ...

"Swanzey, April 12, 1743.

"... Great things are doing in Wales.—An effectual door is opened for preaching the everlasting gospel. Yesterday I preached at Neath, (seven miles from this place) from a balcony, to about three thousand souls in the street. The LORD was with me of a truth. This morning I preached here to about four thousand with great power. About one I preached at Harbrook, four miles off; and am now returned to preach here again ...

"Postscript. Past seven in the evening. I have just now done preaching. Swanzey is taken! I never preached with a more convincing power. Many of the rich and great were present. The congregation larger than in the morning. Free grace for ever!

"Larn, April 15, 1743.

"... On Monday I preached at a place in the way, and afterwards at Neath, a sea port town, to about three thousand people: all was quiet, and the power of JESUS was much there. Then I went to Swanzey seven miles from Neath.—On Tuesday I preached, and the LORD was with me. in the evening I went to Llanelthy, eight miles from Swanzey. There I preached twice on Wednesday with great power to a large congregation; and in the evening near Aberquilley, five miles from thence. On Thursday I preached at Carmarthen, one of the greatest and most polite places in Wales; in the morning from the top of the cross: in the evening from a table near it ...

"Haverfordweft, April, 17, 1743.

"... I went that evening to Narbatt, where I preached to some thousands with great power. On Saturday I preached at Newton, and afterwards at Jefferson to several thousand souls, very like the Kingswood colliers. This morning I preached at Llanwran, and had as it were a Moor-fields congregation; and this afternoon I preached to about the same number near this town. I also read prayers ...

"Carmarthen, April 20, 1743.

"Since I left Haverfordwest, I preached yesterday at eight in the morning to about eight thousand people in this place, and in the afternoon to several thousands at Narbatt, both times with great power. This morning I preached at Larn, and coming over in the ferry had the unexpected compliment paid me, of one ship firing several guns, and of some others hoisting their flags. This afternoon I preached at a little town called Kidwilly, to a large congregation; and came this evening here. One of the ministers preached must against me last Sunday, and mentioned me by name; but, like my other opposers (and like the viper biting the file) he only hurt himself ...

"Bhuadder, April 23, 1743.

"... I preached there twice on Thursday to about ten thousand people, and dear Mr. R—— preached after me. Yesterday we had another blessed association; and have now settled all the counties in Wales ...

"Guensithen, near the Hay in Radnorshire, April 25, 1743.

"... afterwards I preached at Llangathan in the church, to a great congregation; I then went about ten miles, and preached at Landovery in the evening, and on Sunday morning. GOD was with us each time. On Sunday evening I preached to a large and polite auditory at Brecon, fifteen miles from Landovery.—This morning I preached at Trevecka, and just now at this place, with as great freedom, power and melting, almost as we have seen. It is now past seven at night, and I have seven or eight Welsh miles to go ... my body is weak, but I am at the Redeemer's feet, and he reigns king in my heart, and causes me to rejoice and triumph over all ...

"Gloucester, April 29, 1743.

"I am at present strengthening myself in the LORD my GOD. These words have much refreshed me, 'And the LORD was with David, whithersoever he went.' After I wrote my last from a gentlewoman's near the Hay, I went towards Builth, and got into my lodgings about one, and into my bed about two o'clock in the morning. The next day I preached at Builth, with much of the Redeemer's presence. Then I rode to the Gore, the last place I preached at in Wales; and indeed our Saviour kept the good wine till last: he made our cup to overflow.— Between eight and nine at night we set out for Leominster, and reached there between two and three in the morning. At eleven, and three, I preached. It was quite fallow ground ..."4

Thus George Whitefield completed his "circuit of about 400 miles", on horseback, in inclement weather! Sleeping little and preaching often he was like a whirlwind across that craggy, wind-swept land!

He returned to London in May and without any rest he stated, "I purpose staying here about a month, and once more to attack the prince of darkness in Moor-fields, when the holidays come." He said of his itinerancy in Wales, "Dagon hath everywhere fallen before the ark, and the fields are white ready unto harvest."

While in London he handled some long-overdue correspondence with the Orphan House in Georgia by writing letters to both James Habersham and Jonathan Barber. In these few extracts we catch a glimpse of his deep desire to be with them in Savannah once more. He wrote to Habersham on May, 21, 1743 from London. Like the Apostle Paul, we can sense his burden and care for the churches. He wrote:

"My very dear faithful Friend and Brother,

"After watching, and praying, and striving some days for direction and assistance, I now sit down to write you a letter; though I know not well what to say or do. The concern I have felt for you, and my dear family, has had an effect on my body, and increased that weakness, which the season of the year, my constant labours, and continual care upon various accounts, have brought upon me. In the midst of all, my soul I trust grows, and is kept happy in the blessed JESUS. His strength is daily made perfect in my weakness, and I am made more than a conqueror through his love ... I fear I have been sinfully impatient to come over. I think, I could be sold a slave to serve at the gallies, rather than you and my dear Orphan-family should want. Sometimes my wicked heart has said, 'if I know I should have staid so long, I would not have come over to England at all.' But GOD's thoughts are not as our thoughts. It is best to be kept at his feet, waiting to know what he would have us to do ..."5

---

4   Ibid. pp. 12–18.
5   Ibid. pp. 21–22.

On the same day in May (the 21st, and still from London) he wrote an equally tender letter to his friend and helper at the Orphan House—Jonathan Barber. He wrote:

"My very dear Brother Barber,

"Little did I think, when I parted from you at Bethesda, that I should be writing to you at this time in London. But GOD's ways are in the great waters, and his footsteps are not known. I have essayed to come to you more than once, or twice; but I believe I can say, 'the spirit suffered me not.' In thought I am with you daily; when I shall come in person, our Saviour only knows: perhaps, at an hour which neither you nor I think of. You will see what I have wrote (though in much weakness) to my dear Mr. Habersham. The present weakness of my body will not suffer me to enlarge much to you; though, was I to follow the inclinations of my soul, I should fill up many sheets. My dear brother, I love you unfeignedly in the bowels of JESUS CHRIST, and heartily thank you for all your works of faith, and the care you have taken of my dear family. Surely our LORD sent you to Bethesda, and however cloudy the prospect may have been for some time, I am persuaded a glorious sunshine will succeed, and you shall yet see the salvation of our GOD. When our LORD has any thing great to do, he is generally a great while bringing it about, and many unaccountable dark providences generally intervene. Thus it was with Abraham, Jacob, Joseph, Moses, and all the eminent men of GOD in the days of old. Thus our LORD is pleased to deal with me, and my affairs. Many precious promises have been given me in respect to myself, my dear family, and the church of JESUS CHRIST, which I am sure will be fulfilled in due time. I long to be with you, to open our hearts freely, and to tell one another what our good GOD has done for our souls. Great things has he done for me indeed, and greater things is he yet doing, and about to do. The work of GOD is likely to spread far and near, and such are daily added to the church as shall be saved. I am employed every moment for the best of Masters, and only lament that I can do no more. For some days, my body has been much indisposed, but not so as to prevent my preaching. As my day is, so is my strength; and as afflictions abound, consolations much more abound. I know that this will lead you to give thanks on my behalf. I am glad when I hear it goes well with you and yours. I am now like St. Paul, who could have no rest, till he sent a brother to the church, that he might enquire of their affairs, and know how they did ..."[6]

As summer approached the metropolis of London we find Whitefield employed by his blessed Master even more; he recorded on May 31st, "Last Sunday morning, I collected £23 for the orphans in Moorfields. It would amaze you to see the great congregations, and wonderful presence of the LORD. Grace! Grace!" He left London for some itinerant preaching which took him to the districts of Burford, Fairford, and Glanfield. From there he

---

6   Ibid. pp. 22–23.

moved to Gloucester where he wrote to a friend the following amusing anecdote:

"... I must acquaint you, by way of postscript, of the following anecdote of the old Mr. Cole, a most venerable dissenting minister; whom I was always taught to ridicule, and (with shame I write it) used, when a boy, to run into his meeting-house, and cry, *Old Cole! Old Cole! Old Cole!* Being asked once by one of his congregation, what business I would be of? I said, 'a minister, but I would take care never to tell stories in the pulpit, like the old *Cole*.' About twelve years afterwards, the old man heard me preach in one of the churches at Gloucester; and on my telling some story to illustrate the subject I was upon, having been informed what I had before said, made this remark to one of his elders, 'I find that young Whitefield can now tell stories, as well as *old Cole*.' Being affected much with my preaching, he was as it were become young again, and used to say, when coming to and returning from Barn, 'These are days of the Son of Man indeed!' nay, he was so animated, and so humbled, that he used to subscribe himself my Curate, and went about preaching after me in the country, from place to place. But one evening, whilst preaching, he was stuck with death, and then asked for a chair to lean on till he concluded his sermon, when he was carried up stairs and died. O blessed GOD! If it be thy holy will, may my exit be like his!"[7]

Remarkably, when it came time for George Whitefield to die he died in the very same manner! He preached his last sermon (on the stairs of the manse in Newburyport) and went upstairs to die. God honored His faithful servant even in answering his death request.

Up to this point there has been little mention of *Mrs. Whitefield.* We soon learn that she was pregnant with their first child. Evidently as Whitefield moved his preaching labors in the summer of 1743 from Gloucester, to Bristol, to Abergavenny, in Wales, he had his wife in mind for she might have been staying there with her relations (we can only assume this for there is no record). We do know that by the Fall the newly-married couple is back in London. He wrote to a friend from London on September 2, 1743:

"Thousand thanks for your kind solicitude concerning me and mine. My wife has been in trying circumstances, partly through the unskilfulness of a chaise-driver, I mean myself. Being advised to take her out into the air, I drove her as well as myself, though in advertence, into a ditch. Finding that we were falling, she put her hand cross the chaise, and thereby preserved us both from being thrown out. The ditch might be about 14 feet deep, but blessed be GOD, though all that saw us falling, cried out, they are killed, yet, through infinite mercy, we received no great hurt. The place was very narrow near the bottom, and yet the horse went down, as tho' let down by a pulley. A stander-by ran down and catched hold of its head, to prevent its going forwards. I got upon its

_____

7   Ibid. pp. 27–28.

back and was drawn out by a long whip; whilst my wife hanging between the chaise and the bank, was pulled up on the other side by two or three kind assistants. Being both in a comfortable frame, I must own, to my shame, that I felt rather regret than thankfulness in escaping what I thought would be a kind of a translation, to our wished-for haven. But O amazing love! We were so strengthened, that the chaise and horse being taken up, and our bruises being washed with vinegar in a neighbouring house, we went on our intended way, and came home rejoicing in GOD our Saviour. Not expecting my wife's delivery for some time, I intend making a short excursion, and then you may expect further news ..."[8]

Some comments need to be made about this chaise accident. One, Whitefield behaves more like a woman than a man during the accident—it is his wife who has the good sense to save them from further injury or death. Also, his odd attitude of wanting to die so young and at this point in life (with a new wife who is pregnant) and a wide career ahead of him—it is hard to read his words, "that I felt rather regret than thankfulness in escaping what I thought would be a kind of a translation ..."; it also shows his immaturity and insensitivity as a caring husband for he cannot wait to be off again with seemingly little concern for his bruised pregnant wife. By the way, one must wonder if this accident in the ditch had anything to do with the child's early demise soon after.

We learn that Whitefield was not even by his wife's side when their child was born but away on another "short excursion". One must have sympathy for poor Mrs. Whitefield, and realize that any circumstances leading to their marriage withering had to fall heavily upon the slender shoulders of her much-absent husband. One cannot blame her too greatly if she at times, "acted as though she should not."

A brief letter informs us of the birth of their son. Written from London and dated October 5, 1743, it reads:

"My last left me just entering upon another short excursion. Blessed be GOD, it was pleasant because it was profitable to my own, and I trust to many other souls. The last evening of it, I preached from a balcony to many thousands, who stood in the street as comfortable as at noon-day. Upon retiring to my lodgings, news was brought me, that GOD had given me a son. This hastened me up to London, where I now am, and from whence after I have baptized my little one, GOD willing, I purpose to set out again on my Master's public business. You will not fail to pray, that I may be taught how to order the child aright ..."[9]

Through the month of October to the month of January we find Whitefield

8 Ibid. pp. 48–49.
9 Ibid. p. 40.

is busy engaged in itinerancy which took him all around England (Gloucester, Bristol, Hampton, and other areas) to eventually South Wales were he tells us, "... I have been at Abergavenny, and am settled as to my dear wife's coming down. Blessed be GOD, she and the little one are pretty well". Whitefield was back in London by January 18th, 1744, where he commented, "... My brother will receive a letter about my wife's coming. She and the little one are brave and well. But why talk I of wife and little one? Let all be absorbed in the thoughts of the love, sufferings, free and full salvation of the infinitely great and glorious Emmanuel."

By February he received some shocking news—his infant son had died. We try to picture in our minds the first time he held his dear little lamb; how he must have gazed at him in awesome wonder with a heart bursting with thanks to his Creator! Few loved little ones like George Whitefield. It is with great sadness that we read the letter written from Gloucester and dated February 9, 1744, that states:

"Who knows what a day may bring forth? Last night I was called to sacrifice my Isaac; I mean to bury my only child and son about four months old. Many things occurred to make me believe he was not only to be continued to me, but to be a preacher of the everlasting gospel. Pleased with the thought, and ambitious of having a son of my own, so divinely employed, Satan was permitted to give me some wrong impressions, whereby, as I now find, I misapplied several texts of Scripture. Upon these grounds I made no scruple of declaring, 'that I should have a son, and that his name was to be John.' I mentioned the very time of his birth, and fondly hoped, that he was to be great in the fight of the LORD. Every thing happened according to the predictions, and my wife having had several narrow escapes while pregnant, especially by her falling from a high horse, and my driving her into a deep ditch in a one-horse chaise a little before the time of her lying-in, and from which we received little or no hurt, confirmed me in my expectation, that GOD would grant me my heart's desire. I would observe to you, that the child was even born in a room, which the master of the house had prepared as a prison for his wife for coming to hear me. With joy would she often look upon the bars and staples and chains which were fixed in order to keep her in. About a week after his birth, I publickly baptized him in the Tabernacle, and in the company of thousands solemnly gave him up to that GOD, who gave him to me. A hymn, too fondly composed by an aged widow, as suitable to the occasion, was sung, and all went away big with hopes of the child's being hereafter to be employed in the work of GOD; but how soon are all their fond, and as the event hath proved, their ill-grounded expectations blasted, as well as mine. House-keeping being expensive in London, I thought best to send both parent and child to Abergavenny, where my wife had a little house of my own, the furniture of which, as I thought of soon embarking for Georgia, I had partly sold, and partly given away. In their journey thither, they stopped at Gloucester, at the Bell-Inn, which my brother now keeps, and in which I was born. There, my beloved was cut off with a stroke. Upon my coming here, without knowing what had happened, I enquired concerning the welfare of parent and child; and by the answer, found that the flower was cut down. I immediately called all to join in prayer, in which I blessed the Father of mercies for giving me a son, continuing it to me so long, and taking it from me so soon. All joined in desiring that I would decline preaching till the child was buried; but I remembered a saying of good Mr. Henry, 'that weeping must not hinder sowing,' and therefore preached twice the next day, and also the day following; on the evening of which, just as I was closing my sermon, the bell struck out for the funeral. At first, I must acknowledge, it gave nature a little shake, but looking up I recovered strength, and then concluded with saying, that this text on which I had been preaching, namely, 'all things worked together for good to them that love GOD,' made me as willing to go out to my son's funeral, as to hear of his birth. Our parting from him was solemn. We kneeled down, prayed, and shed many tears, but I hope tears of resignation: And then, as he died in the house wherein I was born, he was taken and laid in the church where I was baptized, first communicated, and first preached. All this you may easily guess threw me into very solemn and deep reflection, and I hope deep humiliation; but I was comforted from that passage in the book of Kings, where is recorded the death of the Shunamite's child, which the Prophet said, 'The LORD had hid from him;' and the woman's answer likewise to the Prophet when he asked, 'Is it well with thee? Is it well with thy husband? Is it well with thy child?' And she answered, 'It is well.' This gave me no small satisfaction. I immediately preached upon the text the day following at Gloucester, and then hastened up to London, preached upon the same there; and though disappointed of a living preacher by the death of my son; yet I hope what happened before his birth, and since at his death, hath taught me such lessons, as, if duly improved, may render his mistaken parent more cautious, more sober-minded, more experienced in Satan's devices, and consequently more useful in the future labours to the church of GOD. Thus, 'out of the eater comes forth meat, and out of the strong comes forth sweetness.' Not doubting but our future life will be one continued explanation of this blessed riddle, I commend myself and you to the unerring guidance of GOD's word and spirit ..."[10]

The hymn which was sung on the occasion of the child's birth (mentioned in the previous letter) is presented below. We can only imagine the joy that accompanied the singing of this hymn by Whitefield and then realize the deep sorrow he experienced in realizing the words of the hymn would never be realized. Here now is that hymn:

I.

"Poor helpless babe! dear little child!
John be thy name, thy nature mild;
Great may'st thou be in JESU's sight,
A babe in whom he takes delight.

---

10 Ibid. pp. 50–52.

II.

Be thou made holy from the womb,
By him who sav'd thee from the tomb:*
In JESU's arms still may'st thou rest,
While sucking at thy mother's breast.

(*alluding to the remarkable deliverance that his father and mother had some weeks before
his mother delivered, when she and her husband being riding in a chaise, they were thrown
into a deep ditch, and received no harm as mentioned in previous letter).

III.

Blest be the parents with the son!
Blest be the GOD that gave you one!
We'll magnify the LORD with you!
Share in your joy, we're sure we do.

IV.

O may you both be taught of GOD,
To teach this Child his SAVIOUR's blood:
That thousands in your bliss may share,
In answer to united pray'r.

V.

And may the Lamb, your Master, grant
This grace, that you may never want
A child to stand before his face,
To preach his Love, his Sov'reign Grace!"[11]

About this sad occasion we turn to Dallimore's sensitive remarks:

"We must sympathize more especially, however with Elizabeth, in this loss of
the infant son, particularly since the event occurred so soon after the ordeal of
giving birth.

"Moreover, while at Gloucester she faced the realization that her husband,
large hearted as usual to the poor, had given away much of the furniture from
her cottage at Abergavenny, and had sold apparently all the rest, and was now
borrowing replacement items from his friends. One from whom he sought aid
was his old boyhood companion, Gabriel Harris (now a Magistrate and soon to
become Mayor) and Whitefield closed a letter to him with the remark,

'I bought a second-hand suit of curtains to-day, so you need not send
anything to Abergavenny. "Poor, yet making others rich," shall be my motto
still.'

"After the funeral Whitefield immediately set out on his unrelenting schedule
of preaching. And Elizabeth, replete with her 'second-hand suit of curtains'

---

11 Ibid. p. 53.

(and, surely much more) proceeded on her lonely journey to Wales. It is possible her father still lived at her cottage and at least she had many friends in the area. Nevertheless, a letter she wrote to Harris from Gloucester makes it evident the loss of her child weighed heavily upon her heart."[12]

We find it rather odd that neither Arnold Dallimore nor any other of the Whitefield biographers makes mention of the step-daughter Nancy! Where is this teen-age step-child of Whitefield? Has everyone assumed she has just vanished? She had to be traveling with her saddened mother on the way to Wales. She was probably, in all instances, more of a help and comfort to Elizabeth during this time of grief and sadness than her missing husband was. There is no mention of Nancy ever again, so we too, as others have, leave her memory to the past and not make mention of her again in the rest of the story of Whitefield; for we have no further facts concerning her. We can only assume she either married and moved away from her mother, or continued to live with her and keep her company (remaining an old maid) while Whitefield was off years at a time in itinerancy. Only God knows what happened to poor Nancy.

George Whitefield simply did not have the time to stay at home and grieve the death of his son. For it was only a matter of days after the funeral and he was off again on a extended tour. He buried himself in activity during this time and this must have been his way of reconciling his grief over the loss of his dear son.

---

12 Dallimore, Vol. 2, p. 169.

What a sign and wonder was this man of God in the greatness of his labours! One cannot but stand amazed that his mortal frame could, for the space of near thirty years, without interruption, sustain the weight of them; for what so trying to the human frame, in youth especially, as long-continued, frequent, and violent straining of the lungs? Who that knows their structure would think it possible that a person above the age of manhood could speak in a single week, and that for years—in general forty hours, and in very many weeks sixty—and that to thousands; and after this labour, instead of taking any rest, could be offering up prayers and intercessions, with hymns and spiritual songs, as his manner was, in every house to which he was invited? The truth is, that in point of labour this extraordinary servant of God did as much in a few weeks as most of those who exert themselves are able to do in the space of a year.

Henry Venn

CHAPTER 32

MOB RIOTS AND PRINTED OPPOSITION

Violent mobs were descending upon the Methodist preachers in 1744. The mob scenes and damage which took place in Hampton (England) was now the subject of a trial where Whitefield and his followers were the prosecutors and the rioters were the defendants! The court favored the evangelist and was a major victory for the Methodists at this time. We see this from the following:

"London, March 12, 1744.

"This leaves me just returned from Gloucester assizes, where it has pleased the great Judge of quick and dead to give us the victory over the Hampton rioters ... Matters of fact being proved by a variety of evidence, and the defendants making no reply, the rule was made absolute, and an information filed against them ... Whereupon in a few minutes they gave a verdict for the prosecutors, and brought in all the defendants guilty of the whole information lodged, against them. I then retired to my lodgings, kneeled down, and with my friends gave thanks to our all-conquering Emmanuel ..." [1]

Thus, in the midst of his sorrow and defeat over the loss of his son he has a victory which, at least, momentarily lifts his spirits. We see that his heart was uplifted from his comments, "God was pleased to enlarge my heart much. I was very happy with my friends afterwards."

We also have the following confirmation of these matters from the pen of Luke Tyerman, who stated:

"Whilst Whitefield was burying his child at Gloucester, his friend, Charles Wesley, was preaching, at the peril of his life, in Staffordshire. At Wednesday, the mob 'assaulted, one after another, all the houses of those who were called Methodists.' All the windows were broken, and furniture of every kind was dashed in pieces. At Aldridge and several other villages, many of the houses

---

1   *Works,* Vol. 2, pp 57–58.

were plundered, and the rioters 'loaded themselves with clothes and goods of all sorts, as much as they could carry.'

"… A week after this, Whitefield set out on a visit to his wife at Abergavenny, and took her 'a second-hand suit of curtains,' which he had bought for her humble dwelling.

"At the beginning of the month of March, he returned to Gloucester, to be present at the assizes, at which the Hampton rioters, already mentioned, were tried, and found guilty, the amount of damages to be paid being referred to the King's Bench, London. Whitefield writes:—

'I hear the rioters are hugely alarmed; but they know not that we intend to let them see what we could do, and then to forgive them. This troublesome affair being over, I must now prepare for my intended voyage to America.'

"Nearly seven months, however, elapsed before Whitefield's voyage was begun,—an interval which was partly occupied with what, to Whitefield, was extremely uncongenial, a literary war.

"To understand the controversy, it is needful to remark, that, of late, several publications had been issued, and industriously circulated, attacking the loyalty of Whitefield and his friends. Among others, there was a quarto-sized sheet, of four pages, entitled, 'The Case of the Methodists briefly stated, more particularly in the point of Field-Preaching.' The writer tries to prove that field-preaching is contrary to the Act of Toleration; and then he proceeds to shew, that, because of the largeness of his congregations, Whitefield's preaching in the open air was eminently calculated to promote sedition, and to be a serious danger to the state."[2]

An even larger publication appeared in 1744 which caused great alarm among the Methodists. It was supposedly written by an enemy of Whitefield, Dr. Gibson, Bishop of London, and it was a bitter attack against Methodism; it was entitled, "Observations upon the Conduct and Behaviour of a certain Sect, usually distinguished by the name of Methodists."

Both of these printed pamphlets caused troubled for Whitefield; not because they were the first evidences of opposition in written form published against him (this had been occurring on a regular basis since 1738!), but the main source of concern for Whitefield was that he was being accused of *treason* against the state. The timing of this published attack could not have been worse for Whitefield for at this time the entire nation was in alarm in anticipation of an expected invasion by Prince Charles, the young Pretender. To be labeled a "seceder" at this time was dangerous indeed.

A series of letters written in defense of these verbal attacks were quickly published around London by Whitefield; a major reply to the Bishop of

---

2   Tyerman, Vol. 2, pp. 86–87.

London was committed to the press on the 10th of March. It was entitled, "An Answer to the first part of an anonymous Pamphlet, entitled, 'Observations upon the Conduct and Behaviour of a certain Sect usually distinguished by the name of Methodists.' In a Letter to the Right Reverend the Bishop of London, and the other the Right Reverend the Bishops concerned in the publication thereof." Whitefield's reply to the Bishop consisted of twenty six pages!

Tyerman noted:

"Before the year was ended, Whitefield's 'Letter' passed, at least, through three editions in England, besides being printed and published at Boston in America. The motto on his title-page was Psalm xxxv. 11, 'False witnesses did rise up; they laid to my charge things that I knew not.'

"It is difficult to furnish an outline of Whitefield's pamphlet; but the following extracts will give the reader an idea of its style and spirit:—

"'Young as I am, I know too much of the devices of Satan, and the desperate wickedness and deceitfulness of my own heart, not to be sensible, that I am a man of like passions with others; and that I, consequently, may have sometimes mistaken nature for grace, imagination for revelation, and the fire of my own temper for the pure and sacred flame of holy zeal. If, therefore, upon perusing the pamphlet, I find that I have been blameable in any respect, I will not only confess it, but return hearty thanks both to the compiler and your lordships, *though unknown.* Indeed, it is but of little consequence to the merits of the cause to know who the author is. Only this much may be said, your lordships yourselves being judges, it is not quite fair to *give stabs in the dark.*'

"Whitefield proceeds to say, that the title of the Bishops' pamphlet ought to have run thus:

'Misrepresentations of the Conduct and *Principles* of many Orthodox, well-meaning Ministers and Members of the Church of England, and loyal Subjects to his Majesty, King George, *falsely termed a Sect,* and usually distinguished, *out of contempt,* by the name of Methodists.' He adds:—

"'The principles, as well as conduct, of the Methodists are greatly misrepresented in this pamphlet. Its design is to exhibit their proceedings as dangerous to the Church and State, in order to procure an Act of Parliament against them, or to oblige them to secure themselves by turning Dissenters. But is not such a motion, at such a season as this, both uncharitable and unseasonable? Is not the Administration engaged enough already in other affairs, without troubling themselves with the Methodists? Or, who would now advise them to bring further guilt upon the nation, by persecuting some of the present government's *most hearty* friends? I say, my lords, *the present government's most hearty friends;* for though the Methodists (as the world calls them) disagree in some particulars, yet I venture to affirm that, to *a man,* they all agree in this: namely, to love and honour the king. For my own part, I profess myself a

zealous friend to his present majesty King George, and the present
Administration. Wherever I go, I think it my duty to pray for him and to preach
up obedience to him, and all that are set in authority under him. I have now
been a preacher above seven years, and for six years past have been called to act
in a very public way. Your lordships must have heard of the great numbers who
have attended: sometimes several of the nobility, and, now and then, even some
of the clergy have been present. Did they ever hear me speak a disloyal word?
Are there not thousands, who can testify how fervently and frequently I pray for
his majesty King George, his royal offspring, and the present government? Yes,
my lords, they can; and, I trust, I should be enabled to do so, though surrounded
with popish enemies, and in danger of dying for it as soon as my prayer was
ended."[3]

It is amazing to remind ourselves that this evangelist, who having to defend
himself before King and State, was still only twenty nine years old! This
battle of the "printed word" would continue into late August and still be
active while Whitefield was on the sea and on his way to America once
more. In the end the King and the State felt no threat from young Whitefield
and the matter was eventually forgotten. But we are sure that the Bishop
learned, like others who had tried without success to silence George
Whitefield, that his effort was in vain.

However, these printed mean-spirited attacks by Bishops Gibson and
Lavington did raise some doubts in the public's opinion of Whitefield and
the Methodists and probably added to the persecutions they were yet to
receive.

If the cumulative events of mob scenes, ensuing court trial of the rioters of
Hampton, the vile printed attacks of the spiritually blinded Bishop of
London, were not enough to lay heavily upon the already grieving evangelist
(who had just recently buried his infant son), there was yet ahead a physical
attack upon Whitefield which could have easily resulted in his death!

From March thru June of 1744 Whitefield was busy preaching at
Wellington, Exeter, Bideford, Kingsbridge, and Plymouth. Also, during this
time in the month of April Whitefield met with John Cennick (at Cennick's
house in Tytherton), Howell Harris, Joseph Humphreys, Thomas Adams,
William Humphreys, Isaac Cottle, Thomas Lewis, and Thomas Beswick at
the first formal meeting of the Welsh Methodist Association. So Whitefield's
time (during these busy fifteen weeks from March 15th to June 26th) was
spread out between London, Bristol, and Wiltshire.

In June, while at Portsmouth, he tried to gain passage on a ship bound for
America but the Captain of the vessel refused to let the evangelist on board

---

3   Ibid. pp. 91–92.

the ship lest he "spoil the sailors"! Therefore, Whitefield had to travel to Plymouth to find a vessel there. It was while he was at Plymouth that he was almost murdered in a brutal attack while staying at an inn. On the night of his arrival at Plymouth he tried to preach but was prevented by a "bear and drum" paraded on the ground where he was expected to preach. The next night he did preach but on his return to the inn some ruffians broke into his room and verbally insulted him. This was unsettling to the weak-natured Whitefield; but this verbal abuse paled in comparison to what followed. We have the account from two letters he wrote describing the event in detail:

"Plymouth, June 26, 1744.

"You see by this where I am. Doubtless you'll wonder at the quick transition from Portsmouth to Plymouth. To the former I intended going when I wrote last; but just before I took leave of the dear tabernacle people, a message was sent to me, that the captain in which I was to sail from thence, would not take me for fear of spoiling his sailors. Some interpreted this as a call from providence not to embark at this time; but I enjoined them silence till I had taken my leave, and then, hearing of a mast-ship that was going under convoy from Plymouth, I hastened thither, and have taken a passage in the *Wilmington*, Capt. Dalby, bound to Piscataway, in New England. My first reception here was a little unpromising. A report being spread that I was come, a great number of people assembled upon the Hoe, (a large green for walks and diversions) and somebody brought out a bear and a drum; but I did not come till the following evening, when, under pretence of a hue-and-cry, several broke into the room where I lodged at the inn, and disturbed me very much. I then betook myself to private lodgings, and being gone to rest, after preaching to a large congregation, and visiting the French prisoners, the good woman of the house came and told me, that a well-dressed gentleman desired to speak with me. Imagining that it was some Nicodemite, I desired he might be brought up. He came and sat down by my bedside, told me he was a lieutenant of a man of war, congratulated me on the success of my ministry, and expressed himself much concerned for being detained from hearing me. He then asked me, if I knew him. I answered no. He replied, his name was Cadogan. I rejoined, that I had seen one Mr. Cadogan, who was formerly an officer at Georgia, about a fortnight ago at Bristol. Upon this, he immediately rose up, uttering the most abusive language, calling me dog, rogue, villain, &c. and beat me most unmercifully with his gold-headed cane. As you know I have not much natural courage, guess how surprised I was; being apprehensive that he intended to shoot or stab me, I underwent all the fears of a sudden violent death. But, as it providentially happened, my hostess and her daughter hearing me cry *murder*, rushed into the room and seized him by the collar; however, he immediately disengaged himself from them, and repeated his blows upon me. The cry of *murder* was repeated also, which putting him into some terror, he made towards the chamber-door, from whence the good woman pushed him down stairs. About the bottom of which, a second cry'd out, 'Take courage, I am ready to help you;' accordingly, whilst the other was escaping, he rushed up, and finding one of the women coming down, took her by the heels and threw her upon the stairs, by which her back was almost broken. By this time the neighbourhood was alarmed. Unwilling to add to it, I desired the doors might be shut, and so betook myself to rest, not without reflecting, how indispensibly necessary it was for Christians and Christian ministers to be always upon their guard, and with what great propriety we are taught to pray in our excellent Litany, 'from sudden,' that is, 'from violent and unprepared death, good LORD deliver us.' That this may be our happy lot, is the hearty prayer of, dear Madam,

Yours, &c.

G.W."[4]

When George Whitefield stated, "As you know I have not much natural courage" it reminds us of a story of when Whitefield was facing some persecution from an angry mob and Mrs. Whitefield grabbed the hem of his coat and told him in a stern voice, "Play the man George!"

Obviously he did not "play the man" while being attacked at the inn and had to be rescued by two females! The next letter, explains more of this bizarre incident. He wrote:

"Plymouth, July 4, 1744.

"Since my last, I have had some particular informations about the late odd adventure. It seems, that four gentlemen came to the house of one of my particular friends, kindly enquiring after me, and desired to know where I lodged, that they might come and pay their respects. He directed them. Soon afterwards I received a letter, informing me that the writer was a nephew to Mr. S——, an eminent attorney at New York; that he had the pleasure of supping with me at his uncle's house, and desired my company to sup with him and a few more friends at a tavern. I sent him word, that it was not customary for me to sup out at taverns, but should be glad of his company, out of respect to his uncle, to east a morsel with him at my lodgings. He came; we supped; and I observed that he frequently looked around him, and seemed very absent; but having no suspicion, I continued in conversation with him and my other friends, till we parted. This, I now find, was to have been the *assassin*; and being interrogated by his other companions on his return to the tavern about what he had done, he answered, that being used so civilly, he had not the heart to touch me. Upon which, as I am informed, the person who assaulted me laid a wager of ten guineas that he would do my business for me. Some say, that they took his sword from him, which I suppose they did, for I only saw and felt the weight of his cane. The next morning, I was to expound at a private house, and then to set out for Biddeford. Some urged me to stay and prosecute; but being better employed, I went on my intended journey, was greatly blessed in preaching the

---

4   *Works,* Vol. 2. pp 59–60.

everlasting gospel, and upon my return was well paid for what I had suffered: curiosity having led perhaps two thousand more than ordinary to see and hear a man, that had like to have been murdered in his bed. Thus all things tend to the furtherance of the gospel, and work together for good to those that love GOD.

Thus Satan thwarts, and men object,
And yet the thing they thwart, effect.

Leaving you to add an *Hallelujah,* I subscribe myself,

Ever, ever yours,

G.W."[5]

Luke Tyerman says of this attack upon Whitefield at the inn, "Whitefield seriously believed that this atrocious outrage was a deliberate attempt to murder him; the probability is, that it was a cruel freak, similar to many others for which naval stations have frequently been infamous." Whatever the intent of the attackers was, the beating could very well have killed him if the lady's of the house had not come to his rescue.

Whitefield remained around the environs of Plymouth for another six weeks and occupied himself with preaching and corresponding with the Methodist Societies—news reached Whitefield of some recently martyred Methodist preachers. Two of which were the Rev. David Crossly of Manchester, and well as the Methodist preacher Thomas Beard. The persecution of the Methodists was real indeed!

During Whitefield's time at Plymouth, before embarking for his third visit to America, a happy incident occurred which should be related. It tells of his preaching success amidst his trials at this naval port. We read:

"Thus, at Plymouth, as in other places, did Whitefield triumph in Christ Jesus. One of the conversions, which took place under his marvellous ministry, is too notable to pass unnoticed. Henry Tanner, born at Exeter, was now in the twenty-sixth year of his age, and was working, at Plymouth, as a shipwright. One day, while at work, he heard, from a considerable distance, the voice of Whitefield, who was preaching in the open air; and, concluding that the man was mad, he and half a dozen of his companions filled their pockets with stones, and set off to knock the preacher down. Whitefield's text was Acts xvii. 19,20. Tanner listened with astonishment; and, without using his stones, went home, determined to hear him again next evening. The text, on this occasion, was Luke xxiv. 47; and Tanner was in such agony of soul, that he was forced to cry, 'God be merciful to me a sinner!' The next night, while Whitefield was preaching on 'Jacob's Ladder,' Tanner found peace with God. He at once, joined the Society at Plymouth, which had been formed by Whitefield, and suffered violent persecution from his unconverted wife. To secure time for

---

5   Ibid. pp. 60–61.

prayer and Christian usefulness, he seldom allowed himself more than six hours in bed, and frequently but four. Ten years after his conversion, he removed to Exeter, and began to preach with great success. In 1769, the Tabernacle at Exeter was built, mainly through his exertions, and he became its minister. His labours, however, were not confined to Exeter. At the request of Toplady, he used to preach at Broad Hembury; whilst Moreton, Hampstead, Crediton, Tophsam, and various other places, were favoured with his services. On Sunday morning, March 24, 1805, when he had completed the eighty-sixth year of his age, he was carried, in a chair, to his pulpit, and tried to preach, but was so ill that he was obliged to relinquish the attempt. A week afterwards he peacefully expired."[6]

God's ways are in the waters and though detained from his initial sailing date, and suffering the beating from the man with the cane, Whitefield did what he did best—preach the gospel. Because he faithfully did his part, God faithfully *did His part*, and if for no other reason while he labored in Plymouth before sailing for America George Whitefield would meet a man in heaven one day by the name of Henry Tanner; who, having come to hear him with a pocket full of stones and a stony heart was converted by his preaching and spent the rest of his days as a gospel minister who, only God knows, how many lives were converted under Rev. Tanner's lengthy ministry.

---

6   Tyerman, Vol 2, pp. 104–105.

There can be little doubt that this was the grand scheme now revolving in the mind of the illustrious Countess ... Whitefield tried to raise up converted clergymen and the Countess procured them ordination and [later] built them chapels. The idea was grand—perhaps inspired—and the working it out was unquestionably the principal means of effecting the marvellous change that has taken place since then in the Established Church.

Luke Tyerman

CHAPTER 33

SELINA COUNTESS OF HUNTINGDON

In 1744 an illustrious person of high pedigree and influence would enter George Whitefield's life. Through her contacts with the powerful and rich, Whitefield's audience would broaden to the aristocracy of England. This lady of influence would play a strategic part in the revival. Her Christian friends would include John and Charles Wesley, Howell Harris, Isaac Watts, Phillip Doddridge. Her secular friendships were the who's who of England's society and royalty of the day. This lady was none other than Selina Countess of Huntingdon. Her influence in the life of George Whitefield would continue on after his death; for she not only hired the young evangelist to be her chaplain, she undergirded him financially till his dying day. In his will Whitefield bequeathed his beloved Bethesda to the Countess of Huntingdon—and her portrait hangs at Bethesda to the present day.

Who was this remarkable woman who by marriage gained royalty and who by her conversion to Christianity gained the friendships of men like the Wesley's and Whitefield? Her story is a remarkable one. A study of the life of George Whitefield would be incomplete without a deep study of the Lady who backed him with all her influence and fortune.

George Whitefield had been used of God to preach the gospel to different layers of society. First to the coal-mining colliers of Bristol whose blackened cheeks ran with white gutters of tears; then to everyman in the fields of Moorfields and Kennington Common; across the pond in America Whitefield had preached to the well-heeled in Boston and South Carolina and to the well-known such as Jonathan Edwards and Benjamin Franklin. There would be a door opened to him that had up to now been closed—this was the aristocracy of England. They were too refined to lower themselves to go out to hear the dangerous Methodists. The rich and famous of London were a closed-clique to anyone not in their immediate circle of influence. Lady Huntingdon would change all that!

"Lady Selina Shirley was born on August 24, 1707—seven years before Whitefield—and was married to Theophilus, ninth Earl of Huntingdon, on June 3, 1728. She entered heartily into the pleasures and duties of her high station, was often at Court, took a lively interest in politics, and cared for the poor on her husband's estate ...

"The Earl of Huntingdon ... died on October 13, 1746, leaving the Countess in command of immense wealth, and free to carry out her wishes without interference from any one. Everything favoured her assumption of that position she was soon to gain, and towards which she took her first decisive step, when, in 1748, she appointed Whitefield her chaplain. Liberal to profusion in her gifts, arbitrary in temper, Calvinistic in creed, consummate in administrative ability, devout in spirit, and thoroughly consecrated to the glory of Christ, she was unmistakably the proper leader of the Calvinistic side of the Methodist body, whether in or out of the Established Church ..."[1]

Lady Huntingdon's initial contact with Whitefield occurred in the summer of 1744 before he set sail for his third visit to America. The Countess had a ongoing friendship with Howell Harris who had invited her to hear Whitefield preach at the Moorfields Tabernacle. She liked what she heard and soon became a ardent follower and supporter of Whitefield. She was to befriend both John and Charles Wesley as well, and soon her circle of preaching friends was as famous as her circle of aristocratic friends! Moorfields Tabernacle was in 1744 a temporary wooden structure that housed Whitefield's growing congregations. It was in close proximity to the Foundery, so within walking distance (though royalty dare not walk!) the Countess could visit both Wesley and Whitefield and bring with her some of her influential friends.

Lady Huntingdon, sadly, had a falling out with John Wesley over doctrine. She was a Calvinist and this theology united her with Whitefield and the Calvinistic side of the revival. This work took on new dimensions when she appointed Whitefield her chaplain.

"... A plan had been taking shape in the mind of the Countess of Huntingdon. As a peeress she had the legal right to appoint two private chaplains whose responsibility it was to minister to the spiritual needs of her household wherever she might be living. If she appointed Whitefield to this position she could then invite members of the nobility, politicians and even royalty to her home to listen to her chaplain preach. In this way she could gain a hearing for the gospel of Christ among those of her own rank. Pride, coupled with an apartheid born of social privilege, might otherwise preclude for ever such people from the reach of the evangelical preachers."[2]

This introduction to the rich, royal, and famous in London was what George Whitefield was praying for; he knew these powerful people would never venture out in a field to hear him! So he must go to them—but how? Selina was the answer to that prayer. A list of some of these luminaries is provided for us:

"The Earl and Countess of Huntingdon were constant in their attendance upon his ministry, and were often accompanied by his lordship's sisters, the Ladies Hastings. Occasionally, Sarah, Duchess of Marlborough, and Catherine, Duchess of Buckingham, two of the most celebrated and remarkable women of their day, were among his hearers; so also was Lord Lonsdale, who had been one of the lords of the bedchamber, and constable of the tower. Charles, third Duke of Bolton; Lord Hervey, who had distinguished himself as an orator in both houses of Parliament, and who had held the offices of vice-chamberlain, and keeper of the privy-seal; and Lord Sidney Beauclerk, fifth son of the Duke of St. Albans, were likewise numbered among the young preacher's auditors. Yea, even royalty itself, in the persons of William Augustus, Duke of Cumberland, youngest son of George II., and his brother Frederick, Prince of Wales, helped to swell some of Whitefield's congregations."[3]

Lady Huntingdon also began a prayer meeting which took place at her estate. This was a brilliant idea to broaden the exposure of the gospel to society's elite. Whitefield, when in town, would read prayers and exhort the "Ladies" whose numbers increased remarkably as well as their appetite for the gospel. We see this from the following:

"Under her auspices, a prayer-meeting was established for those females who, from the circles of rank and fashion, became the followers of the Lord. Among these were Lady Frances Gardiner, Lady Mary Hamilton, daughter of the Marquis of Lothian, who had attended the ministry of Whitefield in Scotland, Lady Gertrude Hotham and Countess Delitz, sisters of Lady Chesterfield, Lady Chesterfield herself, and Lady Fanny Shirley, of whom Horace Walpole wrote in his scoffing way to a friend on the continent, 'If you ever think of returning to England, you must prepare yourself with Methodism: this sect increases as fast as ever almost any other religious nonsense did. Lady Fanny Shirley has chosen this way of bestowing the dregs of her beauty, and Mr. Lyttleton is very near making the same sacrifice of the dregs of all those various characters that he has worn. The Methodists love your big sinners, and indeed they have a plentiful harvest.'"[4]

2   Faith Cook, *Selina Countess of Huntingdon* (Edinburgh: The Banner of Truth Trust, 2001), pp. 108–109.

3   A.C.H. Seymour, *The Life and Times of the Countess of Huntingdon,* 2 volumes (London: 1840), Vol. 1, p. 199.

4   Helen C. Knight, *Lady Huntingdon & Her Friends* (Grand Rapids, Baker Book House), p. 59.

These meetings at Lady Huntingdon's soon were blessed of God. Those who before, because of social status, felt religion beneath them were now gladly hearing the Good News! The Countess's circle of influential friends were getting weekly doses of religion. We read:

"'Religion was never so much the subject of conversation as now,' writes Lady Huntingdon to Doddridge. 'Some of the great ones hear with me the gospel patiently, and thus much seed is sown by Mr. Whitefield's preaching. O that it may fall on good ground, and bring forth abundantly.

'I had the pleasure, yesterday, of Mr. Gibbon's and Mr. Crittenden's company to dine with me. Lord Lothian and Lady Frances Gardiner gave them the meeting, and we had truly a most primitive and heavenly day; our hearts and voices praised the Lord, prayed to him, and talked of him. I had another lady present, whose face, since I saw you last, is turned Zionward. Of the "honorable women," I trust there are not a few; patience shall have its proper work: and if we love our Lord, we must be tender over his lambs. I trust He will assist us to keep fanning the flame in every heart; this, my friend, is our joyful task for the best Master we can serve, either in time or eternity. Do not let our hands hang down; we must wrestle for ourselves and for all dead in their sins; till the day break and the shadows of time flee away.'

"While thus solicitous for the spiritual welfare of those of her own rank ..."5

Whitefield had plenty to say of the dear Lady Huntingdon. He trusted her implicitly. He always felt it a high honor to be called her chaplain. Together they did much to further the gospel among the ranks of high society. We have the following letter which attests to his love of their friendship:

"Honoured Madam,   London, Jan. 6, 1750.

"The inclosed letters came to hand on Monday last, as a new-years-fist. As they bring such good news, I must communicate them to your Ladyship. The first writer is a Virginia planter, at whose house I lay, and who with some other gentlemen asked me to play a game at cards: I refused, and retired to pray for him. His present wife is my spiritual child. The letters will shew how GOD was pleased to answer our prayers. This, and other things I meet with, more and more convinces me, that a liberty to range and publish the gospel wherever providence shall call me, is what I am to maintain and preserve. Mr. A—— abides still, and as far as I can judge, disinterested. Blessed be GOD for stripping seasons! I would not lose the privilege of leaning only upon the LORD JESUS for thousands of worlds. He alone can make me happy, and he alone without foreign assistance can bless; and blessed be his name, he daily makes me so. He has been pleased to remove in some degree the pain of my breast, and give me to determine more and more, that every breath I draw by divine assistance shall be his. I thank him ten thousand times that your Ladyship is so well pleased with Mr. B——. He expresses the strong sense he has of the obligations he lies under

---

5   Ibid. p. 60.

to the LORD JESUS CHRIST, and under him, to you Ladyship. O that neither of us may prove ungrateful in any respect! Next week I hope to let your Ladyship know how affairs go at Mrs. K——'s. I expect to see her then. Lately his Majesty seeing Lady Chesterfield at court with a grave gown, pleasantly asked her, 'whether Mr. Whitefield advised her to that colour.' O that all were clothed in the bright and spotless robe of the Redeemer's righteousness! How beautiful would they then appear in the sight of the King of kings! This, honoured Madam, through free grace, is your dress. That your honoured sisters, and all your children, may be adorned in like manner, is the earnest prayer of, honoured Madam,

> Your Ladyship's most obliged and ready servant for CHRIST's sake,
>
> G.W."[6]

There have been some Whitefield biographers who have criticized his letters to Lady Huntingdon, remarking that:

> "Whitefield's letters to Lady Huntingdon, however, have come in for criticism—and not without some justification.

> "Some of his correspondence with her is characterized by a self-abasing attitude which seems servile and which some authors have termed, 'unmanly.' ... Throughout his letters to her there runs this too frequent use of 'your Ladyship' and 'honoured Madam' and in certain of his letters to other people he refers to her as 'the Elect Lady.'

> "... Nevertheless, his manner of address toward the Countess is regrettable and one cannot but agree with Gledstone in his further statement, 'Whitefield used to advise his friends "to be servant-like but not servile;" pity that in this case he did not observe the distinction with due care.'"[7]

We disagree with this consensus. Whitefield had to address Lady Huntingdon by her title for this was how the "commoners" were *expected* to address such nobility. As great a man as George Whitefield was he still was a "commoner" in regard to society's elite. Also, Whitefield felt honored to have such a powerful and influential sponsor and friend as Lady Huntingdon; he was not flattering her but rather paying her the homage that was her due. Whitefield feared no man—nor woman. We see this from an excerpt from another biographer who has a different opinion than Dallimore:

> "Whitefield never sought the patronage of the great, nor ever employed it for any personal end. To the credit of his first noble friends, Lothian, Leven, and Rae, they sought his friendship because they admired his talents, and appreciated his character. They were won by the preaching which won the multitude; and

---

6 *Works,* Vol. 2, pp. 312–313.
7 Dallimore, Vol. 2, pp. 278–280.

when they wrote to him, he answered them just as he did anyone else who sought his counsel or prayers, courteously and faithfully. He paid them, indeed, the current compliments of his times: and if these ever amount to flattery in appearance, they are followed by *warnings* which no real flatterer would have dared to whisper. In his first letters to the Marquis of Lothian, he said, 'You do well, my lord, to fear, lest your convictions should wear off. Your lordship is in a dangerous situation' in the world. 'Come, then, and lay yourself at the feet of Jesus.'—'As for praying in your family, I entreat your, my lord, not to neglect it. You are *bound* to do it. Apply to Christ for strength to overcome your present fears. They are the effects of pride, or infidelity, or of both.' These are not unfair specimens of Whitefield's correspondence with the Scotch nobles, who honoured him with their confidence."[8]

Whatever one's conclusions are regarding Whitefield and *how* he addressed the Countess from time to time we can be sure that he was not afraid to tell truth when it was needed.

The array of nobility, the famous of London, and the powerful, soon were like Mary at the feet of Jesus hearing his word—and we can attribute most of this access through the efforts of Selina Countess of Huntingdon. Many famous people like Chesterfield and Bolingbroke, though complimentary of Whitefield's oratory and genius, were unmoved by the truths of the gospel and remained apart from Christ. *But they did hear the truth preached* and this was all because of the efforts of Lady Huntingdon—had it not been for her many nobility were out of reach of the gospel message. For it was at her house at Chelsea (and other locations) where Whitefield was able to preach to "crowded and fashionable congregations"; and after the Countess made him her domestic chaplain that access to the elite broadened even more. He would preach twice a week at the Countess's house "to the great and noble" with much effect—especially among the ladies.

We must include Luke Tyerman's comments about this time:

"Whitefield mentions his 'brilliant assembly' in the mansion of the Countess of Huntingdon. In a letter to the Countess of Bath, he wrote, 'It would please you to see the assemblies at her ladyship's house. They are brilliant ones indeed. The prospect of catching some of the rich, in the gospel net is very promising. I know you will wish prosperity in the name of the Lord.'

"No wonder that, after one of his first services at Lady Huntingdon's, Whitefield said, 'I went home, never more surprised at any incident in my life.' Such congregations were unique. Nothing like them had heretofore been witnessed. There were gatherings of England's proud nobility, assembled to listen to a young preacher, whose boyhood had been spent in a public-house; whose youth, at the university, had been employed partly in study, and partly in

8   Philip, p. 479.

attending to the wants of fellow-students, who declined to treat him as an equal; and whose manhood life, for the last thirteen years, had been a commingling of marvellous popularity and violent contempt,—a scene of infirmities and errors, and yet of unreserved and unceasing devotion to the cause of Christ and the welfare of his fellow-men. Such was the youthful preacher,—a man of slender learning, of mean origin, without Church preferment, hated by the clergy, and maligned by the public press. Who were his aristocratic hearers? The following list is supplied by the well-informed author of 'The Life and Times of the Countess of Huntingdon':—

"Lady Fanny Shirley, who had long been one of the reigning beauties of the court of George the First; the Duchess of Argyll; Lady Betty Campbell; Lady Ferrers; Lady Sophia Thomas; the Duchess of Montagu, daughter of the great Duke of Marlborough; Lady Cardigan; Lady Lincoln; Mrs. Boscawen; Mrs. Pitt; Miss Rich; Lady Fitzwalter; Lady Caroline Petersham; the Duchess of Queensbury, daughter of the Earl of Clarendon, and celbrated for extraordinary beauty, wit, and sprightliness, by Pope, Swift, and Prior; the Duchess of Manchester; Lady Thanet, daughter of the Marquis of Halifax, and wife of Sackville, Earl of Thanet; Lady St. John, niece of Lady Huntingdon; Lady Luxborough, the friend and correspondent of Shenstone, the poet; Lady Monson, whose husband, in 1760, was created Baron Sondes; Lady Rockingham, the wife of the great statesman, a woman of immense wit and pleasant temper, often at court, and possessed of considerable influence in the higher circle of society; Lady Betty Germain, daughter of the Earl of Berkeley, and through her husband, Sir John Germain, the possessor of enormous wealth; Lady Eleanor Bertie, a member of the noble family of Abingdon; the Dowager-Duchess of Ancaster; the Dowager-Lady Hyndford; the Duchess of Somerset; the Countess Delitz, one of the daughters of the Duchess of Kendal, and the sister of Lady Chesterfield; Lady Hinchinbroke, granddaughter of the Duke of Montagu; and Lady Schaubs.

"Besides these 'honourable women not a few,' there were also the Earl of Burlington, so famed for his admiration of the works of Inigo Jones, and for his architectural expenditure; George Bubb Dodington, afterwards Lord Melcombe, a friend and favourite of the Prince of Wales, and whose costly mansion was often crowded with literary men; George Augustus Selwyn, an eccentric wit to whom nearly all the current *bon-mots* of the day were attributed; the Earl of Holderness; Lord (afterwards Marquess) Townshend, named George, after his godfather, George the First, a distinguished general in the army, member of Parliament for Norfolk, and ultimately a field marshal. Charles Townshend, now a young man of twenty-three, whom Burke described as 'the delight and ornament of the House of Commons, and the charm of every private society he honoured with his presence'; Lord St. John, half-brother to Lord Bolingbroke; the Earl of Aberdeen; the Earl of Lauderdale; the Earl of Hyndford, Envoy Extraordinary to the King of Prussia; the Marquis of Tweeddale, Secretary of State for Scotland; George, afterwards Lord Lyttleton, at one time member for Okehampton, an secretary of Frederick, Prince of

Wales, and who had recently published his well-known book, 'Observations on the Conversion of St. Paul;' William Pitt, the distinguished first Earl of Chatham; Lord North, in his twenty-first year, afterwards First Lord of the Treasury, and ultimately Earl of Guildford; Evelyn, Duke of Kingston; Viscount Trentham (a title borne by the Duke of Sutherland); the Earl of March (one of the titles of the Duke of Richmond); the Earl of Haddington; Edward Hussey, who married a daughter of the Duke of Montagu, and was created Earl of Beaulieu; Hume Campbell, afterwards created Baron Hume; the Earl of Sandwich, subsequently ambassador to the court of Spain, First Lord of the Admiralty, and Secretary of State for the Home Department; and Lord Bolingbroke, the friend of the Pretender, a man of great ability,—a statesman, a philosopher, and an infidel.

"Gillies adds to this long list the name of David Hume, who had recently returned from Italy in great chagrin, because the people of England 'entirely overlooked and neglected' his 'Inquiry concerning Human Understanding.'

"It is said that Hume considered Whitefield the most ingenious preacher he ever listened to, and that twenty miles were not too far to go to hear him. 'Once,' said the great infidel, 'Whitefield addressed his audience thus: "The attendant angel is about to leave us, and ascend to heaven. Shall he ascend and not bear with him the news of one sinner reclaimed from the error of his way?" And, then, stamping with his foot, and lifting up his hands and eyes to heaven, he cried aloud, "Stop, Gabriel, stop, ere you enter the sacred portals, and yet carry with you the tidings of one sinner being saved." This address surpassed anything I ever saw or heard in any other preacher.'

"The foregoing were *some*, not all, of Whitefield's aristocratic hearers."[9]

We marvel, after such a breathtaking list of the Who's Who of Europe, is presented to us and then to have Tyerman comment, "The foregoing were *some*, not all, of Whitefield's aristocratic hearers." We wonder who else is left? We also wonder how many of the aforementioned individuals of rank and royalty actually were converted under Whitefield's preaching. We smile at their titles now as they mean nothing to this present age—all that matters in the end is whose name is written in the Book of Life!

The long list of "movers and shakers" of English society during the eighteenth century does validate one fact: Lady Huntingdon was successful in her endeavors to bring the gospel to her peer group. Not one of those titled individuals had an excuse of never hearing the "truth" when they stood before the King of Kings. As Lady Huntingdon's chaplain, Whitefield had an open door to the rich and famous. The Countess's Chelsea Farm was also a scene of nobility gatherings who came to hear the gospel preached by Whitefield.

---

9   Tyerman, Vol. 2, pp. 209–212.

We see this from the following remarks:

"Throughout 1749 and during the following few years the Countess of Huntingdon's mind was dominated by her new aspiration, and she used every effort to reach these politicians, wits, actors, writers and members of the nobility with the humbling message of the gospel of Christ. And here, her new chaplain George Whitefield was to make a significant contribution. Whenever he was in London Selina arranged for him to preach each Tuesday and Thursday at her Chelsea mansion to as many of her friends and acquaintances as she could gather together—a method of reaching her contemporaries with the gospel that would set a pattern to be copied by a number of her friends. At her request Wesley was also invited to preach at Chelsea Farm, particularly when Whitefield was travelling and preaching in other parts of the country. Glad that his colleague was also to share in this opportunity, Whitefield wrote to the Countess in February 1749:

> The language of my heart is, Lord, send by whom thou wilt, only convert some of the mighty and noble for thy mercy's sake.

"Refreshment on these occasions was limited to drinks of tea or lemonade, but this did not deter some of the most prominent figures of the day from attending. An impressive list of forty or more celebrities was compiled by the Countess's first biographer, Aaron Seymour. Many of these names may mean little or nothing to readers today, yet they were the great and noble of the eighteenth century, men and women who effectively governed the country and to whom all common citizens were expected to show deference.

"… We must try to imagine the scene. The spacious drawing room of Selina's Chelsea home could scarcely contain its titled clientele. Hooped skirts supported by whalebone frames added so much width to each noble lady's person that doorways of many a stately home had to be enlarged to facilitate entry. But it was the height of each figure that would have astounded a modern visitor. Headpieces rose to such an elevation that the men were near dwarfed by their female counterparts. Described as 'enormous erections of wool and horsehair and false curls, overlaid with a paste of powder, ornamented with flowers', they could add many inches to a woman's height. And for the men, the powdered wigs, ostensibly to hid grey hairs or a balding head, also provided their wearers with protection against the ever-present dangers of head lice and similar annoyances. Decorations of war and office were noticeably displayed, with the wearing of a sword as a universal habit.

"Winsome and eloquent, Whitefield was nevertheless unafraid to speak candidly to these showy representatives of high society …"[10]

Actually, Whitefield loved these occasions at the Countess's mansion. He was the kind of man who could address both common and court with the same

---

10 Faith Cook, *Selina Countess of Huntingdon,* pp. 116–118.

ease and familiarity. Here are some extracts from his letters at this period where he is at the Chelsea mansion in his role as chaplain to her ladyship.

"To Mr. Howell Harris.   Chelsea, Jan. 12, 1749.

"... I am now here waiting for Lord Bolingbroke, and some others, who are coming to hear the glorious gospel. Lord L—— is in town. Our good Lady is going on, and every day increasing her reward in heaven ..."

To another he writes:

"The prospect of doing good to the rich that attend her Ladyship's house, is very encouraging. I preach twice a week, and yesterday Lord Bolingbroke was one of my audience. His Lordship was pleased to express very great satisfaction. Who knows what GOD may do? He can never work by a meaner instrument ..."[11]

The work of the Countess increased and soon she was leasing space at another home with more room in London in Park Street near Hyde Park. What good came from these meetings in light of eternity only heaven knows—but it was one of the few times in history where the gospel was presented so faithfully to the rich and powerful of a nation. The female members of these audiences seemed to be more open to the message of the gospel than were the men. Hence, some "despised followers of the Lamb" included: Lady Chesterfield, Lady Gertrude Hotham, Lady Fanny Shirley, and the Countess Delitz each opened their hearts to the Lord and their homes to Whitefield's preaching labors.

But one of Lady Huntingdon's most lasting and far reaching gospel endeavors was the establishing of a "school of prophets" at Trevecca, near to her friend, Howell Harris's home. It would be here at Trevecca College, where John Fletcher, who was called by John Wesley "the most holiest man in all of London," would settle and be president—at the desire of the Countess. And it would be from Trevecca, after the death of George Whitefield, that Lady Huntingdon would send out student missionaries to Georgia to help at Bethesda Orphan House after it was placed in her charge.[12]

Selina Countess of Huntingdon would finish her earthly labors on June 17, 1791 at the age of eighty three; her work of spreading the gospel message

---

11 *Works,* Vol. 2, pp. 220–221.

12 Trevecca College moved to Cheshunt, Hertfordshire (north of London) in 1792 and was renamed Cheshunt College and was primarily, though not exclusively, for training men for the Congregational ministry. This, in turn, moved to Cambridge in 1905. It merged with the Presbyterian Church of England's Westminster College and from 1972 was the training college for ministers of the newly formed United Reformed Church (formed by a merger of the Congregational Chirch in England and Wales and churches of the Presbyterian Church of England). Westminster College library has some correspondence of the Countess of Huntingdon and George Whitefield and some material relating to Bethesda.

covered more than fifty years! On the last day of her life she uttered to a close friend, "My work is done."

Sir, you are first welcome to America; secondly, to New England; thirdly, to all faithful ministers in New England; fourthly, to all the good people in New England; fifthly, to all the good people of York; and sixthly and lastly, to me, dear sir, less than the least of all.

The minister of York, Rev. Moody,
in his welcome of George Whitefield to his parish.

CHAPTER 34

THIRD VOYAGE TO AMERICA

It is interesting to note that in the last years of his life George Whitefield signed all his letters with the quote from humble Rev. Moody, "less than the least of all." And it was with deep humility that he and Mrs. Whitefield embarked for America in the summer of 1744. Before setting sail they had endured already "deep waters" of grief from the loss of their son. Whitefield had been accosted both verbally (in the press) and physically (by the madman with the cane); and both George and Elizabeth Whitefield were looking forward to a "change of scenery" and the placid, calming environment that the Orphan House in Savannah would provide them. Bethesda was not only a "House of Mercy" it was a *setting of tranquility and peace.* It had been three years since Whitefield had set foot in Georgia—his heart ached for his Orphans and he could not wait to show Bethesda to his new wife. He had hopes she would become its headmistress. His hopes would soon be dashed. Elizabeth could not take the heat of the Georgian summers. So, this disqualified her for the one job he hoped she could fill next to being his wife. She would also learn from this visit to America that she was not physically fit to travel such vast distances in a foreign land—this would be her last visit abroad and one of the few times in their whole marriage where the couple would be together for an extended period of time.

We have a brief notice about the voyage from Dr. Gillies. "In the beginning of August, 1744, Whitefield embarked, though in a poor state of health; and after a tedious passage of eleven weeks, arrived at York."

We have a good picture of this voyage from the pen of Philip:

"He sailed from Plymouth, with nearly a hundred and fifty ships, under several convoys. It was, however, "full six weeks" before they reached the Western Islands. This was owing to the want of wind. When the wind did spring up, one of the vessels, which missed stays, drove right upon his ship;

striking her mainsail into the bowsprit. Whitefield's vessel, being large, sustained little damage; but the other received a blow, which disabled and well nigh sunk her. The cries and groans of her crew, he says, "were *awful!*"

"He had been singing a hymn on deck when the concussion took place. This fact, with the news of the concussion, was communicated to the convoy. It drew out, he says, the remark, 'This is your praying and be damned! With many sayings of the like nature.' He adds, 'this, I must own, shocked me more than the striking of the ship.' It did not, however, stop nor intimidate him. 'I called my friends together, and broke out into these words in prayer:—God of the sea and God of the dry land, this is a night of rebuke and blasphemy! Show thyself, O God, and take us under thine own immediate protection. Be thou our Convoy, and make a difference between those who fear thee, and those that fear thee not.'

"Providence soon made a difference! Next day, a 'violent Euroclydon arose,' which 'battered and sent away our convoy, so that we saw him no more all the voyage.' Whitefield, at first, thought this "no loss"; but when two strange sail appeared in the distance, and preparation was made for action by mounting guns, slinging hammocks on the sides of the ship, and encircling the masts with chains, he (being "naturally a coward," as he says) found it 'formidable to have no convoy. The vessels were, however, only part of their own fleet. This was a pleasant discovery to more than the skulking chaplain in the *holes* of the ship.' The captain, on clearing the cabin, said, 'After all, this is the best fighting.' You may be sure I concurred, praying that all our conflicts with spiritual enemies might at last terminate in a thorough cleansing and an eternal purification of the defiled *cabin* of our hearts.'

"No other accident occurred during the voyage. Its tediousness overcame his patience, however, when he saw the port. In order to land a few hours sooner than the vessel, he went on board a smack in the bay; but darkness coming on she missed her course and was tossed about all night. Unfortunately, too, she had no provisions, and he was so hungry that he 'could have gnawed the very boards.' Besides this he was suffering from "nervous cholic." Altogether he was thoroughly mortified, until a man lying at his elbow in the cabin, began to talk of 'one Mr. Whitefield, for whose arrival the *new lights* in New England' were watching and praying. 'This,' he says, 'made me take courage. I continued undiscovered; and in a few hours, in answer, I trust, to new-light prayers, we arrived safe.'

"He was received at York by a physician, once a notorious deist, who had been converted under his ministry. This was a signal providence; for in about half an hour after he entered the doctor's house, he became racked with cholic, and convulsed from the 'waist to the toes.' A 'total convulsion' was apprehended by the physician. He himself dreaded *delirium,* and implored his weeping wife and friends not to be 'surprised if he uttered any thing wrong.' Both fears, however, were soon allayed: but he was brought so low that he could not 'bear the sound of the tread of a foot, or the voice of friends.' Four days elapsed before nature could be relieved; and for weeks he had to be carried like a child. The fact is, he had eaten 'eagerly' of some *potatoes,* during his gnawing hunger on board the smack, and they had remained on the stomach undigested. They were not even 'discoloured,' when they were removed."[1]

After this stomach disorder left him Whitefield was greeted by Mr. Moody of York with the famous line aforementioned—in his welcoming remarks to Whitefield. This welcome was followed by Mr. Moody by a urgent request that Whitefield preach to his congregation. This he did and after sermon he went over to Portsmouth on the ferry. But, while on the ferry in the bitter cold of the evening, he caught cold and this brought him very low once more in his already weakened condition—he came close to dying and three physicians had to tend to him in the night. Such was his distinctive arrival in America! We turn once more to the interesting pen of Philip for the narrative of Whitefield's illness.

"With his usual simplicity, he says, 'My pains returned; but what gave me most concern was, that notice had been give of my being to preach next evening. I felt a divine life *distinct* from my animal life, which made me, as it were, laugh at my pains, though every one thought I was "taken with death". My dear York physician was then about to administer a medicine. I, on a sudden, cried out, Doctor, my pains are suspended; by the help of God, I'll go and preach,—and then come home and die! With some difficulty I reached the pulpit. All looked quite surprised, as though they saw one risen from the dead. Indeed, I was a pale as death, and told them they must look upon me as a dying man, come to bear my dying testimony to the truths I had formerly preached to them. All seemed melted, and were drowned in tears. The cry after me, when I left the pulpit, was like the cry of sincere mourners when attending the funeral of a dear departed friend. Upon my coming home, I was laid on a bed upon the ground, near the fire, and I heard them say, *'He is gone!'* But God was pleased to order it otherwise. I gradually recovered.'"[2]

Whitefield's health had begun to deteriorate as a young man in his twenties; his constant neglect of his body (all in the name of the Lord) was beginning to take its toll on his already-weak constitution and his predisposition to the disease of asthma. Hence, when he caught cold or was exposed to a virus he did not rest until he recovered (like a normal person) he pressed on and pushed himself literally, often, to death's door. At these times of acute sickness he even admits to how close he feels he is near his dissolution. But God kept restoring his servant until the appointed time in 1770.

Dr. Gillies offers a amusing anecdote regarding the aforementioned illness. Gillies records:

---

1   Philip, pp. 304–305.
2   Ibid. p. 306.

"Though wonderfully comforted within, at my return home I thought I was dying indeed. I was laid on a bed upon the ground, near the fire, and I heard my friends say, 'He is gone.' But God was pleased to order it otherwise. I gradually recovered; and soon after, a poor negro woman would see me. She come, sat down upon the ground, and looked earnestly in my face, and then said, in broken language, 'Master, you just go to heaven's gate, but Jesus Christ said, Get you down, you must not come here yet, but go first and call some more poor negroes.' I prayed to the Lord, that if I was to live, this might be the event."[3]

After this event it took Whitefield three weeks, enfeebled and in great weakness, to reach the city of Boston. The ministers of Boston who loved Whitefield noticed how ill he was and they were amazed at his tenacious work ethic in that he did not rest but pushed himself in faithfully laboring for his Master Emmanuel. Not everyone in New England was glad to see Whitefield. As soon as Whitefield reached Boston he found opposition to his labors. He comments, "Testimonies signed by various ministers came out against me, almost every day." This printed opposition added to his distress, "my situation was rendered uncomfortable." But then we have the following cheerful words:

"But amidst all this smoke, a blessed fire broke out. The awakened souls were as eager as ever to hear the word. Having heard that I had expounded early in Scotland, they begged I would do the same in Boston. I complied, and opened a lecture at six in the morning. I seldom preached to less than two thousand. It was delightful to see so many of both sexes, neatly dressed, flocking to hear the word of God, and returning home to family prayer and breakfast before the opposers were out of their beds. So that is was commonly said, that between early rising and tar water the physicians would have no business."[4]

While many ministers published testimonies *against* Whitefield while in he was in Boston, others came out in his *defense*. We have the following account from Dr. Gillies,

"While some published testimonials against Mr. Whitefield, others published testimonials in his favor; as Mr. Hobby, Mr. Loring, fifteen ministers convened at Taunton, March 5, 1745. The following paragraph is in Prince's *Christian History,* No. XCIV:

"Saturday, November 24, 1744, the Rev. Mr. Whitefield was so far revived as to be able to set out from Portsmouth to Boston, whither he came in a very feeble state the Monday evening after; since which, he has been able to preach in several of our largest houses of public worship, particularly the Rev. Dr. Coleman's, Dr. Sewall's, Mr. Webb's, and Mr. Gee's, to crowded assemblies of people, and with great and growing acceptance. At Dr. Coleman's desire, and

3   Gillies, p. 103.
4   Ibid. p. 104.

with the consent of the church, on the Lord's day after his arrival he administered to them the holy communion. And last Lord's day he preached for Mr. Cheever of Chelsea, and administered the holy supper there. The next day he preached for the Rev. Mr. Emerson of Malden. Yesterday he set out to preach in some towns north, and purposes to return hither the next Wednesday evening, and after a few days to comply with the earnest invitations of several ministers to go and preach to their congregations in the southern parts of the province. He comes with the same extraordinary spirit of meekness, sweetness, and universal benevolence, as before. In opposition to the spirit of separation and bigotry, he is still for holding communion with all Protestant churches. In opposition to enthusiasm, he preaches a close adherence to the scriptures, the necessity of trying all impressions by them, and of rejecting whatever is not agreeable to them, as delusions. In opposition to Antinomianism, he preaches up all kinds of relative and religious duties, though to be performed in the strength of Christ; and, in short, the doctrines of the Church of England, and of the first fathers of this country. As before, he first applies himself to the understandings of his hearers, and then to the affections. And the more he preaches, the more he convinces people of their mistakes about him, and increases their satisfaction."[5]

The actual record of Whitefield's labors in his third visit to America are contained in a journal he wrote but never published. We must address this manuscript now and how it was lost and then finally discovered. For we will quote much from it as it is his *last Journal* composed by his hand (apart from a short journal of his time in Bermuda which John Gillies included in his memoir of Whitefield). We have the following account of this "lost manuscript" from the Rev. Iain Murray:

"It was long believed that apart from the autobiographical material already mentioned, Whitefield wrote no further journals except a short account of his visit to Bermuda in 1748. (The latter was never published and the manuscript does not appear to have survived.) This opinion was held by the most thorough writer who has so far written on Whitefield, Luke Tyerman, [this statement was made before Arnold Dallimore's biography on Whitefield was published] who says: 'From his return to England in 1741, he ceased to write Journals.' But sentences in two of Whitefield's letters which Tyerman records should have made him question the above statement; writing from Piscataqua on March 6, 1745, Whitefield says: 'I am writing another New England journal, which I will send when I leave the country. When that will be, I know not.' Again he writes from the same place six days later: 'I am preparing my sermons for the press, and am also writing another Journal.' Nearly two hundred years were to pass before the original manuscript of this forgotten and unpublished Journal was brought to light. It had been lying, unnoticed by Whitefield's biographers, in the Library of Princeton Theological Seminary since 1816.

---

5   Ibid. p. 104.

"… The difficulty arises when we attempt to answer the question, what happened to it between that date and June, 1816, when we know it was given to Princeton Theological Seminary? The letters just mentioned indicated Whitefield's intention to despatch the *Unpublished Journal* to England. Whitefield's usual practice was to have a copy made of all that he wrote (this was Mrs. Whitefield's task when she accompanied him on this third visit to America), but in this case the generally unfinished state of the manuscript, plus the complete absence of any indication that a copy was ever known to have existed in England, leads us to presume that no copy was ever made. Had one been sent to England it can hardly be doubted that it would have been published. The considerable profits made on his earlier published Journals had been devoted to his Orphanage in Georgia—an institution which was again badly in debt in 1745. His English agents who undertook his publishing would surely have been quick to seize an opportunity to increase his income had it been offered them. One is thus driven to the conclusion that Whitefield abandoned his original intention to publish the Journal.

"… Did Whitefield decide that some of the things in his latest Journal would be "better told" after his death and that its immediate publication might restir and rekindle the opposition which had been rampant when he wrote it? … It is apparent that he became increasingly disinclined to publish accounts of his own work and personal experience … it may be that in failing finally to commit it to the press he was to some extent influenced by the feeling he so often expressed, 'Let the name of George Whitefield perish so long as Christ is exalted!'

"A less important difficulty relates to the whereabouts of the manuscript after Whitefield had laid it aside. We know that more than a year after his last reference to it (March, 1745) he was still carrying it with him, for the paper folio on which the *Unpublished Journal* was written also contains three letters in Whitefield's hand: one written at Christian Bride, Delaware, June 12, 1746; the second at Bohemia, Maryland, June 16, 1746; and a third at Philadelphia, August 7, 1746. So the manuscript was still in his possession on that latter date. The next definite thing we know about it is that seventy years later it was given by Dr. John R. Bayard Rodgers to Princeton Theological Seminary.

"The following version of what happened to the manuscript in the intervening period seems to us to be the most probable: when Whitefield left Philadelphia and Pennsylvania at the end of the summer of 1746 and moved southwards towards Georgia, we know from his published letters that he again stopped at Bohemia, Maryland. He often stayed at the mansion owned by his friend 'good old Mrs. Bayard' in this village and regarded it as his 'Headquarters' in Maryland. It was the kind of place where he could safely leave papers which he did not want to carry about with him. Our suggestion is that he left the *Unpublished Journal* here and, as he evidently never collected it again, it was passed into the hands of the Rev. John Rodgers, who was married to Mrs. Bayard's grand-daughter. He in turn entrusted it to his son, Dr. J. R. Bayard Rodgers, who, after preserving it through the Revolutionary Wars, wisely gave it to the recently formed theological seminary at Princeton in 1816. Upon its rediscovery it was transcribed and edited by the Rev. Earnest E. Eells and published in the December, 1938, number of *Church History*—a journal issued by the American Society of Church History ..."[6]

Iain Murray sums up his conclusions with the matter of this Journal with the words, "The whole matter is, however, still an open question, and it may be some future writer will reach firmer conclusions." This writer is puzzled by the following:

1. Why did Whitefield abandon this Journal in 1746 and never touch it again for the next 24 years?

2. Why leave it at Bohemia in Maryland in 1746 when he would revisit America another four times! This was his third visit to America, he would make seven visits total. Why not pick up the manuscript when he returned in 1751?

We can only wonder why he would leave it with the Bayard family when he came back to America time and time again for the next twenty four years. He must have had this manuscript with him at his last visit to America in 1769–1770. He must have entered Bohemia on his way to Newburyport and left it there before he died at Parson's manse. This is a more probable explanation than his just abandoning it for the next twenty four years. Only God knows. We are thankful that we have the manuscript and that it was re-introduced again!

Back to the narrative of Whitefield's life during this third visit to America. Regarding his frail health we have the following support from the pen of Luke Tyerman who states, "Whitefield was now thoroughly disabled." An interesting letter that is preserved is one that Whitefield's wife wrote detailing their rough sea voyage and his illness. Tyerman wrote:

"Hence the following letter from his wife to a friend in England:—

"Portsmouth, New England, November 14, 1744.

"My dear and honoured master has ordered me to send you an account of our sorrowful, yet joyful, voyage.

"Our captain and others say, they never saw such a voyage; for all nature seemed to be turned upside down. We had nothing but storms, calms, and contrary winds. We frequently expected to go into eternity. Our own provision was spent; and Mr. Whitefield was so ill, that he could not take the ship's provision. The winds were such that we expected to be driven off the coast, after we had seen land a week. We prayed to the Lord to send a boat to take us on shore; and, accordingly, a fishing schooner came, that had not been out for a

---

6   *George Whitefield's Journals* (London: The Banner of Truth Trust, 1960), pp. 14–18.

long time before. Into it we went, hoping to get on shore in three or four hours: but the wind arose, and we were out all night.

"On the morrow, being the 26th of October, we landed, about nine in the morning, at York; where the Lord was pleased to visit my dear and honoured master with a nervous colic, which almost took his life. As soon as he was able to go about, he went out and preached twice a day, which was too much for him. We came from York here; and, in the way, he preached in the rain. On reaching Portsmouth, he preached at candle-light. This laid him up again, and the next day he was judged to be dangerously ill; but, when the time he had proposed to preach arrived, finding himself free from pain, he went out and preached. This had like to have cost him his life, for he became as cold as a clod. But the Lord was pleased to hear prayer from him, and he is now in a fair way.

"The Lord is doing great things here. The fields are indeed ready to the harvest, though there is some opposition. Mr. Whitefield has written several things, which will be sent as soon as printed here. We received your letter by Captain Adams, but Mr. Whitefield has not strength to answer it. He desires you will send the contents of this to all friends, and tell them they may expect letters the first opportunity.

"The Lord is with my dear Mr. Whitefield, and has been through his illness. He says, he was frequently in hopes of entering his eternal rest; but, since he is longer detained, he is fully persuaded it will be for the Mediator's glory. I would enlarge, but my dear master's illness, and many other things, oblige me to subscribe myself your sincere friend and affectionate servant,

"Elizabeth Whitefield."[7]

There are some observations which must be made about this letter from Elizabeth Whitefield. She was not in the best of physical health herself, having gone through a difficult delivery and then, four months later, bearing the grief of burying her infant son. One can only imagine the emotional strain and trauma of the sea voyage on top of such existent stress. Add to this her husband's constant illness and his back and forth journey to the brink of death; the strain of all of this must have shook her already tired constitution. And, on top of this, when her husband has the slightest glimmer of strength he is off again preaching until he collapses once again in her arms to be nursed back to life. It is no wonder she did not travel with him on a regular basis, but rather preferred to remain in England or Wales during his long absences. This was too much for her! And who can blame her?

We must now examine some of the "hostile publications" against Whitefield which were beginning to appear in New England after his arrival in Boston. Tyerman states:

---

7   Tyerman, Vol. 2, pp. 122–123.

"Mrs. Whitefield speaks of '*some opposition.*' What was it? Considerable space will have to be occupied in answering this question. The reader will already have observed that some of the Presbyterian and Congregational ministers of America were as bitterly opposed to Whitefield as were any of the clergy of the Church of England. This will become increasingly manifest by the following details. First of all, however, must be given a rampant letter by a quondam [former] Congregationalist, who was now an Episcopalian of the most fervid type.

"Timothy Cutler, after graduating at Harvard College, was ordained in 1709, minister of Stratford, Connecticut, and soon became the most celebrated preacher in the colony. In 1719, he was chosen president of Yale College. Three years afterwards, he renounced his connection with the Congregational churches; and, in consequence, was dismissed from his presidential chair. Embarking for England, he was, in 1723, ordained, first a deacon and then a priest of the Established Church; and, at the same time, was created a doctor of divinity, by the Oxford University. Soon after, he became rector of Christ Church, Boston, where he continued till his death in 1765. Though haughty and overbearing in his manners, he was a man of great ability, and, in addition to his general learning, was one of the best oriental scholars of the age. In the following letter to the Rev. Dr. Zachary Grey, of Houghton Conquest, Bedfordshire, Dr. Cutler, doubtless, represented the Episcopalian animosity too generally cherished by the clergy of New England.

"Boston, New England, September 24, 1743.

"Whitefield has plagued us with a witness. It would be an endless attempt to describe the scene of confusion and disturbance occasioned by him: the divisions of families, neighbourhoods, and towns; the contrariety of husbands and wives; the undutifulness of children and servants; the quarrels among the teachers; the disorders of the night; the intermission of labour and business; the neglect of husbandry and the gathering of the harvest.

"Our presses are forever teeming with books, and our women bastards. Many of the teachers have left their particular cures, and are strolling about the country. Some have been ordained by them *evangelizers.* They all have their *armour-bearers and exhorters.* In many conventicles and places of rendezvous, there has been chequered work—several preaching, and several exhorting, or praying, at the same time,—the rest crying, or laughing, yelping, sprawling, or fainting. This revel, in some places, has been maintained many days and nights together, with intermission, and then there were the 'blessed outpourings of the Spirit!'

"Some of the *New Lights* [a nick-name given to Whitefield's converts and admires in America, and analogous to that of "Methodists" in England] have overdone themselves by ranting and blaspheming, and are quite demolished; others have extremely weakened their interest, and others are terrified from going the lengths they are inclined to. On the other hand, many of the *Old Lights* (thus are they distinguished) have been forced to trim, and some have lost their congregations; but they will soon raise up a new congregation in any new town where they are opposed. I do not know, but we have fifty, in one place or other, and some of them large and much frequented.

"When Mr. Whitefield first arrived here, the whole town was alarmed. He made his first visit to church on a Friday, and conversed with many of our clergy together, and belied them, me especially, when he had gone. Being not invited into our pulpits, the Dissenters were highly pleased, and engrossed him; and immediately the bells rang, and all hands went to lecture. This show kept on all the while he was here. The town was ever alarmed; the streets were filled with people, with coaches, and chaises—all for the benefit of that holy man. The conventicles were crowded; but he rather chose the common, where multitudes might see him in all his awful postures; besides, in one crowded conventicle, six were killed in a fight before he came in. The fellow treated the most venerable with an air of superiority, but he for ever lashed and anathematized the Church of England, and that was enough.

"After him came one Tennent—a monster! Impudent and noisy—and told them they were all *damned! Damned! Damned!* This charmed them; and, in the most dreadful winter I ever saw, people wallowed in snow, night and day, for the benefit of his beastly brayings; and many ended their days under these fatigues. Both of them carried more money out of these parts than the poor could be thankful for."[8]

No matter how learned Whitefield's opponents were, if they like the Pharisees of old, had religion but no *relationship*, they were merely "blind leaders" who missed God in their midst. The Pharisees missed Jesus. Men like Dr. Timothy Cutler, and others, missed God working through his anointed servants such as George Whitefield and Gilbert Tennent.

Another outspoken opponent of Whitefield at this time was the Rev. Charles Chauncy, D. D. He received his first degree from Harvard at the age of sixteen! Rev. Chauncy was Pastor of the first church in Boston and was eminent for his academics; he printed numerous attacks against Whitefield. Chauncy was a prodigious writer and published many volumes against Methodism and particularly Whitefield. We have the following from Tyerman:

"Dr. Chauncy declares that he 'could never see upon what warrant, either from *Scripture or reason,* Mr. Whitefield went about preaching from one province and parish to another, where the gospel was already preached, and by persons as well qualified for the work as he could pretend to be.' He inclines to think, however, that Whitefield was moved by conceit and a love of popular applause."[9]

8   Tyerman, Vol. 2, pp. 123–125.
9   Ibid. p. 126.

It was Dr. Chauncy's aim to put an end to all "itinerant preaching". Fortunately his efforts were as ineffective as his comments were misguided. But it was men like this, of high learning and of high respect by their colleagues, that sneered at Whitefield and bitterly attacked him. Sadly, their hostile publications caused them great loss at the Judgment for they were fighting against God and did not realize it. Also, all of their efforts just led to more crowds pressing to hear the young evangelist to see what the commotion was all about! Men like Chauncy and Cutler, were great advertisements for the preaching of George Whitefield.

But Whitefield's most caustic critics were the men of Harvard. We see this from the following:

> "The professors and tutors of Harvard College, who, on his previous visit, had been his firm friends, were now induced to join with others against him. 'A confederacy! A confederacy!' he exclaims. 'The clergy, amongst whom are a few mistaken, misinformed, good old men, are publishing halfpenny testimonials against me. Even the president, professors, and tutors at Harvard College, where I was received with so much uncommon respect, have joined the confederacy. Some good friends on my side of the question are publishing testimonials in my favour. Thus you see what a militant state we are in at present. Amidst all this the Word runs and is glorified, and many are so enraged at the treatment I meet with, that they came to me lately, assuring me that if I will consent they will erect, in a few weeks' time, the largest place of worship that was ever seen in America. But ceiled houses were never my aim. I therefore thanked them, but begged to decline their kind offer.'"[10]

This opposition from the men of Harvard was a great disappointment to Whitefield for he had preached to the faculty and students with "great power and acceptance" during his last visit to America. But it was the following comment published in his last Journal that enraged the men of Harvard. Whitefield had written, "As for the universities, I believe it may be said their light is now become darkness—darkness that may be felt—and is complained of by the most godly ministers. I pray God these fountains may be purified, and send forth pure streams to water the city of our God ..." These comments evoked a pamphlet from the president of Harvard and the faculty, entitled, "A Testimony from the President and Professors, Tutors, and Hebrew Instructor of Harvard College, against the Rev. Mr. George Whitefield and his Conduct." We read:

> "The 'Testimony' is dated 'December 28, 1744.' The faculty of Harvard College say, 'We look upon Mr. Whitefield's going about in an itinerant way, especially as he has so much of an enthusiastical turn of mind, as being utterly

---

10 J.R. Andrews, *A Light Rising in Obscurity*, pp. 202–203.

inconsistent with the peace and order, if not the very being, of the Churches of Christ.' Whitefield was charged with 'enthusiasm,' and with being 'an uncharitable, censorious, and slanderous man.' The faculty refer to his 'reproachful reflections' on their college, and denounce his 'rashness and his arrogance; his rashness,' say them, 'in publishing such a disadvantageous character of us, because somebody had so informed him; and his arrogance, that such a young man as he should take upon him to tell what books we should allow our pupils to read.' They pronounce Whitefield's assertion that 'the light of the universities had become darkness,' a 'most wicked and libellous falsehood;' and, in reference to his statement that many of the ministers of the country were unconverted, they say his is 'guilty of gross breaches of the ninth commandment of the moral law.' They bear 'testimony' against him as 'a deluder of the people,' in the affair of contributions for the Orphan House; for he had led the people to believe that the orphans would be under his own immediate instruction, and yet 'he had scarce been at the Orphan House for these four years.' And, in conclusion, they condemn his extempore preaching, and his itinerating, as 'by no means proper.'

"Whitefield replied to the 'Testimony,' in a letter, dated 'Boston, January 23, 1745.' He answers the accusation of the college faculty, that 'he *conducted himself by dreams;*' and 'usually governed himself by *sudden impulses and impressions* on his mind.' As to his having slandered Harvard College, he says, he meant no more than President Holyoke did, when, speaking of the degeneracy of the times, in his sermon at the annual convention of ministers, May 28, 1741, he remarked: 'Alas! How is the gold become dim, and the most fine gold changed! We have lost our first love; and, though religion is still in fashion with us, it is evident that the power of it is greatly decayed.' He further replies to the charges that he was 'a deluder of the people,' and had 'extorted money' from them for his Orphan House. He explains in what sense he was an 'extempore preacher;' denies the charge that he was an 'Antinomian;' and justifies his itinerancy. He concludes thus:—

'I am come to New England with no intention to meddle with, much less to destroy, the order of the New England churches; or to turn out the generality of their ministers, and re-settle them with ministers from England, Scotland, and Ireland, as hath been hinted in a late letter written by the Rev. Mr. Clap, rector of Yale College. Such a thought never entered my heart. I have no intention of setting up a party for myself, or to stir up people against their pastors. Had not illness prevented, I had some weeks ago departed from these coasts. But, as it is not a season of the year for me to undertake a very long journey, and as I have reason to think the great God daily blesses my poor labours, I think it my duty to comply with the invitations that are sent to me, and, as I am enabled, to preach the unsearchable riches of Christ. This indeed, I delight in. It is my meat and my drink. I esteem it more than my necessary food. This, I think, I may do, as a minister of the King of kings, and a subject of his present majesty King George, upon whose royal head I pray God the crown may long flourish. And, as I have a right to preach, so, I humbly apprehend, the people have a right to hear … If the pulpits should be shut, blessed be God! The fields are open. I can go without the camp, bearing the Redeemer's sacred reproach. I am used to this, and glory in it. At the same time, I ask public pardon for any rash word I have dropped, or anything I have written or done amiss. This leads me also to ask forgiveness, gentlemen, if I have done you or your society, in my Journal, any wrong. Be pleased to accept unfeigned thanks for all tokens of respect you shewed me when here last. And, if you have injured me and my conduct (as I think you have), it is already forgiven, without asking, by, gentlemen, your affectionate, humble servant,

'George Whitefield.'

"The whole of Whitefield's letter is in his best style of writing. For *him,* it is terse and pointed; and, of course, it is respectful and Christian. Certainly it contains one retort, which, though perfectly fair, must have been especially stinging. The faculty of Harvard College published their 'Testimony' to prove that Whitefield was 'an enthusiast, a censorious, uncharitable person, and a deluder of the people;' and here Whitefield quietly reminds them that, on May 28, 1741, Mr. Holyoke, their president, preached a sermon, which was afterwards published, in which the following paragraph occurs, respecting himself and his friend Gilbert Tennent:—

'Those *two pious and valuable men of God,* who have been lately labouring more abundantly among us, have been greatly instrumental in the hands of God, in reviving His blessed work; and many, no doubt, have been savingly converted from the error of their ways, many more have been convicted, and all have been in some measure roused from their lethargy.'"[11]

Whitefield's response to the men of Harvard did not placate them. And they responded with another "letter" reiterating their charges against Whitefield of "enthusiasm". It would take time to heal these tender wounds. And it would be George Whitefield, who, in a gesture of kindness would come to the rescue of Harvard College's Library when it was destroyed by fire. We see this from the following extract:

"Whitefield lived long enough to requite this offensive imperiousness. Twenty-nine years afterwards, when the library of Harvard College was destroyed by fire, and while Wigglesworth was still divinity professor, Whitefield, forgetful of the past, did his utmost in begging books for the new library; and, four years later still, while Holyoke was yet president, had the noble revenge of being thanked in the following minute, entered in the college records:—

'At a meeting of the President and Fellows of Harvard College, August 22, 1768, the Rev. G. Whitefield having, in addition to his former kindness to

11 Tyerman, Vol. 2, pp. 132–135.

Harvard College, lately presented to the library a new edition of his Journals, and having also procured large benefactions from several benevolent and respectable gentlemen, it was voted that the thanks of this corporation be give to the Rev. Mr. Whitefield, for these instances of candour and generosity.'"[12]

But it was perhaps due to controversies like these which arose from his printed Journals that Whitefield decided to publish them no more. It is a shame for history is lost. We will turn now to the last Journal we have from his pen. We will follow its narrative in the next chapter.

---

12 Ibid. pp. 136–137.

Was there not a heavenly coincidence in the fact that at the very time when the Holy Club at Oxford was sending out the leaders of the Evangelical Revival which spread over Britain and beyond, the Great Awakening in America was getting under way? And George Whitefield, born again in the Holy Club, was the chosen Apostle of the Lord in linking together these two awakenings that finally merged into the vast movement which changed the religious face of the English-speaking world. He came to America just in time to infuse new energy into the languishing work begun under Edwards, and to thrust it forward like a flaming torch into all the Colonies.

Edward Summerfield Ninde

CHAPTER 35

HIS LAST JOURNAL

This period in the eighteenth century was a time of *greatness*. What God did with men like John and Charles Wesley, John Cennick, Howell Harris, Jonathan Edwards, and George Whitefield was truly remarkable. God has seldom in history moved so mightily in the midst of the Nations.

We must remind ourselves that these men, so mightily used of God, were *just men*. They each had their faults and spiritual frailities—some more obvious than others. Whitefield regretted he wrote so candidly in his Journals because it caused many so much pain. Before we are too critical of him we must remind ourselves that he was just *a youth* when he penned them. What were our letters or diaries like when we were still young? Were we more mature than young Whitefield? As we study the lives of these human, but remarkable, men of the eighteenth century we must agree that it was an Almighty God moving *through them* that made them distinguishable. And we must agree with Richard Owen Roberts comments when he writes: "God chose a host of insignificant men like Whitefield, Grimshaw, Harris Rowland, Tennent, Blair, and Davies and made them His implements in leading one of the mightiest acts of God of all time."

George Whitefield in his "unpublished Journal" tones down his *enthusiasm*. In fact, he underplays much of what takes place. Still, from time to time, we hear him say, "Many, very many, were deeply affected ... Everywhere visible tokens of the Divine Presence attended the word." It is with these considerations in mind that we now go to his last journal record. Thank God it was preserved by God's Hand and given to us for our benefit today!

We will pick up the narrative as he records it on Monday, November 6th, 1744:

"Preached this morning by nine o'clock at the desire of Mr. Moody. The

Lord was with us. Was very ill both before and after dinner, but having engaged myself to Mr. Chandler, the minister of Scotland, about four miles from York, I went thither and through the Divine assistance was strengthened to preach with sweetness and freedom to a very crowded Auditory, and, blessed be God, found myself rather better than worse, after my return to York, thanks be to God in and through Christ Jesus, for this and all his tender mercies.

"Tuesday, November 7th.

"Went in a chaise with Mr. Henry Sherburn, an Eminent and wealthy merchant, to Portsmouth, on Piscatauqua, where we designed to land.

"This Mr. Sherburn is a glorious instance of rich and sovereign grace. He told me he received one of his first impressions under my first sermon at Piscatauqua, four years ago, but afterwards was effectually wrought upon under God, by Mr. Gerring and other [faithful] Ministers who [came] went about preaching the Everlasting Gospel. A notable and evident change has been wrought in him. His house is open to all the faithful Ambassadors and followers of the [Lord Jesus] blessed Jesus and he shows that he believes by being careful to maintain good works—

"In our way we called upon Mr. Moody's son who has been under great dejection of spirit and power of melancholy for several Years. Never did I see anybody more resemble holy Job, when his friends stood at a distance and were afraid to speak to him.

"I could have sat by him and held my tongue a considerable time. He often said, 'Look and learn, look and learn.' 'If such a creature as I am can be used as a step for you to step to heaven by I shall be glad,' with many things to the like persuasion—

"He can talk excellently of many things, but cares by no means to talk of himself. Oh that the day of his mourning may be ended and his latter end greatly increase as Job's did! O that I may remember his advice, *Look and learn,* for how know I what may befall me ere I die?—

"About three in the afternoon we reached Piscataqua. The two ministers of the place and many others came to the River's side to give us the meeting. Mr. Sherburn and his wife gladly received us into their house—

"About 6 I preached to a large and affected Auditory: but perceived my disorder of a nervous cholick returning fast upon me as soon as I had done. Lord let thy will be done in, by, and upon me, whether thou hast designed me for life or death—

"Wednesday, November 8th.

"Was very bad all night and exercised the greatest part of this day with extreme pain, but notwithstanding feel a happiness and joy unspeakable and was enabled to talk powerfully of heaven and the invisible realities of another world to those who came to see me—

"I intended to preach in the evening but was unable. However there being great crowds come out of the Country, and God being pleased for a while to suspend my pain, I ventured out in the afternoon and preached with great power to a large Congregation, till the cries of the people, albeit I begged them to refrain themselves, drowned my voice, [indeed the Saviour's presence was amongst us] a more visible alteration I never saw in any people, and I could scarce believe I was preaching to the same persons that behaved like rocks and stones four years agoe, and I saw and felt so much of the divine presence that I could contentedly have went to my lodgings and died. Oh that I may be ready at whatsoever hour my Lord shall come!

"Monday, November 19th.

"Went out for the first after a long and dangerous relapse which threatened my life more than my late visitations at York.

"My pains were more acute and my weakness much more sensible. The help of another Physician was called in. Nothing was wanting that could be necessary. All were officious to attend upon and sit up with me, and above all the Dear Redeemer was please to give me his presence both to support and compose—

"Several times I seemed to be breathing my last, but I really believe the prayers of God's people brought me back. Some spent a whole night in that exercise and others were instant with God by day. O what am I! The Lord humble me, reward my friends, and for his Dear Son's sake grant that I may come out of this furnace like Gold tried seven times in the fire, and that his people may not be disappointed of their hope. Even so Lord Jesus. Amen!

"Thursday, November 22nd.

"Preached in Mr. Fitche's meeting-house this afternoon with a sweet sense of the divine presence. It was a day appointed for a General Annual Thanksgiving. (A laudable custom!). Oh New England, blessed art thou, for thou hast the Lord for thy God!

"Saturday, November 24th.

"Set out this morning from Portsmouth in a Coach sent for that purpose by my Boston Friends. Was accompanied by Mr. Sherburn, and Mr. John Rodgers Minister of Kittery, who tho' He has been in the ministry these 30 years, told me as we rode in the coach, he was not acquainted with real religion, till I was last in New England.

"The words that struck him were these, 'If I was to draw the picture of a natural man I must go to Hell for a picture to draw him by.' This I think was at Hampton. At York, in my discourse upon the Prodigal, He told me I pulled him all to pieces, and razed his false foundation and led him to a Sin forgiving God. He thought I aimed at and spoke particularly to him, and said He should have cried out, only pride prevented him; but he could not refrain after He had come out of the Meeting house. Ever since He has fought the good fight and appeared boldly in defense of the late great and glorious work of God in New England, and even before his conversion was so eminent for his good sense and rational powers that one said, if Mr. John Rogers should become a New Light He should think there was something in it. And yet, when He did become one, that would not do. Such talk is only like the Jews saying to Jesus, come down from the cross, and we will believe, and yet they did not believe though He performed a greater miracle, even died upon the cross and rose again from the grave. Oh how desperately wicked and treacherous above all things is the heart of man! [What hath the Scrip]. God keep me from trusting it, for thy Dear Son's sake!"[1]

It is important for us to take a moment and reflect on this next paragraph in Whitefield's Journal entry: it is his second visit to Newburyport, Ma. His first, back in 1740, was in a blinding snow storm. Now, four years later he returns. It is here he builds a friendship with the Rev. Jonathan Parsons, the minister in whose house Whitefield died twenty six years later. It was in Newburyport that, in 1756, the Old South Presbyterian Church was built to house Whitefield's congregation and to give him a large meeting house in which to preach. This church still stands today. A visit to it will reveal much. The following can be seen and experienced at this remarkable, historic church:

1. The graves of: George Whitefield, Jonathan Parsons, and Joseph Prince.
2. The plaster cast of Whitefield's unusual skull.
3. The box which contained his stolen forearm.
4. A hand-written letter by GW.
5. The Bible from which he preached.
6. The desk from which he preached.
7. The bell tower with the hand-cast bell by Paul Revere and Son.
8. The original wooden structure cut from timber from 1756.

We must also comment upon the ferry landing in Newburyport where Whitefield often landed. Today it is marked by a historical marker. The Public House which Whitefield mentioned was still standing as a private residence in 2007 but has now been demolished. One can stand on the banks of the Merrimack River and see in the mind's eye Whitefield disembarking from the ferry by the river's edge. He mentions in the following extract that on this date (November 24, 1744) there were two hundred people waiting to greet him as he got off the ferry. This shows the popularity of this man! Most of these had to walk great distance to get there to greet him. We return now to the narrative of his Journal:

"Got over New-bury Ferry between four and five in the afternoon and perceived near two hundred on the shore to see us land. The coachman being not ready, I went in to the Publick House. Many crowded in after me and I gave them as I stood a word of exhortation. The Lord was with me. Several wept, and the woman of the house was very much affected. Who would but drop a word for God, whenever opportunity offers! Who would but shoot an arrow at a venture! God may direct it between the joints and the harness of a poor Sinner's heart. Direct and fasten this there my Almighty Lord and God.

"Reached Ipswich about nine at night and was to preach on the Lord's Day following my arrival but was so fatigued with my journey and catched such a cold that I could scarce move off the bed all day and was in great danger of a relapse.

"Abundance of Dear Souls came from New-Bury and other parts to hear me, but God's thoughts are never our thoughts. However I was made abundantly to rejoice in the Good News.

"Mr. Rogers, the Minister of the place, told me what had been done in the parish both for his own and the other Souls. He is brother of Mr. John Rogers that came with me and has had also a new heart given him too in these and Years last past. He has had a glorious harvest. One woman, he informed me, lately died in triumph and left her love to me as being the first under God, that awakened her out of a state of nature.

"At night the people flocked round my room door full of love and exceedingly desirous to see me, but my illness did not admit of it, however one Gracious Man desired me He might sit up with and watch me. I accepted the offer and was refreshed with his conversation. He told me he believed a hundred were converted by the sermons I preached at New-Bury when last at New England, that His wife lately deceased was one, and himself another.

"Oh what reason have I to lie low at the feet of Jesus! Not unto me, not unto me, but unto thy name be all the glory!

"Monday, November 25th.

"Left Ipswich by seven in the morning and called as I went by his house on the Rev. Mr. Rogers, Father to the person where I lay and senior Pastor of the Church. He came out and saluted me most cordially and was ready to weep for joy. He is a Great-Grandson to the famous Mr. John Rogers of Dedham, and is so happy as to have three Sons and one Grandson who have experienced and now preach the truth as it is in Jesus.

"The Lord was good to me in the way and brought me according to my desire, in a private manner, to Boston, just as it began to grow duskish. I was met by and received into the home of Mr. John Smith, a Merchant, a true Disciple of the Lord Jesus. He was the chief instrument under God of bringing me at this time to New England, and gave me an invitation to his house before we embarked.

"A whole room full of Friends that had notice of my coming were ready to welcome me to Boston, which they did in the most cordial affectionate manner. I spent some time with them, as my health would permit, prayed, and retired to rest, blessing God that He had visited me with sickness in order to prepare me for the mercies he had in store for me.

"[Who is like unto our glorious God in holiness] Oh! What good things hath the Lord laid up for them that fear him, even before the sons of men!

"Tuesday, November 27th.

"Could not help remarking the Psalms in the family.

"Had the pleasure of dining today at my lodging with the Rev. Dr. Sewell, Doctor Coleman, Mr. Foxcroft, and Mr. Prince, four of the Seniour Ministers in Boston and very worthy men [who have distinguished themselves in the late]

"Before dinner we had some free conversation together in relation to some passages in my journals and the present posture of religious affairs in New England.

"I found by what they said and by what I had heard by letters that the work of God had went on in a most glorious manner for near two Years after my departure from New England, but then a chill came over the [churches] work, through the imprudence of some Ministers who had been promoters and private persons who had been happy subjects of it.

"They were apprehensive, I found too, that I would promote or encourage separations, and that some would have been encouraged to separate by my saying in my journal that I found the generality of Preachers preached an Unknown Christ, that the Colleges had darkness in them, even darkness that might be felt, and that speaking of the danger of an Unconverted Ministry, I said, How can a Dead man beget a living Child?

"But I told them that these words were not wrote to imply that it was absolutely impossible but that it was highly improbable that an Unconverted man should be made instrumental to beget souls to Christ.

"I said, I was sorry if anything I wrote had been a means of promoting separations for I was of no separating principles, but came to New England to preach the Gospel of peace [to all that were willing to hear] in my way to Georgia, and promote charity and love among all, [several other things].

"We talked freely and friendly [upon] about several other things, [and dined very comfortably] by which their jealousies they had entertained concerning me seemed to be in a great measure ended, and Dr. Coleman invited me to preach the next day at his Meeting house.

"Oh the benefit of free and open dealing! How wise is the Saviour's advice, If thou hast aught against thy Brother go and tell him of it between him and thee. How much mischief, noise, and division would have been prevented through the Christian world, was this one precept but observed. Bind it O Lord as a frontlet about my head. Write it O my God in the table of my heart!

"Wednesday, November 28th.

"Opened my public administration at Boston this afternoon at Dr. Coleman's meeting house from Rom. 1st, 16th. I am not ashamed of the Gospel of Christ for it is the power of God unto salvation to everyone that believeth. The congregation was very large, several ministers were present and the word was attended with sweet power.

"Several things in the Chapter which I hinted at in the preface of my discourse seemed to be appliable to my circumstances and much affected my heart. For I could thank my God through Jesus Christ, (verse 8th) that the faith and revival of religion in New England was spoken of throughout the world—And I could say (verse 9th) God is my witness whom I serve in my spirit in the Gospel of his Son, that without ceasing I had made mention of the Dear New England people always in my prayers, making request (verse 10th) (if by any means now at length I might have a prosperous journey by the Will of God) to come unto them. For I longed to see them (verse 11) that I might be comforted together with them (verse 12) by seeing as well as hearing what good things God had done for their souls. Neither would I have them ignorant (verse 13) that often times I had purposed to come unto them though I had been often prevented putting it in execution. With great sincerity I could say (verse 14) I am a debtor out of love to Jesus, both to the Greeks and Barbarians, both to the wise and unwise, so that as much as in me is (verse 15) I am ready to preach the Gospel once more in New England.

"Also, though the Gospel was faithfully and fully preached in many parts of it as it was in Rome when the Apostle wrote this Epistle.

"My heart, whilst I was preaching, leaped for joy to think what God had done for Dear New England since I spoke from that pulpit last, and the consideration of the Death and the present happiness of my Dear and Honored Friend, Mr. Cooper, who with his worthy Colleague first introduced me into the pulpit, made me cry out with greater vigor, I am not ashamed of the Gospel of Christ, for there were many living witnesses that it had been the power of God unto the salvation of souls.

"Tho my body was weak and my countenance very pale yet the Lord was with me of a truth and Dr. Coleman immediately, as soon as service was over, engaged me to preach his Lecture on Fryday, which I promised to do.

"Blessed be God for such an Entrance into Boston! How does [God] the Lord delight to disappoint fears and overcome hopes! O blessed is the man, O Jesus, that putteth his trust in Thee!

"Saturday, November 30th.

"Preached a preparation sermon, yesterday in the afternoon for the Rev'd

Doctor Coleman, and again in this afternoon for the Rev'd Dr. Webb at his meeting house, where it was observed the Gracious God generally appeared most when I was last in [Boston] New England.

"The Congregations were very large at both places, and many people's prejudices, which had been raised in their minds upon a surmise that I would encourage separations and countenance disorders, I found wore away apace.

"I preached on Fryday upon Christ's Love to us and today upon the marks of our love to Him. Sweet was the power that attended the word preached, and my soul was delighted to hear worthy Mr. Webb (an Israelite indeed) inform me how full his hands were for fiveteen [sic. Ed.] months successively in speaking to souls under concern and how many had been added to his Church during the late Revival of Religion in New England. Surely God has done for them great things. Holy and Reverend be His Name!

"The Lord also comforted my soul by sending many to my lodgings to bless God for what He had done for their souls under my ministry when in Boston, last. My health I perceived also to be more confirmed, and my soul longed (if I must continue here below) to be more than ever upon the full stretch for God. May Jesus make me and all his ministers a flaming fire!

"Sunday, December 1st.

"Heard the Rev'd Dr. Coleman preach a sweet sermon this morning upon these words, 'Behold I bring forth my servant the branch,' and after sermon the Doctor having notified to the Congregation that he had asked me to assist him and nobody making any objection, I administered the holy sacrament, and many, I believe, set under the shadow of God's Servant the Branch with great delight and his fruit was pleasant to taste.

"After having dined with Doctor Coleman I went and heard Dr. Sewell upon the Divinity of Jesus Christ. Blessed be God who has yet left unto his people so many Defenders of the faith [and truth as it is in Jesus] once delivered to the Saints.

"Today the blessing of Joseph come upon them. May they be fruitful boughs even fruitful boughs by a well, and may they bear fruit even in old age. Their branches run over the wall."[2]

In the next journal entry dated December the 8th, we see Whitefield's health and stamina pick up as he began to preach more often. We must remind ourselves he was still a young man of only twenty-nine! Yet he had the constitution of a man much older. He mentioned his sickness and we cannot help but think that this included his asthma. As asthma is a progressive disease that worsens over time this must be the case—he had learned to live with this chronic disorder; he may have been born with it, and it became

---

2   Ibid. pp. 526–532.

more of a problem to him as time waned on. But it is good to see his strength return as he writes:

"Sunday, December 8th.

"Preached four times this last week in several meeting houses to very crowded auditories, and once on Thursday afternoon to the poor people in the Work-House, and had the pleasure of finding that the prejudiced persons were more and more [convinced] reconciled to me, especially by the sermon I preached at Worthy Doctor Sewell's on Tuesday on walking with God. A fire happening in the Town I preached on Fryday on Lot's delivery out of Sodom.

"Waited Yesterday as I rode along to Esq'r Ryall's, who sent his chariot for me, to the aged and venerable Mr. Walter of Roxbury, who I heard had some way or other imbibed prejudices against me. He received me civilly but did not expostulate with me upon any particular nor mention anything to me that was the cause of offense to him I suppose on account of the shortness of my visit, being in haste.

"Dined with Esq'r Ryall and lodged at Captain W...s one of the Council. Preached twice and administered the Holy Sacrament for good old Mr. Chivers the most aged, and perhaps the most hearty minister of his age in all New England. I think He told me He was 87 years of age, and had now and then a little pain in his leg, but not so much He said as He had twenty years agoe. His father was older and continued strong to a miracle almost to his dying day. How beautiful, are Grey hairs when found in the way of righteousness. Jesus was with us both in preaching and in administration of the Lord's Supper, and though it was the first time I had ventured to preach twice in a day, since my sickness yet the Lord was pleased to strengthen and comfort me very much and we closed our Sabbath very sweetly at Esq'r Ryall's. Oh Hasten O Lord that time when we shall spend an eternal Sabbath together in they Kingdom!

"Saturday, December 14th.

"Preached on Monday to a large auditory for the Rev'd Mr. Emerson of Maulden, who has appeared and continued singularly steady and zealous in the late revival of Religion. Gave a word of exhortation at Mr. Ryall's in the Evening.

"On Tuesday at the desire of Rev. Mr. Foxcroft, I ventured to preach in his evening Lecture at Doctor Coleman's Meeting and, blessed be God, found it not so prejudicial to my health as was feared it would be.

"On Wednesday I preached in the forenoon at Mr. Webb's, and in the afternoon for the Rev. Mr. Gee, a [zealous promoter of the Gospel of Christ but] dear minister of Jesus Christ.

"On Thursday for the Rev'd Mr. Morehead, the Presbyterian minister, a hearty Friend to the late work, and whose people [kept] spent a whole night in prayer for my recovery from sickness.

"On Fryday I went to Lyn and preached to a large auditory for the Rev'd Mr. Chivers, grand-son to old Mr. Chivers of Chelsea and I trust like minded with him. In the evening I returned and expounded at Mr. Ryall's and this afternoon came to Concord where I had a kind reception from Mr. Bliss and where with some other Boston Friends we began the Sabbath, as is customary in New England, with praising and blessing God for all past mercies, for the outpouring of the Spirit, since we saw one another last, and in praying that we might yet see greater things than [these] ever we saw or heard yet. Even so Lord Jesus, Come quickly. Amen and amen.

"Saturday, December 21st.

"Preached thrice on the Lord's Day and once on Monday with great sweetness and freedom to large and very affected auditories at Concord. [Had much of the divine presence in conversation] Had much of the divine presence in private conversation both days, and near access to God in our social addresses to Him. I scarce knew how to go away, but having engaged myself before, I rode after sermon in a Chaise, about 14 miles, to Redding, to the house of the Rev'd Mr. Hobby, a person of great abilities; but one that is not ashamed to own [that] (and which indeed is visible to all his Friends) that He has been greatly changed for the better, both as to principles and practise, in the glorious visitation of God's Spirit to New England, and who declared, before I came, that if no other minister would invite me to preach, his pulpit would be open.

"[On Tuesday afternoon as also in the evening]

"On Tuesday [even] afternoon and again in the evening I preached in it to large Auditories. [On Wednesday] My last sermon was very awakening.

"On Wednesday I preached twice at Wooburn, 5 miles from Redding, for the Rev'd Mr. Jackson. It was a snowy day but the congregation was large. My Lord helped me in delivering his word and there seems to be a stirring among the dry bones. After the sermon we went to the seat of Mr. Ryall's who came with some more Friends to hear me at Wooburn. I expounded at his house as usual and went to Boston the Next day and preached at three o'clock in the afternoon at the Meeting house of the Rev'd Mr. Checkly and again in the evening at the Rev'd Doctor Coleman's.

"The Lord was with me at both seasons as well as also on Fryday Evening at the Rev'd Doctor Sewell's. The congregation as well as a sense of the divine presence seemed to increase more and more; and good Doctor Sewell, after sermon, said unto me, "Vive et vige" [Lord] Holy Father send thy Almighty fiat to it for Jesus Christ's sake.

"Set out this morning in a [very] great storm of snow in order to go to [Du] Weymouth, but was obliged to stay by the way on account of the weather, at the home of Treasurer Foy, Father-in-Law of the Rev'd Mr. Cooper, from whom, as well as from several of his family, I received great tokens of civility and respect. May the Lord [reward] return them and all my kind friends ten thousand fold into their bosom!

"Sunday, December 22nd.

"Had a sweet opportunity for a little-wished-for retirement last night at Milton. Publick notice being given and the morning being fair I thought it my duty to gone on to Weymouth where I was engaged to preach for the Rev. Mr. Bayly.

"I rode on horseback, a thing I had not done before for near six months. The weather was very sharp; but the Good Lord preserved me from hurt.

"When I came to Weymouth found Yesterday's violent storm made people think that I would not come. The congregation was small, but there seemed to be a very considerable melting and moving among them.

"After sermon one came to be under awakenings and in the afterpart of the Evening I was sweetly entertained by Mr. Bayly's giving me an account not only of what the Lord had done for his people, but also a gracious turn He himself had met with from the most High about three years agoe. Though he had been settled and reckoned a pious Minister near twenty years.

"O how far may persons go and how long may they be overseers over a flock before they are taught by the Holy Ghost experimentally to feed them! Turn, O Lord, all that preach and do not know Thee as thou hast turned this thy Servant and so shall they be turned!

"[Monday] Thursday, December 26th

"Rode on Monday to Duxbury, 16 miles from Weymouth, whither I was invited by the Rev'd Mr. Veisy, Minister of the place, and who also dates his conversion abut four years back. There I preached in the evening but to a very small congregation, because I was not expected on account of the storm, and many have looked upon Mr. Veisy as their Enemy because since his awakening He has told them the truth.

"The next morning I preached again to a larger and more affected Auditory and went afterwards in company with several Dear Ministers of Jesus Christ to Plymouth, 6 miles from Duxbury, where I was enabled to preach an evening Lecture in loving labour with Freedom and power to a numerous and attentive congregation.

"On Wednesday I preached thrice and on Thursday twice, to yet larger and larger auditories. Many ministers were present, and He that holdeth the stars in his right hand, was peculiarly present also."[3]

Whitefield traveled next to Plymouth, Hallifax, and Bridgewater where while he was preaching at the meeting house of the Rev'd Mr. Porter, he encountered great cries from the people. He wrote, "There was much people and some crying out, and as it did not give offense and as I thought country people could not so well restrain themselves as those of a more polite Education in the Town, I did not so much insist upon them holding their peace, especially as they did not prevent my speaking so as to be heard." Whitefield celebrated New Year in East-town where on New Year's Day he preached twice to "crowded auditories". We pick up the narrative on January 5th, 1745 for it was here that Whitefield named a fellow preacher whom in this edition of the journal (edited by Earnest E. Eells, who published it in 1938) is erroneously identified. Eells identified the "blind boy" as "probably Joseph Amos, the blind Indian preacher"; but Whitefield actually named the preacher, "one Young Prince" and this is none other than the Rev. Joseph Prince, the famous blind preacher who labored with Whitefield across New England. As a matter of fact, this same blind preacher, Joseph Prince, shared the distinction of being buried alongside Whitefield in the crypt at the Old South Church in Newburyport, MA—they lie side-by-side to this day (along with the Rev. Jonathan Parsons, in whose home Whitefield died).

Here now is that narrative of the "Young Prince":

"Saturday, January 5th.

"Preached once this morning for the Rev'd Mr. Fisher, not to a very large Auditory, or so deeply an affected once as was to be seen elsewhere. However we could say, God was with us, and after sermon, I rode near twenty miles in company with a Dear Young Candidate for the ministry and one Young Prince called The Blind Boy in that pamphlet signed A. M. which I answered when last in Scotland.

"He is about 24 years of age, and was first wrought upon, as he told me, when I preached on the Common that day that terrible accident fell out at Mr. Checkly's Meeting-house about four years agoe. I am told he has an excellent memory as well as a sound experience of a change of heart and life. He has been approbated by several Ministers and preached frequently in the late times. He is now chiefly near Trutown and Tiverton where there is no settled [minister] Pastor. He meets with acceptance and if He had proper books and a person to read to Him I think He would make a useful Judicious Preacher of a Crucified Jesus. Well might it be foretold of Emmanual that he was to open the eyes of the Blind. O that all saw so much loveliness in Christ as this Blind Boy does!"4

This blind preacher, Joseph Prince, memorized the Bible by people reading it to him and he went on to be one of the most used men of God during the years after the Awakening. He rode on his horse all over New England preaching the Gospel. It has been said that Rev. Prince preached to

3   Ibid. pp. 532–536.
4   Ibid. pp. 540–541.

thousands during his life. The whole story on this remarkable blind preacher has not been told. Perhaps someday a biography will be written on this remarkable man who lies beside George Whitefield in the tomb awaiting the trump of God! What a magnificent day that will be when the angel blows the heavenly trumpet and the dead in Christ rise first. In that tomb beneath the pulpit at the Old South First Presbyterian Church in Newburyport there will be three who rise up: Jonathan Parsons, George Whitefield, and Joseph Prince!

We now return to the narrative of Whitefield's labors in America in 1745:

"Reached Attleboro, near 20 miles from Deighton, about 8 last night. A place that has been most highly favored indeed, above many others in the present day. Was comforted with a letter I received from Charles-Town which [I heard] informed me of the welfare of the family at Bethesda and that they had heard the news of my arrival. Blessed be God!

"Preached twice and [help] assisted the Rev'd Mr. Wells in administering the Holy Communion of the body and blood of Christ. But a sweeter sacrament I scarce ever saw. King Solomon showed Him in the gallery, nay He sat at his Royal Table. He brought his people into his banqueting house, and his banner over them was love.

"The communicants seemed to be filled as with New wine, and I believe it was a feast of fat things to many souls.

"Under both sermons there was a very great concern and melting among the people, which, together with the account Mr. Wells gave me of what God had done in his parish, was very comforting and confirming to my soul.

"After Evening service and taking some bodily refreshments, I rode 6 miles to Wrentham in as cold an air as ever I felt, but my heart was warmed by stopping at a house of a sick woman who had an exceeding great desire to see me. She seemed to be wailing for the consolation of Israel. At her desire I sung and prayed and the next morning she sent me word God had answered prayer, and given her Himself, so thus she could be content without hearing or seeing the Creature.

"O the happiness of having our all in God! Lord when shall this once be?

"Monday, January 7th.

"[Preached in] Reached Wrentham about ten at night and lay very comfortably at the house of the Rev'd Mr. Messenger, who, with his Son-in-Law that lives near him, has been a Cordial promoter of the Glorious work of God. They seemed to be two downright Nathanaels. I preached twice with but little interval, and I believe it was a convicting time for sinners as well as a day of great consolation to the Saints. Many, very many, were deeply affected. Indeed the concern seemed to be general. There was a very great weeping and crying out, but nothing as I saw that was extravagant. One of the Ministers told me,

Our Lord had kept the good wine until the last, and Mr. Haven said He did not doubt but hundreds felt the power of the Everlasting God. To Him and Him alone be all the Glory.

"About an hour after preaching, as I rode near the meeting-house I heard many continuing their cry after Jesus, and about 10 at night I reached Mr. Foy's at Milton, where many Boston Friends received me with great joy, and I trust we were in some degree thankful for the mercies we and God's people had received since I left that [home] house a few days agoe.

"I do not remember I scarce had a pleasanter circuit since I have been a Preacher. I do not know that we have had one dry meeting. Everywhere visible tokens of the Divine Presence attended the word ..."5

The Great Awakening, which began in 1740, was still in force under Whitefield's preaching in New England as late as 1745. God was still manifesting His Presence among the people under Whitefield and other faithful ministers of His Word. How many today can say with Whitefield, "I do not know that we have had one dry meeting" and that "everywhere visible tokens of the Divine Presence attended the word."

Whitefield reached Boston on January 8th and preached in the evening at Dr. Coleman's meeting-house. The record of Whitefield's labors are somewhat scarce here. He informs us in a journal entry in February (no specific date) that he had been now preaching in Boston for a month. We pick up his comments in the following extract:

"Continued preaching for near a month at Boston, sometimes once, sometimes twice a day to very crowded and affected auditories, and [frequently] with much of the divine Presence, and notwithstanding I preached so often, besides exhorting several times a week in my own Lodging and at private houses, yet the people crowded more and more and would my private business have admitted, I might have spent whole days in talking with souls; but I generally sent them to their own Ministers.

"We had two remarkable Sunday Evening Lectures. In the day I attended on stated sermons, and felt much of the Divine Presence, especially under the Ministry of Mr. Webb, and could not help [thinking] blessing God who had yet left himself so many faithful Witnesses in Boston, who preached the truth as it is in Jesus.

"About the last week I opened a 7 o'clock morning Lecture at the Rev'd Mr. Moorhead's meeting house, which to my great surprise and the surprise of hundreds more was so crowded that numbers were obliged to return home because they could not come in.

"People came from all quarters, some 4 or 5 miles off, and it seems very

5   Ibid. pp. 541–543.

delightful to see those who had been used to lie in bed till 8 or 9 in the morning, running to hear the word in a cold winter season, by break of day, and hearing a sermon before the time they usually got up."[6]

Here, in the winter 1745, while in Boston, Whitefield composed his answer to his enemies at Harvard. The answer is dated, "Boston, January 23rd, 1745". He informs us,

"I did not think of continuing in Boston above a week, but the Gentleman of Harvard College having thought proper to publish a testimony against me, I thought it my duty to stay longer in town and employ what time I could redeem from my public administrations and other more immediate avocations, in writing them the following answer."[7]

Whitefield preached his way north of Boston as he made his way to Newburyport where we learn how the Old South Church was founded. He related how a New Meetinghouse "belonging to an Incorporated Society …" These were the original founders of the First Presbyterian Church who called the Rev. Jonathan Parsons from his pastorate in Lyme, Conn. In fact, it was Whitefield himself who recommended Parsons for the job! He wrote of his time in Newbury,

"Sunday, February:

"Went in the morning to public worship at the Rev'd Mr. T…s, and in the afternoon to hear the Rev'd Mr. Lowell and preached about 5 in the Evening to a very large congregation in a persons Court Yard belonging to the Town, where the Lord met both Preacher and Hearers by his spirit. Afterwards I conversed with several at my lodgings, that had been greatly comforted, and from all I could hear, had reason to believe Our Saviour had much people in and about New-bury who like New-born babes were desirous of being fed the sincere milk of the word. Lord give it to them for the Dear Son's sake, and grant they may grow thereby.

"Saturday, February:

"Left New-bury on Monday morning, tho it was somewhat difficult to part with so many souls. Stopped two places on the way and gave an exhortation at each place at the earnest desire of several. God was with us and also brought me in good season to Portsmouth to dear Mr. S———'s where I expected to have been in a few days after I left Boston, little thinking of having so many invitations on the way. But it is not in man to guide his own steps.

"When I came to my lodgings, my thoughts of what God had done for my body and soul, and the door He Himself had opened for my preaching the Everlasting Gospel since I lay there, in all appearance dying and breathing my

---

6   Ibid. pp. 543–544.
7   Ibid. p. 544.

last, caused me to draw near and breathe out my soul to God. I thought it was like Jacob's coming to his pillar.

"All received me with open hearts. I preached on Tuesday, and so every day, generally twice all the week, and redeemed as much time as I could to write to my Dear Friends at home.

"This day I went to visit General Pepperell and his Lady, who have always expressed great concern for me. At their desire I preached from the words out of Ecclesiastes:

"And then returned to Portsmouth where I preached at their request also, another sermon to the Officers and Soldiers engaged in the Expedition [from these words] I spoke with much freedom, and have thought however some things have been not managed so well as some serious persons could have issue that good will come out of it to the people of God. Many of them were stirred up to God. I trust the Lord will deal with others for their sake.

"A general fast was kept on Thursday, on which I preached twice. Under one sermon our Lord humbled the Hearers very much, and I trust He will send forth a prevailing spirit of repentance ..."[8]

There are few notable events recorded from this point in the journal (only several entries are remaining). One statement by Whitefield grabs our attention. He wrote, "As I went along, one of the Captains, having a gun in his hand, wished that it was loaded for he would then [quick] in a few minutes send me either to heaven or hell." Evidently not everyone was happy to see Whitefield! We will end this chapter with the last two journal entries (existent) of this dear man of God:

"Saturday.

"Preached yesterday twice with much of divine power to large Congregations for the Rev'd Mr. Cushing at ... and today once for the Rev'd Mr. Main of Rochester outermost settlement in the province of New Hampshire, where they fetch Masts for the King of Great Briton. They lie most exposed to the Indians and obliged here and adjacent provinces to build Garrisons for their defense.

"But I thought, the situation was very delightful, and could not help looking over the present uninhabited Woods, between this and Canada, with a believing prospect that these howling wildernesses would, ere long, in God's time, be turned into fruitful fields, and that Jesus would take them as being given Him by the Father into his own possession.

"I thought I felt something of what the Patriarch Abraham felt when he saw the Redeemer's day afar off, and rejoiced. We wait for thy visitation O Lord.

---

8   Ibid. pp. 550–551.

"Monday.

"Preached yesterday twice for the Rev'd Mr. Pike, and this morning once for the Rev'd Mr. Wise, of Berwick. All three Golden seasons whenever Jesus was pleased to lift up the light of his countenance upon many souls. The mentioning of the sudden death of a man lately crushed to death in an instant by the rolling of a great Log over his body, was blessed, I believe, to put many in mind of and to set them upon preaching for the latter end.

"Lord grant that impressions made may be abiding and not prove as alas too too many do, like a morning cloud, or the early dew, that passeth away.

"Set out last Monday, very weak in body, and after many discouragements in my mind, upon a new Circuit, Eastward, where I was under an engagement to go if ever I came again to New England.

"The ground being just about to be broken up and the frost not gone out of it rendered riding dangerous.

"But being apprehensive that, taken altogether, this would be the most convenient season, and Messers. Pike, Rogers, and Wise, with several other Friends being willing to accompany me, we went on in the strength of Jesus Christ, and found everything far beyond expectation.

"By Saturday Evening we got as far as North Yarmouth, about a hundred and thirty miles East from Boston."9 [This ends the unpublished Journal—his last].

9 Ibid. pp. 556–558.

The first Methodists were John and Charles Wesley, Mr. Morgan, commoner of Christ Church, and Mr. Kirkham, of Merton College; but the nickname was fastened on the little company while John was in Lincolnshire, assisting his father, the rector of Epworth. When he returned to Oxford in 1730 he took his brother Charles's place at the head of the band, and became for ever after the chief figure of Methodism. University wits called him the 'Father of the Holy Club.' When Whitefield joined the Methodists, which was about the end of 1734 or early in 1735, they were fifteen in number.

James Patterson Gledstone

CHAPTER 36

THE EARLY METHODISTS

Any biography on George Whitefield must include the impact and magnitude of the men called "Methodists". Their far-reaching effect on world evangelism is unequaled in history. Though the denomination of Methodism resembles little of John Wesley's day it is a fact in history that Methodist ministers have done much for the good of the Church and to the glory of God.

The first Methodist martyr was Whitefield's friend William Seward. He was the first atop a long list of Methodist men and women who gave their lives for their faith through the centuries. It was John Wesley who birthed the itinerant "lay preachers" who became the wild west circuit riders who traversed the American frontier with Bibles and tracts in their saddlebags. These men were dedicated and dutiful. They followed close to their founder, John Wesley. In this chapter we will study the breach that occurred among the Methodists and how they broke away to become the *Arminian* Methodists and the *Calvinistic* Methodists. Though Wesley and Whitefield were both ordained Anglican priests they are known for their Methodism.

We are thankful for a grand discovery of "lost papers"; a treasure cache of correspondence between the early Methodists and preserved by The National Library of Wales. We will rely heavily on this material in this chapter to present the lost history of this early correspondence. Much can be gained from reading these letters of "Whitefield and friends" for they reveal an era and epoch in church history that is both enlightening and entertaining; they enlighten because they shed light on George Whitefield's existing Journals and they entertain with such remarks as: "Mrs. Bray and her sister-in-law, Mrs. Tuner, had sent him a pie." We are sure Whitefield enjoyed this special treat! These letters also bring to light the early formation of the

Societies and how the Calvinistic branch broke away to form its own denomination.

Also, little has been said of William Seward by Whitefield biographers. He was a able man who not only financially backed Whitefield, but carried on his business affairs and traveled with him in an indispensable manner. His early death, through martyrdom, was a shock and a hardship to Whitefield; for it left him with mounting debts. We are fortunate to have newly discovered letters of William Seward relating his activities as he traveled with Whitefield and was an eye witness to the revival. This first hand account, from someone other than Whitefield or Wesley, is priceless and important.

We have the following explanation of the nature of these letters provided for us by The National Library of Wales:

> "The Fetter Lane Society is the key to understanding the nature of this collection of letters. The great majority of them from Whitefield and Seward are to members of this society or to the people in London who might have had connections with it … Whitefield had come into close contact with members of the religious societies in London, especially those that met at the *Bible and Sun*. As John and Charles Wesley had done, Whitefield seems to have lodged with two of its members, John Bray and his wife of Little Britain, Aldersgate Street, and in his letters to Bray, Whitefield addresses him as 'My Kind Dear Host' (letter 8), and 'Dearest Gaius' (letter 15).

> "On 1 May 1738, John and Charles Wesley, James Hutton, Henry Piers, vicar of Bexley, and several others met and reconstituted the society which met at the *Bible and Sun* along improved lines. They had asked the advice of the Moravian missionary, Peter Bohler then in London, in formulating the rules of the new society. The resulting constitution was basically of a Moravian type, e.g. the dividing of the membership into small bands to encourage spiritual fellowship. However, the society as founded in May 1738 was a Church of England society although, unlike other Anglican religious societies, it did not exclude non-Anglicans from membership. The society removed to premises in Fetter Lane and attracted many wealthy business families as members and soon acquired a position of importance. It also became the centre of the activities of the Wesleys, and John retained a say in the running of its affairs, although after visiting the Moravian centres of Hernnhut, Heerendyk, and Marienborn, and meeting Count Von Zinzendorf between June and November 1738, he became disillusioned with them, and in July 1740, he quarrelled with the Moravian leader in England, Philip Henry Molther about doctrine and broke away to form his own society at the Foundery, Windmill Hill. In 1742, the Fetter Lane Society became the Moravian's town church.

> "Whitefield was anxious that a true account of his progress should be recorded and made known to his friends. This was the main reason for his keeping a *Journal*. He also urged his correspondents to circulate his letters amongst

themselves. He had originally intended that they should transcribe the 'historical parts' of his letters and send them to John Thorold who was to act as a kind of chronicler. This role was in fact to be filled by James Hutton. It was to him that Whitefield sent the two parts of his first *Journal* from Gibralter and Savannah and which Hutton published in 1738, and it was to him that Whitefield and his business manager, William Seward, sent letters almost daily recording in detail his first preaching campaign in England and Wales, February 1738/9—July 1739. These letters Hutton was to make available to other friends in London and many of them are still preserved in Moravian House, Muswell Hill, London. The Moravians on the continent observed intercession days for their foreign work when letters of missionaries were read out. Extracts from letters read before the Church of Moravian Brethren at Heerendyk, Holland, are contained in letter 40 (21 December 1738). It is possible that the letters collected by Samuel Mason were intended to be read out at similar intercession days at Fetter Lane.

"Of the 109 letters in the volume, 16 are addressed to Whitefield, 45 are written by Whitefield, 14 by his business manager, William Seward, and 34 are written to and from others ...

"The George Whitefield correspondence in the volume belongs to two periods in his career.

a. Letters written to him between the time of his taking deacon's orders (20 June 1736) and his stay in London, awaiting his embarkation for Georgia, and those written by him on board the *Whitaker* and from Gibraltar and Savannah.

b. Letters written to him and by him and his business manager, William Seward, after his return from America and during his first preaching campaign in Bristol, the West Country, and South Wales until his second voyage to America (November 1738—August 1739)."[1]

The importance of the discovery of this cache of lost letters is of high magnitude. They shed light on the early Methodist societies and give us insights into George Whitefield's labors; plus they add a great deal of excitement and information to the already existing record of his selfless life. One additional benefit which adds greatly to the Whitefield body of work are the letters written by William Seward, his business manager and close friend. For it was Seward's financial backing of Whitefield, especially in the Colonies, that enabled the evangelist to buy land and build his Orphan House. We will examine several of the William Seward letters for they give us great detail on the early excitement caused by Whitefield as he began his ministry. Before now, there has been little written about Seward who figured prominently in Whitefield's life, both as a close friend upon whose

---

1 *The National Library of Wales Journal,* Vol. XXVI, Number 3, Summer 1990, pp. 251–253.

advice Whitefield relied heavily, and as a financial backer of Whitefield's enterprises. Add to this the remarkable fact that William Seward was the *first Methodist martyr.*

William Seward was born into a prominent family. He was the fifth son of John Seward (there were seven sons born to this well-to-do family) of Badsey, Worcestershire. William's father, John was steward of Viscount Windsor's estates in the south of Wales. William had earned much of his fortune as a successful stockbroker with the South Sea House. We see more on his life from the following:

"William Seward appears as a resident of the parish of St. Thomas, the Apostle, London, in a list of residents taken on Lady Day 1733. Here he is described as a 'Clerk at ye South Sea House', and in 1735–6 he unsuccessfully sought a directorship in the South Sea Company. His residence was in Cloak Lane. In 1739 he is described by the earl of Egmont as 'a broker in Exchange Alley, by which business he god 8,000.' He was instrumental in reviving the charity schools in London, especially those in Langbourn, Castle Baynard, Billingsgate, and Vintry Wards in the parish of St. George the Martyr and in Hackney. He experienced a religious conversion in 1738 after hearing Charles Wesley expound *Romans* chapter 7 (see Letter No. 90). Charles Wesley records in his *Journal* for Monday, 23 November 1738 'Charles [Graves] brought Mr. W. Seward; a zealous soul, knowing only the baptism of John' and later on Sunday 19 November 'and dined at Mr. Brockman's, where Mr. Seward testified faith'. He acted as Whitefield's business manager during the latter's first preaching campaign in Bristol, the West Country, and South Wales in 1739, and handled the donations collected for the Orphan-House in Georgia. In August 1739, he accompanied Whitefield on his second voyage to Georgia but returned in 1740. On 22 October 1740, he died as a result of being struck by a stone on the head, while preaching to a crowd at Hay-on-Wye and thus became the first Methodist martyr. At the time of his association with Whitefield, William seems to have been a widower with a daughter, Grace, who was being boarded with Elizabeth Hankinson at Islington (see letters 69, 72). Grace daughter of William and Grace Seward was baptized at St. Thomas the Apostle on 15 May 1732. On hearing of William Seward's death, John Wesley went to see her, then aged eight years old. His diary entry for 29 October 1740 reads, 'at Mrs. Mason's, senr. conversed to Miss Seward.'"[2]

With this account of William Seward we will examine with interest some of his early letters concerning Whitefield and what God was doing through this youthful evangelist. We will examine four letters written by Seward during the start of Whitefield's career—they are filled with wonderful descriptions of Whitefield's early labors. We see from the first:

---

2   Ibid. pp. 262–263.

[Letter 49]

WILLIAM SEWARD TO FRANCIS JUKES

Bristol, 20 February 1738/9.

"Dear Brother Jukes,

"I thank you for your kind letter of the 17th. I beg you'd not pay anymore postage for your letters to Brother Whitefield or me. When we first came here, we were much opposed, but our dear brother triumphed over all. On Sunday and yesterday, he preached at three large churches to vast crowds, and yesterday at one of them, viz St Phillip's, collected £18 for the Orphan-House. He expounds and reads prayers every morning to the prisoners and a large congregation at the Castle, and expounds twice most evenings to crowded societies. No places are big enough to contain the numbers that come. This day, our dear brother was prohibited by the chancellor from preaching or expounding any more in his diocese on pain of suspension and excommunication. But our dear brother, not in the least cast down, resolved by the grace of God to proceed accordingly, after praying for the chancellor and praising God for counting him worthy to be thrust out of the synagogues for his name sake. He went directly and read prayers and expounded at the Castle as usual. At a lecture this evening, there were great crowds expecting to hear him preach, which he designed, but was denied the pulpit. This with the chancellor's affair has, I believe, put the city in a ferment. God grant it all may turn, as doubtless it will, to the furtherance of the Gospel.

"I hope you had our dear brother's letter. We have often prayed for you, and I am sure you would hear more from him had he time, but he is behind even of his *Journal*, being engaged daily to breakfast with one friend and dine with another. I thank you for your prayers for us, which I beg you'll continue, for I have great need of them. I rejoice to find you experience and are daily sensible of the divine goodness. What are we that we should be called, when others are left behind? Oh let us never go back but press forwards in the strength of our God, so that seeing our own weakness and insufficiency we may depend wholly on Christ. Let us not rest till we have attained the prize of our high calling. I must now conclude with salutations to all friends, dear brother, your most affectionate servant in Christ,

Wm Seward

P. S. February 21. This day, our dear brother preached on the Mount at Kings Wood to a great company, perhaps 1500 or 2000. In the morning, the Castle was crowded more than ever and two large societies this evening. I believe Satan's kingdom received a great blow today."[3]

As one can easily see the worth of these letters are priceless! When Seward wrote, 'Let us not rest till we have attained the prize of our high calling' little

---

3 *The National Library of Wales Journal*, Vol. XXVII, Number 1, Summer 1991, pp. 80–81.

did he know he would receive his on October 22, 1740 from a blow to his head while preaching.

The next letter, though shorter, is not short of details which intrigue us as we read it. One catches the absolute thrill of being in the audience as Whitefield preached beneath the sky. These were glorious days indeed and how thankful we are to have such a record of them! This letter reveals God's workings among His people:

Letter 52

WILLIAM SEWARD TO EDWARD NOWERS

Bristol, 24 February 1738/9.

"Dear Brother in Christ,

"We are much obliged to you for your kind correspondence. I refer you to Brother Hutton for news. I wish I had time to be as long as you are; we have matter enough to fill whole sheets of paper. Our dear brother is shut out of the pulpits but the Gospel spreads the wider, for he preached on a mount twice this week. Yesterday was much a concourse as I believe eyes never beheld since the Apostle's day. All glory be to our gracious and good God, who enabled our dear brother to preach at 4 o'clock (though he was in bed at 3) and to expound to three societies afterwards, and this day, though still weak in body, to preach at an almshouse, where he stood on the steps with great power, and had a hill-full behind and almost the court before. 'Twas near the road and being market day, the country people had an opportunity to see this great work. Oh 'tis worth going 100, nay 1000, miles to see what's doing here. Tomorrow, we go to the Mount again, and in the morning, to a village about two miles off, where we are to have the sacrament. Let not learning, politeness, or anything keep us from our true happiness. I wish I had more time; I could write to you till midnight. 'Tis now near 11 and the post just going. Salute our dear brother! From, dear brother, you most affectionate servant.

Wm Seward"[4]

What jumps out from the aforementioned account of William Seward is the account of George Whitefield's preaching at four in the morning when he had just retired to bed at 3am! This mention of Whitefield ignoring his body's need for sleep is a pattern which Whitefield cast in stone for his entire career and it is the main cause of his broken health and early demise. No man, no matter how zealous, can live like Whitefield long. Though, in sacrificing his body for the cause of the spreading of the Gospel, Whitefield was enabled to pack into a brief life span of 55 years the activity and

---

4   Ibid. pp. 82–83.

accomplishment of many life spans. He truly lived by his dictum, "I'd rather wear out than rust out!"

The next letter from William Seward describes an incident we are unaware of from existing Whitefield material (his works, journals, and biographies about him) and this is the accidental fall from his horse. Also we have glimpses of the activities of both Griffith Jones and Howell Harris and the religious societies in Wales. We read:

Letter 64

WILLIAM SEWARD TO DANIEL ABBOT

Bristol, 10 March 1738/9.

"Dear Sir,

"I am desirous of and yet unworthy your correspondence. Our dear Brother Whitefield had yesterday a fall from his horse, whereby he sprained his wrist, and by a great providence it was his left wrist. The fall was so violent it was a miracle his bones were not broken. Our dear brother had been an instrument though God of breaking Satan's head so much in Wales, 'tis not wonder he was permitted to bruise his heel a little. Our dear brother is on this as all other occasions very thankful to that God in whose hands he continually is.

"We met our dear Brother Howel Harris, a clergyman, and two dissenting ministers at Cardiff, who took sweet counsel with us all the time we were there for the furtherance of the Gospel in Wales, where, indeed, it flourishes much more than in England and I believe has never, in late years I mean, been so wholly corrupted as England was. Mr. D. Williams, the dissenting minister of Cardiff, is indefatigable night and day in preaching the Word, not only at his Meeting House but from house to house and sometimes in the fields. He is in constant correspondence with Mr. Griffith Jones in promoting the Welsh Charity Schools, which have this infinite advantage above ours that the masters are teachers of true Christianity and labour more to make their scholars (which are all of ages and both sexes) Christians indeed than scholars. Of this sort, there are about 50 schools already established by the ministry of Griffith Jones and other associates who began with only 13s. or 14s., collected at a country church at the Lord's Table. Such is the mighty power of God to bless such unlikely means beyond human conception.

"Mr. Howel Harris has been an instrument under God of raising about 30 religious societies who all pray extempory and from what we can see of them are filled with the spirit. He goes from place to place and preaches or exhorts on a place like a stage, which they raise for him, and he often appoints his meetings at such times and places where revels, cockfightings, etc., are appointed, whereby he has been a mighty instrument of reformation and of pulling down Satan's strongholds which, you may be sure, makes him rage horribly, so that he, Mr. Howel Harris, has been often openly assaulted like our blessed Master and like him has hitherto escaped their hands, his hour not being yet come [John

7:30]. He is now with us here at Bristol and possibly, if God permit, you may be blessed with seeing him face to face in London.

"He discourses for he doth not call it preaching because he is not in orders, though he was offered himself twice to the bishop and was rejected. I say he discourses often for two, three, or four hours together and sometimes all night. He has a settled hoarseness, notwithstanding which he daily goes on and exerts himself so as to make 1500 or 2000 or more hear him being willing to spend and be spent for the good of souls. How does my heart burn within me to hear him and our dear Brother Whitefield tell their experiences and to see how they resemble each other! Our dear Brother Whitefield preached three times in the Town or Country Hall of Cardiff from the bench where the judge sits to try the country prisoners (the church being refused). At one of our sermons a great man of the town got a dead fox and set his hounds to hunt him round the hall and others threw great stones on the tiles over our dear brother's head. But all this only animated him and the hearers the more, and our dear brother publicly wished the disturbers had been present that he might have offered salvation even to them for whom he also publicly prayed. Our dear brother is going again on duty and being a little hindered by his arm and a multitude of affairs on his hands, you'll excuse his writing this post or however, you'll excuse him if he is but short. I must crave pardon for being so inaccurate and beg you will pray I may grow daily in grace, for I am but young in the school of Christ. You and your dear friends have the most earnest prayers of, dear Mr. Abbot, your unworthy brother in Christ,

Wm Seward"5

The last letter we will present from the pen of William Seward is remarkable for its account and descriptions of Whitefield's preaching at Hanam Mount and Moorfields. He also mentions the faithful collections for the Orphan House in Georgia.

Whitefield's wrist is still on the mend and opposition still is strong from the camp of Satan. We see from the following:

Letter 67

WILLIAM SEWARD TO DANIEL ABBOT

Bristol, 16 March 1738/9.

"Dear Mr. Abbot,

"I thank you for your kind favour of the 13th. Since my last, our dear brother's wrist has mended daily, and, I thank God, is almost whole as the other. His surgeon is the spiritual leader of the chief society here and as soon as he had dressed it, he prayed earnestly for a blessing and next morning, our brother found great relief. Thus we see the benefit of praying for each other.

5   *The National Library of Wales Journal,* Volume XXVII, Number 2, Winter 1991, pp. 175–176.

Sunday last in the morning, we had by computation 4 or 5000 at Hanham Mount but the afternoon being cold and some hail falling, the company was not so great at Rose Green as the Sunday before, though there were more coaches. We collected £10 for the Orphan-House and the collectors being the last of the auditors, they were moved as they returned home to praise the Lord for all the mighty works they had seen and heard and this continued by provoking each other till we came even to our lodging, where our brother was gone before and was singing hymns with those in the dining-room to welcome us home. This bold strike against Satan highly offended his vassals and occasioned a fresh volley of bitter words to be sent against us from all quarters. I was in the midst of this multitude which this unusual triumph caused and I bless God I have found comfort and inward joy from it, though many of our weak brethren were offended. But alas, if this offended them, what if they should see our brother storm the enemy in his strong fortress of balls, assemblies, and playhouses, and give him battle, when he has got his army together in Moorfields and at horse-races. Then shall we see how one shall chase 1,000 and two put 10,000 to fight. Mr. Harris has lead the way in Wales among cockfighters, etc., with great success, and our dear brother is eagerly bent to follow him in England.

"The prison was shut against our brother this week by the joint order of the mayor and sheriffs at the instigation, as we are informed, of the chancellor. 'Tis possible hereafter the chief priest may stir up Pilate to thrust him into the prison. However, Satan is so short-sighted as to his main interest that, when he thinks he has gained the greatest victory, he is most foiled, for by this means the Gospel spreads wider in the suburbs and villages round about, where our brother is daily invited to preach. On Monday, he preached in the fields by Bath, where we went to meet Mr. Jones, Mr. Thomson, etc., on Tuesday, at the Fish Ponds near Stapleton, on Wednesday, at Baptist Mills near this city, and yesterday, had appointed at Sisson Hill but the snow hindered.

"We are just going to two villages 10 miles off, where he is to preach today and tomorrow at the workhouse. Oh, my dear brother, I have offered some weak prayers for you and your friends who, I am sure, will strive with us for our spiritual progress, particularly that our dear Brother Whitefield may go on conquering to conquer [Rev. 6:2] till Satan is dispossessed. That no treaty be made with that grand enemy is the earnest prayer of, dear brother, you most affectionate servant in Christ,

Wm Seward."[6]

Of the early Methodists we must examine letters of John Cennick, and John Wesley. First, is a letter written to John Wesley from John Cennick. The split over theology between Cennick and the Wesley's had not yet occurred (1739) but we catch a glimpse of the brewing storm from the following comments:

6   Ibid. pp. 177–178.

"The correspondence which Samuel Mason has copied into his manuscript was written during the period 1737–9 at the very beginning of the Methodist Revival in England and Wales. It was during this period that both John and Charles Wesley experienced their religious conversions and George Whitefield began his ministry and set the example later adopted by the Wesleys of preaching in the fields and streets. The doctrinal dispute over predestination and election which was to split the Methodist movement into Wesleyan Methodism and Calvinistic Methodism had not yet occurred. However, a portent of the forthcoming divisions between Wesley and Whitefield is seen in the letter (No. 93) supposedly from Jenny, a servant maid at Bristol, informing Whitefield of Wesley's attack on predestination in his sermon on Free Grace, preached in Bristol, three days previously."[7]

The following letter by Cennick to John Wesley is obviously before the fallout between the two men over the doctrine of perfectionism and before Cennick becomes Whitefield's assistant.

Therefore we read with much interest the following letter:

Letter 75

JOHN CENNICK TO JOHN WESLEY

Reading, 29 March 1739.

"Dear Brother,

"Forever blessed be the Lord my strength, because he is not slack in his promise as some men count slackness, for when all fled from me and I was left alone, yet was I not alone, for the spirit of my God was powerful upon me and my dear Saviour excited me to courage. By mere providence I did not receive yours till this morning and I dare say you will praise God with me when I relate my reason. On Saturday last the 24th instant, as I conceive it might be past six in the evening, I was inclined to walk to divert my soul in solemn solitude. It was after I had borne the slanders of an incensed people and the slight carriage of my intimate friends. I can't say but I was entirely composed, though just before a gentlewoman had sent to me to know if I had altered my principles, it not, to forbear to hold friendship with her son. This I weighed whether the love I bore to him, which was great, or the love of my crucified Saviour, was most to be desired, and immediately answered in these words, 'Give my service to Mrs. Pidgeon, and when I see the way I have taken displeases my Redeemer, I will readily decline it and be again fond of my acquaintance, but till then I am glad to loose a friend, knowing it is for my Master's sake.' I had scarce been walking an hour ere I thought on the troubles I was brought out of, the cares I had so lately overcome, when Heaven descended into my calm breast and filled me with unutterable joys and such peace that neither world could give or take away. My soul abode in this transporting enjoyment till near 8 o'clock. All this while I had sweet communion with God and his Christ. I triumphed mightily over all the glory of the world, all the reproaches of Christ I esteemed riches, and all the shame I was to share I trampled on and despised. I looked for Satan to disturb me, but he was gone, for the old man to allure me, but that was silent. Within was love and peace, without thankful adoration, amazement, and rejoicing. I beheld the beauty of the Trinity shining on my soul as the sun in his strength. The Lamb of God embraced me as a son of his love, and the Holy Spirit moved prolific on my spirit, as it did once on the confused waters in the creation. My barren bosom flamed as the altar when the bright rays of the Sun of righteousness shined upon me. My soul was ravished with angelic harmony and my heart danced for joy, for lo! I saw the day of peace dawn, the eyelids of the morning were opened and the promised Star of Jesse arose in his glory. Oh for some angel's tongue to tell the beauties that sparkled in his light! But it sufficeth that we believe hereafter we shall all receive of his fullness and be eternal partakers in boundless felicity. And now I was interrupted with the coming of Mrs. Pidgeon and Mr. Mortimer, both inspired with sparks of infernal rage. It pleased God to give me power, not only to silence their perverse disputes, but they went away all serene and peaceable and thanked me for my good company. So may God calm the fury of every opposer and show his truth and salvation to every enemy that hath [done] evil in his sanctuary.

"Now had I received your letter before I had declared the goodness of the Lord to them of mine acquaintance, then perhaps they had readily concluded it to be mere delusion, because you mentioned intercession for my concerns on Saturday, and your encouraging me to fight manfully under Christ's banner.

John Cennick"[8]

As George Whitefield and John Wesley were co-laborers in the revival, before they had their falling out over doctrinal differences, it is refreshing to find this letter from Whitefield to Wesley whereby George informs John he has just visited his mother, Susanna Wesley. The love between these champions of Christ was still warm as we see from the following letter:

Letter 45

GEORGE WHITEFIELD TO JOHN WESLEY

Staple Aswin, Wiltshire, 13 February 1738/9.

"Honoured Sir,

"Your prayer is heard. This morning, I visited your mother, whose prejudices are entirely removed, and she only longs to be with you in your societies at London. Arguments from Tiverton, I believe, will now have but little weight. We parted with a prayer. Brother Hall rejoiced in spirit and so, methinks, will you and brother Charles. Honoured sir, how shall I express my gratitude to you

8   *The National Library of Wales Journal,* Vol. XXVII, Number 2, Winter 1991, pp. 187–188.

for past favours? I pray for you without ceasing. But that is not enough. I want to give you more substantial proofs. Believe me, I am ready to follow you to prison and to death. Today, I was thinking, suppose my honoured friend was laid in a dungeon for preaching Christ. Oh, how would I visit him! How would I kiss his chain and continue with him till midnight singing psalms. Perhaps our friends may think none of these things shall befall us. That I know not but they may be nigh, even at the door As for my part, I expect to suffer in flesh, I believe I shall be exalted. I know I must be first humbled. I am assured you will not be ashamed of me when I am a prisoner. I only suspect myself. But God's grace will be sufficient for me. Let us then, honoured sir, (if such an one as I may give a word of exhortation) follow our Master without the camp, bearing his reproach. Let us cheerfully suffer the loss of all things and lay down our lives for his sake. I refer you to Brother Hutton for news. I pray continually that as your day is, so your strength may be. I pray that you may not only have peace but joy in the Holy Ghost and be filled with all the fullness of God. I know you pray for, honoured sir, your affectionate son in the faith,

G.W.

"I salute all most kindly"9

The following letter from John Wesley to his brother Charles, though brief, is of great interest. It is of interest because it represents the time (1738) that John Wesley was spending time with the Moravians, here in particular Count Zinzendorf, their leader. The Moravians would have some influence on Wesley's theology at least during this period in his life. Here is the letter:

Letter 31

JOHN WESLEY TO HIS BROTHER CHARLES WESLEY

Utph, 7 July O.S. 1738.

"Dear Brother,

"I am now with the Count at his uncle's, the Count of Solms, five or six hours from Marienborn, and have stole an hour to let you know that God has been very merciful to us in all things. The spirit of the brethren is above our highest expectation. Young and old, they breathe nothing but faith and love at all times and in all places. I do not therefore concern myself with smaller points that touch not the essence of Christianity but endeavour (God being my helper) to grow up in these after the glorious example set before me. Having already seen with my own eyes more than 100 witnesses of that everlasting truth, 'everyone that believeth hath peace with God and is freed from sin and is in Christ a new creature.' [Rom. 1:16, 5:1; 6:7; 2 Cor. 5:17].

"See, therefore, my dear brethren, that none of you receive the grace of God in vain, but be ye also living witnesses of the exceeding great and precious

9   Ibid. pp. 77–78.

promises which are made to every one of us through the blood of Jesus. Adieu."[10]

The next letter is from Whitefield to John Edmonds and it is rich with information concerning Whitefield's delay in Deal whereby John Wesley exhibited peculiar behavior. Wesley was aware as his ship arrived into Deal that Whitefield was there on board *The Whitaker* awaiting to sail for Georgia in answer to Wesley's earlier plea and invitation. But now, the discouraged (and still unsaved) Wesley has changed his mind on whether Whitefield should follow his disastorous footsteps to Georgia—he wrote him to inform him GOD has told him otherwise! Fortunately for the people of Georgia (and America!) Whitefield ignored this strange missive from the lot-casting Wesley. We read with interest the following:

Letter 23

GEORGE WHITEFIELD TO JOHN EDMONDS

Deal, 1 February 1737/8.

"Dearest Mr. Edmonds,

"This is the third or fourth time providence has driven us back to the Downs for wise reasons no doubt, but I rejoice in it especially because I have once more heard from dearest Mr. Edmonds, but what does he tell me?—that the clouds have again overshadowed him. I expected as much. We must not be on the Mount long together in this world. No, we should then say it is good for us to be here. God vouchsafes frequently as helps to the weakness of our faith to give us some short glimpses of his divine presence, but we are not able to bear it long. Be strong, therefore, my good friend, and of a good courage, wait patiently on the Lord and he shall exalt you in his due time [1 Pet. 5:6]. Your seeing why God restrained your writing now, because a letter was coming from me, should confirm your faith at other times and satisfy you that, though you know not what God does to you now, yet you shall know hereafter. If a sparrow falls not to the ground without our heavenly Father's knowledge, much less is our understanding taken from us without the eternal purpose of his will.

"My dear friend, I doubt not, has prayed for humility. God is now answering his prayer, for it's by these trials we must be experimentally taught that we are nothing, and can do nothing. God indeed can do it without, but he will not because this is the most effectual way. I am glad to hear you are so sensible of your moroseness and hastiness of temper that has been observed and complained of in you and doubt not but you will strive sincerely to overcome it. For without this you will bring up an ill report of our good Lord and cause the name of our holy Jesus to be scoffed at and ridiculed. From henceforward then, my dear friend, check every motion to sudden anger and be angry with yourself when

---

10 *The National Library of Wales Journal*, Vol. XXVI. Number 4, Winter 1990, p 392.

you are angry without a cause. Consider that your condition as a servant obliges you to obey, so that should your mistress bid you do a wrong thing, if it be not contrary to the will of God, you should submit; may she not do what she will with her own. Oh, dear Mr. Edmonds, you see how free I am with you, because I love you, love you from my soul, love you in the bowels of Jesus Christ [Phil 1:8], love you so that I am always thinking of you and praying for you. Therefore, excuse and accept my freedom.

"I suppose our dear friends will be returned ere you see this. My hearty love to them and tell them I'll write as soon as possible. Their company refreshed my soul. Oh give thanks for their glad tidings of great joy they bring to your ears and desire Mr. Hutton to write down an account of his journey and send it to Mr. Thorold. Mr. J. Wesley is arrived from Georgia. Surprising! He left Deal this morning. I heard from him but did not see him. He bids me follow him to London. I have answered I cannot charge all friends not to discourage but still to press me on and pray that I may tread the winepress alone [Is. 63:3] and never look back. I have not received Mrs. Thornburough's letter. Bid her write again. Do you pay the postage? I suppose that was the reason the last miscarried. Being in a hurry when we set sail, I forgot to send my dear boy his crown, but I'll make it up another time. I laughed to read what Jephtha told me about your giving thanks in the small beer cellar, a special place. Abound, abound, dear friend, in giving thanks for and in writing to, dearest, dearest Mr. Edmonds, every yours,

G.W.

P.S. Tell Mr. Hutton, Mr. Doble received the sermons but expected a letter. Send to Mr. Bell and ask why he has forgot me. I preach here (God willing) tomorrow. I want some sermons on regeneration."[11]

The next letter is remarkable in that it has great importance in its subject matter on the breach between John Wesley and George Whitefield. It is written by a servant maid (Jenny) and it addresses key issues relating to the coming fallout between Wesley and Whitefield. Regarding this letter we have the following insights:

"John Wesley preached his sermon on free grace in Bristol on 29 April 1739. In it he attacked the Calvinist decree of predestination and election. In a letter to James Hutton, Bristol, 30 April 1739, he wrote, 'On Sunday morning (being so directed again by lot) I declared openly for the first hour against 'the horrible decree'', before about four thousand persons at the Bowling Green.'"[12]

The following letter goes into detail about this historic theological event. We are sure that Whitefield's heart sank as he read this telling letter from his friend Jenny the maid. This would be the second occasion that John Wesley made a major move by the "reading of the lot"; it is regrettable that a man

11 Ibid. pp. 385–386.
12 *The National Library of Wales Journal,* Vol. XXVII, Number 4, Winter 1992, p. 440.

like Wesley, of such genius and holiness, would be a slave to such error as the superstitious practice of casting lots for answers!

Here now is that remarkable letter with its Faulkneresque sentences:

Letter 93

JENNY A SERVANT MAID AT BRISTOL
TO GEORGE WHITEFIELD

2 May 1739.

"Reverend Sir,

"The occasion of my writing to you is on my great Master's account. I understand Mrs. Grevel, your sister, is coming to London very soon. I have no self end in this, no prejudice against Mr. Wesley, for I love him dearly and all people, but for the sake of your sister's soul and he that died for you and I and all that shall believe on him strive to establish, confirm, and strengthen her in the perfect ways of God, if peradventure the gracious God, who is all goodness, gives her faith to lay hold on your words, for if ever she comes to the real birth, she will want a great deal of strength to bring forth, and the thoughts of being in Christ once and forever so is very great encouragement, whereas Mr. Wesley tells her and all people in his sermons the best may finally fall away. He said St. Paul was not sure of his salvation and told me we might be in Christ and out tomorrow. I asked him if God was changeable. He said no, but I was, and I told him God's promises were as firm as his throne to all that received them with power. Now you know this manner of talk is very pernicious to a weak believer, but it did me no harm at all, for none can ever persuade me that after God has received a burnt offering of us and shown us all these things, he will destroy us at last. No, I know on whom I have believed and that the Lord Jehovah is the strength wherein I stand, and I am sure I shall be kept by his mighty power through faith unto salvation, for my life is hid with Christ in God, and whom God loves he loves to the end.

"Another of Mr. Wesley's objections is against an election according to grace. He says all the world is elected alike. Now we know the devil tempts, man consents, and so they are deceived and fall under the condemnation of God. But Christ tells me it is impossible to deceive the elect, and there shall none be able to pluck his sheep out of his hands. I could write all night on texts of scripture to prove our elections and our justification by faith, but that would be troublesome and it is needless, since I am writing to one that doeth the will of our Father, and knoweth of his doctrine, and one that God's grace is not bestowed on in vain. I trust in Christ Mr. Wesley will be turned from a Saul to a Paul, and then I shall rejoice exceedingly, but at present he seems to me a second Apollos. The Lord send another Acquila and Persila, his wife, to take him home and direct him in the ways of God more perfectly, for if an angel from Heaven preached any other doctrine than what has been given I am not to believe him. The faith and knowledge I have, God gave it to me, and none but he can take it away and that I know he never will, for I know he will be with me to the end of the world, though Mr. Wesley tells me that is only a promise to his ministers, but it was one God gave me with as much power as ever he did any, when I was afraid I should not persevere. Besides, St. Peter tells us the promise is to us and to our children and as many as believe on the Lord Jesus, and if the testimony of man is great, the witness of God is greater.

"Mr. Wesley has preached three or four sermons against the seventeenth article of our church and does say, if there is predestination to life, there is no need of ordinances nor of the devil to tempt, not considering the goodness of God in giving us such priviledges, which is the only comfort of life, nor the devil's ignorance, not knowing who is elected, for he does not know things to come nor any of our thoughts, but what he himself puts in us, and if we put them in practice, then he knows they have answered his purpose and the ends he sends them for, but blessed be God I am not ignorant of his devices, and through the strength of Christ am resolved to dash out the brains of his Babylonish brats against the stones. Ignorance was the cause of Satan's transgression; had he known the strength of God that he is no wiser than what he is. Again Mr. Wesley said whoever believed in that article (I almost shudder to name it) made God worse than a devil. Now no man knoweth the will of a man but the spirit of a man. But if the sons of Levi take too much upon them, who can help it? It is my belief and my thoughts are quite the contrary. I have charity for all people. I see nothing but the love of God in all things; he is righteous in all his ways, and holy in all his works, and all that he does is good. If the Lord of the Sabbath had not left us a seed, we should be as Sodom and like to Gomorah, and if any man be tempted to sin, let him not say he is tempted of God, for God cannot tempt any man to do evil; it is not God's rejecting man makes him sin but the devil and his own wicked heart, but be it as it will, it is lawful to do what he pleases with his own, but I never meddle with reprobation at all. I have no business with them that are without, and I know none that have hard thoughts of God but the wicked.

"I am sorry Mr. Wesley's doctrine is so contradictory now to what it was at first. No wonder it takes so much, it being so pleasing to the lower appetites of men. Oh here is a charm in our own wills which makes things appear otherwise than they are, the best cause it ruins, and the worst cause it confirms, truth though in itself inevitable, by it seems to be overcome and error obtains a triumph, but they that are born of God are led by the spirit of God, which is the truth, the life and the way. The Lord give Mr. Wesley a right knowledge of himself, that his essence is entire in all places, yet not terminated in any, that he penetrates all substance yet is mixed with none, that he understands yet receives no ideas in himself, that he wills yet has no motion that carries him out of himself, that in him time has no succession, that which is part is not gone and that which is future is not to come, that he loves without passion, is angry without disturbance, repents without change, and then he will see where Christ spoke after the manner of God, and where after the manner of man, and where he spake to his own, and where to the world, and that it was only to believers salvation was sent, and then he will see in the law where God is so kind to bring things down to our weak capacities to understand, and then he will see God gave man his reason to make use of his ordinances, because it was his command. Oh the ever blessed spirit of God that shows us the things of God here through a glass, the Lord send us all where we shall see him as he is.

"Dear sir, I desire you would please to favour me with an answer, and if I have said anything amiss, smite me kindly and show me my error and pardon me, the unworthiest of your servants and less than the least of all God's mercies, for it was the earnest desire I had to do good to your sister's soul, considering the price she was bought with first and last for Jehovah's sake, knowing the terrors of the Lord, we persuade men, myself, and all our family join in humble duty to you and pray that you may receive the sure mercies of David. Amen. Amen.

Jenny"[13]

The remarks of Whitefield's sister are interesting as well as the content. We wish that all true minsters of the Gospel today had the theological foundations that Jenny the servant maid possessed!

In regard to the early Methodists we must name them. In a footnote to letter #6 the editor of the National Library of Wales has this comment regarding those "friends" who accompanied Whitefield as he first traveled. They are:

"Whitefield left London for Deptford on 28 December 1737 accompanied by four friends (see *Journal* 28 December 1737). This letter [#6] indicates that John Bray was one of them. Charles Wesley wrote to his brother, John, from Gravesend, 3 January 1737/8, 'I am here with G. Whitefield, my brothers Hall and Hutton, and a long etc. of zealous friends'—signed Charles Wesley, Westley Hall, George Whitefield, James Hutton, Thomas Burton, John Hutchings, John Bray, John Doble, Jephthah Harris ..."[14]

The next letter written by Whitefield is important because it clears up the authorship of a well-known statement in Methodism, "The whole world is now my parish". This statement, originally attributed to John Wesley was actually penned by Whitefield and then *quoted* by Wesley. As Wesley's fame grew in history and Whitefield's diminished this statement eventually became one as owned by Wesley.

We see this in the following remarks:

"'The whole world is now my parish'. This well-known Methodist maxim has generally been attributed to John Wesley, who writes in an undated letter 'I look upon all the world as my parish'; see F. Baker, op. cit., pp 614–7, who dates it 28 March 1739 and suggests the recipient was the Rev. John Clayton. Whitefield's letter to Daniel Abbot pre-dates Wesley's by twenty-five days.

---

13 *The National Library of Wales Journal,* Vol. XXVII, Number 3, Summer 1992, pp. 299–301.

14 *The National Library of Wales Journal,* Vol. XXVII, Number 4, Winter 1992, p. 434.

Whitefield repeats this statement in another letter, Philadelphia, 10 November 1739 ..."15

We will now examine the brief letter by Whitefield which contains this famous remark:

Letter 59

GEORGE WHITEFIELD TO DANIEL ABBOT

Bristol, 3 March 1738/9.

"Dear Mr. Abbot,

"You do well to rejoice in my behalf; indeed, I thank you most affectionately. Good God! Was ever such love! What, pray for me, and that for so long a time with so many friends? God reward you for it; indeed, I feel the good effects of them. Otherwise, why do I rejoice with joy unspeakable and full of glory? Go on, go on, my dear friends, hold up you hands and our spiritual Amaleck shall never prevail against me. God knows I go out against him only with my sling and my stone, with foolishness of preaching, and lo, I am made mighty through God to the pulling down his strongholds [2 Cor. 10:4]. At present, he is a little retreated, but pray that I may be always upon my watch. Yet a little while and I expect he will break out with double fury. But I defy him I the name of Jesus of Nazareth. Blessed be God! There is a door opened among the colliers. Tomorrow, I go up farther among them. The whole world is now my parish. 'Tis equal to me whether I preach in field or in a church. I find all things happen for the furtherance of the Gospel. I have begun sifting the hearts of the members of the religious societies and intend establishing them in bands.

"Write next post. On Friday, I hope to return from Cardiff. Give thanks on Brother Seward's behalf; he is become a fisher of men [Mark 1:17]. Lo, his opposing brother is looking towards Christ. God will not work by us till we are despised. Oh rejoice in your prospect of suffering, for I am sure God will then work by the hands of, dearest Mr. Abbot, every yours,

G.W."16

The last letter we will present (from a collection of 107) is written by Whitefield while he is laboring in Bath, early in his remarkable career. The letter is valuable for several reasons: the personal aspect of mention of Whitefield's nieces, as well as his growing success as an open air evangelist. We will conclude the chapter with the following comments and extract:

"(Letter 69: Written from Bath; Whitefield was in Bath from 19–24 March. The recipient, Mrs. Hankinson, seems to have kept a boarding school in Islington. Whitefield was making arrangements for his nieces to be boarded with her. Seward's daughter, Gracy, appears to have been already boarded with

---

15   *The National Library of Wales Journal,* Vol. XXVII, Number 4, Winter 1992, p. 438.
16   *The National Library of Wales Journal,* Vol. XXVII, Number 1, Summer 1991, p. 91.

her. See also letter 72. An Elizabeth Hankinson is listed in the rate books for St. Mary's Islington for 1734 and 1736 under Barnsbury Liberty and in the Land Tax Assessment Book for 1739, p. 5, she is listed under 'The Hedge Row' ... She is mentioned in Charles Wesley's *Journal* 21 August 1738: 'Then Mrs. Hankinson, who told me she had been very uneasy since I said a person must be sure of their forgiveness. I preached faith, as the old instrument of justification. She was quite melted down. We prayed, she rose, and said her heart was set at liberty, her burden taken away, and her spirit joyful in Christ her saviour'; 24 September 1738:'and then Mrs. Hankinson, who has lost several boarders, yet is in nothing terrified by her adversaries ... We sang, rejoiced, and gave thanks at Mr. Stonehouse's: and again at Mrs. Hankinson's. I talked with one of her misses, to whom faith had come by hearing.'"[17]

Here now is the last letter from this collection we will present, written by George Whitefield to this Elizabeth Hankinson.

Letter 69

GEORGE WHITEFIELD TO ELIZABETH HANKINSON

Bath, 20 March 1738/9.

"Dear Mrs. Hankinson,

"I have promised you a line a long while and cannot any longer forbear to perform. Great, unspeakably great blessings does our dear Master bestow on me daily. On Sunday (would you think it?), I preached to 20,000 souls at once, and, so good was the God whom I serve that I was supplied with spiritual bread sufficient to feed so great a multitude. Yesterday, I preached to about 4 or 5,000 here in the fields. When I went out, I was weak, languid, and quite shut up, but being emptied of self, I threw myself into the hands of God and scarce ever spoke with greater freedom and power. Before I began, many scoffed, but God caused them to feel me e'er I had done. The Word was like a hammer, a fire in their hearts, and all were hushed into an aweful silence. Oh give thanks for me, dear Mrs. Ankinson, with your whole heart. I think I am now in one of the devil's strongholds, but I hope the Word will be mighty through God to the pulling down some of them. Many shoot out their arrows, even bitter words [Ps. 64:3], but God fills me with such joy in the Holy Ghost that it is but like throwing chaff against a brass wall. Oh free grace in Christ! I suppose you are not without your share of reproach. If you was, I should question whether or not you was a true disciple of Jesus of Nazareth. But if Christ be with and in us, I am verily persuaded we should willingly be cast into a fiery furnace for his name's sake. May we then always feel him dwelling in our hearts by faith.

"Dear Mrs. Ankinson, in about six weeks, I hope to send you two of my nieces. My brother does not care to go above the ordinary price of a country boarding school, but Brother Seward and I will supply the deficiencies. My sister purposes, God willing, to bring up her daughter. I believe she is a gracious,

17 *The National Library of Wales Journal,* Vol. XXVII, Number 4, Winter 1992, p. 439.

little girl, and the mother, I think, is seeking Christ. Can she lodge conveniently anywhere at Islington? What things are necessary for the little girl?

"Oh, dear Mrs. Ankinson, my heart is full indeed; it is full of a sense of God's love. I am unworthy of his mercies and yet he will be gracious. Oh, dear Mrs. Ankinson, give thanks for your most affectionate brother in Christ,

G.W."[18]

---

18   *The National Library of Wales Journal,* Vol. XXVII, Number 2, Winter 1991, p. 181.

Williams [*Solomon Williams, grandson of Solomon Stoddard*] *was a dedicated friend of Whitefield's and repeatedly invited him to preach from his pulpit. On the last occasion of Whitefield's preaching there, a large number of persons from outside the parish had assembled. Following the main meeting, after Whitefield and the pastor had left, they remained in the church carrying on a Bedlam-like gathering. The leaders were summoned back by a godly deacon. To gain the attention of the boisterous mob, Whitefield stomped violently on the floor and cried, "What means all this tumult and disorder?" The noisy crowd declared they were so filled with the Holy Spirit they could not forbear their demonstrations of joy. To this the saintly evangelist replied, "My dear children, you are like little partridges, just hatched from the egg. You run about with egg shells covering your eyes, and you cannot see and know where you are going." The disorders ceased, and they went quietly home.*

Richard Owen Roberts

CHAPTER 37

PREACHING IN BERMUDA

There is a old chapel in the Bermuda islands where a old plaque reads:

In Memory
Of
The Rev. George Whitefield's
Visit to these islands in 1748
During his brief stay He
"Went everywhere preaching the word and
the hand of the Lord was with him."
Within these walls on eight consecutive Sabbaths He
"Held forth the word of life."
Many got a blessing and
"There was great joy".
"He that winneth souls is wise."
1886

Regarding this inscription on the plaque in Christ Church, Bermuda it is noted in Dallimore's biography on Whitefield that this church is in St. George, Bermuda. We have the following correction:

"The plaque is in Christ Church Presbyterian Church in Warwick, Bermuda (not in St. George as Dallimore incorrectly states on page 224 of Volume 2 of his biography on Whitefield). Warwick is ten miles westward down the island."[1]

Now that the location is established let us examine Whitefield's labors which took place in 1748 on this windswept island. But we first must ask, How did Whitefield end up in Bermuda? An answer is provided by Luke Tyerman who wrote:

---

1   *Whitefield's Works* CD-ROM, Quinta Press.

"Early in the year 1748, Whitefield, instead of embarking for England, set sail for Bermudas. The following letters, to Howell Harris, will explain the reason:—

"Charleston, February 28, 1748.

"By this time, I hoped to have been on my way to England; but, having received no answers to the letters I sent you from New York and elsewhere, and in consequence of other concurring providences, I have been induced to believe it my duty to go to Bermudas. My dear yoke-fellow will stay behind, in these parts; and I purpose to return to her early in the fall. Meanwhile, I expect to hear from you; and, if my way seems clear, I do not despair of seeing you before Christmas next. Think not hard of me, my dear man, for thus deferring to come to you.

"I hope I have now got very near sufficiency for the future support of Bethesda. If my friends in England will help me, I hope my arrears will be paid, and my heart be freed from a load which has lain on me for years. If not, the Friend of all will help me. On Him, my eyes wait; and, in obedience to Him, I go once more upon the mighty waters. My dear wife will have a trial in my being absent so long.

"Yours most affectionately and eternally in Christ Jesus,

"George Whitefield".

"On Board the 'Ann,' (Captain Tucker,) bound from

"Charleston to Bermudas, March 6, 1748.

"My Very Dear, Dear Brother,—Just as I was coming on board, yours, dated October 16, was put into my hands. I have read it, and now believe I shall see you sooner than I expected. I have a great mind to come to you from New England. But what will *Sarah* say? I have left her behind me in the tent; and, should I bring her to England, my two families, in America, must be left without a head. Should I go without her, I fear, the trial will be too hard for her; but, if the Lord calls, I can put both her and myself into His all-bountiful hands.

"I am now going, on a fresh embassage, to Bermudas, after having had a profitable winter in these southern parts. Congregations in Charleston have been greater than ever; and Jesus has helped me to deliver my soul. Had I ten thousand lives, He should have them all. Excuse this scribble; I am just come on board.

"George Whitefield."[2]

Poor Elizabeth! One can only imagine Mrs. Whitefield in a strange land and so far away from home and family (where is her daughter during all this traveling?) and her impetuous husband is now leaving her to fend for herself while he goes off again! We can see from the letter to Howell Harris that it

2   Tyerman, Vol. 2, pp. 179–180.

was Whitefield's hope that his wife become the headmistress of Bethesda. "But what shall Sarah [Elizabeth] say? I have left her behind me in the tent; and, should I bring her to England, my two families, in America, must be left without a head." Meaning head-matron or head-mistress. It is not long that Whitefield learns his wife is not cut out for the hardships of the Georgia heat, nor is she interested in living there as headmistress! Sadly, both parties are disappointed. And their long separations did not produce harmony. We now turn again to the pen of Tyerman who writes:

"As every one knows, the Bermudas are a cluster of small islands, in the Atlantic Ocean, nearly four hundred in number, but, for the greater part, diminutive and barren. They were discovered by Juan Bermudas, a Spaniard, about the year 1522; but were not inhabited till 1609, when Sir George Somers was cast away upon them, and established a small settlement. The length of the colony is less than thirty miles, and the population, even at the present day, is not more than ten thousand, one half of whom are black and coloured persons. The soil of the inhabited islands (about five in number) is exceedingly fertile; vegetation is rapid; spring may be said to be perpetual; and fields and forests are clad with unfading verdure. In these clustered islets, Whitefield landed on March 15; and here he spent eleven weeks, generally preaching once, and often twice, a day. In England, it was reported that he was dead. The *Gentleman's Magazine*, for the month of May, in its 'List of Deaths,' had the following:—

'April.—Rev. Mr. Whitefield, the famous itinerant preacher, and founder of the Methodists in Georgia.'

"Fortunately, the rumour had afterwards to be corrected.

"Whitefield met with the greatest courtesy and kindness in Bermudas. The Rev. Mr. Holiday, clergyman of Spanish-Point, received him in the most affectionate manner, and begged him to become his guest. The governor and the council invited him to dine with them. The Rev. Mr. Paul, an aged Presbyterian minister, offered him his pulpit. Colonels Butterfield, Corbusiers, and Gilbert, Captain Dorrel, and Judge Bascombe, gave him hospitable entertainments. He preached in the churches, in the Presbyterian meeting-house, in mansions, in cottages, and in the open air. Colonel Gilbert lent him his horse during his stay; and the gentlemen of the islands subscribed more than £100 sterling for his Orphan House. Some of the negroes were offended at him, because he reproved 'their cursing, thieving, and lying,' and said, 'their hearts were as black as their faces;' but, as a rule, they flocked to hear him, and were powerfully affected by his discourses."[3]

The most abundant information we have on Whitefield's stay in Bermuda is found in Dr. Gillie's work on him, and fortunately for us it is from Whitefield's own pen! Since Whitefield kept no Journal after 1745 (existing

---

3 Ibid. pp. 180–181.

material ends with 1745—unless there is a manuscript by Whitefield still waiting to be found) and therefore any record of his labors must be considered a treasure. This is the last diary/journal record he kept (except for his correspondence) and therefore it is with great interest we read the following account of his labors in Bermuda in 1748. It is regrettable that Gillies omits important names from the manuscript and that he edited it rather than published it in its entirety—since it is now lost! Bearing that in mind we still are thankful for the material; Dr. Gillies informs us:

"Whitefield met with the kindest reception at the Bermudas, and for about a month he preached generally twice a day, traversing the island from one end to the other; but his activity, treatment, success, will best appear from the following extracts from his manuscript journal of that period.

"The simplicity and plainness of the people, together with the pleasant situation of the island, much delighted me. The Rev. Mr. Holiday, minister of Spanish Point, received me in a most affectionate, Christian manner; and begged I would make his house my home. In the evening I expounded at the house of Mr. Savage, at Port Royal, which was very commodious; and which also he would have me make my home. I went with Mr. Savage, in a boat lent us by Captain ——, to the town of St. George, in order to pay our respects to the governor. All along we had a most pleasant prospect of the other part of the island; a more pleasant one I never saw. One Mrs. Smith, of St. George, for whom I had a letter of recommendation from my dear old friend, Mr. Smith, of Charleston, received me into her house. About noon, with one of the council, and Mr. Savage, I waited upon the governor. He received us courteously, and invited us to dine with him and the council at a tavern. We accepted the invitation, and all behaved with great civility and respect. After the governor rose from the table, he desired, if I staid in town on Sunday, that I would dine with him at his house.

"Sunday, March 20. Read prayers and preached twice this day, to what were esteemed here large auditories—in the morning at Spanish Point church, and in the evening at Brackish Pond church, about two miles distant from each other. In the afternoon I spoke with greater freedom than in the morning; and I trust not altogether in vain. All were attentive—some wept. I dined with Colonel Butterfield, one of the council; and received several invitations to other gentlemen's houses. May God bless and reward them, and incline them to open their hearts to receive the Lord Jesus! Amen and Amen!

"Wednesday, March 23. Dined with Captain Gibbs, and went from thence and expounded at the house of Captain F——le, at Hunbay, about two miles distant. The company was here also large, attentive, and affected. Our Lord gave me utterance. I expounded on the first part of the eighth chapter of Jeremiah. After lecture, Mr. Riddle, a counsellor, invited me to his house; as did Mr. Paul, an aged Presbyterian minister, to his pulpit: which I complied with, upon condition the report was true, that the governor had served the ministers with an injunction that I should not preach in the churches.

"Friday, March 25. Was prevented from preaching yesterday by the rain, which continued from morning till night; but this afternoon, God gave me another opportunity of declaring his eternal truths to a large company at the house of one Mr. B——s, who last night sent me a letter of invitation.

"Sunday, March 27. Glory be to God! I hope this has been a profitable Sabbath to many souls: it has been a pleasant one to mine. Both morning and afternoon I preached to a large auditory, for the Bermudas, in Mr. Paul's meeting house, which I suppose contains about four hundred. Abundance of negroes, and many others, were in the porch, and about the house. The word seemed to be clothed with a convincing power, and to make its way into the hearts of the hearers. Between sermons, I was entertained very civilly in a neighboring house. Judge Bascom, and three more of the council, came thither, and each gave me an invitation to his house. How does the Lord make way for a poor stranger in a strange land! After the second sermon I dined with Mr. Paul; and in the evening expounded to a very large company at Counsellor Riddle's. My body was somewhat weak; but the Lord carried me through, and caused me to go to rest rejoicing. May I thus go to my grave, when my ceaseless and uninterrupted rest shall begin!

"Monday, March 28. Dined this day at Mrs. Dorrel's, mother-in-law to my dear friend the Rev. Mr. Smith; and afterwards preached to more than a large house full of people, on Matthew ix. 12. Towards the conclusion of the sermon, the hearers began to be more affected than I have yet seen them. Surely the Lord Jesus will give me some seals in this island! Grant this, O Redeemer for thy infinite mercy's sake!"[4]

There are dates missing from this journal and we can only assume that Dr. Gillies edited them out for his own personal reasons: Whitefield normally kept a *daily record* of his activities—this was the way of the early Methodists! If Whitefield was traveling, writing correspondence, or ill and confined in bed on these missing dates he would have told us. Now we return back to the narrative which contains mention of Whitefield's preaching in the open air at Bermuda:

"Thursday, March 31. Dined on Tuesday, at Colonel Corbusier's; and on Wednesday, at Colonel Gilbert's, both of the council; and found, by what I could hear, that some good had been done, and many prejudices removed. Who shall hinder, if God will work? Went to an island this afternoon, called Ireland, upon which live a few families; and to my surprise, found a great many gentlemen, and other people, with my friend, Mr. Holiday, who came from different quarters to hear me. Before I began preaching, I went round to see a most remarkable cave, which very much displayed the exquisite workmanship

4   Gillies, pp. 108–109.

of Him, who in his strength setteth fast the mountains, and is girded about with power. While I was in the cave, quite unexpectedly I turned and saw Counsellor Riddle, who with his son, came to hear me: and while we were in the boat, told me, that he had been with the governor, who declared he had no personal prejudice against me—and wondered I did not come to town, and preach there, for it was the desire of the people; and that any house in the town, the court house not excepted, should be at my service. Thanks be to God for so much favor! If his cause requires it, I shall have more. He knows my heart: I value the favor of man no farther, than as it makes room for the gospel, and gives me a larger scope to promote the glory of God. There being no capacious house upon the island, I preached for the first time here in the open air. All heard very attentively; and it was very pleasant after sermon to see so many boats full of people returning from the worship of God. I talked seriously to some in our own boat, and sung a psalm, in which they readily joined.

"Sunday, April 3. Preached twice this day at Mr. Paul's meeting house, as on the last Sabbath, but with greater freedom and power, especially in the morning; and I think to as great, if not greater auditories. Dined with Colonel Harvy, another of the council—visited a sick woman, where many came to hear—and expounded afterwards to a great company, at Captain John Dorrel's, Mrs. Dorrel's son, who with his wife, courteously entertained me, and desired me to make his house my home. So true is that promise of our Lord, 'that whosoever leaves father and mother, houses or lands, shall have in this life a hundred fold with persecution, and in the world to come, life everlasting.' Lord, I have experienced the one: in thy good time grant that I may experience the other also!

"Wednesday, April 6. Preached yesterday at the house of Mr. Anthony Smith, of Baylis Bay, with a considerable degree of warmth; and rode afterwards to St. George, the only town on the Island. The gentlemen of the town had sent me an invitation by Judge Bascom: and he, with several others, came to visit me at my lodgings; and informed me, that the governor desired to see me. About ten I waited upon his excellency, who received me with great civility, and told me he had no objection against my person, or my principles, having never yet heard me; and he knew nothing in respect to my conduct in moral life, that might prejudice him against me; but his intentions were, to let none preach in the island, unless he had a written license to preach somewhere in America, or the West Indies: at the same time he acknowledged that it was but a matter of mere form. I informed his excellency that I had been regularly inducted into the parish of Savannah; that I was ordained priest by letters dismissary from my lord of London, and under no church censure from his lordship; and would always read the church prayers, if the clergy would give me the use of their churches. I added farther, that a minister's pulpit was looked upon as his freehold, and that I knew one clergyman who had denied his own diocesan the use of his pulpit. But I told his excellency, I was satisfied with the liberty he allowed me, and would not act contrary to his injunction. I then begged leave to be dismissed, because I was obliged to preach at eleven o'clock. His excellency said he intended to do himself the pleasure to hear me; at eleven the church bell rung. The church bible, prayer book, and cushion, were sent to the town house. The governor, several of the council, the minister of the parish, and assembly-men, with a great number of the town's people, assembled in great order. I was very sick, through a cold I caught last night; but read the church prayers. The first lesson was the 15th chapter of the 1st book of Samuel. I preached on those words, 'Righteousness exalteth a nation.' Being weak and faint and afflicted much with the head-ache, I did not do that justice to my subject, which I sometimes am enabled to do; but the Lord so helped me, that, as I found afterwards, the governor and the other gentlemen expressed their approbation, and acknowledged they did not expect to be so well entertained. Not unto me, Lord! Not unto me! But unto thy free grace be all the glory!

"After sermon, Dr. F——bs, and Mr. P——t, the collector, came to me, and desired me to favor them and the gentlemen of the town with my company at dinner. I accepted the invitation. The governor and the president, and Judge Bascom were there. All wondered at my speaking so freely and fluently, without notes. The governor asked, whether I used minutes? I answered no. He said it was a great gift. At table, his excellency introduced something of religion, by asking me the meaning of the word HADES? Several other things were started about free will, Adam's fall, predestination, &c., to all which God enabled me to answer so pertinently, and taught me to mix the *utile and dulce* so together, that all at table seemed highly pleased, shook me by the hand, and invited me to their respective houses. The governor, in particular, asked me to dine with him on the morrow; and Dr. F——bs, one of his particular intimates, invited me to drink tea in the afternoon. I thanked all, returned proper respects, and went to my lodgings with some degree of thankfulness for the assistance vouchsafed me, and abased before God at the consideration of my unspeakable unworthiness. In the afternoon, about five o'clock, I expounded the parable of the prodigal son to many people at a private house; and in the evening had liberty to speak freely and closely to those that supped with me. Oh that this may be the beginning of good gospel times to the inhabitants of this town! Lord, teach me to deal prudently with them, and cause them to melt under thy word!

"Friday, April 8. Preached yesterday with great clearness and freedom, to about fourscore people, at a house on David's Island, over against the town of St. George—went and lay at Mr. Holiday's, who came in a boat to fetch me—and this day I heard him preach and read prayers; after which I took the sacrament from him. Honest man! He would have made me administer and officiate; but I chose not to do it, lest I should bring him into trouble after my departure. However, in the afternoon, I preached at Mr. Todd's, in the same parish, to a very large company indeed. The Lord was with me. My heart was warm—and what went from the heart, I trust went to the heart; for many were affected. Oh that they may be converted also! Then will it be a good Friday, indeed, to their souls.

"Sunday, April 10. Dined and conversed yesterday very agreeably with Judge Bascom, who seems to have the greatest insight into the difference between

Arminian and Calvinistic schemes, of any one I have met with upon the island. In the afternoon, I visited a paralytic; and this day preached twice again at Mr. Paul's meeting house. The congregations were rather larger than ever, and the power of God seemed to be more among them. I think I see visible alteration for the better every Lord's day. Blessed be God! In the evening I expounded at Mr. Joseph Dorrel's, where I dined, to a very large company: then went to his kinsman's, my usual lodging on Saturday and Sunday evenings; who with his wife and other friends, seemed kinder and kinder daily. Good measure pressed down, and running over, may the Lord, both as to spirituals and temporals, return into all their bosoms!

"Saturday, April 16. Preached since Lord's day, at five different parts of the island; but was more indisposed one night after going to bed, than I had been for some time. On two of the days of this week, I dined with the president, and Captain Spafford, one of the council, both of whom entertained me with the utmost civility.

"Sunday, April 17. Still God magnifies his power and goodness more and more. This morning we had a pleasing sight at Mr. Paul's meeting house. I began to preach, and the people to hear and be affected as in days of old at home. Indeed, the prospect is encouraging. Praise the Lord, O my soul! After preaching twice to a large congregation in the meeting house, I, at the desire of the parents, preached in the evening a sermon at the funeral of a little boy, about five years of age. A great number of people attended, and the Lord enabled me so to speak, as to affect many of the hearers. Blessed be the Lord for this day's work! Not unto me, O Lord! Not unto me, but unto thy free grace be all the glory!

"Sunday, April 24. The last week being rainy, I preached only five times in private houses; and this day but once in the meeting house; but I hope neither time without effect. This evening expounded at Counsellor Riddle's, who with the other gentlemen treat me with great respect every day. Colonel Gilbert, one of the council, has lent me his horse, during my stay; and Mr. Dorrel, this morning, informed me of a design the gentleman had, to raise a contribution to help me to discharge my arrears, and support my orphan family. Thanks be given to thy name, O God! Thou knowest all things; Though knowest that I want to owe no man any thing, but love; and provide for Bethesda, after my decease. Thou hast promised Thou wilt fulfil the desire of them that fear thee. I believe, Lord help my unbelief, that thou wilt fulfil this desire of my soul. Even so. Amen!"[5]

We must pause in the narrative to make some acute observations on Whitefield's character as a Christian. His desire is to live by his Bible. He did not want to carry debt on the Orphan House in accord with God's Word, "owe no man anything" (Romans 13:8); though he died with the Orphan House in great debt, he labored faithfully all those years to maintain it. He prays for the Lord's help with his unbelief. He never complained to God nor

---

5   Ibid. pp. 109–113.

hardened his heart when circumstances went against him—he always accepted the Sovereignty of God and resigned his own will to it: he lived out his Calvinistic theology and was a great comfort to him throughout his life. Unlike the Israelites who hardened their hearts toward God in the wilderness by their constant complaining and unbelief, Whitefield pressed on, even in fatigue (as we will see in the next journal entry) and always honored his Blessed Emmanuel whom he *modeled so well*. We can learn much from the life of George Whitefield! In 1748 he was 33 and we marvel at his maturity.

As we approach the end of this narrative we are saddened that there exists no further narrative on his daily activities and one can only weep for the loss that the Church has suffered from this lack; but we rejoice in what we have. Praise God! Now we return to his labors in Bermuda:

"Saturday, April 30. Preached since Lord's day, two funeral sermons, and at five different houses in different parts of the island, to still larger and larger auditories, and perceived the people to be affected more and more. Twice or thrice I preached without doors. Riding in the sun and preaching very earnestly, a little fatigued me; so that this evening I was obliged to lie down for some time. *Faint, yet pursuing,* must be my motto still.

"Sunday, May 1. This morning was a little sick; but I trust God gave us a happy beginning of the new month. I preached twice with power, especially in the morning, to a very great congregation in the meeting house; and in the evening, having given previous notice, I preached about four miles distant, in the fields, to a large company of negroes, and a number of white people who came to hear what I had to say to them. I believe in all, there were nearly fifteen hundred people. As the sermon was intended for the negroes, I gave the auditory warning, that my discourse would be chiefly directed to them, and that I should endeavor to imitate the example of Elijah, who, when he was about to raise the child, contracted himself to its length. The negroes seemed very sensible, and attentive. When I asked, if they all did not desire to go to heaven, one of them, with a very audible voice said, 'Yes, sir.' This caused a little smiling; but in general every thing was carried on with great decency; and I believe the Lord enabled me so to discourse, as to touch the negroes, and yet not to give them the least umbrage to slight, or behave imperiously to their masters. If ever a minister in preaching, needs the wisdom of the serpent to be joined with the harmlessness of the dove, it must be when discoursing to negroes. Vouchsafe me this favor, O God, for thy dear Son's sake!

"Monday, May 2. Upon inquiry, I found that some of the negroes did not like my preaching because I told them of their cursing, swearing, thieving, and lying. One or two of the worst of them, as I was informed, went away. Some said, they would not go any more. They liked Mr. M——r better, for he never told them of these things; and I said, their hearts were as black as their faces. They expected, they said, to hear me speak against their masters. Blessed be God, that I was directed not to say any thing, this first time, to the masters at all, though my text led me to it. It might have been of bad consequence, to tell them their duty, or charge them too roundly with the neglect of it, before their slaves. They would mind all I said to their masters, and, perhaps, nothing that I said to them. Every thing is beautiful in its season. Lord, teach me always that due season, wherever I am called, to give either black or white a portion of thy word! However, others of the poor creatures, I hear were very thankful, and came home to their master's houses, saying, that they would strive to sin no more. Poor hearts! These different accounts affected me; and upon the whole, I could not help rejoicing, to find that their consciences were so far awake.

"Saturday, May 7. In my conversation these two days, with some of my friends, I was diverted much, in hearing several things that passed among the poor negroes, since my preaching to them last Sunday. One of the women, it seems, said, 'that if the book I preached out of, was the best book that was ever bought at London, she was sure it had never all that in it, which I spoke to the negroes.' The old man, who spoke out loud last Sunday, and said, 'yes,' when I asked them whether all the negroes would not go to heaven, being questioned by somebody, why he spoke out, answered, 'that the gentleman put the question once or twice to them, and the other fools had not the manners to make me any answer; till, at last, I seemed to point at him, and he was ashamed that nobody should answer me, and therefore he did.' Another, wondering why I said negroes had black hearts; was answered by his black brother thus: 'Ah, thou fool! Dost thou not understand it? He means black with sin.' Two more girls were overheard by their mistress, talking about religion; and they said, 'they knew, if they did not repent, they must be damned.' From all which I infer, that these negroes on the Bermudas are more awake than I supposed; that their consciences are awake, and consequently prepared in a good measure, for hearing the gospel preached unto them.

"Sunday, May 8. This also, I trust, has been a good Sabbath. In the morning I was helped to preach powerfully to a melting, and rather a larger congregation than ever, in Mr. Paul's meeting house; and in the evening, to almost as large a congregation of blacks and whites as last Sunday in the fields, near my hearty friend, Mr. Holiday's house. To see so many black faces was affecting. They heard very attentively, and some of them now began to weep. May God grant them a godly sorrow that worketh repentance not to be repented of!

"Friday, May 13. This afternoon preached over the corpse of Mr. Paul's eldest son, about twenty four years of age; and by all I could hear, and judge of by conversing with him, he did indeed die in the Lord. I visited him twice last Lord's day, and was quite satisfied with what he said, though he had not much of the sensible presence of God. I find he was a preacher upon his death bed: for he exhorted all his companions to love Christ in sincerity; and blessed his brother and sister, and, I think, his father and mother, just before his departure. A great many people attended the funeral. I preached on Luke vii. 13. 'And when the Lord saw her, he had compassion on her, and said unto her, weep not.' Many were affected in the application of my discourse, and, I trust, some will be induced, by this young man's good example, to remember their Redeemer in the days of their youth. Grant it, O Lord, for thy dear Son's sake.

"Sunday, May 15. Praise the Lord, O my soul, and all that is within me praise his holy name! This morning I preached my farewell sermon at Mr. Paul's meeting house—it was quite full; and, as the president said, above one hundred and fifty whites, besides blacks, were around the house. Attention sat on every face; and when I came to take my leave, Oh! What a sweet, unaffected weeping was there to be seen every where. I believe there were few dry eyes. The negroes, likewise, without doors, I heard weep plentifully. My own heart was affected; and though I have parted with friends so often, yet I find every fresh parting almost unmans me, and very much affects my heart. Surely, a great work is begun in some souls at the Bermudas. Carry it on, O Lord! And if it be thy will, send me to this dear people again. Even so, Lord Jesus. Amen!

"After sermon, I dined with three of the council, and other gentlemen and ladies, at Captain Bascom's; and from thence went to a funeral, at which Mr. M——r preached: and after that, I expounded on our Lord's transfiguration, at the house of one Mrs. Harvey, sister to dear Mr. Smith, of Charleston. The house was exceedingly full, and it was supposed above three hundred souls stood in the yard. The Lord enabled me to lift up my voice like a trumpet. Many wept. Mr. M——r returned from the funeral with me, and attended the lecture; as did the three counsellors, with whom I conversed freely. May God reward them, and all the dear people of the island, for those many favors conferred on me, who am the chief of sinners, and less than the least of all saints!

"Sunday, May 22. Blessed be God! The little leven thrown into the three measures of meal, begins to ferment, and work almost every day for the week past. I have conversed with souls loaded with a sense of their sins; and, as far as I can judge, really pricked to the heart. I preached only three times, but to almost three times larger auditories than usual. Indeed the fields are white ready unto harvest. God has been pleased to bless private visits. Go where I will, upon the least notice, houses are crowded, and the poor souls that follow are soon drenched in tears. This day I took, as it were, another farewell. As the ship did not sail, I preached at Somerset in the morning to a large congregation in the fields; and expounded in the evening, at Mr. Harvey's house, around which stood many hundreds of people. But in the morning and evening, how did the poor souls weep! Abundance of prayers and blessings were put up for my safe passage to England, and speedy return to the Bermudas again. May they enter into the ears of the Lord of the Sabaoth! With all humility and thankfulness of heart, will I here, O Lord, set up my *Ebenezer:* for hitherto surely thou hast helped me! Thanks be to the Lord for sending me hither. I have been received in a manner I dared not expect; and have met with little, very little opposition, indeed. The inhabitants seem to be plain and open hearted. They have loaded me with provisions for my sea store; and in the several parishes, by a private voluntary contribution, have raised me upwards of ONE HUNDRED POUNDS sterling. This will pay a little of Bethesda's debt, and enable me to make such a remittance to my dear yoke fellow, as may keep her from being embarrassed, or too much beholden in my absence. Blessed be God, for bringing me out of my embarrassments by degrees! May the Lord reward all my benefactors a thousand fold! I hear that what was given, was given exceedingly heartily; and people only lamented that they could do no more."[6]

We cannot leave this chapter without an answer from Whitefield as to *why* he discontinued the practice of publishing his journals from this point forward. It is found in a letter that he wrote while on board the ship carrying him back to England.

Here are his comments:

"June 24, 1748, (on board). Yesterday I made an end of revising all my Journals. Alas! Alas! In how many things I have judged and acted wrong. I have been too rash and hasty in giving characters both of places and persons. Being fond of scripture language, I have often used a style too apostolical, and at the same time I have been too bitter in my zeal. Wild-fire has been mixed with it, and I find that I frequently wrote and spoke in my own spirit, when I thought I was writing and speaking by the assistance of the Spirit of God. I have, likewise, too much made inward impressions my rule of acting, and too soon and too explicitly published what had been better kept in longer, or told after my death. By these things I have hurt the blessed cause I would defend, and also stirred up needless opposition. This has humbled me much, and made me think of a saying of Mr. Henry—'Joseph had more honesty than he had policy, or he never would have told his dreams.' At the same time, I cannot but praise God, who fills me with so much of his holy fire, and carried me, a poor weak youth, through such a torrent, both of popularity and contempt, and set so many seals to my unworthy ministrations. I bless him for ripening my judgment a little more, for giving me to see and confess, and I hope in some degrees to correct and amend some of my former mistakes."[7]

There is no better explanation than this one from the pen of Whitefield as to why he no longer kept a journal. We must remind ourselves, and it does us well to do so, that when he wrote his Journals he was but a youth; a young man in his twenties! We can forgive him any rashness when we remind ourselves of what *we* were like at that young age.

---

6 Ibid. pp. 113–116.
7 Ibid. p. 117.

John Fawcett was born at Lidget Green, near Bradford, Yorkshire, January 6th, 1740. His early training was in the established church, but it was not until he heard Whitefield preaching in the open air at Bradford in 1755 that he came under deep conviction and found the way of peace in Christ Jesus ... The day after hearing Whitefield preach at Bradford, Fawcett heard him speak at Birstal to a crowd estimated at 20,000 strong. He described his experience saying, "I lay under the scaffold, and it appeared as if all his words were addressed to me, and as if he had known my most secret thoughts from ten years of age. As long as life remains, I shall remember both the text and the sermon."

From Richard Owen Roberts, *Whitefield in Print*

CHAPTER 38

RETURN TO ENGLAND

Whitefield had been absent from his native land for four years and in 1748 he returned. On June 30th he landed at Deal and six days later arrived in London. His congregations in London had sorely missed him and he delayed little in contacting old friends.

We see from the following comments:

"One of his first acts, when he stepped ashore, was to write the following hearty and loving letter 'to the Rev. Mr. John or Charles Wesley.'

Deal, July, 1748.

"Will you not be glad to hear that the God of the seas and of the dry land has brought me to my native country once more? I came last from the Bermudas, where the Friend of sinners was pleased to own my poor labours abundantly. I hope, I come in the spirit of love, desiring to study and pursue those things which make for peace. This is the language of my heart:—

'O let us find the ancient way,
  Our wondering foes to move;
And force the heathen world to say,
  See how these Christians love.'

"I purposed to be in London in a few days. Meanwhile, I salute you and all the followers of the blessed Lamb of God most heartily. Be pleased to pray for, and give thanks in behalf of, reverend and dear brother, yours most affectionately in Christ,

'GEORGE WHITEFIELD."

"Apart from his first visit to America, Whitefield had now spent about four years and a half in itinerant preaching throughout England's transatlantic colonies. Except the religious movement, which began at Northampton in 1734, and declined in 1736, the time spent in Whitefield's second and third visits to America covered the entire period of what has been termed 'the great awakening.' What were the results of that remarkable work of God? In reference to the churches of New England only, it has been carefully estimated that from thirty to forty thousand persons were permanently added to their membership. With these also must be joined a large number who, after a time, 'fell away;' and likewise the multitudes who were 'melted' and made to weep by Whitefield's eloquence, but were not converted. Further, it must be kept in mind, that, up to this period, the practice of admitting to the communion all persons, though unconverted, who were neither heretical nor scandalous, was general in the Presbyterian Church, and prevailed extensively among the Congregational churches; the result being, that a large proportion of the members of these churches, though orthodox and moral, were unregenerated. Multitudes of these were now, for the first time, made the subjects of a saving change. Indeed, in some cases, the revival seems to have been almost wholly within the Church, and to have resulted in the conversion of nearly all the members. These, at the best, had been dead weights to their respective communities; but now they became active and valuable workers."[1]

One cannot help but comment that the state of the Church in New England in the eighteenth century was much like the Church in America today! If a revival were to come it would more than likely remain mostly in the Church and most of the converts would be "dead weights"! It is interesting to note the comments from Tyerman regarding the *ministers* before the awakening in New England and how much that reflection mirrors today's pulpits as well!

We see in the following comments:

"Again: it is useless to deny that there were a large number of unconverted ministers, especially in New England. Young men, without even the appearance of piety, were received into the colleges to prepare for the ministry. Graduates, if found to possess competent knowledge, were ordained as a matter of course, quite irrespective of their being born again. The result was, that in New England and in all the colonies, an unconverted ministry, to a lamentable extent, was the bane of the churches. 'The great awakening,' however, reached not only the pews, but the pulpits and the colleges of the Christian community. In the vicinity of Boston only, there were not fewer than twenty ministers who acknowledged Whitefield as the means of their conversion; and in other parts of the country, there were proportionate numbers. This was an incalculable gain. The great curse of the Church was turned into an equally great blessing. Yea, more than this, the revival fully and finally killed the doctrine that an unconverted ministry might be tolerated; and, henceforth, parents felt that they were not doing a worthy deed by consecrating their unregenerated sons to the office of the Christian ministry, and sending them to colleges to be prepared for it.

"Other immediate results of 'the great awakening' might be mentioned, but these are sufficient to evoke the grateful exclamation, '*What hath God wrought!*'"[2]

---

1   Tyerman, Vol. 2, pp. 184–185.
2   Ibid. p. 185.

As we see George Whitefield return to London in 1748 we have to search writings to locate his wife Elizabeth! It is a odd fact that she did not return with him on board "The Betsy" and we must ask the question why? She had been apart from her husband for nearly the full four years as he ranged about the countryside preaching in the colonies and visiting the Bermudas. Where is she during this protracted time? The answer is: at Bethesda. It was his desire for her to become its headmistress and be a mother to the many orphans—this being one of the large reasons for his marrying her. So when we learn (from him) that he has left her behind in America while he sailed for England it is odd—though explanatory.

We see his following remarks which reveal the fact that he was leaving Elizabeth behind at Georgia. He wrote:

"To Mrs. F———.

On board the Betsy, June 2, 1748.

"... The LORD JESUS has blessed my being at Bermudas very much. A good work I trust is begun in many hearts. I am now on board, and the wind is fair. We expect to sail this day. According to my present view, I intend to return to beloved America next year; which is one of the reasons, why I leave my dear yoke-fellow behind. O that I knew how it was with her! But I see that GOD will make those he loves, to live by faith and not by sense ..."[3]

One can only surmise that Elizabeth Whitefield felt abandoned by her husband. Taken from her kin and home in Wales to be left abandoned in a swamp in Georgia under cruel conditions and as overseer of many individuals who were strangers to her in person and in culture must have been a shock to her system. For we find that when she eventually returned to England she no longer desired to travel with her adventurous husband as he ranged all over many lands. And by making this decision (whether by choice of mind or because of poor health) we learn that the briefly happy couple drifted farther and farther apart until Whitefield seldom even mentioned her in his voluminous correspondence.

His voyage back to England was not without adventure. The Betsy was pursued by a large French vessel and was fired upon three times! Whitefield was caustic in his comments about this episode. He remarked, "We gave up all for lost! We were almost defenceless. I was dressing myself to receive our *visitors*. In the mean time our captain cried, 'The danger is over.'"

Also, while on board on "The Betsy" Whitefield wrote a revealing letter to his mother. We read with interest:

---

3   *The Works of George Whitefield*, Vol. 2, p. 142.

"To Mrs. L——,

Deal, July 5, 1748.

"Very dear and Honoured Mother,

"Are you yet in the land of the living, or rather among the dead? Shall I have the pleasure of receiving one more letter from you, and asking your blessing once more? Next post, I hope that the two former of these will be answered in the affirmative, and in a week or two I trust GOD will grant me the last. About a month ago I left the island of Bermudas, where my poor labours have been honoured with many honours. I am now come once more to see my friends in my native country, and settle some affairs, and then return to America again. My dear yoke-fellow I have left behind, to take care of two families. I have been several times just upon the brink of eternity since I saw you, but am now a little recruited. O that my health and strength may be wholly employed for that JESUS, who has done such great things for me! His blood and cross, my ever honoured mother, I trust are exceeding precious to your soul. O that I may see you laden with holiness, and bringing forth much fruit in your old age! I could say more, but have several other letters to write. As I know not how your outward affairs are situated, or where you live for a certainty, I can only send cordial and general salutations to all friends and relations. I hope you will be pleased to let me know whether you stand in need of any thing, and not cease to pray for, honoured mother,

Your ever dutiful though unworthy son,

G.W."[4]

As Whitefield related in his letters that it was his intention to return to America to labor again and to fetch his wife, we marvel that he failed to go back for poor Elizabeth but rather made her sail *alone* back to her native country and estranged husband. No biographer mentions this and even Luke Tyerman in his detailed work on Whitefield seemed to forget about Elizabeth altogether! One has to search diligently to find the answer: in a letter written from London on July 10, 1749 Whitefield wrote to Mr. Pemberton in America, "... My wife arrived about a fortnight ago ..." We hope it was a cordial reunion!

From his arrival in London on July 1, 1748 to August 29, 1751, Whitefield was engaged in much traveling and activity. For it was about this time (from about 1748 on) that Whitefield gradually pulled away from the Societies in Wales which he helped to form. We learn from the following:

"The plain facts are these: within two months after his return from America, in 1748, Whitefield determined to put an end to his official relationship to the Calvinistic Methodists; this determination was gradually carried out; and,

---

4   Ibid. p. 145.

during the last twenty years of his life, he occupied a new position, which must now be noticed. "The question naturally occurs, Why this change of situation? Was it because of the wild-fire of some of the preachers, and the consequent confusion of some of the Societies, with which Whitefield was officially connected? This is improbable; for, whatever might be Whitefield's failings, shirking difficulties was not one of them. The only way to solve the propounded problem is to remember the close relationship which was now, unexpectedly, created between the Countess of Huntingdon and the great preacher. The Countess had recently been an eye-witness of some of the Societies in Wales, and had been filled with gratitude and praise for what she had seen and heard; but, now she seems to have entertained the idea, that both she and Whitefield might be more usefully employed, than by directly associating themselves with the Calvinistic Methodists, and by using their time, talents, and influence in the multiplication of such Societies. Instead of creating new sects out of the Church of England, was it not possible to reform and amend the Church of England itself? And was not the raising up of evangelical and converted ministers the most likely way to bring about such a reformation? Put the pulpits right, and the pews would certainly improve.

"Though direct evidence may be wanting, there can be little doubt, that, this was the grand scheme now revolving in the mind of the illustrious Countess; and that this scheme, in less or greater detail, was revealed to Whitefield, and led to his separation from the Calvinistic Methodists. At all events, as will be seen hereafter, this was one of the chief objects to which Whitefield and her ladyship devoted their time and energies. Whitefield tried to raise up converted clergymen; and the Countess procured them ordination, and built them chapels. The idea was grand,—perhaps inspired,—and the working it out was unquestionably the principal means of effecting the marvellous change which has taken place, since then, in the Established Church."[5]

In 1748, at the age of thirty three, George Whitefield became the Countess of Huntingdon's chaplain. They would prove to be a remarkable team! It was through her society connections that the evangelist was able to witness to most of the royalty and famous of their day. One story is worth mentioning of the famous infidel Lord Bolingbroke who often came to hear Whitefield preach at Lady Huntingdon's Chelsea mansion. Of Lord Bolingbroke it was said:

"This celebrated infidel and Tory, was one day reading Calvin's Institutes. A clergyman (the Rev. Mr. Church, who died curate of Battersea) of his lordship's acquaintance coming in on a visit, Lord B. said to him, 'You have caught me reading John Calvin; he was indeed a man of great parts, profound sense, and vast learning; he handles the doctrines of grace in a very masterly manner.' 'Doctrines of grace!' replied the clergyman, 'the doctrines of grace have set all mankind together by the ears.' 'I am surprised to hear you say so;' answered Lord B., 'you

---

5 Tyerman, Vol. 2, pp. 191–192.

who profess to believe and to preach christianity. Those doctrines are certainly the doctrines of the Bible, and if I believe the Bible I must believe them. And, let me seriously tell you, that the greatest miracle in the world is the subsistence of christianity, and its continued preservation, as a religion, when the preaching of it is committed to the care of such unchristian wretches as you.'"[6]

In September of that year Whitefield once again visited Scotland. He arrived in Edinburgh on the 14th and remained in Scotland until late October. Of this time, much of it in the capital city of Edinburgh, he related his labors to the Countess; we see this from letters he wrote to her:

"To the Countess of Huntingdon.

"Honoured Madam,   Edinburgh, Sept. 20, 1748.

"I suppose, ere this can reach you, your Ladyship will have heard of my being arrived at Edinburgh, and of another particular or two mentioned in Mr. B—— 's letter. This brings your Ladyship an account of very great multitudes flocking to hear the word; but with what success it is attended, I cannot tell yet. Upon my first coming, I was somewhat discouraged at hearing of the death of many of my valuable and leading friends, and of others losing their first love. Besides, the weather was boisterous, some ministers shy, and GOD was pleased to visit me with a great hoarseness. But the prospect is now more pleasant; and I trust, ere I leave Scotland, your Ladyship will have some good news from a far country ..."

"To the Countess of Huntingdon.

"Honoured Madam,   Sept. 29, 1748.

"Am I not too troublesome in writing to your Ladyship so frequently? I fear I am; and yet I am afraid to break your Ladyship's command, 'Write weekly.' Blessed be GOD, I can yet send your Ladyship word that the glorious *Emmanuel* is with me, and countenances my poor administrations. I have met with some unexpected rubs, but not one more than was absolutely necessary to humble my proud heart. 'O my blessed Redeemer, when shall I learn of thee to be meek and lowly! Thou alone, O Lamb of GOD, canst teach me. Sanctify all thy dispensations to this end, and give me always to lie at thy feet.' There, honoured Madam, I am safe: There I believe this letter will find your Ladyship.—May you every moment hear the Redeemer's voice, and be built up continually in your most holy faith. In about a fortnight I purpose leaving Scotland. Several things concur to make me believe that it was right for me to come here. Particulars your Ladyship may expect at my return to town ..."

"To the Countess of Huntingdon.

"Honoured Madam,   Edinburgh, Oct. 15, 1748.

"Though it is late and nature calls for rest, yet I cannot with satisfaction close my eyes unless I write once more to your Ladyship: and what shall I say? I am

6   Gillies, p. 118.

the chief of sinners, and the LORD JESUS magnifies his grace in being long suffering and infinitely bountiful unto me. At Glasgow he has magnified his strength in my weakness, and out of the eater hath brought forth meat. Next week I purpose, GOD willing, to send your Ladyship the substance of a long debate about poor unworthy me, in the synod of Glasgow. Since that, I find the presbytery of Perth (I mean the new-fashioned part of it) has made an act against employing me. Ill-nature shews itself here, but I feel the benefit of it. Congregations are large, and I am enabled to preach with greater power, and feel unspeakable great comfort in own soul. My hoarseness is quite gone off, my bodily health much repaired, and if my enemies shew themselves, I am persuaded the blessed JESUS will bless me to his people more and more.— Some give out that I am employed by the government to preach against the Pretender; and the Seceders are very angry with me for not preaching up the Scotch Covenant. Blessed be GOD, I preached up the covenant of grace, and I trust many souls are taught to profit. The inclosed, dear Madam, will shew your Ladyship a little how I have been dealt with. Particulars your Ladyship shall have when the LORD is pleased to bring me to London. Next Tuesday sevennight I am to leave Scotland ..."7

It is interesting to note that the fantastic reception Whitefield had experienced in Scotland over four years earlier had waned, as had the revival. Some of the men of the revival had died and many had withered from a lack of abiding in the Vine. It seems that from this third visit to Scotland Whitefield encountered more trouble than blessings. Thus it was with joy he returned to London to pick up his lectures at Chelsea House. He knew the gatherings there, though not all receptive to his gospel message, would be pleasant and agreeable at least to him.

We see from the following:

"On his return to London, he resumed his lectures at Lady Huntingdon's to the 'great ones,' as he calls them. Thirty, and sometimes sixty, persons of rank attended, although the newspapers were full of 'strange lying accounts' of his reception in Scotland. He availed himself of this influence, to forward his intended college: for which his plea was,—'If some such thing be not done, I cannot see how the southern parts will be provided with ministers; for all are afraid to go over.' On this ground he appealed to the trustees of Georgia; reminding them that he had expended £5,000 upon the orphan-house; begging them to relieve it, as a charitable institution, from all quit-rent and taxes; and especially to allow him slaves. 'White hands,' he said, had left his tract of land uncultivated.

"... On his return to London, he found his assemblies at the Countess's 'brilliant indeed,' and Bolingbroke still one in them. It was now winter, and some of his noble friends from Scotland joined them. He felt not only deep interest in Bolingbroke, but had much hope of him at one time, owing to his

7   The Works of Whitefield, Vol. 2, pp. 178,185,194.

declared satisfaction with the doctrines of grace. 'Who knows,' he says, 'what God may do?' If Bolingbroke was hoaxing Whitefield, it is to his everlasting disgrace. It he was not, it was no small item in his advantages, that God gave him a place in Whitefield's heart and prayers. The place *he* held there, had proved the means of salvation to many. Two or three of the nobility were won to Christ at this time.

"Still, they could not keep him from itinerating. In a few weeks he was at Bristol again. 'I long to take the *field*,' he said to the Countess; and he did not take it in vain. 'There was a great stirring among the dry bones at Kingswood and Bristol.' Many new converts were won.

"… It was not all sunshine, however, in Devonshire. He was rudely treated at Tavistock. The rabble brought a bull and dogs, and created much disturbance whilst he was praying. He managed, however, to preach down the uproar. At Exeter, also, a man came prepared to knock him on the head with a stone, whenever the sermon should furnish an offensive expression. He stood with the stone in his hand. He could find no fault. The sermon soon interested him so, that the stone dropped from his hand. Then his heart melted. After the service he went to Whitefield, and said with tears, 'Sir, I came to break your head; but God has given me a broken heart.'"[8]

Time and time again hearers of Whitefield would come to do him harm and end up being converted! With his oratory that could charm birds from trees and the power of God upon him it was a difficult message to resist! But as usual his extreme labors and lack of proper rest wore him out and "in a month he was too ill to hold a pen."

The evangelist was not bedridden for long and soon he was out ranging once more delivering the gospel message to growing crowds. His co-labor with Selina, Countess of Huntingdon was being honored by God. In a letter dated Feb. 9, 1749 he informed her, "Blessed be God, I can inform your Ladyship, that there was a great stirring among the dry bones at Bristol and Kingswood. Last Lord's-day was a great day of the Son of Man. The power of the Lord attended the word, as in the days of old, and several persons, that had never heard me before, were brought under great awakenings." We see that Whitefield was again gaining attention around the areas which surround the metropolis of London. God was moving through him at Exeter, Kingsbridge, and at Plymouth. In March he wrote her, "been moving this week from place to place." His itinerant ministry was once again occupying most of his time.

Besides religion the Countess had a common denominator with her Chaplain—they each suffered from bouts of poor health. Selina off and on

---

8   Philip, pp. 338–341.

would be bedridden and we see this from the following extract of a letter
written to her by Whitefield who was in Portsmouth, May 8, 1749:

"Honoured Madam,

"Glad, very glad was I to hear, in a letter sent me by Mr. Huntingdon, that
your Ladyship was better; and glad am I yea very glad, that I can send your
Ladyship good news from this part of the country. The night after I came here, I
preached to many thousands; a great body of whom was attentive, but some of
the baser sort made a little disturbance. A very great opposer sent for me to his
house immediately and could scarce refrain weeping all the time I was with him.
On the Friday evening I preached at Gofport, where the mob has generally been
very turbulent, but all was hushed and quiet, and as far as I could find, all
approved. Every time the word has seemed to sink deeper and deeper into the
people's hearts, and their affections seem to be more and more drawn out ..."9

At this time, in another letter, Whitefield informed a minister of his
desires to travel to Wales to co-labor with Howell Harris "who tells me
the work is upon the advance." When Whitefield was away from London
on protracted tours it was Harris who preached for him at the Tabernacle.

We finally hear a mention of Elizabeth Whitefield (though there are never
any mentions of the step-daughter Nancy) in a letter from the evangelist to
the Countess—who was in Bath taking the waters for a cure to her ill health.
We read with interest:

"To Lady Huntingdon.

"Honoured Madam,   Abergavenny, May 27, 1749.

"... I earnestly pray the Lord of all Lords to bless the waters, for the recovery
of your health. Though I want to die myself, yet methinks I would have others
live, especially such as, like your Ladyship, are placed upon a pinnacle, and in a
particular manner set up as lights in the world. For two days past I have been at
my wife's house for the sake of a little retirement. It has been sweet, yea very
sweet, so sweet that I should never to be heard of again. But this must not be. A
necessity is laid upon me, and woe is me if I do not preach the gospel of
CHRIST. God willing, I therefore purpose to-morrow to begin a three weeks
circuit, and to see what the LORD will be pleased to do by me. The country is
alarmed, and I hear very numerous congregations are expected ..."10

It sounds as if Whitefield and wife had a happy re-union in Wales. He spoke
of it being, "sweet, yea very sweet, so sweet that I should never be heard of
again." But we are amazed when we discover he was speaking of enjoying
being alone, for his wife is still in America! She did not return to London until
July of 1749. And we wonder how happy that reunion was.

---

9   *Works,* Vol. 2, pp. 250–251.
10 Ibid. p. 258.

We find in another letter to the Countess the success that Whitefield was receiving in Wales as well as his report to her that he has found the Countess a minister to ordain—as part of their co-laboring in building up the Church. Wherever Whitefield went he caused a stir! We read:

"To Lady Huntingdon,

Haverford-west, June 8, 1749.

"Honoured Madam,

"Since my coming into Wales, and leaving Carmarthen, the infinitely great and infinitely condescending Redeemer has been pleased to ride on in the chariot of the everlasting gospel. Congregations grow larger and larger, and all the towns here about are quite open for the word of GOD. Yesterday I preached very near Pembroke, to-day and next LORD'S day I am to preach here, and to-morrow at St. David's. Not a dog stirs a tongue. The mayor and gentlemen at Pembroke were very civil, and the justices here are very fond of having me in Haverford-west. I wish I had more time in these parts. The fields are indeed white, ready unto harvest, and the young men bred up at Carmarthen Academy were much taken. The congregations consist of many thousands, and their behavior is very affecting. Indeed we have blessed seasons. O free grace! Here is a dear young man, just ripe for orders. He has good parts, and hath made some proficiency in the languages, is solid, and of some influence in this town. He can get testimonials, and if ordained I believe would be eminently useful in the church. I wish a way could be found out for his admission: but I fear it is impracticable. However, I thought it my duty just to hint it to your Ladyship. May the great Shepherd and Bishop of souls find out means for sending him, and many more like-minded, into his vineyard! But how is your Ladyship's health? I begin to be quite uneasy, because I have received no letter from my brother. I despair of hearing now till Tuesday sevennight, when I hope to be at Abergavenny again. In the mean while, my prayers are always going to the throne of grace in behalf of your Ladyship, and every branch of your noble family. That they may take root downwards, and bear fruit upwards, is the ardent desire of, honoured Madam,

Your Ladyship's most dutiful, though unworthy servant,

G.W."[11]

By July Whitefield was back in London telling all he had "seen great things in Wales." He picked Elizabeth up at the dock yard and we seldom hear of her again! We see what he desired his epitaph to be in correspondence with a friend, "I am content to wait till the day of judgment for the clearing up of my character: and after I am dead, I desire no other epitaph than this, 'Here lies G.W. what sort of man he was, the great day will discover.'"

---

11   Ibid. pp. 262–263.

It is in July that Whitefield received a letter from his friend Ben Franklin. And in this vitally interesting letter are the remarks of how the College of Philadelphia (which later became the University of Pennsylvania) was founded! We see this from the following:

"[Franklin] ... was proposing to found an academy or college in Philadelphia. Franklin begged about £5,000; the subscribers requested him and Mr. Francis, the Attorney-General, 'to draw up constitutions for the government of the academy;' twenty-four trustees were chosen; a house was hired; masters engaged; and the schools opened. The scholars increasing fast, a large building was found to be indispensable. The meeting-house, which had been built for Whitefield, in 1740, was burdened with an inconvenient debt; Franklin negotiated with the trustees to transfer it to the academy, on condition that the debt was paid, that the large hall should be kept open for occasional preachers, and that a free school should be maintained for the instruction of poor children. In due time, the trustees of the academy were incorporated by a royal charter; the funds were increased by contributions in Great Britain; and thus was established, in Whitefield's meeting-house, by the celebrated Benjamin Franklin, the College of Philadelphia."[12]

There is a stature standing today of George Whitefield at this institution. It is a remarkable likeness of Whitefield and he is pointing skyward and looking downward as if in thought. We will include the letter from Franklin because it has much interest and speaks of the close friendship the two great men shared. When read bear in mind there was no Fourth of July holiday because there was no need to celebrate as yet! We read:

"Philadelphia, July 6, 1749.

"Dear Sir,—Since your being in England, I have received two of your favours, and a box of books to be disposed of. It gives me great pleasure to hear of your welfare, and that you purpose soon to return to America.

"We have no kind of news here worth writing to you. The affair of the building remains in *statu quo,* there having been no new application to the Assembly about it, or anything done, in consequence of the former.

"I have received no money on your account from Mr. Thanklin, or from Boston, Mrs. Read, [Franklin's wife was a Miss Read, before he married her] and your other friends here, in general, are well, and will rejoice to see you again.

"I am glad to hear that you have frequent opportunities of preaching among the great. If you can gain them to a good and exemplary life, wonderful changes will follow in the manners of the lower ranks; for *ad exemplum regis,* etc. On this

12 Tyerman, Vol. 2, p. 228.

principle, Confucius, the famous eastern reformer, proceeded. When he saw his country sunk in vice, and wickedness of all kinds triumphant, he applied himself first to the grandees; and, having, by his doctrine, won them to the cause of virtue, the commons followed in multitudes. The mode has a wonderful influence on mankind; and there are numbers, who, perhaps, fear less the being in hell, than out of the fashion. Our more western reformations began with the ignorant mob; and, when numbers of them were gained, interest and party-views drew in the wise and great. Where both methods can be used, reformations are likely to be more speedy. O that some method could be found to make them lasting! He who discovers that, will, in my opinion, deserve more, ten thousand times, than the inventor of the longitude.

"My wife and family join in the most cordial salutations to you and good Mrs. Whitefield.

"I am, dear sir, your very affectionate friend, and most obliged humble servant,

"BENJAMIN FRANKLIN."[13]

We are certain Franklin's letter brought a smile to Whitefield as he read it, in particular the part concerning Confucius and reformation—all reformation of men is temporary and we see in the correspondence between these two friends a desire on Whitefield's part not to reform his friend but to save him from the fires of hell!

13   Ibid. pp. 228–229.

[*Late in life Whitefield made the acquaintance of the Rev. Richard de Courcy, an Irishman.*] *'On being introduced Whitefield took off his cap, and bending towards Mr. de Courcy, placed his hand in a deep scar on his head, saying, 'Sir, this wound I got in your country for preaching Christ.'"*

Aaron Seymour

CHAPTER 39

FACING OPPOSITION

In the summer of 1749 Whitefield faced serious charges by two Bishops. The first minister is unnamed and referred to as the "Bishop of W——; and it is this man who charges Whitefield with the serious accusation of perjury. The second Bishop who opposes Whitefield becomes one of his fiercest opponents. This was Bishop George Lavington. Lavington was the Bishop of Exeter and "he was one of the most militant anti-Whitefield, anti-Methodist men in the entire kingdom and not always either fair or accurate."[1]

On August 7, 1749 Whitefield wrote a letter to the unnamed Bishop expressing his views of defending his innocence, while at the same time, being cautious not to enrage this minister any further. Whitefield is respectful in his reply and tries not to worsen the situation.

We have the following letter from Whitefield:

"My Lord,   Bristol, Aug. 7, 1749.

"I thank your Lordship for your kind and cordial letter. I shall take care to do you Lordship justice, by shewing it to such persons as I think have been more immediately concerned. This, I imagine, will be as much satisfaction as your Lordship will desire. I suppose the mistake has lain here: your Lordship might have insinuated, that by my present way of acting, I had broken the solemn engagement I had entered into at my ordination: and that might have been interpreted to imply a charge of *Perjury*. The relation in which I stand to the Right Honourable the Countess of Huntingdon, made me desirous to clear myself from such an imputation; and at the same time to give your Lordship an opportunity of vindicating yourself in the manner you have done. Was I not afraid of intruding too much upon your Lordship's time, and of shewing the least inclination to controversy, I would endeavour, in the fear of GOD, to answer the other part of your Lordship's letter; and, as far as lies in me, give your

---

1   Richard Owen Roberts, *Whitefield in Print,* p. 439.

Lordship a satisfactory account of whatever may seem irregular and exceptionable in my present conduct. This I would be glad to do, not only before your Lordship, but all the Right Reverend the Bishops; for I highly honour them on account of the sacred character they sustain, and would make it my daily endeavour to obey all their godly admonitions. This, I presume, my Lord, is the utmost extent of the promise I made at my ordination. If I err or deviate from this, in any respect, it is through ignorance and want of better information, and not (as far as I know my own heart) out of obstinacy or contempt of lawful authority. But I forget myself. I beg your Lordship's pardon for taking up so much of your time; I thank your Lordship for your prayers in my behalf; and beg leave to offer mine in return for your Lordship's present and eternal welfare, who am, my Lord,

Your Lordship's dutiful son, and obliged humble servant,

G.W."[2]

The other Bishop—the more dangerous one to Whitefield—was Lavington. This was a man who fought against God and hurt the cause of Christ. He began publishing pamphlets against Whitefield and the Methodists—but mainly aimed at Whitefield. The first pamphlet was entitled, "The Enthusiasm of Methodists and Papists compared", printed in London in 1749 and consisting of 82 vile pages. Of this pamphlet Richard Owen Roberts wrote, "A very angry work, demonstrating little self-control and even less comprehension of the real issues at stake."[3] The second pamphlet was more venomous and was an eight volume work of two hundred pages. Its rantings were leveled directly at Whitefield.

On this we have the following:

"[regarding this pamphlet by Lavington] It is somewhat difficult to reconcile its levity and buffoonery with Christian piety. At all events, its spirit, tone, and language, are not in harmony with St. Paul's injunction, 'A bishop must not soon be angry, but be sober, just, holy, temperate.' It is needless to give an outline of this episcopal production; but, from the preface of forty-four pages, wholly addressed to Whitefield, the following choice epithets and phrases are taken. 'You are a most deceitful worker, grievously seducing your precious lambs.' 'Your infallible instructions are so many mistakes, blunders, or lies.' 'You have climbed up, and stolen the sacred fire from heaven; have even deified yourself, and put your own spirit in the seat of the Holy Ghost.' 'You have owned yourself a cheat and impostor.'

'... I almost *long* to have a peep at you in your *unexceptionable dress*. I begin to be in an *ecstasy* ..."[4]

2   *Works*, Vol, 2, pp. 271–272.
3   *Whitefield in Print*, p. 439.
4   Tyerman, Vol. 2, pp. 231–232.

Whitefield related these published antics to Lady Huntingdon. He was obviously upset by the Bishop of London's brutal attacks on his character and ministry. He chose not to reply to Lavington's pamphlet directly but instead he decided to preach "in his episcopal city."

We have the following account of his preaching there in which he was physically attacked and injured greatly. We read:

"To Lady Huntingdon.

"Honoured Madam,   London, Sept. 4, 1749.

"By the providence of a good and gracious GOD, I came to town on Thursday evening, after having had a pleasant circuit in the West. The day after I wrote to your Ladyship, I preached twice at Exeter, and in the evening I believe I had near ten thousand hearers. The Bishop and several of his clergy stood very near me, as I am informed. A good season it was. All was quiet, and there was a great solemnity in the congregation; but a drunken man threw at me three great stones. One of them cut my head deeply, and was like to knock me off the table; but, blessed be GOD, I was not discomposed at all. One of the other stones struck a poor man quite down. As I came from Exeter, I visited one John Hayne, the soldier that, under GOD, begun the great awakening in Flanders. He is in Dorchester goal for preaching at Shaftsbury, where there has been, and is now a great awakening. Every where the work is upon the spread; and since I have been here, we have had some of the most awful, solemn, powerful meetings, as I ever saw at the Tabernacle. Congregations have been very large, and I have had several meetings with the preachers. On Saturday I had the honour of being almost all the day long with Lady F——, Lady H——, Lady C——, and the Countess of D——. Lady F—— and the Countess received the blessed sacrament before the others came: and I think they both grow ..."5

Despite all the printed and physical persecution Whitefield endured during this time we see that God was marvelously at work! It is noteworthy that the noble ladies were becoming Whitefield's followers as well! The lectures at Chelsea Mansion were paying off.

The next letter to Selina is from her dutiful chaplain and it precedes an important event in the life of the Wesley brothers. We include it for its record of God's great doings among man and the meeting of Whitefield and Charles Wesley leading up to the strife between John and Charles.

"To Lady Huntingdon,

"Honoured Madam,   Newcastle, Oct. 1, 1749.

"I wrote to your Ladyship lately a few lines under great weariness of body. I then promised to send your Ladyship many pleasing particulars. Till now I have

_____

5   *Works*, Vol. 2, pp. 278–279.

not had opportunity; and now what shall I say to your Ladyship? Never did I see more of the hand of GOD in any of my journies than in this. At Mr. G——'s I believe there were above six thousand hearers. The sacramental occasion was most awful. At Leeds the congregation consisted of about 10,000. In the morning at five I was obliged to preach out of doors. I was invited to Leeds by one of Mr. Wesley's preachers, and by all his people. The gospel was welcome to them. In my way hither I met Mr. Charles Wesley, who returned back with, and introduced me to the pulpit in Newcastle. As I am a debtor to all, and intend to be at the head of no party, I thought it my duty to comply. I have preached now in their rooms four times, and this morning I preached to many thousands in a large close. This evening I am to do the same again. The power of GOD has attended his own word, and there seems to be a quickening and stirring among the souls. To-morrow, GOD willing, we set out for Leeds, and after about a week's stay in those parts I intend returning to London. As it is so late in the year, my Scotch friends advise me to defer my going thither. Had I known that, I should have embarked for America this fall; but I find there were other reasons for my being prevented crossing the waters this winter. I desire to follow the Lamb withersoever he is pleased to lead me. At New-haven there is a great awakening. If any thing offers worthy of notice, your Ladyship shall be sure to hear. In the mean while, I continue to put up my usual prayer, that your Ladyship may be filled with all the fulness of GOD, and to subscribe, myself, honoured Madam,

Your Ladyship's most obliged and willing servant for CHRIST'S sake,

G.W."[6]

There is an important event in the life of the Wesley brothers which we will observe at this time. Whitefield makes no mention of it out of respect toward his friends. However, it gives us insight into the *personal* lives of famous men as the Wesley's. We turn to the following remarks:

"In these and other letters, written while in the north of England, Whitefield makes no mention of an event too important to be entirely omitted. It was now that Charles Wesley succeeded in preventing his brother marrying Grace Murray, by getting her married to John Bennet. This unpleasant, almost romantic, incident occupies so large a space in "The Life and Times of Wesley," [written by Luke Tyerman] that I here purposely refrain from entering into details. The account there introduced has been severely criticised and censured by some of Wesley's admirers, who seem to be unwilling to admit that he shared any of the infirmities common to human beings. I can only say, that while I could add to the details I have already given, I know of nothing that I ought either to retract or to modify. There can be no doubt that Whitefield was cognisant of the intentions of Charles Wesley; for the marriage with Bennet took place in Newcastle, the very day Whitefield left that town for Leeds; and, further, on the night previous to the marriage, Wesley, at Whitehaven, received

---

6   Ibid. p. 283.

a letter from Whitefield, requesting that he would meet him and Charles Wesley, at Leeds, two days afterwards. Nothing more shall be added, except to give Wesley's own account of the distressing interview. He writes:—

'October 4, 1749. At Leeds, I found, not my brother, but Mr. Whitefield. I lay down by him on the bed. He told me my brother would not come till John Bennet and Grace Murray were married. I was troubled; he perceived it; he wept and prayed over me, but I could not shed a tear. He said all that was in his power to comfort me; but it was in vain. He told me it was his judgment that she was *my* wife, (At Dublin, they had made a contract de præsenti, to which Wesley attached great importance, and not without reason. "Any contract made, *per verba de præsenti,* was, before the time of George II, so far a valid marriage, that the parties might be compelled, in the spiritual courts, to celebrate it *in facie ecclesiæ.*") and that he had said so to John Bennet, that he would fain have persuaded them to wait, and not to marry till they had seen me; but that my brother's impetuosity prevailed and bore down all before it. On Thursday, October 5, about eight, one came in from Newcastle, and told us 'They were married on Tuesday.' My brother came an hour after. I felt no anger, yet I did not desire to see him; but Mr. Whitefield constrained me. After a few words had passed, he accosted me with, 'I renounce all intercourse with you, but what I would have with a heathen man or a publican.' I felt little emotion; it was only adding a drop of water to a drowning man; yet I calmly accepted his renunciation, and acquiesced therein. Poor Mr. Whitefield and John Nelson burst into tears. They prayed, cried, and entreated, till the storm passed away. We could not speak, but only fell on each other's neck.'"[7]

It is difficult to read such remarks but it is good that we see the human side of such great men. It is a shame that Charles Wesley was not as successful in preventing his brother John from marrying the next time! Only heaven knows if this first woman would have been better than the shrew John eventually wed to his deep regret!

Out of this personal strife came healing between the three famous friends; the doctrinal difference which had previously separated them is forgiven and God brings the men into a place of peace and renewed friendship. It is with pleasure we read:

"Thus did Whitefield help to prevent a breach of the life-long and ardent friendship of the Wesley brothers. Three days afterwards, Charles Wesley wrote to Mr. Ebenzer Blackwell, the London banker, as follows:—

"Sheffield, Sunday Morning, October 8, 1749.

"George Whitefield, and my brother, and I, are one,—a threefold cord which shall no more be broken. The week before last, I waited on our friend George to our house in Newcastle, and gave him full possession of our pulpit

7 Tyerman, Vol. 2, pp. 234–235.

and people's hearts, as full as was in my power to give. The Lord united all our hearts. I attended his successful ministry for some days. He was never more blessed or better satisfied. Whole troops of the Dissenters he mowed down. They also are so reconciled to us, as you cannot conceive. The world is confounded. The hearts of those who seek the Lord rejoice. At Leeds, we met my brother, who gave honest George the right hand of fellowship, and attended him everywhere to our Societies. Some in London will be alarmed at the news; but it is the Lord's doing, as they, I doubt not, will by-and-by acknowledge."

"It is a fact worth noting, that, on the memorable day, when Whitefield, the two Wesleys, John Bennet and his newly wedded wife met at Leeds, Whitefield preached in that town at five in the morning, and at Birstal, at five in the evening (Tradition says, that when Whitefield preached at Birstal, his voice was heard on Staincliffe Hill, a mile and a half from where he stood, crying, 'O earth, earth, earth, hear the word of the Lord!'—Gledstone.). On both occasions, stricken-hearted Wesley was present, and says, 'God gave Mr. Whitefield both strong and persuasive words (John Wesley's Journal). Five days afterwards, Wesley was in Newcastle, and, in sober language than that used by his brother, pronounced the following judgment on Whitefield's visit there: 'I was now satisfied that God had sent Mr. Whitefield to Newcastle in an acceptable time; many of those who had little thought of God before, still retain the impressions they received from him.'

"On leaving Leeds, Whitefield, accompanied by Ingham, set out on another evangelizing tour through Yorkshire, Lancashire, and Cheshire. 'Go on,' wrote Howell Harris, in a letter to Whitefield, dated, 'October 15, 1749,'—'Go on, and blaze abroad the fame of Jesus, till you take your flight, to bow, among the innumerable company, before His unalterable glory!' And 'go on' Whitefield did."[8]

The year 1750 began with alarm in London and this time it was not from Whitefield's preaching. There was a great earthquake which shook the metropolis and caused much devastation and death. We see this documented by Belcher:

"In the month of March, 1750, a general alarm had been awakened by earthquakes in London, and fears were excited by pretended prophecies of still greater devastation. These signal judgments of Jehovah were preceded by great profligacy of manners, and its fruitful parent, licentiousness of principle. Dr. Horne, afterwards dean of Canterbury and bishop of Bristol, in a sermon preached at the time, says, 'As to faith, is not the doctrine of the Trinity, and that of the divinity of our Lord and Saviour—without which our redemption is absolutely void, and we are yet in our sins, lying under the intolerable burden of the wrath of God—blasphemed and ridiculed openly in conversation and in print? And as to righteousness of life, are not the people of this land dead in trespasses and sins? Idleness, drunkenness, luxury, extravagance, and debauchery; for these things cometh the wrath of God, and disordered nature

---

8   Ibid. pp. 236–237.

proclaims the impending distress and perplexity of nations. And Oh, may we of this nation never read a handwriting upon the wall of heaven, in illuminated capitals of the Almighty, MENE, MENE, TEKEL, UPHARSIN—God hath numbered the kingdom and finished it. Thou art weighed in the balances of heaven, and found wanting the merits of a rejected Redeemer, and therefore the kingdom is divided and given away.'

"The shocks felt in London in February and March of this year, were far more violent than any remembered for a long series of years. The earth moved throughout the whole cities of London and Westminster. It was a strong and jarring motion, attended with a rumbling nose like that of thunder. Multitudes of persons of every class fled from these cities with the utmost haste, and others repaired to the fields and open places in the neighborhood. Towerhill, Moorfields, and Hyde Park were crowded with men, women, and children, who remained a whole night under the most fearful apprehensions. Places of worship were filled with persons in the utmost state of alarm. Especially was this the case with those attached to Methodist congregations, where multitudes came all night knocking at the doors, and for God's sake begging admittance. As convulsions of nature are usually regarded by enthusiasts and fanatics as the sure harbinger of its dissolution, a soldier 'had a revelation,' that a great part of London and Westminster would be destroyed by an earthquake on a certain night, between the hours of twelve and one o'clock. Believing his assertion, thousands fled from the city for fear of being suddenly overwhelmed, and repaired to the fields, where they continued all night, in momentary expectation of seeing the prophecy fulfilled; while thousands of others ran about the streets in the most wild and frantic state of consternation, apparently quite certain that the day of judgment was about to commence. The whole scene was truly awful.

"Under these circumstances, the ministers of Christ preached almost incessantly, and many were awakened to a sense of their awful condition before God, and to rest their hopes of eternal salvation on the Rock of ages. Mr. Whitefield, animated with that burning charity which shone so conspicuously in him, ventured out at midnight to Hyde Park, where he proclaimed to the affrighted and astonished multitudes that there is a Saviour, Christ the Lord. The darkness of the night, and the awful apprehensions of an approaching earthquake, added much to the solemnity of the scene. The sermon was truly sublime, and to the ungodly sinner, the self-righteous pharisee, and the artful hypocrite, strikingly terrific. With a pathos which showed the fervor of his soul, and with a grand majestic voice that commanded attention, he took occasion from the circumstances of the assembly, to call their attention to that most important event in which every one will be interested, the final consummation of all things, the universal wreck of nature, the dissolution of earth, and the eternal sentence of every son and daughter of Adam. The whole scene was one of a most memorable character. Mr. Charles Wesley, Mr. Romaine, and others preached in a similar manner, and with like happy results."9

---

9 Joseph Belcher, D.D, *George Whitefield: A Biography* (New York: American Tract Society), pp. 326–329.

In the midst of this pandemonium clear gospel heads prevailed and the faithful ministers of the Lord proclaimed Him to a shaken world; today when God judges society with natural disasters the blind guides in the pulpits cower in fear of man and ignore such judgments of the Almighty or are too asleep to even recognize them! Heaven help us and send some men like Wesley and Whitefield to awaken this arrogant and ignorant age before it is too late!

Also, at this time in the month of March, Whitefield preached in the district of his arch-enemy Bishop Lavington. With the fear of the Lord still in the air from the recent earthquakes many were flocking to the Lord. We see this in a letter Whitefield wrote to the Countess at this time:

"To Lady Huntingdon.

"Honoured Madam,   Exeter, March 21, 1750.

"I think it is now almost an age since I wrote to your Ladyship, but travelling and preaching have prevented me. Immediately after writing my last, I preached to many thousands, at a place called Gwinnop. The rain dropped gently upon our bodies, and the grace of GOD seemed to fall like a gentle dew and sprinkling rain upon our souls. It was indeed a fine spring shower. In the evening I rode sixteen miles to St Ives, and preached to many that gladly attended to hear the word; a great power seemed to accompany it. On the morrow, being LORD'S day, I preached twice to large auditories, and then rode back again rejoicing to Gwinnop. In my way, I had the pleasure of hearing that good was done, and had fresh calls to preach elsewhere. In the morning I went to church, and heard a virulent sermon from these words, 'Beware of false prophets.' On Saturday the preacher was heard to say, 'Now Whitefield was coming, he must put on his old armour.' It did but little execution, because not scripture proof, and consequently not taken out of GOD's armory. On Monday I preached again at Redruth, at ten in the morning, to near (as they were computed) ten thousand souls. Arrows of conviction seemed to fly fast. In the evening I preached to above five hundred, at twelve miles distant, and then rode about sixteen miles to one Mr. B——'s, a wealthy man, convinced about two years ago. In riding, my horse threw me violently on the ground, but by GOD's providence, I got up without receiving much hurt. The next day we had a most delightful season at St. Mewens, and the day following a like time, at a place called Port-Isaac. In the evening, I met my dear Mr. Thompson again at Mr. Bennet's, a friendly minister aged fourscore, and on Thursday preached in both his churches. Blessed seasons both! On Friday we went to Biddeford, where there is perhaps one of the best little flocks in all England. The power of GOD so came down while I was expounding to them, that Mr. Thompson could scarce stand under it. I preached twice; a commanding, convincing influence went forth a second time, and one came to me the next morning under awakenings. The LORD JESUS has here brought home a lawyer; and one of the youngest but closest reasoners that I ever met with, is now under deep convictions. On Monday evening I came to

Exeter, and with great regret shall stay till Friday. For I think every day lost, that is not spent in field preaching. An unthought of and unexpectedly wide door is opened in Cornwall, so that I have sometimes almost determined to go back again. I beg the continuance of your Ladyship's "prayers, and hope Mr. B——will let me know of your Ladyship's welfare. You will not be forgotten by, honoured Madam,

Your Ladyship's most dutiful, obliged, and chearful servant for CHRIST's sake.

G.W."[10]

This record of correspondence between the Countess and her chaplain Whitefield is one of the best accounts of his daily labors to the end of his life and though he chose to no longer publish a journal we are thankful that "her good Ladyship" encouraged him to write her weekly!

One more comment must be made about the opposition which Whitefield faced during 1749 and 1750; his main opponent continued to be George Lavington, the Bishop of Exeter. So we smile at the following remarks from the pen of Luke Tyerman regarding the Bishop's rantings:

"Thus did Whitefield requite his abusive foe, the Bishop of Exeter. Lavington, in the most scurrilous language, black-guarded Whitefield and the Methodists in the notorious pamphlets which he was now writing and publishing, without having the manliness to acknowledge them as his own; and Whitefield, in return, quietly invaded the bishop's diocese, and, from Land's End to Exeter, tried to revive religion, where it was almost, if not entirely dead. No wonder that the bishop raved!"[11]

10 *Works,* Vol. 2, pp. 340–341.
11 Tyerman, Vol. 2, p. 254.

According to his own account, Cornelius Winter was born at Gray's-Inn-Lane in the parish of St. Andrew, Holborn, on the ninth of October, 1742. His father died when he was nine months old, his mother when he was seven. Cornelius was left in charge of a sister who turned aside to sin, and in consequence, the child was often left to wander the streets and spend his time in idleness and childish dissipation. During these delicate years, Winter had but two years of education, then he became an errand boy, and for a period of sixteen years lived and worked in very unhappy circumstances. In 1755 Winter first heard Whitefield preach, but it was 1760 before he professed to be converted as the result of hearing the evangelist's sermon on I Cor. 15:51–52. In 1767 Winter became Whitefield's travelling companion and was with him in America at the time of his death. While Winter professed great personal attachment to Whitefield, there are some statements in Jay's biography of him which raise the question of loyalty. In the latter years of his life, Cornelius became a preacher of some usefulness and distinction in his own right.

Richard Owen Roberts

CHAPTER 40

CORNELIUS WINTER

To better understand George Whitefield as a orator and preacher one must turn to first hand accounts of those who knew him well. There are few men who knew Whitefield toward the end of his life than his aide Cornelius Winter. Whitefield biographers in the past have been hard on Winter for betraying confidences in the Whitefield household and revealing the great evangelist's weaker points as a human man. We are thankful that the remarks and observations by Cornelius Winter have been preserved through the centuries for they show us the *human side* of Whitefield.

The observations of Winter regarding Whitefield are recorded in a biography on the life and ministry of Winter by William Jay—who was a convert of Winter. We will focus our attention on Cornelius Winter's comments about Whitefield for they shed light not only on the public side of Whitefield's life—his great oratory, but also the private life of a man who towards the end of his life envied those who could eat in a public place with anonymity.

We will start first with the beginning remarks of Cornelius Winter regarding his first impressions of Whitefield then make use of his subsequent observations of the great evangelist. One thing which needs clarification is all of Winter's remarks are given in what appears to be "private letters" to his friend William Jay who has published them in book form. It seems that Rev. Jay has requested Rev. Winter to provide detailed information to him regarding Whitefield; thus the format which exists is in a conversational tone. We begin with how the preaching of Whitefield was used by God to convert Cornelius Winter. All comments are Winter's own words:

> "Mr. Whitefield became increasingly dear to me, and I embraced all opportunities to hear him. Yet I had no knowledge of the evil of sin, and the depravity of my nature. On the 9th of April, 1760, being the Wednesday in the

Easter-week, and the close of the holidays, as I was playing at cards with my fellow-servants; recollecting I might that evening hear Mr. Whitefield, I broke off in the midst of the game, which much discomposed and enraged my companions, who suspected where I was going. It was a night much to be remembered. I have reason to hope the scales of ignorance then fell from my eyes, a sense of my misery opened gradually to me, and I diligently inquired what I should do to be saved. I never more, however, played a game at cards. The text I well remember, was I Cor. xv. 51, 52. The introduction to the sermon, 'Come, my brethren, we have from Sunday till yesterday been meditating upon the resurrection of our Lord, it is now time that we should think about our own.' Could I recite the whole sermon, and it should read acceptably, it would want the energy, *viva voce,* which was so very peculiar to the preacher, that a resemblance is no where to be found. But it was God in the preacher that made the word efficacious; to him be the glory. It is a mercy he is not confined to the abilities of men whose talents are superior to those of their brethren. Much good was at that time doing by the instrumentality of men whose gifts were very inconsiderable; and the Lord could have wrought upon my soul by an inferior preacher. The state of things at the Tabernacle and Tottenham-court chapel, then differed from what it is at the present day, in this, that the supplies were not very considerable, Mr. Kinsman excepted. Hence there was a very great disproportion in the congregation; yet conversions were very frequent, by means of the substitutes provided by Mr. Whitefield in his absence, notwithstanding the inferiority of their gifts to his own. 'It is not by might nor by power,' which is but to say, it is not by human eloquence, but by the Spirit of the Lord, that work is wrought upon the soul which is essential to salvation."[1]

The next letter is a description of how Whitefield approached sermon composition and Bible study. Remember to better understand this document we must remind ourselves that Rev. Winter is writing to Rev. Jay, and in each correspondence he revealed a little more about Whitefield. We see also from the following vivid descriptions of Whitefield's great oratory!

"My very dear Friend,

"In compliance with your request, my own history must be entwined with the history of others. I keep in mind the remark you made to me in a late conversation, namely, that it was the opinion of some, that there had not been sufficient notice taken of Mr. Whitefield as a preacher, and that you wished I would endeavour to exhibit him more particularly in that view. I doubt I shall fail in the attempt; though my close connexion with his person as a private humble friend, as well as the attention I paid to his ministry, may be supposed to give me an advantage in writing upon this head.

"The time he set apart for preparations for the pulpit, during my connexion with him, was not to be distinguished from the time he appropriated to other

---

[1]   William Jay, *Memoirs of the Life and Character of the Late Rev. Cornelius Winter* (New York: Samuel Whiting & Co. 1811), pp. 15–16.

business. If he wanted to write a pamphlet upon any occasion, he was closeted; nor would he allow access to him, but on an emergency, while he was engaged in the work. But I never knew him engaged in the composition of a sermon until he was on board ship, when he employed himself partly in the composition of sermons, and reading very attentively the history of England, written by different authors. He had formed a design of writing the history of Methodism, but never entered upon it. He was never more in retirement on a Saturday than on another day; nor sequestered at any particular time for a period longer than he used for his ordinary devotions. I never met with any thing like the form of a skeleton of a sermon among his papers, with which I was permitted to be very familiar, nor did he ever give me any idea of the importance of being habituated to the planning of a sermon. It is not injustice to his great character to say, I believe he knew nothing about such a kind of exercise.

"Usually for an hour or two before he entered the pulpit, he claimed retirement; and on a sabbath day morning more particularly, he was accustomed to have Clarke's Bible, Matthew Henry's Comment, and Cruden's Concordance within his reach: his frame at that time was more than ordinarily devotional; I say more than ordinarily, because, though there was a vast vein of pleasantry usually in him, the intervals of conversation evidently appeared to be filled up with private ejaculation connected with praise. His rest was much interrupted, and his thoughts were much engaged with God in the night. He has often said at the close of his very warm address, 'This sermon I got when most of you who now hear me were fast asleep.' He made very minute observations, and was much disposed to be conversant with life, from the lowest mechanic to the first characters in the land. He let nothing escape him, but turned all into gold that admitted of improvement; and, in one way or another, the occurrence of the week or the day, furnished him with matter for the pulpit.—A specimen—when an extraordinary trial was going forward, he would be present; and on observing the formality of the judge putting on his black cap to pronounce sentence, I have known him avail himself of it in the close of a sermon; with his eyes full of tears, and his heart almost too big to admit of speech, dropping into a momentary pause—'I am going now to put on my condemning cap: sinner, I must do it; I must pronounce sentence upon you'— and then in a tremendous strain of eloquence, recite our Lord's words, 'Go, ye cursed,' not without a very powerful description of the nature of the curse. I again observe, that it would only be by hearing him, and by beholding his attitude and his tears, that a person could well conceive of the effect; for it was impossible but that solemnity must surround him, who, under God, became the means of making all solemn.

"He had a most peculiar art of speaking personally to you, in a congregation of four thousand people, when no one would suspect his object. If I instance it in an effect upon the servant of the house, I presume it is not unsuitable. She had been remiss in her duty in the morning of the day. In the evening, before the family retired to rest, I found her under great dejection, the reason of which I did not apprehend; for it did not strike me, that in exemplifying a conduct

inconsistent with the Christian's professed fidelity to his blessed Redeemer, he
was drawing it from remissness of duty in a living character; but she felt it so
sensibly as to be greatly distressed by it, until he relieved her mind by his usually
amiable deportment. The next day, being about to leave town, he called out to
her 'Farewell;' she did not make her appearance, which he remarked to a female
friend at dinner, who replied, 'Sir, you have exceedingly wounded poor Betty.'
which excited in him a hearty laugh; and when I shut the coach-door upon
him, he said, 'Be sure to remember me to Betty; tell her the account is settled,
and that I have nothing more against her.'

"The famous comedian, Shuter, who had a great partiality for Mr. Whitefield,
showed him friendship, and often attended his ministry. At one period of his
popularity he was acting in a drama under the character of Ramble. During the
run of the performance he attended service on sabbath at Tottenham-court
chapel, and was seated in the pew exactly opposite to the pulpit, and while Mr.
Whitefield was giving full sally to his soul, and in his energetic address, was
inviting sinners to the Saviour, he fixed himself full against Shuter, with his eye
upon him, adding, to what he had previously said, 'And thou, poor Ramble,
who has long rambled from him, come you also. O end your rambling by
coming to Jesus.' Shuter was exceedingly struck, and coming in to Mr.
Whitefield, said, 'I thought I should have fainted, how could you serve me so?'

"It was truly impressive to see him ascend the pulpit. My intimate knowledge
of him admits of my acquitting him of the charge of affectation. He always
appeared to enter the pulpit with a significance of countenance that indicated he
had something of importance which he wanted to divulge, and was anxious for
the effect of the communication. His gravity on his descent was the same. As
soon as ever he was seated in his chair, nature demanded relief, and gained it by a
vast discharge from the stomach, usually with a considerable quantity of blood,
before he was at liberty to speak. He was averse to much singing after preaching,
supposing it diverted the savour of the subject. Nothing awkward, nothing
careless, appeared about him in the pulpit, nor do I ever recollect his stumbling
upon a word. To his ordinary as well as to his public appearance, this observation
applies; whether he frowned or smiled, whether he looked grave or placid, it
was nature acting in him.

"Professed orators might object to his hands being lifted up too high, and it is
to be lamented that in that attitude, rather than in any other, he is represented in
print. His own reflection upon that picture was, when it was first put into his
hands, 'Sure I do not look such a sour creature as this sets me forth; if I thought I
did, I should hate myself.' It is necessary to remark that the attitude was very
transient, and always accompanied by some expressions which would justify it.
He sometimes had occasion to speak of Peter's going out and weeping bitterly,
and then had had a fold his gown at command, which he put before his face
with as much gracefulness as familiarity.

"I hardly ever knew him go through a sermon without weeping, more or less,
and I truly believe his were the tears of sincerity. His voice was often interrupted

by his affection; and I have heard him say in the pulpit, 'You blame me for weeping, but how can I help it, when you will not weep for yourselves, though your immortal souls are upon the verge of destruction, and for aught you know, you are hearing your last sermon, and may never more have an opportunity to have Christ offered to you.' His freedom in the use of his passions often put my pride to the trial. I could hardly bear such unreserved use of tears, and the scope he gave to his feelings, for sometimes he exceedingly wept, stamped loudly and passionately, and was frequently so overcome, that, for a few seconds, you would suspect he never could recover; and when he did, nature required some little time to compose herself.

"You may be sure from what has been said, that when he treated upon the sufferings of our Saviour, it was not without great pathos. He was very ready at that kind of painting with frequently answered the end of real scenery. As though Gethsemene were within sight, he would say, stretching out his hand—'Look yonder!—What is that is see! It is my agonizing Lord!'—And, as though it were no difficult matter to catch the sound of the Saviour praying, he would exclaim, 'Hark! Hark! Do you not hear?'—You may suppose that as this occurred frequently, the efficacy of it was destroyed; but, no; though we often knew what was coming, it was as new to us as though we had never heard it before.

"That beautiful apostrophe, used by the prophet Jeremiah, 'O earth, earth, earth, hear the word of the Lord,' was very subservient to him, and never used impertinently.

"He abounded with anecdotes, which, though not always recited verbatim, were very just as to the matter of them. One, for instance, I remember, tending to illustrate the efficacy of prayer, though I have not been able to meet with it in the English history—it was the case of the London apprentices before Henry the Eighth, pleading his pardon of their insurrection. The monarch, moved by their sight, and their plea, 'Mercy! Mercy!' cried, 'Take them away, I cannot bear it.' The application you may suppose was, that if an earthly monarch of Henry's description, could be so moved, how forcible is the sinner's plea in the ears of Jesus Christ. The case of two Scotchmen, in the convulsion of the state at the time of Charles the Second, subserved his design; who unavoidably obliged to pass some of the troops, were conceiving of their danger, and meditating what method was to be adopted, to come off safe; one proposed the wearing of a scullcap; the other, supposing that would imply distrust of the providence of God, was determined to proceed bare-headed. The latter, being first laid hold of, and being interrogated, 'Are you for the covenant?' replied, 'Yes;' and being further asked, 'What covenant?' answered, 'The covenant of grace,' by which reply, eluding further inquiry, he was let pass; the other, not answering satisfactorily, received a blow with the sabre, which penetrating through the cap struck him dead. In the application, Mr. Whitefield, warning against vain confidence, cried, 'Beware of your scull-caps.' But here likewise the description upon paper, wanting the reality as exemplified by him with voice and motion, conveys but a very faint idea. However, it is a disadvantage which must be submitted to, especially as coming from my pen.

"The difference of the times in which Mr. Whitefield made his public appearance, materially determined the matter of his sermons, and, in some measure, the manner of his address. He dealt far more in the explanatory and doctrinal mode of preaching on a Sabbath-day morning, than, perhaps, at any other time; and sometimes made a little, but by no means improper, show of learning. If he had read upon astronomy in the course of the week, you would be sure to discover it. He knew how to convert the centripetal motion of the heavenly bodies to the disposition of the Christian toward Christ, and the fatal attraction of the world would be very properly represented by a reference to the centrifugal. Whatever the world might think of him, he had his charms for the learned as well as for the unlearned; and as he held himself to be a debtor both to the wise and to the unwise, each received his due at such times the peer and the peasant alike went away satisfied.

"As though he heard the voice of God ever sounding in his ears the important admonition, 'Work while it is called to-day,' this was his work in London at one period of his life:—After administering the Lord's supper to several hundred communicants, at half an hour after six in the morning; reading the first and second service in the desk, which he did with the greatest propriety, and preaching full an hour, he read prayers and preached in the afternoon, previous to the evening service, at half an hour after five; and afterwards addressed a large society in public. His afternoon sermon used to be more general and exhortatory. In the evening he drew his bow at a venture, vindicated the doctrines of grace, fenced them with articles and homilies, referred to the Martyr's seal, and exemplified the power of divine grace in their sufferings, by quotations from the venerable Fox. Sinners were then closely plied, numbers of whom from curiosity coming to hear a sentence or two, were often compelled to hear the whole sermon. How many in the judgment day will rise to prove that they heard to the salvation of the soul! The society, which after sermon was encircled in the area of the Tabernacle, consisted of widows, married people, young men and spinsters, placed separately; all of whom, when a considerable part of the congregation was resettled, for hundreds used to stay upon the occasion, used to receive from him in the colloquial style, various exhortations comprised in short sentences, and suitable to their various situations. The practice of Christianity in all its branches was then usually inculcated, not without some pertinent anecdote of a character worthy to be held up for an example, and in whose conduct the hints recommended were exemplified. To the young men, for instance—A young man in the mercantile line whose uncle described him as such a jumble of religion and business, that he was fit nor neither. A widow would be held up to view, remarkable for her confidence in God. A young woman would be described commendable for her chastity, prudence, and decorum—in a way that made it desirable for each description of characters to imitate them. Masters of households at these opportunities, parents and children, had their portion, but nothing enforced upon legal principles."[2]

Two things should be noted at this juncture: 1. Cornelius Winter knew

---

2　　Ibid. pp. 16–26.

Whitefield towards the *end* of Whitefield's life; when he was so ill he appeared to John Wesley "as an old worn-out man". It is the more remarkable when we hear about his daily schedule while in his frailest frame. 2. This narrative of Winter's provides a valuable resource for the student of preaching: for if it is carefully studied one could learn much that would seldom be gained from a seminary classroom. Now back to the narrative:

"Perhaps Mr. Whitefield never preached greater sermons than at six in the morning, for at that hour he did preach winter and summer, on Mondays, Tuesdays, Wednesdays, and Thursdays. At these times his congregations were of the select description, and young men received admonitions similar with what were given in the society; and were cautioned, while they neglected the duty required from them under the bond of an indenture, not to anticipate the pleasures and advantages of future life. Beware of being golden apprentices, silver journeymen, and copper masters, was one of the cautions I remember upon those occasions.

His style was now colloquial, with little use of motion; pertinent expositions, with suitable remarks; and all comprehended within the hour. Christian experience principally made the subject of Monday, Tuesday, Wednesday, and Thursday evening lectures; when, frequently having funeral sermons to preach, the character and experience of the dead helped to elucidate the subject, led to press diligence in the Christian course, to reflect upon the blessing of faith on earth and glory in heaven. Mr. Whitefield adopted the custom of the inhabitants of New England in their best days, of beginning the Sabbath at six o'clock on Saturday evenings. The custom could not be observed by many, but it was convenient to a few—a few compared with the multitude, but abstractedly considered, a large and respectable company. Now ministers of every description found a peculiar pleasure in relaxing their minds from the fatigues of study, and were highly entertained by his peculiarly excellent subjects, which were so suitable to the auditory, that I believe it was seldom disappointed. It was an opportunity peculiarly suited to apprentices and journeymen in some businesses, which allowed of their leaving work sooner than on other days, and availing themselves at least of the sermon; from which I also occasionally obtained my blessings. Had my memory been retentive, and had I studiously treasured up his rich remarks, how much more easily might I have met your wishes, and have answered the design of this letter! But though I have lost much of the letter of his sermons, the savour of them yet remains. The peculiar talents he possessed, subservient to great usefulness, can be but faintly guessed from his sermons in print; though, as formerly God has made the reading of them useful, I have no doubt but in future they will have their use. The eighteen taken in short hand, and faithfully transcribed by Mr. Gurney, have been supposed to do discredit to his memory, and therefore they were suppressed. But they who have been accustomed to hear him, may collect from them much of his genuine preaching. They were far from being the best specimens that might have been produced. He preached many of them when, in fact, he was almost incapable of preaching at all. His constitution, long before they were taken, had received its material shock, and they were all, except the two last, the production of a Wednesday evening; when by the current business of the day, he was fatigued and worn out. The 'Good Shepherd' was sent him on board the ship. He was much disgusted with it, and expressed himself to me as in the 1440th letter of the third volume of his works—'It is not verbatim as I delivered it. In some places it makes me speak false concord, and even nonsense; in others the sense and connexion is destroyed by the injudicious disjointed paragraphs, and the whole is entirely unfit for the public review.' His manuscript journal, as quoted by Dr. Gillies, notes— 'September 15. This morning came a surreptitious copy of my Tabernacle farewell sermon, taken, as the short-hand writer professes, verbatim as I spoke it; but surely he is mistaken. The whole is so injudiciously paragraphed, and so wretchedly unconnected, that I owe no thanks to the misguided, though it may be well-meant, zeal of the writer and publisher, be they whom they will. But such conduct is an unavoidable tax upon popularity.' He was then like an ascending Elijah, and many were eager to catch his dropping mantle. In the sermons referred to there are certainly many jewels, though they may not be connected in a proper order.

"Whatever fault criticism may find with his sermons from the press, they were, in the delivery, powerful to command the most devoted attention. I have been informed by good judges, that if many of the speeches in our two houses were to be given in their original state, they would not appear to the first advantage, nor would Mr. Whitefield's sermons have had criminal defects, had they been revised with his own pen. In the fifth and sixth volumes of his works, all the sermons he ever printed are comprised. It is very easy to distinguish them which were pre-composed, from others which were preached extempory. Of the latter, I notice Peter's denial of his Lord, and the true way of beholding the Lamb of God; Abraham's offering up his son Isaac; Christ the believer's husband, and the resurrection of Lazarus. These and others preserve the extemporary style, and fully serve to discover the exactness of the preacher. He shines brightest with a long text, on which fancy has scope to play, and the mind has liberty to range. However exact he may appear in the page, it is impossible for the natural man, who discerneth not the things of the Spirit, to understand him. God may make the page printed, the instrument in his hand to convert the sinner, and then he will no longer ask, 'Doth he not speak parables?' But till then, as living he was, so dead, he is liable to the lash of severity: but the same Providence that preserved his person, will maintain his works: and thus he being dead, yet speaketh, and will continue to speak for a great while to come. Whatever invidious remarks they may make upon his written discourses, they cannot invalidate his preaching. Mr. Toplady called him the prince of preachers, and with good reason, for none in our day preached with the like effect. It is probable I shall have occasion to make further mention of him in the course of the papers I have to communicate to you ...

"My very dear Friend (letter 5),

"Having, in my last letter, taken the liberty to give my free thoughts of my ever honoured and dear friend and father, Mr. Whitefield, by whom, as an instrument in the hand of the Lord, I was brought into newness of life, I would again take up the thread of my own history."[3]

Here Cornelius Winter went into detail of his own life which is interesting but not necessary for our purposes here; we pick up his narrative in letter number 7 which relates how he came to know Whitefield on a personal basis and eventually become his aide, in which capacity he served until Whitefield's death in 1770. We see this from the following:

"... At this period, which was 1766, I was wandering in the parts mentioned already, and waiting for further intimations of the will of God. I had frequently heard Mr. Whitefield lament the want of ministers in America. I knew he had sent some who were equally deficient in point of learning with myself, and I concluded from the kind reception their ministry had met with, my labours, with the blessing of God, might be acceptable also. But a difficulty was before me, which was, how to gain an introduction to Mr. Whitefield. He was accessible but to few. I knew his connexions were very large; and this may be admitted as a reasonable apology for the caution which he used in admitting people to him. He would never be surprised into conversation. You could not knock at his door and be allowed to enter at any time. 'Who is it' 'What is his business?' and such like inquiries usually preceded admission; and if admission were granted, it was thus: 'Tell him to come to-morrow morning at six o'clock, perhaps five, or immediately after preaching; if he is later, I cannot see him.' A person who went to consult him upon going into the ministry, might expect to be treated with severity, if not well recommended, or if he had not something about him particularly engaging. One man saying, in answer to his inquiry, that he was a taylor, was dismissed with, 'Go to rag-fair and buy old clothes.' Another, who afterwards was of the clerical order, but sadly disgraced it, was admitted to preach in the vestry, one winter's morning at six o'clock, as a probationer. When a good domestic came into the study, the question was, 'Well, Betty, what was the text this morning?' 'These that have turned the world upside down have come hither also.'—'That man shall come no more here; if God had called him to preach, he would have furnished him with a proper text.'—A letter well written as to style, orthography, and decency, would prepossess him much in favour of a person.

"By means of a pious young acquaintance, a native of Royston, in Hertfordshire, I had been introduced to Mr. Berridge, Vicar of Everton, whose history is so well known that nothing need be said of him. He had given me countenance, I had gained the attention and esteem of many of his congregation, and he had endeared himself much to me, by his paternal deportment, and apostolic advice, such as I have found of excellent use in every stage of my ministry. I knew from the affection with which Mr. Whitefield always mentioned his name, and the honour in which he held his services, he must have great influence with him. I therefore paid a third visit to him, purposely to acquaint him with my views and wishes, and to beg him to introduce me to Mr.

---

3   Ibid. pp. 26–30.

Whitefield, that I might by him be placed in some situation in America. O how kind did this man of God behave to me upon this occasion!

"After having laid before me the many difficulties he judged I must meet with, and having very seriously exhorted me to pray to God to grant me direction and submission, he complied with my request, and sent me back to London with a letter to Mr. Whitefield. He gave me a mild reception; the interview was short. It was on Wednesday I waited upon him; he said he should expect me to preach at the Tabernacle on the next morning at six o'clock, and appointed the time when I should again come to him. I heard him in the evening, and felt much when he informed the congregation, that a stranger recommended by Mr. Berridge, would preach on the morrow morning at six o'clock. I had little rest that night, and prayed rather than studied for the service. A larger congregation than usual assembled. The sextoness was astonished when she found I was going into the pulpit. When I made my appearance, the people were as much struck by seeing me, for many knew me, as I was by their general whisper. I endeavoured to speak from Eph. iii.4. I was so exceedingly agitated that I knew not what I said. From that morning, however, the prejudice of my religious friends, under whose censure I had lain, was removed, and I found it a blessing to have Mr. Whitefield's suffrage. This was in February, 1767, and I was under promise to pay Portsmouth another visit. Mr. Whitefield desired me to procure him a testimonium of myself from different places, whither I had gone, which I did, and in my absence, to write him some account of the dealings of God with me in his Providence and grace. He said he should have occasion to show it to some friends, and if any thing should turn out favourable, he would let me know; accordingly I wrote him some account, and in a week after was honoured with his first letter, of which the following is an exact copy:

"London, January 29, 1767.

"Dear Mr. Winter,

"Your letter met with a proper acceptance.—The first thing to be done now is to get some knowledge of the Latin—the method to be pursued we can talk of at your return to London. Mr. Green would make a suitable master—no time should be lost—one would hope that the various humiliations you have met with were intended as preparations for future exaltations.—The greatest preferment under heaven, is to be an able, painful, faithful, successful, suffering, cast-out minister of the New Testament. That this may be your happy lot, is the hearty prayer of,

Yours, &c. in our common Lord,

G.W."

"This letter exceedingly animated me, and my expectations began to soar; but by reflection, I was enabled to check them. I considered that the best of men are but men; and thought if by Mr. Whitefield's instrumentality I should be brought into a desirable situation, trials would be answerable to it. At the commencement of my connexion with my honoured friend, and since, I have found it good, neither to seek nor to expect great things.

"The morning after I returned from Portsmouth, I waited early upon Mr. Whitefield. He received me with a mixture of kindness and severity; and for several days kept me in a state of suspense. At last he set me upon a little business, and told me he should expect me to preach two mornings in the week. He appointed me particular times when I was to call upon him; when besides sending me upon some errands, of which he always had a great number, he set me to transcribe some of his manuscripts. He showed himself much dissatisfied with my writing and orthography, both of which certainly stood in need of correction. He desired me to take a lodging near the chapel, where he could conveniently send for me; gave me a little money to defray my expenses, and by degrees brought me into a capacity to be useful to him. I was very enervated, indeed; my scene was new; I was filled with fear, and shocked by the cautious behaviour of Mr. Whitefield, for which I can plead an excuse. He had frequently been imposed upon by people who had very ungenerously served themselves of him, without being of any service to him. In the latter part of his life he was particularly cautious how he disposed of his favours; but, notwithstanding, he was liable to considerable imposition. Soon after, he proposed my going to Mr. Green's for a few hours in the day, to be initiated into the Latin Grammar; but he interrupted the design by requiring a close attention to his own business, and the large demand he made of my pulpit services; for it pleased God to give my ministry a very kind acceptance, and I have met with some instances of its having been useful. A single quarter of a year closed my school exercise, in which I am ashamed, but constrained to say I hardly gained knowledge enough to decline Musa. It was plain, Mr. Whitefield did not intend to promote my literary improvement. Indeed, he said, Latin was of little or no use, and that they who wish to enter upon it late in life, had better endeavour to acquire a good knowledge of their mother-tongue, in which many preachers, while they aim at Latin, are very deficient. Having just at this time attended Mr. Wesley's conference, and having heard him speak to the same effect, he was confirmed in this sentiment, and discouraged any perseverance. Notwithstanding Mr. Whitefield's opinion, thus freely expressed, and his deportment to me corresponding with it, my mind hankered greatly after some smatterings of Latin and Greek; partly that the want of it might be no obstacle in the way of my ordination ..."[4]

The aforementioned is as *priceless* as it is *useful*. We pick up the narrative again when Rev. Winter had passed through a near-fatal illness and was still employed by George Whitefield. The following extracts are taken from "Letter 7". In it we find:

"It pleased the Lord thrice in the year to lay me upon a bed of sickness. In a letter from Mr. Whitefield to Mr. Adams, dated October 12, 1767, stands this sentence—'Heaven is the believer's resting place. There we shall not be

---

4   Ibid. pp. 30–54.

disturbed; I do not know but Mr. Winter will get there soon; at present he is very ill.' The faculty who attended me, said my life was precarious, and advised my being sent into the country ...

"On my return, I found Mr. Whitefield had been busy and successful in getting one and another ordained for the colonies but he made no motion for me; this I thought hard, though I concealed the feeling of my disappointment. I now and then signified to Mr. Whitefield, that my inclinations for America was as strong as ever ... While on a second visit to Bristol, which held four months, Mr. Whitefield wrote me a letter, informing me that a Mr. Wright who was a very principal person with him, had agreed with his relations, to go to Georgia, to put the Orphan-house upon a new plan, and proposed to me whether I should like to go with them, there prosecute my studies, and be considered as domestic chaplain. I returned him answer, after making his motion matter of prayer, that I did not find freedom to go without ordination. This answer was of the Lord, for I was afterwards convinced that my going then and under the circumstances proposed would have involved me in many difficulties. When Mr. Wright embarked for Georgia, I was sent for to London; and to other different capacities, in which I acted, an additional one was to read prayers, and bury the dead at Tottenham-court chapel; an employment that I entered upon only to oblige my most highly esteemed patron ... Having at seasonable opportunities continued still to express my inclination to go to America, Mr. Whitefield one day asked me, if I should have any objection to take the charge of a number of negroes? He informed me at the same time he had received a letter from some gentlemen, requesting him to send them over a proper person for such a charge, and observed, that after entering upon it, and being recommended home for ordination for the service, there was no doubt but I should succeed. This had great weight with me, and though I thought it a tedious method, I was in hopes it would answer a good end at last. I told Mr. Whitefield I would give myself to his disposal, and hoped by him to discover the will of God. Several months past after this, no further notice was taken of the business, though letters had passed between him and the gentlemen upon it. The reason appeared plain to me: Mr. Whitefield had made me very useful to himself, could repose confidence in me, and was unwilling to part with me. He had so delayed the business, that by the time I had arrived at Georgia, the gentlemen had given over all thoughts of my coming. He at last came to a determination that if I would go, I should go with him, and when the time of my departure was at hand, I went out, not knowing whither I went, nor upon what condition. I only knew that I was bound for Georgia, and that I was going to teach the negroes the way of salvation. The necessary preparations for the voyage so engrossed my attention that I had little time to take a formal leave of my friends, nor did I want it, but for the sake of a select few. I had no inclination to preach a farewell sermon, but got off as quietly as I could on Friday, September 2, 1769, with a party of friends in a Gravesend boat, to go to our vessel, laying at Gravesend. Mr. Whitefield came the next day with a very large party, in coaches and chaises, and the next day preached two sermons, one in the morning in the little place called the Tabernacle, for the use of the church was denied him, and in the evening in the Market place. I preached in the afternoon. Several of the company breakfasted with us on board the vessel, on Monday morning, previous to the final leave, which they took immediately after."[5]

Cornelius Winter began the next section of the narrative with what many have felt were a betrayal of confidence. The remarks about Whitefield are not mean-spirited. There is little doubt that Rev. Winter loved and admired his mentor Whitefield immensely—rather, he is being honestly truthful in relating facts to his friend Rev. Jay and he does not color Whitefield into a more attractive portrait because of the greatness of the man; rather, he shows how *human* the great evangelist really was. It is here, Winter tells us that, "he was not happy with his wife". And it is statements like these which have brought on his critics. The reality is every man has his flaws and GW was not without his!

We return now to the narrative:

"By this time I had fully found out dear Mr. Whitefield's complexion, and indeed long before. Not doubting but that by Providence I was introduced to him, highly revering his character, and affectionately loving his person. I was determined to be like Diogenes, who would rather sustain the blows of the stick of his master Antisthenes, than be deprived of the advantage of his school.

"The following are some of the promiscuous traits of his more private character, and I presume this is no improper place in which to give them. He used too much severity to young people, and required too much from them. He connected circumstances too humiliating with public services, in a young man with whom he could take liberty; urging that it was necessary as a curb to the vanity of human nature, and referred to the young Roman orators, who, after being exalted by applauses, were sent upon the most trifling errands. His maxim was, if you love me you will serve me disinterestedly; hence he settled no certain income, or a very slender one, upon his dependents, many of whom were sycophants, and while they professed to serve him, under handedly served themselves effectually. Under this defect his charity in Georgia was materially injured, owing to the wrong conduct of some who insinuated themselves into his favour, by humouring his weakness, and letting him act and speak without contradiction. He was impatient of contradiction; but this is a fault to be charged upon almost all great people. I could mention some.

"He was not happy with his wife, but I fear some, who had not all the religion they professed, contributed to his infelicity. He did not intentionally make his wife unhappy. He always preserved great decency and decorum in his conduct towards her. Her death set his mind much at liberty. She certainly did not behave in all respects as she ought. She could be under no temptation from his conduct towards the sex, for he was a very pure man, a strict example of the chastity he inculcated upon others.

---

5   Ibid. pp. 54–61.

"No time was to be wasted; and his expectations generally went before the ability of his servants to perform his commands. He was very exact to the time appointed for his stated meals; a few minutes delay would be considered a great fault. He was irritable, but soon appeased. Not patient enough one day to receive a reason for his being disappointed under a particular occurrence, he hurt the mind of one who was studious to please; he discovered by the tears it occasioned, and, on reflection, he himself burst into tears, saying, 'I shall live to be a poor peevish old man, and every body will be tired of me.' He frequently broke the force of his passion by saying, 'How could you do so? I would not have served you so.' He never commanded haughtily, and always took care to applaud when a person did right. He never indulged parties at his table; a select few might now and then breakfast with him, dine with him on a Sunday, or sup with him on a Wednesday night. In the latter indulgence he was scrupulously exact to break up in time. In the height of a conversation I have known him abruptly say, 'But we forget ourselves,' and rising from his seat, and advancing to the door, add, 'Come, gentlemen, it is time for all good folks to be at home.'

"Whether only by himself, or having but a second, his table must have been spread elegantly, though it produced but a loaf and a cheese. He was unjustly charged with being given to appetite. His table was never spread with variety. A cow-heel was his favourite dish, and I have known him cheerfully say, 'How surprised would the world be, if they were to peep upon Doctor Squintum, and see a cow heel only upon his table.' He was neat to the extreme in his person and every thing about him. Not a paper must have been out of place, or put up irregularly. Each part of the furniture must have been likewise in its place before we retired to rest. He said he did not think he should die easy, if he thought his gloves were out of their place.

"There was no rest after four in the morning, nor sitting up after ten in the evening. He never made a purchase but he paid the money immediately, for small articles the money was taken in the hand. He was truly generous, and seldom denied relief. More was expected from him than was meet. He was tenacious in his friendship, and when the transition of Providence moved from prosperity to adversity, he moved with it to abide by his friend. He felt sensibly when he was deserted, and would remark, 'The world and the church ring changes.' Disappointed by many, he had not sufficient confidence in mankind; and from hence I believe it was, he dreaded the thought of out-living his usefulness. He often dined among his friends; usually connected a comprehensive prayer with his thanksgiving when the table was dismissed, in which he noticed particular cases relative to the family; and never protracted his visit long after dinner.

"He appeared often tired of popularity; and said, he almost envied the man who could take his choice of food at an eating-house, and pass unnoticed. He apprehended he should not glorify God in his death by any remarkable testimony, and was desirous to die suddenly.

"Thus, my dear friend, I have aimed to gather up the fragments of a character truly excellent, that nothing may be lost. It is the character of a man who had his infirmities, but whose excellencies bore a far greater proportion. He knew himself, and lived under a measure of self-abhorrence; but he knew he was the redeemed of the Lord, and extolled that name by which he was called. Not to detract, but justly to represent, is my object in what I have written concerning him. I had no claim upon him when he took me into his house. I was abundantly indebted to him for his kindness, and his memory will be dear to me while with my hand I can subscribe myself,

Yours, very affectionately,

In our dear Lord Jesus."[6]

There are more references to Whitefield which we will come upon in this rest of this chapter. But we would be remiss if we failed to include the sage advice of Bishop Berridge to Cornelius Winter; for it was Berridge, who was a close, intimate friend of George Whitefield, that allowed the first introduction of the two men. Berridge had one of the greatest minds of his generation and his advice to a young preacher was priceless—therefore, we include a brief letter from Bishop Berridge to Rev. Winter for the sake of preserving our godly heritage handed down from others who have gone before us!

Before we return to Whitefield, we read the following with interest:

"In my situation, hitherto described, letters with which I was favoured from dear Mr. Berridge, were of great use indeed; an extract I will here insert from two of them.

"'Pray frequently, and wait quietly, and the Lord will make your way plain.— Jesus trains up all his servants to waiting, and if you are called to the ministry, he will exercise your soul beforehand with sharp conflicts. Joseph must be cast first into a pit by his own brethren, then into a prison by his master, before he rules the kingdom; and David must be hunted as a flea upon the mountains, before he gets the sceptre. How can you tell what others feel, unless you have felt the same yourself? How can you sympathize with a prisoner, unless your own feet have been fast in the stocks? How can you comfort those who are cast down, unless you have been often at your wit's end? Expect nothing but conflicts, day after day, to humble and prove you, and teach you to speak a word in season to every one that is weary. This is indeed the high road to the kingdom for all, yet a minister's path is not only narrow and stony like others, but covered also with bushes and brakes; and if you labour to remove them by your own hands, they will quickly tear your flesh, and fill your fingers with thorns. Let your master remove them at your request; and remember it is always his work, as it is ever his delight, to clear our way, and lead us on till sin and death are trodden down. Undertake nothing without first seeking direction from the Lord, and when any

---

thing offers, that is plausible and inviting, beg of God to disappoint you, if it be not according to his mind. You cannot safely rely on your own judgment, after God has told you, 'He that trusteth in his own heart is a fool.' This advice relates to all important changes in life. Go no where, settle no where, tarry no where, without frequent usage of this prayer."

"I find your heart is yet looking towards America; this inclines me to think God will some time send you thither; in the mean while, be thankful you have a pulpit in England to preach Jesus Christ in, and health to preach him. Be not in a hurry to go, lest you go without your passport, and then you go on a fool's errand. Do not wish to be any where but where you are, nor any thing but what you are. It is want of communion with God that makes our thoughts run a gadding. Daily beseech the Lord to make your way plain, then leave it to him to direct your steps. Wish not to do good in America next summer, but to do good in England every day you continue here."'[7]

One can only say concerning the above comments: "It is good to be here. Blessed be the name of the Lord!" Regarding Berridge's advice, Cornelius Winter remarks, "Oh that I had never swerved from the good advice of this truly apostolic man!" It is critically important that we study men like Whitefield and those who were his contemporaries. How our pulpits lack today in men like Bishop Berridge!

We now return to more observations about George Whitefield by his close friend and confidant, Rev. Winter. In this next narrative we see "Whitefield in action" as he boarded the ship for America and how he conducted himself with others. We now follow along with the narrative which informs us that the party sailing for America included Rev. Winter and Richard Smith, Whitefield's other companion and aide who was the man in whose arms Whitefield breathed his last in Newburyport in 1770.

"Mr. Whitefield began to familiarize himself to his naval situation, to acquaint himself with the crew and passengers, and proposed to render them all the kindness in his power ... Mr. Whitefield spent his time in largely reading the history of England, composing sermons, writing letters, &c. and sometimes discovered such remarkable lowness and languor, as proved him not very fit to encounter the difficulties of a voyage to sea ... In the course of conversation, Mr. Whitefield had dropped such a hint, as convinced me I might look rather for great crosses than great honours. He told me, what he had concealed while on the English shore, that if I had as many to preach to as his bed-cabin would hold, I might think myself well off, and that I might expect to be whipped off the plantation when I had done ...

"My reception at Charleston was kind and hospitable; I supposed it to have been because I was Mr. Whitefield's friend. Mr. Whitefield's preaching in the

---

7 Ibid. pp. 65–67.

cabin at sea had great energy in it, but it was with additional pleasure I once more heard him in a large congregation on the Sabbath-day."[8]

As the traveling band reached Savannah Rev. Winter's astutely observed a change in George Whitefield's disposition, "Mr. Whitefield was cheerful and easy; he seemed to have lost a weight of care." Bethesda had this very effect upon the great evangelist each time he arrived there; few places on earth placed him so at rest as his beloved Orphan House. We now see the historical aspect of embarking at Savannah as it was in the late eighteenth century.

"What is now the matter of observation, was the matter of experience, when sitting for a little while alone in the canoe, where I was desired to remain, at the bottom of Savannah-bluff, the guardian of our property, while Messrs. Whitefield, Wright, and Smith, ascended to the town. It was dark before I was disengaged and escorted to Mr. Habersham's house, where Mr. Whitefield had preceded me …"[9]

We close this chapter with the observations of the dreadful news which reached the Orphan House in 1770 telling of Whitefield's death. George Whitefield's will was placed into the hands of Cornelius Winter and he was given the grave responsibility of taking it back to England to deliver to Selina, Countess of Huntingdon, for she was the named trustee over Bethesda upon Whitefield's death. We have telling observations of how the town of Savannah received the news of the great evangelist's death. We conclude the chapter with the following remarks:

"I visited the Orphan-house as often as possible, and was in perfect love and harmony with the family. Death made a sad inroad among them in a very little time; but the affliction was completed by the death of Mr. Whitefield. He had left Georgia to go on his northern tour, the latter end of April; and while his return was anticipated, and supposed to be near, his removal was announced. It was opened to me by Mr. Habersham, who was much affected with it. It may be supposed I could not be insensible. As soon as I heard it, I retreated to pray, and pour out my soul to God …

"You have no conception of the effect of Mr. Whitefield's death upon the inhabitants of the province of Georgia. All the black cloth in the stores was bought up; the pulpit and desks of the church, the branches, the organ loft, the pews of the governor and council, were covered with black. The governor and council, in deep mourning, convened at the state-house, and went in procession to church, and were received by the organ playing a funeral dirge. Two funeral sermons were preached, one by Mr. Ellington, which I was desired to compose;

8 Ibid. pp. 67–71.
9 Ibid. p. 72.

the other was preached by Mr. Zubly. All the respect showed to his memory at
his death, kept my sensibility alive."[10]

So ends the observations of George Whitefield by Cornelius Winter and
recorded by William Jay in 1811. We are thankful to the Lord for preserving
the memory of the great itinerant. It is interesting to mention that at the
dissenting meeting house erected at Rodborough for George Whitefield, it
was there that Cornelius Winter preached his *first* and *last* sermons.

---

10 Ibid. pp. 78–81.

The High Church, Glasgow (now Glasgow Cathedral). Whitefield preached in the grounds.

Cambuslang Parish Church

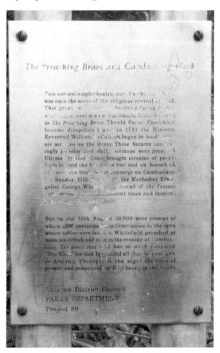

Plaque on the gate leading to the Preaching Braes

Gravestone of William M'Culloch on the side of Cambuslang Parish Church. Badly eroded, the text said "Here rests the remains of the Rev. William M'Culloch, minister of this parish, who died 18th Dec. 1771 in the 80 year of his age and 47th of his ministry. He was eminently successful in preaching the Gospel."

Part of the Preaching Braes, Cambuslang, where 30,000 people attended Whitefield's preaching.

St Mary Redcliffe, Bristol, scene of some of Whitefield's early preaching in Bristol

Whitfield [no middle "e"] Tabernacle, Kingswood, Bristol, near Hanham Mount. The site is dangerous after much neglect, arson attacks and vandalism. The building has presently has no roof. A charitable trust has been set up to rennovate the building.

Side entrance to Wesley's New Rooms in Bristol.

The interior of Wesley's New Rooms in Broadmead, central Bristol

George Whitefield Court, central Bristol, a short street by Broadmead. The area is now being redeveloped.

Imaginative portrayal of Whitefield meeting Wesley outside the Holy Club in Oxford. Note that the diminutive Wesley is standing on the pavement to give him more height.

An imaginative portayal of the first Calvinistic Methodist Association at Watford, near Caerphilly. From left to right: John Cennick, Joseph Humphreys, John Powell, William Williams, George Whitefield, Daniel Rowland and Howell Harris.

Trevecca College, established by the Countess of Huntingdon in 1768 for the training of preachers. Whitefield preached at the opening. After the expiry of the lease the College moved to Cheshunt, north of London, and then to Cambridge. It has now merged with Westminster College, Cambridge. The original building in Trevecca is now a private residence.

Howell Harris's Trevecca College (not the same as that established by the Countess of Huntingdon). It is still in use as a college for the Presbyterian Church of Wales (formerly known as the Calvinistic Methodist Church).

Whitefield preaching at Moorfields. There is a trumpeter in the tree attempting to drown his voice. Below him someone attempting to hit Whitefield with a stick. In the right foreground is a drummer, also attempting to drown him out. In the background are various entertainments.

The *WEEKLY HISTORY:*

O R,

An Account of the most Remarkable Particulars relating to the present Progress of the Gospel.

Printed & Published April 11. 1741.

London: Printed by *J. Lewis* in *Bartholomew-Close*, near *West-Smithfield.*
[Price One Penny.]

Those who are willing to take in this Paper Weekly, may have all the following Numbers; and such Persons are desired to send in their Names and Places of Abode to the Printer above mentioned, in order to be regularly served.

New CONVERTS exhorted to cleave to the *LORD.*

A Sermon on Acts xi. 23. *Preached* July 30, 1740, *at a* Wednesday Evening Lecture, *in* Charles-town, *set up at the Motion, and by the Desire of the Rev. Mr.* Whitefield; *with a brief Introduction relating to the Character of that excellent Man. By* Isaac Chanler, *Minister of the Gospel on* Ashley-River, *in the Province of* South-Carolina. *With a Preface by the Rev. Mr.* Cooper *of* Boston *in* New-England.
Acts xi. 21. 'And the Hand of the Lord was with them: and a great Number believed and turned to the Lord.'

The Reverend Mr. Cooper's *Preface.*

THE successful Progress of the Gospel of Christ, and its saving Efficacy on the Hearts of Men, is Matter of Joy to all *that love the Lord Jesus in Sincerity.* The Increase of *the Houshold of Faith* is acceptable to all that already belong to it. And how much is their divine Master honour'd and pleas'd, when the *Members* of this his Family live united in the Bonds of Love and Charity; and if they can't be one in Judgment in every *lesser Matter,* are yet one in Disposition and Affection, in Aim and Design.----More especially is the Unity of *Ministers* the Beauty and Strength of the *Church.*

It was therefore no small Pleasure to me when in a late Letter from a most valued Friend and Correspondent, giving me a refreshing Account of the Success with which God has been pleas'd to crown the Ministry of the dear and admir'd WHITEFIELD in *Charles-town* in *South-Carolina,* I read the following Passage, " Under the Influence of *His* Preaching, the *Baptist Ministers* have join'd *us* in a stated weekly Lecture, to which the People shew a surprising Disposition and Affection; and I sometimes shed Tears of Joy in my Retirements."

The following SERMON was preach'd at *that* Lecture, in the first Course of it, by one of *those* Ministers. And as it has been put into my Hands in its

[*The Second Impression.*]

Saturday   March 15th 1734/5

4 ... 66   8·1·7·3·4·9·
5 ... 6 5 & 3   4·1·
6 ...

7 ...ch nr. to Brom   66   8·9·1·
                          6 6   8·9·3·4·
8 ...wt to ...

to Whit... ch ...   66   8·3·9·4·
9 ...Br... Extracts from ... 66   8·3·15·4·1·
10 ...M. Rat   6 6   8·3·4·9·1a
11 ...Pup. m. 6. Libr... 6 6   9·3·4·1·
12 ...light. fire...   6 6   9·3·1·15·9·10·
1 ...   6 6   8·3·4·
2 ...ex out f ...   6 6   8·3·4·
3 ...   6 6   8·3·1·4·9·
4 ...wt to Chap 6 m...
   ...   6 6   8·3·4·9·
5 ...   6 5 8·1· 3·4·9
6 6m... w Freman...
   ...wt to Hav...
   ...   66   8·3·9·4·
7 ... Snowball...   6 6
   ...   6 5 8· 3·15·9·
8 ...   6 5 8·1· 3·
9 ...
   ...kn. about   6 6   8·3·4·1·
10 ...

                          8·4
                          1·2

The Revd Mr George Whitefield
of Pembroke College Oxford.

Portraits of Whitefield at various times of life. The one on the following page is perhaps the best known, though Whitefield is said to have disclaimed the habit of raising both hands together.

Below left: A portrait medallion of Whitefield.

Whitefield preaching in the open air for the first time at Islington, painted by Gustave Sintzennich. This hung in the Tottenham Court Road Chapel and is assumed destroyed when the building was bombed in World War II.

Yours most affectionately
in S.t Jesus

George Whitefield

The first sight of his countenance struck me. There was an immense multitude, and his voice was like a trumpet. His text was Romans xiii. 11, "It is high time to awake out of sleep." The whole of the discourse was attended with an amazing power, I believe, to many. I am sure it was to me. When he addressed himself to people of several ages in the large congregation before him, and among the rest, to the young people, that took great hold of me. I did not observe anything extraordinary in what he said, as to his matter; but there was such an unction in his word as I have never felt before.

Thomas Taylor
member of John Wesley's inner circle.

CHAPTER 41

MOUNTAINS AND VALLEYS

The close of the year 1750 was a great accomplishment to George Whitefield. He had done much in the name of the Lord. The beginning of 1751 brought many personal trials.

In 1750 James Hervey visited Whitefield. A member of the Holy Club and warm friend of Whitefield, James Hervey was a well received author whose writings influenced many. We have this about him:

"Hervey and Whitefield remained intimate until the former's death on Christmas day in 1758. No less a giant than William Romaine preached his funeral sermon. Hervey wrote to Whitefield, 'Your journals and sermons, and especially that sweet sermon on "What think ye of Christ" were a means of bringing me to a knowledge of the truth.' Whitefield in turn felt the warmest attachment to Hervey, and when he introduced some of his works in America, wrote, 'The author is my old friend; a most heavenly-minded creature; one of the first Methodists, who is contented with a small cure, and gives all he has to the poor. We correspond with, though we cannot see each other.' Hervey was among the most gentle, pious, and Christ-like men of all times. As Whitefield indicated, all the profits from the vast sale of his books were dedicated to the Lord's work. His memory, while largely lost to the church of this age, well deserves restoration."[1]

We see the description of this meeting of James Hervey and Whitefield in 1750 from the pen of Whitefield biographer, Joseph Belcher. We will let Belcher describe to us in brief the range of activities of George Whitefield in 1750, beginning with some meetings of other famous individuals whose lives crossed the path of the great evangelist, including that of James Hervey and his comments and description of George Whitefield at this time:

"At the beginning of the year 1750, Whitefield was still in London. At this time his intended college at Bethesda occupied much of his attention. He wrote

---

1   Richard Owen Roberts, *Whitefield in Print,* p. 380.

to his friends in every quarter for help. His usual appeal was, 'We propose having an academy or college at the orphan-house. The house is large, and will hold a hundred. My *heart*, I trust, is larger, and will hold ten thousand.' Though in London, his heart was in America. He says, 'Ranging seems my province; and methinks I hear a voice behind me saying, "This is the way, walk in it." My heart echoes back, "Lord, let thy presence go with me, and then send me where thou pleasest." In the midst of all, America, *dear* America, is not forgotten. I begin to count the days, and to say to the months, "Fly fast away, that I may spread the gospel-net once more in dear America."'

"Be it here mentioned, that amid the busy scenes of his life, and while surrounded with the flatteries of the great and noble, Whitefield did not forget the duties he owed to his mother. A person whom he had employed to obtain some comforts for her, had neglected the duty, so that the now aged matron might have felt a week's anxiety. He wrote to her, 'I should never forgive myself, was I, by negligence or any wrong conduct, to give you a moment's needless pain. Alas, how little have I done for you. Christ's care for his mother excites me to wish I could do any thing for you. If you would have any thing more brought, pray write, honoured mother ... Tomorrow it will be *thirty-five* years since you brought unworthy me into the world. O that my heart were waters, and mine eyes fountains of tears, that I might bewail my barrenness and unfruitfulness in the church of God.'

"While he was now fully engaged in preaching, and was surrounded with flatteries, he did not forget his duty to conflict with sin. He writes, 'I find a love of power sometimes intoxicates even God's dear children. It is much easier for me to obey than govern. This makes me fly from that which, at our first setting out, we are apt to court. I cannot well buy humility at too dear a rate.'

"Dr. Philip Doddridge, as every reader knows, was one of the most pious and accomplished preachers and writers of the Non-conformists of England in his day. Nor was his *missionary zeal* small in its degree. Though he died as early as 1751, he had said, 'I am now intent on having something done among the dissenters, in a more public manner, for propagating the gospel abroad, which lies near my heart. I wish to live to see this design brought into execution, at least into some forwardness, and then I should die the more cheerfully.' It was indeed the passion of his life to promote the interests of evangelical truth, and save the souls of men. And though, as his recent eulogist, the Rev. John Stoughton, has said, condemned by some, and suspected by others for so doing, he took a deep and sympathetic interest in the evangelical labors of Whitefield. It seems strange in our day to think of Whitefield being regarded as an enthusiast by orthodox dissenters. Yet there were those who did thus regard him. Bradbury poured on him streams of wit; Baker regarded his sermons as low and coarse; and another in writing calls him, 'honest, crazy, confident Mr. Whitefield.' But Doddridge regarded him as far otherwise, and spoke of him as 'a flaming servant of Christ.' He prayed on one occasion at the Tabernacle, but Dr. Watts was much grieved by it; and when, on Whitefield's visiting Northampton,

Doddridge gave him the use of his pulpit, the managers of the college of which he was president remonstrated with him for so doing.

"The visit of Whitefield to Doddridge was in February, 1750, where he met the Rev. Dr. Sir James Stonehouse, and the Rev. Messrs. Hartley and Hervey. The latter eminent clergyman [Hervey] thus writes, 'I have lately seen that most excellent minister of the ever-blessed Jesus, Mr. Whitefield. I dined, supped, and spent the evening with him at Northampton, in company with Dr. Doddridge, and two pious, ingenious clergyman of the church of England, both of them known to the learned world by their valuable writings. And surely I never spent a more delightful evening, or saw one that seemed to make nearer approaches to the felicity of heaven. A gentleman of great worth and rank in the town invited us to his house, and gave us an elegant treat; but how mean was his provision, how coarse his delicacies, compared with the fruit of my friend's lips: they dropped as honey from the honey-comb, and were a well of life. Surely people do not know that amiable and exemplary man, or else, I cannot but think, instead of depreciating, they would applaud and love him. For my part, I never beheld so fair a copy of our Lord, such a living image of the Saviour, such exalted delight in God, such enlarged benevolence to man, such a steady faith in the divine promises, and such a fervent zeal for the divine glory; and all this without the least moroseness of humor, or extravagance of behavior, sweetened with the most engaging cheerfulness of temper, and regulated by all the sobriety of reason and wisdom of Scripture; insomuch that I cannot forbear applying the wise man's encomium of an illustrious woman to this eminent minister of the everlasting gospel: 'Many sons have done virtuously, but thou excellest them all.'"[2]

It is easier to swallow such accolades of George Whitefield when we can balance them with the remarks of a Cornelius Winter. Nevertheless, all of the remarks made by James Hervey regarding George Whitefield were true. He was an unique, elegant, special, holy man of God. There are too many like observations of him by others to argue this point.

Whitefield's activities hit their peak by summer of 1750. He had just finished a preaching tour of many towns and had literally preached to many thousands. We see this from a letter he wrote to his friend James Hervey, it is dated, June 21, 1750. It reads:

"Reverend and very dear Sir,   Kendal, June 21, 1750.

"I guess this will find you returned from good Lady Huntingdon, with whom undoubtedly you have taken sweet counsel, and been mightily refreshed in talking about the things which belong to the kingdom of GOD. This leaves me at Kendal, where I arrived this morning, and where, GOD willing, I shall preach the everlasting gospel this evening. An entrance is now made into Westmoreland; and pen cannot well describe what glorious scenes have opened

2   Joseph Belcher, D.D., *George Whitefield: A Biography*, pp. 323–326.

in Yorkshire, &c. Perhaps, since I saw you, seventy or eighty thousand have attended the word preached in divers places. At Howarth, and Whitsunday, the church was almost thrice filled with communicants, and at Kirby-Steven the people behaved exceedingly well ...

"In my way, I have read Mr. Law's second part of 'The Spirit of Prayer.' His scheme about the fall is quite chimerical; but he says many noble things. The sun has its spots, and so have the best of men. I want to see my own faults more, and those of others lesss ... Next week I hope to reach Edinburgh ..."[3]

On the heels of hurried and non-stop activity Whitefield traveled to Scotland in July. Scotland had previously been for him a scene of both glory (in revival) and hostility (in the many pamphlets printed against him by the Seceders). The Erskine brothers had turned against him and he had felt the sting of several former friends who were set against him because of party politics and doctrine.

We see how he was received in Scotland by the following extracts:

"Whitefield reached Edinburgh on Friday, July 6th, having preached, since he left London, two months before, above ninety times, and, as he estimated, to a hundred and forty thousand people. He, at once, commenced preaching in his open-air cathedral, the Orphan-Hospital Park; and, on July 12th, wrote, as follows, to the Countess of Huntingdon:—

'Though I am burning with a fever, and have a violent cold, I must send your ladyship a few lines. They bring good news. People flock rather more than ever, and earnestly entreat me not to leave them soon. I preach generally twice a day,—early in the morning, and at six in the evening. Great multitudes attend. Praise the Lord, O my soul! Mr. Nimmo and his family are in the number of those who are left in Sardis, and have not defiled their garments. Your ladyship's health is drunk every day.'

"... Having preached twenty times in Edinburgh, Whitefield, on the 19th of July, set out for Glasgow, where, on the 23rd, he wrote:—

'Friends here received me most kindly, and the congregations, I think, are larger than ever. Yesterday [Sunday] besides preaching twice in the field, I preached in the College Kirk, being forced by Mr. Gillies. It was a blessed season. I have met and shaken hands with Mr. Ralph Erskine. Oh, when shall God's people learn war no more?'

"On July 27, he returned to Edinburgh; and, two days later, wrote to Lady Huntingdon:—

'No one can well describe the order, attention, and earnestness of the Scotch congregations. They are unwearied in hearing the gospel. I left thousands sorrowful at Glasgow; and here I was again most gladly received

---

3   *Works*, Vol. 2, pp. 358–359.

last night. By preaching always twice, and once thrice, and once four times in a day, I am quite weakened; but I hope to recruit again, and get fresh strength to work for Jesus.'"4

After finishing his labors in Scotland Whitefield left for London on August 3rd. Important events await him in the metropolis for he united with the Wesleys and preached in their chapel. He was weary from his superhuman labors but joyful in what the Lord had done. We see the enormity of both his popularity and the magnitude of his labors in the following:

"On August 3rd, Whitefield set out for London, and, at Berwick, wrote again to the Countess:—

'Berwick, August 4, 1750.

'I have taken a very sorrowful leave of Scotland. The longer I continued there, the more the congregations, and the power that attended the word, increased. I have reason to think that many are under convictions, and am assured that hundreds have received great benefit and consolation. I shall have reason to bless God to all eternity for this last visit to Scotland. Not a dog moved his tongue all the while I was there, and many enemies were glad to be at peace with me. Preaching so frequently, and paying so many religious visits, weakened me very much; but I am already better for my riding thus far. One of the ministers here has sent me an offer of his pulpit, and I hear of about ten more round the town who would do the same. I came here this evening [Friday] and purpose to set out for Newcastle on Monday morning.'

"Such extracts as these are fragments; but, put together, they form sort of diary, and exhibit Whitefield's enormous labours, and his marvellous popularity and success.

"When Whitefield arrived in London, Hervey had become an inmate of his house, and wrote: 'Great care is taken of me. The house is very open and airy, and has no bugs, a sort of city gentry for which I have no fondness.' The two friends visited Lady Gertrude Hotham, one of whose daughters was dying; and, by their joint instrumentality, the sufferer was led to the Saviour. Hervey attended Whitefield's ministry at the Tabernacle, and speaks of him as being, 'in labours more abundant,' 'a pattern of zeal and ministerial fidelity.'

'Though Whitefield had been four months from home, the time had not come for him to settle in his *"winter quarters."* First of all, he ran off to Portsmouth, and was there when Miss Hotham died. At his return to London, he wrote:—

'September 14. I was received with great joy, and our Lord has manifested His glory in the great congregation. I have preached in Mr. Wesley's chapel several times. Mr. Wesley breakfasted and prayed with me this morning; and Mr. Hervey was so kind as to come up and be with me in my house. He is a

---

4   Tyerman, Vol. 2, pp. 259–262.

dear man; and, I trust, will yet be spared to write much for the Redeemer's glory.'

"On the same day, Charles Wesley wrote, in his Journal: 'I met James Hervey at the Tabernacle, and in the fellowship of the spirit of love.'

"Never since they had left Oxford had the four old friends met together till now. Fifteen years had elapsed since then,—years full of strange and unforeseen adventures."[5]

Odd how Whitefield's biographers fail to make mention of poor Elizabeth. When they do it is to introduce change or tragedy. Here we see George Whitefield gone from home four months (away from his wife) and still longing to range again!

It is at this time that Whitefield reached his thirty-seventh year. All between his forceful labors are serious bouts of illness which lay him low, but oddly do not cease his labors—he kept pushing his human body until it could not be pushed along by mere effort anymore. Gradually, he began to become an old man before his time. No one, not even George Whitefield, can deny taking care of the mortal frame by proper rest and nourishment.

So it is no surprise to find him ill once more:

"Shortly after this, Whitefield had a serious illness, which he called a 'violent fever,' and which kept him confined to his room nearly a fortnight. As soon as he was able, he resumed his preaching, and also his correspondence. To one of his friends, he wrote: 'December 17th. Yesterday, I entered upon my seven-and-thirtieth year. I am ashamed to think I have lived so long, and done so little.' To another: 'December 21. I have been near the gates of death, which has hindered my answering your kind letter as soon as I proposed. I shall be glad to know your friend's answer about Georgia. If the Lord raises up a solid, heavenly-minded, learned young man for a tutor, I shall be glad. Nothing, I believe, but sickness or death, will prevent my going over next year. Methinks the winter is long. I want to take the field again.'

"Whitefield longed to be in America; and, notwithstanding past revivals, America was in need of him. Hence the following extract ...

'Philadelphia, December 15, 1750.

'Reverend And Dear Brother,—Religion, at present, is very low in general in this country. A great deadness prevails, and few appear to be converted; but the Church of Christ I trust, is in some measure, edified by the word of God. We wish and hope for better times. I am glad that you are able to continue your itinerancy, and that with such encouragement and success. May your life and labours be long continued, and be blessed to the great increase of Christ's kingdom on earth, and the brightening of our own crown in heaven!

5   Ibid. pp. 262–263.

'I am much obliged to you, dear sir, for the hope you gave me, in a letter I received from you, of doing something among your friends to assist us in completing the new house of public worship, which we are erecting. Some time ago, I told you of the difficult and necessitous state of our case; and I may now add, that we are likely to lose many hundreds of pounds that were promised. This is very discouraging. However, we have got the house covered, and hope to have the pleasure of hearing you preach in it next fall. Dear sir, as I know your hearty good-will towards the interests of religion in general, and towards us in particular, I cannot but believe that you will compassionate us, and will use your best endeavours for us. I forbear incitements to a mind that needs them not. I salute yourself and your consort with cordial respect; and remain yours as formerly,

'Gilbert Tennent.'

"Whitefield was always ready to assist his friends, both at home and abroad ...

"To Whitefield, the year 1751 opened sadly. It is true, he speaks of have had 'blessed seasons' in London, and of many being awakened to a consciousness of their sins and danger; but his own health was shaken, his wife was 'expecting an hour of travail,' and death was entering the mansion of the Countess of Huntingdon. During the whole of December, the Countess had been dangerously ill; and, at the beginning of 1751, her health declined so rapidly, that Whitefield was requested to hasten to Ashby with all the speed he could. He obeyed the summons; but, before his arrival, death had claimed a victim,— not, however, Whitefield's honoured patroness; she was spared to the Church and the world forty years longer; but Lady Frances Hastings, sister of her late husband, was taken to the rest of the righteous; and Lady Selina, the Countess's daughter, was extremely ill, though slowly recovering from a fever. Extracts from two of Whitefield's letters will tell all that is needful to relate:—

'Ashby, January 29, 1751. I rode post to Ashby, not knowing whether I should see good Lady Huntingdon alive. Blessed be God! She is somewhat better. Entreat all our friends to pray for her. Her sister-in-law, Lady Frances Hastings, lies dead in the house. She was a retired Christian, lived silently, and died suddenly, without a groan. May my exit be like hers! Whether right or not, I cannot help wishing that I may go off in the same manner. To me it is worse than death, to live to be nursed, and see friends weeping about one. Sudden death is sudden glory. But all this must be left to our heavenly Father.'

"Strangely enough, Whitefield's wish, so often uttered, was literally fulfilled. To Lady Mary Hamilton, Whitefield wrote:—

'Ashby, January 30, 1751. I found good Lady Huntingdon very sick, though, I trust, not unto death. The death of Lady Frances was a translation. Almost all the family have been sick. Lady Selina has had a fever, but is better. Lady Betty is more affected than ever I saw her. Lady Ann bears up pretty well, but Miss Wheeler is unconsolable. The corpse is to be interred on

Friday [February 1] evening. May all who follow it, look and learn! I mean
learn to live, and learn to die.'

"Whitefield remained some days after the funeral, and then returned to
London, where, to use his own expression, his wife was 'exceeding bad.' Three
weeks afterwards, he wrote the following to Lady Huntingdon; but makes no
mention, in any of his letters, of the accouchement of his wife. It is probable,
that, like her last, the present child was dead:"[6]

This time of mourning for the Whitefields lies silent in history. It is as if he
fails to acknowledge the death of their baby; at least, to his friends by his
correspondence. He did not even remain in London long to help his grieving
and ailing wife, but in just a few days was off again to visit with Lady
Huntingdon in Bristol, "where the Countess of Huntingdon was then
staying for the benefit of her health." We can only imagine the pain and
suffering that Elizabeth endured; once again, she was denied the role of
being a mother; once again, she has to bury another child; once again, she
was left to her loneliness while her spouse was off ranging away from hearth
and home. What George Whitefield felt about all this is not known. We
assume it was a great shock to his constitution as was the death of his four-
month-old son. This was not the last of the couple's sorrows for Elizabeth
endured yet other miscarriages and still births and remained childless with
her present husband—though she was able to bring into the world her
daughter Nancy by her first husband. Nancy is an enigma at this juncture
and we never learn what happened to her.

To add to the great evangelist's aforementioned trials and tribulations he
began to receive some bitter opposition once again in the press. Two public
attacks were brought upon him in this manner at this time, they came in the
spring of 1751. The first was a controversial letter published by *Gentleman's
Magazine* (of which they were anything but!) and the second was another
round of Bishop Lavington's rantings published in this third part of his
"Enthusiasm of Methodists and Papists compared."

We see this from the following where George Whitefield was wrapping
up a preaching circuit where he hoped he would catch "some great fish in
the gospel net." From the following we see:

"After about a fortnight's stay in Bristol, he started for Plymouth, preaching at
Taunton and Wellington on his way. On his return, he wrote to Hervey, dating
his letter, 'Exeter, April 11, 1751.' He tells the amiable invalid that he would
count it 'a great honour and privilege' to have him as his guest for the remainder
of his life. During the last month, he had 'some trying exercises;' but he had
'preached about forty times,' and, in several instances, had ridden forty miles a

---

6   Ibid. pp. 267–269.

day. He had been among Hervey's old friends at Bideford; and had been blessed with 'sweet seasons at Plymouth.'

"It is impossible to determine what were the 'trying exercises,' which Whitefield mentions. One was the affliction of his wife. Perhaps, another was occasioned by the insertion of a letter in the *Gentleman's Magazine*, proposing that, because 'Whitefield preached that man, the chief work of God in this lower world, *by nature is half brute and half devil,*' the following lines should be inscribed on the door of Whitefield's house, and should not be removed until he 'recanted his shocking account of human nature, and declared that man is the *offspring of God,* and formed *by nature* to approve and love what is *just and good*':—

'Here lives one by nature half brute and half devil.
Avoid him, ye wise, though he speak kind and civil.
The devil can seem like an *angel of light,*
And *dogs* look *demure*, the better to bite.'

"It is rather surprising that a squib so paltry ... gave birth to a controversy, in that periodical, which lasted until the month of October next ensuing, not fewer than six different articles, for and against, being published on the subject.

"Probably, another cause of Whitefield's 'trying exercises' was the publication, about this period, of the third part of Lavington's 'Enthusiasm of Methodists and Papists compared,' an 8vo. volume of four hundred and twenty pages. This was the bishop's big gun, pointed at Wesley almost altogether, but discharging a few stray shots at Whitefield. It was not pleasant, for instance, to find the author perverting Whitefield's honest acknowledgment of the errors into which he had unwittingly fallen, by declaring, 'Whitefield has *confessed* that he has *imposed* upon the world by many *untruths*' (p. 263). Whitefield never confessed anything of the sort; and Dr. Lavington, Bishop of Exeter, knew, when he wrote these words, that he himself was writing an *untruth.*

"Lampoons, and episcopal mendacity like this, were, without doubt, annoying. It was also a matter of profound grief that, in the bulky volume just mentioned, his friend Wesley should be made the butt of all the sneering sarcasm which Lavington could bring to bear against him ...

"In the midst of all this worry and vexation, Whitefield found comfort and cause of exultation in a fact which ought to have augmented the severity of his 'trying exercises:' slavery was authorised in Georgia! Read in the light of the last hundred years, the following letter, addressed to a minister in America, is, to say the least, a curious production:—

'Bristol, March 22, 1751.

'Reverend and very dear Sir,—My wife has been in pitiable circumstances for some time. The Lord only knows what will be the issue of them. This is my comfort, "All things work together for good to those that love God." He is the Father of mercies, and the God of all consolation. He can bring light out of darkness, and cause the barren wilderness to smile.

'This will be verified in Georgia. Thanks be to God! That the time for favouring that colony seems to be come. Now is the season for us to exert ourselves to the utmost for the good of the poor Ethiopians. We are told, that, even they are soon to stretch out their hands unto God. And who knows but that their being settled in Georgia may be over-ruled for this great end?

'As to the lawfulness of keeping slaves, I have no doubt, since I hear of some that were bought with Abraham's money, and some that were born in his house. I, also, cannot help thinking, that some of those servants mentioned by the apostles, in their epistles, were or had been and, though liberty is a sweet thing to such as are born free, yet to those who never knew the sweets of it, slavery perhaps may not be so irksome.

'However this be, it is plain to a demonstration, that hot countries cannot be cultivated without negroes. What a flourishing country might Georgia have been, had the use of them been permitted years ago! How many white people have been destroyed for want of them, and how many thousands of pounds spent to no purpose at all! Had Mr. Henry been in America, I believe he would have seen the lawfulness and necessity of having negroes there. And, though it is true that they are brought in a wrong way from their native country, and it is a trade not to be approved of, yet, as it will be carried on whether we will or not, I should think myself highly favoured if I could purchase a good number of them, to make their lives comfortable, and lay a foundation for breeding up their posterity in the nurture and admonition of the Lord.

'You know, dear sir, that I had no hand in bringing them into Georgia. Though my judgment was for it, and so much money was yearly spent to no purpose, and I was strongly importuned thereto, yet I would have no negro upon my plantation, till the use of them was publicly allowed in the colony. Now this is done, let us reason no more about it, but diligently improve the present opportunity for their instruction. The Trustees favour it, and we may never have a like prospect. It rejoiced my soul, to hear that one of my poor negroes in Carolina was made a brother in Christ. How know we but we may have many such instances in Georgia before long? By mixing with your people, I trust many of them will be brought to Jesus; and this consideration, as to us, swallows up all temporal inconveniences whatsoever.'

"Whitefield's letter is a distracting compound of good and evil principles. Probably it will lower his character in the estimation of not a few who read it. Be it so. The letter exists, and it would not be honest to withhold it."[7]

Luke Tyerman was quite happy to present the above letter for by its lowering Whitefield it automatically raised John Wesley—who made no mention of his bias towards slavery. In a biography it is wrong to leave out the black marks on the subject's character; therefore we have included the letter in its

---

7   Ibid. pp. 270–273.

base form and simply leave it to history. We will add this on the subject of slavery and Whitefield's favoring it—he really believed he could bring the gospel to the slaves if they were in Georgia, whereas there was no missionary work existing at this time in history which would bring the gospel to darkest Africa. Though his bias towards slavery was absolutely in error, at least part of his reasoning was altruistic.

The mention of George Whitefield's wife captures our interest. And his comments of "My wife has been in pitiable circumstances for some time" is somewhat revealing. It tells us that the emotional grief and physical suffering from the loss of the child *lingered*. Apparently George Whitefield did not know how to properly console her and he committed her to the hands of his Blessed Lord. It is seen in observing him during these times of sorrow that his medicine for his soul is to take to the fields and throw himself into vigorous labor for his Lord. Non-stop preaching occupied him fully and thus made his own grieving easier to bear as it was lost in busyness.

On May 24, 1751, Whitefield set foot in Ireland. On his way to the Emerald Isle he passed through Wales where he "in about three weeks rode above five hundred miles, and generally preached twice a day, and that his congregations were as large as usual". We see that he began his labors in Dublin:

> "He began his labour in Dublin, and found at once large congregations hearing 'as for eternity.' In Limerick and Cork, also, his commanding eloquence overawed the old persecutors. The public cry was, 'Methodism is revived again;' but it was the signal of welcome, not of war, as formerly. At this time he was both very weak in body, and subject to daily vomiting. During this visit, he preached eighty times, and with great success. 'Providence,' says he, 'has wonderfully prepared my way, and overruled every thing for my greater acceptance. Every where there seems to be a shaking among the dry bones, and the trembling lamps of God's people have been supplied with fresh oil. The word ran and was glorified.' 'Hundreds,' says Dr. Southey, 'prayed for him, when he left Cork; and many of the Catholics said, that, if he would stay, they would leave their priests.'"[8]

We have some extracts of some letters he wrote while laboring in Ireland at this time:

"Dublin, June 1, 1751.

"My very dear Friend,

"... After being about five days on the water, I arrived here the 24th ult. At first the greatness and hurry of the place surprized me; but thanks be to the

---

8   Philip, p. 354.

LORD of the harvest, here as well as elsewhere the fields are white ready unto harvest. I have now preached about fourteen times, and find great freedom in dealing out the bread of life. Congregations are large, and hear as for eternity. Perhaps last LORD's day upwards of ten thousand attended. It much resembled a Moor-fields auditory. Next Monday, GOD willing, I leave Dublin, and set out on a circuit to Limerick, Cork, Athlone, Waterford, &c. I now lodge at a banker's who purposes to come to London shortly ..."

"To Lady Huntingdon.

"Athlone, June 10, 1751.

"This morning I had the wished-for favour and honour of you Ladyship's letter. O that it had acquainted me of your Ladyship's better health! But our LORD knows what is best. May patience have its perfect work, and your Ladyship come out of the furnace like gold tried seven times in the fire! Every day I can sympathize with your Ladyship. As the weather grows warmer, my body grows weaker, and my vomitings follow me continually. But all is little enough to keep me down, and prepare me for the service in which I am engaged. My last from Dublin, acquainted your Ladyship of my being owned of GOD there. By a letter from Mr. L——, I am informed, that Dublin is in a ferment, and that my hearers will be much more numerous at my return. Oh the blessedness of leaving all for JESUS! For this week past, I have been preaching twice almost every day in some country towns, and yesterday I sounded the gospel trumpet here ..."

"Limerick, June 14, 1751.

"... At Athlone I preached four times, and last night was gladly received here at Limerick. Every where our LORD hath vouchsafed us his blessed presence. That supports me under the heat of the weather, the weakness of my body, and the various trials which exercise my mind. I am now earnestly asking counsel from above. A wide open door is open in Dublin; but after I have visited Cork, I believe I must cut short my circuit, lest I should have a winter's voyage ..."

"To Lady Huntingdon.

"Ever-honoured Madam,   Dublin, June 28, 1751.

"... One to whom I had been represented in black colours, writes thus from Dublin to a preacher in Cork,—'What blessed seasons have we had since Mr. Whitefield came,—his coming hath been unspeakably blest to many. Thousands constantly attended the word. His word is attended with power. I never heard a man preach holiness of heart in a clearer manner.—He powerfully preaches CHRIST for us and in us. I confess I had strange ideas about him, but blessed be GOD, I have not now. GOD be praised that ever I saw his face ... ' Thus it hath been elsewhere. O that I was humble! O that I was thankful! Not unto me, O LORD, not unto me, but to thy free unmerited grace be all the glory! ...

"To Lady Huntingdon.

"Ever-honoured Madam,   Belfast, July 7, 1751.

"Last Monday about noon I left Dublin, but with what concern in respect to many poor weeping souls, cannot well be exprest. On Wednesday evening I came hither, and intended to embark immediately for Scotland, but the people by their importunity prevailed on me to stay. In about an hour's time, thousands were gathered to hear the word. I preached morning and evening, and since that have preached at Lisburn, Lurgun, the Maize, and Lambag, towns and places adjacent. So many attended, and the prospect of doing good is so promising, that I am grieved I came to the north no sooner. The country round about is like Yorkshire in England, and quite different from the most southern parts of Ireland. I am now waiting for a passage to Scotland, which I hope to get either to-morrow or on Tuesday. From thence your Ladyship shall hear from me again; in the mean while, having preached to many thousands again this morning, I must content myself with praying, that the best of blessings may descend on your Ladyship …"9

This celebrated itinerant preacher, when he visited America, like a comet drew the attention of all classes of people. The blaze of his ministration was extended through the continent, and he became the common topic of conversation from Georgia to New Hampshire. All the newspapers were filled with paragraphs of information respecting him, or with pieces of animated disputation pro and con; and the press groaned with pamphlets written in favor of, or against, his person and ministry. In short, his early visits to America excited a great and general agitation throughout the country, which did not wholly subside when he returned to Europe. Each succeeding visit occasioned a renewal of zeal and ardor in his advocates and opponents; and, it has been said, that from his example American preachers became more animated in their manner.

Isaiah Thomas

CHAPTER 42

BRIEF FOURTH VISIT TO AMERICA

It is a great wonder why, after he lamented his absence from America in so many letters, he merely stayed a total of six months! It was that very length of time he spent on the turbulent seas to travel to and from there! Oddly, we have little explanation for George Whitefield's peculiar behavior regarding his brief stay in America—we can only surmise that some urgency brought him back to England so soon: was it Elizabeth? Business? The affairs of the Orphan House?

Dr. Gillies tells us little about this brief episode in the evangelist's life. We read:

"October 27, he arrived at Savannah, and had the consolation to find the Orphan-house in a flourishing state. 'Thanks be to God,' says he, 'all is well at Bethesda. A most excellent tract of land is granted to me, very near the house, which in a few years, I hope, will make a sufficient provision for it.'

From November 1751, to the beginning of April 1752, he was partly at Bethesda, and partly in South Carolina, still upon the stretch in his Master's work. 'I intend, (says he) by his assistance, now to begin; for as yet, alas! I have done nothing.' And again, 'O that I may begin to be in earnest! It is a new year; GOD quicken my tardy pace, and help me to do much work in a little time! this is my highest ambition.'

"Being warned by what had happened to him formerly, he did not venture to stay the summer season in America; but took his passage in the end of April for London." [1]

These remarks by Gillies do not satisfy. And, they make no sense. Why did not Whitefield venture up to New England, as was his previous custom (he always labored in New England in the summer, as it was cooler there, and then headed south for Savannah in the winter—as the weather was more

---

1   Gillies, p. 140.

agreeable there)? Why did he not spend time with Gilbert Tennent and the rest of his good New England friends? Surely, Ben Franklin had desire to see him as well. It simply makes no sense for George Whitefield to endure the rigors of a total of six months at sea (three months each way in crossing the Atlantic) to only remain in America for the same duration. Something urgent in England drew him back and changed his plans—because he does not mention it we can only assume it was family related. Not only does Whitefield not mention the explanation for his sudden return to England, Whitefield biographer Arnold Dallimore makes no mention whatsoever of George Whitefield's fourth visit to America, considering it too brief and without merit to record. Another Whitefield biographer, J.P. Gledstone ignores the fourth visit to America as well merely stating:

> "From January, 1751, to December, 1752, there occurred nothing that deserves detailed record in a life like this, where effort was generally at the full stretch, and where sufferings, both mental and bodily, as well as joys, abounded."[2]

Philip makes no mention of this fourth return to America. And Belcher only remarks:

> "He took a hasty leave of his friends, and set sail for Georgia, in the Antelope, Captain M'Lellan, taking several orphans with him. He arrived at Savannah Oct. 27, and had the happiness of finding the orphan-house in a prosperous condition. Here, however, he did not stay long; as in November we hear of him in his usual labors, and with his usual ardor engaged in his constant work of preaching. Having formerly suffered much from the climate of America in the summer, he determined again to embark for London, which he did in April."[3]

It is quite obvious the only research Joseph Belcher did in this regard on reporting of Whitefield's fourth journey to America was to *copy* what Gillies had already mentioned. Our only next reliable source to turn to is Luke Tyerman (reliable meaning thorough). We read his comments about the fourth visit to America by George Whitefield:

> "Whitefield's sojourn in America was of short duration. He landed in October, 1751, and seven months afterwards was again in England. His time on land seems to have been spent chiefly in Georgia and South Carolina. Very little, however, is known of his proceedings. There was an urgent need to recruit his health. His business affairs, also, required attention. Still, he preached, at least, occasionally. With him, preaching was almost an element of life. His departure from England was abrupt; and his return was unexpected. All that is know of his brief visit is contained in half a dozen letters."[4]

---

2 Gledstone, p. 283.
3 Belcher, p. 340.
4 Tyerman, Vol. 2, p. 278.

At least Tyerman points us to his letters. And it is *there* we will turn. Sadly, George Whitefield's failure to keep a diary or journal at this time in his life is our loss (if he did keep one it was never intended to be published and it has been lost). At least we have his recorded activities that exist in these few letters. It was a significant event that Whitefield visited America for the fourth time and it needs to be dealt with adequately. We will now turn our attention to this history found in his letters of 1751–1752. We regret that Gillies removed the identities of the letter's recipients:

"To the Reverend Mr. G———.

"On board the Antelope, Sept. 2, 1751.

"Reverend and very dear Sir,

"Though I could not, through hurry of business, write to you on shore, yet I would fain send you a few lines from on board. We are now near the *Downs*, and, I trust, shall sail comfortably on.—The Captain is civil; and the cabin passengers seem to be very agreeable company. Parting seasons of late have been to me dying seasons.—Surely they have broken my very heart: but it is for JESUS, and therefore all is well. Remember, my dear, dear Sir, a floating pilgrim.—If possible, send me a line.—Young Mr. T———r knows how to direct. I shall rejoice to hear of your prosperity. Before my embarkation, I ordered forty of *Aaron's* pictures, and the folio book concerning the *Moravians,* to be sent to Mr. ———. They will be committed to the care of Mr. T———, in *Edinburgh.* And now, my dear Mr. G———, farewel, farewel! The LORD be with you and Mr.———, Mr.———, Mr. S———, and all my dear, very dear *Glasgow* friends. I salute you all much in the LORD, and beg the continuance of your most earnest prayers in behalf of, very dear Sir,

Yours most affectionately in our blessed JESUS,

G.W.

"Dear Sir,   On board the Antelope, Oct. 6, 1751.

"I have been just writing to one, to whom I know you will gladly convey the inclosed. I must now send you a few lines: may the Redeemer attend them with his blessing! At the great day, you shall know how often you have been remembered by me at the throne of grace, this voyage. Blessed be GOD, hitherto it has been a short and easy one! We are now within a few hundred miles of shore; and He that hath hitherto helped, I trust will help us even to the end. O that the blessings bestowed upon us, may, through the thanksgiving of many, redound to thy glory, O GOD! O that I could do something to promote this! As yet alas! Alas! How little have I done! Stir up then, my sluggish soul, and begin to exert thyself for Him, who hath shed his dear and precious heart's blood for thee! O my dear Sir, is it not strange that we should forget this love? Strange, that a little silver dust, should blind our eyes, and divert us from beholding Him, who indeed is altogether lovely! A word to the wise is enough.

Our LORD hath dealt wonderously kind with each of us, with us, and with ours. What shall we render unto him? My obligations are much increased by the mercies of this voyage. Your kind present was very useful. I pray the LORD of all lords to reward you ten thousand-fold. You will remember me to your dear partner, and all enquiring friends. That grace, mercy, and peace may be multiplied on you all, is the earnest prayer of, dear Sir,

Yours most affectionately in our common LORD,

G.W.

"To Mr. T——.

"Bethesda, in Georgia, Nov. 20. 1751.

"My dear Mr. T——,

"Ere this can reach you, I suppose you will have heard of our safe arrival in *Georgia*; for which, I trust, you and my other dear friends will be thankful in our behalf. Blessed be GOD, I found the Orphan-house in as good a situation as could be expected. The children have much improved in their learning; and I hope a foundation is now laid for a future useful seminary. I want to know what answer Mr. W——'s hath given. I expect letters by C——, when I go to *Charlestown* next month. I was there about ten days ago, and had some close talk with Mr. L——, and several of Mr. S——'s congregation concerning you. All seemed to be unanimous, in giving you a call. I need only observe, that if GOD should direct your course to them, you will find a generous, loving people, who will study to make your labours profitable and delightful to you. I doubt not but in the congregation there are many dear children of GOD. And as there will be such harmony between you and Mr. L——, I hope you will be an happy instrument of promoting peace between all parties, and adding such to the church as shall be finally saved. Very near you, are several pious ministers of other denominations, who will be glad to keep up a Christian correspondence with you, and strengthen your hands in the work of the LORD. As far as I can judge of your disposition, and all other concurring circumstances, your situation will be very agreeable to others, and to yourself. However, a trial can do no hurt to either side. A voyage to sea, and the seeing and conversing with many of GOD's people and ministers on this side the water, will make it worth your while to leave your native country. Travelling improved, will enlarge your ideas, and promote your future usefulness. May the glorious *Emmanuel* direct your goings in his way! If it should appear to be the divine will that you should come over to *Charles-town*, I am persuaded, the good old man your father will chearfully let his *Benjamin* go; and he will find his blessed Master to be better to him then seven sons. Pray salute him and all dear friends in the kindest manner. I would write to many, but as yet have not time. Brethren, pray for us. My very dear friend,

Yours most affectionately in our common LORD,

G.W.

"To Mr. K———.

"Charles-town, Dec. 26, 1751.

"My dear Mr. K———,

"May this find you getting out of your eclipse, and determining, through the strength of CHRIST, that the earth shall never get in between your soul and the Son of Righteousness any more! What mercies, signal mercies hath the LORD JESUS conferred on you and me! What shall we render unto the LORD? Shall we not give him our whole hearts? O let us not follow afar off. Let his love constrain us to an holy, universal, chearful obedience to all his commands. You have a wife that will provoke you to love, and to good works. Make much of her; and present her, and your mother, and all her children, with my most cordial salutations. I do not forget them, or you, or dear Mr. R———. For CHRIST's sake forget not unworthy me. I am now returning to the Orphan-house, which I trust will be like the burning bush indeed. My poor labours are accepted here; and in the Spring I purpose going to the *Bermudas*. JESUS is very good to me. Help me to praise him; and believe me to be, my dear Sir,

Your affectionate friend for CHRIST's sake,

G.W."[5]

It is necessary to pause here to make an important statement concerning Whitefield's *intentions* to remain on this side of the Atlantic to pursue good and continue in his labors for the Lord among His people. He had previously enjoyed a remarkable season of blessings while in the Bermuda islands. It was his intention to *return there* as was his practice in ministry. He made it a habit to return to an area a year or several years later to see if he could find *evidences* of the salvation which had taken place during his earlier visits. He also believed in making personal contact with the new friends he made on each journey—Whitefield was a "people person" and enjoyed the company of others—especially ministers. So it is the information found in this letter that lends support to our theory that he had full intentions of remaining in America for a longer period than just six months. And it was *not due to the heat of the climate nor his poor health* as Gillies alludes to that made him return. We even see misinformation again from Whitefield biographer, John Richard Andrews who, regarding George Whitefield's quick return, mistakenly concludes:

"Whitefield's fourth visit to America was a very short one, for he returned in the following April. The principle object he had in going at this time was to convert the orphan house into a seminary for training young men for the ministry. On his arrival he found everything going on satisfactorily. Additional land had been granted close to the house, and on this he determined to grow all

---

5   *Works,* Vol. 2, pp. 423–426.

the produce necessary for the institution, and then to part with the plantation in Carolina, which had proved a failure. These matters being speedily arranged, he left Georgia and ... arrived in London in May, 1752.[6]

Again, there is no mention of Whitefield planning to return to the Bermudas and no mention of a "Spring campaign". From all of this we make the following observations: One must be careful in biography not to copy remarks of other biographers without first doing the necessary research to prove the remarks true or factual. Hence this misinformation of the reason *why* George Whitefield returned to England so quickly was bad information first from Dr. Gillies, and then passed on by others like Belcher and others; each successor erroneously quoting from the previous writer without looking at all the facts: let this be a warning to each of us as we approach our subjects to—get the facts straight and not just rely on comments of others. It is in the very next letter that we find Whitefield's own intentions of continued labors in America when he states, "am almost ready to enter upon my Spring campaign." Something, urgent interrupted this "Spring campaign". We know not, but at least now, *we know of it.*

Now back to the narrative of Whitefield's letters!

"To Mr. William L———.

"Very dear Sir,   Bethesda, Jan. 25, 1752.

"Man appoints, but GOD disappoints. Though we missed seeing each other on earth, yet if JESUS CHRIST be our life, we shall meet never to part again in the kingdom of Heaven. Your kind letter found me employed for the fatherless, in this wilderness, and am almost ready to enter upon my Spring campaign. The news from *Ireland*, does not at all surprize me. Weak minds soon grow giddy with power; and then they become pests, instead of helps to the church of GOD. You have done well Sir, not to desist from doing good, on account of some rubs you meet with in the way. *Benefacere et male pati, vere christianum est.* Go on, therefore, to lay up treasures in heaven; and let the world see, that you have been with JESUS, by imitating him in going about doing good. I intend, by his assistance, now to begin; for as yet alas! I have done nothing. Continue to pray for me; and be pleased to assure our *Irish* friends, that they are not forgotten by me. Who knows but I may see them once more on this side eternity? As soon as possible, some of them shall hear from me. Thanks be to GOD, the Orphan-house flourishes. That the work of CHRIST may flourish amongst all persons of all denominations, and that you and yours may be always abounding in the work of the LORD, is the earnest prayer of, very dear Sir,

Your most affectionately in our common LORD,

G.W.

6   John Richard Andrews, *George Whitefield, A Light Rising in Obscurity*, pp. 253–254.

"To the Rev. Mr. H——.

"My very dear Friend,   Charles-town, Feb. 1, 1752.

"I long to write to, and inform you, that I love you in the bowels of JESUS
CHRIST, and earnestly pray, that you may go on from strength to strength, and
increase with all the increase of GOD. This leaves unworthy me, endeavouring
to do something for Him on this side the water. Glory be to his great name, he
causes his work to prosper in my worthless hands. The Orphan-house is in a
flourishing way, and I hope will yet become a useful seminary. My poor labours
in this place meet with acceptance; and after one more trip to *Georgia*, I purpose
setting out upon my Spring campaign. Follow me with your prayers; and who
knows but we may meet once more on this side heaven. Our dear Mr. H—— I
find is to be detained longer from thence. I think he will live to bury many
stronger men. I wish *Lisbon* may be blessed to Dr. D——; and O how do I wish
that dear Dr. S—— was fully employed in preaching the everlasting gospel!
Pray salute him tenderly in my name, and beg him to renounce the world for
CHRIST. I hope you both write to, and see our good Lady Huntingdon
frequently. I was rejoiced to hear, from my dear yoke-fellow, that her Ladyship
was bravely: this was joy indeed. May the long live to be a blessing! That is all in
all. O that I may begin to be in earnest! It is a new year; GOD quicken my tardy
pace, and help me to do much work in a little time! This is my highest ambition.
The LORD JESUS fill me with this ambition more and more! For the present,
adieu. Accept this as a token of your not being forgotten by, reverend and very
dear Sir,

Yours most affectionately in our dear LORD JESUS,

G.W."[7]

It is interesting to take note that the above letter is included in a *select few* that
make mention of his wife Elizabeth, "my dear yoke-fellow". What is striking
also from this letter is the repeated comments of George Whitefield's
"unworthy me"; "my poor labors"; "my tardy pace"; his humility is rare for
one who has already commanded the attention of two continents!

It is strikingly clear in this last letter of Whitefield's (while in America on
his fourth visit) that he had already made plans to travel up to New England
to see friends such as, Gilbert Tennent and Ben Franklin. This was to be his
"Spring campaign" which was never realized because of his abrupt return to
England. But notice in this last letters his comments, "After one more trip to
the Orphan-house, I purpose going to the *Northward*." This desire was cut
short by an unexpected call to England—of what nature we finally learn
about from a *letter* provided for us by Tyerman which we will examine in the
next chapter, "Return to England"; it is there we learn the reason!

---

7   *Works*, Vol. 2, pp. 426–427.

Now we examine this last letter from his brief time in the Colonies in 1751–1752. It is a rare specimen for it talks in detail about the doctrinal differences which still remain between him and John Wesley. It also speaks of his desire to leave no denomination behind him. It is truly one of his greatest letters and therefore, it is with great interest that we read:

"To Mr. S—— C——.

Charles-Town, Feb. 5, 1752.

"As I love you most tenderly in the bowels of JESUS CHRIST, you may easily guess, what great pleasure both your kind letters gave me. They came attended with a great blessing, and knit my heart, if possible nearer to you than ever. Part of the first, indeed, I mean that which respected the Tabernacle-house, gave me uneasiness; but your last removed it, and made me thankful to our common Redeemer, who in spite of all opposition, I find will cause his word to run and be glorified. Poor Mr. Wesley is striving against the stream; strong assertions will not go for proofs, and those who are acquainted with the divine life, and are sealed by the Holy Spirit even to the day of redemption. They know, that their stock is now put into safe hands; that the covenant of grace is not built upon the faithfulness of a poor fallible, changeable creature, but upon the never-failing faithfulness of an unchangeable GOD. This is the foundation whereon I build. 'LORD JESUS, I believe, help my unbelief! Having once loved me, thou wilt love me to the end; thou wilt keep that safe, which I have committed unto thee: establish thy people more and more in this glorious truth; and grant that it may have this blessed effect upon us all, that we may love thee more, and serve thee better!' All truths, unless productive of holiness and love, are of no avail. They may float upon the surface of the understanding; but this is to no purpose, unless they transform the heart. This, I trust, the dear Tabernacle preachers and people will always have deeply impressed upon their minds. Let us not dispute, but love. Truth is great, and will prevail. I am quite willing that all our hearers shall hear for themselves. The Spirit of CHRIST is a Spirit of liberty. You remember what I have often told you about *Calvin*. He was turned out of *Geneva* for several years; but in less than twelve years time they wished for their *Calvin* again. But what is *Calvin*, or what is *Luther*? Let us look above names and parties; let JESUS, the ever-loving, the ever-lovely JESUS, be our all in all.—So that he be preached, and his divine image stamped more and more upon people's souls, I care not who is uppermost. I know my place, (LORD JESUS enable me to keep it!) even to be the servant of all. I want not to have a people called after my name, and therefore act as I do. The cause is CHRIST's, and he will take care of it. I rejoice that you go on so well at the Tabernacle. May the shout of a king be always in the midst of you, and the glory of GOD be your reward. I am apt to believe you will pray me over. But future things belong to him, whose I am, and whom I endeavour to serve. After one more trip to the Orphan-house, I purpose going to the *Northward*, where I expect more letters by Captain *Grant*. Thanks be to GOD, all is well at *Bethesda*. A most excellent tract of land is granted to me very near the house, which in a few years I hope will make a sufficient provision for it. Pray give my tenderest and most hearty love to all your dear family, and all the Tabernacle people, and all enquiring friends. Entreat them, I pray you, to be mindful of a poor pilgrim, who night and day is never unmindful of you or them. Doctor *Doddridge* I find is gone; LORD JESUS prepare me to follow after!—With real and great affection, I subscribe myself, very dear Jemmy,

Yours, &c.

G.W."[8]

So this chapter closes in the life of George Whitefield on his fourth visit to America! In the next chapter we will see what mystery brought George Whitefield back to England so soon.

---

8   Ibid. pp. 428–429.

The prejudices of most that set themselves against him before his coming, seem to be in a great measure abated, and in some, to be wholly removed; and there is no open opposition made to him. I have frequent opportunities of being with him, and there always appears in him such a concern for the advancement of the Redeemer's kingdom and the good of souls, such a care to employ his whole time to these purposes, such sweetness of disposition, and so much of the temper of his great Lord and master, that every time I see him, I find my heart further drawn out towards him.

William Shurtleff
minister of Portsmouth, New Hampshire.

CHAPTER 43

RETURN TO ENGLAND

Back in England Whitefield lost no time in throwing himself back into his busy labors. The members of the Tabernacle were shocked to see him return so soon but elated that he had. Sad news reached his ears: his mother was dead. Much mystery is cleared up for us by the following comments of "old reliable Tyerman":

"Whitefield did not go to 'the Bermudas,' nor yet 'northward,' as he intended. About two months after the date of the foregoing letter, he suddenly set sail for England. Why was this? Nothing has yet been published to explain it. The following letter, now for the first time printed, solves the difficulty. It was addressed, 'To Mr. Blackwell, banker, in Lombard Street, London':—

'Portsmouth, May 21, 1752.

'My Dear Mr. Blackwell,—I fully purposed to have written you when I was at Charleston, in South Carolina; but my sudden resolution to embark for England prevented me. God has vouchsafed to bless me, in respect to the Orphan House, in a very unexpected manner. To put it upon a proper footing, and to apply for some privileges, before the time of the Trustees' Charter be expired, is what has called me home so speedily. Home, did I say? I trust heaven is my home; and it is my comfort that it is not far off. Surely this body will not hold out always. Yet a little while, and our Lord will come, and take us to Himself, that where He is, there we may be also.

'There pain and sin and sorrow cease,
And all is calm and joy and peace.'

'I wish you and yours much of this heaven upon earth. Looking unto Jesus is the only way of drawing it down into our souls. Out of His fulness, we all receive grace for grace. We have an open-handed, an open-hearted Redeemer. He giveth liberally, and upbraideth not. O for power from on high to set forth the riches of redeeming love! In a few days I hope to attempt a little of this in London. I beg your prayers. I thank you heartily for all favours; and, with cordial salutations to your *whole self*, subscribe myself, dear sir, yours most affectionately in our common Lord,

G. Whitefield.'"[1]

So with those remarks by Whitefield and dependable Luke Tyerman (though at times biased in favor of Wesley) the great mystery of why George Whitefield's fourth visit to America was cut so short: it had to do with an expiring document (the Trustees' Charter) that required immediate attention!

It was also the Hand of Providence that called him back to his native country. For he soon learns his dear mother is dead. We see this in the following:

> "During his absence, Whitefield's beloved mother had exchanged mortality for life; but this was not the reason of his sudden return to England. The affairs of the Orphan House brought him back ..."[2]

After paying respects to his mother's grave and staying in the Metropolis for a month, in June he hit the road again; writing to a friend on June 9th he states, "May I die preaching! Next Thursday se'nnight I leave London, and purpose to take a long circuit." First going to Portsmouth then to Bath, George Whitefield joined his good friend and patroness the Countess whose health had improved and Whitefield labored in the town of Bath for three weeks where he "preached every evening to great numbers of the nobility". We see in a letter to Selina her Chaplain's ministerial intentions:

"To Lady Huntingdon.

"Ever-honoured Madam,   London, June 12, 1752.

> "This day about noon I received your Ladyship's wished-for letter, which brought me the welcome news of your Ladyship's safe arrival at *Bath.* May the waters be abundantly blessed to the restoring of your bodily health, and may the comforts of the ever-loving, ever-lovely JESUS, fill and refresh your soul! ... Next week, GOD willing, I shall go to *Portsmouth,* from thence to *Bath,* then to the West, then to *Wales,* and from thence, may be to *Scotland* and *Ireland.* O that I could fly from pole to pole publishing the everlasting gospel! Every day we hear of fresh conquests gained. Grace! Grace! Yesterday I had several pleasing particulars told me about *Georgia.* The having my work so divided, is a great trial to me; but what is undertaken for GOD, ought to be carried on for him. He can and will do wonders for those who put their trust in him. O for faith, precious faith! It is all in all. Old times seem to be coming about here. My body is much enfeebled, but the joy of the LORD is my strength ..."[3]

In another letter to a friend Whitefield revealed some details of the colony in

---

1   Tyerman, Vol. 2, pp. 280–281.
2   Ibid. p. 281.
3   *Works,* Vol. 2, p. 433.

Georgia and his desire to visit it again the following year. He writes from Portsmouth, on June 19, 1752:

"... We have had blessed seasons in *London*; there I must be again in about a fortnight. On next *Tuesday* the Trustees give up *Georgia* to the King; the King of Kings has appeared for *Bethesda*. I cannot think of seeing it again, till next year ..."[4]

In July we find the great evangelist in Wales. From Cardiff, on July 17th he writes to a friend the following:

"... I was at Bristol four days, and preached nine times. To my great surprize, thousands (very near as many as attended at *Moorfields*) came out every evening to hear the word. A blessed influence attended it; and I have reason to believe much good was done. Old times seemed to be revived again. Praise the LORD, O my soul! The last evening it rained a little, but few moved. I was wet, and contracted a cold and hoarseness; but I trust, that preaching will cure me again. This is my grand Catholicon. O that I may drop and die in my blessed master's work!

"For this let men revile my name,
I'll shun no cross, I'll fear no shame;
All hail reproach, and welcome pain;
Only thy terrors, LORD, refrain.

"I am now entering upon *Wales*. What success my Master gives me, you may hear some time hence. I beg your prayers, that I may be kept from robbing GOD of his glory, or of any more of my precious time ..."[5]

Both Whitefield and Howell Harris had relinquished their positions of office with the Welsh Calvinists but not their friendships with them. Whitefield was no longer their official moderator and Harris had withdrawn from the "Association" to form and begin (in April of 1752) his "family" at Trevecca. Later, in 1768, Lady Huntingdon would throw her money and influence behind establishing a college for the training of preachers close by to Harris's home. It would be missionary graduates from Trevecca who would be sent to Georgia after Whitefield's death to labor at his beloved Bethesda.

We have news of the Welsh circuit and its attendant success from George Whitefield to the Countess in the following letter written from Haverford-west, on July 25, 1752.

"Ever-honoured Madam,

"As this is the first day of rest from journeying, since my coming into *Wales*, and also the extent of my *Welch* circuit, I must not omit sending your Ladyship a few lines. They inform your Ladyship of the continued goodness of my blessed

4   Ibid. p. 435.
5   Ibid. pp. 436–437.

master, to the most unworthy servant he ever sent forth. As my day, so hath my strength been. Abundance of souls, especially in *Pembrokeshire*, have attended; and I hope that seed hath been sown, which will spring up to eternal life. On *Monday* next, I shall begin to return back, and some time this day sevennight hope to wait upon your Ladyship at *Clifton*. On the following day, I propose to preach at *Bristol*, and the next day shall set out for *Gloucestershire*, to keep an association there. The LORD help me to hold on and hold out unto the end! I dread the thoughts of flagging in the latter stages of my road. JESUS is able to keep me from being either weary or faint in my mind. In him, and in him alone is all my strength found ..."[6]

We see the full scope of George Whitefield's labors in Wales, including his meeting with the Calvinist Methodists where he was present at an Association with nine of their clergy, in another letter written to a friend. It is dated August 1, 1752 and written from Bristol. Here are some extracts from it:

"The glorious *Emmanuel* hath carried me through the *Welch* circuit in peace and comfort. In the fortnight past, from my leaving this place, I preached twenty times, and have travelled above three hundred miles. Congregations were very large Last Lord's day was a high day indeed; the number of hearers at seven in the morning, as well as in the evening, at *Haverford-west*, was almost incredible. The LORD was in the midst of them. My body was weak in speaking to them, but JESUS hath strengthened me again. O that I was humble and thankful! In my way hither, we held an association; there were present about nine clergy, and near forty other labourers ..."[7]

Back in London in August we see the growing friendship between Whitefield and Benjamin Franklin. Franklin, who was growing famous in Europe for his scientific discoveries, had in 1752 "established the identity between lightning and the electric fluid". He had recently successfully explained the phenomena of the Leyden Jar and as these discoveries became more known so did his fame. We have the following letter that George Whitefield wrote to Franklin at this time. It is dated August 17, 1752 and was written from London.

"Dear Mr. Franklin,

"... I find that you grow more and more famous in the learned world. As you have made a pretty considerable progress in the mysteries of electricity, I would now humbly recommend to your diligent unprejudiced pursuit and study the mystery of the new-birth. It is a most important, interesting study, and when mastered, will richly answer and repay you for all your pains. One at whose bar we are shortly to appear, hath solemnly declared, that without it, 'we cannot

6   Ibid. pp. 437–438.
7   Ibid. p. 439.

enter the kingdom of heaven.' You will excuse this freedom. I must have *aliqid Christi* in all my letters. I am yet a willing pilgrim for his great name sake, and I trust a blessing attends my poor feeble labours. To the giver of every good gift be all the glory ..."[8]

Though the friendship between Whitefield and Franklin was discussed in Part One of this volume we will include further comments about their unique friendship by Luke Tyerman:

"The long continued friendship, existing between Whitefield and Franklin, was an odd incident in the great preacher's life. In addressing Franklin, Whitefield never fawned; he was always faithful. Franklin disbelieved the chief doctrines Whitefield preached; but he respected the good intentions, the zeal, the benevolence, the honesty of the man ..."[9]

We are sure that if Ben Franklin died apart from saving faith in Christ he has in hell continually lamented his time spent on the pursuits of life and not of God.

Toward the end of August Whitefield once more visited Scotland and his labors there were truly blessed of God. We are thankful that the Countess of Huntingdon instructed her chaplain to make weekly contact with her while on his itinerancies for it is these records of correspondence that enable us to keep track of his fantastic labors. The following two letters addressed to the Countess reveal much of his activity in Scotland including being pelted with turnips!

"To Lady Huntingdon.

"Ever-honoured Madam, Edinburgh, Sept. 22, 1752.

"The day after I wrote to your Ladyship, I left *London*, and in my way to *Scotland* I preached twice at *Lutterworth.*—The auditories were very numerous, and very quiet; but at *Leicester* some turnips were thrown at me during the first sermon; at the second all was hushed, and I hear since that good was done. Some of the *Ashby* society came thither to hear me. At *Aberford* I called on Lady *Margaret*, who behaved very friendly, and enquired much after your Ladyship's welfare. At *Newcastle* I was, as it were, arrested to stay. I preached four times and indeed a whole shower of divine blessings descended from heaven on the great congregations. I came hither last *Wednesday* was sevennight, and have preached twice a day in the open air, to very large and polite auditories. Abundance of the better sort constantly attend. Next *Tuesday* I thought to move, but they have prevailed upon me to stay a little longer. I hope the great GOD will give me a useful journey back again to *London*. I design keeping from thence as long as I can, before I go into my Winter quarters. Alas, how little is to be done even in the Summer season! One had need work whilst it is day; the night comes on a

8   Ibid. p. 440.
9   Tyerman, Vol. 2, p. 283.

pace, when no man can work. I need not tell your Ladyship of this, who are always employed for your GOD. O that the rich and great would learn to copy after your example! Surely all your Ladyship's efforts will not be lost upon them! ..."

"To Lady Huntingdon.

Newcastle, Oct. 15, 1752.

"Ever-honoured Madam,

"Thus far hath a never-failing Redeemer brought me in my way towards *London*. With all humility and thankfulness of heart I desire to set up my *Ebenezer:* for surely hitherto hath the LORD helped me. Since my writing last to your Ladyship, I went and preached for about a week at *Glasgow*, where the word of the LORD ran and was glorified. I preached twice a day, and rather more attended than at *Edinburgh*. We had a sorrowful parting at both places. For about twenty-eight days, I suppose I did not preach to less than ten thousand every day. This hath weakened my body, but the Redeemer knows how to renew my strength. At present, I am as well as a pilgrim can expect to be. About seventy pounds were collected for the *Edinburgh* orphans, and I hear that near a dozen young men that were awakened about ten years ago, have since entered upon the ministry, and are likely to prove very useful. Praise the LORD, O my soul!—In my way hither, I preached at *Berwick, Alnwick and Morpeth;* and next *Monday*, after preaching at *Sunderland*, as is intended, I am to go into *Yorkshire* ..."[10]

Regarding these seasons of abounding blessings from heaven upon the people of Scotland we have the following observations by Whitefield's good friend and biographer Dr. Gillies, who made it a habit to attend Whitefield's preaching each time he came to Scotland. We read:

"Though after the years 1741 and 1742 there were no such extensive new awakenings, Mr. Whitefield's coming was always refreshing to serious persons, and seemed to put new life into them, and also to be the means of increasing their number. His preaching was still eminently useful in various respects. In the first place, it had an excellent tendency to destroy the hurtful spirit of bigotry, and excessive zeal for smaller matters, and to turn men's attention to the great and substantial things of religion. Another effect was, that it drew several persons to hear the gospel, who seldom went to hear it from other ministers. Again, young people in general, were much benefitted by his ministry, and particularly young students, who became afterwards serious evangelical preachers. Lastly, his morning discourses, which were mostly intended for sincere but disconsolate souls, were peculiarly fitted to direct and encourage all such in the Christian life. And his addresses in the evening to the promiscuous multitudes who then attended him, were of a very alarming kind. There was something exceedingly striking in the solemnity of his evening congregation in

---

10 *Works*, Vol. 2, pp 443, 447–448.

the Orphan-house park at Edinburgh, and High churchyard of Glasgow, especially towards the conclusion of his sermons (which were commonly very long, though they seemed short to the hearers) when the whole multitude stood fixed, and, like one man, hung upon his lips with silent attention, and many under deep impressions of the great objects of religion, and the concerns of eternity. These things will not soon be forgotten; and it is hoped the many good effects which, by the divine blessing attended them, never will.

"His conversation was no less reviving than his sermons ... His friends in Scotland, among whom were many of all ranks, from the highest to the lowest, were very constant and steady in their great regard for him. And his opposers grew more and more mild. Some anonymous pamphlets were written against him at his first coming, but these soon died and were forgotten. Afterwards a number of stories were handed about to his disadvantage; but, upon inquiry, it was found either that matters were misrepresented or exaggerated, or that there was no foundation for such reports at all: in short, when they were traced to their origin, they rather turned out to his honor ...

"But, indeed, Mr. Whitefield's whole behavior was so open to the eyes of the world, and his character, after it had stood many attacks from all quarters, came at last to be so thoroughly established, that several of his opposers in Scotland seemed rather to acquire a certain degree of esteem for him at least, they all thought proper to give over speaking against him.

"When he was at Glasgow, he always lodged with Mr. James Neven, merchant, above the Cross; till, towards the end of his life, his asthmatic disorder made the town air disagree with him. And then he went out in the evenings, and stayed with his good friend Mr. M'Culloch, at Cambuslang.

"A person of eminence, whom a sincere esteem of Mr. Whitefield made attentive to his reception and ministrations in Scotland, from first to last, writes thus to the compiler:

'Edinburgh, January, 1772. I think more might be said, with great justice, concerning the effects of his ministry in Scotland, after the first two years; as there was always a remarkable revival following each of his visits; which many of the ministers testified to from their particular knowledge, especially by the number of new communicants. Mention might be made of the great number of ministers in Scotland that employed him, and of the many affectionate letters he received from them, of which there were a good many printed, both in London and Glasgow Weekly Histories, from some of the most eminent men in the church, who had employed him to preach in their pulpits, and continued so to do, when opportunity offered; except in the Presbytery of Edinburgh; and even there the magistrates always allowed him a church to preach in, every time he came.'"[11]

It would do well to include a true incident recorded by Dr. Gillies that

11 Gillies, pp. 138–139.

speaks volumes to the *supernatural power* that attended the preaching of George Whitefield. What made him so strikingly singular as a preacher were two things: his great oratory and the unction which so accompanied it. Though the following account took place in England and not in Scotland it is still pertinent to this period for it occurred soon after George Whitefield left Scotland and was preaching in the environs of Norwich. Here is this remarkable account:

'A young man of the city of Norwich, of about eighteen years of age, was walking one morning, with a party of other young men, who had all agreed to make that day a holiday. The first object that attracted their attention was an old woman, who pretended to tell fortunes. They immediately employed her to tell theirs, and that they might fully qualify her for their undertaking, first made her thoroughly intoxicated with spiritous liquor. The young man of whom mention was first made, was informed, among other things, that he would live to a very old age, and see his children, grand children, and great grand children, growing up around him. Though he had assisted in qualifying the old woman for the fraud, by intoxicating her, yet he had credulity enough to be struck with these parts of her predictions which related to himself. 'And so,' quoth he, when alone, 'I am to see children, grand children, and great grand children! At that age I must be a burden to the young people. What shall I do? There is no way for an old man to render himself more agreeable to youth, than by sitting and telling them pleasant and profitable stories. I will then, thought he, during my youth, endeavor to store my mind with all kinds of knowledge. I will see and hear, and note down every thing that is rare and wonderful, that I may sit, when incapable of other employment, and entertain my descendants. Thus shall my company be rendered pleasant, and I shall be respected rather than neglected in old age. Let me see what I can acquire first? Oh! Here is the famous Methodist preacher, Whitefield; he is to preach, they say, to-night. I will go and hear him.'

"From these strange motives the young man declared he went to hear Whitefield. He preached that evening from Matthew iii.7. 'But when he saw many of the Pharisees and Sadducees come to his baptism, he said unto them, O generation of vipers, who hath warned you to flee from the wrath to come?' 'Mr. Whitefield,' said the young man, 'described the sadducean character; this did not touch me. I thought myself as good a christian as any man in England. From this he went to that of the pharisees. He described their exterior decency, but observed that the poison of the viper rankled in their hearts. This rather shook me. At length, in the course of his sermon, he abruptly broke off; paused for a few moments; then burst into a flood of tears; lifted up his hands and eyes, and exclaimed, 'O my hearers! *The wrath's to come! The wrath's to come!*' These words sunk into my heart, like lead in the waters. I wept, and when the sermon was ended, retired alone. For days and weeks I could think of little else. Those awful words would follow me, wherever I went, '*The wrath's to come! The wrath's to come!*'" The issue was, that the young man, soon after made a public profession of religion, and in a little time became a considerable preacher. He himself related the foregoing circumstances a few years since, to the Rev. Andrew Fuller, of Kettering."[12]

Time after time we see incidents like the one just related where someone goes to hear the great evangelist out of mere curiosity and then that person returns home changed for eternity. This is God's doings through His obedient servant!

Regarding Whitefield's preaching, it is noteworthy (from Gillies' remarks) that his morning preaching encouraged the saints—those who were sincere enough to attend a service at 5am!; whereas his evening service (attended more by lost sinners) was not to encourage but to alarm and awaken. Such is the distinguishing mark of good preaching!

As the great evangelist closes the year of 1752 we see he is in the metropolis and busy as usual. He relates in a letter to The Countess dated Dec. 15, 1752, "My hands are full of work … has your Ladyship read the awful account of the hurricane in South Carolina?" No doubt this brought his attention to his plantation there and on January 7, 1753 he decides to sell "Providence Plantation". Writing to a friend in America he states, "By this conveyance, I send you a power of attorney to dispose of Providence plantation. I leave it to your discretion to sell at what price you please …" It was George Whitefield's intention to take the proceeds from the land in South Carolina and apply it to buy more land for Bethesda. This additional money would help the Orphan House become a working plantation and hopefully be self-supporting. At least these were his intentions.

Whitefield ends 1752 in London with his wife whom he mentions in a letter to a friend. We learn that Elizabeth Whitefield has been sick. He writes from London, Dec. 22, 1752, "… I am much indebted to you, and hope to see you in London soon. My wife longs to have you under our roof; she hath been ill, but bless be GOD is now better … A variety of business obliges me to hasten to subscribe myself, Yours &c. G.W."

---

12 Ibid. p. 143.

As converts increased in Bristol and its neighborhood, Mr. Whitefield felt compelled to erect there also a "tabernacle." Lady Huntingdon was one of the earliest contributors to this important object, and through her influence Lord Chesterfield gave twenty pounds to it. He had no taste for religion, but he well understood oratory, and in his letter to Lady Huntingdon covering his remittance, he said, "Mr. Whitefield's eloquence is unrivalled, his zeal inexhaustible."

Joseph Belcher, D.D.

CHAPTER 44

HIS TABERNACLES AND GREAT LABORS OF 1753

As Whitefield entered the year of 1753 there was much activity and eagerness to greet the new year. We get a sense of George Whitefield's plans as he entered another year of serving his Blessed Emmanuel from a letter to "Honoured Madam", Selina. We read:

"To Lady Huntingdon.

"Honoured Madam, London, Jan. 1, 1753.

"... Eternity! Eternity! The very writing or hearing this word, is enough to make one dead to the world, and alive unto GOD. The LORD quicken my tardy pace! I am now thirty-eight years of age, and entering upon another new year; Alas! Alas! How little have I done for that JESUS, who hath done and suffered so much for me! I want to begin to begin to act and preach for GOD. Blessed be his name, that his spirit is moving on precious souls at *Bristol*. For ever adored be his rich, free, and unmerited grace, the same be said of *London*. We have had blessed holidays, and I have had good news from the Orphan-house.

A life that all things casts behind,
Spring forth obedient at his call.

"Had I a thousand lives, the LORD JESUS should have them. I with your Ladyship, and honoured daughters, much of his divine love shed abroad in your hearts. That is the best new year's compliment, and the best new year's gift. I hope, the young ladies through grace are kept unspotted from the world. I would come and wait upon our elect Lady at *Clifton*, but am engaged in forwarding the building of a new tabernacle; I hope it will be accomplished, and that GOD's presence will fill it when erected. I could enlarge, but am called away, and therefore subscribe myself,

Your Ladyship's most dutiful, obliged, and ready servant for CHRIST's sake.

G.W."[1]

---

1   *Works*, Vol. 2, pp. 468–469.

We gain insights into this vast building project which so occupied the young
evangelist from the following comments:

> "The wooden meeting-house, in Moorfields, had now stood the storms of a
> dozen winters. At the best, it was but a huge, ugly shed; and, of course, signs of
> decay were becoming visible. Still, the uncouth fabric was a sacred one. Many
> were the mighty sermons preached by Whitefield beneath its roof; and countless
> were the blessings which had fallen upon its crowds of worshippers. A more
> durable edifice, however, was greatly needed; and, in the summer of 1751,
> while at Lady Huntingdon's residence at Ashby-de-la-Zouch, the project had
> been discussed, in the presence of her ladyship, Doddridge, Hervey, Hartley,
> and Stonehouse, all of whom were "most cordial in their approval and promise
> of support." Towards the end of 1752, the subject was renewed at the house of
> Lady Frances Shirley, in South Audley Street; and, in compliance with the
> urgent entreaties of her ladyship and of the Countess of Huntingdon, Whitefield
> now began to exert himself in collecting money. He resolved not to begin
> building till he had £1,000 in hand. That amount he soon obtained; the first
> brick was laid on the 1st of March, 1753; and, withing fifteen weeks afterwards,
> the structure was opened for public worship; the congregations, during that
> interval, still continuing to assemble in the wooden tabernacle, which was left
> standing within the shell of the building in course of erection. The new
> Tabernacle needs no description; for, though a third was within the last few
> years been built upon its site, there are thousands still living who have often
> gazed with reverence at the low, unpretentious edifice where Whitefield so
> often mounted his pulpit throne, and not a few who found salvation within its
> walls."[2]

It is only fitting at this juncture in the great evangelists's life to produce a
sermon specimen which so captures his great eloquence and preaching style.
It is a little known sermon and has not been made available until recently.
We will present only a portion of it but enough to show his great oratory
and line of persuasion to his hearers. Sadly, it is without the thunder, and the
lightning and the rainbow—but mere words on the printed page, yet it is
representative of him.

Sermon on Romans 4:16

> "… II. *How valuable and useful are the Doctrines of free Grace!* No Doctrines but
> these have any Suitableness, or Tendency, to produce, or excite, that most
> necessary important, and precious Grace of Faith. We acknowledge indeed, that
> the most evangelical Discourses have no Power, or Influence in themselves to
> work Faith: 'Tis the divine Spirit alone that can give them an Efficacy; but there
> is, and ought to be a Suitableness between the Means and the End. And how
> well adapted the Doctrine of free Grace is, to answer this End, is plain to those
> that have felt the Power of them, and may be learn'd from the very Nature of
> the Truths themselves.

---

2   Tyerman, Vol. 2, pp. 290–291.

"That we might be instrumental in the hands of the divine Spirit, to lead you out of yourselves to fly to, and trust upon the Lord *Jesus Christ* by Faith, we *on the one hand* are obliged as Ministers of the Word, to inform you of, and declare unto you, your deplorable, and in itself desperate Condition by Nature; to assure you, that no Works of your own can atone for your Sins, satisfy divine Justice, or make the least Amends for your past Iniquities. For this End we assure you, that you cannot work any saving Change in your Hearts, or make any saving Alteration in your State towards God. For this End we frequently set forth before you, the Corruption of your Natures, the Deceitfulness of your Hearts, the Guilt and Malignity of your Sins, the Purity and Spirituality of the divine Law, and the Strictness of divine Justice. We are obliged faithfully to insist upon such Truths as these; not to drive you into absolute Despair, or to make you more miserable than you are; but to shut you up unto the Faith of the Gospel; to hedge up every false Way of Peace with Thorns, and to deter you from receiving any other Help, and from being satisfied with any other Hope, but that which the Gospel presents before you.

"*On the other hand*; for this End we preach to you *Jesus Christ*, in his *Person, Offices,* and *Benefits.* We preach him as GOD, and so *able* to save; as *Man,* and so *suited* to save as *Mediator,* and so *appointed* and *designed* to save.

"For this Cause we preach him as the only atoning Sacrifice, as the LORD our Righteousness and Strength; as the Trustee, and Repository of all saving Blessings. For this Cause we proclaim, in the Name of *Christ,* all this Grace that is treasured up in him, as entirely free: If by any Means you may be led out of yourselves, and be engaged to trust in *Christ,* and live upon him, for all you really need; and may learn by direct Acts of Faith, *to receive of his Fullness, and Grace for Grace.*

"III. *How dangerous are any Tenets that contradict the Doctrines of Free Grace in Jesus Christ!* Consider, *Christians,* that Errors of this kind, are not merely speculative, such as may be received, or rejected with equal Safety; but they are dangerous in their very Nature, and must be pernicious in their Tendency; and that for this Reason. Because the Scripture is full of this Doctrine; that Remission, Justification, and all Salvation are by Faith; and that the Way in which a Soul acts in the Reception of Christ, and his Salvation, is by *trusting, relying, and depending* upon him. Now observe, whatsoever Doctrines have a Tendency in their own Nature, to cloud, or hinder, to overturn, pervert, or contradict these most important, and spiritual Actings, have a real Tendency to destroy Souls. Think a little, and you may see, how ever other Doctrine naturally leads us away from *Christ.* Were we to tell you, that Salvation is by Works; this would lead you to trust in your own Performances. Did we tell you, that sincere, though imperfect Obedience, is accepted in the Room of perfect; this directly tends to lead you to trust in, and lay the Stress of your Souls upon your Sincerity: Nay, were we to tell you, that your Repentance and Faith, were properly Conditions of Justification to Life; this would lead you to trust in your Repentance and Faith, whereby the very Nature of both would be contradicted. For what is Repentance, but a Soul's going out of itself, under a humble Sense

of Sin and Guilt? And what is Faith, but the Soul's going to Christ, and relying
upon him? If therefore we lead you to rely on your Repentance, we in effect bid
you trust in yourselves, instead of directing you to go out of yourselves. And if
by any Doctrine we should induce you to trust in your Faith; what is this? but to
make Faith its own Object, which contradicts its very Nature and Tendency;
since its Business and Office is to trust in another?

"In, a Word, did we give you any, even, the least Ground, by our Preaching,
to think that any Thing, done by you is the Matter of your Justification, or the
proper Condition thereof, you would be hereby induced to trust in *that Thing*,
whatever it be; and so would fall short of a direct and absolute Trust in Christ;
which would be ruinous to your precious and immortal Souls. And therefore, as
we have a pure Design to advance the Glory of *Christ*, as we highly prize, and
value the Method of Grace, and as we have a tender Concern for the Good of
your Souls; we would not, we cannot, we dare not declare any Thing in the
Name of the Lord, that should have any Tendency to turn your Hopes, or
Desires, your Confidences, or Expectations, any other Way, than towards him,
in whom all Fullness dwells.

"IV. *What an admirable Tendency is there in these Doctrines to produce true Holiness!*
The more we look into this Scheme of Grace, the more our Souls will be
surprised at it, and ravished by it. There is not any, the least Flaw or Imperfection
to be found in it; but under every Consideration, it recommends itself both to
the rational Mind, and to the awakened, inquiring Conscience. Nor can there
be any Room for the holy Tendency of this Doctrine to be suspected. 'Tis only
when Persons trifle with it, that they pervert it, and so turn the Doctrine of
Grace into Lasciviousness. But let us now seriously consider the Case of a poor
Soul, that is really wrought upon to see its own Misery and Helplessness, and is
truly led to behold and receive the Grace of God in *Christ*, as entirely free, and
then observe; what Effect such Convictions, Persuasions, and Impressions, must
necessarily produce. Tho' such a Faith, as has been described, is only *instrumental*
in our Justification; yet 'tis greatly *influential* into our Sanctification. Such a
spiritual Persuasion of the *Free Grace* of God, not only produces the Acts of
trusting, relying, and the like; but, at the same Time, it forms the Heart, for
Holiness, and fills it with an Aversion to Sin. Can we suppose a Soul to have
been in Distress upon the Account of Sin, and to have had realising Views of
Christ, and the free Promises; and not be in some Measure roused from its
natural Carelessness about Salvation; purged from its Fondness for Sin, and
drawn forth into a real Love of God in *Christ*? And will not this Love operate in
the fearing of his Name, in obeying his Precepts, and delighting in the Law of
God after the inward Man?

"Nay, father; did we really and truly consider what *holiness* is; we should upon
close Examination find; that nothing has a direct Tendency to produce it, but
the powerful Impression of the *Free-Grace* of God. For true Holiness includes,
not merely the Regulation of the Tongue, or an outward Reformation of Life;
but likewise a Rectification of the Heart and Conscience. A good Temper,
moral Honesty, extensive Knowledge, natural Abilities, and learned

Acquirements, may render a Man fit for civil Societies, and in some measure useful in religious Societies; but all this may be without true Holiness; for this consists in an inward, hearty Love, and Fear of God; in a inward Hatred of Sin, and a Delight in the Law of God after the inward Man. Nothing short of this can justly be called a real Renovation of Soul, or a spiritual Conformity to God, or be any proper Meetness for Heaven. Now how shall this be brought about? 'Tis true, Precepts may bind us, conditional Promises may excite us to some Good; and Threatenings may deter us from some Evil; but without something farther than all this, there is no true Holiness; for after all the Amendment that can be wrought by these Means alone, the Heart, the Spirit of the Mind, remains the same as before. But true Faith in *Christ*, being an Impression of the Grace of God upon the Heart, and an Application of it to the Conscience, never fails of making a gracious, holy Alteration in the Soul itself.

"Do we therefore desire true Holiness; let us not expect it from the Law, but from *Christ*: Let us daily meditate upon the Doctrines of *Free-Grace*, and beg that the holy Spirit may make an effectual Application of them to our Souls, and write them upon our Hearts; and if this be done, we shall find that our whole Souls are going out to *Christ*, in a way of Dependence and Love; and our Hearts will be more and more formed averse to Sin, and furnished out for every good Word and Work.

"*Fifthly*, and Lastly, *How exactly suited is this Doctrine to our necessitous Circumstances!* Let us here be persuaded to look a little into our Case as *Sinners*. 'Tis not so small a Matter to be Sinners as we are ready to imagine. We have naturally slight Thoughts of Sin, of the Law, and Justice of God. But after all our Excuses and Evasions; to *sin* is no less than to break the divine Law, to affront the divine Holiness, to inflame the divine Justice, and to subject ourselves to the divine Wrath and Displeasure. And what Hope is there now for us? Will the divine Justice give up its Strictness, or the divine Law give up its Purity and Spirituality; or God infringe upon the Faithfulness of his Threatnings; or can we make Atonement for our own Sins, or satisfy the Justice of God? Or can we do any Thing to engage the great God to lay aside his Holiness, Justice, Law, and Faithfulness, in order to save us?

"Again, are we Sinners, and are not our Hearts corrupted, our Natures defiled, our Affections vitiated? And can we purge all this away? Oh *Christians*, did we truly know the Plague of our Hearts, we should be forced to acknowledge, that all this is beyond our Power. How great then is our Need of a complete Atonement, a perfect Righteousness, and the most powerful Grace!

"Now behold: all this is contained in the Lord *Jesus Christ*; he is the Repository of all spiritual Blessings, and in him is a complete Fulness of Grace; surely then this Thought should recommend this Scheme to us; for here is sufficient Provision made for our Deliverance, both from the Curse of the Law, and the Bondage of Corruption. Surely none that knows himself, could ever be offended at these Things, or think the Power of *Christ too great*, or his Grace *too full*.

"But farther, as we need all this Help from another; so we likewise need that it should be given freely; and unless the Exhibition was suited in this Respect, all the Declarations signify nothing to us; for as for Conditions, we can of ourselves perform none, that are suited to the Blessings to be bestowed, or fit for God to require. If we could indeed truly repent and believe, there would then be Room for Conditions; but how can an hard Heart repent, or a blind Mind believe, or a depraved Nature obey? But now in this Perplexity and Difficulty, how incouraging, exciting, and suitable, is the Proposal and Exhibition of free, powerful, and saving Grace?

"Are there any Souls sensible of their Need, through the Corruption and Depravity of Nature, the Hardness of their Hearts; the Guilt of their Sins, and the Wrath of God upon them? Do they see their Condition to be in itself hopeless and desperate? Let me assure you, that all the Grace of *Christ* is held forth in such a free Form as to answer your Need directly. Through *Christ* is preached unto you *Wisdom, Righteousness, Sanctification and Redemption*. Are you guilty? With *Christ* is free pardon. Are you filthy? With him is free Cleansing. Are you helpless? In him your Help is found. Are you weak? With him is everlasting Strength. Indulge thy Discouragements and Fears no longer; see all in *Christ* thou needest, and all to be freely given: Hesitate no longer, look up and live, Thou mayest, poor Soul, whosoever thou art, how sinful, guilty, or polluted soever; thou mayest and oughtest immediately to fly to *Christ* and receive him for thy Salvation. Now if such a Proclamation as this be brought home to the Conscience, and applied to the Soul by the Spirit; this will satisfy the doubting Soul, incourage the trembling Soul, strengthen the weak Soul; and it will see and feel that this answers all its Desire. Now there is nothing between *Christ* and it; but is enabled to receive, embrace, and rest upon *Christ* as freely held forth in the Gospel. Such a Representation as this, will sometimes make the Heart of a poor Sinner to leap for joy.

"Oh that the Spirit of Grace did more frequently and powerfully apply the Word of Grace; then careless Sinners would be roused from their Stupidity; self-righteous Sinners would be drawn off from their vain Confidences; and convinced, despairing Sinners, would receive the Hope and Joy of Faith!

"In the hope and Expectation, of this, we would be found frequently insisting upon the Doctrines of *Free-Grace*; knowing their wonderful Tendency to beget and promote true Faith and Holiness; looking up and waiting for the divine Spirit, that he would set his Seal to those Doctrines, which so much humble the Creature, and advance the Glory of God, Father, Son, and Spirit, in the Scheme, of Redemption, and the Method of Grace."³

It is acutely apparent that back in Whitefield's day preachers took no offence in preaching the great Doctrines of Scripture. Also, it is readily apparent how much there has been since the eighteenth century a dumbing down of society, particularly in the pulpits of our churches. If someone today took the message of George Whitefield and the Bible and preached it today with

---

3   Sermon provided by Dr. Digby James, Quinta Press, Shropshire, England.

unction and fearlessness how much our congregations and society would benefit is immeasurable!

We see from the following letter of Whitefield's an announcement of a book of hymns for public worship and the laying of the first brick for the Tabernacle. There is much in this letter of value. He is still battling health problems but illness does not keep him from preaching. He has a desire to die in his work (which God honors in 1770). Therefore we read with interest:

"To Mr. G——.

"Reverend and very dear Sir,   London, Feb. 19, 1753.

"I have two of your kind letters lying by me unanswered.—I am not usually so dilatory, but business and bodily weakness have prevented me. At present, I have a cold and fever upon me, but I preach on, hoping one day or another to die in my work. One Mr. Steward, a dear minister of CHRIST, that began to be popular in the church, entered into his rest last week. I saw him just before he expired. Methinks I hear him say, 'LOVE CHRIST more, and serve him better.' O that I may do so in earnest! For indeed my obligations increase continually. We have had a blessed winter. Many have been added to our flock.—Next week I intend, GOD willing, to lay the first brick of our new tabernacle. I am now looking up for directions about my removal.—Which are the best seasons for the north? I should be glad to know speedily. Have you the first account you wrote of your conversion? Or have you leisure to draw up a short narrative of the rise and progress of the work of GOD in your parts? A dear christian minister in Scotland, is about to publish two volumes, relative to the late awakenings in various places. Such things should be transmitted to posterity; in heaven all will be known. Thanks be to GOD that there is such a rest remaining for his dear people. I am too impatient to get at it. But who can help longing to see JESUS? What but a hope and prospect of furthering his glorious gospel, can reconcile us to this *aceldama*, this wide howling wilderness? If we had not our beloved to lean on, what should we do? Go on, my dear Sir, in his strength; I wish you much, yea very much prosperity. The LORD bless you, and all the dear souls in your parts with all spiritual blessings. I am glad you have received the books. I am now publishing two more sermons, and a small collection of hymns for public worship ..."[4]

We have a description of the first service in the new building of the Tabernacle from a letter written to Charles Wesley and dated from London, March 3, 1753. Here is that interesting letter:

"My dear Friend,

"I thank you and your brother most heartily for the loan of the chapel. Blessed be GOD, the work goes on well.

"... On *Thursday* morning, the first brick of our new tabernacle was laid with

---

4   *Works,* Vol. 3, Edward and Charles Dilly, in the Poultry, compiled by Gillies, pp. 5–6.

awful solemnity. I preached from *Exodus* the twentieth, and the latter part of the twenty-fourth verse; 'In all places where I record my name, I will come unto thee and bless thee.' Afterwards we sung, and prayed for GOD's blessing in all places, where his glorious name is recorded. The wall is now about a yard high. The building is to be eighty feet square. It is upon the old spot. We have purchased the house, and if we finish what we have begun, shall be rent-free for forty-six years. We have above eleven hundred pounds in hands. This I think is the best way to build. Mr. *Seward's* death so affected me, that when I met the workmen that night to contract about the building, I could scarce bear to think of building tabernacles. Strange! That so many should be so soon discharged, and we continued! Eighteen years have I been waiting for the coming of the son of GOD; but I find we are immortal till our work is done O that we may never live to be ministered unto, but to minister! Mr. *Seward* spoke for his LORD as long as he could speak at all. He had no clouds nor darkness. I was with him, till a few minutes before he slept in JESUS. I have good news from several parts; a door is opening at *Winchester*. Surely the little leaven will ferment, till the whole kingdom be leavened. Even so, LORD JESUS, Amen! Pray how does our elect Lady? I hope to write to her Ladyship next post. Joint love attends you and yours, and your brother and his household.—That all may increase with all the increase of GOD, is still the earnest prayer of, my dear Sir,

Yours most affectionately in our common LORD,

G.W."[5]

Whitefield and the Wesley brothers were friends again and though they no longer co-labored in the work of the Lord they still helped one another now and then as it is evident in the words from George Whitefield to Charles Wesley, "I thank you and your brother most heartily for the loan of the chapel." Though friendships were renewed, old passions concerning doctrinal differences still remained. We see this clearly from the following letter which Whitefield wrote to a friend that is dated March 10, 1753. We read:

"... I have preached at *Spitalfields* chapel twice. Both the Mr. Wesleys are agreed, as the younger brother writes me word, in answer to my letter. Let brotherly love continue! I do not like writing against any body, but I think, that wisdom which dwells with prudence, should direct you not to fill Mr. Wesley's people (who expect you will serve them) with needless jealousies. He that believeth does not make haste.—I therefore wait, being assured of this, that every plant which our heavenly Father hath not planted shall be rooted out. I hope to see the time, when you will talk less of persons and things, and more of Him, who is the common head of his whole mystical body. This, and this alone can make and keep you steady in yourself, and extensively useful to others. I am glad you know when persons are justified. It is a lesson I have not yet learnt. There are so many stony-ground hearers that receive the word with joy, that I

5   Ibid. pp. 6–7.

have determined to suspend my judgment, till I know the tree by its fruits. You will excuse this freedom. I love you with a disinterested love ..."[6]

We have paid notice to the first of Whitefield's ambitious designs during the year of 1753, the erecting of his tabernacle, now we will focus on the second project he took on which was his *hymn book*. We have a description of it from the following:

"Whitefield's hymn-book was entitled, 'Hymns for Social Worship, collected from various Authors, and more particularly designed for the use of the Tabernacle congregation in London. By George Whitefield, A.B., late of Pembroke College, Oxford, and Chaplain to the Right Hon. the Countess of Huntigdon. London: printed by William Strahan, and to be sold at the Tabernacle, near Moorfields. 1753.' (16mo. 144pp).

"The hymns are a hundred and seventy in number, besides several short doxologies. At least twenty-one of them are hymns by John and Charles Wesley. The largest number are by Watts. Most of the others were written by Cennick, Seagrave, Hammond, and Humphreys. Mr. Daniel Sedgwick, a high authority on such a subject, says, between the years 1753 and 1796, Whitefield's hymn-book passed through thirty-six editions, a good number of them containing additions to the hymns published in 1753. Want of space renders it impossible to give a minute description of Whitefield's collection; but the following preface is too characteristic to be omitted:—

'COURTEOUS READER,—If thou art acquainted with the divine life, I need not inform thee that, although all the acts and exercises of devotion are sweet and delightful, yet we never resemble the blessed worshippers above more when we are joining together in public devotions, and, with hearts and lips unfeigned, singing praises to Him who sitteth upon the throne for ever. Consequently, hymns, composed for such a purpose, ought to abound much in thanksgiving, and to be of such a nature, that all who attend may join in them, without being obliged to sing lies, or not sing at all.

'Upon this plan, the following collection of hymns is founded. They are intended purely for social worship, and so altered, in some particulars, that I think all may safely concur in using them. They are short, because I think three or four stanzas, with a doxology, are sufficient to be sung at one time. I am no great friend to long sermons, long prayers, or long hymns. They generally weary, instead of edifying, and, therefore, I think, should be avoided by those who preside in any public worshipping assembly. Besides, as the generality of those who receive the gospel are commonly the poor of the flock, I have studied cheapness, as well as conciseness. Much in a little is what God gives us in His word; and the more we imitate such a method, in our public performances and devotions, the nearer we come up to the pattern given us in the Mount.

6   Ibid. pp. 7–8.

'I think myself justified in publishing some hymns, by way of dialogue, for the use of the Society, because something like it is practised in our cathedral churches, but much more so because the celestial choir is represented, in the Book of Revelation, as answering one another in their heavenly anthems.

'That we all may be inspired and warmed with a like divine fire, whilst singing below, and be translated, after death, to join with them in singing the song of Moses and the Lamb above, is the earnest prayer of, courteous reader,

'Thy ready servant, for Christ's sake,

G.W.'"[7]

When one examines a copy of this collection of hymns compiled by Whitefield one is awed by both their voluminous and care of arrangement. The amount of time that Whitefield put into this hymn book is unbelievable given his already cramped schedule of preaching daily. This collection of hymns became so popular with the Tabernacle and members that before the great evangelist's death he had edited the twenty-third edition! We will now present some hymn specimens:

HYMN XCVII

Sitting at JESU's Feet.

SWEET the Moments, rich in Blessing,
Which before the Cross I spend;
Life, and Health, and Peace possessing,
From the Sinner's dying Friend.
Here I'll sit, for ever viewing
Mercy's Streams in Streams of Blood:
Precious Drops my Soul bedewing,
Plead and claim my Peace with God.

Truly blessed is this Station,
Low before his Cross to lie:
While I see divine Compassion
Floating in his languid Eye.
Here it is I find my Heaven,
While upon the Lamb I gaze;
Love I much, I've much forgiven,
I'm a Miracle of Grace.

Love and Grief my Heart dividing,
With my Tears his Feet I'll bathe;
Constant still in Faith abiding,
Life deriving from his Death.

7   Tyerman, Vol, 2, pp. 294–295.

May I still enjoy this Feeling,
   In all Need to Jesus go!
Prove his Wounds each Day more healing,
   And himself more deeply know.

HYMN CXI.

At the coming of a Minister.

WELCOME, welcome, blessed Servant,
   Messenger of Jesu's Grace!
O how beautiful the Feet of
   Him that brings good News of Peace.
Welcome Herald, welcome Herald, &c.
   Priest of God, thy People's Joy.

Saviour, bless his Message to us,
   Give us Hearts to hear the Sound
Of Redemption, dearly purchas'd
   By thy Death and precious Wounds,
O reveal it, O reveal it, &c.
   To our poor and helpless Souls.

Give reward of Grace and Glory
   To thy faithful Labourer dear,
Let the Incense of our Hearts be
   Offer'd up in Faith and Prayer,
Bless, O bless him; bless, O bless him, &c.
   Now henceforth for evermore.

HYMN CXV.

For a Public Fast.

LORD, look on all assembled here;
   Who in thy Presence stand,
To offer up united Pray'r
   For this our sinful Land.

Oft have we, each in private, pray'd,
   Our Country might find Grace,
Now hear the same Petitions made
   In this appointed Place.

Or, if amongst us some be met,
   So careless of their Sin,
They have not cry'd for Mercy yet;
   Lord let them now begin.

Thou, by whose Death poor Sinners live,
   By whom their Pray'rs succeed,

Thy Spir't of Supplication give,
　　And we shall pray indeed.

We will not slack; nor give thee rest;
　　But importune thee so,
That, 'till we shall be by thee blest,
　　We will not let thee go.

Great God of Hosts, Deliv'rance bring,
　　Guide those that hold the Helm;
Support the State; preserve the King;
　　And spare the guilty Realm.

Or should the dread Decree be past,
　　And we must feel thy Rod;
May Faith and Patience hold us fast
　　To our correcting God.

Whatever be our destin'd Case,
　　Accept us in thy Son;
Give us his Gospel, and his Grace;
　　And then thy Will be done.

HYMN CXXIV.

Before Sermon.

SOURCE of Light and Pow'r divine,
Deign upon thy Truth to shine.
Lord, behold thy Servant stands;
Lo! To Thee his lifts his Hands;
Satisfy his Soul's Desire;
Touch his Lip with holy Fire.

Ope thy Treasures! so shall fall
Unction sweet on him, on All.
Till by Odours scatter'd round,
Christ Himself be trac'd and found.
Then shall ev'ry raptur'd Heart,
Rich in Peace and Joy depart.

HYMN XXXI.

At Parting.

BLEST be the dear uniting Love,
　　That will not let us part;
Our Bodies may far off remove,
　　We still are join'd in Heart.

Join'd in one Spirit to our Head,
　　Where he appoints we go,

And still in Jesu's Footsteps tread,
   And do his Work below.

O let us ever walk in him,
   And nothing know beside,
Nothing desire, nothing esteem,
   But Jesus crucify'd.

Closer and closer let us cleave,
   To his belov'd Embrace,
Expect his Fulness to receive,
   And Grace to answer Grace.

But let us hasten to the Day,
   Which shall our Flesh restore,
When Death shall all be done away,
   And Bodies part no more."[8]

What more can we say "that has been said"? Oh for the old paths again!

Whitefield spent the spring of 1753 battling the Moravians in print. George Whitefield printed a letter to the Moravians attacking their ritualism and community. Both Peter Bohler and Count Zinzendorf were angry and responded in letters to Whitefield and public denouncements. Peter Bohler "declared publicly, in the pulpit, that Whitefield's letter was all a lie". This feud lasted through the month of May. We see from the following:

"About the middle of the month of May, he left London for a tour in Wales, and made 'a circuit of about seven hundred miles.' He preached above twenty times, at Narberth, Pembroke, Haverfordwest, and other places; and was again in London on the 7th of June. The Moravian controversy filled his mind and crushed his heart. To his old secretary, John Syms, who had joined the Moravians, and who had basely threatened a revelation of some of Whitefield's secret affairs, he wrote:—

"Haverfordwest, May 27, 1753.

"MY DEAR MAN,—Though my wife has not forwarded the letter, she says you have sent me a threatening one. I thank you for it, though unseen, and say unto thee, if thou art thus minded, "What thou doest, do quickly.' Blessed be God, I am ready to receive the most traitorous blow, and to confess, before God and man, all my weaknesses and failings, whether in public or private life. I laid my account of such treatment, before I published my 'Expostulatory Letter.' Your writing in such a manner convinces me more and more, that Moravianism leads men to break through the most sacred ties of nature, friendship, and disinterested love.

---

8   *A Collection of Hymns for Social Worship* (23rd Edition, London: printed by Henry Cock. republished on *The Works of George Whitefield* CD-ROM by Quinta Press.

"My wife says, you write, that, '*I am drunk with power and approbation.*' Wast thou with me so long, my dear man, and hast thou not known me better? What power didst thou know me ever to grasp at? or, what power am I now invested with? None, that I know of, except that of being a poor pilgrim. As for approbation, God knows, I have had little else besides the cross to glory in, since my first setting out. May that be my glory still!

"My wife says, you write, that 'I promised not to print.' I remember no such thing. I know you advised me not to do so, but I know of no promise made. If I rightly remember, I had not then read Rimius; but, after that, I both heard and saw so many things, that I could not, with a safe conscience, be silent.

"My wife says, you write, 'the bulk of my letter is not truth.' So says Mr. Peter Bohler; nay, he says, 'it is all a lie;' and, I hear, he declares me so in the pulpit; so that, whether I will or not, he obliges me to clear myself in print. If he goes on in this manner, he will not only constrain me to print a third edition, but also to publish a dreadful heap that remains behind. My answers to him, the Count, and my old friend Hutton, are almost ready. I cannot send them this post, but may have time before long.

"O, my dear man, let me tell thee, that the God of truth and love hates lies. That cause can never be good, that needs equivocations and falsehoods to support it. You shall have none from me. I have naked truth. I write out of pure love. The Lord Jesus only knows what unspeakable grief I feel, when I think how many of my friends have so involved themselves. If anything stops my pen, it will be concern for them, not myself. I value neither name nor life itself, when the cause of God calls me to venture both. Thanks be to His great name, I can truly say, that, for many years past, no sin has had dominion over me; neither have I slept with the guilt of any known, unrepented sin lying upon my heart.

"I wish thee well in body and soul, and subscribe myself, my dear John, your very affectionate, though injured, friend for Christ's sake,

"GEORGE WHITEFIELD."9

This breach between Whitefield and the Moravians pained him since they had earlier shared so much labor together, especially in America where he worked with them in the spring of 1740. Peter Bohler and some other Moravians had left Savannah to go northward to join some others who had settled in Pennsylvania. There, under Whitefield's direction, they were employed to build Nazareth, a school for the Negro children in that township. All was harmony then between them—but no longer! The great evangelist was a true defender of the gospel and if he felt anyone or any sect was compromising the plain truth he would challenge them on it—as he had done earlier with the Wesleys. Nevertheless, all this was a source of much

9   Tyerman, Vol. 2, pp. 308–309.

consternation to him as we see from excerpts of a letter which he wrote to a friend at this time. It is dated, "London, June 8, 1753." He wrote:

"... Mr. S—— can tell you what concern the Brethren's awful conduct hath given me. Surely if the Redeemer had not supported me, I should within these two months have died with grief. But I will say no more:—JESUS knows all things. He will not long bear with guile. You know my temper. The LORD help me in simplicity and godly sincerity to have my conversation in the world, and in the church! ... I am glad to hear Mr. Tennent is coming over with Mr. Davies. If they come with their old fire, I trust they will be enabled to do wonders. I and Messrs. Wesley's are very friendly. I like them, because they go out and let the world see what they are at once; I suspect something wrong, when so much secrecy is required. But I must have done. Only let me tell you, that the Redeemer still owns my feeble labours. I have been a circuit of about 700 miles, and preached to many thousands. My body yet is upheld, and my soul rejoices in GOD my Saviour ..."[10]

In the month of June we see the great evangelist "take the field" once more. His gospel ranging's take him from Portsmouth to Scotland with a return in November to England. We see this stated in the following account of his labors. We must remind ourselves, that his preaching exploits are anything but normal in relation to anyone or anything else. His incredible schedule of activity is joined with crowds of hearers who are continually growing under the hand of God. This is no normal man. He is human. But his activities for this year of 1753 are indeed superhuman! Therefore it is with great interest that we read:

"Two days after writing this, [letter of June 8,] Whitefield opened his new Tabernacle, on which occasion he preached, in the morning, from Solomon's prayer at the dedication of the temple; and, in the evening, from I Chron. xxix. 9: 'Then the people rejoiced, for that they offered willingly, because with perfect heart they offered willingly to the Lord: and David the king also rejoiced with great joy.' It is needless to add, that the building, 'was crowded almost to suffocation in every part.'

"The Tabernacle being built and opened, Whitefield felt himself at liberty to 'take the field.' Accordingly, on June 20, he started off to Portsmouth, where he spent about a week. Having fulfilled his mission there, he set out for the north of England. He had 'two good meetings' at Olney. At Northampton, 'several thousands attended.' Leicester was 'a cold place; but the people stood very attentive, and some were affected.' At Nottingham, 'a great multitude came to hear, but a son of Belial endeavoured to disturb them.' At Sheffield, he had 'two good meetings,' and a congregation 'consisting of several thousands.' At Rotherham, 'after preaching, a young man was set at liberty, who had been groaning under the spirit of bondage for four years.' At Leeds, thousands

10 *Works*, Vol. 3, pp. 15–16.

attended daily; and, on the Lord's day, it was computed that near twenty thousand were present. At Birstal and Bradford, 'many thousands flocked together.'

"Benjamin Rhodes, now a boy of eleven years of age, but afterwards one of the best of Wesley's itinerant preachers, was present at Birstal. He writes, 'I went with my father to Birstal to hear Mr. Whitefield. I found my soul deeply affected under the word. At first, I had a kind of terror; but, before the sermon was ended, my heart was melted into tenderness, and sweetly drawn after God.'

"At York, he says, 'I preached four times; twice we were disturbed, and twice we had sweet seasons.' Thus did he preach all the way from London to Newcastle where he arrived on Saturday, July 14. Three days afterwards, he wrote to the Countess of Huntingdon:—

'Newcastle, July 17, 1753.

'I wrote to your ladyship just before I set out for Portsmouth, and thought to have written again at my return, but was hindered by staying only one night in London. Ever since, I have been on the range for lost sinners; and, blessed be God! I have been much owned by Him who delights to work by the meanest instruments. Sometimes I have scarce known whether I have been in heaven or on earth. I came hither on Saturday, and have preached seven times, and once at Sunderland, where a great multitude attended, and were deeply impressed. At five in the morning, the great room is filled [no doubt Wesley's old chapel, the Orphan House]; and, on the Lord's-day, the congregation out of doors was great indeed. Surely the shout of a King has been amongst us. All is harmony and love. I am now going to a place called Sheep-hill, and shall return to preach here again in the evening. To-morrow I set forward to Scotland. This may be communicated to Mr. Charles Wesley, to whom I would write if I had time.'"[11]

Whitefield always enjoyed his trips to Scotland but this time he dreaded leaving the crowds which were attending the Word as he ranged around the countryside of England. Still, he felt led to go and arrived in Scotland on July 20th. The *Scots' Magazine* ran an article announcing his arrival in Edinburgh:

"Mr. George Whitefield arrived at Edinburgh July 20th; went thence to Glasgow on the 27th; returned to Edinburgh August 3rd; and set out for London on the 7th. He preached daily, morning and evening, when at Edinburgh, in the Orphan House Park; and, when at Glasgow, in the Castle-yard, to numerous audiences. In his sermons at Glasgow, he declaimed warmly against a play-house, lately erected, with the enclosure in which he preached. The consequence was, that, before his departure, workmen were employed to take it down, to prevent its being done by ruder hands."[12]

11 Tyerman, Vol. 2, pp. 310–311.
12 Ibid. p. 311.

Whitefield's great friend Dr. Gillies was glad to see his old friend and offered him his pulpit in Glasgow. From Edinburgh Whitefield writes to his friend that revival had been attending the places in England where the great evangelist roamed and this movement of God was something he did not wish to cease. The revival blessings were not so in Scotland and he missed them! So thus he shared his heart feelings and his discouragements with his Scottish friend; and as he trusted him with his heart it is only fitting that God trusted Gillies with George Whitefield's personal papers after his demise. Therefore we read with great interest the following letter preserved by Gillies:

"To Mr. Gillies, at Glasgow.

"Edinburgh, July 21, 1753.

"YOURS I just now received, but know not what to say by way of answer. The inward discouragements I have felt for above a week, against coming to *Scotland*, have been very many. I have left a people full of fire. Thousands and thousands flocked to hear the glorious gospel. Awakenings I have heard of in every place; saints have been revived, and heaven as it were come down on earth. We have enjoyed perpetual *Cambuslang* seasons. My eyes gush out with tears of joy, (and I trust at the same time with godly sorrow for my vileness) at the very thought of it. My heart is quite broken, to think poor *Scotland* is so dead. O how gloomy hath been the aspect! I have been afraid of catching cold, though, alas! I am too cold towards Him, who out of warm love bled and died for me. O that *Glasgow* friends, if I do come, may pray for me! I could scarce believe your letter, that your people would be glad to see such an ill and hell-deserving, good for nothing creature as I am. If I lose the opportunity of seeing you, I shall be disappointed indeed. I believe I shall keep to the time proposed. O time, time, how slowly dost though go on! When shall I be wafted to an happy eternity? Often within these three weeks have I hoped to die in the embraces of my GOD. Had I a thousand souls and bodies they should be all *itinerants* for JESUS CHRIST. I want to see all on a flame of fire. You know, dear Sir, what fire I mean. O! Break heart strings, break, and let the imprisoned soul be set at liberty. I want to go where I shall neither sin myself, nor see others sin any more. My tender love to all. I can no more for weeping. When I forget to pray for my ungrateful vile self,—then will my worthy and dear friend cease to be remembered by, reverend and very dear Sir,

Yours most affectionately in our common LORD,

G.W."[13]

It is odd to see George Whitefield so filled with doom and gloom! Everyone has their *blue days!* What is striking from this letter is how *dead* Scotland had

---

become since the revival days. This was a great concern to the evangelist. And it should be a concern to us to keep the coals warm on the altar of our hearts. Despite these seasons of discouragement we soon see that the great evangelist was back in the saddle and God was moving once again!

Whitefield wrote to a friend from Glasgow, on July 25, 1753 the following:

"... And will the high and lofty one then continue to honour such a wretch as I am? Then, through the divine strength, let me now begin to preach more than ever. Yesterday I was enabled to preach five times, and I suppose the last time to near twenty thousand, and almost to as many in the morning. People flock and are more fond than ever to hear; at *Edinburgh* also, I preached twice every day to many thousands; among whom are many of the noble and polite.—Attention sits upon the faces of all ..."[14]

Since we included a depressing letter from George Whitefield to his friend Dr. Gillies of Glasgow, it is only fitting we include a lighter one which speaks volumes of his great success in Scotland in 1753. In it we see George Whitefield doing street preaching and pressing on for Christ's sake: It is dated from Newcastle, Aug. 12, 1753:

"I would have answered your kind letter before I left *Edinburgh*, but I had not a moment's leisure. With great difficulty I got away, after a heart-breaking parting on *Tuesday* about noon. On *Wednesday* evening, and the *Thursday* morning, I preached at *Berwick*, and on *Thursday* evening at *Alnwick*, in the street. It being the time of the races, I discoursed on these words, 'So run that ye may obtain.' Whilst I was discoursing, the gentlemen came down from the race, and surrounded the congregation, and heard very attentively. The next morning at five I preached again, and about noon at a place called *Placy*, and in the evening about nine at *Newcastle*, where a great number expected me. My text was 'At midnight a cry was made, behold the bridegroom cometh.' The next morning I received the following note, 'Dearly beloved in the LORD, I write to you good news. Your labour was not in vain last night, for my wife answered to the midnight cry, and received CHRIST into her soul.' O that we may all praise the Three in One! Last night I prepared for, and this morning I opened the gospel fair from these words, 'Ho! Every one that thirsteth.' Much of the divine presence was in the congregation, and I believe many tasted of CHRIST's wine. I am to preach three times almost every day this week. This promise supports me. 'As thy day is, so shall thy strength be.' By the inclosed, you will see the devil owes me a grudge for what was done at *Glasgow*. Would it not be proper to insert a paragraph to contradict it? Thousands and thousands come to hear notwithstanding. LORD, what am I? A poor hell-deserving creature; and yet the LORD makes use of such to thresh the mountains with. May the LORD help me so to do, and then let him deal with me as seemeth good in his sight ... My lot is to be a pilgrim, a run-about for CHRIST ..."[15]

---

14 Ibid. p. 24.
15 Ibid. pp. 25–26.

The "pilgrim" and "run-about for Christ" finishes his labors in Scotland and returns to London by way of Leeds and York. He describes the blessings he has seen to his patroness and friend Selina in the following letter:

"Ever-honoured Madam,   York, Sept. 11, 1753.

"Last *Saturday* I returned to *Leeds*, from whence I had been absent a fortnight. But what the glorious *Emmanuel* gave us to see and feel, is indeed inexpressible. What a sacrament at *Howarth!* We used thirty-five bottles of wine on the occasion. I have been as far as *Bolton, Manchester and Stockport.* At the last place so much of the divine presence came amongst us, that is was almost too much for our frail natures to bear; at the former, our cup was also made to run over. Every where the congregation looked like swarms of bees, and the more I preached the more eager they seemed to be. At *Bustall* last Lord's day, perhaps there were near twenty thousand, and on *Monday* morning at *Leeds,* the parting was the most affecting I ever saw: it has been almost too much for me. I have not as yet half recovered it. LORD, hasten the time when thy people shall part no more! Last night I came hither, and preached with quietness. This morning I am setting out for *Lincolnshire,* and have some thoughts of taking a trip to *Ireland.* LORD JESUS, what am I that I should be called to go out into the highways and hedges? Besides travelling, I have been enabled to preach thrice a day frequently. Arrows of conviction have fled, and of souls I hear scores have been awakened; they tell me that a hundred have been added to *Sunderland* society. O that the leaven may ferment till the whole be leavened! Never did I see the work more promising. GOD be merciful to me a sinner, and give me, for his infinite mercy's sake, an humble thankful and resigned heart! Surely I am viler than the vilest, and stand amazed at his employing such a wretch as I am; but his name is LOVE. I could enlarge, but must away to preach ..."[16]

As George Whitefield reaches the metropolis he stayed in London only a few days (much to the regret of lonely Elizabeth we are sure). But before we record his labors for the remainder of this remarkable year in the life of this busy evangelist we must look at his labors up to this point! We will use a brief extract from a letter to The Countess dated from London, Sept. 26, 1753:

"Ever-honoured Madam,

"Yesterday about noon, a good and never-failing Redeemer brought me and mine in safety to town, where I expect to stay only a few days. Thanks be to GOD for this last circuit! I thinks this day three months I left *London*; since which time I have been enabled to travel about twelve hundred miles, and to preach about one hundred and eighty sermons to many, very many thousands of souls. More glorious seasons I never saw; parting has almost killed me. My last excursion hath been to *York, Lincolnshire, Rotheram, Sheffield, Nottingham, Northampton,* where I believe near ten thousand souls came to hear last Lord's day. It was a Lord's day indeed ..."[17]

---

16 Ibid. p. 29.
17 Ibid. p. 30.

We see George Whitefield's reluctance to take time to rest his weary frame and spend time with his wife. We are amazed he spent ten days in London before ranging once more! We see this from the following comments:

> "Though Whitefield had built and opened his new Tabernacle, he was not inclined to '*nestle*' in it. Within ten days after his arrival in London, he resumed his itinerancy. On Saturday, October 6th, he had 'a blessed season at Olney;' and, next day, 'two glorious opportunities' at Northampton. On Monday, October 8th, he preached at Oxenden and Bosworth; on Tuesday, at Kettering and Bedford; and on Wednesday, at Bedford and Olney. He then set out for Staffordshire, and preached 'at Birmingham and several adjacent places.'"[18]

Whitefield's further excursions round the countryside encountered opposition and he and his friends were attacked by mobs. At a place near Dudley he learned that many individuals had been affected by his written sermons. "I heard of a whole company awakened by reading my poor sermons." His incessant labors are continued and we see the account of them in a letter to a friend dated from Wolverhampton, Oct. 27, 1753:

> "... the ever-loving, ever-lovely JESUS, hath vouchsafed to employ me in breaking up new ground. I have preached four times at *Alperam in Cheshire*, where the LORD was with us of a truth, and where he had sweetly prepared my way, by blessing several of my poor writings. At *Chester* I preached four times; a great concourse attended; all was hushed and quiet, several of the clergy were present, and the word came with power. I have since heard, that the most noted rebel in town, was brought under deep conviction, and could not sleep night or day. Within doors, where I preached early in the morning, conviction seemed to go through the whole congregation. At *Liverpool*, the way was equally prepared.—A person who had been wrought on by some of my printed sermons, met me at landing, and took me to his house; a great number at a short notice was convened; all was quiet here also. Some came under immediate conviction; and I could wish to have stayed much longer, but notice was given for my preaching at *Wrexham*, which I find since, hath been a rude place indeed. Upon my coming; the town was alarmed, and several thousands came to hear. Several of the baser sort made a great noise, and threw stones, but none touched me, and I trust I can say, our LORD got himself the victory. The next day, near *Alperam*, we had another heaven upon earth. A divine power descended among the people, and we could say, how awfully sweet is this place! The next morning I intended to preach near *Nantwich*, where a Methodist meeting-house hath lately been pulled down. Here Satan roared.—The mob pelted Mr. D—— and others much, but I got off pretty free, and had opportunity of preaching quietly a little out of town. Last night I preached here in the dark, to a great body of hearers, for this country, and am now bound for *Wednesbury, Dudley and Kidderminster*. From thence, perhaps I may come to *London* for a few days ..."[19]

---

18 Tyerman, Vol. 2, p. 315.
19 *Works*, Vol. 3, pp. 34–35.

We find it odd that given the remarkable exploits of George Whitefield for the year 1753 it is ignored and passed over by his other biographers (with the exception of Tyerman), except for an occasional mention of the erecting of the Tabernacle. We must assume that George Whitefield's life for this year was so similar to his other years they did not feel it necessary to include it or enumerate upon it! This speaks volumes to this man's life of remarkable labor—it is altogether too much for one biographer to grasp!

Whitefield ranged to Gloucester and the west of England and it is from there he wrote a letter to his friend Dr. Gillies of Glasgow. It is an important letter and worth including for in it George Whitefield answered the request of Gillies to elaborate on those sections of his Journals which he had intended to insert in the *Historical Collections*. In this letter we see George Whitefield's great humility—it is dated from Gloucester, November 16, 1753.

> "Your kind letter I received, and would have answered it during my stay in *London* (which was only a few days) but really I was almost killed with a multiplicity of business. The journals also I would have sent immediately, but knew not how.—My wife promised me to embrace the first opportunity that offered, and I hope ere long they will come safe to hand. As for my pointing out particular passages, it is impracticable; I have neither leisure nor inclination so to do. At present, my doings and writings appear to me in so mean a light, that I think they deserve no other treatment than to be buried in eternal oblivion. 'Behold, I am vile, I am vile,' is all I can say to GOD or man. And yet, amazing love! Vile as I am, the high and lofty One that inhabiteth eternity, still delights to honour me, by owning and succeeding my poor feeble labours ... CHRIST is in our ship, and therefore it will not sink ..."[20]

In November of the year George Whitefield wrote to a friend from Bristol and made mention of erecting a new Tabernacle there as well. He wrote, "... I came here [Bristol] on Monday evening, and, to my great disappointment, found that the new Tabernacle is not finished, so that I know not well what to do." Of this new Tabernacle (in addition to the one already opened earlier in the year at London) we have the following explanation:

> "Then, in reference to the Bristol Tabernacle. Almost from the commencement of their career, the followers of Whitefield and of Wesley had held separate services at Bristol. Wesley had had a chapel there ever since the year 1739. Up to the present, Whitefield had none. Considering the peculiar position held by Whitefield, as belonging to no party and yet the friend of all, it is difficult to imagine why he now sanctioned the erection of a chapel for himself, except that he and his special adherents were well aware that many belonging to the upper classes of society, who were in the habit of visiting the

---

20 Ibid. pp. 37–38.

Hotwells, would not attend Wesley's meeting-house, but would be likely to sit under the more popular ministry of his friend Whitefield. Be that as it may, the Countess of Huntingdon exerted her influence to obtain the necessary funds for a new erection. Lord Chesterfield sent her £20; but added, 'I must beg *my name* not to appear *in any way.*' …

"It is a curious fact that this remarkable man [Chesterfield] was sometimes almost fascinated by Whitefield's preaching. On one occasion, when the great preacher was representing the sinner under the figure of a blind beggar, whose dog had broken from him, and who was groping on the brink of a precipice, over which he stepped, and was lost, Chesterfield was so excited by the graphic description, that he bounded from his seat, and exclaimed, 'By heavens, the beggar's gone.' It is also related, that when it was proposed in the Privy Council that some method should be used to stop Whitefield's preaching, Chesterfield, who was present, turned upon his heels and said, 'Make him a bishop, and you will silence him at once.'"[21]

During this time Whitefield received the alarming news that his dear friend John Wesley was near death with galloping consumption. Wesley had already written his epitaph. In a letter written by George Whitefield to the Countess on December 3rd we read, "I am now hastening to London, to pay my last respects to my dying friend." Wesley not only recovered, he lived another forty years and even preached his concerned friend's funeral sermon!

Toward the close of the year the great roaming evangelist had some welcome company come from America; his two dear friends, Gilbert Tennent and Samuel Davies. We hear about this visit from a letter to Gillies on Dec. 27th, "Perhaps it will please you to hear that Messrs. Tennent and Davies supped with me last night." Whitefield biographer, J.B. Wakeley has the following account of the Christmas time visit. He wrote:

"Mr. Whitefield invited Mr. Davies to come to England for the purpose of raising funds for Princeton College, promising to open the way for his success. Mr. Davies, having corresponded with John Wesley on the same subject, was thereupon, together with Gilbert Tennent, appointed by the Synod of New York to visit England for that purpose. They arrived in London on Christmas-day, 1753, and were cordially welcomed by Mr. Whitefield. Their visit proved a very successful one, for, while not expecting to be able to raise more than £300, they succeeded in collecting over £1,200.

"Mr. Davies kept a diary, from which the following extract is made: '*Wednesday,* Dec. 26. Mr. Whitefield, having sent us an invitation to make his house our home during our stay here, we were perplexed what to do, lest we should blast the success of our mission among the Dissenters, who are generally disaffected to him. We at length concluded, with the advice of our friends and his, that a public intercourse with him would be imprudent in our present situation, and visited him privately this evening, and the kind reception he gave us revived dear Mr. Tennent. He spoke in the most encouraging manner of the success of our mission, and in all his conversation discovered so much zeal and candor that I could not but admire the man as the wonder of the age. When we returned Mr. Tennent's heart was all on fire, and after we had gone to bed he suggested that we should watch and pray, and we arose and prayed together till about three in the morning."[22]

As our examination of the year 1753 draws to a close we marvel at a man who in it built two tabernacles, compiled and edited a huge hymn book, accomplished his seventh visit to Scotland with incredible blessings of God there; who in his itinerant preaching had a vast impact in the countryside of England, and ended the year assisting the College of New Jersey by raising funds for it. And, if this year in the life of this man is ordinary for him, we walk far behind being careful not to tread upon his vast shadow.

---

22 J.B. Wakeley, *A Portraiture of Rev. George Whitefield M.A.*, (New York: Carlton & Lanahan, 1871), pp. 257–258.

A torpid community was aroused, as by the trump of God, from its long and heavy slumber; ministers and people were converted; the style of preaching, and the tone of individual piety were improved; a cold, cadaverous formalism gave place to the living energy of experimental godliness; the doctrines of the Gospel were brought out from their concealment, and made to reassert their claims to a cordial, practical credence, and all the interests of truth and holiness received new homage from regenerated thousands.

Baron Stow
in describing Whitefield's preaching.

CHAPTER 45

FIFTH VISIT TO AMERICA

After his great labors of 1753 Whitefield did not look back but pressed on! He was never one to rest on his laurels. New Years Day, 1754, found him preaching in his new Tabernacle in London to a crowded congregation. George Whitefield was glad to have his two American friends, Gilbert Tennent and Samuel Davies with him for the memorable occasion.

We see from the following:

"On the 1st of January, 1754, Davies and Tennent went to hear Mr. Whitefield preach in the Tabernacle, which was a large spacious building, and on this occasion was densely crowded. His theme was the barren fig-tree. Mr. Davies says: 'And though the discourse was incoherent, yet it seemed to me better calculated to do good to mankind than all the accurate, languid discourses I had ever heard. After the sermon I enjoyed his pleasing conversation at his house.'

"Mr. Davies says in his diary, January 25, 1754, 'Mr. Tennent and myself dined with the Rev. Mr. Bradbury, who had been in the ministry fifty-seven years. He read us some letters that passed between Whitefield and himself in 1741. Whitefield had reproved Mr. Bradbury for singing a song at a tavern, in a large company, in praise of old English beef. The old gentleman then sang it for us, and we found it was partly composed by himself in the high-flying style of the days of Queen Anne. He is a man of singular turn, which would be offensive to the greater number of serious people; but for my part I could say,

'I knew 'twas his peculiar whim,
Nor took it ill as 't came from him.'"[1]

Few today are familiar with the great men of revival from New England during the eighteenth century. They were remarkable men distinguishable

1   J.B. Wakeley, *A Portraiture of George Whitefield, M.A.*, pp. 258–259.

by both academics and God's Hand upon them. A story about Rev. Samuel Davies is worth including here only to more introduce him as a man who kept company with George Whitefield. Therefore we read:

"When in England Mr. Davies was listened to with great delight, and crowds attended his frequent ministrations. The following anecdote is related of him. King George II., being curious to hear a preacher from the wilds of America, attended on one occasion, and was so much struck with his commanding eloquence that he expressed his astonishment loud enough to be heard half way over the house. Davies, observing that the King was attracting more attention than himself, paused, and, looking his Majesty full in the face, gave him in an emphatic tone the following rebuke: '*When the lion roareth let the beasts of the forest tremble; and when the Lord speaketh let the kings of the earth keep silence.*' The King shrank back in his seat and remained quiet during the remainder of his discourse, and the next day sent for Mr. Davies and gave him fifty guineas for the college, observing at the same time to his courtiers, 'He is an honest man! An honest man!'

"In 1755 Davies was chosen to succeed Jonathan Edwards as President of the college of New Jersey. This appointment he declined, but it being renewed the following year, he, in accordance with the judgment of the Synod, accepted it. He did not, however, long enjoy this high honor, for he died in February, 1762, when but thirty-six years of age. He was interred in the burying-ground at Princeton, where sleep Edwards, Burr, Witherspoon, Finlay, and others of the mighty dead."[2]

The great evangelist prepared to sail to America for the fifth time, the Orphan House was on his mind and heart and he was bringing with him a dozen "destitute orphans" for Bethesda. This trip to the Colonies would last longer than his previous abrupt one and after this fifth visit to his beloved Bethesda it would be another *eight years* before he returned again.

We will look at his activities in the metropolis before he set sail. We see that his first two months were spent in London:

"Whitefield spent the first two months of 1754 in London, and was fully occupied, partly in preaching, and partly in preparing for his intended voyage to America. He wrote: 'I meet with my share of trials. Every sermon preached this winter has been fetched out of the furnace. But what are we to expect, as Christians and ministers, but afflictions? Our new Tabernacle is completed, and the workmen all paid. What is best of all, the Redeemer manifests His glory in it. Every day, souls come crying, "What shall I do to be saved?" I expect, in a fortnight, once more to launch into the great deep, with about ten or twelve destitute orphans under my care.' He embarked at Gravesend, on the 7th of March."[3]

2   Ibid. p. 260.
3   Tyerman, Vol. 2, p. 324.

We have Dr. Gillies brief comments about this voyage and his statement that George Whitefield brought more than a dozen orphans with him to Savannah.

> "March 7, 1754, having got about twenty poor children under his care, he embarked for America, but put in at Lisbon, where he stayed from the 20th of March, to the 13th of April."[4]

Before we detail the adventure of Whitefield's time in Lisbon we must make a comment about his wife Elizabeth. She has been living in London alone for most of the year 1753 since he was out itinerating, and when he did come back to their home it was only for a week or two at the longest until the first part of 1754 where he was there for two months. Now he was off again on a long voyage to America—but without her. He made no mention of her nor do many of his biographers at this point with the exception of the insightful remarks of Gledstone under the chapter heading, "His Wife's Loneliness". We read:

> "His wife was not with him this voyage, indeed she seems to have performed but one long journey with him after their marriage. Her health was unequal to the trials of an American summer; and it would have been useless for her to have travelled with him as a companion from place to place. He could but leave her to her own resources and the kindness of his friends—not a pleasant position for a wife, but the best in which he could place her, unless he relinquished his evangelistic work, and that would simply have overturned his whole plan of life, and violated his most solemn convictions. He implored one of his London friends to visit his wife frequently. 'Add to my obligations,' he said, 'by frequently visiting my poor wife. Kindness shown to her in my absence will be double kindness.'
>
> "With a family, but not with his wife, he arrived at Bethseda ..."[5]

Intrigued by the superstitions of the church of Rome, Whitefield decided to spend time in the country of Portugal in the capital of Lisbon. His friend Doddridge had died there but this was apparently not the reason for his visit, there is no existing record of any visit to his friend's tomb. We cannot say with accuracy that he chose to stay in Lisbon a month but rather it seems that the ship in which he was traveling had some extended business there. We have Tyerman's explanation:

> "Nine days after leaving England, the ship, in which Whitefield sailed, anchored in Lisbon harbour, where it remained about a month. This was a long detention for Whitefield and his 'destitute orphans;' but he usefully employed the time in making himself acquainted with the full-blown Popery of the

---

4   Gillies, p. 148.
5   Gledstone, p. 293.

metropolis of Portugal. His letters on this subject fill twenty-four closely printed pages, in his collected works."[6]

The thirty-nine-year-old Whitefield wrote to a friend from Lisbon Harbor on March 19th, the following:

"How soon does the scene shift? At what a distance, in a few days, may we be removed from each other! On the sixteenth instant, that GOD whom I desire to serve in the gospel of his dear Son, brought me and my orphan charge to this harbour. As yet I have not been on shore, but expect to go to-morrow ...

"The bank of heaven is a sure bank. I have drawn thousands of bills upon it, and never had one sent back protested. GOD helping me, I purpose lodging my little earthly all there. I hope my present poor but valuable cargo, will make some additions to my heavenly inheritance. O free grace! That ever such an ill and hell-deserving wretch as I am, should ever be called out to leave his carnal and spiritual friends, for that friend of sinners the Lamb of GOD! These partings are indeed trying to nature ..."[7]

Of this visit to Lisbon we have this from the pen of Dallimore:

"After a week of sailing the vessel put in at Lisbon in Portugal, where it remained for a month.

"A wealthy merchant residing in the city invited Whitefield to his home. Spring had arrived—it was now the middle of April—and the weather was pleasant. Moreover, because of the language barrier there was no one to whom Whitefield could preach and thus he was forced to accept the rest he so badly needed.

"He busied himself, however, in observing the Roman Catholic Lenten practices and writing an account of them. He described a series of processions that were carried on throughout the Holy Week, with highly dramatic representations of the life of St. Francis of Assisi, and of the crucifixion of Christ ...

"After a month at Lisbon the vessel continued its journey to America. Six weeks of sailing—the smoothest of all Whitefield's crossings of the Atlantic— brought it to harbour in South Carolina. The date was May 26 (1754).

"The arrival ended a period that stood alone in Whitefield's life thus far. It was now eleven weeks since he had left England and during that time he had not once preached. Never since the first months of his ministry had there been a time of such inactivity and he reached the American shore well rested and in better health than he had known for some years."[8]

The ceremonial religiosity of the Papists in Lisbon caused Whitefield to comment, "What a spirit must Martin Luther, and the first Reformers be

6   Tyerman, Vol. 2, p. 325.
7   *Works,* Vol, 3, pp. 66–67.
8   Dallimore, Vol. 2, pp. 365, 367.

endued with, that dared to appear as they did for GOD!" Observing these rites and rituals of the Catholics made George Whitefield marvel and he states he was "... so taken up in seeing the ecclesiastical curiosities of the place ..." that he wrote about his experiences and observations while in Lisbon and had them printed in London on his return in 1755. The pamphlet was entitled, "A brief Account of some Lent and other Extraordinary Processions and Ecclesiastical Entertainments, seen last Year at Lisbon. In four Letters to an English Friend. By George Whitefield". Of this commentary of Roman Catholicism in Lisbon we have a summary of what George Whitefield felt and thought as he witnessed the Papal processions through the streets of the city during Holy Week. He wrote:

> "... the image of the Virgin Mary was placed upon the front of the stage, in order to be kissed, adored, and worshipped by the people. Thus ended this Good Friday's tragic-comical, superstitious, idolatrous farce."9

Before moving on to Whitefield's activities in America we must include Luke Tyerman's comments of George Whitefield's time in Lisbon for they are both historical and worthwhile. It is also interesting to note that in Tyerman's day it was quite common for believers to connect great natural disasters as the Hand of God meting out His Wrath upon the people. Unlike the Deism of today which claims a natural calamity is due to the quirks of "Mother Nature" or "global warming". Thus we read with interest the following comments:

> "Thus terminated Whitefield's visit to the city of Lisbon, a city containing 36,000 houses, 350,000 inhabitants, a cathedral, forty parish churches, as many monasteries, and a royal palace; and yet a city which a year and a half afterwards, by an earthquake, which shook almost the whole of Europe, was reduced to a heap of ruins, and in which, in six minutes, not fewer than 60,000 persons met with an untimely death. The terrific judgment was not unmerited. No act of the Supreme Ruler is capricious. Some of the sights which Whitefield witnessed were hateful, hideous caricatures of the greatest and most solemn truths and facts ever made know to human beings. They were theatrical idolatries, which no system, except Paganism and Popery, would dare to practise. Popery in Lisbon was unchecked, and, therefore, undisguised. In England and America, it chiefly existed in lurking-places. The thing, as it really is, Whitefield had never seen till he went to the Portuguese metropolis. Favourable circumstances are always needful for its full development. The system is essentially *semper idem*; and if the sights seen by Whitefield are not *at present* seen in England, the reason is, not because the Popish hierarchy deem them wrong, but, because such profanities are impracticable.

---

9 *Works,* Vol. 3, p. 88.

"Whitefield was about a month in Lisbon, without preaching a single sermon. Why? To have attempted preaching would have ensured his immediate expulsion or imprisonment. His heart yearned over the deluded inhabitants, but he was powerless to afford them help. On hearing of the just judgment of 1755, he wrote, 'O that all who were lately destroyed in Portugal had known the Divine Redeemer! Then the earthquake would have been only a rumbling chariot to carry them to God. Poor Lisbon! How soon are all thy riches and superstitious pageantry swallowed up!'

"Whitefield, for once in his life, was gagged and silent; but his time was not unprofitably spent. He was learning lessons which could not be learned in England or America, and which, he hoped, would make him a better man and a better preacher, to the end of life. He became a stauncher Protestant, and felt more than ever how invaluable were the privileges enjoyed by the inhabitants of Great Britain. 'Every day,' said he, 'I have seen or heard something that has a tendency to make me thankful for the glorious Reformation. O that our people were equally reformed in their lives, as they are in their doctrines and manner of worship! But alas! Alas! O for another Luther! O for that wished-for season, when everything that is antichristian shall be totally destroyed by the breath of the Redeemer's mouth, and the brightness of His appearing!"[10]

Regarding America there were several things which kept drawing the great evangelist back to its shores. One, was his beloved Bethesda and the continual care and concern for the Orphan House there in Savannah. Debts continued to mount and thus so did his labors in his itinerant preaching to further gain financial support for its continuation. Secondly, was the aftermath of the Great Awakening, which had resulted in many new meeting houses being erected and in thousands of conversions. Also, from this great movement of God in the Colonies was the added pulpit dimension of this: the New England pastors who were a part of the revival continued to preach revival messages long after the event. Thus, Whitefield was drawn to America to re-visit the places where God had used him mightily in revival and to spend time in fellowship with his dear friends and colleagues in the ministry. Men such as: Gilbert Tennet, Samuel Davies, Jonathan Parsons, Thomas Prince, Dickenson and others. Not to mention the likes of Benjamin Franklin who George Whitefield had become not only close friends, but who was also now publishing his Journals in the Colonies. So it was with great anticipation that he set foot on American soil in 1754, especially since he had left it so suddenly his last visit.

We see some of this thought in the following observations by Philip:

"Whitefield's former visits to America, although not unwelcome to her spiritual churches, were, in some measure, unsought for by them, as churches. I mean, he consulted his own sense of duty, and the interest of his orphan-house, and the urgency of private friends, rather than public opinion, on either side of the Atlantic. On the present occasion, besides his ordinary reasons for ranging America, he had many pressing invitations 'to cross-plough' his old grounds, and to water where he had planted. He had also a *home* reason. He wished to come back upon England and Scotland again, in the power of an *American* unction; a savour he had found to be 'of life unto life,' in all his movements through his native land. Hence he said on his voyage, 'After a short tour through America, I hope to see my native country, and begin to *begin* to ramble after poor sinners again.' It was there he learned to range, and there he discovered how much he *could* range, as well as how much good ranging did; and therefore he was unwilling to forget the lesson. And no wonder. Had he not hunted in the American woods and wilds, he would not have done nor dared what he attempted at home. And he was an *apt* scholar. It must have been a strange place indeed, where Whitefield could pick up nothing useful. Every where his maxim was, 'I would fain be one of Christ's *bees*, and learn to extract honey from every flower;'—whilst every where his feeling was, 'Alas, I am a *drone*, and deserve to be stung out of God's hive.'

"He arrived in safety with his orphans at Bethesda, after an easy voyage; and found himself at the head of a family of a hundred and six members, 'black and white,' all dependent upon his personal efforts and influence. But he had no fears. He regarded his charge as a stewardship of Providence, and hoped and begged accordingly, nothing doubting. Having arranged his household, he started to his work, and traversed Carolina. It was now high summer, and besides the oppressive heat, 'great thunders, violent lightnings, and heavy rains,' frequently beat upon him as he journeyed from town to town; but his health improved and his spirits rose as he advanced. One reason of this was that he chiefly travelled by night. 'In spite of thunder, lightning, rain, and heat, God is pleased,' he says, 'to hold my soul in life, and to let me see his glorious work prosper in my unworthy hands ...'

"Having 'fully preached the gospel' in the regions of Carolina, he went to New York and Philadelphia, and found at both 'prejudices removed, and a more effectual door than ever.' for labour."[11]

We see in his letters written during this time that George Whitefield is not only watering old ground but planting! We will use his correspondence as a narrative not unlike his Journals of earlier years. We will not make use of *all* the letters but include extracts from most of them. We pick up his labors in South Carolina where he writes:

---

11 Philip, pp. 417–418.

"Charles-Town, July 10, 1754.

"Since I have left *Bethesda*, I have been out two nights by land, and one by water, and though wearied, am preserved in as good health as can in any wise be expected. To-morrow or *Monday*, I expect to embark again for *New-York*. The prospect of being ere long at the new *Jerusalem*, makes all things easy ...

"On board the Deborah, July 20, 1754.

"... hurrying from place to place, and settling my orphan-charge, hath almost put it out of my power to perform it; however, I am now once more on the great deep in my way to *New-York*; ... we had a pleasant passage to *Carolina*, and since that I found and left my orphan family comfortably settled at *Georgia*. The colony, as well as *Bethesda*, is now in a thriving situation. Black and white persons I have now a hundred and six to provide for. The GOD whom I desire to serve, will enable me to do it for his great name's sake. At *Charles-Town*, and in other parts of *Carolina*, my poor labours have met with the usual acceptance, and I have reason to hope a clergyman hath been brought under very serious impressions. Not unto me, O LORD, not unto me, but unto thy free grace be all the glory! What will befall me at the northward, I know not; this I know, that JESUS CHRIST will suffer nothing to pluck me out of his hands. My health is wonderfully preserved.—My wonted vomitings have left me, and though I ride whole nights, and have been frequently exposed to great thunders, violent lightnings, and heavy rains, yet I am rather better than usual, and as far as I can judge, am not yet to die. O that I may at length learn to begin to live. I am ashamed of my sloth and lukewarmness, and long to be on the stretch for GOD ...

"New-York, July 27, 1754.

"Here will I set up my *Ebenezer*—for hitherto the LORD hath helped me. Through his divine goodness, I left *Georgia and Bethesda* in growing circumstances, and am come once more to pay a short visit to the northward ... Strange! That I should be in this dying world till now. What changes have I seen! What changes must I expect to see before my final departure, if the Redeemer is pleased to lengthen out this span of life. Welcome, welcome, my LORD and my GOD, whatever cup thou shalt see meet to put into my hands! Only sweeten it with thy love, and then, though bitter in itself, I cannot but be salutary. Alas! How little do we know of ourselves, till we are tried, and how hard doth the old man die! Well! Blessed be GOD, die he shall. JESUS hath given him his deadly blow, and at the best he only lives a dying life. Thanks be to GOD for such a Saviour! O for a thousand tongues to shew forth his praise! LORD JESUS, cloath me with humility, that I may every day know more and more the honour conferred upon me in being made a poor pilgrim for thee! Keep me travelling, keep me working, or at least beginning to begin to work for thee till I die! ...

"New-York, July 28, 1754.

"... Some time next month, I hope to come as far as *Boston* ... What is to befall me I know not; Father, into thy hands I commend my spirit! Fain would I be as clay in they hands. LORD JESUS, when shall it once be? But I am a stubborn, ill and hell-deserving creature. Less than the least of all, shall be my motto still. Amazing,—that the Redeemer should suffer such a wretch to speak or travel for him. Sure his name and nature is Love. O That I could but begin to begin to love him! My obligations increase daily ... O that the Redeemer may provide for the dear *New-York* people! The residue of the spirit is in his hands ...

"Here our LORD brought me two days ago, and last night I had an opportunity of preaching on his dying, living, ascending, and interceding love, to a large and attentive auditory. Next week I purpose going to *Philadelphia,* and then shall come back again here in my way to *Boston* ... His presence keeps me company, and I find it sweet to run about for him. I find the door all along the continent is as open as ever, and the way seems clearing up for the neighbouring islands. What a pity is it, that we can only be at one place at once, for the ever-loving, ever-lovely JESUS.

"New-York, July 30, 1754.

"... Yesterday I preached thrice; this morning I feel it. Welcome weariness for JESUS! O how little can I do for him! I blush and am confounded ...

"Philadelphia, August 7, 1754.

"... Yesterday I was taken with a violent cholera morbus, and hoped ere now to have been where the inhabitants shall no more say, 'I am sick.' But I am brought back again. May it be in order to bring some more precious souls to the ever-blessed JESUS! This is all my desire. O that GOD should ever make use of such a worthless creature as I am! But his grace is free, he yet blesses me, and rather more than ever. My poor labours, seemed to be owned here, as well as at *New-York.* I received the sacrament at church on *Sunday,* and have preached in the academy, but I find Mr. *Tennent's* house abundantly more commodious ...

"Philadelphia, August 15, 1754.

"Once more, after having my cables out ready (as I thought) to cast anchor within the port, I am constrained to put out to sea again. My late sickness, though violent, hath not been unto death. O that it may be to the glory of GOD! With some difficulty I can preach once a-day. Congregations rather increase than decrease; and many, O strange! are desirous of my making a longer stay. But the time is fixed for next *Tuesday*; and all the following days till *Sunday,* are to be employed between this and *New-Brunswick.* There I am informed some execution was done. Whilst I live, LORD JESUS, grant I may not live I vain ...

"Philadelphia, August 17, 1754.

"... Here's a glorious range in the *American* woods. It is pleasant hunting for sinners. Thousands flock daily to hear the word preached ...

"New-York, Sept. 2, 1754.

"... We had pleasant seasons in our way hither, and here people attend gladly. Some time this week I expect to sail for *Rhode Island* ...

"Newark, Sept. 27, 1754.

"... Providence, and the circumstances of the Southern provinces, point directly towards *Virginia* and the Orphan-house. In the former, I am told, the door is opening in earnest; and the business of the latter requires my presence this Winter. These being dispatched, my mind will be disburdened, and my heart free for a large range in *New-England* ... I will not go hence to the *West Indies*, because I cannot go without a companion, and that companion (if possible) is to be Captain Gladding ...

"To Lady Huntingdon.

"Elizabeth-Town (New-Jersey), Sept. 30, 1754.

"... Every where a divine power accompanies the word, prejudices have been removed, and a more effectual door opened than ever for preaching the everlasting gospel. I am now at Governor Belcher's, who sends your Ladyship the most cordial respects. His outward man decays, but his inward man seems to be renewed day by day. I think he ripens for heaven apace. This last week was at the *New-Jersey* commencement, at which the President and Trustees were pleased to present me with the degree of A.M. The synod succeeded.—But such a number of simple hearted, united ministers, I never saw before. I preached to them several times, and the great Master of assemblies was in the midst of us. To-morrow, GOD willing, I shall set out with the worthy President for *New-England*, and expect to return back to the Orphan-house through *Virginia*, where the gospel I trust will have free course and be glorified. This will be about a two thousand mile circuit; but the Redeemer's strength will be more than sufficient. Once this Summer, I thought my discharge was come; but it seems the shattered bark must put out to sea again. Father, thy will be done! ...

"Boston, October 14, 1754.

"Surely my coming here was of GOD. At *Rhode-Island* I preached five times. People convened immediately, and flocked to hear more eagerly than ever. The same scene opens at *Boston*. Thousands waited for, and thousands attended on the word preached. At the *Old North*, at seven in the morning, we generally have three thousand hearers, and many cannot come in. Convictions I hear do fasten, and many souls are comforted. Doctor Sewall hath engaged me once to preach his lecture. The polite, I hear, are taken, and opposition falls. What are thou, O mountain? before our great *Zerubbable* thou shalt become a plain. I preach at the *Old* and the *New North* ... At *Rhode Island* and this place souls fly to the gospel like doves to the windows. A divine power hath hitherto accompanied the word, and opposition seems to fall daily ... I have preached in four large meeting-houses, and the prospect of doing good is very promising ...

"Portsmouth (New-Hampshire), October 24, 1754.

"... I am advanced about three hundred miles further northward. But what have I seen? *Dagon* falling every where before the ark; enemies silenced, or made to own the finger of GOD; and the friends of JESUS triumphing in his glorious conquest. At *Boston* a most lovely scene hath opened. In the morning before seven o'clock, though the meeting-house will hold about four thousand, yet many were obliged to go away, and I was helped in through the window. The prospect is most promising indeed. In the country a like scene opens; I am enabled to preach always twice, and sometimes thrice a day. Thousands flock to hear, and JESUS manifests forth his glory ... I now come to the end of my *northward* line, and in a day or two purpose to turn back, in order to preach all the way to *Georgia*. It is about a sixteen hundred miles journey. JESUS is able to carry me through ...

"Portsmouth, October 25, 1754.

"... Still the LORD of all lords stoops to accompany my feeble labours with his divine presence. At *Salem* we were favoured with a sweet and divine influence. Sunday was a high day at *Ipswich*; twice I preached for Mr. R——, and once for Mr. W——. Hundreds were without the doors. On Monday at *Newbury* the like scene opened twice ... Too many came to meet and bring me into *Portsmouth*, where I preached on Tuesday evening, also twice the next day, and just now I have taken my leave. The blessed Spirit vouchsafed to be with us each time. Yesterday I preached at *York and Kittery:* at both places the Redeemer manifested forth his glory ... I am now going to *Greenland* and *Durham*, and to-morrow shall preach at *Exeter*. The sabbath is to be kept at *Newbury* ..."[12]

It is important to pause here in the narrative of his travels to comment. This last mention by George Whitefield of his preaching his way from Boston up to Portsmouth and then back down through Exeter on Saturday and then on to Newbury (Newburyport) on Sunday. Was a set pattern of ministry for him while in New England and one he repeated each time his visited America. For it was at Exeter on his last trip to America that he preached in the field with his chest heaving and near death and he then moved down to Newburyport with the intention of preaching at his friend, Jonathan Parson's, church the Old South. This itinerary laid out for us by Whitefield in 1754 is the exact one of his last visit in 1770 when he died in Newburyport, and is there buried today beneath the pulpit of the Old South First Presbyterian Church on Federal Street.

Now back to the narrative:

"... Monday I am to preach thrice,—at Rowley, Byfield, and Ipswich; Tuesday, at Cape Ann, and Wednesday night or Thursday morning at Boston ...

"Rhode Island, Nov. 22, 1754.

"... A more effectual door I never saw opened, than lately at Boston, and indeed at every place where I have been in New-England; not a hundreth part can well be told ... With great difficulty I am got to this place, where people, as

12 *Works*, Vol. 3, pp. 92–108.

I am informed, are athirst to hear the word of GOD. I shall therefore stay, GOD willing, till Monday, and then set forward to Connecticut in my way to New-York ... O what a friend is JESUS! A friend that sticks closer than a brother. He is indeed the pilgrim's stay and staff; few choose to try him in such a station. This be my happy lot! ...

To the Rev. Mr. Gillies.

"Rhode-Island, Nov. 25, 1754.

"... This shews you where I am at present, going towards *Georgia* from *Boston*; where my reception hath been far superior to that fourteen years ago. In that and other places in *New-England*, I have been enabled to preach near a hundred times since the beginning of October, and thanks be to GOD, we scarce had so much as one dry meeting. Not a hundredth part can be told you. In *Philadelphia*, *New-Jersey*, and at *New-York* also, the great Redeemer caused his word to run and be glorified. I am now returning through those and the other Southward provinces again, in my way to *Georgia*, where I expect to see our new Governor. Blessed be GOD, *Bethesda* is in growing circumstances, and, I trust, will more and more answer the end of its institution. I was exceedingly delighted at *New-Jersey* commencement. Surely that college is of GOD. The worthy president [Mr. Burr] intends to correspond with you. O that I could do it oftener: but it is impracticable. Traveling, and preaching always twice, and frequently thrice, engrosseth almost all my time. However, neither you nor any of my dear *Glasgow* friends, are forgotten by me. No, no: they are engraven upon the very tables of my heart. O that the LORD of all lords, whose mercy endureth for ever, may give you hearts ro remember poor sinful, ill, and hell-deserving me! Fain would I continue a pilgrim for life.

Christ's presence doth my pains beguile,
And make each wilderness to smile.

I have a fourteen hundred miles ride before me ...[13]

Here we must pause from the narrative. Whitefield had a second home in America (at least a place where he could kick off his shoes and relax and be at ease) to which he arrived in the month of December—this was Bohemia. His first home was Bethesda. When not in Georgia George Whitefield would seek the tranquility of Bohemia, an estate owned by his dear friend Mrs. Bayard. We see from the following:

"Bohemia Manor was the mansion of the elderly Mrs. Bayard. She was the descendant of two of the great patrician Colonial families and her late husband was the grandson of Anna Stuyvesant Bayard, the sister of Governor Stuyvesant. Mrs. Bayard's son, Colonel Peter Bayard and his family, also made their home at the Manor.

---

13 Ibid. pp. 108–111.

"Mrs. Bayard 'was a Greek and Latin scholar and could converse in several languages, and was a woman of exceptional talents and intelligence.' She was also a most earnest Christian, and after arriving at her home in time to spend Christmas there Whitefield said in a letter:

'I am at length got into Maryland, and into a family out of which, I trust, five have been born of God.'

"... Moreover, Whitefield now had still more extensive plans in mind. He intended to sail from Charleston to the West Indies and since several of these islands had large English-speaking populations but little Gospel ministry, he longed to visit them. But his responsibilities at Bethesda made the trip impossible at the time.

"Accordingly, he made his way to Georgia and to the Orphan House. The institution which for seventeen years had been so great a care was also his chief delight, and after the visit ended he declared, 'I could almost say that the few last hours I was there, were superior in satisfaction to any hours I ever enjoyed.'

"Nevertheless, during these last weeks in America certain events took place which brought him profound grief. He does not tell us what they were but merely refers to them in the words,

'The trials I have met with on various accounts, have brought my old vomitings upon me, and my soul hath been pierced with many sorrows.'

"And thus, in this mixture of joy and sorrow, on March 27, (1755) Whitefield brought this fifth visit to America to a close and set sail for England."[14]

Before we leave George Whitefield's labors for the year 1754 we must also look at what another says about him during this time:

"More than a month intervenes between the date of this letter to Mr. Gillies [Nov. 25th], and the next preserved letter of Whitefield. The reader must try to imagine the great preacher gradually pursuing his immense horseback-ride, making the primeval forests ring with his songs of praise, and preaching the gospel of his Master, twice or thrice every day. His Christmas was spent in Maryland. Hence the following:—

'Bohemia, Maryland, December 27.

'I have been travelling and preaching in the northern provinces for nearly five months. I suppose I have ridden near two thousand miles, and preached about two hundred and thirty times; but to how many thousands of people cannot well be told. O what days of the Son of man have I seen! God be merciful to me an ungrateful sinner!

'I am now forty years of age, and would gladly spend the day in retirement and deep humiliation before that Jesus, for whom I have done so little, though He had done and suffered so much for me.

14 Dallimore, Vol. 2, pp. 372–373.

'About February, I hope to reach Georgia; and, at spring, to embark for England ...'"[15]

Early in 1755 George Whitefield wrote some letters to his friend Charles Wesley and it is from these extracts that we learn about his activities in the month of January 1755, for two months later Whitefield set sail for England. We read with interest:

"'January 14, 1755. I suppose my circuit already has been two thousand miles; and, before I reach Bethesda, a journey of six hundred more lies before me. Scenes of wonder have opened all the way. A thousandth part cannot be told. In Virginia, the prospect is very promising. I have preached in two churches, and, this morning, am to preach in a third. Rich and poor seem quite ready to hear. Many have been truly awakened.

'Virginia, January 13. I have not been here a week, and have had the comfort of seeing many impressed under the word every day. Two churches have been opened, and a third (Richmond) I am to preach in to-morrow. I find prejudices subside, and some of the rich and great begin to think favourably of the work of God. Several of the lower class have been with me, acknowledging what the Lord did for them when I was here before.

'Virginia, January 17. I am now on the borders of North Carolina, and, after preaching to-morrow in a neighbouring church, I purpose to take my leave of Virginia. Had I not been detained so long northward, what a wide and effectual door might have been opened. Here, as well as elsewhere, rich and poor flock to hear the everlasting gospel. Many have come forty or fifty miles; and a spirit of conviction and consolation seemed to go through all the assemblies ...'

"Of Whitefield's ride from Virginia to Georgia, no record now exists; neither is there any information respecting his work at Bethesda. As usual, his sojourn at the Orphan House was brief; for, on February 26th, he had returned to Charleston, whence, towards the end of March, he embarked for England. The following are extracts from two letters addressed to his housekeeper at Bethesda:—

'Charleston, March 3, 1755. Through Divine goodness, we arrived here last Wednesday afternoon. On Thursday, Mr. E—— was solemnly ordained. The trials I have met with have brought my old vomitings upon me. My soul has been pierced with many sorrows. But, I believe, all is intended for my good. Amidst all, I am comforted at the present situation of Bethesda. I hope you will walk in love, and that the children will grow in years and grace. I pray for you all, night and day.'

'Charleston, March 17, 1755. Had I wings like a dove, how often would I have fled to Bethesda, since my departure from it! I could almost say, that the last few hours I was there were superior in satisfaction to any hours I ever

---

15 Tyerman, Vol. 2, p. 337.

enjoyed. But I must go about my heavenly Father's business. For this, I am a poor, but willing pilgrim, and give up all that is near and dear to me on this side of eternity. This week, I expect to embark in the *Friendship*, Captain Ball; but am glad of the letters from Bethesda before I start. They made me weep, and caused me to throw myself prostrate before the prayer-hearing and promise-keeping God. He will give strength, He will give power. Fear not. You are now, I believe, where the Lord would have you be, and all will be well. I repose the utmost confidence in you, and believe I shall not be disappointed of my hope. I should have been glad if the apples had been sent in the boat; they would have been useful in the voyage. But Jesus can stay me with better apples. May you and all my dear family have plenty of these! I imagine it will not be long before I return from England.'

"Whitefield set sail about March 27th; and, after a six weeks' voyage, landed at Newhaven, on the 8th of May. More than eight years elapsed before his next visit to America."[16]

So ends the great evangelist's fifth visit to America. His receptions had been as warm as his wanderings extensive. The congregations at his two tabernacles in England were glad to see him!

---

16 Ibid. pp. 339–340.

I wish I could say anything to add to the best impressions of my late dear friend Mr. Whitefield. One part of his character, ever the most to be admired by me, was the most artless mind—an Israelite indeed in whom there was no guile ... There is not one soul living either in temporals or spirituals who he ever meant to deceive for any purpose, and that it was his great point ever in godly sincerity and simplicity to have his whole life approved in this world. No prospect of pretended good could make him do evil—this is my testimony of him in this respect. I account for this from the clear revelation of Jesus Christ to his soul by the Holy Ghost ... He had a single eye for the Lord and whatever was mistaken for this end was deficiency in judgment, considered rationally and temporally. Anyone that knew as well as I his true spiritual knowledge of eternal things must be absolutely sure of this. My dear friend, believe me, there is little of this left in the world ...

Selina, Countess of Huntingdon
in a letter to John Wesley. Nov. 20, 1770.

CHAPTER 46

A RUN-ABOUT FOR CHRIST

Whitefield wrote in a letter to his good friend Gillies in Glasgow on May 10th, 1755, as he was settling once again into the metropolis. He had arrived in London on the 8th of May and what stands out in this correspondence is the statement, "... I left America with regret.—Never was the door opened wider in those parts for preaching the everlasting gospel, than now."

We see the following remarks about his return to his native land:

"'On his return from America, the first thing he took notice of,' says Gillies, 'was the success of religion in his native country.' He was delighted to find 'the poor Methodists as lively as ever; the gospel preached with power in many churches; some fresh ministers, almost every week, determining to know nothing but Jesus Christ, and him crucified; and many at Oxford awakened to the knowledge of the truth.'

"Almost the first thing he did on his arrival was, to use his influence with the Marquis of Lothian, for a *diploma* to his friend, President Burr of New Jersey ..."[1]

We find the explanation to this request in the following observations:

"During his recent visit to America, the Rev. Aaron Burr and the trustees of New Jersey College conferred on Whitefield an M. A. degree. Within a week after his return to England, Whitefield commenced an endeavour to return the compliment. He had formed a high opinion of Mr. Burr, and wished him to be honoured; but, apart from this, he doubtless thought that the college would be helped if its president were made a doctor of divinity. The Marquis of Lothian had been a generous benefactor of the college, and, through him, Whitefield hoped to procure the coveted distinction. In a letter to the Marquis, he spoke of the college as 'the purest seminary' he had known, and added, 'If the degree of doctor of divinity could be procured for Mr. Burr, the present president, it would make an addition to its honours.'"[2]

---

1   Philip, p. 422.
2   Tyerman, Vol. 2, p. 342.

The great evangelist wasted no time in resuming his title of "a run-about for Christ". He labored in London for six weeks preaching to growing crowds— his absence in America had not diminished his great popularity! In addition to his labors in continual preaching we see that in 1755 he published another written work which he called "my little communion book." A description of this publication is necessary:

"The 'little Communion book' here mentioned was a 12mo. volume, of 140 pages, with the following title: 'A Communion Morning's Companion. By George Whitefield, A.B. late of Pembroke College, Oxford, and Chaplain to the Right Honourable the Countess of Huntingdon. London, 1755.' The book consists of: 1. Meditations on the five last Questions and Answers of the Catechism of the Church of England. Extracted from Bishop Ken. 2. The Order for Administration of the Lord's Supper. After the pattern of Bishop Wilson. 3. Fifty-nine Sacramental Hymns, and seventeen Doxologies, extracted from several authors ... The book had an extensive sale. As early as 1758, it had passed through a third edition."[3]

During all these immense labors we hear no mention of Elizabeth Whitefield and wonder how much felicity was in their little home and if the burden of a marriage was weighing upon his already wearied frame. We see his exhaustion from a letter written to The Countess, it is dated from London, July 11, 1755.

We read:

"Yesterday about noon, after being worn down with travelling, and preaching twice and thrice a day in *Gloucestershire, at Bath, and Bristol,* a gracious and never-failing Providence brought me to town, where I had the pleasure of receiving two kind, very kind and undeserved letters from your Ladyship's hand. Had I the least leisure or strength, I should have written a letter of condolence to your Ladyship from *Bristol.* There I heard of the death of good Lady Ann, and was glad to find that Miss. W—— bore the news of it with so much composure. Alas! How many have your Ladyship lived to see go before you! An earnest this, I hope, that you are to live to a good old age, and be more and more a mother in *Israel.* A short, but sweet character. GOD knows how long I am to drag this crazy load, my body, along. Blessed be his holy name, I have not one attachment to this inferior earth. I am sick of myself, sick of the world, sick of the church, and am panting daily after the full enjoyment of my GOD. John Cennick is now added to the happy number of those who are called to see him as he is. I do not envy, but I want to follow after him. Give my patience, holy JESUS, to wait till my appointed time shall come. In the mean while, if it be thy holy will, improve me to promote, in some small degree, thy glory and the good of souls! Thanks be to his adorable majesty, the fields at *Bristol and Kingswood* were whiter, and more ready to harvest than for many years last past. Was the new Tabernacle at *Bristol* as large as that in *London,* it would be filled. Thrice last Sunday, and twice

3   Ibid. p. 344.

the Sunday before, I preached in the fields to many, many thousands ... I am
now looking up for direction what course to steer next. I suppose it will be
northward. I wish your Ladyship's plan may do; but I fear the parts about your
Ladyship are too cold. O how unworthy of such a guest! ... I must away to
preach the everlasting gospel. O how unworthy of such a divine employ!
Pardon, honoured Madam, this poor, and too prolix scribble ..."[4]

Whitefield left London in late August to be "a run-about for Christ" once
more. He ventured to the north of England spending a few days with his old
Oxford friend Hervey. But in addition to the evangelist's labors an event
began that would prevent him from visiting his beloved Bethesda or America
again for *eight long years*. This of course was the start of what became known
as "The Seven Years' War". We see from the following:

"Just at the time when Whitefield left America, the ministers of George the
Second announced to Parliament that a war with France was inevitable. The
Committee of Supply eagerly voted a million of money for the defence of their
American possessions; and Admiral Boscawen was sent with a fleet towards the
Gulf of St. Lawrence, to intercept a French fleet which had been prepared in the
forts of Rochefort and Brest, and which was carrying reinforcements to the
French Canadians. America was now in martial confusion. Among others,
Whitefield's old friend Sir William Pepperell had gone to the field of action; and
Whitefield, while a guest at Hervey's wrote to Lady Pepperell and her daughter,
to cheer them in the colonel's absence, as follows:—

'Weston-Favell, August 30, 1755.

'Dear Miss,—A few days past, as I was going into the Tabernacle to read
letters, yours came to hand. Immediately, I read it among the rest, and you
and my other New England friends had the prayers of thousands. How did I
wish to be transported to America! How did I long to stir up all against the
common enemy, and to be made instrumental of doing my dear country
some little service! Dear New England,—dear Boston lies upon my heart!
Surely the Lord will not give it over into the hands of the enemy. He has too
many praying ministers and praying people there, for such a dreadful
catastrophe.'

"Such were Whitefield's feelings at the commencement of the Seven Years'
War, which was ended by the Peace of Paris, February 10, 1763. The terrific
strife kept Whitefield from his beloved America for the space of eight long
years, and, during this lengthened period, many and great were his anxieties
concerning his Orphan House, and his transatlantic friends ..."[5]

George Whitefield remained busy ranging for the good of the gospel and we
pick up his labors through some letters written to friends at this time. He had

---

4   *Works,* Vol. 3, pp. 128–129.
5   Tyerman, Vol. 2, pp. 350–351.

preached both in and out of doors in the northern parts of England and God was accompanying the preaching of his word by his faithful servant!

We read of this wondrous activity from the following extracts of his steady correspondence between his friends:

"Northampton, Sept. 1, 1755.

"... Every where the fields are white ready unto harvest. At *London, Bristol, Bath, in Gloucestershire, at Norwich, Bury, Braintree,* and yesterday twice here, we had blessed seasons ...

"To Lady Huntingdon.

"Ever-honoured Madam,   Newcastle, Sept. 24, 1755.

"I know not how long it is since I left your Ladyship; but this I know, a sense of the satisfaction I felt when at *Donington,* still lies upon my heart. Surely, I was not called out to publc work, waiting upon and administering to your Ladyship in holy offices would be my choice and highest privilege. But JESUS calls, and therefore I travel to do or suffer thy will, O GOD! The only new ground that hath been broken up, I think is *Liverpool;* there the prospect is promising. I preached in a great square on the Lord's day, and the alarm I hear went through the town. At *Bolton* the cup of GOD's people ran over; and at *Manchester* we had large auditories and blessed seasons. At *Leeds* we felt what is unutterable, and at *Bradford,* I believe, last Sunday the congregation consisted of at least ten thousand. But O how hath my pleasure been alloyed at *Leeds!* I rejoiced there with trembling; for unknown to me, they had almost finished a large house in order to form a separate congregation. If this scheme succeeds, an awful separation I fear will take place amongst the societies. I have written to Mr. Wesley, and have done all I could to prevent it. O this self-love, this self-will! It is the devil of devils. LORD JESUS, may thy blessed spirit purge it out of all our hearts! But O how must the divine Paraclete sit as a refiner's fire upon the heart, in order to bring this about! Few choose such fiery purgations, and therefore so few make the progress that might justly be expected of them in the divine life. Make me, O GOD, willing to be made, willing to be, to do, or suffer what thou pleasest, and then—what then?—this foolish fluttering heart will sweetly be moulded into the divine image.

"This I write from *Newcastle,* where the people twice a day hear the gospel gladly. At *York* I hope a fine gentleman was touched, and several I find were awakened there, and here also, at my last visit. What to do now, I know not. Calls on all sides are very loud, and it is too late to go either to *Ireland or Scotland.* O my GOD!—Winter is at hand, and in the summer how little hath been done for thee! I cannot bear to live at this poor dying rate. My good and ever-honoured Lady, add, for CHRIST's sake add to my already innumerable obligations, by praying for a poor and unfruitful and ungrateful dwarf. I am sick of my vileness, and yet just comes in a letter acquainting me, that my preaching hath been blessed to many this morning. Good GOD, what is this? Grace! Grace! I am lost, I am lost.

Take me Uriel, take me hence,
And bear my soul to GOD.

"Your Ladyship sees I am running into my old fault. I cannot well help it, when writing to your Ladyship ..."[6]

It is interesting to note that throughout all the great labors under God that George Whitefield accomplished he "remained little in his own eyes." Humility always attended him. It was one of his greatest marks as a man of God; for it is God Himself who states, "I dwell in the high and holy place, with him also that is of a contrite and humble spirit, to revive the spirit of the humble, and to revive the heart of the contrite one" (Isaiah 57:15).

About this time, as the great evangelist entered his forties, he became rather corpulent. It was not attributed to over-eating for he always lived his life "by the rule of the Methodists" keeping his body under subjection. Regardless of his moderations at the table he was no longer the slender frame of his youthful days. He comments about his weight condition in a letter to a friend:

"London, Oct. 31, 1755. Last night, a never-failing GOD brought me from the north of *England*, where I have been enabled to preach twice and thrice a day, to many, many thousands for these two months past. And yet I cannot die.—Nay they tell me, 'I grow fat.' O that I may grow in grace, especially in humility! Then would the LORD delight to honour me. Vile as I am, this he continues to do. Never did I see the word more blessed, or so many thousands run after it with greater greediness. Next to inviting them to CHRIST, I have always taken care to exhort them to pray for King George, and our dear friends in America. I trust, that thousands are now engaged this way, and whatever dark providences may intervene, I hope to hear they have been more than conquerors ..."[7]

Whitefield was busy, more active than usual, because he knew that winter would soon be settling upon the land of England—then little ranging would be done. So like a comet burning its last embers before it crashes down he pushed himself into vast labor for God before colder weather prevented him! We will narrate his labors from letters written from November through December 1755.

"To Lady Huntingdon.

"Ever-honoured Madam, London, Nov. 1, 1755.

"What shall I say? Indeed and indeed, it hath given me great concern, that I could not perform my promise to return to *Donnington-park* so soon as I

---

6   *Works*, Vol. 3, pp. 143–144.
7   Ibid. pp. 145–146.

expected.—But had I done so, I must have failed preaching at least to above fifty thousand souls, who at different places ran most greedily many miles after the everlasting gospel. This I thought you Ladyship would by no means approve of, and therefore acquiesced. On Thursday evening, with no small regret I came to town, after having preached about a hundred times, and travelled about eight hundred miles in the country. Blessed be GOD, my feeble carcase was strengthened to hold out, though for more than ten days together, I preached thrice a day.—O that I could preach three hundred times! All would be little enough, (alas, alas, infinitely too little) to testify my feeble love to the ever-loving, ever-lovely JESUS. I hope that your Ladyship, and the other elect Ladies, will enjoy much of his blessed spirit, in your present sweet retreat. After about a week's stay here, I hope to move westward. O winter, winter! Haste and fly, that I may again set out, and begin to spring for my GOD! ..."[8]

One searches in vain to find any reference to Elizabeth Whitefield in his letters. We see that the itinerant is in London (his home is there—and supposedly his wife!) for only one week before he is off again in other labors. We also see his health is broken from his vast physical efforts: his crying out at the top of his voice in fields and pulpits, his long difficult rides on horseback in inclement weather, his poor eating habits from being out on the road, are all catching up to him. He laments to a friend about his current illness:

"Bristol, Nov. 30, 1755 ... For near ten days past I have preached in pain, occasioned by a sore throat, which I find now is the beginning of an inflammatory quinsey. Silence and warmth, the doctor tells me, under GOD, may cure me, but heaven (if I had my will) is my choice, especially if I can speak no longer on earth for my GOD. However, painful and expensive as, in a spiritual sense, the medicine of silence is, I have promised to be very obedient, and therefore I have not preached this morning ..."[9]

Because of his illness and weakened condition George Whitefield returned to London and to his home, and to his wife. He closed the year in busying himself with catching up on his correspondence. We see from the following letter written to The Countess that he has been resting. But he also makes mention of the Long Acre Chapel. This chapel became a scene of great controversy which we will cover in the next chapter. We will conclude this present chapter of the life of George Whitefield in 1755 with his last letter of the year written to his dear friend, Selina. It is with great interest that we read:

"To Lady Huntingdon.

"Ever-honoured Madam,   London, Dec. 31, 1755.

"Your Ladyship's kind and condescending letter should not have lain so long by me, had not bodily weakness, and my Christmas labours, prevented my

---

8   Ibid. pp. 147–148.
9   Ibid. p. 151.

writing. Indeed and indeed my good Lady, it hath been a joyful mournful season to my inward man. For exclusive of a pretty sharp outward trial, Saturday last being my birth-day, my soul was deeply exercised from morning till evening, in thinking how much in one-and-forty years I have sinned against, and how little I have done for an infinitely good and ever-blessed GOD. This impression yet lies deep upon my heart, and therefore, through divine assistance, I purpose to end the old year in preaching on those words, 'I abhor myself, and repent in dust and ashes' O that all things belonging to the new man live and grow in me! But alas, this is a work of time. Every day and every hour must we be passing from death to life. Mortification and vivification make up the whole of the divine work in the newborn soul. Come, LORD JESUS, come quickly; have compassion on this barren fig-tree, and if it is to be spared another year, so dig and dung round it, that it may bring forth much fruit unto GOD! But shall I conceal the goodness of my long-suffering Master? No: I dare not;—for in spite of my unworthiness, he still continues to smile upon my poor ministrations, and gives me to see his stately steps in the great congregations. A noble chapel is now opened in *Long-acre,* where I am to read prayers and preach twice a week. Hundreds went away last night, who could not come in; but those that could, I trust, met with JESUS. Mr. C—— and I have met twice, and hope for a third interview very soon. LORD JESUS, make me a peace-maker! I am obliged to Mrs. W—— and the other Ladies for their kind remembrance of an unworthy worm ..."[10]

10 Ibid. pp. 153–154.

I pray that it may be a soul-trap indeed, to many wandering sinners.

George Whitefield
on his Tottenham Court Road Chapel

CHAPTER 47

LONG ACRE RIOTS AND THE SOUL TRAP

The year 1756 brought much persecution to the forty-one-year old evangelist. The center of the controversy lay in the already mentioned area outside of London, called "Long Acre". Whitefield was a bitter opponent to theater districts for he believed them to be instruments of Satan himself, causing much harm to the believing body of Christ by both their content and character. Being vocal about this in his sermons it is not surprising to find the great evangelist in the middle of deep controversy over this issue. The first real physical attacks relating to the theater come from this area known as "Long Acre". We see the following comments:

> "Long Acre has just been mentioned.—Long Acre, with the London theatres on the left, and Wesley's West Street chapel on the right,—then a fashionable street; now, to a great extent, consisting of workshops for making and exhibiting all kinds of carriages. In the theatres, John Rich, the harlequin, with a kind of dumb eloquence, was electrifying his audiences by the mere gesticulations of his body. Catherine Clive was cleverly acting the characters of chambermaids, fashionable ladies, country girls, romps, hoydens, dowdies, superannuated beauties, viragoes, and humorists. David Garrick, who once said, 'I would give a hundred guineas if I could only say, "Oh!" like Mr. Whitefield,' was the celebrated manager of the theatre in Drury Lane. Margaret Woffington was an admired favourite at Covent Garden. And Samuel Foote was at the height of his popularity.

> "The chapel in Long Acre was rented by the Rev. John Barnard, one of Whitefield's early converts, who was now an Independent minister ... Whitefield had long wished to have a West-end chapel, which might serve as the meeting-house, not only of the rich in general, but especially of the distinguished persons who were accustomed to assemble in the mansions of the Countess of Huntingdon, Lady Frances Shirley, and Lady Gertrude Hotham ..."[1]

We have two letters which detail the beginnings of trouble at Long Acre.

---

1   Tyerman, Vol. 2, pp. 355–356.

The first letter is to Dr. Gillies and in it is a detailing of the great work God was doing at this township. We will take an extract from it to show how wonderfully God was working despite Whitefield's ill health.

"London, Jan. 22, 1756. Enclosed you have some extracts, which perhaps may afford you comfort, and I trust will excite you to pray for one, who is indeed less than the least of all saints. Ever since I came from the North, it hath pleased a sovereign LORD to visit me with a violent cold and sore throat, which threatened an inflammatory quinsey ... One physician prescribed a *perpetual blister*, but I have found *perpetual preaching* to be a better remedy ... Every day brings us fresh news of newly awakened souls. Both at this and the other end of town, (where I now preach at a chapel twice a week) there is a glorious stirring amongst the dry bones ..."[2]

The second letter is to Lady Huntingdon and in it is described a scene whereby the great evangelist is being harassed by some hecklers in the crowd each time he preaches. Whitefield informs The Countess that, "The sons of *Jubal and Cain* continue to serenade me at Long Acre chapel. They have been called before a justice; and, yesterday, the Bishop of Bangor sent for them ..." A friend sympathetic to Whitefield had brought some of the hecklers before the local magistrate but the Bishop in charge of the district, Bishop Pearce barred Whitefield from preaching in the district of the Long Acre chapel. We see the storm clouds brewing from the following observations:

"But for the meddling of Bishop Pearce, it is possible, perhaps probable, that these disreputable disturbances might have ceased; but, two days after writing thus to the gentleman who had commenced a prosecution of the noisy musicians, Whitefield received a letter from the Bishop, in which he prohibited Whitefield's further preaching in the Long Acre chapel. This led to an important correspondence between the prelate and the preacher. Whether his lordship had a legal right to issue such a prohibition, ecclesiastical lawyers must determine; but, to say the least, his action had the appearance of episcopal persecution. The Bishop's letters to Whitefield have not been published; for, with contemptible cowardice, Pearce informed Whitefield that, if he dared to publish them, he must be prepared to undergo the penalty due to the infringement of 'the privilege of a peer!' Still, the substance of his letters may be gathered from Whitefield's answers; and, as these answers contain an explanation and a defence of the course of conduct which Whitefield had pursued for nearly the last twenty years, they are inserted here at greater length, than, under other circumstances they would have been.

'Tabernacle House, February 2, 1756.

'My Lord,—A few weeks ago, several serious persons, chosen to be a committee for one Mr. Barnard, applied to me, in the name of Jesus Christ,

---

2   *Works,* Vol. 3, p. 155.

and a multitude of souls desirous of hearing the gospel, to preach at a place commonly called Long Acre chapel. At the same time, they acquainted me, that the place was licensed; that Mr. Barnard either had taken or was to take it for a certain term of years; that he had preached in it for a considerable time, as a Protestant Dissenting minister; but that, notwithstanding this, I might use the Liturgy if I thought proper, so that I would but come and preach once or twice a week.

'Looking upon this as a providential call from Him, who, in the days of His flesh, taught all who were willing to hear, *on a mount, in a ship, or by the seaside*, I readily complied; and I humbly hope that my feeble labours have not been altogether vain.

'This being the case, I was somewhat surprised at the prohibition I received from your lordship this evening. For, I looked upon the place as a particular person's property; and being, as I was informed, not only unconsecrated, but also licensed according to law, I thought I might innocently preach the love of the crucified Redeemer, and loyalty to the best of princes, our dread sovereign King George, without giving any just offence to Jew or Gentile, much less to any bishop or overseer of the Church of God. As I have, therefore, given notice of preaching tomorrow evening, and every Tuesday and Thursday whilst I am in town, I hope your lordship will not look upon it as *contumacy*, if I persist in prosecuting my design, till I am more particularly apprized wherein I have erred.

'Controversy, my lord is what I abhor; and, as raising popular clamours and ecclesiastical dissensions must be quite unseasonable, especially at this juncture, when *France* and *Rome*, and *hell* ought to be the common butt of our resentment, I hope your lordship will be so good as to inform yourself and me more particularly about this matter; and, upon due consideration, as I have no design but to do good to precious souls, I promise to submit. But, if your lordship should judge it best to decline this method, and I should be called to answer for my conduct, either before a spiritual court, or from the press, I trust the irregularity I am charged with will appear justifiable to every true lover of English liberty, and (what is *all* to me) will be approved of at the awful and impartial tribunal of the great Shepherd and Bishop of souls, in obedience to whom I beg leave to subscribe myself, your lordship's most dutiful son and servant,

GEORGE WHITEFIELD.'

"The Bishop of Bangor replied to this straightforward letter; but, of course, his threat, as a peer of the realm, suppressed his communication. Whitefield's next letter was as follows:"3

This long letter from Whitefield which follows is important for *several reasons*:

---

3   Tyerman, Vol. 2, pp. 357–358.

1. It is a defense of his call from God to preach in the open air as well as in Dissenting meeting houses.

2. It is an apologetic, much like the Apostle Paul's letter to the Corinthians, where he defends his right to preach in the manner in which God called him as well as present his history of his faithful service which bears no refutation.

3. It exhibits George Whitefield's strengths as a defender of the faith and shows the historicity of his ministry as a ordained minister of the Church of England.

4. Lastly, it shows Whitefield's indefatigable labor. Here he has commenced and completed a harried week of busy preaching, he is ill, tired, and ready for bed—but duty calls and he *must answer* this letter and defend his right to preach the gospel in the manner in which God has called him!

These reasons mentioned it is worthwhile to include the letter in its entirety. We now continue:

"Tabernacle House, February 16, 1756.

"My Lord,—I this evening received your lordship's kind letter; and, though it is late, and nature calls for rest, I now sit down to give your lordship an explicit answer.

"God can witness, that I entered into holy orders, according to the form of ordination of the Church of England, with a disinterested view to promote His glory, and the welfare of precious and immortal souls. For now twenty years, as thousands can testify, I have conscientiously defended her Homilies and Articles, and, upon all occasions, have spoken well of her Liturgy. So far from renouncing these, together with her discipline, I earnestly pray for the due restoration of the one, and daily lament the departure of too many from the other. But, my lord, what can I do?

"When I acted in the most regular manner, and when I was bringing multitudes, even of Dissenters, to crowd the churches, without any other reason being given than that too many followed after me, I was denied the use of the churches. Being thus excluded, and many thousands of ignorant souls, that perhaps would neither go to church nor meeting-houses, being very hungry after the gospel, I thought myself bound in duty to deal out to them the bread of life.

"Being further ambitious to serve my God, my king, and my country, I sacrificed my affections, and left my native soil, in order to begin and carry on an Orphan House in the infant colony of Georgia, which is now put upon a good foundation. This served as an introduction, though without design, to my visiting the other parts of his Majesty's dominions in North America; and I humbly hope that many in that foreign clime will be my joy and crown of rejoicing in the day of the Lord Jesus.

"Nay, my lord, if I were not assured that the blessed Redeemer has owned me for the real conversion and turning of many from darkness to light, the weakness of my decaying body, the temptations that have beset my soul, and the violent opposition with which I have met, would long since have led me to accept some of those offers that have been made me to nestle, and by accepting which I might have screened myself from the obloquy and contempt which, in some degree or other, I meet with every day. But, hitherto, without eating a morsel of the Church of England's bread, I still continue to use her Liturgy, wherever a church or chapel is allowed me, and preach up her Articles, and enforce her Homilies. Your lordship, therefore, judgeth me exceeding right, when you say, 'I presume you do not mean to declare any dissent from the Church of England.' Far be it from me. No, my lord, unless thrust out, I shall never leave her; and even then I shall still adhere to her doctrines, and pray for the restoration of her discipline, to my dying day.

"Fond of displaying her truly protestant and orthodox principles, especially when Church and State are in danger from a cruel and popish enemy, I am glad of an opportunity of preaching, though it should be in a meeting-house; and I think it discovers a good and moderate spirit in the Dissenters, who quietly attend on the Church service, as many have done, and continue to do at Long Acre chapel, while many, who style themselves the faithful sons of the Church, have endeavoured to disturb and molest us.

"If the lessor of this chapel has no power to let it, or if it be not legally licensed, I have been deceived; and if, upon enquiry, I find this to be the case, I shall soon declare, in the most public manner, how I have been imposed upon. But if it appears that the lessor has a right to dispose of his own property, and that the place is licensed, and as some good, I trust, has been done by this foolishness of preaching, surely your lordship's candour will overlook a little irregularity, since, I fear, that, in these dregs of time wherein we live, we must be obliged to be irregular, or we must do no good at all.

"My lord, I remember well (and O that I may more than ever obey your lordship's admonition!) that awful day, wherein I was ordained priest, and when authority was give me, by my honoured friend and father, good Bishop Benson, to preach the word of God; but never did I so much as dream that this was only a local commission, or that the condition annexed, 'Where you shall be lawfully appointed thereunto,' was to confine me to any particular place, and that it would be unlawful for me to preach out of it. It is plain my Lord Bishop of Gloucester did not think so; for when his secretary brought a license for me, his lordship said, it would cost me thirty shillings, and therefore I should not have it. And when, after being presented to the late Bishop of London, I applied to him for a license, his lordship was pleased to say I was going to Georgia, and needed none. Accordingly, I preached in most of the London churches, under his lordship's immediate inspection; and why any other license than my letters of orders should now be required, I believe no substantial, I am positive no scriptural, reason can be assigned.

"It is true, as your lordship observes, there is one canon that says, 'No curate or minister shall be permitted to serve in any place, without examination and admission of the Bishop of the Diocese.' And there is another, as quoted by your lordship, which tells us, 'Neither minister, churchwarden, nor any other officers of the Church shall suffer any man to preach within their chapels, but such as, by shewing their license to preach, shall appear unto them to be sufficiently authorised thereunto.' But my lord, what curacy or parsonage have I desired, or do I desire to be admitted to serve in? or, into what church or chapel do I attempt to intrude myself, without leave from the churchwardens or other officers? Being as I think, without cause, denied admission into the churches, I am content to take the field, and, when the weather will permit, with a table for my pulpit, and the heavens for my sounding-board, I desire to proclaim to all the unsearchable riches of Jesus Christ. Besides, my lord, if this canon should be always put into full execution, I humbly presume, no bishop or presbyter can legally preach at any time out of the diocese in which he is appointed to serve; and, consequently, no city incumbent can even occasionally be lawfully permitted to preach a charity sermon out of his own diocese, without a special license for so doing.

"As for the other canon which your lordship mentions, and which runs thus, 'Neither shall any minister, not licensed as is aforesaid, presume to appoint or hold any meetings for sermons, commonly termed, by some, prophecies or exercises, in market towns or other places, under the said pains,'—I need not inform your lordship, that it was originally levelled against those who would not conform to the Church of England, and that, too, in such high-flying times as not one of the present moderate bench of bishops would wish to see restored. If this be so, how, my lord, does this canon belong to me, who am episcopally ordained, and have very lately published a small tract recommending the communion office of the Church of England?

"But, my lord, to come nearer to the point in hand. And, for Christ's sake, let not your lordship be offended with my using such plainness of speech. As in the presence of the living God, I would put it to your lordship's conscience, whether there is one bishop or presbyter, in England, Wales, or Ireland, who looks upon our canons as his rule of action? If this opinion be true, we are all perjured with a witness, and, in a very bad sense of the word, *irregular indeed*. If the canons of our Church are to be implicitly obeyed, may I not say, 'He, who is without the sin of acting illegally, let him cast the first stone at me, and welcome.' Your lordship knows full well, that canons and other Church laws are good and obligatory, when conformable to the laws of Christ, and agreeable to the liberties of a free people; but, when invented and compiled by men of little hearts and bigotted principles, to hinder persons of more enlarged souls from doing good, or being more extensively useful, they become mere *bruta fulmina*; and, when made use of as cords to bind the hands of a zealous few, who honestly appear for their king, their country, and their God, they may, in my opinion, like the withes with which the Philistines bound Samson, very legally be broken. As I have not the canons at present before me, I cannot tell what pains and penalties are to be incurred for such offence; but, if any penalty is incurred, or any pain to be inflicted on me, for preaching against sin, the Pope, and the devil, and for recommending the strictest loyalty to the best of princes, his Majesty King George, in this metropolis, or in any other part of his Majesty's dominions, I trust, through grace, I shall be enabled to say,—

'All hail reproach, and welcome pain!'

"There now remains but one more particular in your lordship's letter to be answered,—your lordship's truly apostolical canon, taken out of 2 Cor. x. 16,—upon reading of which, I could not help thinking of a passage in good Mr. Philip Henry's life. It was this. Being ejected out of the Church, and yet thinking it his duty to preach, Mr. Henry used now and then, to give the people of Broad-Oaks, where he lived, a gospel sermon; and one day, as he was coming from his exercise, he met with the incumbent, and thus addressed him: 'Sir, I have been taking the liberty of throwing a handful of seed into your field.' 'Have you?' said the good man. 'May God give it His blessing! There is work enough for us both.' This, my lord, I humbly conceive, is the case, not only of your lordship, but of every minister's parish in London, and of every bishop's diocese in England; and, therefore, as good is done, and souls are benefited, I hope your lordship will not regard a little irregularity, since, at the worst, it is only the irregularity of doing well. But, supposing this should not be admitted as an excuse at other seasons, I hope it will have its weight at this critical juncture, wherein, if there were ten thousand sound preachers, and each preacher had a thousand tongues, they could not be too frequently employed in calling upon the inhabitants of Great Britain to be upon their guard against the cruel and malicious designs of *France, of Rome, and of hell.*

"After all, my lord, if your lordship will be pleased to apply to Mr. Barnard himself, who, I suppose, knows where the place is registered; or if, upon enquiry, I shall find that the lessor has no power to let it, as I abhor every dishonourable action, after my setting out for Bristol, which I expect to do in a few days, I shall decline preaching in the chapel any more. But, if the case should appear to be otherwise, I hope your lordship will not be angry, if I persist in this, I trust, not unpardonable irregularity; for, if I decline preaching in every place, merely because the incumbent may be unwilling I should come into his parish, I fear I should seldom or never preach at all. This, my lord, especially at the present juncture, when all our civil and religious liberties are at stake, would to me be worse than death itself.

'I humbly ask pardon for detaining your lordship so long; but, being willing to give your lordship all the satisfaction I could, I have chosen rather to sit up and deny myself proper repose, than to let your lordship's candid letter by me one moment longer than was absolutely necessary.

'I return your lordship a thousand thanks for your favourable opinion of me, and for your good wishes; and, begging the continuance of your lordship's blessing, and earnestly praying that, whenever your lordship shall be called hence, you may give up your account with joy, I beg leave to subscribe myself, my lord, your lordship's most dutiful son and servant,

GEORGE WHITEFIELD.'

"Such was Whitefield's midnight letter to Bishop Pearce. Its length is gigantic, but, throughout, it is pointed, manly, and respectful; and, because of its historical facts, and its statement of the principles which regulated Whitefield's life, it is of great importance. A summary of it could not have done it justice."[4]

Having written this letter to the Bishop, George Whitefield felt free to carry on his spring campaign. So on March 14th, in Bristol he commenced his preaching labors, "by preaching thrice in the fields to many thousands, in Gloucestshire."

Upon his return to London George Whitefield wrote another letter to the Bishop for the disturbances at Long Acre grew worse. He wrote:

"Tabernacle-House, March 20, 1756.

"... On Thursday evening last, when I preached there myself, they were rather increased. Notwithstanding some of the windows were stopped up, to prevent in some degree the congregations being disturbed by the unhallowed noise, yet large stones were thrown in at another window, and one young person sadly wounded. This constrains me to trouble your Lordship once more, and to beg the favour of your Lordship so far to interpose ..."[5]

The Bishop wrote Whitefield back, and intimating from George Whitefield's response we can conclude that the Bishop was not too concerned about the trouble maker's for they *were just making noise*. To this Whitefield went onto describe more of the trouble at Long Acre chapel in another response to the Bishop's letter. We see this from the following:

"London, March 25, 1756.

"... Indeed, my Lord, it is more than noise. It deserves no milder a name than *premeditated rioting*. Drummers, soldiers, and many of the baser sort, have been hired by subscription.—A copper-furnace, bells, drums, clappers, marrow bones and cleavers, and such like instruments of reformation, have been provided for, and made use of, by them repeatedly, from the moment I have begun preaching, to the end of my sermon. By these horrid noises, many women have been almost frightened to death, and mobbers encouraged thereby to come and riot at the chapel door during the time of divine service, and then insult and abuse me and the congregation after it hath been over. Not content with this, the chapel windows, while I have been preaching, have repeatedly

4   Ibid. pp. 358–362.
5   *Works*, Vol. 3, p. 166.

been broken by large stones of almost a pound weight (some now lying by me) which though levelled at, providentially missed me, but at the same time sadly wounded some of my hearers ..."[6]

Regardless of the evangelist's efforts to reach the Bishop's heart over these disturbances they still increased. And on top of the disturbances during worship time at Long Acre chapel, George Whitefield began to receive death threats in the form of three anonymous letters, "threatening him with 'a certain, sudden, and unavoidable stroke.' unless he desisted from preaching, and refrained from prosecuting the rioters of Long Acre."

The end result of all this was that the great evangelist was forced to erect his own chapel (the Tottenham Court Road chapel) where his congregation could worship in peace. The following description of this famous chapel is worth including for it importance to religious history:

"The site of Whitefields' new chapel was surrounded by fields and gardens. On the north side of it, there were but two houses. The next after them, half a mile further, was the 'Adam and Eve' public-house; and thence to Hampstead, there were only the inns of 'Mother Red Cap' and 'Black Cap.' The chapel, when first erected, was seventy feet square within the walls. Two years after it was opened, twelve almshouses and a minister's house were added. About a year after that, the chapel was found to be too small, and it was enlarged to its present dimensions of a hundred and twenty-seven feet long, and seventy feet broad, with a dome a hundred and fourteen feet in height. Beneath it were vaults for the burial of the dead; and in which Whitefield intended that himself and his friends, John and Charles Wesley, should be interred. 'I have prepared a vault in this chapel,' Whitefield used to say to his somewhat bigotted congregation, 'where I intend to be buried, and Messrs. John and Charles Wesley shall also be buried there. We will all lie together. You will not let them enter your chapel while they are alive. They can do you no harm when they are dead.' ... The foundation-stone of the chapel was laid in the beginning of June, 1756, when Whitefield preached from the words, 'They sang together by course in praising and giving thanks unto the Lord; because He is good, for His mercy endureth for ever toward Israel. And all the people shouted with a great shout, when they praised the Lord, because the foundation of the house of the Lord was laid.' (Ezra iii. 11.) ... The chapel was opened for divine worship on November, 7, 1756, when Whitefield selected, as his text, the words, 'Other foundation can no man lay than that is laid, which is Jesus Christ.' (I Cor. iii. 11).

"Tottenham Court Road chapel has a history well worthy of being written. From this venerable sanctuary sprang separate congregations ... Much also might be said of the distinguished preachers who, in olden days, occupied its pulpit: Dr. Peckwell, De Courcy, Berridge, Walter Shirley, Piercy, chaplain to General Washington, Rowland Hill, ... and many others ... Whitefield's

6   Ibid. pp. 168–169.

Tottenham Court Road chapel is now his only erection in the great metropolis;
and long may it stand as a grand old monument, in memory of the man who
founded it! Thousands have been converted within its walls ..."7

Good came out of the riots at Long Acre—the need for a new chapel!
Tottenham Court Road Chapel was referred to by many as a *soul-trap*.
Indeed, this is how George Whitefield himself described it! We see his
comments about the chapel to a friend at the end of the year, dated,
December 30th:

"... God is doing wonders at the new chapel. Hundreds went away last
Sunday morning that could not come in. On Christmas-Day, and last Tuesday
night (the first time of burning candles) the power of the LORD was present,
both to wound and to heal. A neighbouring Doctor hath baptized the place,
calling it, '*Whitefield's Soul-trap.*' ... pray the friend of sinners to make the chapel
a *soul-trap* indeed."8

The disturbances at Long Acre chapel were replaced by rejoicing at
Tottenham Court Chapel. And although, for the most part the year had
been full of turmoil, it was on this happier note that the great evangelist
ended the year 1756.

7   Tyerman, Vol. 2, pp. 373–374.
8   *Works*, Vol. 3, p. 196–197.

Whitefield was desirous of the honors of martyrdom. He said, "It would be sweet to wear a martyr's crown." He came near having his wish gratified ... when he received honorable scars that he carried with him to the grave. It was while preaching in Dublin Ireland.

J.B. Wakeley

CHAPTER 48

HONORS IN SCOTLAND
AND ROCKS IN IRELAND

The year 1757 was to be a memorable one for George Whitefield. The great evangelist would be both praised and persecuted! One large wound, near his temple, was the result of a near-fatal blow from a rock. In 1757 the "run-about for Christ" once more took to the fields—this time the focus of his labor was Scotland (his ninth) and Ireland (his third).

Scotland had become dear to him, though as he grew older his asthma kept him from staying there long for the climate was not agreeable to his troubled lungs. But though his health was usually poor in Edinburgh, his preaching was rich and full of power! The infidel Hume came to hear the great evangelist preach in Edinburgh, for the capital was well regarded as an intellectual city full of great minds. We have the following story:

"An intimate friend of the infidel Hume, asked him what he thought of Mr. Whitefield's preaching; for he had listened to the latter part of one of his sermons at Edinburgh. 'He is sir,' said Mr. Hume, 'the most ingenious preacher I ever heard. It is worth while to go twenty miles to hear him.' He then repeated the following passage which he heard towards the close of that discourse. 'After a solemn pause, Mr. Whitefield thus addressed his numerous auditory:—"The attendant angel is just about to leave the threshold, and ascend to heaven. And shall he ascend and not bear with him the news of one sinner, among all this multitude, reclaimed from the error of his ways?" To give the greater effect to this exclamation, he stamped with his foot, lifted up his hands and eyes to heaven, and with gushing tears, cried aloud, "Stop Gabriel! Stop Gabriel! Stop, ere you enter the sacred portals, and yet carry with you the news of one sinner converted to God." He then in the most simple, but energetic language, described what he called a Savior's dying love to sinful man; so that almost the whole assembley melted into tears. This address was accompanied with such animated, yet natural action that it surpassed any thing I ever saw or heard in any other preacher.'" [1]

---

1   Gillies, pp. 167–168.

Scotland has always been a land of great preaching and one of the best countries to hear great preachers. So it was not surprising to find that many ministers attended Whitefield's services and we see this from the following remarks by Dr. Gillies:

"In 1757, he again took his circuit northward, and came to Edinburgh some time in the month of May, and at the time of the annual meeting of the general assembly, a circumstance which afforded him much satisfaction. His preaching was attended by many ministers; it is said, a hundred at a time. Many of them appeared to be deeply affected; and thus their prejudices were removed. About thirty of them, as a proof of their regard, invited him to a public entertainment ..."[2]

About this trip to Scotland we have also the following:

"On Monday, April 25, Whitefield set out for Scotland. Sixteen days afterwards, he arrived in Edinburgh, where he at once commenced preaching in his old open-air cathedral, the Orphan House Park, and, for nearly a month, preached twice a day, morning and evening, 'to very numerous audiences.' In all respects, this was a memorable visit."[3]

We have a limited account of his labors there (there are only two known letters which speak of his activities at this time); we will turn to the letter with the fuller account which details some of the extent of his labors. We read:

"Glasgow, June 9, 1757.

"... at Edinburgh I was so taken up all day, and kept up so late at night, that writing was almost impracticable. Surely my going thither was of GOD. I came thither the twelfth of May, and left it the sixth of June, and preached just fifty times. To what purpose, the great day will discover. I have reason to believe to very good purpose. Being the time of the general assembly (at which I was much pleased) many ministers attended, perhaps a hundred at a time. Thereby prejudices were removed, and many of their hearts were deeply impressed. About thirty of them, as a token of respect, invited me to a public entertainment. The Lord High Commissioner also invited me to his table, and many persons of credit and religion did the same in a public manner. Thousands and thousands, among whom were a great many of the best rank, daily attended on the word preached, and the longer I staid, the more the congregations and divine influence increased. Twice I preached in my way to Glasgow, and last night opened my campaign here. The cloud seems to move towards Ireland. How the Redeemer vouchsafes to deal with me there, you shall know hereafter ..."[4]

The only other reliable information we have from this trip to Scotland (that differs from what we have already seen) is from the pen of trustworthy Tyerman:

2   Ibid. p. 168.
3   Tyerman, Vol. 2, p. 391.
4   *Works*, Vol. 3, pp. 203–204.

"At Whitefield's farewell sermon in the Orphan Hospital Park, Edinburgh, there was a young Scotchman present, who afterwards became one of Wesley's most faithful and sturdy itinerants. Thomas Rankin, born at Dunbar, was now resident at Leith, and came to Edinburgh to hear the great preacher. He wrote:—

'I had often before had thoughts of hearing Mr. Whitefield; but so many things had been said to me of him, that I was afraid I should be deceived. He preached in the field adjoining the Orphan House yard. His text was Isaiah xxxiii. 13–17. The sermon exceeded all the sermons I ever heard. About the middle of it, I ventured to look up, and saw all the crowds around Mr. Whitefield bathed in tears. I listened with wonder and surprise, and had such a discovery of the plan of salvation as I had never known before. I was astonished at myself that I had listened to the idle tales concerning him, and thereby have been kept from hearing a burning and shining light, who had been instrumental in the hand of God for the good of so many thousands of souls. When I understood he was about to leave Edinburgh, I was distressed. I remembered more of that sermon than of all the sermons I had ever heard. I had a discovery of the unsearchable riches of the grace of God in Christ Jesus; as also of how a lost sinner was to come to God, and obtain mercy through the Redeemer. From this time, I was truly convinced of the necessity of a change of heart.'

"As already stated, Thomas Rankin became one of Wesley's most valuable preachers. His labours, both in England and in America, were of great importance; and, if no other end had been accomplished by Whitefield's present visit to the Scotch metropolis, the conversion of Rankin was an ample compensation for all his toil and travelling."[5]

Though his labors were appreciated by many in Edinburgh and Glasgow this would not be the case in Ireland. Mobs attacked him with a vehemence of the like he had not encountered before! Though much of his visit to Ireland was positive (some of his previous converts had begun a vibrant Moravian church and others had formed a Baptist congregation), the result of the trip almost took his life! How little did he realize how prophetic were his words before he left, "The cloud seems to move towards Ireland. How the Redeemer vouchsafes to deal with me there, you shall know hereafter." The clouds of opposition were black and ominous! Gillies has the following comment:

"He used to say, in speaking of this event, that in England, Scotland and America, he had been treated only as a common minister of the gospel, but that in Ireland he had been elevated to the rank of an *Apostle*, in having had the honor of being stoned."[6]

To get a clearer picture of George Whitefield's labors in Ireland we will turn

5   Tyerman, Vol. 2, p. 393.
6   Gillies, p. 169.

to the narrative of his correspondence and allow the action of his record
speak for itself:

"Dublin, June 30, 1757 ... Here in Dublin the congregations are very large,
and very much impressed. The Redeemer vouchsafes to give me great freedom
in preaching, and arrows of conviction fly and fasten. One of the Bishops told a
nobleman, 'He was glad I was come to rouse the people' ... Not one clergyman
in all Ireland yet stirred up to come out singularly for GOD! Pity, LORD, for
they mercy's sake! I think GOD will yet appear for the protestant interest. My
route now is to Athlone, Limerick, Cork, and to return here about July 21 ...

"Dublin, July 9, 1757. Many attacks have I had from Satan's children, but
yesterday, you would have thought he had been permitted to have given me an
effectual parting blow ... When here last, I preached in a more confined place in
the week days, and once or twice ventured out to *Oxminton-Green*, a large place
like *Moorfields*, situated very near the barracks, where the *Ormond and Liberty*,
that is, *high and low party boys*, generally assemble ever Sunday, to fight with each
other. The congregations then were very numerous, the word seemed to come
with power; and no noise or disturbance ensued. This encouraged me to give
notice, that I would preach there again last Sunday afternoon. I went through
the barracks, the door of which opens into the green, and pitched my tent near
the barrack walls, not doubting of the protection, or at least interposition of the
officers and soldier, if there should be occasion. But how vain is the help of man!
Vast was the multitude that attended; we sang, prayed, and preached, without
much molestation; only now and then a few stones and clods of dirt were
thrown at me. It being war time, as is my usual practice, I exhorted my hearers
not only to fear GOD, but to honour the best of kings, and after sermon I
prayed for success to the Prussian arms. All being over, I thought to return home
the way I came; but to my great surprize access was denied, so that I had to go
near half a mile from one end of the green to the other, through hundreds and
hundreds of papists, &c. Finding me unattended, (for a soldier and four
methodist preachers, who came with me, had forsook me and fled) I was left to
their mercy; but their mercy, as you may easily guess, was perfect cruelty.

"Vollies of hard stones came from all quarters, and every step I took a fresh
stone struck, and made me reel backwards and forwards, till I was almost
breathless, and all over a gore of blood. My strong beaver hat served me as it
were for a scull cap for a while; but at last that was knocked off, and my head left
quite defenseless. I received many blows and wounds; one was particularly large
and near my temples. I thought of Stephen, and as I believed that I received
more blows, I was in great hopes that like him I should be dispatched, and go off
in this bloody triumph to the immediate presence of my master. But
providentially, a minister's house lay next door to the green; and with great
difficulty I staggered to the door, which was kindly opened to, and shut upon
me. Some of the mob in the mean time having broke part of the boards of the
pulpit into large splinters, they beat and wounded my servant grievously in his
head and arms, and then came and drove him from the door. For a while I
continued speechless, panting for and expecting every breath to be my last; two

or three of the hearers, my friends, by some means or other got admission, and kindly with weeping eyes washed my bloody wounds, and gave me something to smell and to drink. I gradually revived, but soon found the lady of the house desired my absence, for fear the house should be pulled down. What to do, I knew not, being near two miles from Mr. W——'s place; some advised one thing, and some another. At length, a carpenter, one of the friends that came in, offered me his wig and coat, that I might go off in disguise. I accepted of, and put them on, but was soon ashamed of not trusting my master to secure me in my proper habit, and threw them off with disdain. I determined to go out (since I found my presence was so troublesome) in my proper habit; immediately deliverance came. A methodist preacher, with two friends, brought a coach; I leaped into it, and rid in gospel triumph through the oaths, curses, and imprecations of whole streets of papists unhurt, though threatened every step of the ground. None but those who were spectators of the scene, can form an idea of the affection with which I was received by the weeping, mourning, but now joyful methodists. A christian surgeon was ready to dress our wounds, which being done, I went into the preaching place, and after giving a word of exhortation, join'd in a hymn of praise and thanksgiving, to him who makes our extremity his opportunity, who stills the noise of the waves, and the madness of the most malignant people. The next morning I set out for port Arlington, and left my persecutors to his mercy, who out of persecutors hath often made preachers ..."7

In a another letter, this time sent to his dear friend in Glasgow, Dr. Gillies, George Whitefield wrote from Staffordshire, on August 7, 1757 the following comments, "... At Athlone, Limerick, Cork, and especially at Dublin, where I preached near fifty times, we had Cambuslang seasons ... The blows I received some time ago, were like to send me, where all partings would have been over. But I find we are immortal till our work is done ..."

Whitefield arrived back in London in late August. We are amazed that, rather than rest from his vast labors and grievous injuries (at home with his wife) we find him again ranging from the first of September to the second week of October. Only the winter weather slowed him down! He wrote from Exeter on September 28, 1757:

"... Blessed be GOD, I can send you good news from Plymouth.—The scene was like that of Bristol; only more extraordinary, to see officers, soldiers, sailors, and the dock-men, attending with the utmost solemnity upon the word preached. Arrows of conviction fled and fastened, and I left all GOD's people upon the wing for heaven. Blessed be the LORD JESUS for ordering me the lot of a *cast-out!*

For this let men revile my name,
I'd shun no cross, I'd fear no shame;
All hail reproach!

---

7   *Works,* Vol. 3, pp. 207–209.

"… If the weather should alter I may be in town; if not, I may range further.—
This spiritual hunting is delightful sport …"[8]

By the end of 1757 we see George Whitefield writing to Lady Huntingdon
about his recent labors at the Tottenham Court chapel. He is ever-occupied
in the service of his Master and continually planning expansions to the
ministry. We read:

"London, Dec. 15, 1757. "… At Tottenham-Court the word runs and is
glorified. By new-year's day I hope the debt will be discharged. Several have
proposed building some alms-houses for godly widows, on each side of the
chapel. I have a plan for twelve … May that GOD, whom I desire to serve in the
gospel of his dear Son, direct and bless us in this and every thing we undertake
for his glory …"[9]

---

8   Ibid. p. 212.
9   Ibid. p. 224.

His health now failed sadly. He was brought to live on the "short allowance of preaching but once a day, and thrice on the Sunday." He was so feeble, that he could not bear to drive nor ride in a one-horse chaise ... "Every thing," he says, "wearies this shattered bark now! ... Oh for a hearse to carry my weary carcass to the wished-for grave!" During all this tour, he was unable to sit up in company even once.

Robert Philip

CHAPTER 49

WHITEFIELD'S BROKEN HEALTH

A human body can only take so much neglect before it breaks down—sometimes permanently. Such was the case of George Whitefield's "shattered bark", he had simply worn himself out. The numerous rides on horseback in inclement weather, the profound lack of needed rest, the strain of preaching many times a week, the burdens of the Orphan House, and opposition, had finally taken its collective toll on his physical frame. John Wesley said that his friend Whitefield now appeared "as a frail old man". Nevertheless, this did not cease his labors—he merely pressed on, often preaching, ill much of the time. The year 1758 gave him rest from persecution but not the physical rest he so needed.

We begin to see this failing health from his letters.

"… my nightly rests are continually broken; … to my great mortification, through continual vomitings, want of rest, and of appetite, I have been reduced, for some time, to the short allowance of preaching only once a day, except Sundays, when I generally preach thrice … Long, long before now did I think of entering into my wish'd-for rest. Times without number hath this tabernacle groaned; but having obtained help from GOD, I yet continue, in my poor way, to preach to all that are willing to hear, the unsearchable riches of JESUS CHRIST …"[1]

Desirous to preach the "unsearchable riches of Jesus Christ" and due to the necessity for him to continue to range about collecting money for the Orphan House in Georgia (though he was unable to travel there he was still accountable for its financial survival) we see the great evangelist press on. Being confined to London because of the winter weather he preached locally. But once spring arrived he was out itinerating once again! We catch up to him in Gloucester in the month of May—he was now aged 43. He wrote:

---

1   *Works,* Vol. 3, pp. 227–229.

"... I am now writing in the room where I was born. Blessed be GOD, I know there is a place where I was born again! That is my native city indeed. After finishing this, I shall set out for *Bristol*, where I propose staying over Sunday: then for *Wales* ... This tabernacle makes me to groan. The one-horse chaise will not do for me. As it will not quarter I am shaken to pieces. Driving likewise wearies me, and prevents my reading; and if the road be bad, my servant that rides in the fore-horse is dirtied exceedingly ...

"Bristol, May 24, 1758 ... On Sunday we opened the summer campaign in *Gloucestershire*. Yesterday I came hither. In both places the fields are white ready unto harvest ...

"Bristol, May 26, 1758 ... Ever since Tuesday evening, I have been preaching here twice daily. Multitudes fly like doves to the windows ...

"Bristol, June 16, 1758. The Welch roads have almost demolished my open one-horse chaise, as well as me. But it is in JESUS's cause. Grace! Grace! ... I trust some lasting blessings have been left behind in *Wales*. Welcome shocks, both of body and mind. In such a case it is worth dying for ... I must away to preach ..."[2]

Despite his health problems and "frequent vomitings" (which only grew more frequent as time went on) Whitefield has great preaching success on his ranging. We find him relating his recent activities to his favored friend, Lady Huntingdon. He wrote to her:

"To Lady Huntingdon.

"Ever-honoured Madam,   Bristol, June 17, 1758.

"This leaves me returned from *Wales*. It proved a most delightful trying circuit. I suppose your Ladyship hath heard how low I have been in body, scarce ever lower; not able to sit up in company all the time, yet strengthened to travel without bodily food, and to preach to thousands every day. Never were the fields whiter, and more ready to harvest. The LORD JESUS seemed to ride in triumph through the great congregation in *Haverford-west*. Perhaps the auditory consisted of near fifteen thousand. Tears flowed like water from the stony rock. The cup of GOD's people quite runs over. Many were sick of love. Welcome then bodily pain, and bodily sickness! O for a hearse to carry my weary carcase to the wished for grave! 'There the wicked cease from troubling, there the weary are at rest.' But, perhaps I must see *London* first. With regret I turn my back on this blessed itinerating weather, but Mr. Dav— must be released. O for some disinterested soul to help at the chapel during the summer season! Spiritual, divine ambition, whither art thou fled! But I see such honours are reserved for few. I rejoice at the increase of your Ladyship's spiritual routs. I can guess at the consolations such uncommon scenes must afford to your Ladyship's new-born soul. No wonder you are distressed from other quarters. Indeed, my most noble

2   Ibid. pp. 231–237.

and ever-honoured patroness, thus it must be. CHRIST's witnesses must be purged at home. Inward domestic trials, fit for outward public work. Nature recoils, when constrained to take the cup; and it may be from a near and dear relation's hand but infinite Wisdom knows what is best. O that I could be more passive! O that I could let the good and all-wise Physician choose my medicines, and the hands that shall convey them to me! But I am a stubborn reasoning creature, and thereby force almighty love frequently to drench me. O, I am sick! I am sick! Sick in body, but infinitely more so in my mind,—to see what dross yet remains in, and surrounds my soul. Blessed be GOD, there is one, who will sit as a refiner's fire, and purify the sons of Levi. O for an heart to bear its scorching, soul purging heat! When I am tried, I shall come forth as gold. I write this to your Ladyship out of the burning bush. Blessed place! CHRIST is there! CHRIST is there! To his never-failing mercy do I most humbly commend your Ladyship, and with ten thousand thousand thanks for honouring such a unfruitful unworthy worm with your unmerited patronage, I beg to leave to subscribe myself, ever-honoured Madam,

Your Ladyship's most dutiful, and ready servant, for CHRIST's sake,

G.W."[3]

During the month of July Whitefield was involved in *enormous* labor. How he managed to do so much in such ill health is but a marvel. George Whitefield was like a comet. One which knew it would soon crash to earth and so it burned faster and brighter the closer it got to the ground. We stand amazed at the following report of his labors:

"Newcastle, July 31, 1758. Thus far, a never failing Redeemer hath brought on the most worthless and weak pilgrim, that was ever employed in publishing his everlasting gospel. All the last week was taken up in preaching at *Everton, Saint Neots, Knyfo, Bedford, Oulney, Weston, Underwood, Ravenstone and Northampton.* Four clergymen lent me their churches, and three read prayers for me in one day. I preached also in Mr. Bunyan's pulpit, and at Northampton I took the field. Good seasons at all the places. Mr. Berridge, who was lately awakened at *Everton*, promises to be a burning and shining light. Yesterday we had good times here, and to-morrow, GOD willing, I shall set off for *Edinburgh*. My bodily strength increases but very little. Sometimes I am almost tempted to turn back, but through divine strength I hope to go forward, and shall strive, as much as in me lies, to die in this glorious work ..."[4]

And go forward in the work he did. He traveled to Scotland and was received warmly. We must make mention that part of Whitefield's physical troubles may have been related to the stoning he received in Ireland. The blow on the head could have weakened his constitution further. His asthma was a besetting disease that continually grew worse as he aged. Add to all this lack

3   Ibid. pp. 237–238.
4   Ibid. p. 238.

of proper food and rest and it is easy to see how sick he really was. We have an account of his arrival in Scotland (his eleventh visit to this country) from the following:

"Whitefield arrived at Edinburgh on August 4, and, despite physical weakness, preached, for nearly a month, in the Orphan Hospital Park, to enormous congregations, morning and evening, every day ...

"On August 29, he went to Glasgow, where he remained a week. Here, after one of his sermons, he made a collection, amounting to nearly £60, on behalf of a Society, established in 1727, for educating and putting to trades the sons of Highlanders, and of which the Duke of Argyll was the principal member ... On September 6, Whitefield returned to Edinburgh, and, during another week, preached twice every day ... These fragmentary records are truly marvellous. How a man, in such health, performed such labours, for months together, it is difficult to imagine."[5]

We have a narrative of his Scottish labors in three letters to his friend Dr. Gillies. In them we find accounts of his work in Scotland but also, that he preached his way all back to London! We read the following correspondence to Dr. Gillies of Glasgow with great interest:

"My very dear Friend,   Edinburgh, Aug. 10, 1758.

"I thank you most heartily for your kind letter of invitation to Glasgow. But alas! What shall I say?—I fear it cannot be complied with. For above these three months last past, I have been so weak in my animal frame, that I can scarcely drag the crazy load along. With great difficulty I came here, and if I should stay to come westward, it would make my journey to London too far in the year, as I have many places to call upon in the way. Blessed be GOD, the work prospers in London more than ever. I am strengthened to preach here twice a day; but alas, I grow weaker and weaker in preaching, and in all I do for the ever-loving and altogether lovely JESUS. I suppose you have heard of the death of Mr. Jonathan Edwards.—Happy he!—You will add to my obligations, by continuing to pray, that the divine strength may be magnified in my weakness, and that I may speedily (if it be the divine will) be sent for to my wished-for heaven! ...

"Reverend and very dear Sir,   Edinburgh, Aug. 24, 1758.

"After long meditation and earnest prayer, I cannot come to any determination about my journey to *Glasgow*. For these four months last past, I have been brought so exceeding low in my body, that I was in hopes every sermon I preached would waft me to my wish'd-for home. *Scotland*, I hoped, would finish my warfare; but it hath rather driven me back to sea again. By force I have been detained here this race week; but if I come to *Glasgow*, I shall be detained in *Scotland* a fortnight longer, which will greatly hinder me in my

5   Tyerman, Vol. 2, pp. 410–412.

English work. However, I will continue to look up; and by Saturday's post my dear Gaius may expect a positive answer. LORD JESUS, direct my goings in thy way! I am much obliged to you and other dear *Glasgow* friends for taking notice of such a worthless creature ...

"Reverend and very dear Sir,   Rotherham, October 15, 1758.

"Since my leaving *Scotland*, in various parts of the north of *England, as at Alnwick, Newcastle, Leeds,* &c. the ever-loving, altogether-lovely JESUS hath manifested forth his glory. Thousands and thousands have flocked twice, and sometimes thrice a day to hear the word. Never did I see the fields whiter, or more ripe for a spiritual harvest. Praise the LORD, O our souls! If the weather continues fair, I hope to prolong my Summer's campaign. It shocks me to think of Winter quarters yet. LORD, help me! How soon does the year roll round! LORD JESUS, quicken my tardy pace! ..."[6]

Whitefield returned to London in October after preaching at Bath. He closed the year of 1758 with attention paid to his Orphan House in Georgia by paying off some of its debts. We see this from the following:

"Once again in London, his Orphan House demanded his attention. The family had been reduced, and he now had it in his 'power to pay off all Bethesda's arrears.' He sent a number of 'Bibles and other books.' 'He longed for an opportunity' to go himself; but the war prevented him, and he knew not how to get supplies for his two London chapels. He was, however, quite satisfied with the management of his housekeeper, and sent her 'ten thousand thousand thanks.' He wished his superintendent to consign him 'a little rice and indigo,' that his 'friends might see some of the Orphan House produce.' Taken altogether, his affairs in Georgia were less embarrassing than usual.

"During the year, Whitefield had gained a new clerical friend, in Berridge of Everton; but, before it ended, he lost a friend, whom he dearly loved. James Hervey died on Christmas-day, 1758. Within a week of this mournful occurrence, Whitefield wrote the following pathetic letter to the dying rector of Weston-Favel:—

'London, December 19, 1758.

'And is my dear friend indeed about to take his last flight? I dare not wish your return into this vale of tears. But our prayers are continually ascending to the Father of our spirits that you may die in the embraces of a never-failing JESUS, and in all the fulness of an exalted faith. O when will my time come! I groan in this tabernacle, being burdened, and long to be clothed with my house from heaven. Farewell! My very dear friend, f-a-r-e-well! Yet a little while, and we shall meet,—

'Where sin, and strife, and sorrow cease,
And all is love, and joy, and peace.'

6   *Works,* Vol. 3, pp. 241–244.

'There JESUS will reward you for all the tokens of love which you have showed, for His great name's sake, to yours most affectionately in our common Lord,

'GEORGE WHITEFIELD.'

'P.S. God comfort your mother, and relations, and thousands and thousands more who will bewail your departure!'"[7]

It was with sadness at the loss of his dear friend that George Whitefield ended the year. Though his health was poor his labors were great!

---

7   Tyerman, Vol. 2, p. 413.

In the thirty-four years of his ministry it is reckoned that he preached publicly eighteen thousand times. His journeyings were prodigious, when the roads and conveyances of his time are considered. He was familiar with "perils in the wilderness and perils in the seas," if ever man was in modern times. He visited Scotland fourteen times, and was nowhere more acceptable or useful than he was in that Bible-loving country. He crossed the Atlantic seven times, backward and forward, in miserable slow sailing ships, and arrested the attention of thousands in Boston, New York, and Philadelphia. He went over to Ireland twice, and on one occasion was almost murdered by an ignorant Popish mob in Dublin. As to England and Wales, he traversed every county in them ... His regular ministerial work in London for the winter season, when field preaching was necessarily suspended, was something prodigious. His weekly engagements at the Tabernacle in Tottenham Court Road comprised the following work:—Every Sunday morning he administered the Lord's Supper to several hundred communicants at half-past six. After this he read prayers, and preached both morning and afternoon. Then he preached again in the evening at half-past five, and concluded by addressing a large society of widows, married people, young men and spinsters, all sitting separately in the area of the Tabernacle, with exhortations suitable to their respective stations. On Monday, Tuesday, Wednesday, and Thursday mornings, he preached regularly at six. On Monday, Tuesday, Wednesday, Thursday, and Saturday evenings, he delivered lectures. This, it will be observed, made thirteen sermons a week! And all this time he was carrying on a large correspondence with people in almost every part of the world. That any human frame could so long endure the labours that Whitefield went through does indeed seem wonderful. That his life was not cut short by violence, to which he was frequently exposed, is no less wonderful. But he was immortal till his work was done.

Bishop J.C. Ryle, D.D.

CHAPTER 50

A BRIGHT AND SHINING LIGHT

When one stands back and surveys the life and labors of George Whitefield one is left entirely breathless. How could one man accomplish so much? How could one man reach so many people (before automobiles, jet planes, and television)? Even D.L. Moody relied on the train to forward his constant labors! Billy Graham has reached so many through television broadcasts. But when reviewing the life of George Whitefield we see a man *on a horse, on a sailing ship, on a table in a field*. He broke his body like the alabaster box for the Lord.

Besides his preaching labors George Whitefield was active in publishing Christian material. In the year 1759 he was responsible for republishing two important works. To each one he wrote a preface. The first was a sermon by John Foxe (author of the "Book of Martyrs"); the second publication was a favorite Bible commentary of Whitefield's, "Samuel Clarke's *Commentary on the Old and New Testaments.*" Both of these publications were added greatly to God's kingdom work.

The beginning of the year 1759 finds the great evangelist doing what he did best: preaching! We see this from the following remarks:

"Little is known respecting Whitefield's health, labours, and success, during the fist four months of 1759.

"On the 4th of January, the Countess of Huntingdon went to Bristol to meet Wesley, who accompanied her to Bath, and preached, to several of the nobility, in her house. Early in February, her ladyship returned to London, and, on Friday, the 16th, the day appointed for a public fast, she went to the Tabernacle, where Whitefield addressed an immense congregation from the words, 'Rend your hearts, and not your garments.' ... Her ladyship, profoundly impressed with a conviction of the necessity and power of prayer, arranged for a series of intercession meetings in her own mansion. On Wednesday, February 21, the officiating ministers were Whitefield, Charles Wesley, Venn and Thomas

Maxfield ... On Tuesday, the 27th, [John] Wesley writes: " I walked with my brother and Mr. Maxfield to Lady Huntingdon's. After breakfast, came in Messrs. Whitefield, Madan, Romaine, Jones, Downing, and Venn, with some persons of quality, and a few others. Mr. Whitefield, I found, was to have administered the sacrament; but he insisted upon my doing it: after which, at the request of Lady Huntingdon, I preached on I Cor. xiii. 13. O what are the greatest men, to the great God! As the small dust of the balance.' Charles Wesley adds to this account, by saying, 'My brother preached, and won all our hearts. I never liked him better, and was never more united to him since his unhappy marriage ...'

"These remarkable meetings seem to have been concluded on Tuesday, March 6, when, besides the clergymen already mentioned, there was another present, who afterwards attained a distinguished eminence—John Fletcher, the immortal Vicar of Madeley. First of all, the sacrament was administered by Whitefield. ... Whitefield addressed the communicants; 'and all were touched to the heart,' said Lady Huntingdon, 'and dissolved in tears.' Whitefield, Romaine, and Madan prayed. The sacramental service being ended, the Earls of Chesterfield and Holderness, and several others of distinction, were admitted. Whitefield preached, with his accustomed eloquence and energy, from 'Him that cometh unto me, I will in no wise cast out.' The word, remarked Lady Huntingdon, 'drew sighs from every heart, and tears from every eye ...'"[1]

Though busy with his labors in London, Whitefield had not forgotten about his Orphan House in Georgia. In the month of March he writes a letter to his housekeeper at Bethesda and informs her, "... Bethesda's God liveth for ever and ever. His word runs and is glorified daily, especially at Tottenham-Court ... O that Bethesda's little flock may take deep root downward, and bear fruit upwards!"

The great evangelist began a large task of labor in the latter part of May as he started his "Spring Campaign". While in Bristol he wrote the following report to a friend:

"This day se'nnight, through divine goodness, I came hither. The next day the Spring campaign was opened: on the Lord's-day we took the field. Thousands and thousands attended: full as many as in *London*. The power of the LORD was present at the three meetings, as well as at the holy communion. Some cups were made to run over. Ever since I have been enabled to preach twice, and sometimes thrice a day. Never did I see the *Bristol* people more attentive or impressed. My body feels the heat: but no matter. If souls are benefitted, all is well. Would to GOD I could begin to so something for JESUS! ..."[2]

---

1 Tyerman, Vol. 2, pp. 414–416.
2 *Works,* Vol. 3, pp. 250–251.

After his immense preaching labors in Bristol Whitefield traveled once more to Scotland. He arrived in Edinburgh on the 30th of June, 1759. He wasted no time in preaching and we have the following remarks about this time in Scotland:

"... Whitefield made his way to Scotland, arriving at Edinburgh on Saturday, the 30th of June. Three days afterwards, he wrote as follows:—

'Edinburgh, July 3, 1759. There has been a long interval between my last and this. My quick motions and frequent preaching have been the causes. O what am I that I should be employed for Jesus! In Gloucestershire, the cup of many of His people ran over. In Yorkshire, I preached for a week twice a day. Great congregations! Great power! Blessed be the name of the Great God for ever and ever! Here, also, people, high and low, rich and poor, flock as usual, morning and evening. I am growing fat; but, as I take it to be a disease, I hope I shall go home the sooner. Happy are they who are safe in harbour.'

"Whitefield spent nearly seven weeks in Scotland, a fortnight in Glasgow, and the remainder of the time in Edinburgh. Of course, his cathedral in the latter city was the Orphan Hospital Park, as usual, where he preached every morning and evening without exception. He did the same in Glasgow, only on the two Sundays that he was there, he preached ten times!"[3]

One of the closest friends the great evangelist had in Scotland was the Reverend John Gillies of Glasgow. Often George Whitefield would preach in his pulpit and stay in his home. Many of the letters written to Gillies over the years reveal a transparency only a best friend would reveal. The following is a letter from Whitefield to Gillies and it is dated, July 7, 1759:

"GOD willing, I purpose to see Glasgow; but cannot as yet fix the day. I preach, and people flock as usual; but *Scotland* is not *London*. The Redeemer is doing wonders there. Every post brings fresh good news. GOD's Spirit blows when and where it listeth. O for a gale before the storm! I expect one is at hand. The refuge is as near. JESUS is our hiding-place. O for a hiding-place in heaven! When will my turn come? Some say, not yet; for (would you think it?) I am growing fat: so did Mr. Darracot a little before he died. O that my latter end may be like his! You will not forget a worthless but willing pilgrim. Hearty love to all.

Yours, &c. &c. in the best bonds,

G.W."[4]

It was at this time, Whitefield was entering his mid-forties, that he put on weight. The extra pounds drastically altered his appearance and

3   Tyerman, Vol. 2, p. 419.
4   *Works,* Vol. 3, p. 252.

unfortunately most of the existing portraits of him are from this time period and not when he was a slender youth. There is one portrait of him in his slender days, and it is of this portrait that Dr. Gillies claims to be his best likeness. We hear his own regrets on growing fat in a letter to a friend:

"Dear Mrs. W——,　　　　　　　　　　　Glasgow, July 18, 1759.

"... I want the purgation most of all. I dread a corpulent body. But it breaks upon me like an armed man. O that my heart may not wax gross at the same time! I would fain not flag, but rather begin at least to begin in the latter stages of my road. Congregations in *Scotland* are very large ..."[5]

Little can be learned of his activities once back in London; his existing correspondence is slight and even Tyerman is mystified by the untraceable footsteps, "It is a remarkable fact, that hardly anything is known of Whitefield's public ministry for the next five months." We must assume that George Whitefield was busy with the Samuel Clarke *Commentary* for we read Tyermans's comments: "During this interval, however, he is not entirely shrouded from the public eye." Tyerman went on to describe the work that Whitefield was actively preparing for publication and the following is a extract from the Preface to that work which was published in 1759. Here is Whitefield's preface:

"In my poor opinion, next to holy Mr. Matthew Henry's incomparable Comment upon the Bible, the Rev. Samuel Clarke's Annotations seem to be the best calculated for universal edification. Though short, they contain, generally speaking, a full and spiritual interpretation of the most difficult words and phrases. A great many parallel scriptures are most judiciously inserted. And an analysis of the contents of every book and chapter is added. It may be, that, the curious and very critical reader may meet with a few exceptionable expressions; but, alas! If we forbear reading any book or comment, till we meet with one that will suit every taste, and is liable to no exception, I fear, we must never read at all. The best of men's books, as well as the best of men themselves, are but men and the books of men, at the best. It is the peculiar property of Thy life, and of Thy Book, O blessed Jesus! to be exempt from all imperfections."[6]

This annotated work of Rev. Clarke must have taken up much of George Whitefield's time in preparing it for publication and helps to explain his absence in other ways. We do know that in late October of 1759 Whitefield preached in celebration and thanksgiving of the news received that there had been a surrender of Quebec. We close the year 1759 with the following remarks:

5　Ibid. p. 254.
6　Tyerman, Vol. 2, p. 422.

"... the Rev. Mr. Whitefield preached three thanksgiving sermons, two in the morning at the Tabernacle, and one at his chapel at Tottenham Court, to numerous audiences of persons of distinction."[7]

---

7   Ibid. p. 422.

Samuel Foote, actor and dramatist, was born in Truro in 1720. He studied at Worcester College, Oxford, but did not finish. He took up law and left it. He married and forsook his wife. He took up his delights as a comic and depreciator of what many others held sacred and in this ignoble profession he spent his time and talents. But thirty years of riotous living caught up with him, and he died suddenly at Dover on October 21, 1777. Some called what he had talent; others simply labeled it vice. Foote made heavy use of outlandish lies to gain his desired end including, "I have heard George Whitefield's mother frequently declare that he was a dull, stupid, heavy boy, totally incapable" of their business at the Bell,' the principle inn at Gloucester.

From *Whitefield in Print.*

CHAPTER 51

AN OBJECT OF RIDICULE

The year 1760 introduced one of the most agonizing trials in the life of George Whitefield. A cruel man by the name of Samuel Foote, brought a disgraceful theatrical production to popularity. It was called "The Minor". Foote was both the author of this base production and the primary actor in it. "The Minor" was billed as a comedy and it soon became a rage in all of London. It played in a theatre called "the Hog-Market" and this typified the content for it was fit only for swine. Through this theatrical production the great evangelist got the nickname, "Dr. Squintum".

The play's actors not only degraded the evangelist and all he stood for but took free liberty of making fun of his physical defect of which was the squint in his eye. This play took a physical toll on the sensitive Whitefield and it caused him immense anguish.

An explanation of the origin of this play and its impact is presented by Dallimore:

"... a new and particularly vicious form of opposition appeared. The theatre people, angry that the rioting at Long Acre had been frustrated by the move to Tottenham Court Road, found a powerful vent for their hatred. One of their number, Samuel Foote, a talented comic actor, wrote and performed a play, in which Whitefield was held up to derision in a most cruel and lewd manner.

"The play, entitled *The Minor*, had four major characters, 'Shift', 'Shirk', 'Mrs. Cole', and 'Dr. Squintum', the latter being Foote's name for Whitefield in mockery of the misfocus of his eyes. The attraction of the play lay as much in its foulness as in its ridicule. Lady Huntingdon made a strong protest to the Lord Chamberlain, the governmental authority in such matters, but while he professed to be offended by the play, he also claimed he could do nothing about it. She then carried her complaint to David Garrick, yet though he also admitted the play to be offensive, he soon gave it increased prominency by allowing it to be performed at His Majesty's Theatre Royal of which he was the manager ...

"But the matter did not end there. *The Minor* was a financial success and therefore one theatre after another soon boasted similar plays, many of which sought to outdo *The Minor* in foul mockery. Moreover a stream of filthy pamphlets appeared and ballads were sung in the pubs and on the streets, carrying the vilest tales about Whitefield. Several horrible portraits were turned out and one was flanked by that of an imaginary American Indian princess with whom the ballads attempted to link Whitefield's name.

"Whitefield makes no mention whatsoever of this affair except that he says in a letter, 'I am now mimicked and burlesqued upon the public stage. All hail such contempt!'"

"Nevertheless, despite this outward unconcern he undoubtedly suffered inwardly. He could not but have been hurt when, as he walked the streets, he was accosted by some filthy jibe about 'Mrs. Cole', or as he heard a group of children singing some vile song about 'Dr. Squintum'.

"There is no record of his ever speaking of Foote, but he was probably referring to him when, in the midst of a sermon on heaven, he expressed his longing for its bliss, and exclaimed, 'There, there, the ungodly foot will trample upon the saint no more!'

"This difficult experience, however, coming as it did immediately on the heels of the previous series of trials, weakened Whitefield still further." [1]

Another biographer of Whitefield stated aptly:

"While Whitefield's ministry at the Tabernacle was at its height of popularity, Foote, a comedian of eminent talent for mimicry, who was frequently in difficulties on account of his love of ridicule, by which indeed his life was shortened, employed his wit to bring the distinguished preacher into contempt. One of his biographers says, that 'very pressing embarrassments in his affairs compelled him to bring out his comedy of *The Minor* in 1760, to ridicule Methodism, which, though successful, gave great offence, and was at last suppressed.' Of this miserable piece of buffoonery, it may be enough to say, that Foote, and the agents employed at the Tabernacle and Tottenham Court-road chapel to collect materials from Whitefield for the accomplishment of their object, were so disgracefully ignorant of the inspired writings, as not to know that what they took for Mr. Whitefield's peculiar language was that of the word of God." [2]

One can imagine the hurt that the gentle evangelist felt deep inside by this public humiliation! Obviously the one behind it all was Satan, he was using his human dupes to accomplish his vile attacks on Whitefield and hinder the gospel. But through it all George Whitefield never lashed out at the production by trying to sue or shut it down, he like Christ, just *endured public reproach*.

1   Arnold Dallimore, *George Whitefield,* vol. 2, pp. 407–409.
2   Joseph Belcher, *George Whitefield A Biography*, p. 373.

Of this difficult time in the life of the great evangelist we have descriptions from the following extracts:

"It is a remarkable fact, that, though the burlesquing of Whitefield, in 1760, was a most disgraceful, and almost unparalleled outrage against all propriety ... the subject is disgusting; but it must be noticed ... Foote continued to select, for the entertainment of the town, such public characters as seemed most likely to amuse the attendants at his theatre. In 1760, he published and performed, 'The Minor,' a filthy and profane burlesque of Whitefield and his followers. Six years afterwards, he broke his leg, and was compelled to undergo an amputation ... Foote grew in wickedness, as he grew in years. He was charged with an unnatural crime, but was acquitted.

"This profane and filthy-minded comedian was the author of the infamous production, which brought upon Whitefield an unequalled torrent of abuse and ridicule. 'The Minor' was first acted early in July, 1760. It would be far worse than offensive to give an outline of it in a work like this. How educated and respectable people could listen to such ribald and blasphemous outpourings it is difficult to imagine. The whole thing is so steeped in lewdness, that it would be criminal even to reproduce the plot. Suffice it to say, that Foote was not only the author of the piece, but its chief actor ...

"A month later, was published a 4to. shilling pamphlet, entitled, 'A Satyrical Dialogue between the celebrated Mr. Foote and Dr. Squintum,' which the *Monthly Review* pronounced, 'Dirty trash: intended to vilify Mr. Whitefield.'"[3]

Unfortunately more public attacks surfaced against George Whitefield. A London publication called, *Lloyd's Evening Post* published a scurrilous letter praising Foote and attacking Whitefield. Then more pamphlets appeared (written by Foote) humiliating Whitefield further. Finally the *Monthly Review* came to the evangelist's aid:

"The impudence of our low dirty, hedge-publishers is risen to a most shameful height. To take such scandalous liberties with names, as is here done with that of Mr. Whitefield, is surely insufferable in any well-regulated community. If it is not in that gentleman's power to procure redress of such a flagrant injury, it is high time to provide the means of punishing such audacious proceedings for the future."[4]

Some extracts from Foote's published pamphlets must be inserted if only to show how damaging they were in content and what duress they must have plagued Whitefield with. Here are some extracts:

"I am extremely puzzled in what manner to address you; it being impossible to determine, from the title you assume, whether you are an authorised pastor, or a peruke-maker,—a real clergyman, or a corn-cutter ... The force and

---

3 Tyerman, Vol. 2, p. 431.
4 Ibid. p. 432.

miserable effects of Whitefield's mystic doctrines are obvious enough. *Bedlam* loudly proclaims the power of your preacher, and scarce a street in town but boasts its tabernacle; where some, from interested views, and others—unhappy creatures! Mistaking the idle offspring of a distempered brain for divine inspiration, broach such doctrines as are not only repugnant to Christianity, but destructive even to civil society.

"I believe Whitefield is too cunning to let anybody into the secret as to the quantity of wealth he has amassed; but, from your own computation of males fit to carry arms, who are listed in his service, and the price they are well known to pay for admittance, even into the gallery of his theatre, I should suppose his annual income must double the primate's."[5]

If this wasn't bad enough more trouble arose in the month of November and it is sad to see that this public harassment lasted the entire year while the sick evangelist remained silent to this hostile opposition. We read the following with a saddened heart for the evangelist:

"The reader must pardon these long extracts from such a writer; for, without them, it is difficult to convey an adequate idea of what a sensitive man like Whitefield must have suffered from the publication of such falsehoods and abuse. Unfortunately more must follow.

"In the month of November, Garrick permitted 'The Minor' to be acted in Drury Lane Theatre, but with some insignificant alterations, the chief of which was, in lieu of a filthy and profane sentence, which cannot be quoted, Mrs. Cole the bawd, was represented as saying, 'Dr. Squintum washed me with the soapsuds and scouring sand of the Tabernacle, and I became as clean and bright as a pewter-platter.' The theatre was crowded, and thus even Garrick, as well as Foote, began to make money by holding up Whitefield to the ridicule of the large and fashionable assemblies of the Theatre Royal in Drury Lane ... it might be added, that portraits—hideous ones—of Whitefield were published with the offensive words, 'Dr. Squintum' underneath them. One lies before me ...

"These lengthened details may be somewhat tedious; but they shew the terrible *fracas* in which Whitefield was involved during the year 1760. This certainly was one of the most painful years of his eventful life. The persecution also was novel. He had been abused by clergymen in England, Scotland, and America, by pamphleteers learned and illiterate, and by mobs; but now, for the first time, he was ridiculed by theatrical comedians and their friends. Other opponents had been severe; but, as a rule, they had not been ribald and profane. Now it was otherwise. The farce of Foote, and the ballads in the streets, were steeped in blasphemy and filth. And yet, with the exception already mentioned, they are never noticed in any of Whitefield's published letters. That he suffered—keenly suffered—it is impossible to doubt; but there is no evidence that he murmured or complained. No man more fully realized the truth and meaning of the Saviour's beatitude, 'Blessed are ye, when men shall revile you,

---

5   Ibid. p. 433.

and persecute you, and shall say all manner of evil against you *falsely*, for my sake.' 'The Minor' was not the only farce published against Whitefield. At least, three other kindred productions were printed during the ensuing year ...

"It is mournful to relate, that the wretched Foote hunted Whitefield, with undiminshed hatred, to the end of Whitefield's life. Two months after the great preacher's death, in 1770, Foote was acting 'The Minor' in the theatre at Edinburgh. The first night's audience was large; but the indecency of the piece so shocked the people, that, at the following night's performance, only ten of the female sex had effrontery sufficient to witness such profane impurity. Meanwhile, the news arrived of Whitefield's decease, and loud was the outcry against ridiculing the man after he was dead. The Revs. Dr. Erskine, Dr. Walker, and Mr. Baine denounced Foote's outrageous behaviour from their respective pulpits. 'How base and ungrateful,' exclaimed the last-mentioned minister, 'is such treatment of the dead! and that, too, so very nigh to a family of orphans, the records of whose hospital will transmit Mr. Whitefield's name to posterity with honour, when the memory of others will rot. How illiberal such usage of one, whose seasonable good services for his king and country are well known; and whose indefatigable labours for his beloved Master were countenanced by heaven!'

"Here, while the buffoon, as it were, gesticulates, capers, and makes grimaces over Whitefield's corpse, we take our leave of Foote for ever."[6]

With those apt remarks we close this year of turmoil for the great evangelist.

---

6   Ibid. pp. 433–439.

I breakfasted with Mr. Whitefield, who seemed to be an old, old man, being fairly worn out in his Master's service, though he has hardly seen fifty years: And yet it pleases God, that I, who am now in my sixty-third year, find no disorder, no weakness, no decay, no difference from what I was at five-and-twenty; only that I have fewer teeth, and more grey hairs.

John Wesley
in his journal, dated Dec. 21st, 1765.

CHAPTER 52

A BED-RIDDEN INVALID

It is extremely painful to learn after Whitefield suffered so much emotional turmoil in the previous year that he enters 1761 as an invalid, one whose diagnoses is bleak, and one who is confined to bed for nearly twelve months. It is true that he pushed his mortal body way past the breaking point from his indefatigable labor. It is also true he carried the emotional burden of his Orphan House (along with its constant debts and cares) with him until his death. Add to this the foul, lewd attacks on his public persona by the theatrical crowd, add to this a wife who was more of a burden than a helpmeet, and it is easy to see how he ended up a convalescent for nearly a year.

Much can be learned of a man from his correspondence with others. In the study of biography one of the most revealing aspects of the subject oftentimes are his/her letters; for they speak of *the desires of the heart, the aspirations of the individual, and the character of the man.* Whitefield's most revealing aspects of his life are found in his letters. Therefore we will pay close attention to them as we proceed to the end of his life's journey. Regarding the importance of letters we turn to the following comments regarding the letters of Samuel Rutherford:

> "Rutherford's greatest legacy to the church was his *Letters*. These have a place in the hearts and minds of Christians perhaps above all because they express a quality and ardour of devotion that we instinctively yearn after, because we recognize it as authentic biblical religion. Throughout the *Letters* a number of themes surface again and again: The *Letters* are supremely Christ-centered; they reveal a deep concern for the souls of Rutherford's people; they show a deep sense of the sinfulness of sin; they are full of counsel to afflicted saints; and they are full of eagerness for heaven. But if we desire to know what made this extraordinary Christian 'tick', we will need to see him through the lens of his dying words: 'Dear brethren, do all for Christ. Pray for Christ. Preach for

Christ. Do all for him; beware of men-pleasing. The Chief-Shepherd will shortly appear.'"[1]

The same is true about the letters of George Whitefield for in them we hear his prayers, see his great labors, listen to his heart-cries, and share in his disappointments. With this in mind we read the following letters from George Whitefield. In the first we learn of a near-fatal accident in a chaise and then of a solemn fast day he led at his chapels. We see that Bishop Berridge has begun to help out as a preacher at the Tabernacle with great success. We receive the sad news that Dr. Gillies had lost his young daughter. We also learn that his wife Elizabeth has shared in her husband's poor health. What terrible timing! Here, in 1761, both George and Elizabeth are laid low with ill health. Therefore we read with great interest the following:

"London, Feb. 21, 1761 ... I returned in post-haste, last month, from *Bristol*. Both in going and coming, dear Mr. H——y and I were in great jeopardy. Once the machine fell over, and at another time we were obliged to leap out of the post-chaise, though going very fast. Blessed be GOD, we received little hurt. Good was to be done. On the fast-day, near six hundred pounds were collected for the German and Boston sufferers. Grace! Grace! ... I want my wife to ride as far as *Plymouth*. Nothing but exercise will do with her ...

"London, Feb. 23, 1761 ... A new instrument is raised up out of Cambridge university. He has been here preaching like an angel of the churches indeed. My wife is poorly, but joins in sending hearty love ...

"To the Reverend Mr. Gillies.

"My dear Sir,   London, March 14, 1761.

"I hear that your little daughter is gone to heaven: a fine flower soon cropped. I thought she was too fine to continue long in this bad soil. She is now transplanted to an infinitely better. O that I may have patience to wait till my wish'd for change to come! Every day almost we hear of persons dying in triumph. The awakening is rather greater than ever. Satan's artillery hath done but little execution.

Thoughts are vain against the LORD,
All subserves his standing word;
Wheels encircling wheels must run,
Each in course to bring it on.
    Hallelujah!

"I hope you prosper at Glasgow. My kindest respects await all your dear

1   Ian Hamilton, Banner of Truth Magazine, August/September issue.

reverend brethren that honour me with their countenance, your whole self, and all who are so kind as to enquire after, my dear Sir,

Yours, &c. in our common LORD,

G.W.

P.S. One Mr. Berridge, lately Moderator of Cambridge, hath been preaching here with great flame."[2]

We must elaborate on one item mentioned by Whitefield; this was the *fast day*. It was not uncommon in the Church of years ago to recognize war victories or national disasters with a day of solemn assembly: which meant a time set aside for prayer, fasting, and the word of God. On this we have further explanation:

"The general fast, here mentioned, was held on Friday, February 13. On that day, Whitefield preached early in the morning, at the Tabernacle, from Exodus xxxiv. I, etc., and collected £112. In the forenoon, at Tottenham Court Road, he selected as his text, 'Blow the trumpet in Zion, sanctify a fast, call a solemn assemble.' Here the collection was £242. In the evening, he preached again in the Tabernacle, choosing for his text, 'The Lord said unto Noah, Come thou and all thy house into the ark; for thee have I seen righteous before me in this generation.' The third collection amounted to £210. The ridicule of Foote, so far from lessening, had increased Whitefield's popularity. On the day in question, not only did his congregations crowd the two chapels, but comprised an assemblage of the aristocracy of England rarely witnessed in a Methodist meeting-house. Among others present, there were the Countess of Huntingdon, Lady Chesterfield, Lady Gertrude Hotham, Lady Fanny Shirley, Lord Halifax ...

"The collections, made on the occasion, were for a twofold purpose, partly for the benefit of the plundered Protestants in the Marche of Brandenburg, and partly to relieve the distresses of the inhabitants of Boston, in New England, where a fire had destroyed nearly four hundred dwelling-houses."[3]

After this great burst of activity and energy on Whitefield's part his body gave out. He caught a cold that had gone deep into his chest and disabled him. We begin to hear about it from his correspondence in the month of April. We see this from the following:

"During his late visit to the city of Bristol, he had caught a cold, which so seriously affected his health, that, in one of the London newspapers, it was announced that he was dead. His illness disabled him during the whole of the months of March and April."[4]

2 *Works*, Vol. 3, pp. 263–265.
3 Tyerman, Vol. 2, pp. 440–441.
4 Ibid. pp. 441–442.

Many in the metropolis were concerned about Whitefield's grave illness. Even the press published notices when he would surface here and there:

"April 13. The Rev. Mr. Whitefield is so well recovered from his late illness, that he appeared abroad on Saturday last.

"April 29. The Rev. Mr. Whitefield was so well on Sunday, as to assist in administering the sacrament of the Lord's supper."[5]

But we soon learn that these few public appearances of George Whitefield became more infrequent as his health deteriorated further. Going to the existent source of his letters we find the following extracts relating to his declining health:

"Cannonbury-House, April 27, 1761.

"Accept a few lines of love unfeigned from a worthless worm, just returning from the borders of an eternal world. O into what a world was I launching! But the prayers of GOD'S people have brought me back. LORD JESUS, let it be for thy glory and the welfare of precious and immortal souls! Thou hast been digging and dunging round me. O that the barren fig-tree may at length begin to bring forth some fruit! O, my dear man, how ought ministers to work before the night of sickness and death comes, when no man can work! LORD JESUS, quicken my tardy pace, according to the multitude of thy tender mercies! You will not cease to pray for me, who am indeed less than the least of all. Weakness forbids my enlarging. ...

"To the Reverend Mr. Gillies.

"Cannonbury-House, May 2, 1761.

"Surprizing, that any friends of Zion should be solicitous for the welfare of such a worthless worm! Indeed my dear friend, the news you have heard was true. I have been at the very gates of what is commonly called death. They seemed opening to admit me, through the alone righteousness of the blessed JESUS, into everlasting life. But at present they are closed again: for what end, an all-wise Redeemer can only tell. I have, since my illness, once assisted a little at the Lord's-supper, and once spoke a little in publick. But, my locks are cut; natural strength fails: JESUS can renew: JESUS can cause to grow again. By his divine permission, I have thoughts of seeing *Scotland*. If I relapse, that will be a desirable place to go to heaven from ..."[6]

It is not surprising to learn the following:

"For the next twelve months, Whitefield was an invalid, and, with a few exceptions, was obliged to refrain from preaching ... His health was gone, and yet, when he could, he tried to preach."[7]

---

5   *Lloyd's Evening Post,* 1761, April issues.
6   *Works,* Vol. 3, pp. 266–267.
7   Tyerman, Vol. 2, p. 443.

We have glimpses of his slight activity here and there. Gradually, in time, he began to regain his strength and health. In July he wrote, "Through Divine mercy, I am somewhat improved in my health since my leaving London. At Bristol, I grew sensibly better, but hurt myself by too long journeys to Exeter and hither ..." From Bristol he wrote a pain-filled letter that was also full of disappointment, "... I strive to put out to sea as usual, but my shattered bark will not bear it. If this air does not agree with me, I think of returning, in a few days, to my old nurses and physicians ..." By July we find George Whitefield back in London. We have no word of Elizabeth, whether she is still in ill health herself or what her whereabouts are. The peculiar absence of mention of her in his correspondence only adds to the mystery.

On July 6, he seems to be improving through bed rest for he wrote, "Blessed be God, I am better! ... Who knows what rest and time may produce?" Though the glimmer of hope is soon extinguished for we learn:

"Wesley was now in Yorkshire, and was anxious about the health of his old and much-loved friend ... in a letter to Ebenezer Blackwell, the London banker, Wesley wrote:—

'Bradford, July 16, 1761. Mr. Venn informs me that Mr. Whitefield continues very weak. I was in hope, when he wrote to me lately, that he was swiftly recovering strength. Perhaps, sir, you can send me better news concerning him ...'

"For weeks after this, Whitefield was almost entirely silent. To an afflicted friend, he wrote:—

'My Dear Fellow-Prisoner,—I hope the all-wise Redeemer is teaching us to be content to be buried ourselves, and to bury our friends. This is a hard but important lesson. I have not preached a single sermon for some weeks. Last Sunday, I spoke a little; but I have felt its effects ever since.'

"Immediately after this, Whitefield set out for Edinburgh, to obtain medical advice ... Five days later, Whitefield had reached Newcastle, where he wrote the following to Mr. Robert Keen, of London:—

'... I bear riding sixty miles a day in a post-chaise quite well. Friends, both here and at Leeds, are prudent, and do not press me to preach much. But, I hope, I am travelling in order to preach.

If not, Lord Jesus help me to drink the bitter cup of a continued silence with a holy resignation, believing that what is, is best!"[8]

Dr. Gillies described this difficult season in his old friend's life:

"But his bodily health, which had often been very bad, now grew worse and

8   Ibid. pp. 444–445.

worse; so that, in August, 1761, he was brought to the very gates; yet the Lord was pleased to raise him again. It was happy for him, that he frequently obtained the assistance of clergymen from the country at this time; particularly of the Rev. John Berridge, vicar of Everton ... Mr. Berridge, preached at the Tabernacle and Tottenham Court chapel, and continued to do so annually till 1793 ...

"Accordingly he journeyed slowly to Edinburgh and Glasgow; and was in London till the month of December; when he was much recovered, which he attributed instrumentally to his following the advice and prescriptions of several eminent physicians in Edinburgh; being convinced, as he said, 'that their directions had been more blessed, than all the medicines and advice he had elsewhere.'"9

Praise God for the doctors of Edinburgh! There is little information concerning George Whitefield for the remainder of 1761. He wrote to Dr. Gillies while in Edinburgh and states, "Little, very little, can be expected from a dying man." However, one item must be mentioned. Though he lay dying his enemies still hunted him and printed vile pamphlets against him. We see this from the following:

"The poor fellow apparently was dying; but, even under such circumstances, his enemies could not restrain their malice. It is a painful thing to advert again to hostile publications, but Whitefield's history cannot be fully told without it. Some, belonging to 1761, have been already noticed; others, unfortunately, are, as yet, unmentioned:—

"1. 'A Funeral Discourse, occasioned by the much-lamented Death of Mr. Yorick.' It is enough to say that this profane and filthy production was dedicated to 'the Right Honourable the Lord F——g, and *to the very facetious Mr. Foote!*

"2. 'A Journal of the Travels of Nathaniel Snip, a Methodist Teacher of the Word.' This was an infamous production, full of burlesque and banter; but the foot-note, at the end of it, will be quite enough to satisfy the reader's craving:—

'As Snip's manuscript concludes thus abruptly, I beg leave to finish the whole with an account of what I observed at a puppet show, exhibited at one of the principal towns in the west of Yorkshire. Punch was introduced in the character of Parson Squintum, the field-preacher, holding forth to a number of wooden-headed puppets, mostly composed of old women and ungartered journeymen of different callings. The more noise Punch (alias Squintum) made, the more the audience sighed and groaned. At last, Squintum said something about a woman with the moon under her feet, and pointed up to the sky, on which he desired them to fix their eyes with steadfastness. They did so; and, while their eyes were thus fixed, he fairly picked all their pockets, and stole off.'

9   Gillies, pp. 177–178.

"3. A third of these malignant productions *professed* to have for its author the most notorious quack of the age ... The purport of this bantering tract was a proposal that, as Rock and Whitefield were both quacks, they should enter into partnership.

"4. 'The Crooked Disciple's Remarks upon the Blind Guide's Method of Preaching ... made use of the by the Reverend Dr. Squintum ... ' This was one of the vilest pamphlets ever published. Its trash cannot be quoted.

"5. 'The Spiritual Minor. A Comedy.' Another infamous production with an 'Epilogue,' by Dr. Squintum. All this is extremely loathsome, and worthy of Foote, the comedian.

"6. A pamphlet by 'Jonas Hanway' ... who had the courage to be the first who appeared in the streets of London carrying an umbrella, will, perhaps, amuse the reader.

'... When he began his sermon, the oddness of some of his conceits, his manner, and turn of expression, had I not been in a place of public worship, would have excited my laughter. As he went on, I became serious, then astonished, and at length confounded. My confusion arose from a mixture of sorrow and indignation, that any man bearing the name of a minister of our meek and blessed Redeemer, or the dignity of the Christian priesthood, should demean himself like an inhabitant of Bedlam ...'

"7. Another pamphleteer must now be introduced. Whitefield had already been attacked by the Bishop of London, the Bishop of Lichfield, and the Bishop of Exeter. Now he came under the lash of the Rev. John Green, D.D., Bishop of Lincoln. The Bishop wrote with great ability. The chief fault to be found with him is, that, he based his strictures upon the first editions of Whitefield's Journals ... This was hardly fair, because Whitefield, since then, had, more than once, publicly expressed his regret for having used certain loose and extravagant expressions ... Anyhow, remembering that such apologies had been made, and that Whitefield's health was now even dangerously affected, paragraphs like the following, were neither courteous nor fair:—

'All the exalted things you have said, and all the wonderful things you have done, will pass, I fear, with many, only for the frenzy and rant of fanaticism ... Though possessed of so happy a talent at opening the hearts and purses of the people, that you were traduced under the name of the Spiritual Pickpocket ...'

"These were taunts unworthy of a bishop of the Established Church, and undeserved by poor afflicted Whitefield. Doubtless they were painful; but they were patiently endured."[10]

We end this sad chapter with the last letter George Whitefield wrote during this troublesome year. It is dated, "Leeds, Dec. 1, 1761." We read with interest:

---

10 Tyerman, Vol. 2, pp. 445–452.

"It is near ten at night, and I am to set off to-morrow in the *Leeds* stage for *London* ... Silence is enjoined me for a while by the *Edinburgh* physicians. They say my case is recoverable. The great physician will direct ..."[11]

We can happily report that the forty-six-year old's health soon grew somewhat better in the new year. Though, for the rest of his life, his energy, his life force, was a mere shadow of his younger days. He simply had become a physically handicapped man.

---

11 *Works,* Vol. 3, p. 273.

He loved the Church in which he had been ordained; he gloried in her Articles; he used her Prayer-book with pleasure. But the Church did not love him, and so lost the use of his services. The plain truth is, that the Church of England of that day was not ready for a man like Whitefield. The Church was too much asleep to understand him, and was vexed at a man who would not keep still and let the devil alone … He was once married to a widow named James of Abergavenny, who died before him. If we may judge from the little mention made of his wife in his letters, the marriage does not seem to have contributed much to his happiness. He left no children, but he left a name far better than that of sons and daughters. Never perhaps was there a man of whom it could be so truly said that he spent and was spent for Christ than George Whitefield.

Bishop J. C. Ryle

CHAPTER 53

THE SCARRED LION

Whatever trial or tribulation beset the great evangelist he always rose above it much like the rising phoenix of Egyptian mythology. Though as Whitefield rose from his ash heap time and time again he remained charred from the burns. This however did not handicap his great power in preaching. Though limping like the Patriarch Jacob he still could *roar as a lion*. We find George Whitefield at the opening of the year 1762 in improved health—at least he was no longer dying and was enabled to preach once more. Seasoned from his many battles he had so much more to offer his hearers as he could relate to almost any personal trial they had encountered and therefore gripped their attention even more than before with his oratory and stories. They now saw a man standing before them who was no longer the handsome, slight youth of grace and energy but a man, like a soldier, who now bore on his chest the colored medallions of conflicts and wars. Whether one liked him or not there was at least a level of respect gained from his seasoned presence in the pulpit. He had become a public figure hailed and vilified on both continents. There was hardly a man alive in the eighteenth century in Great Britain or America that had not heard the name *George Whitefield*.

We have news of the forty-seven-year old's activity from a letter dated from London, Jan. 8, 1762. It reads:

"I thought my wife had written many letters to you before this time. Blessed be GOD, I am better. The *Scotch* journey did me service. I preached on new-year's day, and am to do so again, GOD willing, to-morrow. Who knows? Who knows?—I may again see *Plymouth*. Is there any thing too hard for the LORD? ... I had a violent fall upon my head from my horse last Thursday, but was neither surprized nor hurt. Help me to praise Him whose mercy endureth for ever. Mr. Berridge is here, and preaches with power. Blessed be GOD that some can speak, though I be laid aside ..."[1]

---

1   *Works*, Vol. 3, pp. 273–274.

We hear no more from George Whitefield until late April, his whereabouts and labor for the first three months of the year are a mystery. We are not surprised to learn that he was still the victim of the printing press and another foul pamphlet was published at the beginning of 1762 which lampooned him. Of it was reported:

> "It is contemptible for its stupidity. It is a filthy, obscene thing, for which the dirty author ought to be washed in a horse-pond."[2]

We find him in April at Bristol doing what he does best—*preaching*. And we are pleased to learn his health is enabling him to do more of it! We follow his month of preaching labor with the following narrative:

> "Bristol, April 17, 1762. Will not my dear steady friend be glad to hear that *Bristol* air agrees with me, and that I have been enabled to preach five times this last week without being hurt? LORD JESUS, make me truly and humbly thankful! Was the door open for an *American* voyage, I verily believe it would be very serviceable towards bracing up my relaxed tabernacle. But he who knoweth all things, knows what is best. Fain would I say, from whatever quarter trials come, 'Father, not my will, but thine be done!' I see more and more, that grace must be tried. But this is our comfort, when we are tried, we shall come forth like gold. In how many fires is that precious metal purified? O for a heart to be willing to be made willing to be nothing, yea less than nothing, that GOD, even a GOD in CHRIST, may be all in all!"

> "Bristol, April 18, 1762 ... Since my coming here, my health hath improved. The last week I was enabled to preach five times. This morning I have been administering the ordinance; and this evening I hope to be upon my throne again. Our LORD vouchsafes to smile upon my feeble labours; and the people seem to feel a refreshing from his divine presence. Who knows but I may yet be restored so far as to sound the gospel trumpet for my GOD? The quietness I enjoy here, with daily riding out; seems to be one very proper means. Be this as it will, I know ere long I shall serve our LORD without weariness. A few more blows from friends, and from foes, and the pitcher will be broken. Then the wicked one will cease from troubling, and the weary traveller arrive at his wish'd-for rest ..."

> "Bristol, April 29, 1762 ... Surely a sea voyage would help to brace up this relaxed tabernacle. Blessed be GOD, I am now enabled to preach four or five times a week; but it is with much weakness ...

> "Bristol, May 4, 1762 ... The archers have of late shot sorely at me and grieved me. Job's friends were his greatest trials, when GOD's hand pressed his body sore. So it hath been with me. But if we are brought out when tried like gold, we shall only lose our dross. O that this may be my happy case! LORD, I believe, help thou my unbelief! Blessed be his name for a little revival in my bondage! For these three weeks past, I have been enabled to preach four or five times. Not

---

once without a special blessing. Join with me in crying, Grace, grace! But my body still continues weak ...

> "Bristol, May 4, 1762 ... With some difficulty I preach four or five times a week; but you would scarce know me, I am so swoln with wind, and so corpulent. Blessed be GOD for the prospect of a glorious resurrection! ..."[3]

Whitefield makes comment in his correspondence toward the end of May that his "country excursion" has helped his health. From this day forward George Whitefield pressed forward with his itinerant ministry with the belief that "a few days riding and preaching will brace me up again" and so he acted upon this belief until his dying day. Though his health was now broken forever (this side of heaven) he remained obedient to the call of preaching the Gospel!

As the great evangelist moved from his country labors in Bristol toward the metropolis (and home) in London we see how God still accompanied his "feeble efforts". We read with interest:

> "Rodborough, May 21, 1762 ... Through divine mercy, preaching four or five times a week did not hurt me; and twice or thrice I have been enabled to take the field ... I hope soon to slip away and get strength, and then hunt for precious souls again. How gladly would I bid adieu to cieled houses, and vaulted roofs! Mounts are the best pulpits, and the heavens the best sounding boards. O for power equal to my will! I would fly from pole to pole, publishing the everlasting gospel of the SON of GOD ..."

> "London, May 28, 1762. I am just now come to town for a few days, sensibly better by my country excursion. Once more I have had the honour of taking the field, and have now some hopes of not being as yet quite thrown aside as a broken vessel ..."[4]

It is interesting to note that in the month of June George Whitefield sailed to Holland and while there his health continued to improve. We have no account of his activity in Holland, we merely see the benefits of it—by his improved strength. While preaching at Norwich he wrote to a friend:

> "Norwich, July 31, 1762 ... Holland last month, was, I trust, profitable to myself and others; and if ever my usefulness is to be continued at London, I must be prepared for it, by a longer itineration both by land and water. At present, blessed be GOD, I can preach once a day, and it would do your heart good to see what an influence attends the word. All my old times are revived again ..."[5]

Shortly after this Whitefield traveled to the town of Leeds to attend a Methodist conference conducted by John and Charles Wesley. And then

---

3   *Works,* Vol. 3, pp. 274–277.
4   Ibid. pp. 278–279.
5   Ibid. p. 279.

from Leeds George Whitefield set his face toward Scotland once more! His stay there was brief and so was the record of it. We find from the following:

"Edinburgh, Sept. 2, 1762. I am just this moment returned from *Glasgow*, where I have been enabled to preach every day, and twice at *Cambuslang*. Auditories were large, and JESUS smiled upon my feeble labours ...

"Edinburgh, Sept. 9, 1762 ... I have been helped to preach every day. The Kirk has been a Bethel. Grace! Grace! On Monday, GOD willing, I shall set off."[6]

On his way back to London George Whitefield stopped off to preach in Sunderland and Leeds. We find news of this as well as some interesting developments in the Seven Years War. He wrote to friends:

"Sunderland, Sept. 19, 1762 ... You will be glad to hear that I can preach once a day, and that I have now a prospect of embarking soon. We expect peace, and I hope the places in London will be provided for ... Sickness lowers my circumstances. But JESUS is all in all ...

"Leeds, Sept. 25, 1762 ... I am just now setting towards London, but fear I cannot reach it before Sunday. My chaise wanted repairing here. O how good hath JESUS been to a worthless worm! Once a day preaching, I can bear well; more hurts me. What shall I do with the chapel and tabernacle? LORD JESUS, be thou my guide and helper! He will! He will ..."[7]

We see the prospects of visiting America now opening again to Whitefield as the war came to an end. It had been seven long years indeed to the grand itinerant who often wished to visit his beloved Bethesda but was prevented by War. We see this history play out in the following observations:

"The 'Seven Years' War' was now nearly ended. The campaign of 1762 was eminently successful. Frederick the Great and Prince Ferdinand had been victorious in Germany; Burgoyne had aided Portugal in repelling the Spaniards; and the English fleet and army in the West Indies had taken the Carribbean Islands and Havannah ... the negotiations proceeded with such rapidity, that *preliminaries* for peace were signed at Fontainebleau on the 3rd of November following.

"In consequence of these events, Whitefield now had a prospect of carrying out his long-cherished wish to visit his Orphan House, and his numerous friends, across the Atlantic ...

"In November, Whitefield went to Bristol, where his 'congregations were large, and a most gracious gale of Divine influence attended the word preached.'"[8]

---

6   Ibid. p. 280.
7   Ibid. p. 281.
8   Tyerman, Vol. 2, pp. 454–455.

It was on a visit to Plymouth in the month of December that we have a charming story which depicts George Whitefield's great gift of warm-heartedness. This event occurred while George Whitefield was visiting his good friend Andrew Kinsman. It is with great interest that we read:

"Kind-heartedness was a prominent trait in Whitefield's character. It was during this, or some other visit to Plymouth, that an incident occurred which is worth telling. 'Come,' said Whitefield to his friend and host, Andrew Kinsman, 'come, let us go to some of the poor and afflicted of your flock. It is not enough that we labour in the pulpit; we must endeavour to be useful out of it.' Away the two friends went, and Whitefield not only gave counsel to those they visited, but monetary aid. Kinsman reminded him that his finances were low, and that he was more bountiful than he could afford. 'Young man, replied Whitefield, 'it is not enough to pray, and to put on a serious countenance: " pure religion and undefiled is this, to visit the fatherless and widows in their affliction," and to administer to their wants. My stock, I grant, is nearly exhausted, but God will soon send me a fresh supply.' In the evening, a gentleman called, and asked to see Whitefield. 'Sir,' said he, 'I heard you preach yesterday: you are on a journey, as well as myself; and, as travelling is expensive, will you do me the honour of accepting this?' The present was five guineas, and came from a man noted for his penuriousness. 'Young man,' cried Whitefield, on his return to Kinsman, 'young man, God has soon repaid what I bestowed. Learn, in future, not to withhold when it is in the power of your hand to give.'"9

George Whitefield ended the year with a preaching excursion to the country. He wrote from Plymouth, on Dec. 5th to a friend, "Though I preach in much weakness, an infinitely condescending JESUS vouchsafes to come down in glorious gales of his blessed Spirit." A week later we find him at Bristol on Dec. 12th, where he advised a friend to rise early to have devotions, "Mind and get up in a morning to pray, before you get into shop." The great evangelist ended the year as usual in London, administering the sacrament and preaching at his chapels.

Whitefield began the year 1763 with plans to embark for America. He arranged for his two chapels (the Tabernacle and Tottenham Court) to be settled with trustees in the event of his death.

We see this concern for his chapels in the following letter:

"Jan. 15, 1763 ... as trustees, to take upon you the whole care, both inward and outward, of the affairs of Totenham-court chapel and tabernacle, and all other my concerns in *England*: this one thing being settled, I have nothing to retard my visit to *America*, to which I think there is a manifest call at this time, both as to the bracing up my poor feeble crazy body, and adjusting all things relating to Bethesda ..."10

---

9   Ibid. p. 456.
10   *Works,* Vol. 3, p. 285.

Whitefield always believed that a sea journey would benefit his poor health—and it often did just that. So having the affairs of the chapels settled he sets his sights on America once more. This would be his *sixth visit* to the colonies. The forty-eight-year old evangelist was *worn out*. Still he arranged a preaching schedule fit for a healthy man; he made plans to preach his way to Scotland and then sail for America from there. As we will observe, his asthma continued to deteriorate to the point where he was a semi-invalid. At this stage in his life, Whitefield lacked all the energy which he had possessed in such great measure in his earlier days—his asthma limited his labors. It is not unrealistic to believe that George Whitefield's asthma was developing into the disease of emphysema. We mention this because this is often a normal progression and as we study the great evangelist as he aged he was more and more prone to infection and labored breathing which are both symptoms of the disease of emphysema. With emphysema one often suffocates to death; which seems to be similar to Whitefield's last hours in Newburyport before he died. At this deathly hour he stumbled from window to window trying to catch his breath. Enough of this for now. We will study his labors until he sets sail for America and his beloved Bethesda.

The great evangelist preached his farewell sermons at his London chapels on February 23, 1763. The title of the sermon was "The grace of our Lord Jesus Christ be with you all." We have the following sermon specimens, though they are not entirely accurate (for they were taken down in shorthand by Joseph Gurney, and published without George Whitefield's permission), they are representative of his preaching style at this period in his life. When Whitefield saw these sermons in print he commented disapprovingly, "It is not *verbatim*, in some places Mr. Gurney makes me to speak false concord, and even nonsense." Of these sermons Luke Tyerman states, "they serve to show the declamatory and colloquial style used by Whitefield in the latter period of his ministry. His sermons were *earnest talk,* full of anecdotes, and ejaculatory prayers." We see this from the following:

"In the earlier parts of this biography, lengthened extracts were given from Whitefield's sermons, for the purpose of conveying an idea of the character of his preaching, at that period of his ministry. For the same purpose, other extracts from sermons, belonging to the present date, may be given here.

"In the sermon, preached on February 23, 1763, Whitefield is reported as having said:—

'The grace of our Lord Jesus Christ be with you *all*. It is not said, all ministers, or all of this or that particular people; but with all believers. Mr. Henry said, he desired to be a Catholic, but not a Roman Catholic. There is a great reservoir of water from which this great city is supplied; but how is it supplied? Why, by hundreds and hundreds of pipes. Does the water go only to the Dissenters, or to the Church people,—only to this or that people? No: the pipes convey the water to all; and, I remember, when I saw the reservoir, it put me in mind of the great reservoir of grace, the living water that is in Christ Jesus.

'What a horrid blunder has the Bishop of Gloucester been guilty of! What do you think his lordship says, in order to expose the fanaticism of the Methodists? "Why," says he, "they say they cannot understand the Scriptures without the Spirit of God." Can any man understand the Scriptures without the Spirit of God helps him? Jesus Christ must open our understanding to understand them. The Spirit of God must take of the things of Christ, and shew them unto us. So, also, with respect to all ordinances. What signifies my preaching, and your hearing, if the Spirit of God does not enlighten? I declare I would not preach again, if I did not think that God would accompany the word by His Spirit.

'Are any of you here unconverted? No doubt too many. Are any of you come this morning, out of curiosity, to hear what the babbler has to say? Many, perhaps, are glad it is my last sermon, and that London is to be rid of such a monster; but surely you cannot be angry with me for my wishing that the grace of God may be with you all. O that it may be with every unconverted soul! O man! What wilt thou do if the grace of God is not with thee? My brethren, you cannot do without the grace of God when you come to die. Do you know that without this you are nothing but devils incarnate? Do you know that every moment you are liable to eternal pains? Don't say I part with you in an ill humour. Don't say that a madman left you with a curse. Blessed be God! When I first became a field-preacher, I proclaimed the grace of God to the worst of sinners; and I proclaim it now to the vilest sinner under heaven. Could I speak so loud that the whole world might hear me, I would declare that the grace of God is free for all who are willing to accept of it by Christ. God make you all willing this day!'"[11]

Tyerman observes from this sermon, "Was Whitefield still a Calvinist? Language like this can hardly be harmonized with Whitefield's holding the doctrine of election, and, by consequence, the doctrine of reprobation." We observe, that George Whitefield was a *moderate Calvinist*. He strongly believed in the great Doctrines of the Bible, especially the Doctrines of Grace. He also believed in calling sinners to repentance, and he did this with all his life-force!

Brief extracts from a couple of George Whitefield's sermons preached at this time are now presented for review:

'Woe! Woe! Woe! To those who, in the hour of death, cannot say, "God is

---

11 Tyerman, Vol. 2, pp. 459–460.

my refuge." O what will you do, when the elements shall melt with fervent heat? When the earth with all its furniture shall be burnt up? When the archangel shall proclaim, "Time shall be no more!" Whither then, ye wicked ones, ye unconverted ones, will ye flee for refuge? "O," says one, "I will flee to the mountains." Silly fool! Flee to the mountains, that are themselves to be burnt up! "O," says you, "I will flee to the sea." That will be boiling! "I will flee to the elements." They will be melting with fervent heat. I know of but one place you can go to, that is to the devil. God keep you from that! Make God your refuge. If you stop short of this, you will only be a sport for devils. There is no river to make glad the inhabitants of hell: no streams to cool them in that scorching element. Were those in hell to have such an offer of mercy as you have, how would their chains rattle! How would they come with the flames of hell about their ears! Fly! Sinner, fly! God help thee to fly to Himself for refuge! Hark! Hear the word of the Lord! See the world consumed! See the avenger of blood at they heels! If thou dost not take refuge in God to-night, thou mayest to-morrow be damned for ever.'

'Tremble for fear God should remove His candlestick from you. Labourers are sick. Those who did once labour are almost worn out; and others bring themselves into a narrow sphere, and so confine their usefulness. There are few who like to go out into the fields. Broken heads and dead cats are no longer the ornaments of a Methodist. These honourable badges are now no more. Languor has got from the ministers to the people; and, if you don't take care, we shall all be dead together. The Lord Jesus rouse us! Ye Methodists of many years' standing, shew the young ones, who have not the cross to bear as we once had, what ancient Methodism was.'

'Don't be angry with a poor minister for weeping over them who will not weep for themselves. If you laugh at me I know Jesus smiles. I am free from the blood of you all. If you are damned for want of conversion, remember you are not damned for want of warning. You are gospel-proof; and, if there is one place in hell deeper than another, God will order a gospel-despising Methodist to be put there. God convert you from lying a-bed in the morning! God convert you from conformity to the world! God convert you from lukewarmness! Do not get into a cursed Antinomian way of thinking, and say, "I thank God, I have the root of the matter in me! I thank God, I was converted twenty or thirty years ago; and, though I can go to a public-house, and play at cards, yet, I am converted; for once in Christ, always in Christ." Whether you were converted formerly or not, you are perverted now. Would you have Jesus Christ catch you napping, with your lamps untrimmed? Suffer the word of exhortation. I preach feelingly. I could be glad to preach till I preached myself dead, if God would convert you. I seldom sleep after three in the morning; and I pray every morning, "Lord, convert me, and make more a new creature to-day!"'[12]

From these sermon specimens we can see *why* God used this dear man so *greatly*. Is there any preaching like this today? We mourn over the vacuum.

---

12 Ibid. pp. 460–461.

Still these specimens of Whitefield's preaching display the style he used up until his dying day. He did indeed describe himself accurately when he exclaimed, "I preach feelingly."

After the farewell sermon was preached at the Tabernacle he began his journey toward Scotland. Along the way he preached for his dear friend Bishop Berridge at Everton. He then preached in John Wesley's chapel in Sheffield. In early March he preached in Leeds. On March 13th, he recorded in a letter to a friend that he had just finished preaching at: Everton, Leeds, Kippax, Aberford, and this place (Newcastle). Once in Scotland he hoped to sail on the ship *Jenny* which was to set out from Greenock to Boston the middle of April. For various reasons he did not set sail until June 4th. We learn why from the following:

> "Whitefield arrived at Edinburgh, as he expected; but, instead of sailing in the middle of April, his embarkation was deferred until the 4th of June. During this unexpected detention, his old friend Wesley came to Scotland, and wrote: 'Sunday, May 22. At Edinburgh, I had the satisfaction of spending a little time with Mr. Whitefield. Humanly speaking, he is worn out; but we have to do with Him who hath all power in heaven and earth.' Though 'worn out,' Whitefield continued preaching, as often as he could. He spent eleven weeks in Scotland, and, towards the end of that interval, had an alarming illness. In *Lloyd's Evening Post*, for June 6, it was announced, 'The Rev. Mr. Whitefield is so ill in Scotland, as not to be able to embark for America.' But, four days later, the same journal contained the following: 'Last week, the Rev. Mr. Whitefield, being recovered from his indisposition, sailed from Greenock, on board the *Fanny*, Captain Galbraith, bound to Rappahanock, in Virginia.'
>
> "The best glimpses of Whitefield, during his stay in Scotland, will be obtained by brief extracts from his letters."[13]

With those remarks made we will turn to some extracts from his brief correspondence from this time:

> "Edinburgh, March 19, 1763 … We have had good seasons at Everton, Leeds, Newcastle, &c. in the way. Grace! Grace! In about a month I expect to sail …
>
> "Edinburgh, March 26, 1763 … My poor tabernacle is so far restored, as to mount the gospel throne once a day. Perhaps the sea air may brace me up a little more: but after all, it is only like the glimmering of a candle before it goes out. Death will light it up in a better world. Work on, my dear son, work on. The night cometh when no man can work. O that I had done more for the blessed JESUS! O that I could think more of what he hath done for me! …"
>
> "Leith, May 14, 1763 … though disappointed in embarking, by reason of sickness, I can read, and write, and hope (notwithstanding a little cold, which threw me somewhat back this week) soon to get upon my throne again …"

---

13 Ibid. pp. 464–465.

"Greenock, June 4, 1763 ... JESUS is kind. I am better, and just going on board the *Fanny*, bound to *Rapanoch* in *Virginia*. Yours to good Lady Huntingdon is taken care of. I hear her daughter died well, and that her Ladyship is comforted and resigned ..."[14]

The "Scarred Lion" is now aboard his vessel and headed for America. We end this chapter with insightful comments from Luke Tyerman who observed:

"Thus ended Whitefield's eight years' wanderings in the United Kingdom of Great Britain and Ireland. During this interval, he had reached the zenith of his usefulness and fame. His health was now broken; and, though he lived for seven years afterwards, he, comparatively speaking, continued to be, what Wesley called him, a 'worn-out' man."[15]

---

14 *Works,* Vol. 3, pp. 289–292.
15 Tyerman, Vol. 2, p. 466.

It was more than eight years since he had last been in America, and we may well suppose that the people could not but have been amazed at the change in his appearance. The Whitefield they had known during his first visits to the Colonies had been a slim and lithe young man, marked by an easy dignity of person, a radiant countenance and a strong alacrity of movement.

But now the slim figure had given place to a rather ungainly corpulence, his movement seemed sluggish, his whole person appeared feeble and his countenance was very much that of a worn-out man. Only when he became greatly aroused in preaching did he recapture something of his former strength, and seem again, to some extent, the George Whitefield of earlier years.

Arnold Dallimore

CHAPTER 54

WHITEFIELD'S SIXTH VISIT TO AMERICA

The *Jenny* was at sea a long time. It was on the waters for nearly three long months and the last "six weeks were very trying to my shattered bark". Robert Philip claims the ocean voyage did him good, we see otherwise from his letters. However, we will turn to Philip's remarks about this trip to America for his comments are noteworthy:

"He had sailed 'with but little hopes of further public usefulness,' owing to his *asthma*: but after being six weeks at sea, he wrote to a friend, 'Who knows but our latter end may *yet* increase?' He was, however, afraid of presuming, and added—'If not in public usefulness, Lord Jesus, let it be in heart-holiness! I know who says, Amen. I add, Amen and Amen.'

"On his arrival, he found many Christian friends, of whom he had 'never heard before,' waiting to welcome him. They were the fruits of his former visit to Virginia; and the more welcome to him, because he was not very sure that he had won any souls upon the voyage. It was with great difficulty, however, that he preached to them; his breathing was so bad, although his general health was better. At Philadelphia, also a still higher gratification awaited him: not less than 'forty *new-creature* ministers, of various denominations,' visited him; some of them 'young and bright witnesses' for Christ. He heard, also, that sixteen students had been converted last year, at New Jersey college. This was medicine to him for every thing but his asthma …"[1]

It is true the people of New England had been waiting eight long years in anticipation of seeing Whitefield again and once more hearing his great oratory. Though shocked at his obesity and "shattered bark" they still loved him greatly. Many had already received news of his altered appearance and brushes with death and this made them attend his preaching more zealously for they knew it may be the last time they heard him.

---

1   Philip, p. 442.

George Whitefield's hopes that the sea voyage would "brace me up" did not occur—it seemed to be the very opposite. He was too disabled to travel such a great distance on such slow-moving vessels and upon such rough waters. All of this took its toll upon him. We see this from the following:

"Whitefield's days on the ocean did not bring the physical improvement he desired. During the first weeks under sail the passage was smooth and he spoke of experiencing 'that quietness which I have in vain sought after for some years'. But thereafter conditions changed: the weather became boisterous and the seas rough. Above all, the voyage seemed endless—it lasted for most of June, July and August, 1763—and he declared 'the last six week were very trying to my shattered bark.'

"While on board he wrote a letter which reveals something of both the outer and inner man at the time. It reads:

'... my breath is short, and I have little hopes, since my late relapse, of much further public usefulness. A few exertions, like the last struggles of a dying man, or glimmering flashes of a taper just burning out, is all that can be expected from me.

'But blessed be God, the taper will be lighted up again in heaven. The sun, when setting here, only sets to rise in another clime. Such is the death of all God's saints ...

'We had need of patience, especially when the evil days of sickness and declining age come. But we serve a Master who will not forsake his servants when grey headed. When heart and flesh fail, God, even our God in Christ, will be our portion and confidence for ever.'

"His words, 'the last struggles of a dying man, or glimmering flashes of a taper just burning out' are a poignant description of the efforts that lay before him during this visit to America, and indeed, of all his endeavours throughout the few remaining years of his life."[2]

Reading his letters makes one think of a frail old, grey-headed senior who is ready for the grave—we must remind ourselves that George Whitefield was only forty eight! We hear him speak of "his old disorder" (his asthma) in the following letter. While on board the *Fanny* Whitefield wrote two letters to his congregations in London; one to the Tabernacle Hearers and the other to the Tottenham-Court Hearers. We will exhibit the first letter in its entirety for it is priceless as it captures the transparent heart of its author. The second letter is too similar to include. This letter is rare for it is one of Whitefield's few existing "Pastoral Letters". We read with interest:

2   Dallimore, Vol. 2, p. 425.

"To all my dear Tabernacle Hearers, that love the LORD JESUS CHRIST in Sincerity.

"Dearly Beloved in the LORD,   Virginia, Sept. 1, 1763.

"Though absent in body, the Searcher of hearts knows that I have been present with you in spirit ever since I left *London*. Glad, very glad was I to hear from time to time whilst ashore that the shout of a king was among you; and it was my continual prayer whilst at sea, that the glory of the LORD may so fill the Tabernacle, that all who come to hear the word, may be constrained to say, 'Surely GOD is in this place.' I doubt not of your wrestling in my behalf. Certainly it must be in answer to your cryings unto the LORD, that I have been dealt with so bountifully. For some weeks I was enabled to preach once a day when in *Scotland*, and I trust not without some divine efficacy. But my late disorder kept me silent for some weeks afterwards, and put me upon thinking sometimes, that my intended voyage would be retarded, at least for one year longer. Having obtained a little more bodily strength, I ventured upon the mighty waters, and thanks, eternal thanks to a never-failing Redeemer, I have not been laid by an hour through sickness since I came on board. Every thing hath been providentially ordered, suitable to my low estate. A large and commodious cabin, a kind Captain, and a most orderly and quiet ship's company, who gladly attended when I had breath to preach. Scarce an oath have I heard upon deck, during a twelve weeks voyage; and such a stillness through the whole ship, both on week days and the Lord's day, as hath from time to time surprized me. Some concern hath appeared, but of what kind or duration the event alone can discover. The spiritual bread hath been cast on the waters: who knows but it may be found after many days. How it shall please my all-bountiful Master to dispose of me when I get on shore, you shall know hereafter. All that I can say is, (if I know any thing of my unspeakably deceitful, and desperately wicked heart) LORD JESUS,

> *A life that all things casts behind*
> *Springs forth obedient to thy call;*
> *A heart, that no desire can move,*
> *But still t'adore, resign, and love,*
> *Give me, my LORD, my life, my all!*

"You will not forget to persevere in praying for a poor, worthless, but willing pilgrim, who dearly loves you, and daily rejoices in the pleasing reflection, that he shall ere long meet you in a better world, where the inhabitants shall no more say, 'I am sick.' Blessed prospect! Surely on the very mentioning it, you will break forth in singing,

> *Rejoice, the LORD is king, &c.*

"I will not interrupt you. Adieu. The LORD JESUS be with your spirits. Only when you have done singing, my dear fellow-labourers, my dear Tabernacle-hearers, forget not to subjoin at least one petition, that whether absent or present, JESUS may be more and more precious to,

Your affectionate friend, and willing servant, for his great name's sake,

G.W."[3]

As we follow Whitefield in America this time we must continually remind ourselves of his wearied and feeble condition for this will help underline that the tremendous effort of the evangelist can only be explained by supernatural aid—God was indeed with him wherever he went. Even Whitefield biographer, J. P. Gledstone, in his chapter entitled "An Old Man At Fifty" says of the great evangelist:

"Work and sickness had wrought a striking change in his appearance when he ended his twelfth voyage. That his health must have been grievously broken is evident from his touching appeal to his friends Keen and Hardy: 'Stand, my friends,' he said, 'and insist upon my not being brought into action too soon. The poor old shattered barque hath not been in dock one week, for a long while. I scarce know what I write. Tender love to all.' Asthma had now firmly seated itself in his constitution, and he felt sure that he should never breathe as he would, till he breathed in yonder heaven."[4]

After Whitefield disembarked in Virginia he struggled with two things: the great preaching task which lays before him (with all its difficult travel on hard roads) and the great hindrance of his poor health which delayed him. Still, he preached four times in Virginia but stated, "still visited with my old disorder." He bemoaned in a letter from Philadelphia written on September 7, 1763, "I have been here above a week; but am still an invalid." The great evangelist spent two months in the city of Philadelphia. James Habersham came up to visit him and he wrote, "If possible, I intend returning with Mr. Habersham (now here) to Georgia." The following comments are helpful in our understanding as to why George Whitefield was so slow getting around the Colonies this visit:

"Poor Whitefield was not able to fulfil his intentions. Instead of visiting his Orphan House, he was, for more than a year, obliged to content himself with writing to its managers. The following is an extract from the first of these letters:—

'Philadelphia, November 8, 1763. My very dear Friends,—Man appoints; and God, for wise reasons disappoints. All was ready for my coming, by land, to you at Bethesda, with Mr. Habersham; but several things concurred to prevent me; and the physicians all agree, that the only chance I have for growing better, is to stay and see what the cold weather will do for me. At present, I make a shift to preach twice a week; but, alas! My strength is perfect weakness. What a mercy that Jesus is all in all! You will let me hear from you very particularly. I want to know the present state of all your affairs in every respect.'

---

3   *Works,* Vol. 3, pp. 295–296.
4   Gledstone, p. 323.

"There was, however, another reason, besides his state of health, why he deferred his visit to Bethesda. True, after the long 'Seven Years' War,' peace had been proclaimed between France and England; but, during the war, the opponents had cruelly employed the Indians in carrying out their purposes; and now it was far from easy to keep the Indians quiet. Hence the following, addressed to Mr. Robert Keen:—

'Philadelphia, November 14, 1763. I am about to make my first excursion, to the New Jersey College. Twice a week preaching, is my present allowance. Many, of various ranks, seem to be brought under real concern. Physicians are absolutely against my going to Georgia, till I get more strength. Besides, it is doubtful whether the southern Indians will not break out; and, therefore, a little stay in these parts may, on that account, be most prudent.'

"Towards the end of November, Whitefield and Habersham started from Philadelphia; but, instead of getting to Georgia, Whitefield was obliged to halt at New York, where he remained about two months."[5]

It is sad to see the great evangelist in this pitiful physical condition. He was once a man who could preach twice a day and oftentimes "thrice"; now he was reduced to preaching *twice a week*. This physical hindrance to his work must have bore heavily upon his mind—for he was a man who wanted to be engaged for Christ every moment! To be prevented from preaching more than two times a week must have been hard for him emotionally.

The Orphan House in Georgia was put on hold once more as George Whitefield was unable to travel there by December. The fact that he was being prevented from visiting his dear orphans and Bethesda weighed heavily upon him. We can see this from the following letter written to his beloved friends at the Orphan House:

"My very dear Friends,   New York, Dec. 7, 1763.

What a mortification do you think it must be to me, to part thus from, and not to accompany my dear Mr. Habersham to Bethesda. Thus it was near twenty years ago, and yet I came, though he left me so ill at *New-England*. Assure yourselves, I shall come as soon as possible. In the mean while, I have desired Mr. Habersham to assist in supervising and settling the accounts, and to give his advice in respect to the house, plantation, &c. &c. I beg you will be so good as to let me have an inventory of every individual thing, the names and number of the negroes. I would only observe in general, that I would have the family lessened as much as may be, and all things contracted into as small a compass as possible. And now once more adieu, though I trust but for a short season. My heart is too full to enlarge. I have not got the account of the children taken in since the first institution; it is left I believe in *New-England*. I purpose going thither now from the southward. But it will be better to go to heaven ..."[6]

5   Tyerman, Vol. 2, pp. 468–469.
6   *Works*, Vol. 3, p. 302.

Whitefield's strength picked up somewhat in New York and he was enabled to preach three times a week. In a letter dated December 8th, he wrote, "Blessed be God, I am enabled to preach thrice a week." He wrote to a friend in London at the Tabernacle the following letter dated from New York, Dec. 16, 1763:

> "I see by what you have done lately for the tabernacle, that you do not forget absent friends. I think you and yours are not forgotten by them, neither I believe are forgotten by the Friend of all. He remembers us, though he is advanced to so great a kingdom; remembers us in our low estate, and remembers that we are but dust. What a blessing this to worthless, ill and helldeserving me! What a mercy, to meet with such a friend in the latter stages of our road! Surely he is altogether lovely. Having loved his own, he loves them to the end; witness his yet continuing to own the feeble labours of an almost worn out pilgrim. Every day the thirst for hearing the word increases, and the better sort come home to hear more of it. I must now go soon to New-England. Cold weather and a warm heart suit my tottering tabernacle best."[7]

In a letter written on December 18th his spirits seem improved. We see that his health has as well, "I am in better health than when I wrote last. Preaching thrice a week agrees pretty well with me this cold season of the year. I am apt to believe my disorder will be periodical."

Whitefield spent Christmas with friends in New York. The next day he wrote to his friend Charles Wesley the following letter:

> "My Dear Old Friend,—Once more I write to you from this dying world. Through infinite, unmerited mercy, I am helped to preach twice or thrice a week, and never saw people of all ranks more eager in Philadelphia, and in this place, than now. Lasting impressions, I trust, are made. At New Jersey College we had sweet seasons among the sons of the prophets, and I have had the pleasure of conversing with new-creature ministers of various denominations. Ere long, we shall join the elders about the throne. Then shall we all greatly marvel, and try who can shout loudest, 'He hath done all things well.' Neither you, nor your brother, nor the highest archangel in heaven, shall, if possible, outdo even me, though less than the least of all."[8]

Regarding the ministers of various denominations which Whitefield called "new-creature ministers" it is noteworthy to include the following comments:

> "In more than one of these extracts, Whitefield makes grateful mention of his conversing with what he calls *new-creature ministers*. This is a notable fact. Compared with his first visits to America, the difference, in this respect, was great. It ought always to be remembered, that the revival, in the days of Whitefield and the Wesleys, was remarkable, not only for the quickening of churches and the saving of sinners, but also for the raising up of a host of

---

7   Ibid. p. 303.
8   Luke Tyerman, *Life of Charles Wesley*, Vol. 2, p. 221.

converted ministers, in England, Wales, Scotland, Ireland, and America. This was not the least of its glorious results."9

The year 1763 closed with GW in New York. Though he was not in the *rare form* of younger days he still was causing a commotion in the city and he was in the newspapers with the following report of his recent activity at the beginning of 1764:

> "New York, January 23, 1764. The Rev. Mr. George Whitefield has spent seven weeks with us, preaching twice a week, with more general acceptance than ever. He has been treated with great respect by many of the gentleman and merchants of this place. During his stay, he preached two charity sermons: one on the occasion of the annual collection for the poor, when double the sum was collected that ever was upon the like occasion; the other for the benefit of Mr. Wheelock's Indian School, at Lebanon, in New England, for which he collected (notwithstanding the prejudices of many people against the Indians) the sum of £120. In his last sermon, he took a very affectionate leave of the people of this city, who expressed great concern at his departure. May God restore this great and good man (in whom the gentleman, the Christian, and the accomplished orator shine forth with such lustre) to a perfect state of health, and continue him long a blessing to the world, and the Church of Christ!"10

The forty-nine-year old Whitefield received a warm welcome in Boston. He was honored by the citizens of Boston for enlisting aid for them in 1761 to help with the terrible tragedy of the great Boston fire of 1760. A committee of the city's fathers presented George Whitefield with a certificate of appreciation. To which the great evangelist wrote the following letter of appreciation:

> "Gentleman,—This vote of thanks for so small an instance of my goodwill to Boston, as it was entirely unexpected, quite surprises me. Often have I been much concerned that I could do no more upon such a distressing occasion. That the Redeemer may ever preserve the town from such-like melancholy events, and sanctify the present afflictive circumstances to the spiritual welfare of all its inhabitants, is the hearty prayer of,
>
> Gentleman, your ready servant in our common Lord,
>
> George Whitefield."11

We note similar circumstance in 1764 whereby Whitefield once again came to the aid of victims of a fire. This time it was the Harvard College Library which burnt down. We see that he came to their aid in the following letter written to a friend:

> "Concord, 20 miles from Boston, March 10, 1764 ... I also wish you could give some useful puritanical books to Harvard-college library, lately burnt

---

9   Tyerman, Vol. 2, p. 471.
10 *Boston Gazette*, extract.
11 *Lloyd's Evening Post*, issue dated, April 16, 1764.

down. Few perhaps will give such; and yet a collection of that kind is absolutely necessary for future students and poor neighbouring ministers, to whom I find the books belonging to the library are freely lent out from time to time. You will not be angry with me for these hints … my wings are clipped. I can only preach twice or thrice a week with comfort. And yet a wider door than ever is opened all along the continent. A beginning is made in *Boston*. But as the small-pox is spreading there, I purpose preaching for a while in adjacent places …"[12]

During this time in New England God was doing wonders through the feeble preacher. A church in Newburyport was borne under the preaching of Whitefield. As its congregation grew they required a larger meeting house. The Old South First Presbyterian Church is built in 1756 and George Whitefield recommended to the congregation a close friend of his to be their new pastor. This man was Jonathan Parsons, from Lyme, Conn. Jonathan Parsons had been a co-laborer with Whitefield ranging around New England together during the Great Awakening. Parsons had studied under Jonathan Edwards and was a dynamic and forceful preacher in his own right. From Whitefield's journal entry of March 23rd, 1764 we have the following report from the Grand Itinerant regarding the Old South Church, "At Newbury, which I left yesterday, there is a stir indeed." And inside the walls of the Old South Church Whitefield's magnificent voice would ring often—as this was one of his favorite preaching places.

In April Whitefield desired to head southward towards Georgia to see his Orphan House but the people of Boston would not let him go—just yet. They were gathering at six in the morning to hear him and he was willing to delay his trip to Bethesda to preach to such willing hearts. In a letter dated from Boston, April 25th, 1764 he stated, "I was meditating an escape to the southward last week; but Boston people sent a gospel hue and cry after me, and really brought me back."

We find that George Whitefield was still there in June! In another letter we see the following:

"Boston, June 1, 1764 … Friends have even constrained me to stay here, for fear of running into the Summer's heat. Hitherto I find the benefit of it. Whatever it is owing to, through mercy, I am much better in health than I was this time twelvemonth, and can now preach thrice a week to very large auditories without hurt. Every day I hear of some brought under concern; and I trust; whenever I remove, a blessing will be left behind. This is all of grace. To the glorious giver, purchaser, and applier of it, be all the glory. All was well at *Georgia* in April, and I hope to be carried comfortably through the southern journey that lies before me …"[13]

---

12 *Works*, Vol. 3, p. 307.
13 Ibid. p. 311.

It was Whitefield's desire to spend the winter at Bethesda. He could not wait to get there for he missed his favorite spot on earth. In the meantime he preached his way to New York where stayed for three months. His health was so improved he took to the fields once more in early August and preached beneath the New York sky twice with great success. We see this from the following letter:

"New York, August 25, 1764. Still am I kept as it were a prisoner in these parts, by the heat of the weather. All dissuade me from proceeding southward till the latter end of September. My late excursions upon *Long-Island*, I trust have been blessed. It would surprize you to see above a hundred carriages at every sermon in this new world ..."[14]

The great evangelist moved to Philadelphia in September where he wrote on September 21st, "I am come thus far in my way to Georgia. There I hope to be about Christmas; and in Spring, God willing, to embark for England ... I have only preached twice here, but the influence was deep indeed." While in Philadelphia he preached at the commencement of a new term at the College of Philadelphia, an institution he helped to found.

On September 25, 1764 George Whitefield answered a letter to Wesley and it is noteworthy to include it in our study:

"Rev. and Dear Sir,—Your kind letter, dated in January last, did not reach me till a few days ago. It found me here, just returned from my northern circuit; and waiting only for cooler weather to set forwards for Georgia. Perhaps that may be my *ne plus ultra*. But the gospel range is of such large extent, that I have, as it were, scarce begun to begin. Surely nothing but a very loud call of Providence could make me so much as think of returning to England as yet. I have been mercifully carried through the summer's heat; and, had strength permitted, I might have preached to thousands and thousands thrice every day. Zealous ministers are not so rare in this new world as in other parts. Here is room for a hundred itinerants. Lord Jesus, send by whom Thou wilt send! Fain would I end my life in rambling after those who have rambled away from Jesus Christ.

'For this let men despise my name;
I'd shun no cross; I'd fear no shame;
All hail reproach!'

"I am persuaded you are like-minded. I wish you and all your dear fellow-labourers great prosperity. O to be kept from turning to the right hand or the left! Methinks, for many years, *we* have heard a voice behind us, saying, 'This is the way; walk ye in it.' I do not repent being a poor, despised, cast-out, and now almost worn-out itinerant. I would do it again, if I had my choice. Having loved His own, the altogether lovely Jesus loves them to the end. Even the last glimmerings of an expiring taper, He blesses to guide some wandering souls to

---

14 Ibid. p. 314.

Himself. In New England, New York, and Pennsylvania, the word has run and been glorified. Scarce one dry meeting since my arrival. All this is of grace. In various places, there has been a great stirring among the dry bones.

"If you and all yours would join in praying over a poor worthless, but willing pilgrim, it would be a very great act of charity, he being, though less than the least of all, Rev. and very dear sir,

"Ever yours in Jesus,

GEORGE WHITEFIELD."[15]

The great itinerant ranged to Virginia in early November where he preached at Newburn and he wrote, "... good impressions were made. Several gentlemen after sermon escorted me out of town." He then ventured through North and South Carolina finally reaching Charleston by the first of December. He preached a sermon there and then departed for Georgia on December 3rd. We pick up his whereabouts and activity from the following information:

"On December 3, he left Charleston for Georgia, and about a week afterwards, reached Savannah,—more than a year and a half from the time of his embarkation for America. His detention, in the northern colonies, had been long; but no time was wasted after his arrival. Within a week, he had the boldness to ask the governor of Georgia, and the two Houses of Assembly, for a grant of two thousand acres of land, to enable him to convert his Orphan House into a college. The story will be best told by the insertion of Whitefield's 'Memorial,' and the answers it evoked:—

'To His Excellency James Wright, Esq., Captain-General and Governor-in-Chief of His Majesty's Province of Georgia, and to the Members of His Majesty's Council in the said Province.

'The Memorial of George Whitefield, Clerk,

'Sheweth,—That about twenty-five years ago, your memorialist, assisted by the voluntary contributions of charitable and well-disposed persons, at a very great expense, and under many disadvantages, did erect a commodious house, with necessary out-buildings, suitable for the reception of orphans, and other poor and deserted children; and that with the repair of the buildings, purchase of negroes, and supporting a large orphan family for so many years, he hath expended upwards of £12,000 sterling, as appears by the accounts, which from time to time have been audited by the magistrates of Savannah.

'That your memorialist, since the commencement of this institution, hath had the satisfaction of finding, that, by the money expended thereon, not only many poor families were assisted, and thereby kept from leaving the

15 *Arminian Magazine*, p. 440, issued in 1782.

Colony in its infant state, but also that a considerable number of poor helpless children have been trained up; who have been, and now are, useful settlers in this and the neighbouring Provinces.

'That in order to render the institution aforesaid more extensively useful, your memorialist, as he perceived the colony gradually increasing, hath for some years past designed within himself, to improve the original plan, by making further provision for the education of persons of superior rank; who thereby might be qualified to serve their king, their country, or their God, either in Church or State. That he doth with inexpressible pleasure see the present very flourishing state of the Province; but with concern perceives that several gentlemen have been obliged to send their sons to the northern Provinces; who would much rather have had them educated nearer home, and thereby prevent their affections being alienated from their native country, and also considerable sums of money from being carried out of this into other Provinces.

'Your memorialist further observes, that there is no seminary for academical studies as yet founded southward of Virginia; and consequently if a College could be established here (especially as the late addition of the two Floridas renders Georgia more central for the southern district) it would not only be highly serviceable to the rising generation of the Colony, but would occasion many youths to be sent from the British West India Islands and other parts. The many advantages accruing thereby to this Province must be very considerable.

'From these considerations, your memorialist is induced to believe, that the time is now approaching, when his long-projected design for further service this his beloved Colony, shall be carried into execution.

'That a considerable sum of money is intended speedily to be laid out in purchasing a large number of negroes, for the further cultivation of the present Orphan House and other additional lands, and for the future support of a worthy, able president, and for professors, and tutors, and other good purposes intended.

'Your memorialist therefore prays your Excellency and Honours to grant to him in *trust*, for the purposes aforesaid, two thousand acres of land, on the north fork of the Turtle River, called the Lesser Swamp, if vacant, or where lands may be found vacant, south of the River Altamaha.

GEORGE WHITEFIELD.

'Savannah, in Georgia, December 18, 1764."[16]

It was within George Whitefield's makeup that young persons should be given opportunity to advance themselves in life. He always gave a "hand up" to those who needed it. The idea for a college in Georgia was visionary to

---

16 Tyerman, Vol. 2, pp. 479–480.

say the least! Had the Orphan House been turned into a college (which it never was) it would have joined Harvard, Princeton, and the College of Philadelphia as one of the oldest academic institutions in the land. Still, Bethesda today is the *oldest* orphanage in America. And its tradition should remain and be well supported.

We see what was on the itinerant's heart while in Savannah as we study excerpts from his correspondence while there; there were few places on earth which gave this dear persecuted man more comfort and peace than Bethesda. Whitefield was now fifty, he had only five more years left of his earthly pilgrimage. He hoped that the work he had accomplished would remain after he was gone. We see this and more from the following narrative of his relaxed winter repose while there:

"Bethesda, Jan. 14, 1765. Through tender mercy, I have been in this province above five weeks. All things, in respect to Bethesda, went on successfully. GOD hath given me great favour in the sight of the governor, council, and assembly. A memorial was presented for an additional grant of lands, consisting of two thousand acres. It was immediately complied with. Both houses addressed the Governor in behalf of the intended college. As warm an answer was given; and I am now putting all in repair, and getting every thing ready for that purpose. Every heart seems to leap for joy, at the prospect of its future utility to this and the neighbouring colonies. The only question now is, whether I should embark directly for *England*, or take one tour more to the northward? He that holdeth the stars in his right hand, will direct in due time. I am here in delightful winter quarters. Peace and plenty reign at Bethesda. His Excellency dined with me yesterday, and expressed his satisfaction in the warmest terms. Who knows how many youths may be raised up for the service of the ever-loving and altogether lovely JESUS? Thus far however we may set up our Ebenezer. Hitherto the bush hath been burning, but not consumed.

Blest is faith that waits GOD's hour,
Blest are saints that trust his power.

"Bethesda, Feb. 3, 1765. We have love feasts every day. Nothing but peace and plenty reign in Bethesda, this house of mercy. GOD be praised, for making the chapel such a Bethel. I believe it will yet be a gate of heaven to many souls. Whether we live or die, we shall see greater things. Remember, my dear friend, to ask something worthy of a GOD to give. Be content with nothing short of himself. His presence alone, can fill and satisfy the renewed soul. Trials only empty the heart, and thereby make way for further communications from above. Seed time and harvest, summer and winter, will always succeed each other here ...

"Bethesda, Feb. 13, 1765. A few days more, and then farewell Bethesda, perhaps for ever. Affairs, as to me, I trust are now brought near a close. The within audit I sent to the Governor. Next day came Lord F.A. G——n, to pay his Excellency a visit. Yesterday morning, they with several other gentlemen favoured me with their company to breakfast. But how was my Lord surprized and delighted! After expressing himself in the strongest terms, he took me aside, and informed me, 'that the Governor had shewn him the accompts, by which he found what a great benefactor I had been: that the intended college would be of the utmost utility to this and the neighbouring provinces; that the plan was beautiful, rational, and practicable; and that he was persuaded his Majesty would highly approve of, and also favour it, with some peculiar marks of his royal bounty.' At their desire I went to town, and dined with him and the Governor at *Savannah*. On Tuesday next, GOD willing, I move towards *Charles-Town*, leaving all arrears paid off, and some cash in hand, beside the last year's whole crop of rice, some lumber, the house repaired, painted, furnished with plenty of clothing, and provision till next crop comes in, and perhaps some for sale. Messrs. D——n, S——k, and their wives, stay till my successors come to supply their places. Only a few boys will be left, and two of them are intended for the foundation. So that this year they will be getting rather than expending. Near ten boys and girls have been put out, and the small-pox hath gone through the house, with the loss of about six negroes and four orphans. Before which, I think not above four children have been taken off these twenty-four years ... It is for JESUS, who shed his dear and precious blood for ill and hell-deserving me. And now it may be, I may see *England* this summer. But still I cry, who shall roll away the stone? JESUS will do it for me. And now farewell, my beloved Bethesda; surely the most delightfully situated place in all the southern parts of *America*. I do not forget your dear relations. What a blessed winter have I had!

"Savannah, Feb. 18, 1765. Yesterday we had a most cutting parting at Bethesda; but blessed be GOD, for giving me to part from it in such comfortable circumstances! All arrears are paid off, cash, stock, and plenty of all kinds of provision before hand, and under GOD, no danger, at least for this year, of going back; so that one great load is taken off. What shall I render unto the LORD of all Lords for this and all other his mercies?

Praise GOD, my soul, even unto death,
And raise a song with every breath.

"And now my thoughts turn toward *England* ..."[17]

George Whitefield arrived at Charleston on February 21st, 1765. A month later he was in Philadelphia in hope of sailing for England from there. However, he did not sail from Philadelphia for reasons unknown; in actuality he did not sail for England until June 9th, when he boarded a ship in New York and landed in his native country twenty-eight days later on July 7th, 1765.

---

17 *Works*, Vol. 3, pp. 320–323.

He would not return to America again until his last visit in 1770—the year he died. His work in the Colonies under God was drawing to a close; as was his great journey in life.

Illness was an old adversary; he suffered from convulsions and vomiting, respiratory pains, and for one short period, from nervous depression. He began to look much older than he was; the slim youth, preaching like a lion, now began to assume the bulky, middle-aged appearance, familiar from so many portraits. His greater bulk, if anything, added to the authority of his manner.

Anthony Beaurepaire

CHAPTER 55

THE WORN-OUT ITINERANT

His congregations were glad to have him home though they were disappointed by his being prevented of preaching to them because of his failing health. Two years had passed between them and time had not improved his physical condition but worsened it. The burden of his two London chapels was too much for him now and he gave the management of them over to others with more energy than himself. The two men (Keen and Hardy) in charge of the management of his chapels in his absence now were told by Whitefield to keep their positions as the tired evangelist had no life force to occupy their pulpits on a regular basis any longer; but he did feel obliged to find able men to preach in his place.

We see that the trip to America had worsened his already weakened condition from the following observations:

"Upon the whole, Whitefield's health was not improved by his visit to America. He had worked when others would have rested. If he had them with him, which perhaps is doubtful, he had worn 'gown and cassock,' when it would have been more prudent to have lounged and travelled in a tourist's dress. No doubt, his preaching in America had been of inestimable service; but he came back to England scarcely able to preach at all. On his arrival, he thus wrote to Mr. Keen:—

'Plymouth, July 12, 1765. I left Halifax packet, from New York, near the Lizard; and, by the blunder of a drunken fellow, misssed the post of the 8th inst. I want a gown and cassock. Child, in Chancery Lane, used to make for me, and perhaps knows my measure. Amazing, that I have not been measured for a coffin long ago! I am very low in body, and, as yet, undetermined what to do. Perhaps, on the whole, it may be best to come on leisurely, to see if my spirits can be a little recruited. You may write a few lines, at a venture, to Bristol. Had I bodily strength, you would find me coming upon you unawares; but that fails me much. I must have a little rest, or I shall be able to do nothing at all.'

"Six days after this, he was at Bristol, in 'a fine commodious house, and kept from much company,' but still begging 'not to be brought into action too soon.' He wrote, 'The poor old shattered bark has not been in dock one week for a long while.'" [1]

There was an odd absence of Elizabeth Whitefield. Where was she? He had returned to London on the 7th of July. There is no mention of her until he made mention of her in a letter written from London on September 6th, 1765. And in the letter we discover she had been away in the country! He commented, "My wife is gone for a little while into the country." This odd marriage mystifies any serious student of his life. We read the following with interest:

"London, Sept. 20, 1765 ... LORD JESUS quicken my tardy pace! Through his never-failing mercy, I have been better in health for a week past, than I have been for these four years. O for a thankful and an humble heart! My wife also returned well, last night, from *Bury*. She indulges this morning, being weary. But I take it for granted, that you and I rise at five ... I shall never breathe as I would, till I breathe in yonder heaven ..."[2]

Luke Tyerman's comments on this letter regarding Elizabeth Whitefield are insightful: "Notwithstanding Whitefield's long absence, and the recentness of his return, she had been a fortnight in the country!" Evidently Elizabeth has been in declining health as well and perhaps her visit to the country was for health reasons. She was to die in three years.

Once George Whitefield had gained some strength we find him reunited to his old friend and benefactor, Selina the Countess of Huntingdon. The Countess had been busy in Whitefields' absence building chapels, her choice of location had been where the wealthy and famous gather. Hence her efforts had been largely focused on Bath and its environs which were the haunts of the rich in the eighteenth century.

In the month of October, with his health somewhat improved, he traveled to Bath to resume his duties as the Countess's chaplain and co-laborer in the faith. We see much of this from the following comments:

"On October 1, Whitefield set out for Bath. For twenty-five years, the Countess of Huntingdon had been accustomed to visit that fashionable city. Wherever she went, she took her religion with her, for her religion was a part of herself. Her position, in many respects, was new and peculiar. She seemed to be a combination of Puritan, Churchman, Dissenter, and Reformer. Her chief characteristic, however, was heartfelt and practical religion. Her lighted 'candle' was never 'put under a bushel.' On all suitable occasions, she was ready to speak

---

1   Tyerman, Vol. 2, p. 487.
2   *Works,* Vol. 3, p. 331.

of the sins and errors of her early life, and to tell of her conversion to God, and to insist that the same change is necessary in all. At Bath, she had conversed on religious subjects, with many of the most distinguished personages of the time. Whitefield, Charles Wesley, and others, had conducted religious services in her lodgings, and the services had been attended by considerable numbers of the aristocracy, who would have declined to enter an ordinary Methodist meeting-house. To meet the case of such, her ladyship, years ago, had built chapels of her own at Brighton, and at Bristol; and now she erected a third at Bath; and, soon afterwards, built a forth at Tunbridge Wells,—all of them places of fashionable resort."[3]

A description of this Bath chapel and the activities of the men who preached there is given in the following observations:

"On 6 October 1765 the new chapel in Bath was at last ready and opened for worship. Three magnificent eagles with outspread wings—still to be seen today—formed a trio of lecterns at the front of the chapel, one on each side of the central lectern or pulpit. On the pedestal of each eagle-lectern a set of initials was engraved, WS, TH and SH, representing three whom the Countess had loved dearly: her father, Washington Shirley, her husband, Theophilus Hastings and her daughter, Selina Hastings.

"Among her friends, Whitefield, Venn, Shirley and Townsend accepted the invitation to participate in the opening services. Whitefield preached in the morning and Townsend at night. Reporting on the occasion Whitefield wrote, 'the great Shepherd and Bishop of souls consecrated and made it holy ground by his presence.' Crowded with both aristocracy and ordinary citizens, with the curious and the concerned, the opening of the Vineyards chapel in Bath was a source of widespread interest in the city."[4]

This was the momentous occasion that George Whitefield could not miss! He was honored by her "Ladyship's" invitation and it would be an opportunity to see his old friends. The great evangelist preached with power at the new chapel in Bath and commented on its beauty, "The Chapel is extremely plain, and yet equally grand. A most beautiful original!" After a few days at Bath the great man returned to London where he spent the remainder of the year as he was too tired to travel any further.

The year 1766 opened up with sadness for Whitefield. The fifty-one-year old was feeling his own mortality as he received the devastating news of his brother's death. Oddly, he died at Bath with the Countess of Huntingdon near him at the time of his departure. We read:

"Lately died suddenly, at the Countess of Huntingdon's, at Bath, Mr. James

3 Tyerman, Vol. 2, pp. 489–490.
4 Faith Cook, *Selina Countess of Huntingdon* (Edinburgh: Banner of Truth Trust, 2001), p. 225.

Me:

Whitefield, formerly a merchant of Bristol, and brother of the Rev. Mr. George Whitefield."[5]

After burying his brother, George Whitefield had the strength to do some "ranging" and he was enabled to preach at both Bath and Bristol in March of the year. His care of the two chapels in London was becoming too much for him and he was thankful to be away from their burden. We see this in a letter written to a friend, dated from Bristol, March 17, 1766. He wrote:

"The uncertainty of my motions hath made me slow in writing, and a desire to be a while free from *London* cares, hath made me indifferent about frequent hearing from thence ... Last Friday evening, and twice yesterday, I preached at *Bath*, to very thronged and brilliant auditories. I am told it was a very high day. The glory of the Lord filled the house. To-morrow, GOD willing, I return thither again ..."[6]

It is obvious that George Whitefield is now a mere *shadow* of his former self in regard to both labors and preaching. However, he still has a commanding presence in the pulpit and God was still attending his preaching. We see some of this from the following observations:

"Although Whitefield's last days were not 'his best days,' either at home or abroad, they were both happy and useful days. The very *evening* of his life includes more labour and success than the *whole* day of ordinary men. After opening the Countess's chapel at Bath, the care of his own chapels in London quite absorbed him for some months. He could neither range nor revisit, because of the difficulty of supplying his pulpits. Besides, he was too weak 'to do now as he had done.' He thought himself fit only to 'stand by an *old gun* or two in a garrison,' instead of leading the battle. But such thoughts did not last long in his mind. His 'old ambition' soon returned, whenever his strength or spirits rallied for a day. A very slight improvement in his health would make him exclaim,—'Who knows but this feeble arm may yet be strengthened to annoy the enemy?'

"In the spring of 1766, he was assisted by Occum, the Indian preacher, who came over with Whitaker, to collect for Dr. Wheelock's college. He was much pleased with Occum's spirit, and with his preaching; for both the noble and the poor heard him gladly, and contributed liberally. Whitefield threw all his soul into this enterprise, and nearly a thousand pounds were soon raised for it. Even the king, through the influence of Lord Dartmouth, contributed to the fund. Occum, as well as his object, deserved the welcome. He was a superior man and a popular preacher in his own country, both in the woods and in the cities. He died in 1792, at New Stockbridge, and was followed to the grave by three hundred weeping Indians.

"In the spring and summer of 1766, Whitefield paid some visits to Bath and

5   *Lloyd's Evening Post*, issue of February 10, 1766.
6   *Works*, Vol. 3, p. 334.

Bristol, for the benefit of the waters, and in the hope of making excursions. But both the weather and his health were bad, and he could seldom preach in these cities, except at *six* in the morning. But even at that hour he had large audiences."7

With his preaching labors in Bath and Bristol concluded George Whitefield met with John and Charles Wesley to promote a more agreeable union between themselves and the Countess of Huntingdon. It is good to see these three friends reunited and co-laboring whenever possible. The meetings resulted in broadening opportunities for the Wesley's to preach more frequently in the Countess's chapels. We see this from the following:

"One of their arrangements was, that the Wesleys should preach in the chapels of the Countess of Huntingdon, as Whitefield, for many years, had been accustomed to preach in theirs. Charles Wesley was delighted. In a letter to his wife, he wrote:—

'London, August 21, 1766. Last night, my brother came. This morning, we spent two blessed hours with George Whitefield. The three-fold cord, we trust, will never more be broken. On Tuesday next, my brother is to preach in Lady Huntingdon's Chapel at Bath. that and all her chapels (not to say, as I might, herself also) are now put into the hands of us three.'

"... the Countess of Huntingdon approved of the arrangements made. In a letter to Wesley, she wrote:—

'September 14, 1766. I am most highly obliged by your kind offer of serving the chapel at Bath during your stay at Bristol. *I do trust that this union which is commenced* will be for the furtherance of our faith and mutual love to each other. It is for the interest of the best of causes that we should all be found, first, faithful to the Lord, and then to each other. I find something wanting, and that is, a meeting now and then agreed upon, that you, your brother, Mr. Whitefield, and I, should, at times, regularly communicate our observations upon the general state of the work. Light might follow, and would be a kind of guide to me, as I am connected with many.'

"This 'quadruple alliance,' as Charles Wesley called it, lasted till Whitefield's death."8

This "quadruple alliance" also introduced John Fletcher to Whitefield's London chapels and as odd a couple as Fletcher and Whitefield were, (they were at opposite extremes in doctrine) they each respected the other. John Fletcher was described by John Wesley as "the holiest man in all of England." And George Whitefield said of John Fletcher in a letter dated London, November 1, 1766, "Dear Mr. Fletcher is become a scandalous Tottenham

---

7   Philip, p. 458.
8   Tyerman, Vol. 2, pp. 496–497.

Court preacher. I trust he will come down into your parts, baptized with the Holy Ghost." And of Whitefield, John Fletcher had this to say:

"Mr. Whitefield was not a flighty orator, but spoke the words of soberness and truth, with divine pathos, and floods of tears declarative of his sincerity."9

We see the great evangelist's strength improve somewhat as he is enabled to travel more and preach more frequently—at times three times a week. This still is little labor from a man who was accustomed to preaching three times a day. We catch up with him in Bath in the month of November. Here are some excerpts from his correspondence at this time:

"Bath, Nov. 12, 1766 ... have been low ever since my coming here. *Bath* air, I believe, will never agree with me long. However, if good is done, all will be well. They tell me, that Sunday and last night were seasons of power. Some we trust were made willing. I hope you enjoy much of GOD in town. Surely *London* is the *Jerusalem* of *England*. Happy they who know the day of their visitation! ... As I am so poorly, I question whether I shall go to *Bristol* at all. GOD help us to look up, and look out, and our path will be made plain before us. Remember me to all at Tabernacle. I hope to write to Mr. Fletcher to-morrow or next day ...

"Bath, Nov. 20, 1766. On Tuesday evening I preached at *Bristol* to a very crowded auditory, though the weather was very foul. Last night I administered the sacrament there also. We used near eight bottles of wine. I trust some tasted of the new wine of the kingdom ... I hope at farthest to be in *London* by next Tuesday se'nnight, and to preach at Tabernacle the following evening. I was afraid my wife would get cold by her late excursions, as at other times she is so confined ...

"Bristol, Nov. 23, 1766. Such a numerous brilliant assembly of the mighty and noble, I never saw attend before at *Bath*. Every thing is so promising, that I was constrained to give notice of preaching next Sunday ... Congregations have been very large and very solemn. O what Bethels hath JESUS given to us! We were filled as with new wine! O that GOD would make my way into every town in *England*! Methinks I long to break up fresh ground, and to begin to begin to do something for JESUS. I am just come here weary, but am going to speak a few words ..."10

The worn-out evangelist spent the remainder of the year enlisting aid for his pulpits at his London chapels. Along with John Fletcher and John Berridge we encounter distinguished names such as Captain Scott, Rowland Hill. Of the last mentioned, Rowland Hill asked George Whitefield for advice regarding persecution as he was beginning to encounter it from his college. In the following we have a letter of George Whitefield written to young

9   *The Works of John Fletcher,* Vol. 1 (reprint, Ohio: Schmul Publishers, 1974), p. 298.
10   *Works,* Vol. 3, pp. 340–342.

Rowland Hill with some parental advice regarding persecution. Here is a brief excerpt:

> "... If opposition did not so much abound, your consolations would not so abound. Blind as he is, Satan sees some great good coming. We never prospered so much at Oxford, as when we were hissed at and reproached as we walked along the street. Go on, therefore, my dear man, go on. Old Berridge, I believe, would give you the same advice. You are honoured in sharing his reproach and name ... Good Lady Huntingdon is in town. She will rejoice to hear you are under the cross ..."[11]

In regard to persecution, the end of the year 1766 brought more printed abuse upon the sickly Whitefield. This opposition came in the form of published pamphlets both cruel and obscene. As Tyerman stated, "He was still hunted by the hatred of his enemies." Of the first pamphlet it was "too coarse and blasphemous to be quoted." The second was a "foul publication" entitled, *The Methodist and Mimic*, which linked Whitefield and Foote in tasteless banter. The last will be presented more fully as it captures the mean-spiritedness of his enemies and displays how tasteless they were in presenting the ill evangelist as a object or ridicule.

The following is an example of this printed opposition against George Whitefield:

> "*The Methodist. A Poem. By the Author of the Powers of the Pen, and the Curate.* London, 1766. (4to. pp. 54). Some parts of this impious publication are obscene, and attribute to Whitefield behaviour of the most infamous and impure description. The general purport of it is to describe the devil making a tour of discovery, to find some one to manage his affairs on earth, so that he himself might have leisure to attend to his government in hell ... But nowhere could he find an agent suited to his mind, till he got to Tottenham Court Road chapel, where he discovered Whitefield. For the sake of gold, Whitefield became his terrestrial viceroy, and swore fealty to him. One of the devil's requirements was, that, because what Whitefield *did* was contrary to what he *said*, his eyes ought to look different ways; and, accordingly, they were twisted. Describing Whitefield's sermons, the writer says:—

> > 'He knows his *Master's* realm so well,
> > His sermons are a *map* of hell,
> > An *Ollio* made of conflagration,
> > Of *gulphs* of brimstone, and *damnation*,
> > *Eternal torments, furnace, worm,*
> > *Hell-fire, a whirlwind, and a storm.*

> "An apology is almost needed for the insertion of such profanity as this, and yet, without it, it is impossible to convey to the reader an adequate idea of the

---

11 *Life of Rowland Hill*, p. 25, as quoted in Tyerman, Vol. 2, p. 504.

ridicule and odium cast upon dying Whitefield. Vile as are the extracts given, much viler remain unquoted."[12]

It is hard to read such items without feeling sorry for the deathly ill man who had done so much good for the kingdom of God. Yet, this persecution began with his early ministry and followed him to the grave—even persisting after his death!

The last record of George Whitefield for the year 1766 is found in a letter written to a friend, Thomas Powys, who was hosting four Methodist preachers in his mansion over Christmas. Thus we end this chapter with this letter by George Whitefield:

"At My Tottenham Court Bethel, Six in the Morning, December, 30, 1766.

"The Christmas holiday season hath prevented my sending an immediate answer to your last kind letter. The order therein given shall be readily complied with, and the love therein expressed, returned, by praying for the writer's whole self, and the honourable, Christian, and ministerial circle with which they are at present happily surrounded with, *four Methodist parsons*. Honourable title! So long as attended with the cross. When fashionable, (and blessed be GOD there is not much danger of that) we will drop it. *Four Methodist parsons!* Enough (when JESUS says, Loose them and let them go) to set a whole kingdom on fire for GOD. I wish them prosperity in the name of the LORD ... Fy upon me, fy upon me, fifty-two years old last Saturday; and yet, O loving, ever-loving, altogether lovely JESUS, how little, yea how very little have I done and suffered for thee! Indeed and indeed, my dear and honoured friends, I am ashamed of myself: I blush and am confounded. To-morrow, GOD willing, and Thursday also, with many hundreds more, I intend to take the sacrament upon it, that I will begin to begin to be a Christian. Though I long to go to heaven to see my glorious Master, what a poor figure shall I make among the saints, confessors, and martyrs, that surround his throne, without some deeper signatures of his divine impress, without more scars of Christian honour. Our truly noble mother in *Israel*, is come to *London* full of them ... She is come out of her cell, with her face shining again. Happy they who have the honour of her acquaintance! Highly honoured are those ministers, who have the honour of preaching for and serving her ... O this single eye, this disinterested spirit, this freedom from worldly hopes and worldly fears, this flaming zeal, this daring to be singularly good, this holy laudable ambition to lead the van; O it is, what? an heaven on earth! O for a plerophory of faith! To be filled with the Holy Ghost. This is the grand point. GOD be praised that you have it in view! All our lukewarmness, all our timidity, all our backwardness to do good, to spend and be spent for GOD, is all owing to our want of more of that faith, which is the inward, heart-felt, self-evident demonstration of things not seen. But whither am I going? Pardon me, good Sir: I keep you from better company. Praying that all (if you live to be

12 Tyerman, Vol. 2, pp. 505–506.

fifty-two) may not be such dwarfs in the divine life as I am, I hasten to subscribe myself, most honoured friends,

Yours, &c. &c. &c. in JESUS,

G.W."13

---

13 *Works,* Vol. 3, pp. 342–343.

By the time Whitefield and the pastor reached Baskingridge some 3,000 people had gathered. When Whitefield preached, standing on a wagon, a tremendous wave of feeling passed across the audience. A little boy who was weeping as if his heart would break was lifted up to the wagon. Whitefield was so touched at the sight of him that he turned from his subject to dwell on the sovereignty of God in melting a child and in leaving so many other older persons in carnal security. A universal concern immediately appeared, and many were brought to faith in Christ.

Richard Owen Roberts
in *Whitefield In Print*

CHAPTER 56

LABORS OF 1767

Of the first three months of 1767 little is revealed of George Whitefield's labors. His time seems to be occupied and he commented in a letter that his "feeble hands were full of work." Some of this work was his writing a preface to a third edition of the collected works of John Bunyan, whom Whitefield called "Bishop Bunyan." The preface by Whitefield was dated January 3rd, 1767 and the following extract from the preface are characteristically Whitefield:

> "Ministers never write or preach so well as when under the cross. The Spirit of Christ and of glory then rests upon them. It was this, no doubt, that made the Puritans of the last century such burning and shining lights. When cast out by the black Bartholomew Act, and driven from their respective charges to preach in barns and fields, in the highways and hedges, they, in an especial manner, wrote and preached as men having authority. Though dead, by their writings they yet speak. A peculiar unction attends them to this very hour. For these thirty years past, I have remarked that the more true and vital religion has revived, either at home or abroad, the more the good old Puritanical writings, or the authors of a like stamp, who lived and died in the communion of the Church of England, have been called for. I must own that what more particularly endears Mr. Bunyan to my heart is this, he was of a catholic spirit ..." [1]

The collected works of Bunyan were published in two large, quality folio volumes and sold by advertisements in the London papers. Whitefield believed deeply in preserving the legacy of those saints who have gone before us!

In chapter 40 we dealt with the subject of Cornelius Winter, the young man who had become a personal aide to the aging evangelist and who wrote frankly about George Whitefield after his demise. It was at this period of

---

1   Tyerman, Vol. 2, p. 508.

time that Cornelius Winter entered the life of George Whitefield and we hear Winter comment, "My fidelity being proved, I became one of the family, slept in the room of my honoured patron, and had the privilege to sit at his table." About Winter and his close relationship to Whitefield we have the following:

> "Just at this period, Whitefield took under his patronage a young man, who, if not a tinker, was quite as poor as the 'immortal dreamer.' Cornelius Winter, the son of a shoemaker, and bred in a workhouse, was now in the twenty-fifth year of his age. For twelve long years, he had been the drudge and the butt of a drunken brute in Bunhill Row. The poor workhouse lad had been converted by attending Whitefield's Tabernacle, and had become a member of its Society … The quondam workhouse boy seems to have been an inmate of Whitefield's house for about eighteen months; and as he is the only one, *thus privileged*, who has left behind him … an account of Whitefield's domestic habits and public life …
>
> "In some of his statements, Winter may have been, unconsciously to himself, somewhat swayed by his relationship to Whitefield; but, generally speaking, his description of Whitefield's preaching, and of his spirit and habits in domestic life, is the most exact that has ever yet been published. The foregoing extracts were written by a man who, during Whitefield's last two years in England, read prayers in Whitefield's Tottenham Court Road chapel, assisted in Whitefield's study, sat at Whitefield's table, and occupied a bed in the same room as Whitefield did. The man knew his master, and wrote with the utmost frankness concerning him."[2]

Winter has been criticized by Whitefield biographers for his frankness regarding George Whitefield's wife Elizabeth and the evangelist's personal idiosyncrasies. However we are grateful to Jay's account of Winter's life which contains such a valuable record of the habits of George Whitefield.

In the month of March of 1767 we find Whitefield engaged in re-opening a chapel for the Countess of Huntingdon. The chapel was at Brighton and her Ladyship had "all her chaplains around her." It seems that his energy level has picked up for we find him active in field preaching once again. Of this we have the following observations:

> "In the spring of 1767, Whitefield visited Cambridge and Norwich, and preached with something of his *old* power for some time. He left London, intending a '*large* plan of operations;' but his 'inward fever' returned upon him, and checked him. Lady Huntingdon then took him to Rodborough by easy stages, and he was soon in the *fields* again. This encouraged him to enter into Wales also; for he had great faith in the 'thirty-year-old methodistical medicine,' of preaching in the *open air*; and the Welsh liked him best in that element. 'Thousands on thousands,' therefore, now met him around his '*field throne*,' and

---

2   Ibid. pp. 508, 515.

light and life flew in all directions, as in the days of old. This was, however, more than he could stand long. Both the work and the reward were too much for his strength to sustain. He was soon as thankful to be again on '*this* side of the Welsh mountains,' as he had been to get to 'the *other* side' of them, although they *rung* with the cry, 'Evermore give this bread of life.'"3

We find that George Whitefield can only get around by traveling in a carriage for he was seldom able to ride a horse because of his poor health. Therefore we read in a letter dated from Gloucester in May, "I am just setting out in a post-chaise for Haverford-west." Also we see him comment, "This tabernacle often groans under the weight of my feeble labours." He was making do with his limited activities and was happy to still be employed by his Blessed Emmanuel. He preached at Gloucester in the month of May; he writes on May 21, 1767, "I am going to preach here this morning in my native city." We pick up the narrative of his travels with the following:

"Haverfordwest, May 31, 1767, Sunday. My route is not yet fixed. I am just come from my field throne. Thousands and thousands attended by eight in the morning. Life and light seemed to fly all around. On Tuesday, GOD willing, I am to preach at *Woodstock*; on Friday, at *Pembroke*; here again next Sunday by eight, and then for *England*.

"Haverfordwest, June 1, 1767 … I have strength to preach in the fields. They are white ready unto harvest. Hoping to put forth the gospel sickle again in my beloved *America* …"

"Gloucester, June 10, 1767. Blessed be GOD, I am got on this side the *Welsh* mountains! Blessed be GOD, I have been on the other side. What a scene last Sunday! What a cry for more of the bread of life! But I was quite worn down."4

The fifty-two-year old is still capable of great efforts—even if they are merely a fraction of his former ones. Though his feeble frame will allow him only so much activity at one time, George Whitefield was thankful for what God was still doing and how God was still using him!

During the summer of 1767 we find Whitefield once again using his influence to transform Bethesda into a College. The correspondence between George Whitefield and the Archbishop of Canterbury is interesting. The Archbishop desired the president of the proposed college in Georgia to be a licensed priest with the Church of England and that there should be a daily use of the liturgy of the Church of England in the proposed college and

---

3   Philip, p. 460.
4   *Works*, Vol. 3, pp. 347–349.

that the Church's doctrines be taught there as well. Whitefield was opposed to all of this for he felt this would hinder the progress and purpose of the college, therefore he wrote:

"I cannot in honour and conscience *oblige* the master of the Georgia College to be a member or minister of the Church of England. Such an obligation has greatly retarded the progress of the College of New York ... For the same reasons, I dare not enjoin the daily use of our Church liturgy. I myself love to use it. I have fallen a martyr, in respect to bodily health, to the frequent reading it in Tottenham Court chapel. It has, also, been constantly read twice every Sunday in the Orphan House, from its first institution to this very day ... But I cannot enjoin it by charter ...

"This being the case, I would humbly appeal to the Lord President, whether I can answer it to my God, my conscience, my king, my country, my constituents, and Orphan House benefactors and contributors, both at home, and abroad, to betray my trust, forfeit my word, act contrary to my own convictions, and greatly retard and prejudice the growth and progress of the institution, by narrowing its foundation, and thereby letting it fall upon such a bottom, as will occasion general disgust, and most justly open the mouths of persons of all denominations against me. This is what I dare not do."[5]

The Orphan House needed improvements—and money! Whitefield also, in his reply to the Archbishop asked for assistance in improving the house and grounds of the estate which had been neglected for three years. Unfortunately, all of this fell upon deaf ears as the Church of England would not budge from their statements in regard to the charter for the College. The result of this was the Orphan House was never converted into a college. It is however, an academic institution to this very day!

Apparently George Whitefield had a boost of energy come summer for we find the following report:

"During the summer of 1767 he visited Northampton, Sheffield, Leeds, Newcastle, Thirsk, and Huddersfield. 'Let me enjoy myself,' he wrote to Mr. Keen, 'in my delightful itinerancy, it is good both for soul and body.'

"He was now able to preach in the open air occasionally; 'golden seasons,' he exclaims: traveling was found very fatiguing, 'but', he adds, 'comforts in the soul over-balance it. Every stage more and more convinces me that old Methodism is the thing.'

"To another correspondent he wrote: 'O to be instrumental in bringing some with us! This excursion, I trust, will be overruled for that blessed purpose. I have been enabled to go forth into the highways and hedges, into the lanes and streets of the towns and cities. Good old work, good old seasons. Help to praise Him whose mercy endureth for ever ... Field and street preaching hath rather bettered me than hurt me.'"6

George Whitefield returned to London in June and caught up on his massive correspondence with friends in England, Scotland, and America. We have glimpses of his activity from these existing letters. He resumed his traveling ministry in late August. Here now are some extracts telling of his labors while "ranging". He wrote:

"Leeds, Sept. 11, 1767. Through the tender mercies of our GOD, we arrived here last night about six o'clock. In the way, I was enabled to preach both at *Northampton and Sheffield*. Good seasons! ...

"Newcastle, Sept. 20, 1767. Preaching and travelling prevent writing. Through unmerited mercy, I am well. Upon the maturest deliberation, after earnest prayer, and for several peculiar reasons, which you shall know hereafter, I decline going to *Scotland* this fall. I have now a blessed methodist field street-preaching plan before me. This afternoon in the *Castle-Garth*, to-morrow for *Sunderland*, next day at Mr. R——'s mother's door, then to *Yarm*, &c. &c. ... Let me enjoy myself in my delightful itineracy. It is good, both for my body and soul. I have been enabled to preach in the street, at several places, and hope to go to *Gesborough, Whitby, Scarborough, New Malton, York, Leeds, Liverpool, Chester, Manchester*, &c. &c ...

"Thirsk, Sept. 28, 1767. Never was I so long a stranger to *London* affairs before ... My body feels much fatigue in travelling; comforts in the soul over-balance. Every stage, more and more convinces me, that old methodism is the thing ...

"Leeds, Sept. 30, 1767 ... I have been enabled to go forth into the highways and hedges, into the lanes and streets, of the towns and cities. Good old work, good old seasons! ...

"Leeds, Oct. 1, 1767 ... By his divine permission, I purpose preaching the society sermon. It may be on the Wednesday, or Thursday before the 31st of this month ..."7

During this time of his "ranging" Whitefield had attended John Wesley's annual Conference in London and had officiated at some Society meetings. Speaking of Whitefield helping with the Societies under Wesley the following comment needs to be made. George Whitefield was a man of *selfless* purposes—he built no denomination to leave after his demise. He gladly worked with the Wesleys and others to help build the Kingdom of God. Whitefield did not "pen his sheep" as Wesley had. Regarding his selfless labor in the Methodist cause we read with interest:

6 John Richard Andrews, pp. 359–360.
7 *Works*, Vol. 3, pp. 353–355.

"While Mr. Whitefield lived, he was glad to confirm his love to the members of Mr. Wesley's Societies, by preaching in their chapels, by sitting at their tables, by lying in their beds, and by conversing with them, late and early, in the most friendly and Christian manner. When he preached in Mr. Wesley's pulpits, in the north of England, he several times did me the honour of making my house his home. On all such occasions, multitudes can tell what expressions of the highest esteem he frequently made use of, in exhorting Mr. Wesley's Societies; in keeping lovefeasts, and watch-nights with them; in his table talk; and as he travelled with them by the way. Nay, strange as it may seem, he has been known to say, that he found *more Christian freedom* among Mr. Wesley's people than he did among his own in London. As to the preachers in connexion with Mr. Wesley, these have frequently received very great marks of Mr. Whitefield's esteem. In private, he conversed with them, as with *brethren and fellow-laborers*. In public, he frequently said far greater things in their favour than Mr. Wesley thought it prudent to say. He never seemed happier than when he had a number of them about him. When he had opportunity, he gladly attended our Conferences; sometimes *listening* to our debates, and at others *joining* in them. On these occasions, he more than once favoured us with a suitable sermon; and often said such things in our behalf, as decency forbids me to mention."[8]

The breach that had broken the friendship between George Whitefield and the Wesley's was healed and they remained friends until his death—even though much is commented upon their doctrinal differences. Regarding their lasting friendship we have the following:

"It ought to be kept in mind, that, in all the towns mentioned in the foregoing extracts, Wesley and his preachers had already formed Societies and that Whitefield went among them, not as Wesley's rival, but as his helper. For many years, in his country excursions, Whitefield, without ostentatiously professing it, acted in this capacity,—an important fact, which Whitefield's biographers, for some reason, have not noticed. Whitefield and Wesley were never firmer friends than now. Writing to Mrs. Moon, of Yarm, a few weeks after Whitefield's return to London, Wesley says:—

'In every place where Mr. Whitefield has been, he has laboured in the same friendly, Christian manner. God has indeed effectually broken down the wall of partition which was between us. Thirty years ago we were one; then the sower of tares rent us assunder; but now a stronger than he has made us one again.'"[9]

We catch up with the traveling evangelist in London in October. He had just returned from a northern circuit where he had been doing what he enjoyed best—ranging and preaching. He wrote to a friend the following letter, in it was concern for Cornelius Winter who was thought to be dying (he recovered, outliving George Whitefield). We read:

---

8   Thomas Olivers, *Rod for a Reviler* (1777), p. 58.
9   Tyerman, Vol. 2, p. 534.

"London, October 12, 1767 ... I am just returned from my northern circuit. It hath been pleasant, and I trust profitable. Praise the LORD, O our souls! Every where the fields have been white ready unto harvest. I am become a downright street and field preacher. I wish the city, and want of riding, may not hurt me. No nestling, no nestling, on this side Jordan. Heaven is the believer's only resting place. There we shall not be disturbed. I do not know but Mr. Winter will get there soon. At present he is very ill ..."[10]

Apparently Whitefield was still active with London labors for the rest of the year—it is a supreme wonder how a man who felt as bad physically as he did was able to do all that he did! All one can say is "God did it!" We find the following report of him preaching to a large crowd at the end of October:

"Wednesday morning, October 28, was preached by the Rev. Mr. Whitefield, at his Tabernacle near Moorfields, a sermon, for the benefit of the Society for Promoting Christian Knowledge among the Poor, by distributing Bibles and other good books, before a very polite audience of upwards of six thousand people, and above forty ministers of different persuasions. Near £200 was collected."[11]

On December 1st, 1767 a good friend of the Countess of Huntingdon died. The Earl of Buchan was converted at one of her Ladyship's chapels in Bath and it was there that he died in the knowledge of Jesus Christ. He was a jewel in her Ladyship's spiritual coronet and his last words were "I have no foundation of hope whatever, but in the sacrifice of the Son of God." Because of the importance of the funeral Whitefield (acting as her Ladyship's chaplain) was summoned to Bath from London. He arrived early December and of this we have the following report:

"The corpse of the late Earl of Buchan lay in state, at the Countess of Huntingdon's chapel, from Sunday to Thursday night. Two sermons on the occasion were preached each day by the Rev. Mr. Whitefield and others."[12]

The Earl was an important man in English society and it is noteworthy that he had become such a Christian influence. Therefore it is wise to include Whitefield's letter describing this morbid scene for it is interesting from historical standpoints as well:

"Bath, Dec. 9, 1767. All hath been awful, and more than awful. On Saturday evening, before the corpse was taken from Buchan House, a word of exhortation was given, and a hymn sung, in the room where the corpse lay. The young Earl stood with his hands on the head of the coffin; the Countess Dowager on his right hand; Lady Ann and Lady Isabella on his left; and their brother Thomas

---

10 *Works,* Vol. 3, p. 357.
11 *Lloyd's Evening Post,* issue month of October, 30th, 1767.
12 *Lloyd's Evening Post,* issue of December 16, 1767.

(Afterwards Lord High Chancellor of Great Britain) next to their mother, with Miss Orton, Miss Wheeler, and Miss Goddle on one side. All the domestics, with a few friends, were on the other. The word of exhortation was received with great solemnity, and most wept under the parting prayer. At ten, the corpse was removed to good Lady Huntingdon's chapel, where it was deposited (within a place railed in for that purpose), covered with black baize and the usual funeral concomitants, except escutcheons.

"On Sunday morning all attended, in mourning, at early sacrament. They were seated by themselves, at the feet of the corpse; and, with their head servants, received first, and a particular address was made to them. Immediately after receiving, these verses were sung for them:—

'Our lives, our blood, we here present,
If for Thy truths they may be spent;
Fulfil Thy sovereign counsel, Lord,—
Thy will be done, Thy name ador'd!

Give them Thy strength, O God of pow'r!
Then let men rave or devils roar,
Thy faithful witnesses they'll be;
'Tis fixed—they can do all through Thee.'

"Then they received this blessing: 'The Lord bless you and keep you! The Lord lift up the light of His countenance upon you! The Lord cause His face to shine upon you, and give you peace!' and so returned to their places. Sacrament being ended, the noble mourners returned to good Lady Huntingdon's house, which was lent them for the day.

"At eleven, public service began. The bereaved relations sat in order within, and the domestics around the outside of the rail. The chapel was more than crowded. Near three hundred tickets, signed by the present Earl, were given out to the nobility and gentry, to be admitted. All was hushed and solemn. Proper hymns were sung, and I preached on these words, 'I heard a voice from heaven, saying unto me, Write, blessed are the dead that die in the Lord.' Attention sat on every face, and deep and almost universal impressions were made.

"The like scene, and if possible more solemn, was exhibited in the evening; and I was enabled to preach a second time. A like power attended the word, as in the morning.

"Ever since, there has been public service and preaching twice a day. This is to be continued till Friday morning. Then all is to be removed to Bristol, in order to be shipped for Scotland. The inscription on the coffin runs thus:—

'His life was honourable,
His death blessed;
He sought earnestly peace with God;—
He found it,

With unspeakable joy,
Alone in the merits of Christ Jesus,
Witnessed by the Holy Spirit to his soul.
He yet speaketh;
"Go thou, and do likewise.'"

"... Congregations are very large, attentive, and deeply impressed. Surely the
death of this noble Earl, thus improved, will prove the life of many ..."[13]

While Whitefield was at Bath he took the opportunity to preach also at
Bristol and Kingswood until December 21st when he returned for London.
Of this preaching route we have the following incredible account from the
weakened evangelist:

"Bristol, Dec. 16, 1767 ... We have been favoured with golden seasons here.
I have been enabled to preach thrice, and to administer the holy sacrament.
Thousands went away on Sunday because they could not come in. The word
hath been attended with great power. Grace! Grace! What a pity that we cannot
stay a week or two longer! But I must away to *Bath* to preach to-morrow, and
the next Lord's-day ... We come in the two days post-coach ... Pray tell my
wife, that I intend doing myself the pleasure of dining at Tabernacle-house next
Wednesday ..."[14]

It was from London that George Whitefield wrote to his old friend in
Glasgow, Dr. John Gillies. In it we learn of Whitefield's birthday. We will
close this chapter of the year 1767 with a brief extract from that letter dated,
December 28, 1767:

"Why do you and I exchange letters so seldom? Perhaps it would be better
to correspond more frequently. This brings you the good news of the
triumphant death of the late Earl of Buchan. He behaved like the patriarch
Jacob, when by faith leaning upon his staff, he blessed his children ...

"I am now fifty-three years old. Did you ever hear of such a fifty-three
years old barren fig-tree? So much digging, so much dunging, and yet so little
fruit. GOD be merciful to me a sinner! A sinner—a sinner—a sinner. He is
merciful; he is gracious: his mercy endureth for ever. He yet vouchsafes to
bless my feeble labours. You would have been delighted to have seen the
awful scene exhibited at *Bath*, whilst the late noble Earl lay in state. Two
sermons every day; life and power attended the word; and I verily believe
many dead souls were made to hear the voice of the Son of GOD. Since that
we have been favoured with comfortable seasons in town. I hope you are
blessed in *Glasgow*. Who knows but we may have one more interview in
Spring?

13 *Works,* Vol. 3, pp. 363–365. Also, Tyerman, Vol. 2, p. 537 for names of individuals.
14 Ibid. p. 366.

Whether we meet next on earth or in heaven, you will find that with great sincerity I subscribe myself, reverend and very dear Sir,

Yours, &c. &c &c. in our glorious JESUS,

G.W."[15]

---

15 Ibid. p. 367.

I knew him intimately upward of thirty years. *His integrity, disinterestedness, and indefatigable zeal in prosecuting every good work I have never seen equaled, I shall never see excelled.*

Benjamin Franklin

CHAPTER 57

1768 LABORS AND THE DEATH OF HIS WIFE

The year 1768 was a busy year for George Whitefield and a sad year; much was accomplished for God's Kingdom and his wife entered into it. The fifty-three-year old evangelist had only two more years of life himself. And he would finally be in "that wished-for grave". The last years of George Whitefield's life were full of activity even though he was obviously a dying man.

His old friend Benjamin Franklin was becoming famous around the world and the two men corresponded in the early part of the year. On Franklin's rise to prominence we have the following:

"Benjamin Franklin, the poor printer, was now a man of great distinction. He had visited Holland, Germany, and France; and, for the last two year, had been in England. The degree of LL.D. had been conferred upon him by the three Universities of St. Andrew's, Edinburgh, and Oxford. In France Louis XV. had shown him marked attention. But, in the midst of all his honours, he still respected his old friend Whitefield."[1]

George Whitefield contacted his old friend in January. The following letter written to Franklin reveals that Whitefield is bedridden once again with illness. We read with great interest the letter as well as the following comments:

"Through the courtesy of a friend we are permitted to furnish to the reader an original letter of Whitefield's never before published. It was written to Dr. Franklin when he was in England, about a year and a half prior to Whitefield's death. Though on business, the writer does not forget the interests of eternity."

'Tottenham Court, January 21, 1768. My Dear Doctor,—When will it suit you to have another interview? The college affair is dormant. For above a week, I have been dethroned, by a violent cold and hoarseness. Who but would work

---

1 Tyerman, Vol. 2, p. 540.

413

and speak for God while it is day! "The night [of sickness and death] cometh when no man can work." Through rich grace, I can sing, "O death, where is thy sting?" But only through JESUS of Nazareth. Your daughter, I find, is beginning the world. I wish you joy from the bottom of my heart. You and I shall soon go out of it. Ere long we shall see it burst. Angels shall summon us to attend on the funeral of time. And (O transporting thought!) we shall see eternity rising out of its ashes. That you and I may be in the happy number of those who, in the midst of the tremendous final blaze, shall cry Amen, Hallelujah! is the hearty prayer of, my dear doctor,

Yours, etc., etc., G. WHITEFIELD.'

"What increases the value of this letter is that it is indorsed on the back in Franklin's own handwriting, 'Mr. Whitefield.'"[2]

It is interesting to note that George Whitefield was constant in his gospel witness to his dear lost friend. It is important to include the following observations about these two men as well as a letter written by Franklin to Whitefield. In it is news of the impending Revolutionary War and Franklin's prophetic words. Hence, we observe with great interest:

"That the friendship of Dr. Franklin towards Mr. Whitefield was sincere, cannot be doubted; there is, however, somewhat painful in the thought, that even in this connection Franklin could not conceal his scepticism. In 1769 both these eminent men were in London, and every one knows that the state of our country was very trying. Franklin thus wrote to Whitefield:

'I am under continued apprehensions that we may have bad news from America. The sending soldiers to Boston always appeared to me a dangerous step; they could do no good, they might occasion mischief. When I consider the warm resentment of a people who think themselves injured and oppressed, and the common insolence of the soldiery, who are taught to consider that people as in rebellion, I cannot but fear the consequences of bringing them together. It seems like setting up a smith's forge in a magazine of gunpowder. I *see* with you that our affairs are not well managed by our rulers here below; I wish I could *believe* with you, that they are well attended to by those above: I rather suspect from certain circumstances, that though the general government of the universe is well administered, our particular little affairs are perhaps below notice, and left to take the chance of human prudence or imprudence, as either may happen to be uppermost. It is, however, an uncomfortable thought, and I leave it.'

"It would have been strange indeed if Whitefield had allowed a letter closing in this manner to pass without a remark; hence we are prepared to find that, in his own handwriting, at the foot of the autograph letter, he wrote, '*Uncomfortable* indeed! and, blessed be God, *unscriptural*; for we are fully assured that "the Lord reigneth," and are directed to cast *all* our own care on him, because he careth for us.'

"Could Dr. Franklin have seen the splendid results of that management which he thought indicated the absence of a particular providence—could he have beheld the vast Republic, the abode of liberty, commerce, literature, and religion, which in less than a century has grown out of the insurgent colonies— he would surely have exclaimed, in the language of the prophet, 'Verily there is a God in the earth!'"3

We witness next the founding of Trevecca, the training school for ministers begun by Countess Huntingdon to train men to fill her multiplying chapels. This school figures in importance to Whitefield and Bethesda, for after George Whitefield's death several Trevecca graduates went to Georgia as missionaries to help at the Orphan House! On this remarkable school we have the following:

"Lady Huntingdon was multyplying her chapels; but none of them were episcopally consecrated. Whitefield, the Wesleys, Romaine, Madan, Fletcher, and other Methodist clergymen preached in them as far as they had opportunity; but, it was evident, that, without lay evangelists, the work would be impeded. Captain Scott, Captain Joss, Thomas Adams, and others rendered efficient help to Whitefield in his London chapels; but they were not sufficient to meet the growing wants of himself and the Countess. Hence, her ladyship began to make preparation for the training of converted and zealous men to supply the existing pulpits, and to extend the work. At Trevecca, not far from the residence of Howell Harris, stood an ancient structure, part of an old castle, erected in the reign of Henry II. The date over the entrance is 1176. This venerable ruin belonged to Harris, who rented it to the Countess, for the purpose of its being turned into a sort of ministerial college."4

This "school of the prophets" was the breeding ground for many noteworthy ministers who long after graduation conducted significant ministries and its early direction was under the leadership of the saintly John Fletcher. Of this early life at this famous school we have the following:

"Towards the middle of April 1767 Selina set out together with Jenetta Orton and another young friend, Lady Anne Erskine. They spent a few days near Gloucester on the way, and discovering Whitefield in the area, would have enjoyed hearing him preach once more. Soon after arriving at Trevecca, the party was joined by John Fletcher who had also been taking a lively interest in all the Countess's plans for a college."5

---

3   Joseph Belcher, D.D., *George Whitefield A Biography* (American Tract Society, 1862), pp. 414–415.
4   Tyerman, Vol. 2, p. 541.
5   Faith Cook, *Selina Countess of Huntingdon* (Edinburgh: Banner of Truth Trust, 2001), p. 235.

The first four months of 1768 reveal little to us about Whitefield's broader activities. He did in March attend to a prisoner who was sentenced to death in Newgate prison and administered to him the holy sacrament as the man professed to be a believer. The next burst of activity from George Whitefield was when he visited Tunbridge Wells then preached as well in Lewes, and Brighton. We have a description of this from the following:

"At Whitsuntide, Whitefield visited Tunbridge Wells, Lewes, and Brighton. At the first of these places, Lady Huntingdon had procured a permanent residence, on Mount Ephraim; and Whitefield preached there twice in the open air. 'Very man,' says her ladyship, 'were cut to the heart. Sinners trembled exceedingly before the Lord, and a universal impression seemed to abide upon the multitude. Truly God was in the midst of us to wound and to heal.'"[6]

In the month of June the busy evangelist traveled once more to Scotland; this would be his *fifteenth and last* visit to the land that he loved so dearly. Of this last visit we have a short narrative of his labors there from his correspondence and we learn that Elizabeth Whitefield was deathly ill. Now to his last labors in Scotland:

"Edinburgh, June 15, 1768 ... You would be delighted to see our Orphan-house park assemblies; as large, attentive, and affectionate as ever. Twenty-seven year old friends and spiritual children, remember the days of old; they are seeking after their first love, and there seems to be a stirring among the dry bones ... I must away to my throne ...

"Edinburgh, July 2, 1768 ... My journey hither was certainly of GOD. Could I preach ten times a day, thousands and thousands would attend. I have been confined for a few days, but on Monday or Tuesday next hope to mount my throne again. O to die there! ... I am here only in danger of being hugged to death. Friends of all ranks seem heartier and more friendly than ever. All of is grace. Grace! Grace! ...

"Edinburgh, July 4, 1768. What various interruptions do we meet with in this lower world! Sickness, preaching, and company, have prevented my answering your kind letter more speedily. I strive to stir and fly as formerly; but the earthly house of this tabernacle pulls me down.

Strange, that a harp of thousand strings,
Should keep in tune so long!

"However, this is my comfort, the Redeemer still vouchsafes to smile upon my feeble efforts. In *London* the word runs and is glorified, and in *Edinburgh*, I trust, the prospect is promising. The fields are white ready unto harvest. Who knows but some wheat may be gathered into the heavenly garner? ... A week or fortnight, at most, is the longest time I can stay here. I desire to move, till I can move no more. O to die in the field! I pray GOD to send Mrs. T—— a safe delivery. My wife is as well as can be expected. Both descending in order to ascend ...

"Edinburgh, July 9, 1768 ... Every thing goes on better and better here. But I am so worn down by preaching abroad, and by talking at home almost all the day long, that I have determined, GOD willing, to set off for *London* next Tuesday noon ... As you do not mention my wife, I suppose she is out of town ..."7

Regarding Elizabeth Whitefield we learn that her condition was grave at best. It must have been difficult for her to be dying and her husband absent. Whitefield returned to London by early August. On August 9th, 1768 Elizabeth Whitefield died as the result of a fever which lasted for five days— she was sixty-five years of age. It is bizarre that the only reference made to his wife's decease from his correspondence is found in a letter dated from London, Aug. 16, 1768 in which he announces in a nondescript manner:

"The late very unexpected breach, is a fresh proof that the night soon cometh when no man can work. Pray where may I find that grand promise made to Abraham after Sarah's death? May it be fulfilled in you, whilst your Sarah is still alive! Sweet bereavements, when GOD himself fills up the chasm! Through mercy I find it so. Adieu ..."8

The above quoted letter was written two days after George Whitefield preached his wife's funeral sermon. On this momentous occasion we have several observations: the first is from the pen of Tyerman who wrote:

"On his return to London, she was attacked with fever, and died on August 9. Five days afterwards, he preached her funeral sermon; and, noticing her fortitude, remarked,—

'Do you remember my preaching in those fields by the old stump of a tree? The multitude was great, and many were disposed to be riotous. At first, I addressed them firmly; but when a desperate gang drew near, with the most ferocious and horrid imprecations and menaces, my courage began to fail. My wife was then standing behind me, as I stood on the table. I think I hear her now. She pulled my gown, and, looking up, said, "George, play the man for your God." My confidence returned. I spoke to the multitude with boldness and affection. They became still, and many were deeply affected.' A monument to the memory of Whitefield's wife was put up in Tottenham Court Road chapel, with the following inscription:—

'To the memory of Mrs. Whitefield, who, after thirty years' strong and frequent manifestations of her Redeemer's love, mixed with strong and frequent strugglings against the buffetings of Satan, and many sicknesses and indwellings of sin, was joyfully released, August 9, 1768.'"9

---

7   *Works*, Vol. 3, pp. 370–372.
8   Ibid. p. 373.
9   Tyerman, Vol. 2, pp. 554–555.

The next observation comes from John Berridge, friend of Whitefield who often preached in his chapels. Berridge was known for his formidable wit and he wrote to the Countess of Huntingdon after Elizabeth Whitefield's death the following comments on their marriage:

> "Matrimony has quite maimed poor Charles and might have spoiled John and George if a wise Master had not graciously sent them a brace of ferrets."[10]

Of course, the witty Berridge is naming John Wesley, Charles Wesley and George Whitefield and commenting on their unhappy unions. Add to these comments the one's by Cornelius Winter whereby he stated, "He was not happy with his wife ... She certainly did not behave in all respects as she ought"; and we add to these the infrequent mentions of Elizabeth by George in his vast correspondence and well—it is very sad indeed. We feel even worse when we read about the hardships that Elizabeth Whitefield endured during their long marriage. We see some of this from the following statements:

> "There were difficulties in Elizabeth Whitefield's life of which these critics knew little or nothing. We have already noted the loss of her infant son, followed by four miscarriages, and her nearness to death in 1746. Then came the unplanned two years of separation from her husband, which, despite her courage, was no doubt too much for her nervous strength. Thereafter, once back in England, she did not travel with him again."[11]

Needless to say, as George Whitefield threw himself into his preaching labors so soon after the death of his four-month-old son, so now, did he resume his intense labors once more to help him in his bereavement. We find him on August 24th at Trevecca where he opened the College for the Countess of Huntingdon with a sermon and exhortation to the students. Then on Sunday August 28th he preached in the court of the College. We see this from Dr. Gillies:

> "In his memorandum book, he wrote as follows: 'August 24, 1768, opened good Lady Huntingdon's chapel and college, in the parish of Talgarth, Brecknockshire, South Wales—preached from Exodus XX. 24. *In all places where I record my name, I will come unto thee, and I will bless thee.*

> 'August 25. Gave an exhortation to the students in the college chapel, from Luke I. 15. *He shall be great in the sight of the Lord.*

> 'Sunday, August 28. Preached in the court before the college, the congregation consisting of some thousands, from I Cor. iii. 11. *Other foundation can no man lay, than that is laid, which is Jesus Christ.*'

10 Rev. Richard Whittingham, vicar of Potton, Bedfordshire, *The Works of the Rev. John Berridge, A. M.,* p. 20.
11 Dallimore, Vol. 2, p. 472.

"Thus we see him incessantly *doing the work of an evangelist*. Well would it be for the church of Christ, if there were more of his brethren inclined to follow his steps, even as he followed Christ!"[12]

But in Bristol we see that the great evangelist was in poor health again. He wrote on August 30th, "My disorder has returned." This was a dying man though he did not realize it. On more of his deteriorating health and last labors of 1768 we have the following:

"He then hurried back to London, where he arrived on September 1. His health was broken, and he was again an invalid. In a letter, dated September 6, he wrote to a sick and suffering friend:—

'Why should not one invalid write to another? What if we should meet in our way to heaven unembodied,—freed from everything that at present weighs down our precious and immortal souls? For these two days past I have been almost unable to write: to-day, I am, what they call better.'

"Immediately after this, he ruptured a blood-vessel; and, on September 12, remarked:—

'I have been in hopes of my departure. Through hard riding, and frequent preaching, I have burst a vein. The flux is, in a great measure, stopped; but rest and quietness are strictly enjoined.'

"Rashly enough, Whitefield re-commenced preaching before the month was ended … Whitefield set out for Bath and Bristol; and began to have a longing to go to his orphans at Bethesda. He writes:—

'Bristol, November 12, 1768. Bethesda lies upon my heart night and day …'

"By the end of November, he was back in London, and wrote:—

'November 30, 1768. Many thought I should not hold out from Bath to London; but I cannot as yet go to Him whom my soul loveth. Last Sunday, I creeped up to my gospel-throne; this evening, the same honour is to be conferred upon me. Mr. Wright is going with his brothers to Georgia to finish the wings of the intended College, and repair the present buildings.'

"Whitefield's weakness continued; but he preached as often as he was able. 'I love the open bracing air;' said he, on December 14; 'preaching within doors, and especially to crowded auditories, is apt to make us nervous.'"[13]

We end the turbulent though victorious year for the great evangelist with his last two letters written in December of 1768. The first letter refers to a recent portrait made of George Whitefield (the portrait was done by Hone and displays the corpulent likeness of Whitefield's later years) and the letter is

---

12 Gillies, pp. 191–192.
13 Tyerman, Vol. 2, pp. 555–557.

one full of hope for future fields and more labor, the other reveals that he is now fifty-four years of age and speaks of his great humility with an ending line that now frequents most of his letters until the day he dies: "Less then the least of all". We close this chapter with these last two letters of 1768:

"London, Dec. 15, 1768. You will see the contents of my letter to Dr. Erskine. I have considered the affair of the picture. What think you? A limner who lately drew me, and hung the picture up in the exhibition, asks forty guineas for a copy. I shall not mind him, but send a bust taken several years ago. It shall be paid for here, and presented as a token of my hearty, hearty love to the Orphan-house at *Edinburgh*, and its never-to-be forgotten friends. Nothing but my disorder of body, GOD willing, shall prevent my engagement in the plains of *Philippi*: But, I fear, that will be an obstruction to so long a journey. You cannot tell how low my late excursion only to *Bristol* and *Bath* brought me. But I serve a GOD who killeth and maketh alive. I would leave future events to Him, and like you merchants improve the present Now: time is short; eternity is endless. The Judge hath sent this awful message, 'Behold, I come quickly.' That we all may be ready to go forth to meet him, earnestly prays, my dear friend,

Less then the least of all,

G.W."

"London, Dec. 29, 1768. Many thanks for your kind sympathetic congratulatory letter. Mr. Wright is gone, or rather lies yet in the *Downs*. He is gone to build for Him, who shed his precious heart's-blood for ill and hell-deserving me. Whether the unworthy Founder lives or dies, Bethesda affair, I trust, will now be completed. Strange, that I am now living! Fifty-four years old last Thursday. GOD be merciful to me a sinner! A sinner! A sinner! Less then the least of all, must be my motto still …"[14]

The "Scarred Lion" lives only two more years; but what years they turn out to be! George Whitefield planned and succeeded in a last trip to America where he died and lies still until the resurrection!

---

14 *Works,* Vol. 3, p. 380.

It is here we touch the unique splendour of George Whitefield, the greatest evangelist of the British race. Whilst Wesley was the steady light of revival, Whitefield was the raging flame, the kindling torch whose fiery zeal caused him to run ahead of others in his time and blaze a new trail of more daring endeavour for Christ. Without that pioneer achievement there might well have been no Evangelical Revival, no Methodist Church, no mighty social emancipation such as resulted therefrom. Indeed there is much to be said in favour of Southey's verdict: "If the Wesleys had never existed Whitefield would have given birth to Methodism." ... Through thirty-four years of ceaseless labour, George Whitefield knew no abatement of evangelistic passion. From end to end of that remarkable career his soul was a furnace of burning zeal for the salvation of men ... No preacher of the Gospel before or since has gathered such audiences, no evangelist has achieved such magnitude in results, no single life has had a wider impact upon our English speaking race.

Albert D. Beldon, D. D.

CHAPTER 58

HIS LAST LABORS IN GREAT BRITAIN

George Whitefield had a deep desire to see his beloved Bethesda once again and re-visit his dear friends in America. Though he wondered if his "shattered bark" could survive another sea voyage he trusted his God would get him there—one last time. As the fifty-four year old made preparations to sail for America he had much to do in London in regard to the managing of his two chapels and their care after his departure. Deep inside he knew he would not see his London friends again—the parting was painful to him. He did not know, however, that he would have only one more year to live.

We see a gathering of "old friends" before this last voyage to America. From the following we observe:

"It is the last interview between Whitefield and Wesley that Wesley records in his journal on Monday (their old meeting day), February 27, 1769. He says, 'I had one more agreeable conversation with my old friend and fellow-labourer, George Whitefield. His soul appeared to be vigorous still, but his body was sinking apace; and unless God interposes with His mighty hand, he must soon finish his labours.' And this is a pleasant picture of the now aged, grey-headed evangelists, who in their youth had fired the nation with religious enthusiasm, which is sketched by Charles Wesley in a letter to his wife: 'Last Friday I dined with my brother at George's chapel. Mrs. Herritage was mistress, and provided the dinner. Hearty Mr. Adams was there; and to complete our band, Howell Harris. It was indeed a feast of love. My brother and George prayed: we all sang an hymn in the chapel.' They were never all together again in this world." [1]

Such was this remarkable and memorable scene! We will look at George Whitefield's labors up to his sailing for America in September of 1769. The record of his labors is quite astonishing as he began 1769 with unusual energy—he was preaching three times a week in London and was planning a

---

1   Gledstone, pp. 335–336.

"gospel range" to the country! The following are extracts from his correspondence at this time detailing the narrative of his labors:

"London, March 11, 1769 ... Through infinite mercy, I am enabled to preach thrice a week, besides other occasional exercises; and indeed (O amazing condescension!) the shout of the King of kings is amongst us. After Easter, I hope to make an elopement to *Gloucestershire*, and some western parts ...

"London, March 17, 1769 ... It is not time to think of leaving a *happy wilderness now*. There's more noise in great cities. I am every day, every hour, almost every moment, thinking of and preparing for *America*. A pilgrim life to me is the sweetest on this side eternity. I am daily expecting Bethesda accompts. I am daily waiting for the kingdom of GOD ...

"London, March 31, 1769. You will be glad to hear, that frequent preaching hath prevented writing. Through infinite mercy I have been enabled to preach four days successively. And indeed we have been favoured with a blessed passover season. All to make us shout louder and louder, Grace! Grace! I have some thoughts of making *Gloucestershire* my first excursion: but at present, the cloud abides over *London*. LORD JESUS, direct my goings in thy way! ...

"London, April 1, 1769 ... The shout of the King of kings is still heard in the midst of our Methodist camps; and the shout of Grace, grace! resounds from many quarters. Our almighty JESUS knows how to build his temple in troublous times. His work prospers in the hands of the elect Countess, who is now gone to *Bath*, much recovered from her late indisposition ...

"Bath, April 18, 1769. Hitherto GOD hath helped us. A good opening at *Chippenham*. A precious season here on Sunday morning. This evening I am to preach again. To-morrow, GOD willing, I shall set out for *Bristol* ...

"Bristol, May 4, 1769. This evening we are to have a love feast; yesterday had a good field preaching at *Kingswood*. The night before I preached here. GOD willing, to-morrow here again. Sunday morning at *Bradford*. Monday at *Frome*. Then *Chippenham,* and other parts of *Gloucestshire*. I designed to go to *Plymouth*, but I have such a cold, and the weather begins to be so warm, that I know not how the issue will be ..."[2]

It is interesting to note that the more Whitefield preached in the open air the more strength he seemed to gain! Also, the crowds were growing and growing just like old times. It is no wonder that he was excited beyond measure and pressing on despite his bad health and terrible chest cold. This man literally spent himself out for God—all before his challenging journey across rough seas!

"Frome, May 8, 1769 ... A blessed day yesterday in *Bradford* church. A blessed day here in the fields; thousands attended, all more than solemn ... Glorious

---

2   *Works*, Vol. 3, pp. 382–386.

prospect in these parts. Grace! Grace! I am now going to *Chippenham*, *Castlecomb*, *Dursley*, *Rodborough*, *Painswick*, *Gloucester*, *Cheltenam*, in my way to *London*. The west circuit must be deferred, on account of the opening of the chapel at *Tunbridge* ...

"Rodborough, May 11, 1769. Ebenezer, Ebenezer! Through infinite mercy, I just now arrived here. Blessed seasons at *Chippenham*, *Castlecomb and Dursley*, in our way from *Frome*. Have been enabled to preach five times this week. It is good to go into the highways and hedges. Field-preaching, field-preaching for ever! Cannot yet determine what course to steer next. At present a very heavy cold lies upon me. JESUS's warm love more than makes amends for all ..."3

The great evangelist is back in London by the middle of May and finished with his "country circuit". Great has been his labor and the results under the Hand of God. We see notice of a remarkable movement of God at Rodborough; he wrote:

"London, May 18, 1769 ... Through infinite mercy, we got safe to town. *Ebenezer, Ebenezer!* My cold is about the same as when we parted. But who knows what the Father of mercies may do for less than the least of all his children, by next Lord's-day morning? Perhaps we may be favoured with another *Rodborough* pentecost. Never was that place so endeared to me, as at this last visit. Old friends, old gospel wine, and the great Governor ordering to fill to the brim! ..."4

We see from the following correspondence that George Whitefield had worn himself out by travel and preaching and he was bed-ridden again. He stated on May 26th, "I suppose you have heard of my hoarseness, gotten through mercy, in the highways and hedges. A delightful spring campaign." He was still ill come June 10th, for he wrote, "This leaves me a little recovering from my late indisposition, consequently it leaves me singing ... *O happy, happy rod, That brought us hither to our GOD!*"

George Whitefield now turned his face toward America and began to settle his affairs in London. But before he set sail come September he had another remarkable season of blessed activity. We have this from the following account:

"One of his last public services was the opening of the Countess of Huntingdon's chapel at Tunbridge Wells. This took place on Sunday, July 23. The Countess, Lady Anne Erskine, Lady Buchan, and Miss Orton went with him. Early in the morning, a large number of persons assembled at the front of Lady Huntingdon's residence, and, in the open air, sang hymns and prayed, till the time announced for the commencement of public service in the chapel. 'Never, said her ladyship, 'can I forget the sensation of pleasure I felt, on being

---

3 Ibid. pp. 386–387.
4 Ibid. pp. 386–388.

awoke by the voice of praise and thanksgiving.' The chapel, of course, was
thronged. De Courcy read the prayers of the Established Church; and, then, a
large crowd not being able to get inside the chapel, Whitefield came out,
followed by those who had joined in the reading of the liturgy, and preached to
the assembled thousands, from 'How dreadful is this place! This is none other
but the house of God, and this is the gate of heaven.' The sermon was said to be
'a perfect piece of oratory.'

"'Look yonder!' cried the preacher, as he stretched out his hands 'Look
yonder! What is that I see? It is my agonizing Lord! Hark! Hark! Hark! Do not
you hear? O earth, earth, earth, hear the word of the Lord!' Simple words, but
producing effects which cannot be described. In connection with these and all
Whitefield's utterances, the reader must bear in mind that Whitefield's face was
language, his intonation music, and his action passion. Garrick used to say of
him, that he could make men weep or tremble by his varied pronunciation of
the word 'Mesopotamia.' This was an exaggeration; but it expressed the opinion
of the greatest of theatrical orators concerning the power of Whitefield's
eloquence."5

That day in May at Tunbridge Wells went down in history as a remarkable
day of the blessings of the Lord upon His people! George Whitefield had yet
to preach his farewell sermons at his London chapels! As his last days in Great
Britain were drawing to a close he prepared to say good-bye to his
congregations and friends. On a Friday evening in late August (the 25th) the
great evangelist performed one of his last sacramental services in his native
country. He gave out the sacrament to two thousand communicants at his
Moorfields Tabernacle.

The following Sunday was a momentous occasion for he preached his last
sermon to his beloved congregation in Tottenham Court Road chapel. Of
this memorable occasion we have the following description:

"The text was, Genesis xxviii. 12–15. A few extracts must be given. Besides
the interest they possess as being among Whitefield's *last words* in England, they
will help to illustrate his style of preaching, when his work was nearly ended.

'When we are travelling in the woods of America, we are obliged to light a
fire; and that keeps off the beasts from us. I have often got up in the night, and
said to them that were with me (and God forbid I should ever travel with any
one, even a quarter of an hour, without speaking something of Jesus!)—"This
fire," said I, "is like the fire of God's love which keeps off the devil and our
own lusts from hurting our souls."

'It comforts me much, I assure you, to think that, whenever God shall call
for me, angels will carry me into the bosom of Abraham; but it comforts me
more to think, that, as soon as they lay hold of me, my first question to them

5   Tyerman, Vol, 2, pp. 560–561.

will be, "Where is my *Master*? Where is my *Jesus*?" And that, after all my tossings and tumblings here, I shall be brought to see His face at last.

'It is now high time for me to preach my own *funeral sermon*. I am going, for the thirteenth time, to cross the Atlantic. When I came from America last, my health was so bad that I took leave of all friends on the continent, from one end to the other, without the least design of returning to them again. But, to my great surprise, God has been pleased to restore to me some measure of strength; and, though I intended to give up the Orphan House into other hands, God has so ordered it, that his Grace the late Archbishop of Canterbury refused me a charter, unless I would confine it to episcopacy. I could not, in honour, comply with this, as Dissenters, and other serious people of different denominations, had contributed towards its support. I would sooner cut off my head than betray my trust. I always meant the Orphan House to be kept upon a broad bottom, for people of all denominations. I hope, by the 25th of March next, all intended alterations and additions will be completed, and a blessed provision be made for many hundreds; and a comfortable support for poor orphans and poor students. This is my only design in going. I intend to travel all along the continent. I am going in no public capacity. I am going trusting in God to bear my charges. I call heaven and earth to witness that I have never had the love of the world one quarter of an hour in my heart. I might have been rich; but now, though this chapel is built, and though I have a comfortable room to live in, I assure you I built that room at my own expense. It cost nobody but myself anything, and I shall leave it with an easy mind. I have thought of these words with pleasure, "I will bring thee again to this land." I know not whether that will be my experience; but, blessed be God! I have a better land in view. I do not look upon myself at home till I land in my Father's house. My greatest trial is to part with those who are as dear to me as my own soul. O keep close to God, my dear London friends. I do not bid you keep close to chapel. You have always done that. I shall endeavour to keep up the word of God among you during my absence. I might have had a thousand a year out of this place, if I had chosen it. When I am gone to heaven, you will see what I have got on earth. I do not like to speak now, because it might be thought boasting.'[6]

One can be sure that faces were wet as their dear pastor said good-bye to them; they could tell by looking at his worn-out and dying frame that they would never see him again. He knew it as well and this made the parting of friends much harder. On these tearful scenes we see:

"Thus the only thing which really oppressed him, on leaving, was the pain of parting from his friends for a time. But this was nothing new with him. What he said now, he had said often; 'Oh these partings! Without a divine support they would be intolerable. Talk not of taking *personal* leave: you know my *make*. Paul could stand a *whipping*—but not a weeping farewell.'

6   Ibid. pp. 562–563.

"The parting scene at the Tabernacle and Tottenham Court was awful, and seems to have been repeated: for he says, in his own manuscript journal, that he preached on the vision of Jacob's ladder, at both places; and Winter says, that 'The Good Shepherd' was his farewell sermon. Indeed, Whitefield himself in a letter, calls this his 'last sermon.' Thus there must have been 'more last words' than his journal records. He himself was 'disgusted' with the manner in which this farewell sermon was reported and printed."[7]

One can only imagine in the mind's eye the scene of this great evangelist leaving England for the last time; on the docks there are coaches and chaises, weeping throngs waving good-bye to a man they have loved so dearly! On deck of the ship the *Friendship* the worn-out Whitefield raised his arm and in his hand was a white handkerchief which he waved tirelessly until he couldn't take the farewell any longer—he knew well the words which he spoke that "Paul could stand a *whipping* but not a weeping farewell." As he descended into his cabin with Richard Smith and Cornelius Winter (his traveling aides) he completed what God had for him in Great Britain and closed the door on all his vast labors in that land. Never again would he set eyes on his native land.

---

7   Philip, pp. 470–471.

This is the thirteenth time of my crossing the mighty waters. It is a little difficult at this time of life; but I delight in the cause, and God fills me with a peace that is unutterable. I expect many trials while on board. Satan always meets me there; but God, I believe, will keep me. I thank God, I have the honour of leaving everything quite well and easy at both ends of the town. If I am drowned, I will say, if I can, while I am drowning, "Lord, take care of my English friends!"

George Whitefield's last public remarks in England

CHAPTER 59

HIS SEVENTH AND LAST VISIT TO AMERICA

It was with a heavy heart, a worn-out physical frame, but with great expectations that George Whitefield set sail for America aboard the *Friendship* on September 4th, 1769. The Orphan House was on his mind—his desire was that it be established into a college—and it would be good to see his many friends in New England again and to take to the fields once more with "another Gospel range". The sea voyage was stormy and rough but God preserved his faithful servant who could remark upon disembarking in Charleston, South Carolina, "I am in better health than at the end of any voyage I have made for some years." In fact, he felt so rested he preached on the very day he landed! Whitefield and party landed at Charleston on November 30th, 1769 receiving a warm welcome from friends as well as several invitations to preach. Of this we have the following:

"Arriving at Charleston on Thursday, November 30, he commenced preaching on the following afternoon, and, for ten days, continued to delight and profit large congregations. Mr. Wright, his manager at Bethesda, met him; and, on Sunday, December 10, he and his party set sail for Georgia. Hence the following, addressed to Mr. Keen:—

'Charleston, December 9, 1769. So much company crowds in, that, together with my preaching every other day, etc., I have scarce the least leisure. To-morrow, I set off by water to Georgia, the roads being almost impassable by land. Mr. Wright is come to go with me, and acquaints me that all is in great forwardness at Bethesda.'

"The voyage to Savannah was made in an open boat. Cornelius Winter writes:—'We had a pleasant passage through the Sounds, and frequently went on shore, and regaled ourselves in the woods. The simplicity of the negroes, who rowed us, was very diverting. We stopped at a plantation called Port Royal, where we were most kindly refreshed and entertained; and safely arrived at Savannah on December 14. Mr. Whitefield was cheerful and easy, and seemed to have lost a weight of care.'"[1]

Such was the effect of his beloved Bethesda! In 1765 George Whitefield was quoted as saying, "My beloved Bethesda; surely the most delightfully situated place in all the southern parts of America." He might as well have added, "in all the world" for to him it was the happiest place on earth. What a contrast from a few months ago where the evangelist was barely able to preach once a week and now he preached for ten days straight in Charleston! The remarks of Cornelius Winter were true indeed for George Whitefield "seemed to have lost a weight of care." It is obvious that Whitefield's spirits had lifted since his arrival in America (he had suffered from depression on board the *Friendship*) and he felt physically better to plan a "gospel range." We confirm this from some correspondence of Whitefield at this time. Hence the following:

"Savannah, Dec. 24, 1769 ... I write this at my old friends Mr. Habersham's. I am to preach here this morning, and to-morrow, and purpose in a few days to pay a visit to *Charles-Town*. Blessed be GOD, all things are in a most promising way. But I am obliged to leave Mr. Winter behind, for the work's sake. Mr. Smith goes with me. He is attentive, hath behaved well, and been useful in the house. Never was I blessed with so many proper industrious workmen and helpers before. Grace! Grace! Next Wednesday I am fifty-five years old. GOD be merciful to me a sinner, a sinner, a sinner! As such, continue to pray, my dear steady friend, for,

Less than the least of all,

G.W."[2]

Two observations must be made at this time. 1. George Whitefield refered to Mr. Smith and compliments this young man's usefulness to him. This traveling aide was none other than Richard Smith the man who not only witnessed the death of Whitefield, in the manse at Newburyport, but in whose very arms the great evangelist died. 2. George Whitefield commented that in a week he was to turn fifty five. This would be his last birthday on earth and it is the sweet mercy of God that the evangelist got to celebrate it at his happiest location—The Orphan House. What a birthday party that must have been with all his beloved Orphan family around him!

George Whitefield wrote from his beloved Bethesda on January 11th the following letter of which some interesting extracts are taken regarding progress at the Orphan House:

1   Tyerman, Vol. 2, p. 573.
2   *Works*, Vol. 3, p. 411.

"Bethesda, Jan. 11, 1770 ... This prospect gives songs in the night; this makes *Georgia and Bethesda* to more than smile: and indeed you and yours would smile too, were you to see what a lasting foundation is laying for the support and education of many yet unborn. All admire the work already done. In a few months the topstone, I trust, will be brought forth, with shouting, Grace! Grace! In the mean while I must range northward ... If I thought you did not, or would not use your globes, I would beg them for our infant library. The increase of this colony is almost incredible. Real good, I trust, is doing; and a blessed door is opening for Mr. Winter's usefulness. Blessed be GOD! Blessed be GOD!

Less than the least of all,

G.W."[3]

We have a splendid description of the goings on at the Orphan House in January of 1770 from the following extracts:

"An official paper of the Georgia legislature will show the esteem in which Whitefield was held by that body.

'Commons House of Assembly, Monday, Jan. 29, 1770. Mr. Speaker reported, that he, with the house, having waited on the Rev. Mr. Whitefield, in consequence of his invitation, at the orphan-house academy, heard him preach a very suitable and pious sermon on the occasion; and with great pleasure observed the promising appearance of improvement towards the good purposes intended, and the decency and propriety of behavior of the several residents there; and were sensibly affected, when they saw the happy success which has attended Whitefield's indefatigable zeal for promoting the welfare of the province in general, and the orphan-house in particular. Ordered, that this report be printed in the Gazette.

John Simpson, Clerk.'

"In pursuance of this vote, we find in the Georgia Gazette as follows: 'Savannah, January 31, 1770. Last Sunday, his Excellency the Governor, Council, and Assembly, having been invited by the Rev. Mr. Whitefield, attended divine service in the chapel of the orphan-house academy, where prayers were read by the Rev. Mr. Ellington, and a very suitable sermon was preached by the Rev. Mr. Whitefield, from Zechariah 4:10, "For who hath despised the day of small things?" to the great satisfaction of the auditory; in which he took occasion to mention the many discouragements he met with, well known to many there, in carrying on the institution for upwards of thirty years past, and the present promising prospect of its future and more extensive usefulness. After divine service, the company were very politely entertained with a handsome and plentiful dinner; and were greatly pleased to see the useful improvements made in the house, the two additional wings of apartments for students, one hundred and fifty feet each in length, and other lesser buildings, in so much forwardness; and the whole executed with taste, and in so masterly a

---

3   Ibid. pp. 411–412.

manner; and being sensible of the truly generous and disinterested benefactions derived to the province through his means, they expressed their gratitude in the most respectful terms.'"4

This sermon preached by Bethesda's Founder is a wonderful example of George Whitefield's prowess as an orator and it reveals his many labors and obstacles in continuing the institution. It was preached on January 28th, 1770 at the Orphan House before the Governor, and Council, and the House of Assembly, in Georgia; this sermon is found in its entirety in Part One: chapter 16; Bethesda.

Because of this momentous and historical occasion we must include a more detailed description of the days' proceedings for it is a last glimpse of glory for the Orphan House with its Founder there in rare form amidst such a distinguished gathering. Henceforth we have the following description of this blessed day found in a letter addressed to someone in London by an attendee of this grand social function: we also get a glimpse of what the *inside* of Bethesda looked like. It is with great interest therefore that we read the following:

"Savannah, January 29, 1770, Monday morning.

"You would have been pleased to have been at the Orphan House Academy yesterday, where his Excellency our Governor, the Hon. the Council, and the Commons House of Assembly, were agreeably entertained in consequence of an invitation given them by the Founder, the Rev. Mr. Whitefield. Everything was conducted with much decency and order. His Excellency was received at the bottom door by the officers, orphans, and other domestics; and was then escorted upstairs by Mr. Whitefield, through a gallery near sixty feet long, into a large room thirty feet in length, with six windows, canvassed and made ready for blue paper hangings. In a room of the same extent over against it (intended for the library, and in which a considerable number of books is already deposited), was prepared, on a long table and adjacent side-board, cold tongue, ham, teas, etc., for the gentleman to refresh themselves with, after their ten miles' ride, from Savannah. Between eleven and twelve, the bell rung for public worship. A procession was formed in the long gallery, and moved forward to the chapel in the following order: The orphans, in round, black, flat caps, and black gowns; the chaplain in his gown; the workmen and assistants; the steward and superintendent, with their white wands; the clerk of the chapel; the Founder in his university square cap, with the Rev. Mr. Ellington, now missionary at Augusta, and designed to be chaplain, and teacher of English and elocution at the Orphan House Academy; then his Excellency, followed by his Council and the Chief Justice; then the Speaker, succeeded by the other Commons, and a number of gentlemen and strangers, among whom were the Governor's two sons. As the procession moved along, the clerk of the chapel began a doxology, the singing of

---

4   Belcher, pp. 423–425.

which was harmonious and striking. At the chapel door, the orphans, officers, and domestics broke into ranks on the right hand and the left; and, as his Excellency with his train went up the chapel stairs, the orphans sang,—

'Live by heaven and earth ador'd,
Three in One, and One in Three,
Holy, holy, holy Lord
All glory be to Thee!'

"The Governor being seated fronting the chapel door, in a great chair, with tapestry hangings behind, and a covered desk before him, divine service began. Mr. Ellington read prayers; and then Mr. Whitefield enlarged, for about three-quarters of an hour, on 'The hands of Zerubbabel have laid the foundation of this house; his hands shall also furnish it; and thou shalt know that the Lord of hosts hath sent me unto you. For who hath despised the day of small things?' (Zech. iv. 9, 10.) His whole paraphrase was pertinent and affecting; but when he came to give us an account of the small beginnings of our now flourishing Province, of which he was an eye-witness; and also of the trials and hardships, obloquy and contempt, he had undergone in maintaining, for so long a term, such a numerous orphan family, in such a desert; as well as the remarkable supports and providences that had attended him in laying the foundation, and raising the superstructure of the Orphan House Academy to its present promising height; especially when he came to address his Excellency, the Council, Speaker, etc., etc.,—the whole auditory seemed to be deeply affected; and his own heart seemed too big to speak, and unable to give itself proper vent. Sermon being ended, all returned in the same manner as they came, the clerk, orphans, etc., singing as they walked,—

'This God is the God we adore,
Our faithful, unchangeable friend,
Whose love is as large as His power,
And neither knows measure nor end.
'Tis Jesus, the first and the last,
Whose Spirit shall guide us safe home;
We'll praise Him for all that is past,
And trust Him for all that's to come.'

"In about half an hour the bell rung for dinner. All went down, in order, to a large dining room, intended hereafter for academical exercises. It is forty feet long, with eight sash windows, and the Founder's picture, at full length, at the upper end. Two tables, the one long and the other oval, were well covered with a proper variety of plain and well-dressed dishes. After dinner, two toasts were given by his Excellency, viz., 'The King,' and 'Success to the Orphan House College.' The whole company broke up, and went away, in their several carriages, about five in the afternoon. One thing gave me particular pleasure: when the Governor drank, 'The King,' Mr. Whitefield added, 'And let all the people say, Amen;' upon which a loud amen was repeated from one end of the room to the other.

"Upon the whole, all seemed most surprisingly pleased with their spiritual and bodily entertainment, as well as with the elegance, firmness, and dispatch of the late repairs, and additional buildings and improvements. The situation is most salubrious and inviting; the air free and open; and a salt-water creek, which will bring up a large schooner east and west, ebb and flows at a small distance from the house. I suppose there might be above twenty carriages, besides horsemen; and there would have been as many more, had not the invitation been confined, by way of compliment, to the Governor, Council, and Commons House of Assembly. A strange sight this, in the once despised, deserted Province of Georgia, where, as Mr. Whitefield told us in his discourse, about thirty years ago, scarce any person of property lived; and lands, which now sell for £3 an acre, might have been purchased almost for threepence.

"But I must have done. Excuse me for being so prolix. Yesterday's scene so lies before me, that, to tell you the truth, I wanted to vent my feelings. If Mr. Whitefield intends, as I am informed he does, to give a more general invitation to the gentlemen in and about Savannah, I will endeavour to be amongst them. Accept this hasty scribble (as I hear the ship sails to-morrow), as a mark of my being, dear sir, your obliged friend and servant."[5]

Regarding this "more general invitation" Whitefield placed an advertisement in the local newspaper. Here is an extract from the *Georgia Gazette:*

"Bethesda, January 29, 1770. A more particular application being impracticable, the Rev. Mr. Whitefield takes this method of begging the favour of the company of as many gentlemen and captains of ships in and about Savannah, as it may suit to accept this invitation, to dine with him at the Orphan House Academy next Sunday. Public service to begin exactly at eleven o'clock."

GEORGE WHITEFIELD."

It is to our loss that no record of this second memorable event exists. It is important at this time to include a letter which George Whitefield wrote to his old friend Charles Wesley. The letter is valuable for several reasons including its warm-heartedness towards Wesley and the fact that this was the very last letter Whitefield wrote to Charles Wesley. The letter acknowledges their more than thirty year friendship. Here now is this important letter:

"Bethesda, January 15, 1770.

"MY VERY DEAR OLD FRIEND,—I wrote to your honoured brother from on board ship. Since then what wonders have I seen! What innumerable mercies have I received!—a long, trying, but, I humbly hope, profitable passage.

"My poor, feeble labours were owned in Charlestown; and everything is more than promising in Georgia. The increase of this once so much despised

5   Tyerman, Vol. 2, pp. 575–577.

colony is indescribable. Good, I trust, is doing at Savannah, and Bethesda is like to blossom as the rose; the situation most delightful, very salubrious, and everything excellently adapted for the intended purpose. All admire the goodness, strength, and beauty of the late improvements. In a few months, the intended plan, I hope, will be completed, and a solid, lasting foundation laid for the support and education of many as yet unborn. Nothing is wanted but a judicious and moderately learned single-hearted master. Surely the glorious Emmanuel will point out one in His own due time. Do pray. I am sure, prayers put up above thirty years ago are now being answered; and, I am persuaded, we shall yet see greater things than these. Who would have thought that such a worthless creature as this letter-writer should live to be fifty-five years old? I can only sit down and cry, 'What hath God wrought!' My bodily health is much improved, and my soul is on the wing for another gospel range.

"You and all your connexions will not cease to pray for me. I would fain begin to do something for my God. My heart's desire and incessant prayer to the God of my life is, that the word of the Lord may prosper in your hands, and run and be glorified more and more. O to work while it is day! O to be found on the full stretch for Him who was stretched and who groaned, and bled, and died for us! Unutterable love! I am lost in wonder and amazement, and, therefore, although with regret, I must hasten to subscribe myself, my very dear sir, less than the least of all,

GEORGE WHITEFIELD.

"P.S. Cordial love awaits your whole self, and enquiring friends, and all that love the ever-living, altogether-lovely Jesus in sincerity. I hope to write to your honoured brother soon. Brethren, pray for us."[6]

Since the purpose of George Whitefield's last visit to America was primarily to settle the Orphan House accounts and prepare this institution for it's transformation into a college we will take a look at several facts relating to his beloved Bethesda and then examine George Whitefield's proposed "rules" for the students of the new college. There is much of interest and history in each account. First, we notice that George Whitefield and Thomas Dixon (the manager of Bethesda) appeared before "the Honourable Noble Jones, Esq., Senior Assistant Justice for the Province of Georgia," for the "purpose of being sworn that the Orphan House accounts" were in order from 1765 to the present (1770). This notable document contains a complete balance and income statement for the Orphan House which had been built thirty years earlier and had been continuously maintained. It is interesting to note that "not a penny had been paid out of the general fund to either Whitefield or any of his managers; and Whitefield himself, out of his own private means, had contributed £3,299!" This document stood against any false

---

6   *Life of Charles Wesley*, Vol. 2, p. 244.

claims that George Whitefield had enriched himself through public collections for the Orphan House.

Also of interest is the following:

"During the thirty years that had elapsed since the Orphan House was built, 140 boys and 43 girls had been 'clothed, educated, maintained, and suitably provided for;' and, besides these, 'many other poor children had been *occasionally* received, educated and maintained.'

"The Orphan House family now consisted of *whites*: Managers and carpenters, 9; boys, 15; girl, 1; total, 25. And of *negroes*: Men 24, of whom 16 were fit for any labour; 7 old, but capable of some service; and 1 so old as to be useless; women, 11, of whom 8 were capable of the usual labour; 2 old, but able to assist in the business of the house; and 1 almost incapable of any service; children 15, all employed as far as their strength permitted; total, 50.

"The lands granted to Whitefield, in *trust* for his Orphan House, were a tract of 500 acres, called Bethesda, on which the Orphan House was erected; another of 419 acres, called Nazareth; a third of 419 acres, called Ephratah, on which were the principal planting improvements; and a fourth of 500 acres, adjoining Ephratah, and called Huntingdon. Besides these, three other tracts, amounting to 2,000 acres, and contiguous to the former, had been granted to him *in trust*, for the endowment of his College.

"As one object of Whitefield's present visit to America was to start his College, or, to speak more properly, his Academy, he drew up a set of Rules, to be observed by the inmates of his establishment, of which the following is a summary:—

1. Morning Prayer was to begin constantly, every day in the year, at half-past five o 'clock. Evening Prayer every night. On every Sunday, besides a short prayer with a psalm or hymn early in the morning, full Prayers and a Sermon at ten; the same at three in the afternoon; a short prayer and a hymn at half-past six in the evening; the first Lesson to be read at dinner; the same at supper; and a short hymn at each meal.

2. Great care to be taken, that all read, write, speak, and behave properly.

3. All the statutes to be read to every student at admission, and thrice a year, at Easter, Whitsuntide, and Christmas, publicly.

4. No cards, dice, or gaming of any kind to be allowed, on pain of expulsion; and no music but divine psalmody.

5. All to be taught *Bland's Manual Exercise*, but not bound to attend on musters or other exercises, unless on account of an alarm.

6. No one to be suffered to run into arrears for above half a year; and a certain amount of caution money to be paid.

7. All students to furnish their own rooms, and to sleep on mattresses.

8. No one suffered to go to Savannah without leave.

9. Breakfast at seven; dinner at twelve; supper at six, through all the year; and the utmost neatness to be observed and maintained in every room.

10. All orphans and students to learn and repeat the Thirty-nine Articles.

11. The Homilies to be read publicly, every year, by the students in rotation.

12. All to be thoroughly instructed in the history of Georgia, and the constitution of England, before being taught the history of Greece and Rome.

13. The young negro boys to be baptized and taught to read; the young negro girls to be taught to work with the needle.

14. The following divinity books to be read:—The Commentaries of Henry, Doddridge, Guise, Burkit, and Clarke; Wilson's Dictionary, Professor Francke's Manuductio, Doddridge's Rise and Progress, Boston's Fourfold State, and his book on the Covenant, Jenks on the Righteousness of Christ, and also his Meditations, Hervey's Theron and Aspasio, Hall's Contemplations, and other works, Edward's Preacher, Trapp on the Old and New Testament, Poole's Annotations, Warner's Tracts, Leighton's Comment on the first Epistle of Peter, Pearson on the Creed, Edwards' Veritas Redux, and Owen and Bunyan's Works."[7]

To say that Whitefield ran a tight ship is an understatement! All of this, of course, was an outflow of the "Oxford Methodists" and their strict disciplines which they placed upon themselves. If John Wesley were to have begun a college his list of "rules" would more than likely been the same or similar. Such was religious training back in the eighteenth century!

With the auditing of Bethesda's accounts behind him and the hope in his heart of the Orphan House becoming a useful College, George Whitefield left Savannah and traveled to Charleston where he labored for a month—preaching almost every day! We will now begin the narrative of his labors as he preached his way northward to New England. Using his correspondence from this time we will use extracts to form "the narrative" of his labors during this last year of his life. These letters reveal, how at the end of his life, the great evangelist viewed himself—"unworthy worm, less than the least of all" and so forth, all speaking of his great humility! Here now is the narrative of his last labors:

"Charles-Town, Feb. 10, 1770 ... Through infinite mercy, this leaves me enjoying a greater share of bodily health than I have known for many years. I am now enabled to preach almost every day and my poor feeble labours seem not to be in vain in the LORD ... Since my being in *Charles-Town*, I have shewn the draught to some persons of great eminence and influence ... and as my name is

7 Tyerman, Vol. 2, pp. 581–583.

to be annihilated, they may accept the trust without expecting much trouble, or suffering contempt for being connected with me ...

Less then the least of all,

G.W.

"Charles-Town, Feb. 22, 1770 ... I have been in *Charles-Town* near a fortnight, am to preach at a neighbouring country parish church next Sunday, and hope to see *Georgia* the week following ... I am blessed with bodily health, and an enabled to go on my way rejoicing. Grace! Grace! ... I am happier than words can express: which I take, in a great measure, to be owing to the prayers of my dear *English* friends, which are daily put up for, and I hope daily returned by, an unworthy worm ...

Less then the least of all,

G.W.

"Charles-Town, Feb. 27, 1770 ... All things at Bethesda go on quite well. My bodily health is upon the advance, and the word, I trust, runs and is glorified ... Next week, GOD willing, I return to *Georgia*, and soon after I purpose to go northward ... O this pilgrim way of life! To me it is life indeed! ... Ere long we shall sing,

All our sorrows left below,
And earth exchang'd for heav'n.

Less than the least of all,

G.W.

"Charles-Town, March 4, 1770 ... It leaves me almost ready to return to Bethesda, from a place where, I trust, the word hath run and been glorified. Matters are now drawing near to a wished-for close. All things have succeeded beyond my most sanguine expectation. I expect to come according to the appointed time. But future things belong to Him who orders all things well. Through mercy I enjoy more bodily health than for many years last past. You will join in crying, Grace! Grace! Next month, I purpose moving to the northward. As Mr. Wright is the main spring at the Orphan-house, I must leave him behind. Mr. Smith is with me: he behaves well, and is diligent and attentive ...

Less than the least of all,

G.W."[8]

Whitefield returned to Savannah the second week of March and resumed his duties at the Orphan House; though his face was now set northward and to his New England friends. He remained at Bethesda until the 24th of April.

---

8 *Works,* Vol. 3, pp. 413–416.

We must pause and picture him there amongst his beloved orphan family, in his study at Bethesda planning his northern spring campaign, this would be his last enjoyments at the Orphan House. The quietude of the majestic oaks lining the peaceful plantation which lay on the still backwaters of the river; Bethesda was more than a life-work to Whitefield—it was *his home*. This would be the last time he ever saw it again. Let us follow him from the letters which he wrote there from this place of tranquility and peace:

"Savannah, March 11, 1770. Blessed be GOD, the good wine seemed to be kept till the last at *Charles-Town*. Last Thursday I returned, and found all well at Bethesda. I am come to town to preach this morning, though somewhat fatigued with being on the water three nights: upon the whole, however, I am better in health than I have been for many years. Praise the LORD, O my soul!

Less than the least of all,

G.W.

"Bethesda, April 6, 1770. I am waiting here for a brig that is to carry me northward, and for a letter and news from *England* ... How glad would many be to see our Goshen, our Bethel, our Bethesda! Never did I enjoy such domestic peace, comfort, and joy during my whole pilgrimage. It is unspeakable, it is full of glory. Peace, peace unutterable attends our paths, and a pleasing prospect of increasing, useful prosperity is continually rising to our view. I have lately taken six poor children, and, GOD willing, purpose to add greatly to their number ...

Less than the least of all,

G.W.

"Bethesda, April 16, 1770. HALLELUJAH! Praise the LORD! The books and letters both by Ball and Sunbury, are come safe ... Mr. Smith (the clerk) was much rejoiced by receiving a letter. Next week, GOD willing, we sail for *Philadelphia*. I shall leave letters behind me to come by Mr. D——n. All is well, all more than well here! Never, never did I enjoy such an era of domestic peace and happiness. I have taken in about ten orphans. Prizes! Prizes! *Hallelujah!* Join, my very dear friends, join in praising Him whose mercy endureth for ever. If possible, I shall write a line to the Welch brethren. They have sustained a loss indeed, in the death of Mr. Howell Davies. GOD sanctify it! Surely my turn will come by and by ...

Less than the least of all,

G.W."9

Little did Whitefield realize that in just five months he would be dead. It is surely the mercy and good pleasure of God that he gave the great evangelist a season of peace and good health before his time came! Reading these letters

---

9 Ibid. pp. 417–418.

one is struck with the mention of his never before domestic happiness—this is a revealing statement concerning his marriage and his now deceased wife Elizabeth. He should never have married for he was married to God. Now back to his Edenic existence while at Bethesda:

"Bethesda, April 20, 1770 ... We enjoy a little heaven upon earth here. With regret I go northward, as far as *Philadelphia* at least, next Monday. Though I am persuaded, as the house is now altered, I should be cooler here, during the summer's heat, than at any other place I know of, where I used to go ... Everything concurs to shew me, that Bethesda affairs must go on as yet in their old channel. A few months may open strange scenes. O for a spirit of love and moderation on all sides, and on both sides the water! I wish some books might be procured for our infant library. But more of this in my next. Letters may now be sent by way of *Boston, New York, and Philadelphia*. I should be glad to hear often, if it be but a line. In all probability I shall not return hither till November. Was ever any man blest with such a set of skillful, peaceful, laborious helpers! O *Bethesda*, my *Bethel*, my *Peniel*! My happiness is inconceivable. A few hundreds, besides what is already devoted, would finish all. I do not in the least doubt. I have had nine or ten prizes lately. You know what I mean. Nine or ten orphans have been lately taken in. *Hallelujah! Hallelujah!* Let Chapel, Tabernacle, heaven, and earth, rebound with *Hallelujah!* I can no more. My heart is too big to speak or add more, than my old name,

Less than the least of all,

G.W.

"Bethesda, April 21, 1770 ... This comes to inform you, that the Father of mercies hath not forgotten to be gracious to the chief of sinners, and less than the least of all saints. On the contrary, he daily loads us with his benefits. Bethesda is a place, that the LORD doth and will bless. Dear Mr. D——n and his wife, will inform you of particulars. Among other things, they will tell you of our new chapel. I have sent for sundries for its use and completion. O help me to praise Him, whose loving kindness is better than life!

Less than the least of all,

G.W.

"Bethesda, April, 21, 1770. No such good news yet. Less than the least of all, is not drowned to this very day. Perhaps he may live to see his *London* friends in *England*, or at *Bethesda*. How would many rejoice to be in such a peaceful, commodious, and comfortable habitation! I cannot tell you half. Blessed be GOD, I was never better, at this season of the year, in bodily health; never more comfortable in my soul. Grace! Grace! *Hallelujah!* Praise the LORD! ... Happy Bethesda! ...

Less than the least of all,

G.W.

"Bethesda, April 21, 1770 ... My bodily strength seems to be renewed, and every thing at Bethesda is in a most promising way ... Never did I spend such a comfortable domestic winter, as the last ...

Less than the least of all,

G.W.

"Savannah, April 24, 1770, five in the morning. I am just going into the boat, in order to embark for *Philadelphia* ... Such a set of helpers I never met with. They will go on with the buildings, while I take my gospel range to the northward. It is for thee, O JESUS, even for thee, thou never-failing *Bethesda*'s GOD! But I can do no more at present ...

Less than the least of all,

G.W."[10]

We catch up with George Whitefield in Philadelphia in the month of May. He was still enjoying good health and he was glad to see his New England friends. There are three existing letters that George Whitefield wrote while in Philadelphia in 1770, here are some extracts from them:

"Philadelphia, May, 9, 1770. This leaves me a two days inhabitant of *Philadelphia*. I embarked at *Savannah*, in the *Georgia* packet, on the 24th and arrived here the 6th instant. The evening following, I was enabled to preach to a large auditory, and am to repeat the delightful task this evening. Pulpits hearts, and affections, seem to be as open and enlarged towards me, as ever ... As yet I have my old plan in view, to travel in these northern parts all summer, and return late in the fall to *Georgia* ... Through infinite mercy, I still continue in good health, and more and more in love every day with a pilgrim life ...

Less than the least of all,

G.W.

"Philadelphia, May 24, 1770 ... I have now been here near three weeks, and in about a week more I purpose to set off for *New-York* in my way to *Boston*. A wide and effectual door, I trust, hath been opened in this city. People of all ranks flock as much as ever. Impressions are made on many, and I trust they will abide. To all the episcopal churches, as well as most of the other places of worship, I have free access. My bodily health is preserved, and notwithstanding I preach twice on the Lord's-day, and three or four times a week besides, yet I am rather better than I have been for many years. This is the LORD's doing. To this long-suffering, never-failing LORD, be all the glory! ...

Less than the least of all,

G.W.

10 Ibid. pp. 418–422.

"Philadelphia, June 14, 1770. This leaves me just returned from a hundred and fifty miles circuit, in which, blessed be GOD! I have been enabled to preach every day. So many new as well as old doors are open, and so many invitations sent from various quarters, that I know not which way to turn myself. However, at present I am bound to *New-York*, and so on further northward. Help me to praise Him whose mercy endureth for ever. As yet I am enabled to ride and travel cheerfully; the heat not greater than yours in *England* ... The ship I find is going ...

Less than the least of all,

G.W."[11]

It is remarkable to find the great evangelist in such rare form and physical strength to where he was preaching nearly every day! In addition to this he seemed to be able to ride a horse! This was a far cry from the invalid who in England could barely ride in a post chaise and preach once a week! Of the reception George Whitefield received in Philadelphia we have some following observations:

"Whilst Whitefield was rejoicing over Georgia, applications were pouring in upon him from all quarters, to hasten again to the cities and wildernesses of America. He hardly knew which call was loudest, or 'which way to turn' himself. He went, however, first to Philadelphia, after having preached the gospel fully in Savannah. On his arrival he found, he says, 'pulpits, hearts, affections as open and enlarged as ever' towards him. Philadelphia could not have given him a more cordial welcome, had she even foreseen that she was to see his face no more: for all the churches as well as the chapels were willingly opened to him, and all ranks vied in flocking to hear him. This free access to the episcopal churches delighted him much, wherever it occurred. He never fails to record both his gratitude and gratification, when he obtains, on any tour, access even to one church. It always did him *good* too. I have often been struck with this, whilst tracing his steps. True; he was at *home* wherever there were souls around him; but he was most at home in a church, except, indeed, when he had a mountain for his pulpit, and the heavens for his sounding-board, and half a county for his congregation. Then, neither St. Paul's nor Westminster had any attractions for him. The fact is, Whitefield both admired and loved the liturgy. He had the spirit of its compilers and of its best prayers in his own bosom, and therefore it was no *form* to him. It had been the channel upon which the first mighty spring-tides of his devotion flowed, and the chief medium of his communion with heaven, when he was most successful at Tottenham Court and Bath. All his great 'days of the Son of Man' there, were associated with the church service. He was, therefore, most in his element *with* it; although he was often equally and more successful *without* it. Accordingly, it would be difficult to say, whether the gospel triumphed most, at this time, in the churches or the chapels of Philadelphia. His prayers for the outpouring of the Holy Spirit went,

11 Ibid. pp. 422–424.

in an equally 'direct line, to heaven,' and were equally answered, whether with or without book."[12]

From Philadelphia the great evangelist took upon himself one of his largest American campaigns; his labor was indefatigable and his old passions for lost souls enlarged as he preached through the colony of New York. God's Hand was upon him and the impact of his preaching was astounding. It was the last fire of the comet as it blazed toward earth—never to blaze again. But what an impact it made when it landed! We catch some of the excitement from a letter he wrote from New York in July to his old friend Robert Keen. The letter is as follows:

"New-York, July 29, 1770. Since my last, and during this month, I have been above a five hundred miles circuit, and have been enabled to preach and travel through the heat every day. The congregations have been very large, attentive, and affected, particularly at *Albany, Schenecdady, Great Barrington, Norfolk, Salisbury, Sharon, Smithfield, Powkeepsy, Fishkill, New Rumburt, New Windsor, and Peckshill.* Last night I returned hither, and hope to set out for *Boston* in two or three days. O what a new scene of usefulness is opening in various parts of this new world! All fresh work, where I have been. The divine influence hath been as at the first. Invitations crowd upon me both from ministers and people, from many, many quarters.

"A very peculiar providence led me lately to a place, where a horse-stealer was executed. Thousands attended. The poor criminal had sent me several letters, hearing I was in the country. The Sheriff allowed him to come and hear a sermon under an adjacent tree. Solemn, solemn! After being by himself about an hour, I walked half a mile with him to the gallows. His heart had been softened before my first visit. He seemed full of solid divine consolations. An instructive walk. I went up with him into the cart. He gave a short exhortation. I then stood upon the coffin, added, I trust, a word in season, prayed, gave the blessing, and took my leave. Effectual good, I hope, was done to the hearers and spectators. Grace! Grace! But I must not enlarge. The Ship is going, and I keep at home to write this ... traveling and preaching entirely prevent my writing as I would. All are continually remembered by, my very dear friend,

Less than the least of all,

G.W."[13]

The scene described of George Whitefield standing upon the coffin while the doomed man faced the gallows is strong! There is evidence here in the above quoted letter as to why the *volume* of his correspondence is so slight during these last few months of his life—he was busy "traveling and preaching" which reveals that these activities "entirely prevent my writing

12 Philip, pp. 491–492.
13 *Works*, Vol. 3, pp. 424–425.

as I would." We wish there were more letters describing the incredible scenes of his preaching activities but we must be thankful for what exists! Regarding this five hundred mile circuit we have some interesting anecdotes from the following:

"While traveling this 'five hundred miles' circuit,' Whitefield, one day, dined, with a number of ministers, at the manse of his old friend, the Rev. William Tennent. After dinner, as often happened, Whitefield expressed his joy at the thought of soon dying and being admitted into heaven; and, then, appealing to the ministers present, he asked if his joy was shared by them. Generally they assented; but Tennent continued silent. 'Brother Tennent,' said Whitefield, 'you are the oldest man among us. Do you not rejoice that your being called home is so near at hand?' 'I have no wish about it,' bluntly answered Tennent. Whitefield pressed his question, and Tennent again replied, 'No, sir, it is no pleasure to me at all; and, if you knew your duty, it would be none to you. I have nothing to do with death. My business is to live as *long* as I can, and as *well* as I can.' Whitefield was not satisfied, and a third time urged the good old man to state, whether he would not choose to die, if death were left to his own choice. 'Sir,' answered Tennent, 'I have no choice about it. I am God's servant, and have engaged to do His business as long as He pleases to continue me therein. But now, brother Whitefield, let me ask you a question. What do you think I would say, if I were to send my man Tom into the field to plough, and if at noon I should find him lounging under a tree, and complaining, 'Master, the sun is hot, and the ploughing hard, and I am weary of my work, and overdone with heat: do, master, let me go home and rest'? What would I say? Why that he was a lazy fellow, and that it was his business to do the work I had appointed him, until I should think fit to call him home.' For the present, at least, Whitefield was silenced, and was taught, that it is every Christian man's duty to say, 'All the days of my appointed time will I wait till my change come.'"[14]

Three more anecdotes must be included of Whitefield during this last trip to America. Each typifies his eloquence and oratory skills. The first is as follows:

"Whitefield was the 'old man eloquent.' In July, 1770, he visited Sharon, Conn. There was some opposition to him, and yet Rev. Cotton Mather Smith, a descendant of Cotton Mather, invited him into his pulpit, and he preached on his favorite theme, the *New Birth*, from 'Ye must be born again.' The sermon was preached to an immense multitude with astonishing power and eloquence, and there was a moving and a melting time. He thus concluded his eloquent discourse: 'Awake, O north wind, and come, thou south; blow upon this garden that the spices thereof may flow out. Let my beloved come into this garden, and eat his pleasant fruits.' The sermon made a life-time impression on those who heard it. It was an era in the history of the place, and was talked of as a day of wonder till that generation had passed away. So impressed were the people of Sharon with his great oratorical powers that it is no wonder they followed him

---

14 Tyerman, Vol. 2, pp. 590–591.

into the adjoining towns for several successive days in order to hear him again and again."[15]

The second anecdote speaks of his ability to move an entire congregation with his pathos. In this story George Whitefield used a thunderstorm to wax eloquent!

"The grander the occasion the more sublime was Whitefield. The majestic thunder, the vivid lightning, the terrific storm fired his soul, and inspired him with sentiments grand, sublime, and magnificent. On such occasions he transcended himself, and was superlatively eloquent.

"At one time Whitefield was preaching in Boston, his theme being, 'The Wonders of Creation, Providence, and Redemption.' The theme was grand, and the sermon of almost unrivaled sublimity. In the midst of the discourse a violent storm arose, the clouds gathered thick and heavy, the rain descended in torrents, the lightnings flashed, deep-toned thunder rolled over their heads. The audience was deeply affected. They were awe-stricken, and anxiety was depicted on every countenance.

"He closed his book and went into one of the wings of the pulpit, and kneeling down, he with the deepest feeling and exquisite taste repeated,

'Hark, the Eternal rends the sky!
A mighty voice before him goes—
A voice of music to his friends,
But threat'ning thunder to his foes:
Come, children, to your Father's arms;
Hide in the chambers of my grace
Till the fierce storm be overblown,
And my revenging fury cease.'

"Then said he, 'Let us rise and devoutly sing to the praise and glory of God this hymn to the tune of "Old Hundred."' The whole audience instantly arose and poured forth the sacred song in a style of simple grandeur and heartfelt devotion seldom equaled, perhaps never surpassed. By the time they had finished singing the hymn the storm was over, the rain had ceased, the thunders were hushed, the lightnings still, the clouds were dispersed, and the sun shone forth in beauty and splendor. He proceeded with the remainder of the services, which were calculated to still further deepen the impressions made by the storm. He then pronounced the benediction, which the audience received with devotional feelings, and hearts overflowing with gratitude to the God of creation, whose wonders they had been called upon to contemplate."[16]

This last anecdote of George Whitefield involves an aged elm tree on the campus of Harvard College.

Regarding this magnificent ancient elm we have the following story:

15 Wakeley, pp. 357–358.
16 Ibid. pp. 358–360.

"It has defied the storms of hundreds of winters. It is a curiosity not only on account of its antiquity, but also for the historical incidents which cluster around it. Under its branches Washington first drew his sword and took command of the armies of the Revolution. Hence it is called the 'Washington Elm.' But it is also the Whitefield Elm, Whitefield having on one occasion when on a visit to Cambridge preached under its shade a sermon of uncommon brilliancy and power to the multitudes who had gathered to hear the man who was the wonder of those times.

"When the late Dr. Holyoke, of Salem—then nearly a hundred years old—visited Cambridge for the last time, he, while passing this tree with a friend, remarked that he had, when a student in Harvard College, heard the sermon Whitefield delivered under that tree. Washington and his army and Whitefield and his audience have long since passed away, but the old tree still stands in all its original grandeur, a living monument to true patriotism and genuine eloquence."[17]

From New York, at the end of July, Whitefield began which was to be his *last circuit*. It was a whirlwind of activity and the further he traveled north and the more frequently he preached the sicker he became—he was dying and this was his last blaze of glory before he died out. We will present his itinerary and then some letters he wrote toward the last days of his life. First, we will display his remarkable record of last labor:

"Whitefield sailed from New York on Tuesday, July 31st, and arrived at New Port on the Friday following. With the exception of six days, on five of which he was seriously ill, he preached daily until he died. From August 4th to 8th inclusive, he preached at New Port; August 9th to 12th, at Providence; August 13th, at Attleborough; and 14th, at Wrentham. With the exception of the 19th, when he discoursed at Malden, he officiated every day at Boston, from the 15th to the 25th. On August 26th, he preached at Medford; on the 27th, at Charlestown; and on the 28th, at Cambridge. The next two days were employed at Boston; August 31st, at Roxbury Plain; September 1st, at Milton; 2nd, at Roxbury; 3rd, at Boston; 5th, at Salem; 6th, at Marble Head; 7th, at Salem; 8th, at Cape Ann; 9th; at Ipswich; 10th and 11th, at Newbury Port; and 12th and 13th, at Rowley. On the 14th and two following days, he was disabled by violent diarrhoea. From September 17th to 19th, he again preached at Boston; and on the 20th, at Newton. The next two days he was ill, but managed to travel from Boston to Portsmouth, where he preached on the 23rd to the 25th. The 26th, he employed at Kittery; the 27th, at Old York; the 28th, at Portsmouth; and the 29th, at Exeter. At six o'clock in the morning of the 30th, he died."[18]

From Dr. John Gillies record of this last circuit of labor we have the following observations:

"From the 17th to the 20th of September, Whitefield preached every day in

17   Ibid. p. 310.
18   Tyerman, Vol. 2, pp. 592–593.

Boston; on the 20th of September, at Newton; and proceeded from Boston, September the 21st, on an excursion to the eastward, although at the time indisposed. At Portsmouth, in New Hampshire, he preached daily from the 23rd to the 29th of September; also once at Kittery, and once at York; and, on Saturday morning, September 29th, he set out for Boston; but before he came to Newburyport, where he had engaged to preach next morning, he was importuned to preach by the way, at Exeter. At the last he preached in the open air, to accommodate the multitudes that came to hear him, no house being able to contain them. He continued his discourse nearly two hours, by which he was greatly fatigued; notwithstanding which in the afternoon, he set off for Newburyport, where he arrived that evening; and soon after retired to rest, being Saturday night, fully intent on preaching the next day. His rest was much broken, and he awoke many times in the night, and complained very much of an oppression at his lungs, breathing with much difficulty. And at length, about six o'clock on the Lord's day morning, he departed this life, in a fit of asthma. Thus died this faithful laborer in the gospel vineyard, who finished his course with joy, and is now singing the praises of that Jesus whom he so many years delighted to preach."[19]

We will now look at the great evangelist's last labors in life through *his eyes* taken from his correspondence. Even though it is an incomplete record as it consists of only two letters (the last being written on Sept. 23rd—he died the 30th) it will serve as a narrative of his last labors in his own words. Here now are those two last letters, the first written to Mr. Wright of the Orphan House, it is a tender love letter to his dear orphan family, the second letter is written to Robert Keen in London. We read with great interest:

"Boston, Sept. 17, 1770. I am afraid, as Mr. E——n mentioned your writing, that you letter hath miscarried. But, blessed be GOD! I find all was well; only I want to know what things are wanted, that I might order them from *Philadelphia*, by Captain Souder. Fain would I contrive to come by him, but people are so importunate for my stay in these parts, that I fear it will be impracticable. LORD JESUS, direct my goings in thy way! He will, he will! My GOD will supply all my wants, according to the riches of his grace in CHRIST JESUS. By a letter, received last night from Mr. W——y, of July 5, I find that Mr. D——n was arrived, Anderson sailed, and that all orders would be immediately complied with. Two or three evenings ago, I was taken in the night with a violent lax, attended with retching and shivering, so that I was obliged to return from *Newbury*, &c. &c.; but, through infinite mercy, I am restored, and to-morrow morning hope to begin to begin again. Never was the word received with greater eagerness than now. All opposition seems as it were for a while to cease. I find GOD's time is the best. The season is critical as to outward circumstances. But when sorts are given up, the LORD JESUS can appoint salvation for walls and for bulwarks; he hath promised to be a wall of fire round about his people. This comforts me concerning Bethesda, though we should have a *Spanish* war.

---

19 Gillies, p. 210.

You will be pleased to hear I never was carried through the summer's heat so well; I hope it hath been so with you, and all my family. Hoping, ere long, to see you, I must hasten to subscribe myself, my dear Mr. Wright,

Yours, &c. &c. &c.

G.W.

"Portsmouth, New Hampshire, Sept. 23, 1770. Your letters, of May 2 and 22, came to hand. *New-York* packet is always the surest and most centrical medium of conveyance. Before I left *Boston*, on Friday afternoon, I left a large packet in the hands of a young man, who promised to deliver it to you safely. You and Mr. H———y may peruse all, and communicate what you think proper. By this time I thought to be moving southward. But never was greater importunity used to detain me longer in these northern parts. Poor *New England* is much to be pitied; *Boston* people most of all. How falsely misrepresented! What a mercy, that our *christian character* cannot be dissolved! Blessed be GOD for an unchangeable JESUS! You will see, by the many invitations, what a door is opened for preaching his everlasting gospel. I was so ill on Friday, that I could not preach, though thousands were waiting to hear. Well, the day of release will shortly come, but it does not seem yet; for, by riding sixty miles, I am better, and hope to preach here to-morrow. I trust, my blessed Master will accept of these poor efforts to serve him. O for a warm heart!; O to stand fast in the faith, to quit ourselves like men, and be strong! May this be the happy experience of you and yours! I suppose letters are gone for me, in *Anderson to Georgia*. If spared so long, I expect to see it about Christmas. Still pray and praise. I am so poorly, and so engaged when able to preach, that this must apologize for not writing to more friends. It is quite impracticable. Hoping to see all dear friends about the time proposed, and earnestly desiring a continued interest in all your prayers, I must hasten to subscribe myself, my dear, very dear Sir,

Less than the least of all,

G.W."[20]

It is noteworthy to record that the very last words George Whitefield wrote for public perusal were, "Less than the least of all". His humility before man and God was truly remarkable. The narrative of his last preaching labors in Exeter and Newburyport has already been mentioned in chapter 1. It should be noted that during the last six months of his eventful life America was in political turmoil—the American Rebellion had already begun and many "angry discontents" were part of his auditories. The inhabitants of the British colonies were rebelling at taxes imposed upon them from their Mother Country. The famous phrase was coined, "Taxation, without representation, is tyranny." So amidst this political turmoil we see George

---

20 *Works*, Vol. 3, pp. 425–427.

Whitefield faithfully preaching the word of God though he is aware of the impending conflicts for he states, "Poor New England is much to be pitied; Boston people most of all." Whitefield would not live to see the great war that would divide the colonies from his native land; he would not live to see the blood spilt on American shores for the sake of liberty—God in his mercy would take his dear, choice servant far away to a place where no cannon fire could be heard; a place of rest and peace for eternity.

Have we read or heard of any person since the Apostles, who testified the gospel of the grace of God through so widely extended a space, through so large a part of the habitable world? Have we read or heard of any person who called so many thousands, so many myriads, of sinners to repentance? Above all, have we read or heard of any who had been a blessed instrument in his hand of bringing so many sinners from "darkness to light, and from the power of Satan unto God?"

John Wesley
preaching the funeral of George Whitefield

CHAPTER 60

HIS FUNERAL

The news of the death of George Whitefield was a great shock to a great many—though few were surprised. The loss of such a man unworthy of the world was great; great also were the tears shed in his memory. Funeral sermons were prepared on both continents. Many towns and cities were draped with black cloth and a solemnity that is often rare and reserved for only the most famous and noteworthy of men. George Whitefield lived life to the fullest he was "All wing and all force" to quote Charles Spurgeon. In his death he was mourned deeply and missed greatly.

Funeral sermons and eulogies were preached on both continents. We will present two full funeral sermons preached at his funeral: one delivered by the Rev. Jonathan Parsons (in whose house Whitefield died) and the other by John Wesley, given at a later date honoring the memory of George Whitefield. Both are noteworthy and catch the spirit and essence of George Whitefield and therefore need to be included in a full study of his life; for the first represents him as he was known in *America*, the second as he was known in *England*.

The actual funeral was a memorable event as was the decision to bury him beneath the pulpit of The Old South Church in Newburyport—where his remains lie to this day. The vault may be visited by appointment. There are many of Whitefield's personal artifacts in the church where he is buried: his bible, a signed hand-written letter, a nail from his coffin, the coffin lid, the box in which his stolen forearm was returned! But most interesting of all is the plaster cast of his skull on view in the crypt.

George Whitefield was buried on October 2, 1770 and the following gives an accurate account of that eventful day:

"Early on the morning after his death, Mr. Sherburne of Portsmouth sent Mr. Clarkson and Dr. Haven, with a message to Mr. Parsons, desiring that

Whitefield's remains might be buried in his own new tomb, at his own expense; and in the evening several gentlemen from Boston, came to Mr. Parsons, desiring that the body might be carried there. But as Whitefield had repeatedly desired that he might be buried before Mr. Parsons' pulpit, if he died at Newburyport, Mr. Parsons thought himself obliged to deny both of their requests.

"The following account of his interment is subjoined to this sermon, viz:— October 2, 1770. At one o'clock all the bells in the town were tolled for an hour, and all the vessels in the harbor gave their proper signals of mourning. At two o'clock, the bells tolled a second time. At three, the bells called to attend a funeral. The Rev. Dr. Haven of Portsmouth, the Rev. Messrs. Daniel Rogers of Exeter, Jedediah Jewet, and James Chandler, of Rowley, Moses Parsons, of Newbury, and Edward Bass, of Newburyport, were pall bearers. The procession was from the Rev. Mr. Parsons of Newburyport, where Whitefield died. Mr. Parsons and his family, together with many other respectable persons, followed the corpse in mourning. The procession reached only one mile, when the corpse was carried into the Presbyterian church, and placed on a bier in the broad aisle, over which the Rev. Mr. Rogers made a very suitable prayer in the presence of about six thousand persons, within the walls of the church, while many thousands were on the outside, not being able to find admittance."[1]

Regarding the aforementioned, upon visiting the Old South Church today it is hard to fathom how six thousand people could fit inside its doors. The original church has not been structurally modified in size and it is more accurate to say that the church can *realistically* contain around two thousand people and no more—unless the pews are removed and people stand shoulder to shoulder which is highly unlikely to have occurred on that somber day. Also, the length of the funeral procession is somewhat exaggerated by Gillies, there is no way it stretched a mile, for the manse in which Whitefield died is merely three houses down from the church—no more than three hundred yards.

Despite these two inaccuracies the following is a detailed account of the somber activities of that day in October 1770:

"The corpse being placed at the foot of the pulpit, the Rev. Daniel Rogers offered prayer, in which he confessed that he owed his conversion to Whitefield's ministry, and then exclaiming, 'O my Father! my Father!' stopped and wept as though his heart was breaking. The scene was one never to be forgotten. The crowded congregation were bathed in tears. Rogers recovered himself, finished his prayer, sat down, and sobbed. One of the deacons gave out the hymn beginning with the line,—

'Why do we mourn departing friends?'

---

1   Gillies, p. 219.

"Some of the people stood, and some wept, and others sang and wept alternately. The coffin was then put into a newly prepared tomb, beneath the pulpit; and, before the tomb was sealed, the Rev. Jedediah Jewet delivered a suitable address, in the course of which he spoke of Whitefield's 'peculiar and eminent gifts for the gospel ministry, and his fervour, diligence, and success in the work of it.' 'What a friend,' cried Jewet, 'he has been to us, and our interests, religious and civil; to New England, and to all the British colonies on the continent!' After this, another prayer was offered, and the immense crowd departed weeping through the streets, as in mournful groups they wended their way to their respective homes.

"The sensation occasioned by the sudden decease of the 'man greatly beloved' was enormous. The people came in crowds, begging to be allowed to see his corpse. Ministers of all denominations hastened to the house of Mr. Parsons, where several of them related how his ministry had been the means of their conversion ...

"The effect of Whitefield's death upon the inhabitants of Georgia was indescribable. All the black cloth in the colony was bought up. The pulpit and desk, the chandeliers and organ, the pews of the Governor and Council in the church at Savannah were draped with mourning; and the Governor and members of the two Houses of Assembly went in procession to the church, and were received by the organ playing a funeral dirge. A sum of money also was unanimously voted for the removal of Whitefield's remains to Georgia, to be interred at his Orphan House; but the people of Newbury Port strongly objected, and the design had to be relinquished ...

"Jesse Lee, in his *History of the American Methodists,* remarks: 'Mr. Whitefield, had often felt his soul so much comforted in preaching in the Presbyterian meeting-house at Newbury Port, that he told his friends long before his death, that, if he died in that part of the world, he wished to be buried under the pulpit of that house. The people, who remembered his request, had it now in their power to grant it; and they prepared a vault under the pulpit, where they laid his body.' During the last hundred years, [written in the 1870s] thousands of persons have visited that vault; and, as time flows on, the numbers still increase. The *Christian's Magazine,* for 1790, inserted a startling letter, written by 'J. Brown, of Epping, Essex,' to the following effect:—

'In 1784, I visited my friends in New England, and, hearing that Whitefield's body was undecayed, I went to see it. A lantern and candle being provided, we entered the tomb. Our guide opened the coffin lid down to Whitefield's breast. His body was perfect. I felt his cheeks, his breast, etc.; and the skin immediately rose after I had touched it. Even his lips were not consumed, nor his nose. His skin was considerably discoloured through dust and age, but there was no effluvium; and even his gown was not much impaired, nor his wig.'

"If this were true in 1784, it had ceased to be a fact in 1796. In a letter dated 'Newbury Port, August, 15, 1801,' William Mason remarks: 'About five years

ago, a few friends were permitted to open Whitefield's coffin. We found the
flesh totally consumed, but the gown, cassock, and bands were almost the same
as when he was buried in them ...

"An instinctive awe pervades thoughtful men when in the presence of the
last earthly remains of those who wielded a controlling influence upon their
times. Napoleon lingered thoughtfully and reverently in the tomb of Frederick
the Great. The Prince of Wales took off his hat at the grave of Washington.
This may be a sort of hero-worship, but it is not a weakness. Thousands have
entered the vault beneath the pulpit at Newbury Port, to look at the open
coffin of Whitefield, the good and eloquent. The coffin, apparently of oak, is
yet undecayed, and rests upon the coffin of Mr. Prince, a blind preacher, and
one of the first pastors of the church. The skull, the bones of the arms, the
backbone, and the ribs are in good preservation. Many years ago, Mr. Bolton,
an Englishman, and one of Whitefield's great admirers, wished to obtain a small
memento of the great preacher. A friend of Bolton's stole the main bone of
Whitefield's right arm, and sent it to England in a parcel. Bolton was horrified
with his friend's sacrilegious act, and carefully returned the bone, in 1837, to
the Rev. Dr. Stearns, then pastor of the church at Newbury Port. Great interest
was created by the restoration of Whitefield's relic; a procession of two
thousand people followed it to the grave; and it was restored to its original
position ...

"Of the numerous descriptions published by those whose curiosity or piety
had brought them to Whitefield's resting-place, one only shall suffice,—and
that by an outsider. Henry Vincent, the eloquent English lecturer, thus described
his visit in 1867:—

'We descended into a cellar, through a trap-door behind the pulpit, and
entered the tomb of the great preacher. The upper part of the lid of
Whitefield's coffin opens upon hinges. We opened the coffin carefully, and
saw all that was mortal of the eloquent divine. The bones are blackened, as
though charred by fire. The skull is perfect. I placed my hand upon the
forehead, and thought of the time when the active brain within throbbed
with love to God and man; and when those silent lips swayed the people of
England, from the churchyard in Islington to Kennington Common,—from
the hills and valleys of Gloucestershire to the mouths of the Cornish mines,
and on through the growing colonies of America. In these days of High
Church pantomime, would it not be well to turn our attention to the times of
Whitefield and his glorious friend Wesley? Not by new decorations and
scenery,—not by candles and crosses,—not by what Wycliffe boldly called
the 'priests' rags,'—not by Pan-Anglican Synods, or by moaning out bits of
Scripture in unearthly chants; but by such lives as those of Whitefield and
Wesley, are the people to be reached and won. I confess that, as an
Englishman, I envy America the possession of the earthly remains of dear
George Whitefield; but perhaps it is appropriate that, while England claims
the dust of Wesley, the great republic should be the guardian of the dust of his
holy brother.'

"The Americans are proud of their possession, and, to this day, not only preserve his sepulchre, but, at Newbury Port, still use in the pulpit the old Bible out of which Whitefield was wont to read his texts, and still keep the old chair in which he died, and still shew the ring taken from the finger of his corpse."[2]

Though there is much of interest to see at the Old South First Presbyterian Church in Newburyport, one will not find the chair in which he died nor the ring taken from his finger (the same ring with the diamond that wrote on the window pane of the rich man's house, "One Thing Is Needful"). These two items have mysteriously disappeared—more than likely in someone's personal possession. Yet, one can still visit the crypt beneath the pulpit and see other Whitefield artifacts!

The life of George Whitefield was one of *excitement*. He did great things for God—rather God did great things *through* him. He was indefatigable in labor, forever humble, and used of God like no man since the Apostle Paul. He and Paul had much in common: they shared the same zeal for lost souls, the passion to be Christ-like, and each bore the physical scars of persecution. The world was changed in Paul's day because of him, and the same can be said of Whitefield. Few times in history has God manifested his presence so closely with one man. What qualities did Whitefield possess that made him so used of God? He was first a *man of prayer*, second a man of *holiness and purity*; he was warm-hearted toward his fellow-man—especially the poor; he pursued God like few men before or after him; in his belly was a forever burning fire for the salvation of lost souls; yet in the end he was an ordinary man with God-given talents and oratorical gifts, the summation of his life was that he continually viewed himself, "less than the least of all".

We close this account of his remarkable life, the life of the "Young Phenomenon" and the life of the "Scarred Lion" with the following two funeral sermons preached by two of his dearest friends; one an American (Jonathan Parsons) the other an Englishman (John Wesley). Let their words end this tribute to this man whom the world was *not worthy*.

---

2   Tyerman, Vol. 2, pp. 600–607.

FUNERAL SERMON GIVEN BY JONATHAN PARSONS,
OCT. 2ND, 1770.

PHIL. 1:21 "FOR ME TO LIVE IS CHRIST, AND TO DIE IS GAIN."
(Sermon preached at The Old South Presbyterian Church with the body of
George Whitefield lying before the pulpit in an open coffin.)

" Christ became a principle of spiritual life in his soul, while he was an
under-graduate at the university in Oxford. Before his conversion,
he was a pharisee of the pharisees, as strict as ever Paul was, before God
met him on his way to Damascus, according to his own declaration in his
last sermon, which I heard him preach at Exeter, yesterday. He was, by
means of reading, a very searching puritanical writer; convinced of the
rottenness of all duties he had done, and the danger of a self-righteous
foundation of hope. When he heard Christ speak to him in the gospel, he
cried, 'Lord, what wilt thou have me to do?' And it seems as if, at that
time, It had been made known to him, that he was a chosen vessel, to bear
the name of Jesus Christ through the British nation, and her colonies; to
stand before kings and nobles, and all sorts of people, to preach Christ, and
him crucified. From that time, the dawn of salvation had living power in
his heart, and he had an ardent desire to furnish himself for the gospel
ministry. To this end, besides the usual studies at the college, he gave
himself to reading the holy scriptures, to meditation and prayer; and
particularly, he read Mr. Henry's Annotations on the Bible, upon his
knees before God.

"Since my first acquaintance with him, which is about thirty years ago, I
have highly esteemed him, as an excellent christian, and an eminent
minister of the gospel. A heart so bent for Christ, with such a sprightly,
active genius, could not admit of a stated fixed residence in one place, as
the pastor of a particular congregation; and therefore, he chose to itinerate
from place to place, and from one country to another; which indeed, was
much better suited to his talents, than a fixed abode would have been. I
often considered him as an angel flying through the midst of heaven, with
the everlasting gospel, to preach unto them that dwell on the earth; for he
preached the uncorrupted word of God, and gave solemn warnings against
all corruptions of the gospel of Christ. The late Dr. Grosvenor, upon
hearing Whitefield preach at Charles-square, Hoxton, expressed himself
thus:—'That if the apostle Paul had preached to this auditory, he would
have preached in the same manner.' When he came the first time to

Boston, the venerable Dr. Coleman, with whom I had a small acquaintance, condescended to write to me, 'that the wonderful man was come, and they had a week of sabbaths; that his zeal for Christ was extraordinary; and yet he recommended himself to his many thousand hearers by his engagedness for holiness and souls.' I soon had opportunity to observe, that wherever he flew, like a flame of fire, his ministry gave a general alarm to all sorts of people, though before they had, for a long time, been amazingly sunk into dead formality. It was then a time in New England, when real christians generally had slackened their zeal for Christ, and fallen into a remiss and careless frame of spirit; and hypocritical professors were sunk into a deep sleep of carnal security. Ministers, and their congregations seemed to be at ease. But his preaching appeared to be from the heart, though too many, who spake the same things, preached as if it were indifferent, whether they were received or rejected. We were convinced that he believed the message he brought us, to be of the last importance. Nevertheless, as soon as there was time for reflection, the enemies of Christ began to cavil, and hold up some of his sallies as if they were unpardonable faults. By such means he met with a storm as tempestuous as the troubled sea, that casts up mire and dirt. Some of every station were too fond of their old way of formality, to part with it, for such a despised cause as living religion. But the spirit of Christ sent home the message of Lord upon the conscience of some, and shook them off from their false hopes: but many began to find fault, and some to write against his evangelizing through the country, while others threatened fire brands, arrows, and death. Yet God gave room for his intense zeal to operate, and fit objects appeared, wherever he went, to engage him in preaching Christ, and him crucified.

"In his repeated visits to America, when his services had almost exhausted his animal spirits, and his friends were ready to cry, 'Spare thyself,' his hope of serving Christ, and winning souls to him, animated and engaged him to run almost any risk. Neither did he ever cross the Atlantic, on an itinerating visitation, without visiting his numerous brethren here, to see how religion prospered amongst them; and we know that his labors have been unwearied among us, and to the applause of all his hearers; and, through the infinite mercy of God, his labors have sometimes been crowned with great success, in the conversion of sinners, and the edification of saints. And though he often returned from the pulpit, very feeble after public preaching, yet his engaging sweetness of conversation, changed the suspicions of many into passionate love and friendship.

"In many things, his example is worthy of imitation; and if in anything he exceeded, or came short, his integrity, zeal for God, and love to Christ and his gospel, rendered him, in extensive usefulness, more than equal to any of his brethren. In preaching here, and through most parts of America, he has been in labors more abundant, approving himself a minister of God, in much patience, in afflictions, in watchings, in fastings, by pureness, by the Holy Ghost, by love unfeigned; as sorrowful, yet always rejoicing; as having nothing, yet possessing all things. And God, that comforteth those that are cast down, has often comforted us by his coming; and not by his coming only, but by the consolation wherewith he was comforted in us, so that we could rejoice the more.

"His popularity exceeded all that ever I knew; and though the asthma was sometimes an obstruction to him, his delivery and entertaining method was so inviting to the last, that it would command the attention of the vast multitudes of his hearers. An apprehension of his concern to serve the Lord Jesus Christ, and do good to the souls of men drew many thousands after him, who never embraced the doctrines he taught. He had something so peculiar in his manner, expressive of sincerity in all he delivered, that it constrained the most abandoned to think he believed what he said was not only true, but of the last importance to souls; and by adapted texts adduced, and instances of the grace of God related agreeable thereto, often surprised his most judicious hearers.

"His labors extended not only to New England, and many other colonies in British America, but were eminent and more abundant in Great Britain. Many thousands at his chapel and Tabernacle, and in other places were witnesses that he faithfully endeavored to restore the interesting doctrines of the reformation, and the purity of the church to its primitive glory. Some among the learned, some of the mighty and noble, have been called by his ministry, to testify for the gospel of the grace of God. The force of his reasonings against corrupt principles, and the easy method he had of exposing the danger of them, have astonished the most that heard him, in all places where he preached. How did he lament and withstand the modern unscriptural notions of religion and salvation, that were palmed upon the churches of every denomination! The affecting change from primitive purity to fatal heresy, together with the sad effects of it in mere formality and open wickedness, would often make him cry, as the prophet did in another case, 'How is the gold become dim, and the most fine gold changed! How has the Lord covered the daughter of Zion with a cloud in his anger, and cast down from heaven to earth, the beauty of Israel.'

"It is no wonder that this man of God should meet with enemies and with great opposition to his ministry; for hell trembled before him. It is not more than may be always expected of the devil, that he should stir up his servants, to load the most eminent ministers of Christ with calumny and most impudent lies; and represent them as the filth and offscouring of all things. All this may be, and often has been done, under a pretense of great concern for the honor of Christ, and the preservation of the gospel order. When Satan totters and begins to fall, he can find men enough to cry, 'the church is in danger;' and that he knows is sufficient with many, to hide his cloven foot, and make him appear as an angel of light.

"Through a variety of such labors and trials, our worthy friend, and extensively useful servant of Christ, Mr. Whitefield, passed both in England and America; but the Lord was his sun to guide and animate him, and his shield to defend and help him unto the end: neither did he count his own life dear, so that he might finish his course with joy, and the ministry that he had received of the Lord Jesus, to testify the gospel of the grace of God.

"The last sermon that he preached, though under the disadvantage of a stage in the open air, was delivered with such clearness, pathos, and eloquence, as to please and surprise the surrounding thousands. And as he had been confirmed by the grace of God, many years before, and had been waiting and hoping for his last change, he then declared, that he hoped it was the last time he should ever preach. Doubtless, he then had such clear views of the blessedness of open vision, and the complete fruition of God in Christ, that he felt the pleasures of heaven in his raptured soul, which made his countenance shine like the unclouded sun."[3]

3   Gillies, pp. 221–225.

ON THE DEATH OF THE REV. MR. GEORGE WHITEFIELD

PREACHED BY THE REV. JOHN WESLEY, AT THE CHAPEL IN TOTTENHAM-COURT ROAD, AND AT THE TABERNACLE NEAR MOORFIELDS, ON SUNDAY, NOV. 18, 1770.

Numbers 23:10, "Let me die the death of the righteous, and let my last end be like his!"

"1. 'Let my last end be like his!' How many of you join in this wish? Perhaps there are few of you who do not, even in this numerous congregation! And O that his wish may rest upon your minds!—that it may not die away till your souls also are lodged 'where the wicked cease from troubling, and where the weary are at rest.'

"2. An elaborate exposition of the text will not be expected on this occasion. It would detain you too long from the sadly-pleasing thought of your beloved brother, friend, and pastor; yea, and father too: For how many are here whom he hath 'begotten in the Lord!' Will it not, then, be more suitable to your inclinations, as well as to this solemnity, directly to speak of this man of God, whom you have so often heard speaking in this place?—the end of whose conversation ye know, 'Jesus Christ, the same yesterday, and to-day, and for ever.'

"And may we not,

"I. Observe a few particulars of his life and death?

"II. Take some view of his character? And,

"III. Inquire how we may improve this awful providence, his sudden removal from us?

"I. 1. We may, in the First place, observe a few particulars of his life and death. He was born at Gloucester, in December, 1714, and put to a grammar-school there, when about twelve years old. When he was seventeen, he began to be seriously religious, and served God to the best of his knowledge. About eighteen he removed to the University, and was admitted at Pembroke College, in Oxford; and about a year after he became acquainted with the Methodists, (so called,) whom from that time he loved as his own soul.

"2. By them he was convinced that we 'must be born again,' or outward religion will profit us nothing. He joined with them in fasting on Wednesdays and Fridays; in visiting the sick and the prisoners; and in gathering up the very fragments of time, that no moment might be lost: And he changed the course of his studies; reading chiefly such books as entered into the heart of religion, and led directly to an experimental knowledge of Jesus Christ, and him crucified.

"3. He was soon tried as with fire. Not only his reputation was lost, and some of his dearest friends forsook him; but he was exercised with inward trials, and those of the severest kind. Many nights he lay sleepless upon his bed; many days, prostrate on the ground. But after he had groaned several months under 'the spirit of bondage,' God was pleased to remove the heavy load, by giving him 'the Spirit of adoption;' enabling him, through a living faith, to lay hold on 'the Son of his love.'

"4. However, it was thought needful, for the recovery of his health, which was much impaired, that he should go into the country. He accordingly went to Gloucester, where God enabled him to awaken several young persons. These soon formed themselves into a little society, and were some of the first fruits of his labour. Shortly after, he began to read, twice or thrice a week, to some poor people in the town; and every day to read to and pray with the prisoners in the county gaol.

"5. Being now about twenty-one years of age, he was solicited to enter into holy orders. Of this he was greatly afraid, being deeply sensible of his own insufficiency. But the Bishop himself sending for him, and telling him, 'Though I had purposed to ordain none under three-and-twenty, yet I will ordain you whenever you come,'—and several other providential circumstances concurring,—he submitted, and was ordained on Trinity Sunday, 1736. The next Sunday he preached to a crowded auditory, in the church wherein he was baptized. The week following he returned to Oxford, and took his Bachelor's degree: And he was now fully employed; the care of the prisoners and the poor lying chiefly on him.

"6. But it was not long before he was invited to London, to serve the cure of a friend going into the country. He continued there two months, lodging in the Tower, reading Prayers in the chapel twice a week, catechising and preaching once, beside visiting the soldiers in the barracks and the infirmary. He also read Prayers every evening at Wapping chapel, and preached at Ludgate prison every Tuesday. While he was here, letters came from his friends in Georgia, which made him long to go and help them: But not seeing his call clear, at the appointed time he returned to his little charge at Oxford, where several youths met daily at his room, to build up each other in their most holy faith.

"7. But he was quickly called from hence again, to supply the cure of Dummer, in Hampshire. Here he read Prayers twice a day; early in the morning, and in the evening after the people came from work. He also daily catechised the children, and visited from house to house. He now divided the day into three parts, allotting eight hours for sleep and meals, eight for study and retirement, and eight for reading Prayers, catechising, and visiting the people.—Is there a more excellent way for a servant of Christ and his Church? If not, who will 'go and do likewise?'

"8. Yet his mind still ran on going abroad; and being now fully convinced he was called of God thereto, he set all things in order, and, in January, 1737, went down to take leave of his friends in Gloucester. It was in this journey that God began to bless his ministry in an uncommon manner. Wherever he preached, amazing multitudes of hearers flocked together, in Gloucester, in Stonehouse, in Bath, in Bristol; so that the heat of the churches was scarce supportable: And the impressions made on the minds of many were no less extraordinary. After his return to London, while he was detained by General Oglethorpe, from week to week, and from month to month, it pleased God to bless his word still more. And he was indefatigable in his labour: Generally on Sunday he preached four times, to exceeding large auditories; beside reading Prayers twice or thrice, and walking to and fro often ten or twelve miles.

"9. On December 28, he left London. It was on the 29th that he first preached without notes. December 30, he went on board; but it was above a month before they cleared the land. One happy effect of their very slow passage he mentions in April following:—'Blessed be God, we now live very comfortably in the great cabin. We talk of little else but God and Christ; and scarce a word is heard among us when together, but what has reference to our fall in the first, and our new birth in the Second, Adam.' It seems, likewise, to have been a peculiar providence, that he should spend a little time at Gibralter; where both citizens and soldiers, high and low, young and old, acknowledged the day of their visitation.

"10. From Sunday, May 7, 1738, till the latter end of August following, he 'made full proof of his ministry' in Georgia, particularly at Savannah: He read Prayers and expounded twice a day, and visited the sick daily. On Sunday he expounded at five in the morning; at ten read Prayers and preached, and at three in the afternoon; and at seven in the evening expounded the Church Catechism. How much easier it is for our brethren in the ministry, either in England, Scotland, or Ireland, to find fault with such a labourer in our Lord's vineyard, than to tread in his steps!

"11. It was now that he observed the deplorable condition of many children here; and that God put into his heart the first thought of founding an Orphan-House, for which he determined to raise contributions in England, if God should give him a safe return thither. In December following, he did return to London; and on Sunday, January 14th, 1739, he was ordained Priest at Christ Church, Oxford. The next day he came to London again; and on Sunday, the 21st, preached twice. But though the churches were large, and crowded exceedingly, yet many hundreds stood in the church-yard, and hundreds more returned home. This put him upon the first thought of preaching in the open air. But when he mentioned it to some of his friends, they judged it to be mere madness: So he did not carry it into execution till after he had left London. It was on Wednesday, February 21, that, finding all the church doors to be shut in Bristol, (beside, that no church was able to contain one half of the congregation,) at three in the afternoon he went to Kingswood, and preached abroad to near two thousand people. On Friday he preached there to four or five thousand; and on Sunday to, it was supposed, ten thousand! The number continually increased all the time he stayed at Bristol; and a flame of holy love was kindled, which will not easily be put out. The same was afterwards kindled in various parts of Wales, of Gloucestershire, and Worcestershire. Indeed, wherever he went, God abundantly confirmed the word of his messenger.

"12. On Sunday, April 29, he preached the first time in Moorfields, and on Kennington Common; and the thousands of hearers were as quiet as they could have been in a church. Being again detained in England from month to month, he made little excursions into several counties, and received the contributions of willing multitudes for an Orphan-House in Georgia. The embargo which was now laid on the shipping gave him leisure for more journeys through various parts of England, for which many will have reason to bless God to all eternity. At length, on August 14, he embarked: But he did not land in Pennsylvania till October 30. Afterwards he went through Pennsylvania, the Jerseys, New-York, Maryland, Virginia, North and South Carolina; preaching all along to immense congregations, with full as great effect as in England. On January 10, 1740, he arrived at Savannah.

"13. January 29, he added three desolate orphans to near twenty which he had in his House before. The next day he laid out the ground for the House, about ten miles from Savannah. February 11, he took in four orphans more; and set out for Frederica, in order to fetch the orphans that were in the southern parts of the colony. In his return he fixed a school, both for children and grown persons, at Darien, and took four orphans thence. March 25, he laid the first stone of the Orphan-House; to which, with great propriety, he gave the name of Bethesda; a work for which the children yet unborn shall praise the Lord. He had now about forty orphans, so that there were near a hundred mouths to be fed daily. But he was 'careful for nothing,' casting his care on Him who feedeth the young ravens that call upon Him.

"14. In April he made another tour through Pennsylvania, the Jerseys, and New-York. Incredible multitudes flocked to hear, among whom were abundance of Negroes. In all places the greater part of the hearers were affected to an amazing degree. Many were deeply convinced of their lost state; many, truly converted to God. In some places, thousands cried out aloud; many as in the agonies of death; most were drowned in tears; some turned pale as death; others were wringing their hands; others lying on the ground; others sinking into the arms of their friends; almost all lifting up their eyes, and calling for mercy.

"15. He returned to Savannah, June 5. The next evening, during the public service, the whole congregation, young and old, were dissolved into tears: After service, several of the parishioners, and all his family, particularly the little children, returned home crying along the streets, and some could not help praying aloud. The groans and cries of the children continued all night, and great part of the next day.

"16. In August he set out again, and through various provinces came to Boston. While he was here, and in the neighbouring places, he was extremely weak in body: Yet the multitudes of hearers were so great, and the effects wrought on them so astonishing, as the oldest men then alive in the town had never seen before. The same power attended his preaching at New-York, particularly on Sunday, November 2: Almost as soon as he began, crying, weeping, and wailing were to be heard on every side. Many sunk down to the ground, cut to the heart; and many were filled with divine consolation. Toward the close of his journey he made this reflection:—'It is the seventy-fifth day since I arrived at Rhode-Island, exceeding weak in body: Yet God has enabled me to preach a hundred and seventy-five times in public, besides exhorting frequently in private! Never did God vouchsafe me greater comforts: Never did I perform my journeys with less fatigue, or see such a continuance of the divine presence in the congregations to whom I preached.' In December he returned to Savannah, and in the March following arrived in England.

"17. You may easily observe, that the preceding account is chiefly extracted from his own Journals, which, for their artless and unaffected simplicity, may vie with any writings of the kind. And how exact a specimen is this of his labours both in Europe and America, for the honour of his beloved Master, during the thirty years that followed, as well as of the uninterrupted shower of blessings wherewith God was pleased to succeed his labours! Is it not much to be lamented, that anything should have prevented his continuing this account, till at least near the time when he was called by his Lord to enjoy the fruit of his labour?—If he has left any papers of this kind, and his friends account me worthy of the honour, it would be my glory and joy to methodize, transcribe, and prepare them for the public view.

"18. A particular account of the last scene of his life is thus given by a gentleman of Boston:—

'After being about a month with us in Boston and its vicinity, and preaching every day, he went to Old-York; preached on Thursday, September 27, there; proceeded to Portsmouth, and preached there on Friday. On Saturday morning he set out for Boston; but before he came to Newbury, where he had engaged to preach the next morning, he was importuned to preach by the way. The house not being large enough to contain the people, he preached in the open field. But having been infirm for several weeks, this so exhausted his strength, that when he came to Newbury he could not get out of the ferry-boat without the help of two men. In the evening, however, he recovered his spirits, and appeared with his usual cheerfulness. He went to his chamber at nine, his fixed time, which no company could divert him from, and slept better than he had done for some weeks before. He rose at four in the morning, September 30, and went into his closet; and his companion observed he was unusually long in private. He left his closet, returned to his companion, threw himself on the bed, and lay about ten minutes. Then he fell upon his knees, and prayed most fervently to God that, if it was consistent with his will, he might that day finish his Master's work. He then desired his man to call Mr. Parsons, the Clergyman, at whose house he was; but, in a minute, before Mr. Parsons could reach him, died, without sigh or groan. On the news of his death, six gentleman set out for Newbury, in order to bring his remains hither: But he could not be moved; so that his precious ashes must remain at Newbury. Hundreds would have gone from this town to attend his funeral, had they not expected he would have been interred here.—May this stroke be sanctified to the Church of God in general, and to this province in particular!'

"II. 1. We are, in the Second place, to take some view of his character. A little sketch of this was soon after published in the Boston Gazette; and extract of which is subjoined:—

'In his public labours he has, for many years, astonished the world with his eloquence and devotion. With what divine pathos did he persuade the impenitent sinner to embrace the practice of piety and virtue! He spoke from the heart, and with a fervency of zeal perhaps unequaled since the days of the Apostles. From the pulpit he was unrivaled in the command of an ever-crowded auditory. Nor was he less agreeable and instructive in his private conversation;—happy in a remarkable case of address, willing to communicate, studious to edify. May the rising generation catch a spark of that flame which shone, with such distinguished luster, in the spirit and practice of this faithful servant of the most high God!'

"2. A more particular, and equally just, character of him has appeared in one of the English papers. It may not be disagreeable to you to add the substance of this likewise:—

'The character of this truly pious person must be impressed on the heart of every friend to vital religion. In spite of a tender constitution, he continued, to the last day of his life, preaching with a frequency and fervour that seemed to exceed the natural strength of the most robust. Being called to the exercise of his function at an age when most young men are only beginning to qualify themselves for it, he had not time to make a very considerable progress in the learned languages. But this defect was amply supplied by a lively and fertile genius, by fervent zeal, and by a forcible and most persuasive delivery. And though in the pulpit he often found it needful by "the terrors of the Lord" to "persuade me," he had nothing gloomy in his nature; being singularly cheerful, as charitable and tender-hearted. He was as ready to relieve the bodily as the spiritual necessities of those that applied to him. It ought also to be observed, that he constantly enforced upon his audience every moral duty; particularly industry in their several callings, and obedience to their superiors. He endeavoured, by the most extraordinary efforts of preaching, in different places, and even in the open fields, to rouse the lower class of people from the last degree of inattention and ignorance to a sense of religion. For this, and his other labours, the name of GEORGE WHITEFIELD will long be remembered with esteem and veneration.'

"3. That both these accounts are just and impartial will readily be allowed; that is, as far as they go. But they go little farther than the outside of his character. They show you the Preacher, but not the man, the Christian, the saint of God. May I be permitted to add a little on this head, from a personal knowledge of near forty years? Indeed, I am thoroughly sensible how difficult it is to speak on so delicate a subject;—what prudence is required, to avoid both extremes, to say neither too little nor too much! Nay, I know it is impossible to speak at all, to say either less or more, without incurring from some the former, from others the latter censure. Some will seriously think that too little is said; and others, that it is too much. But without attending to this, I will speak just what I know, before Him to whom we are all to give an account.

"4. Mention has already been made of his unparalleled zeal, his indefatigable activity, his tender-heartedness to the afflicted, and charitableness toward the poor. But should we not likewise mention his deep *gratitude* to all whom God had used as instruments of good to him?—of whom he did not cease to speak in the most respectful manner, even to his dying day. Should we not mention, that he had a heart susceptible of the most generous and the most tender *friendship*? I have frequently thought that this, of all others, was the distinguishing part of his character. How few have we known of so kind a temper, of such large and flowing affections! Was it not principally by this, that the hearts of others were so strangely drawn and knit to him? Can anything but love beget love? This shone in his very countenance and continually breathed in all his words, whether in public or private. Was it not this, which, quick and penetrating as lightning, flew from heart to heart? Which gave that life to his sermons, his conversation, his letters? Ye are witnesses!

"5. But away with the vile misconstruction of men of corrupt minds, who know of no love but what is earthly and sensual! Be it remembered, at the same time, that he was endued with the most nice and unblemished *modesty*. His office called him to converse very frequently and largely with women as well as men; and those of every age and condition. But his whole behaviour toward them was a practical comment on that advice of St. Paul to Timothy: 'Entreat the elder women as mothers, the younger as sisters, with all purity.'

"6. Meantime, how suitable to the friendliness of his spirit was the *frankness* and *openness* of his conversation!—although it was as far removed from rudeness on the one hand, as from guile on the other. Was not this frankness at once a fruit and a proof of his *courage* and *intrepidity*? Armed with these, he feared not the faces of men, but 'used great plainness of speech' to persons of every rank and condition, high and low, rich and poor; endeavouring only 'by manifestation of the truth to commend himself to every man's conscience in the sight of God.'

"7. Neither was he afraid of labour or pain, any more than of 'what man can do unto him;' being equally *Patient* in bearing ill and doing well.

"And this appeared in the *steadiness* wherewith he pursued what ever he undertook for his Master's sake. Witness one instance for all,—the Orphan-House in Georgia; which he began and perfected, in spite of all discouragements. Indeed, in whatever concerned himself he was pliant and flexible. In this case he was 'easy to be entreated;' easy to be either convinced or persuaded. But he was immovable in the things of God, or wherever his conscience was concerned. None could persuade, any more than affright, him to vary, in the least point, from that *integrity* which was inseparable from his whole character, and regulated all his words and actions. Herein he did

Stand as an iron pillar strong,
And steadfast as a wall of brass.

"8. If it be inquired what was the foundation of this integrity, or of his
sincerity, courage, patience, and every other valuable and amiable quality; it
is easy to give the answer:—It was not the excellence of his natural temper,
not the strength of his understanding; it was not the force of education; no,
nor the advice of his friends: It was no other than faith in a bleeding Lord;
'faith of the operation of God.' It was 'a lively hope of an inheritance
incorruptible, undefiled, and that fadeth not away.' It was 'the love of God
shed abroad in his heart by the Holy Ghost which was given unto him,'
filling his soul with tender, disinterested love to every child of man. From
this source arose that torrent of eloquence, which frequently bore down all
before it; from this, that astounding force of persuasion, which the most
hardened sinners could not resist. This it was which often made his 'head as
waters, and his eyes a fountain of tears.' This it was which enabled him to
pour out his soul in prayer, in a manner peculiar to himself, with such fulness
and ease united together, with such strength and variety both of sentiment
and expression.

"9. I may close this head with observing what an honour it pleased God to
put upon his faithful servant, by allowing him to declare his everlasting
gospel in so many various countries, to such numbers of people, and with so
great an effect on so many of their precious souls! Have we read or heard of
any person since the Apostles, who testified the gospel of the grace of God
through so widely extended a space, through so large a part of the habitable
world? Have we read or heard of any person who called so many thousands,
so many myriads, of sinners to repentance? Above all, have we read or heard
of any who has been a blessed instrument in his hand of bringing so many
sinners from 'darkness to light, and from the power of Satan unto God?' It is
true, were we to talk thus to the gay world, we should be judged to speak as
barbarians. But *you* understand the language of the country to which you are
going, and whither our dear friend is gone a little before us.

"III. But how shall we improve this awful providence? This is the Third
thing which we have to consider. And the answer to this important question
is easy: (May God write it in all our hearts!) By keeping close to the grand
doctrines which he delivered; and by drinking into his spirit.

"1. Add, First, let us keep close to the grand scriptural doctrines which he
everywhere delivered. There are many doctrines of a less essential nature,
with regard to which even the sincere children of God (such is the present
weakness of human understanding) are and have been divided for many

ages. In these we may think and let think; we may 'agree to disagree.' But, meantime, let us hold fast the essentials of 'the faith which was once delivered to the saints;' and which this champion of God so strongly insisted on, at all times, and in all places!

"2. His fundamental point was, 'Give God all the glory of whatever is good in man;' and, 'In the business of salvation, set Christ as high and man as low as possible.' With this point he and his friends at Oxford, the original Methodists, so called, set out. Their grand principle was, There is *no power* (by nature) and *no merit* in man. They insisted, all power to think, speak, or act aright, is in and from the Spirit of Christ; and all merit is (not in man, how high soever in grace, but merely) in the blood of Christ. So he and they taught: There is no power in man, till it is given him from above, to do one good work, to speak one good word, or to form one good desire. For it is not enough to say, all men are *sick of sin*: No, we are all *'dead* in trespasses and sins.' It follows, that all the children of men are, 'by nature, children of wrath.' We are all 'guilty before God,' liable to death temporal and eternal.

"3. And we are all helpless, both with regard to the power and to the guilt of sin. For 'who can bring a clean thing out of an unclean?' None less than the Almighty. Who can raise those that are *dead*, spiritually dead in sin? None but He who raised us from the dust of the earth. But on what consideration will he do this? 'Not for works of righteousness that we have done.' 'The dead cannot praise thee, O Lord;' nor do any thing for the sake of which they should be raised to life. Whatever, therefore, God does, he does it merely for the sake of his well-beloved Son: 'He was wounded for our transgressions, he was bruised for our iniquities.' He himself, 'bore' all 'our sins in his own body upon the tree.' 'He was delivered for our offences, and was raised again for our justification.' Here then is the sole meritorious cause of every blessing we do or can enjoy;—in particular of our pardon and acceptance with God, or our full and free justification. But by what means do we become interested in what Christ has done and suffered? 'Not by works, lest any man should boast;' but by faith alone. 'We conclude,' says the Apostle, 'that a man is justified by faith, without the works of the law.' And 'to as many as thus receive Him, giveth he power to become the sons of God, even to those who believe in his name; who are born, not of the will of man, but of God.'

"4. And 'except a man be' thus 'born again, he cannot see the kingdom of God.' But all who are thus 'born of the Spirit' have 'the kingdom of God within them.' Christ sets up his kingdom in their hearts; 'righteousness, peace, and joy in the Holy Ghost.' That 'mind is in them which was in Christ Jesus,' enabling them to 'walk as Christ also walked.' His indwelling Spirit makes them both holy in heart, and 'holy to all manner of conversation.' But still, seeing all this is a free gift, through the righteousness and blood of Christ, there is eternally the same reason to remember, 'He that glorieth, let him glory in the Lord.'

"5. You are not ignorant that these are the fundamental doctrines which he every where insisted on. And may they not be summed up, as it were, in two words,—the new birth, and justification by faith? These let us insist upon with all boldness, at all times, and in all places;—in public, (those of us who are called thereto,) and at all opportunities in private. Keep close to these good, old, unfashionable doctrines, how many soever contradict and blaspheme. Go on, my brethren, in the 'name of the Lord, and in the power of his might.' With all care and diligence, 'keep that safe which is committed to your trust:' knowing that 'heaven and earth shall pass away, but this truth shall not pass away.'

"6. But will it be sufficient to keep close to his doctrines, how pure soever they are? Is there not a point of still greater importance than this, namely, to drink into his spirit?—herein to be a follower of him, even as he was of Christ? Without this, the purity of our doctrines would only increase our condemnation. This, therefore, is the principle thing,—to copy after his spirit. And allowing that in some points we must be content to admire what we cannot imitate; yet in many others we may, through the same free grace, be partakers of the same blessing. Conscious then of your own wants and of His bounteous love, who 'giveth liberally and upbraideth not,' cry to Him that worketh all in all for a measure of the same precious faith; of the same zeal and activity; the same tender-heartedness, charitableness, bowels of mercies. Wrestle with God for some degree of the same grateful, friendly, affectionate temper; of the same openness, simplicity, and godly sincerity! 'love without dissimulation.' Wrestle on, till the power from on high works in you the same steady courage and patience; and above all, because it is the crown of all, the same invariable integrity.

"7. Is there any other fruit of the grace of God with which he was eminently endowed, and the want of which among the children of God he frequently and passionately lamented? There is one, that is, catholic love; that sincere and tender affection which is due to all those who, we have reason to believe, are children of God by faith;—in other words, all those, in every persuasion, who, 'fear God and work righteousness.' He longed to see all who had 'tasted of the good word,' of a true catholic spirit: a word little understood, and still less experienced, by many who have it frequently in their mouth. Who is he that answers this character? Who is a man of a catholic spirit? One who loves as friends, as brethren in the Lord, as joint partakers of the present kingdom of heaven, and fellow-heirs of his eternal kingdom, all, of whatever opinion, mode of worship, or congregation, who believe in the Lord Jesus; who love God and man; who, rejoicing to please and fearing to offend God, are careful to abstain from evil, and zealous of good works. He is a man of a truly catholic spirit, who bears all these continually upon his heart; who, having an unspeakable tenderness for their persons, and an earnest desire of their welfare, does not cease to commend them to God in prayer, as well as to plead their cause before men; who speaks comfortably to them, and labours, by all his words, to strengthen their hands in God. He assists them to the uttermost of his power, in all things, spiritual and temporal; he is ready to 'spend and be spent' for them; yea, 'to lay down his life for his brethren.'

"8. How amiable a character is this! How desirable to every child of God! But why is it then so rarely found? How is it that there are so few instances of it? Indeed, supposing we have tasted of the love of God, how can any of us rest till it is our own? Why, there is a delicate device, whereby Satan persuades thousands that they may stop short of it and yet be guiltless. It is well if many here present are not in this 'snare of the devil, taken captive at his will.' 'O yes,' says one, 'I have all this love for those I believe to be children of God; but I will never believe he is a child of God, who belongs to that vile congregation! Can he, do you think, be a child of God, who holds such detestable opinions? or he that joins in such senseless and superstitious, if not idolatrous, worship?' So we may justify ourselves in one sin by adding a second to it! We excuse the want of love in ourselves by laying the blame on others! To color our own devilish temper, we pronounce our brethren children of the devil! O beware of this!—and if you are already taken in the snare, escape out of it as soon as possible! Go and learn that truly catholic love which 'is not rash,' or hasty in judging; that love which 'thinketh no evil;' which 'believeth and hopeth all things;' which makes all the allowance for others that we desire others should make for us! Then we shall take knowledge of the grace of God which is in every man, whatever be his opinion or mode of worship: Then will all that fear God be near and dear unto us 'in the bowels of Jesus Christ.'

"9. Was not this the spirit of our dear friend? And why should it not be ours? O thou God of love, how long shall thy people be a by-word among the Heathen? How long shall they laugh us to scorn, and say, 'See how *these*

Christians love one another!' When wilt thou roll away our reproach? Shall the sword devour for ever? How long will it be ere thou bid thy people return from 'following each other?' Now, at least, 'let all the people stand still, and pursue after their brethren no more!' But whatever others do, let all of us, my brethren, hear the voice of him that, being dead, yet speaketh! Suppose ye hear him say, 'Now, at least, be ye followers of me as I was of Christ!' Let brother 'no more lift up sword against brother, neither know ye war any more!' Rather put ye on, as the elect of God, bowels of mercies, humbleness of mind, brotherly kindness, gentleness, longsuffering, forbearing one another in love. Let the time past suffice for strife, envy, contention; for biting and devouring one another. Blessed be God, that ye have not long ago been consumed one of another! From henceforth hold ye the unity of the Spirit in the bond of peace.'

"10. O God, with thee no word is impossible! Thou doest whatsoever pleaseth thee! O that thou wouldest cause the mantle of thy prophet, whom thou hast taken up, now to fall upon us that remain! 'Where is the Lord God of Elijah?' Let his spirit rest upon these thy servants! Show thou art the God that answers by fire! Let the fire of thy love fall on every heart! And because we love thee, let us love one another with a 'love stronger than death!' Take away from us 'all anger, and wrath, and bitterness; all clamour and evil-speaking!' Let thy Spirit so rest upon us, that from this hour we may be 'kind to each other, tender-hearted, forgiving one another, even as God for Christ's sake hath forgiven us!'"

AN HYMN

1. SERVANT of God, well done!
   Thy glorious warfare's past,
   The battle's fought, the race is won,
   And thou art crown'd at last;
   Of all thy heart's desire
   Triumphantly possess'd,
   Lodged by the ministerial choir
   In thy Redeemer's breast.

2. In condescending love,
   Thy ceaseless prayer be heard;
   And bade thee suddenly remove
   To thy complete reward:
   Ready to bring the peace,
   Thy beauteous feet were shod,
   When mercy sign'd thy soul's release,
   And caught thee up to God.

3. With saints enthroned on high,
   Thou dost thy Lord proclaim,
   And still *To God salvation cry,*
   Salvation to the Lamb!
   O happy, happy soul!
   In ecstasies of praise,
   Long as eternal ages roll,
   Thou seest they Saviour's face!

4. Redeem'd from earth and pain,
   Ah! When shall we ascend,
   And all in Jesu's presence reign
   With our translated friend?
   Come Lord, and quickly come!
   And, when in thee complete,
   Receive thy longing servant's home
   To triumph at thy feet!"[4]

---

4 *The Works of John Wesley,* Vol. 5 (Grand Rapids: Baker Books, 2002), pp. 167–182.

The only statue of Whitefield in the world in the quadrangle of the University of Pennsylvania, Philadelphia, which he had a hand in founding. Access to the quadrangle is restricted and permission must be granted in advance.

Rock outside West Brookfield, central Massachusetts, which Whitefield used as a pulpit in 1740.

GEORGE WHITEFIELD
EARLY METHODIST EVANGELIST
PREACHED FROM THIS ROCK
OCTOBER 16, 1740
ON HIS FIRST TOUR OF AMERICA

300TH ANNIVERSARY, QUABOAG PLANTATION
SEPTEMBER, 1960

NEW ENGLAND METHODIST HISTORICAL SOCIETY

Pulpit Rock, near Ipswich, north of Boston, Massachusetts. The sign-writer changed Whitefield to Whitehouse towarsd the end of the text (below).

PULPIT ROCK

REV. GEORGE LESSLIE WAS THE FIRST PASTOR FOR THE LINEBROOK PARISH THAT BEGAN ON NOVEMBER 15, 1749. THE MEETING HOUSE FOR LINEBROOK PARISH WAS BUILT JUST INSIDE THE ROWLEY BOUNDARY ON LESLIE ROAD. THE SITE IS MARKED WITH A SIGN DOWN THE ROAD. THE LINEBROOK CHURCH WAS TAKEN DOWN IN 1847 AND REBUILT IN IPSWICH ON LINEBROOK ROAD. IT WAS PUT INTO USE AGAIN IN 1848.

PULPIT ROCK WAS NEXT DOOR TO THE CHURCH BUILDING IN ROWLEY. REV. GEORGE WHITEFIELD, ON ONE OF THE IMPORTANT CHURCH CELEBRATIONS, PREACHED TO MORE THAN 2000 PEOPLE FROM PULPIT ROCK. THE CONGREGATION WAS TOO LARGE FOR THE CHURCH SO THE PEOPLE SAT OUTSIDE AND LISTENED AS REV. WHITEHOUSE GAVE HIS SERMON WHILE STANDING ON TOP OF THE HUGE ROCK. PULPIT ROCK IS STILL USED TODAY AS A SPECIAL MEETING PLACE FOR LOCAL CHURCHES.

XXI   Moorfields Tabernacle, from an early print

Moorfields Tabernacle as originally built in 1753. It was taken down and the building below erected in 1868, with the stone on the opposite page embedded in the wall.

Tottenham Court Chapel as extended later in Whitefield's life.

The Whitefield Memorial Church, Tottenham Court Road, London, rebuilt on the site of the Tottenham Court Road Chapel following the destruction of its predecessor by the last V2 attack of the Second World War.

This stone outside the former Baptist manse in Exeter, New Hampshire, marks the spot where Whitefield preached his last sermon on 29 September 1770.

Formerly an inn at the former ferry crossing, Newburyport, this inn was used by Whitefield and he exhorted there. After many years of neglect, the building has been condemned and is due for demolition.

Display cabinet in the Old South Presbyterian Church, Newburyport, Massachusetts where Whitefield is buried. The bust was very common. Some were unpainted white, some painted black and some painted in colour. The box was used to return Whitefield's right forearm which was removed from the grave and taken to England.

First Presbyterian Church, on Federal Street, Newburyport, Massachusetts. Founded as a result of Whitefield's preaching in the area in the early 1740s, the church adopted presbyterian principles in 1746. It moved into this building in 1756. Whitefield is buried in the crypt beneath the pulpit.

Jonathan Parsons, minister of First Presbyterian Church, Newburyport, 1746–1776. He was a friend of Whitefield and is buried next to him

The former parsonage at Newburyport, where Whitefield died early in the morning of 30 September 1770 in an upstairs bedroom. The house has been extensively rennovated in recent years. It is now a private dwelling with no connection to the church.

The interior of First Presbyterian Church, Newburyport. Whitefield is buried in the crypt which lies below the pulpit.

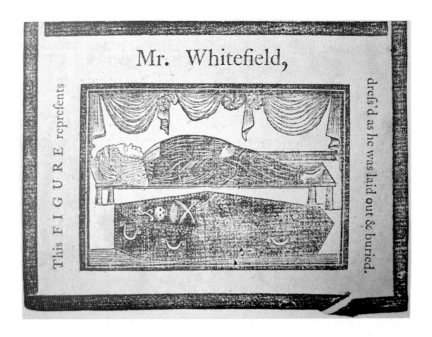

Cenotaph commemorating the life of George Whitefield in First Presbyterian Church, Newburyport

Between sixteen and twenty designs of medals were struck in honour of Whitefield at his death. This photograph of one example is shown with thanks to its owner, Darrin Brooker.

Whitefield's grave. The coffin was covered with slate in about 1930 to prevent theft of body parts and clothing. The skull is a cast of Whitefield's. On the left is the grave of Jonathan Parsons and on the right Joseph Prince.

The crypt where Whitefield is buried with Dr Digby L. James (left), Rob John, pastor of First Presbyterian Church, Newburyport (centre) and the author (right). Photographed by Marianne James.

APPENDIX 1

"Northampton in New-England, Feb. 12, 1739/40.

"Rev. Sir,

"My Request to you is, that in your intended Journey through New-England the next Summer, you would be pleased to visit Northampton. I hope it is not wholly from Curiosity that I desire to see and hear you in this Place; But I apprehend, from what I have heard, that you are one that has the Blessing of Heaven attending you wherever you go: and I have a great desire, if it may be the will of God, that Such a Blessing as attends your Person and Labours may descend on this Town, and may enter mine own House, and that I may receive it in my own Soul. Indeed I am fearful whether you will not be disappointed in New-England, and will have less Success here than in other Places: we who have dwelt in a Land that has been distinguished with Light, and have long enjoyed the Gospel, and have been glutted with it, and have despised it, are I fear more hardend than most of those places where you have preached hitherto. But yet I hope in that Power and mercy of God that has appeared So triumphant in the Success of your Labours in other places, that he will send a Blessing with you even to us, tho' we are unworthy of it. I hope, if God preserves my Life, to see something of that Salvation of God in New-England which he has now begun, in a benighted, wicked and miserable world and age and in the most guilty of all nations. It has been with refreshment of Soul that I have heard of one raised up in the Church of England to revive the mysterious, Spiritual, despised and exploded Doctrines of the Gospel, and full of a Spirit of zeal for the promotion of real vital piety, whose Labours have been attended with such Success. Blessed be God that hath done it! who is with you, and helps you, and makes the weapons of your warfare mighty. We see that God is faithful, and never will forget

491

the promises that he has made to his Church; and that he will not Suffer the smoking flax to be quenched, even when the floods seem to be overwhelming it; but will revive the flame again, even in the darkest times. I hope this is the dawning of a day of God's mighty Power and glorious grace to the world of mankind. May you go on Rev. Sir! and may God be with you more and more abundantly, that the work of God many be carried on by a Blessing on your Labours still, with that Swift Progress that it has been hitherto, and rise to a greater height, and extend further and further, with an irresistable Power bearing down all opposition! and may the Gates of Hell never be able to prevail against you! and may God send forth more Labourers into his Harvest of a Like Spirit, until the Kingdom of Satan shall shake, and his proud Empire fall throughout the Earth and the Kingdom of Christ, that glorious Kingdom of Light, holiness, Peace and Love, shall be Established from one end of the Earth unto the other!

"Give my love to Mr. Seward: I hope to see him here with you. I believe I may venture to say that what has been heard of your Labours and Success has not been taken notice of more more [sic] in any place in New-England than here, or received with fuller credit. I hope therefore if we have opportunity, we shall hear you with greater attention. The way from New-York to Boston through Northampton is but little further than the nearest that is; and I think leads through as populous a part of the Country as any. I desire that you and Mr. Seward would come directly to my house. I shall account it a Great favour and Smile of Providence to have opportunity to Entertain such Guests under my Roof, and to have some Acquaintance with such Persons.

"I fear it is too much for me to desire a particular Remembrance in your prayers, when I consider how many thousands do doubtless desire it, who can't all be particularly mention'd; and I am far from thinking my self worthy to be distinguished. But pray Sir Let your heart be lifted up to God for me among others, that God would bestow much of that blessed Spirit on me that he has bestowed on you, and make me also an instrument of his Glory. I am Rev. Sir

> unworthy to be called your
> fellow Labourer,
Jonathan Edwards.
To the Rev. Mr. George Whitefield"[1]

---

1   *William and Mary Quarterly,* 3rd Series, Vol. 29 (1972), pp. 487–489.

APPENDIX 2

1739

Works by Whitefield

"Franklin sold each of the following three editions of Whitefield's journals as individual publications; he also published them together in 1740 as the first volume of his subscription publication:

1a. *A Journal Of A Voyage From Gibraltar to Georgia ... Containing Many curious Observations, and Edifying Reflections, on the several Occurrences that happen'd in the Voyage.* pp. 45.

1b. 2nd Title: *A Continuation Of the Reverend Mr. Whitefield's Journal From His Arrival at Savannah, To His Return to London.* pp. 47–102.

1c. 3rd Title: *A Continuation Of the Reverend Mr. Whitefield's Journal From His Arrival at London, To His Departure from Thence, on His Way to Georgia.* pp. 103–252. Evans 4453. Miller 180.

Works for Whitefield

None

Works against Whitefield

None

1740

Works by Whitefield

2. *A Brief and General Account Of the First Part Of The Life Of the Reverend Mr. Geo. Whitefield, From his Birth, to his Entering into Holy Orders.* Evans 4626. Miller 214.

3. *Journal Of A Voyage From London to Gibralter ... Containing Many curious Observations, and Edifying Reflections, on the several Occurrences that happen'd in the Voyage.* The Sixth Edition. Evans 4630. Miller 219.

4a. *A Continuation Of the Reverend Mr. Whitefield's Journal During the Time he was detained in England, by the Embargo.* Vol. II. Evans 4633. Miller 215a.

4b. 2nd Title: *A Continuation Of the Reverend Mr. Whitefield's Journal From His Embarking after the Embargo. To His Arrival at Savannah in Georgia.* Evans 4633. Miller 216.

5 A second edition of *A Continuation Of the Reverend Mr. Whitefield's Journal From His Embarking after the Embargo. To His Arrival at Savannah in Georgia.* Evans 4634. Miller 216.

6. *A Continuation Of the Reverend Mr. Whitefield's Journal From A few Days after his Arrival at Georgia, To His second Return thither from Pennsylvania.* Evans 4636. Miller 217.

7. *A Letter From the Reverend Mr. Whitefield To A Friend In London, Shewing the Fundamental Error of the Book, Entitled, The Whole Duty of Man.* Evans 4643. Miller 220.

8. *A Letter from the Rev. Mr. Whitefield, to some Church-Members of the Presbyterian Perswasion, in answer to certain Scruples lately Proposed in proper Queries raised on each Remark.* Evans 4646. Miller 221.

9. *Sermons on Various Subjects. In Two Volumes.* Evans 4650. Miller 222, 223.

10. *Three Letters From The Reverend Mr. G. Whitefield: Viz. Letter I. To a Friend in London, concerning Archbishop Tillotson. Letter II. To the same, on the same Subject. Letter III. To the Inhabitants of Maryland, Virginia, North and South-Carolina, concerning their Negroes.* Evans 4651. Miller 224.

11. *Voorbidding ein Ieder Christen's Plicht, in de Wyze and Dwaaze Maagden, Vertoont in Twe Predicaties* [with J. Peter Zenger] Evans 4657. Miller B21.

12. *A Journal of a Voyage from Gibraltar to Georgia.* Second printing of the first section of Whitefield's Journal. A reset.

Works for Whitefield

13. Erskine, Ralph. *Gospel Sonnets, Or Spiritual Songs. In Six Parts.* Franklin advertised in the September 25 *Pennsylvania Gazette* that the Erskine reprint was "Particularly recommended by the Rev. Mr. Whitefield." Evans 4506. Miller 187.

14. Finley, Samuel. *A Letter to a Friend, Concerning Mr. Whitefield, Messrs. Tennents, etc. and Their Opposers ...* Evans 4509. Miller 189.

15. Gillespie, George. *A Letter to the Rev. Brethren of the Presbytery of New York, or of Elizabeth-Town* ... By the time Whitefield returned to Pennsylvania in 1745 on his third American journey, Gillespie had become an opponent of revivalism. Evans 4520. Miller 282.

16. *A Letter to Mr. Ebenezer Kinnersley from his Friends in the Country, In Answer to His Two Letters Lately Published.* A Baptist lay preacher, Kinnersley provoked a controversy in a sermon against what he considered to be emotional excesses of revivalists. Evans 4542. Miller 196.

17. Smith, J[osiah]. *The Character, Preaching, &c. Of The Reverend Mr. Geo. Whitefield, Impartially represented and Supported, in a Sermon Preach'd in Charlestown, South-Carolina, March 26. Anno Domini 1740.* Evans 4601. Miller 209.

18. *Some Observations on the Rev. Mr. Whitefield, And His Opposers. Printed for the Benefit of the Orphan House in Georgia.* Evans 4603. Miller B17.

Works against Whitefield

19. *The Querists, Or An Extract of sundry Passages taken out of Mr. Whitefield's printed Sermons, Journals and Letters: Together With Some Scruples propos'd in proper Queries raised on each Remark. By Some Church-Members of the Presbyterian Persuasion.* Evans 4586. Miller 206.

20. *Remarks on Several Passages of Mr. Whitefield's Sermons, Journals and Letters, Which Seem Unsound and Erroneous and Very Liable to Exceptions; with Several Queries by Some Friends to the Truth of the Gospel.* Evans 4591. Miller B16.

1741

Works by Whitefield

21. *An Account of the Money Received and Disbursed For the Orphan House in Georgia. By the Rev. Mr. George Whitefield.* Evans 4843. Miller B26.

22. *A Continuation Of the Reverend Mr. Whitfield's Journal, From a few Days after his Arrival at Savannah, June the Fourth, To His leaving Stanford, the last Town in New-England, October 29, 1740.* Evans 4846. Miller 269.

23. *A Continuation of the Reverend Mr. Whitefield's Journal From Savannah, June 25, 1740. To His Arrival at Rhode-Island, His Travels in the Other Governments of New-England, To His Departure from Stanford for New-York* [New England edition]. Evans 4850. Miller B28.

24. *A Continuation of the Reverend Mr. Whitefield's Journal, From His Leaving Stanford in New-England, To His Arrival at Falmouth, in England, March 11, 1741. Containing An Account of the Work of God at New-York, Pennsylvania and South-Carolina* [Pennsylvania edition]. Evans 4854. Miller B27.

25. *A Letter From The Reverend Mr. George Whitefield, To The Reverend Mr. John Wesley, In Answer To His Sermon, Entitled, Free Grace.* Evans 4856. Miller 270.

Works for Whitefield

26. Blair, Samuel. *A Particular Consideration Of A Piece, Entitled, The Querists: Wherein sundry Passages ... of the Rev. Mr. Whitefield are vindicated ...* Evans 4675. Miller 270.

27. Erskine, Ralph. *A Letter From The Reverend Mr. Ralph Erskine To The Reverend Mr. Geo. Whitefield.* Evans 4714. Miller 234.

28. Finley, Samuel. *Christ Triumphing, and Satan Raging. A Sermon On Matth. XIII. 28.* Evans 4716. Miller 235.

29. *Free Grace indeed! A Letter To The Reverend Mr. John Wesley, Relating to His Sermon Against Absolute Election ...* Originally published in London, this unsigned letter sides with Whitefield in his theological dispute with John Wesley over predestination. Evans 4857. Miller 238.

30. Tennent, Gilbert. *Remarks Upon a Protestation Presented to the Synod of Philadelphia, June 1, 1741.* Evans 4820. Miller 263.

Works against Whitefield

31. [Cross, Robert, et al.]. *A Protestation Presented To The Synod Of Philadelphia, June 1, 1741.* Evans 4704. Miller 230.

32. [The Querists]. *A Short Reply To Mr. Whitefield's Letter ...* Evans 4805. Miller 260.

Sources: Charles Evans, ed., *American Bibliography: A Chronological Dictionary* ... (New York, 1941), II, 149–150, 170–173, 195–197; C. William Miller, *Benjamin Franklin's Philadelphia Printing, 1728–1766: A Descriptive Bibliography* (Philadelphia, 1974). Miller does not consider the entries prefixed with B to be authentic. See also Roger Pattrell Bristol, ed., *Supplement to Charles Evans' American Bibliography* (Charlottesville, Va., 1970), 62, 65, 68.

ANDREW BRADFORD'S PUBLICATIONS OF WORKS BY, FOR, AND AGAINST WHITEFIELD

1739

Works by Whitefield

1. *A Letter From the Reverend Mr. Whitefield, To the Religious Societies lately form'd in England and Wales. Printed for the Benefit of the Orphan House in Georgia.* Evans 4455.

2. *What think ye of Christ. A Sermon Preached at Kensington-Common, near London, and at Philadelphia,* 1739. Evans 4458.

3. *The Rev. Mr. Whitefield's Answer to the Bishop of London's Last Pastoral Letter.* Evans 4457.

Works for Whitefield

4. [Coleman, Benjamin, and others]. *Three Letters to The Reverend Mr. George Whitefield.* Evans 4354.

Works for Whitefield
None

Works against Whitefield
None

1740

Works by Whitefield

5. Another edition of Whitefield's Life. See Franklin's 1740 edition. *A Brief and General Account, Of the First Part of the Life of the Reverend Mr. George Whitefield, From His Birth, to his Entering into Holy-Orders.* Evans 4627.

6. *Directions How to Hear Sermons, Preach'd by the Reverend Mr. George Whitefield, A. B.* 3d ed. Evans 4638.

7. *Five Sermons, viz.* A collection of previously published sermons. Evans 4639.

8. *The Heinous Sin of Drunkenness. A Sermon Preached by George Whitefield, A.B. of Pembroke College, Oxford.* Evans 4640.

9. *The Indwelling of the Spirit the Common Privilege of all Believers. A Sermon at Bexley, in Kent, on Whitsunday,* 1739. Evans 4641.

10. *A Sermon, Entitled, The Wise and Foolish Virgins.* Evans 4649.

11. *Worldly Business No Plea for the Neglect of Religion. A Sermon.* Evans 4652.

Works for Whitefield

12. Seagrave, Robert. *Remarks Upon The Bishop of London's Pastoral Letter. In Vindication of Mr. Whitefield. And His Particular Doctrines.* The Fourth Edition. Evans 4594.

Works against Whitefield

13. Cummings, Archibald. *Faith absolutely necessary, but not sufficient to Salvation without good works. In Two Sermons, Preached at Christ-Church in Philadelphia, April 20, 1740.* Evans 4499.

14. Gibson, Edmund. *The Bishop of London's Last Pastoral Letter, Against Lukewarmness and Enthusiasm.* Bradford reprinted this strongly worded attack on Whitefield that was first published in London in 1740. Evans 4518.

15. Kinnersley, Ebenezer. *A Letter to the Rev. Jenkins Jones from Ebenezer Kinnersley Occasioned by a Late Anonymous Paper* ... Bradford published this anti-revivalist's pamphlets while Franklin printed pro-revivalist responses. Evans 4538.

16. Kinnersley, Ebenezer, *A Second Letter From Ebenezer Kinnersley, To His Friend in the Country.* Evans 4537.

Source: Evans, *American Bibliography, II,* 149–150, 170–173, 195–197. See also Bristol, ed., *Supplement to Charles Evans' American Bibliography,* 62, 65, 68."[1]

---

[1]   *William And Mary Quarterly,* 3rd Series, Vol. L (1993), Frank Lambert, pp 549-554.

APPENDIX 3

NOTEWORTHY INFORMATION ON WHITEFIELD

It should be noted that there is a historical building in Newburyport, MA which is called "The Dalton House", named after a prominent and wealthy businessman of the mid-eighteenth century in New England. For it was in this home that many famous men visited including, George Washington, John Quincy Adams, Thomas Jefferson, John Hancock, and George Whitefield. As one studies the life and ministry of George Whitefield it is noticed that in each town wherein he preached he often visited or lodged at the most prominent person in town. In Newburyport in 1770 he visited this house on his way up to Portland. This home was a favorite of the pastors of the Old South Church (Jonathan Parsons, and John "fire and brimstone" Murray). Visiting the house today (now a private club) one steps back in time to the eighteenth century; the front room with the large inviting hearth (with the parson's cabinet—where the liquor was hid in the event of the minister's coming!) gives a clear picture of what it was like in Whitefield's day. The room is conducive to relaxing by the fire and sharing warm fellowship with host and guests. It is easy to picture George Whitefield sitting by the glowing fire with a glass of rum in hand relating his recent preaching routes to interested guests. There is a portrait of Whitefield hanging in one of the many rooms of this mansion as is typical of each important visitor with noted brass nameplate detailing the year of the VIP's visit.

In the town of Exeter, New Hampshire there is a stone marker which commemorates the exact spot where Whitefield preached his last open-air sermon whereby the comments were made by a bystander as George Whitefield made his way to the hastily made pulpit (more than likely consisting of two hogheads with a broad board across the tops): "Sir, you

look more fit for bed than for preaching". "Quite true Sir," replied
Whitefield, "but I'd rather wear out than rust out."

The stone has Whitefield's name on it and it is difficult to picture the scene
that day where thousands stood beneath the sky in an open field which is a
busy paved street today. However, it is easy to find and the trip is quite
worthwhile and the town of Exeter is delightful.

There is a piece of Whitefieldian history that has recently come to light
and it has surprised many George Whitefield scholars. There is evidence that
one of George Whitefield's thumbs is not in his casket! But in another
location altogether—the thumb resides in the Methodist Archives at Drew
University in a reliquary alongside personal items of the Methodist preacher
Francis Asbury. This isn't the first time a Whitefield relic has been
transported to various locations (his arm being stolen in the nineteenth
century, taken to London and later returned—the box it was shipped in is on
display at the Old South Church in Newburyport).

There is also an interesting piece of Colonial history which occurred in
Newburyport, MA at the Old South First Presbyterian church on September
16th, 1775. The church historian of the Old South related in a tour of the
church that a band of Continental Army soldiers arrived at the church on
their way to Quebec. What is noteworthy about this is that the commander
of this little band was the infamous Benedict Arnold! Benedict Arnold
wished to see the crypt where Whitefield lay and he and a few soldiers made
the descent to the tomb beneath the historic pulpit. They ordered the sexton
to open the coffin containing George Whitefield's remains, the soldiers then
defiled the tomb by cutting off pieces of the great evangelist's collar and
wristbands. They carried these with them for their dangerous journey into
Canada hoping the articles to be good luck charms (it did not work for their
mission was a disaster!).

In Ipswich, Massachusetts, is the historic house of John Whipple.
Contained within its walls are a portrait of an under forty George Whitefield
by an unknown artist and his leather bound 1615 edition of the Geneva
Bible that he used when preaching.

Dallimore mentions an incident where Whitefield was staying at a
merchant's house (Thomas Fanning) in Southold, Long Island, wherein he
wrote on a pane of glass, "One Thing Is Needful". Through research I have
located this pane of glass! It is in a box in the attic of the Oysterponds
Historical Society on Long Island, New York. Amy Folk, the historian there
climbed into the attic and found the following inscription attached to the
old pane of glass:

"About the year 1765 the Rev. George Whitefield visited the Township, (Southold). He lodged one night at the house then occupied by a Mr. Thomas Fanning, who was possessed of an abundance of the good things of this life yet to him seemed to be destitute of that which is preferred before all temples, "The upright heart and pure'. In the morning Mr. Whitefield arose, and ere he left the room in which he had lodged, wrote with a diamond on the pane of glass those important words which appear upon its face. Since that time, the house has been occupied by a number of different occupants: it has several times been repaired; nearly every pane of glass has been broken, yet this distinguished one remains entire to this day, being a period of more than sixty years." This explanatory note was attached to the pane in 1828.

How did this pane of glass with Whitefield's inscription wind up in the Oysterponds Historical Society? The answer is provided by Southold historian, Antonia Booth, who writes:

"Thomas Fanning did own what is called the Orange Webb House now in Orient, New York, and originally situated at Sterling Creek and Main Street in the Village of Greenport (originally called Sterling). The house was built by Captain William Booth around 1720 and it is supposed to have been his son Lieutenant Constant Booth who succeeded him upon his death in 1723, who entertained Reverend George Whitefield in 1763 and also Colonel George Washington (not at the same date). The pane of glass upon which Whitefield is said to have etched the words, 'But one thing is needful' was removed from the window in 1828 and presented by a Miss Fanny Booth to Augustus Griffin of Southold. The pane of glass was lost for a long time and turned up in the archives of the then named Long Island Historical Society in Brooklyn (now called the Brooklyn Historical Society). The Booth House was moved to Oyster ponds (Orient) on a barge in 1955 where it overlooks Orient Harbor and is part of the Oysterponds Historical Society."

Any study of the life and ministry of George Whitefield, evangelist, has its rewards. For to read his life history is to take hot embers and place them on the altar of one's heart. The power of God burned through the obedient vessel of George Whitefield and its fire is still contagious!

It is the author's hope that if a serious student of George Whitefield took Arnold Dallimore's fine two volume biography on Whitefield and added this present one to it there would form a composite of the great itinerant that would come close to the full portrait of the man that is humanly possible this side of heaven. Men like Whitefield *need to be studied* to preserve the legacy of our faith. It is our prayer that God raises up men like George Whitefield for this critical chapter in Church History and that by His grace He pours out His Spirit once again in revival upon a thirsty Church and spiritually dry society. What God has done before He can do again!

APPENDIX 4

PACKER ON WHITEFIELD

The following is an essay written by Dr. J.I. Packer entitled, "The Spirit with the Word: the Reformational Revivalism Of George Whitefield". It is included in its entirety for few men understand George Whitefield's theology and ministry better than James Packer. It is one of the wisest pieces ever written on Whitefield hence its inclusion in this definitive biography of the great evangelist.

If you ask an English Christian today who was the central figure of the mid-eighteenth-century revival, he or she will probably name John Wesley, the ex-Oxford don who for half a century led the network of societies which after his death became the Methodist Church, and whose Journal remains a classic of inspirational literature.[1] If you ask a modern American Christian to identify the central figure in New England's Great Awakening (1739–42), he or she is likely to point to Jonathan Edwards, still, perhaps, America's greatest theologian, whose *Narrative of a Surprising Work of God in the Conversion of Many Hundred Souls in Northampton and the Neighbouring towns and Villages* (1735) became the model for all subsequent revival histories, and whose theology of the matter, set out in a series of masterful treatises published after the Awakening had subsided,[2] has commanded virtually unanimous evangelical assent from that day to this. But if these two questions had been put in Edward's and Wesley's own

---

[1]   Wesley's *Journal* (actually, a sequence of 21 Journals) fills the first four volumes of his *Works* (ed. T. Jackson; 14 vols.; repr. Grand Rapids: Baker Book House, 1986). See also *The Journal of John Wesley* (ed. N. Curnock; 8 vols.; London: Epworth Press, 1938).

[2]   The writings in question are *A History of the Work of Redemption* (sermons preached in 1739; book published in 1744); *The Distinguishing Marks of a Work of the Spirit of God* (1741); *Thoughts on the Revival of Religion in New England in 1740* (1742); *A Treatise on the Religious Affections* (1746); all contained in *Works* (ed. E. Hickman; 2 vols.; repr. Edinburgh: Banner of Truth, 1974).

lifetime to anyone with the least knowledge of either movement, it is as
certain as anything can be that the same name would have been given in
reply to both, and it would not have been either of theirs; it would have
been the name of George Whitefield, the 'Grand Itinerant', whose preaching
sparked off and sustained revival religion of the Puritan type—reflective,
assured, joyful, powerful, life-transforming—in tens of thousands of lives
both sides of the Atlantic for more than thirty years, from the time of his
ordination in 1736 to his death in 1770.

"Preaching the grace of God in Christ was Whitefield's life, both
metaphorically and literally. He kept a record of over 18,000 formal
preaching occasions, and if the informal 'exhorting' (his term) which he
regularly did in private homes be added in it is probably true to say that he
preached twice that number of times. Three stated sermons a day was
common; four was not unknown; and the 'exhorting' was done on top of
that. 'Who would think it possible', wrote Henry Venn, vicar of
Huddersfield, who knew Whitefield well,

> that a person ... should speak in the compass of a single week (and that for
> years) in general forty hours, and in very many, sixty, and that to thousands; and
> after this labour, instead of taking any rest, should be offering up prayers and
> intercessions, with hymns and spiritual songs, as his manner was, in every house
> to which he was invited.[3]

"Whitefield squandered himself unstintingly, and it is no wonder that in
1765, when he was fifty-one, John Wesley, eleven years his senior, should
have noted after a breakfast meeting with him: 'Mr. Whitefield ... seemed to
be an old, old man, being fairly worn out in his Master's service'.[4] The
wonder is, rather, that Whitefield was able to maintain his non-stop
preaching routine for nearly five more years, constantly testifying that the
preaching which exhausted his body energized his heart.

"To the last, a visit from Whitefield to any location was a major event, and
he drew much larger crowds on his tours than did any other revival
spokesman. Often over 10,000, sometimes more than 20,000, attended his
open-air orations, and all heard his huge voice distinctly, even in the two-
hour message he gave at Exeter, New Hampshire, the afternoon before the
cardiac asthma attack that ended his life. It has been estimated that during his
ministry he preached to combined audiences of over ten million, and that
four-fifths of America's colonists, from Georgia to New Hampshire, heard

3   A. Dallimore, *George Whitefield* (2 vols.: Banner of Truth, 1970, 1980), II. p 521.
4   Wesley, *Works*, III, p. 238. Other similar comments: 'Humanly speaking, he is worn
out' (133; May, 1763). 'His soul appeared to be vigorous still, but his body was sinking apace'
(354; March, 1769). Whitefield died on Sept. 30, 1770.

him at least once—something that could be said of no other person. About eight years of his life were spent in America, where he died in the middle of his seventh tour; otherwise, apart from two months in Bermuda in 1748, the British Isles were his stamping-ground, and he criss-crossed them again and again as a messenger of the gospel of Christ. Cried John Wesley in his memorial sermon for Whitefield, which he preached in both the London centres (Moorfields Tabernacle and Tottenham Court Chapel) that had been put up as stations for Whitefield's ministry:

> Have we read or heard of any person since the Apostles, who testified the gospel of the grace of God … through so large a part of the habitable world? Have we read or heard of any person who called so many thousands, so many myriads, of sinners to repentance? Above all, have we read or heard of any who has been a blessed instrument in his [God's] hand of bringing so many sinners from 'darkness to light, and from the power of Satan unto God?'[5]

"The expected answer, of course, was no; and the same answer would have had to be given through the next two centuries, right up to the glory days of electronically-boosted Billy Graham.

"In Whitefield's own lifetime he had celebrity status as a preaching phenomenon, and was recognized as the pioneer of all the distinctives that marked the revival in Britain: use of the name 'Methodist';[6] evangelistic preaching in the open air as well as in churches, and on planned tours as well as in response to direct invitations; forming local Methodist societies and lining up lay circuit riders to provide them with regular evangelical instruction and exhortation;[7] publishing news of the ongoing revival in a weekly paper;[8] and printing his journals, a personal record of his life and ministry, as he did between 1737 and 1741. It is usual to credit Wesley with these procedural innovations, but in fact at each point Wesley did no more than follow the younger man's example.[9] Today, however, Whitefield's pastoral pioneering, like so much else about him, is largely forgotten; which is, to say the least, an injustice and a pity.

"When I became a Christian in 1944, Whitefield's role in the evangelical life of his day was unknown to those who nurtured me. But I knew his

5 Wesley, *Works*, VI, p. 177.
6 Dallimore, *George Whitefield*, I, pp. 381–83.
7 Dallimore, *George Whitefield*, II. pp. 149–59.
8 H. S. Stout, *The Divine Dramatist: George Whitefield and the Rise of Modern Evangelicalism* (Grand Rapids: Eerdmans, 1991), pp. 144–47. Whitefield's paper was called *The Weekly History; or, An Account of the Most Remarkable Particulars Relating to the Present Progress of the Gospel*.
9 Dallimore, *George Whitefield*, II, p. 531.

name, for I had attended his old school, the Crypt School, Gloucester,[10] and
had seen him represented in a school pageant (not very accurately, as I later
learned) hammering sabbath-breakers. Three months after my conversion,
lying in bed with bronchitis, I read both volumes of Luke Tyerman's 1876
biography, and the career of the great Gloucestrian made a tremendous
impression on me, securing him pride of place in my private heroes' gallery.
I subsequently found that Whitefield had made a similar impact on C.H.
Spurgeon, the nineteenth century's greatest pastoral evangelist,[11] and on
Martyn Lloyd-Jones, Spurgeons' nearest twentieth-century counterpart.[12]
Interest in Whitefield has grown in recent years, as witness the publishing of
the first collected edition of his journals,[13] the facsimile reprint of his letters
up to 1742 from the edition of 1771,[14] the big and painstaking 'filiopietistic'
life of Whitefield by Arnold Dallimore, *George Whitefield: The Life and Times
of the Great Evangelist of the Eighteenth-Century Revival,*[15] John Pollock's vivid
and racy *George Whitefield and the Great Awakening,*[16] and Harry S. Stout's
not-so-filiopietistic but shrewd biography, *The Divine Dramatist: George
Whitefield and the Rise of Modern Evangelicalism,*[17] plus most recently the
Spring 1993 number of the widely circulated journal of popular scholarship,
Christian History.[18] Perhaps the recognition of greatness and significance that
is Whitefield's due is coming to him at last. In any case, however, I am
confident that my honoured friend James Atkinson, who is himself as much
a preacher of the gospel as he is a historical scholar and theologian, will have
some interest in the attempt of this essay to determine Whitefield's place in
the Reformation succession for which he cares so deeply.

---

10 Dallimore calls it 'St Mary's' (*George Whitefield,* I, p. 50) and 'the de Crypt School'
simpliciter. Stout, *The Divine Dramatist,* p. 2, moves the school, with the Bell Inn, Whitefield's
home (almost next door), and Southgate Street, where both stood, from Gloucester to
Bristol—a spectacular slip.
11 'There is no end to the interest which attaches to such a man as Whitefield. Often as I
have read his life, I am conscious of a distinct quickening whenever I turn to it. *He lived.* Other
men seem to be only half alive; but Whitefield was all life, fire, wing, force. My own model, if
I may have such a thing in due subordination to my Lord, is George Whitefield' (quoted from
L. Drummond, *Spurgeon Prince of Preachers* [Grand Rapids: Kregel, 1992], p. 219).
12 See Lloyd-Jones's appreciation of Whitefield, 'John Calvin and George Whitefield', in
The Puritans: Their Origins and Successors (Edinburgh: Banner of Truth, 1987), pp. 101–28. 'I
could imagine no greater privilege, than to speak on George Whitefield', p. 102.
13 *George Whitefield's Journals* (London: Banner of Truth Trust, 1960).
14 *George Whitefield's Letters,* 1734–42 (Edinburgh: Banner of Truth, 1976).
15 See n. 3 above. The adjective 'filiopietistic' comes from Stout.
16 John Pollack, *George Whitefield and the Great Awakening* (London: Hodder & Stoughton,
1973).
17 See n. 8 above.
18 Published quarterly by Christianity Today, Inc., 465 Gundersen Drive, Carol Stream, IL
60188.

II

"With his Oxford education, natural ease of manner, and slight West-country twang, which made him seem attractively human (his resonant speech was always somewhat nasal, and he pronounced 'Christ' as 'Chroist' all his life), Whitefield, having been ordained at twenty-one in 1736, shot quickly into prominence as a Bible-preaching pastoral evangelist on the grand scale. At a time when other Anglican clergy were writing and reading flat sermons of a mildly moralistic and apologetic sort, Whitefield preached extempore about heaven and hell, sin and salvation, the dying love of Christ, and the new birth, clothing his simple expository outlines with glowing dramatic conscience-challenging rhetoric, and reinforcing his vocal alternations of soothing and punching with a great deal of body movement and gesture, thereby adding great energy to the things he was saying. At a time when other Anglican clergy were watching their churches empty, Whitefield went out to preach in the open air, loved the experience, and saw vast crowds gather to hear him and many come to faith through his messages. To put his extraordinary ministry in perspective, we need to note that he was, first, a born orator; secondly, a natural actor; thirdly, an English Protestant pietist; fourthly, an Anglican Calvinist of the older Puritan type; fifthly, a disciplined, somewhat ascetic clergyman of inflexible single-mindedness and integrity, childlike in humility and passionately devoted to his Lord; sixthly, a transparent friendly, forthcoming, care-giving man, as far from stand-offishness as could be, to whose spontaneous good will was added the evangelist's gift of making all the members of the crowd feel they were being addressed personally in what he said;[19] and seventhly, a Christian of catholic and ecumenical spirit whose vision of continuous revival throughout the English-speaking world led him to renounce all forms of institutional leadership and control, so that he might be entirely at the service of all. Each of these points calls for separate comment.

"*First*, on Whitefield as an orator, the most insightful remarks come from a transcribed address by one who was himself a notable pulpit orator, and thus knew what he was talking about, Martyn Lloyd-Jones, I quote him at some length.

A man is born an orator. You cannot make orators. You are either an orator or you are not. And this man was a born orator. He could not help it ... and like all orators, he was characterized by the great freedom and appropriateness of his

---

19 'He had a most peculiar art of speaking personally to you, in a congregation of four thousand people' (Cornelius Winter, who was Whitefield's factotum and travelling companion, 1767–70: in Dallimore, *George Whitefield*, II, p. 482).

gestures. The pedantic John Wesley was not an orator, and he sometimes tended to be a bit critical of George Whitefield in this respect. I remember reading in Wesley's *Journal* of how once they both happened to be in Dublin at the same time and how John Wesley went to listen to Whitefield. In his account of the service, Wesley refers to his gestures, and says that it seemed to him that Whitefield was a little bit too much like a Frenchman in a box. He means that Whitefield tended to speak with his hands as much as with his lips and mouth. But that is oratory. One of the greatest orators of all time was Demosthenes. Somebody asked Demosthenes one day, 'What is the first great rule of oratory?' And Demosthenes answered, 'The first great rule of oratory is—action; and the second great rule of oratory is—action; and the third great rule of oratory is—action' ... We are living in evil days; we know nothing about oratory. George Whitefield was a born orator. Have you heard what David Garrick is reported to have said? David Garrick was the leading actor in London in those times and whenever he had an opportunity he always went to listen to Whitefield. He was not so much interested in the gospel as in the speaking and the gestures ... Garrick is reported to have said that he would give a hundred guineas if could only say 'Oh!' as George Whitefield said it ...[20]

"*Secondly,* Whitefield was an actor—'a born actor', in Lloyd-Jones's phrase[21]—who, as his contemporaries sometimes observed, might have been equal or superior to Garrick had he gone on the stage. As a boy, he had excelled in school theatricals, where evidently he had mastered the actor's two arts, expression and projection. Stout underlines the significance of this actor's training. Acting manuals of Whitefield's day, he tells us, pinpointed

> ten dramatic passions to which appropriate actions and facial expressions were attached: joy, grief, fear, anger, pity, scorn, hatred, jealousy, wonder, and love. With these ten tools the actor could play any part, for they encompassed the sum and substance of the human condition. Of Whitefield's great contemporary David Garrick it was said that he could entertain guests by 'throwing his features into the representation of Love, Hatred, Terror, Pity, Jealousy, Desire and Joy in so rapid and striking a manner [as to] astound the whole country' ... In place of thinking man the manuals substituted impassioned man ...[22]

"All this Whitefield absorbed in his youth, and as a result his public style was that of 'an actor-preacher, as opposed to a scholar-preacher'.[23]

---

20 Lloyd-Jones, 'John Calvin and George Whitefield', p. 117. I cannot track down Lloyd-Jones's reference to Wesley; but his Journal for February 1750 contains this equally condescending comment: 'Mr. Whitefield preached ... Even the little improprieties both of his language and manner were a means of profiting many, who would not have been touched by a more correct discourse, or a more calm and regular manner of speaking' (Wesley, *Works*, II. p. 172). And later that year: 'I have sometimes thought Mr. Whitefield's action was violent' (Wesley, *Works*, II. p. 195).
21 Lloyd-Jones, 'John Calvin and George Whitefield', p. 117.
22 Stout, *The Divine Dramatist*, pp. 9–10.
23 Stout, *The Divine Dramatist*, p. xix.

"As a born actor, now trained to wear his heart on his face and to pour it into his voice, Whitefield's instinct was for performance.[24] He lived to evangelize and nurture, and 'his private life shrank into a small and relatively insignificant interlude between the big performances'.[25] Stout, with others, speaks of Whitefield's 'shameless' self-promotion,[26] but the adjective does not fit ('uninhibited' might do): no pride, self-aggrandizement or exploitation of others entered into what he did at any stage of his career to publicise his preaching of the gospel. As God's anointed barnstormer, he simply advertised coming performances, looking to God to cause each congregation to pull out of him fresh dramatic creativity in communicating the material he knew so well. It is in these terms that we should understand his statement, in a letter of 1750: 'The more we do, the more we may do; every act strengthens the habit; the best preparation for preaching on Sunday is to preach every day of the week'.[27] We need to remember that for an actor every performance is, among other things, a rehearsal for the next one.

"*Thirdly,* Whitefield was a pietist, that is, one who saw practical personal devotion to the Father and the Son through the Spirit as always the Christian's top priority. Mark Noll types pietism in terms of

(1) its experiential character—pietists are people of the heart for whom Christian living is the fundamental concern; (2) its biblical focus—pietists … take standards and goals from the pages of Scripture; (3) its perfectionist bent— pietists are serious about holy living and expend every effort to follow God's law, spread the gospel, and provide aid for the needy; (4) its reforming interest— pietists usually oppose what they regard as coldness and sterility in established church forms and practices.[28]

"The pietism of Whitefield's day grew out of the devotional revival that broke surface in both Protestantism and Roman Catholicism in the

---

24 Compare Winter's observations, from the end of Whitefield's life: 'It was truly impressive to see him ascend the pulpit. My intimate knowledge of him admits of my acquitting him of the charge of affectation. He always appeared to enter the pulpit with a significance of countenance, that indicated he had something of importance which he wanted to divulge, and was anxious for the effect of the communication'. 'I hardly ever knew him go through a sermon without weeping, and I truly believe his tears were the tears of sincerity. His voice was often interrupted by his affection.' 'His freedom in the use of his passions often put my pride to the trial [i.e embarrassed me]. I could hardly bear such unreserved use of tears, and the scope he gave to his feelings, for sometimes he exceedingly wept, stamped loudly and passionately, and was frequently so overcome, that for a few seconds, you would suspect he never could recover' (Dallimore, *George Whitefield,* II. pp. 482–83).

25 Stout, *The Divine Dramatist,* p. xxii.

26 Stout, *The Divine Dramatist,* p. xxiii.

27 Dallimore, *George Whitefield,* II, p. 286.

28 *Evangelical Dictionary of Theology* (ed. W. Elwell; Grand Rapids: Baker Book House, 1984), *s.v.* 'Pietism', pp. 855–56.

seventeenth century, partly as a reaction against the hard-shell controversialist, imperialist and formalist mind-sets that the Reformation conflicts had left behind, partly as a renewed perception of biblical Christianity in its own terms. In Protestant England, this seventeenth-century movement was channelled mainly through Puritanism, where justification by faith and regeneration and assurance through the Holy Spirit were set in a clear and classic Augustinian frame of sovereign grace. The High Church devotional development, fed more by the Greek fathers, was at first less influential, just as it was doctrinally less clear. But it was High Church pietists who developed the religious societies (midweek gatherings for devotional exercises) in Restoration times, and it was as a participant in one of these, John Wesley's 'Holy Club', whose members were called 'Methodists' because of their methodical rule of life, that Whitefield first realized his need of the characteristic pietist experience, namely the new birth.

"Through a long and painful conversion process Whitefield finally found the new birth that he sought—assurance of sins forgiven and Christ's love set upon him, newness of heart, and an overflow of joy in God. One of his first acts then was to buy and devour Matthew Henry's commentary, a brilliant pietistic exposition of Scripture that draws on a century of Puritan theology, Bible study and homiletics. This classic became his lifelong companion,[29] and, reinforced by subsequent association with America's latter-day Puritans, Jonathan Edwards and the Tennents, it established his pietism in the Puritan mould. Thereafter all the marks of pietism as Noll profiles it—devotional ardour, Bible-centredness, holiness with evangelism and philanthropy, hostility to cold and formal religion—became marks of Whitefield's life and ministry. His printed sermons and pastoral letters, the latter numbering over 1400, show that he concentrated throughout his ministry on the basics of personal religion—new birth, faith, repentance, righteousness and good works, praise of God, and love to Christ. No breath of scandal ever touched his personal life; the lures of sex, shekels and empire-building never enmeshed him. The pietism of his outlook was given credibility by the piety of his life.

---

29 See D. Crump, 'The Preaching of George Whitefield and his Use of Matthew Henry's Commentary', *Crux* 25.3 (September 1989), pp. 19–28. 'Usually, for an hour or two, before he entered the pulpit, he claimed retirement; and on a sabbath morning more particularly [when in London, where he had two pulpits to serve, and a new sermon was needed each Sunday], he was accustomed to have [Samuel] Clarke's Bible [a Puritan product, reprinted in 1759 with 'A Preface to the Serious Reader' by Whitefield: see *Works of George Whitefield* (ed. J. Gillies; London, 1771), IV, pp. 275ff.], Matthew Henry's Comment, and Cruden's Concordance within his reach' (Winter, in Dallimore's *George Whitefield*, II. p. 481).

"*Fourthly*, he was an Anglican Calvinist of the Puritan type. He embraced the sovereign-grace teaching of the Thirty-nine Articles with regard to personal salvation (see especially Articles 9–13 and 17), affirmed the developed federal theology of the seventeenth century, and insisted that sovereign-grace teaching, with its rejection of salvation by self-effort in all its forms, bears directly on the purity or otherwise of the believer's devotion. Two extracts from his letters show this.

> This ... is my comfort, 'Jesus Christ, the same yesterday, today, and for ever'. He saw me from all eternity; He gave me being; He called me in time; He has freely justified me through faith in his blood; He has in part sanctified me by His Spirit; He will preserve me underneath His everlasting arms till time shall be no more. Oh the blessedness of these evangelical truths! These are indeed Gospel; they are glad tidings of great joy to all that have ears to hear. These, bring the creature out of himself. These, make him hang upon the promise, and cause his obedience to flow from a principle of love.

> The doctrines of our election, and free justification in Christ Jesus are daily more and more pressed upon my heart. They fill my soul with a holy fire and afford me great confidence in God my Saviour.[30]

"Whitefield constantly maintained these doctrines and the spirituality of dependent gratitude that flowed from them, declaring: 'I embrace the Calvinistic scheme, not because of Calvin, but Jesus Christ has taught it to me',[31] and insisting that Anglicanism's historic formularies and best theologians were on his side at this point.

"Whitefield's identification with the Puritan type of theology, both in and outside the Church of England, is apparent from his 'Recommendatory Preface' to the 1767 reprint of the works of the Baptist John Bunyan, which contained the following sentences:

> Ministers never write or preach so well as when under the cross: the sprit of CHRIST and of glory then rests upon them.

> It was this, no doubt, that made the *Puritans* of the last century such burning and shining lights. When cast out by the black *Bartholomew-act* [the 1662 Act of Uniformity, which triggered 2000 ejections from the ministry of the Church of England] ... they in an especial manner preached and wrote as men having authority. Though dead, by their writings they yet speak: a peculiar unction attends them to this very hour; and for these thirty years past I have remarked, that the more, true and vital religion hath revived either at home or abroad, the more the good old puritanical writings, or the authors of a like stamp who lived and died in the communion of the church of *England*, have been called for.[32]

---

30 *George Whitefield's Letters*, 1734–42, pp. 98, 79.
31 *George Whitefield's Letters*, 1734–42, p. 442.
32 *Works*, IV, p. 306.

"When in 1829 selections from Whitefield's works were published under
the title *The Revived Puritan*, the phrase was uncannily apt.[33] That, precisely,
is what Whitefield was. *"Fifthly* and *sixthly*, Whitefield displayed qualities of
Christian character that added credibility to his public ministrations. He was
no hypocrite, nor did those closest to him find great flaws and weaknesses in
him. They found him, rather, to be a person of real genuineness, integrity,
humility, poise and charm, affable and courteous in all company, with a
genius for friendship, great practical wisdom, simple tastes, and much joy in
living for God. To illustrate this properly would require virtually a retelling
of his life story, which is not possible here,[34] but a few facts may be
mentioned.

"In 1738 Whitefield committed himself to fund Bethesda, Georgia's
orphan house which he himself had founded. He carried this responsibility
for the rest of his life, and nearly ruined himself in the process of discharging
it.

"In 1739 he and Benjamin Franklin became friends, though neither then
nor thereafter did Franklin embrace his message of salvation from sin
through new birth. But Franklin wrote of him in 1747: 'He is a good man
and I love him',[35] and after his death: 'I knew him intimately upwards of
30 years. His Integrity, Disinterestedness and indefatigable Zeal in
prosecuting every good Work, I have never seen equalled, I shall never see
excelled.'[36]

"In 1739 Whitefield also became friends with Howell Harris, the
dynamic Welsh exhorter, and the friendship was lifelong, despite a period
during which Harris' behavioural aberrations strained it to its limit.[37] In
1743 Whitefield was chosen as moderator for life of the Calvinistic
Methodist Association of Wales, a body founded to regulate the evangelical
religious societies that Harris and others had formed throughout the
country, and Harris' praise for Whitefield's handling of his role was
unstinting.[38]

---

33 *The Revived Puritan*. Select Works of the Rev. George Whitefield, Containing a Memoir
... Thirty Sermons ... Fourty Seven Discourses ... A Compendium of his Epistolary
Correspondence ... In One Volume (Lewes: Sussex Press, John Baxter, 1829).
34 See the biographies, especially those of Tyerman, Pollock and Dallimore. All the
biographers are captivated, more of less, by Whitefield's personal qualities.
35 Dallimore, *George Whitefield*, II, p. 222.
36 Dallimore, *George Whitefield*, II, p. 453.
37 Dallimore, *George Whitefield*, II, pp. 295–303.
38 'I was stunned to see his amazing wisdom, wherein he is taught to manage the Church,
doing all calmly and wisely, following the Lord' (*Howell Harris Reformer and Soldier* [ed. T.
Beynon; Caernarvon: Calvinistic Methodist Bookroom, 1958], p. 41).

"In 1748, aged thirty-three, having reviewed the journals he published[39] at twenty-three, he wrote in a letter:

Alas! alas! In how many things have I judged and acted wrong ... I frequently wrote and spoke in my own spirit, when I thought I was writing and speaking by the assistance of the Spirit of God ... I have likewise too much made inward impressions my rule of acting, and too soon and too explicitly published what had been better kept in longer, or told after my death. By these things I have given some wrong touches to God's ark, and hurt the blessed cause I would defend, and also stirred up needless opposition. This has humbled me much ... I bless him [God] for ripening my judgment a little more, for giving me to see and confess, and I hope in some degree to correct and amend, some of my mistakes.[40]

"Whitefield in maturity was able to see and eliminate the imprudences of his youthful zeal; they did not recur during the last twenty-two years of his life.

"Finally, Whitefield distinguished himself as 'the peace-maker' (John Fletcher's description)[41] between John Wesley and himself, bending over backwards to heal the breach after Wesley and he had diverged in print over the meaning of predestination and 'free grace' (1740–41). Wesley's imperious single-mindedness and donnish didacticism, plus his eleven-year seniority to Whitefield and his fixed habit of treating Whitefield as his pupil and protege, as he does most unbeautifully throughout his printed journals, made him a difficult man for Whitefield to get back on terms with; but he managed it, at the cost of renouncing all his leadership roles in England and Wales in 1748 and operating thereafter from time to time as one of Wesley's assistants.[42] It was a triumph of humility on the part of the public celebrity who at the close of his life was signing his letters, 'Less than the least of all, George Whitefield'.[43]

"The *seventh* key fact about Whitefield, his passion for Christian unity as part of his vision of sustained spiritual vitality undergirding and transforming

---

39 It should be noted that the publishing of Whitefield's Journals began without his consent. On his return to England from Georgia in 1738 he found that James Hutton, an ardent supporter, had at this point jumped the gun. 'Whitefield had sent his diary of the journey from London to Gibraltar, for private circulation. A printer called Cooper saw it, scented profits and put it in print; but as he could not always decipher Whitefield's handwriting the text was corrupt and Printer Hutton had decided the absent author would approve if he published an accurate version' (Pollock, *George Whitefield*, p. 69). Finding this Journal already a best-seller, Whitefield followed it up over the next three years with half a dozen more. For more details, see Iain Murray's introduction to *Whitefield's Journals*, pp. 13–19.

40 Dallimore, *George Whitefield*, II, p. 241.

41 Dallimore, *George Whitefield*, II, p. 352.

42 Dallimore, *George Whitefield*, chs. 17, 23, II, pp. 247ff., 335ff.

43 To John Wesley, 12 Sept. 1769; to Robert Keen (Whitefield's last letter), 23 Sept. 1770; Dallimore, *George Whitefield*, II, pp. 475, 498.

514   GEORGE WHITEFIELD

community life both sides of the Atlantic, is sufficiently illustrated by the foregoing paragraph, and need not be further displayed here.

III

"We learn Whitefield's theology from his tracts and letters, and also from his seventy-five printed sermons.[44] These vary in style and provenance. They are all based on biblical texts, expounded, however sketchily, in context, but 46 of them were printed before Whitefield was twenty-five, and some were written out after being preached rather than before, and some were transcribed *viva voce* from Whitefield's lips as he orated and put in print sometimes with and sometimes without his approval. Such material needs to be handled with care, but theologically it is all homogeneous, and in no way innovative. We have already noted that, like all England's evangelical clergy then and since, Whitefield insisted that the religion he modelled and taught was a straightforward application of Anglican doctrine as defined in the Articles, the Homilies and the Prayer Book. We have seen that he took his interpretations of Scripture mainly if not entirely from the 'unparalleled', 'incomparable'[45] Matthew Henry. His developed understanding of justification by faith only through the imputed righteousness of Christ, and of the federal plan of salvation that five-point Calvinism spells out, came to him from Puritan and Scottish sources.[46] But the things he took from the Reformed tradition came out in his own way, cast into meditations and messages that called for present response, and located every such response, or refusal of it, as part of the drama which the Puritans had already mapped with great skill, namely the personal drama of the soul's ongoing journey to heaven or to hell. 'Dramatize! Dramatize!' urged Henry James; plots and characters of novels should be full of 'felt life'. Whitefield's instinct for drama led him to preach sermon after sermon that dramatized the issues of eternity,

---

44 Reprinted in one volume, *Sermons on Important Subjects* (London: Henry Fisher, Son, and P. Jackson, 1832).

45 *Works*, IV, pp. 307, 278.

46 For details, see Dallimore, *George Whitefield*, I. p. 405. Dallimore corrects the mistake, traceable to Tyerman, of supposing that Whitefield learned his Calvinism from Jonathan Edwards, whom he first met in 1740. On the voyage to America, a year before, he recorded that he had been 'greatly strengthened by perusing some paragraphs out of a book called *The Preacher*, written by Dr. [John] Edwards, of Cambridge, and extracted by Mr Jonathan Warn, in his books entitled, *The Church of England-Man turned Dissenter,* and *Arminianism the Backdoor to Popery*. There are such noble testimonies ... of justification by faith only, the imputed righteousness of Christ, our having no free-will, &c., that they deserve to be written in letters of gold' (*Journals*, p. 335). Tyerman and others seem to have confused Jonathan with John Edwards.

and summoned his hearers to seek, in his phrase, a 'felt Christ'. We can sum up the substance of Whitefield's sermons in a series of imperatives, as follows.

"*First, Face God.* People live thoughtlessly, drifting through their days, never thinking of eternity. But God the Creator, our lawgiver and holy judge, who made us for himself and holds us in his hands every moment, has revealed in Scripture that a day of judgment is coming when he will either welcome us into heaven's eternal joy or banish us for ever to hell's misery. So—*wake up! and reckon, here and now, with God!* Whitefield repeatedly shed tears of agonized compassion as he preached about the ruinous, suicidal, self-hating folly of those who would not do this.

"*Secondly, Know Yourself.* We mortals all see in ourselves, and in our children, and in all our fellow-humans, self-centered, self-pleasing, worldly-minded, really vicious dispositions. These bespeak the universal corruption of nature called original sin. G.K. Chesterton called original sin the one Christian doctrine that admits of demonstrative proof, and that was how Whitefield presented it. From Genesis 3 and Romans 5 he analyzed it in the standard Reformed way: the sin of Adam, our progenitor and covenant head, was imputed to us, his posterity, in the sense that we all now share the penal deprivations that his sin incurred for himself—bodily decay and mortality, plus a morally twisted disposition that makes faith, love and obedience God-ward a natural impossibility, just as it flaws all the godliness of those whose hearts God supernaturally renews. The doctrine of original sin thus answers the question: why am I no better than I am? It does not excuse us by letting us shift the blame for our perversities on to Adam; it just confirms to us that we are all naturally lost, spiritually impotent and helpless, without hope of commending ourselves to God by anything we do. This is the bad news that we must accept and internalize before we can appreciate the good news of salvation.

"*Thirdly, See Jesus.* Whitefield's preaching, like his personal faith, centred upon the person of 'the dear Jesus', the once-crucified, now glorified God-man, the gift of the Father's love and the embodiment of divine mercy. From Scripture Whitefield would set forth with rhapsodic rhetoric and arms-lifted, foot-stamping passion the incarnation, Jesus's friendship with sinners, his pity for the needy, his agonizing death for our sins, his bodily resurrection and ascension, his present heavenly reign and coming return to judgment, and then he would go to town, as we would say, on the invitations to faith, promises of justification, preservation and glorification, and guarantees of his own fidelity that comprise Jesus' word to the world. It was said of Charles Finney that in his evangelistic preaching he rode sinners down with a calvary charge; Whitefield's way, however, was to sweep them off their feet with an overflow of compassionate affection, modelling his Master's good will towards the lost. Thus by word and action Whitefield enabled his hearers mentally and spiritually to see Jesus, with constantly overwhelming effect.

"*Fourthly, Understand Justification.* Following the Restoration many Anglican minds, recoiling from all things Calvinistic, took up with a moralistic, indeed legalistic, recasting of justification by faith. Faith ceased to be thought of as self-despairing trust in the person, work, promises and love of Jesus Christ the Mediator, and became, in the words of the influential Bishop Bull, 'virtually the whole of evangelical obedience'—in other words, a moral life of good works lived in hope of acceptance for it at the last day, despite its actual shortcomings. The significance of the cross in the process of salvation was that, in Jeremy Taylor's grotesque phrase, Christ has 'brought down the market'—that is, made it possible to secure final salvation through a devotion that is far from flawless. The bottom-line effect of Christ's death was thus to rehabilitate self-righteousness. Works are the way to heaven, after all.[47]

"This was in essence the theology of John Wesley during his Holy Club period, as it was of conventional Anglicanism all through Whitefield's life. It produced a religion of aspiration, perspiration, and, in sensitive souls, periodic desperation. Whitefield came to see it as blasphemous impiety, the religion of the natural man masquerading as Christianity, and he laboured constantly to wean people away from it. So he denounced self-righteousness, insisted that nothing we do is free from sin, and called on his hearers to come to Christ as guilty, helpless, hell-deserving offenders, and find righteousness and life in him.

"Put your trust in Jesus Christ, said Whitefield, over and over again, and present justification (pardon and acceptance, both lasting for ever) will be yours—not because of what you are or have done, but because Christ's righteousness wrought out by his active and passive obedience, his law-keeping and sin-bearing, is now imputed to you. The Holy Spirit will help you to believe if you are willing to believe and show your willingness by asking to be helped to do so, and the Spirit will witness to your justification and God's fatherly love for you once a true change of heart has taken place. Keep seeking through prayer to turn fully to Christ till you know you have been enabled to do just that, so that the gift of righteousness is now yours,

---

47 See, on this, C.F. Allison, *The Rise of Moralism* (London: SPCK, 1966).

and then you will worship and obey your God and Saviour out of unending gratitude for being saved.

"I quote at length the peroration of one of Whitefield's sermons, to give the flavour of this:

> Are any of you depending upon a righteousness of your own? Do any of you here think to save yourselves by your own doings? I say to you ... your righteousness shall perish with you. Poor miserable creatures! What is there in your tears? What in your prayers? What in your performances, to appease the wrath of an angry God? Away from the trees of the garden; come, ye guilty wretches, come as poor, lost, undone, and wretched creatures, and accept of a better righteousness than your own. As I said before, so I tell you again, the righteousness of Jesus Christ is an everlasting righteousness; it is wrought out for the very chief of sinners. Ho, every one that thirsteth, let him come and drink of this water of life freely. Are any of you wounded by sin? Do any of you feel you have no righteousness of your own? Are any of you perishing for hunger? Are any of you afraid you will perish for ever? Come, dear souls, in all your rags; come, thou poor man; come, thou poor distressed woman; you, who think God will never forgive you, and that your sins are too great to be forgiven; come, thou doubting creature, who art afraid thou wilt never get comfort; arise, take comfort, the Lord Jesus Christ, the Lord of life, the Lord of glory, calls for thee ... O let not one poor soul stand at a distance from the Saviour ... O come, come! Now, since it is brought into the world by Christ, so, in the name, in the strength, and by the assistance of the great God, I bring it now to the pulpit; I now offer this righteousness, this free, this imputed, this everlasting righteousness, to all poor sinners who will accept of it ... Think, I pray you, therefore, on these things; go home, go home, go home, pray over the text, and say, 'Lord God, thou hast brought an everlasting righteousness into the world by the Lord Jesus Christ; by the blessed Spirit bring it into my heart!' then, die when ye will, ye are safe; if it be tomorrow, ye shall be immediately translated into the presence of the everlasting God; that will be sweet! Happy they who have got this robe on; happy they that can say, 'My God hath loved me, and I shall be loved by him with an everlasting love!' That every one of you may be able to say so, may God grant, for the sake of Jesus Christ, the dear Redeemer; to whom be glory for ever ... Amen.[48]

"*Fifthly, Welcome the Spirit.* When Whitefield burst on the Anglican scene, very little was being said about the Holy Spirit, and it was commonly affirmed that the Spirit's activity in Christians' lives was something of which they would not be conscious. At the cost of being accused over and over of 'enthusiasm' (meaning, the fanaticism that thinks it receives direct revelations from God), Whitefield ridiculed this idea, and insisted that the Holy Spirit's presence in human lives would always be consciously felt, because of the

---

48 'The Righteousness of Christ, an Everlasting Righteousness' in *Sermons on Important Subjects*, pp. 207ff.

change in experience that the Spirit would bring about. This change, which the Bible calls regeneration, new birth, new creation, sanctification, transition from death to life, and Christ being formed in us, and which expresses itself in a sense of one's sin, leading to self-despair, leading one out of oneself to look to Christ and trust him alone for salvation, as was described above, is wrought only by the Holy Spirit; therefore we should desire, seek, and be ready for the Spirit's ministry in our lives, bringing about and continually deepening the change itself. In a sermon on conversion, Whitefield expounds the matter as follows:

> They that are truly converted to Jesus, and are justified by faith in the Son of God, will take care to evidence their conversion, not only by the having grace implanted in their hearts, but by that grace diffusing itself through every faculty of the soul, and making a universal change in the whole man ... The author of this conversion is the Holy Ghost ... nothing short of the influence of the Spirit of the living God can effect this change in our hearts ... and though there is and will be a contest between these two opposites, flesh and spirit, yet if we are truly converted, the spirit will get the ascendency ... God grant we may all thus prove that we are converted. This conversion, however it begins at home, will soon walk abroad; as the Virgin Mary was soon found out to be with child, so it will be soon found out whether Christ is formed in the heart. There will be new principles, new ways, new company, new works; there will be a thorough change in the heart and life ... first we are in bondage, afterwards we receive the Spirit of adoption to long and thirst for God, because he has been pleased to let us know that he will take us to heaven. Conversion means a being turned from hell to heaven ... the heart once touched with the magnet of divine love, ever after turns to the pole ...
>
> What say you to this change, my dear souls? is it not godlike, is it not divine, is it not heaven brought down to the soul? Have you felt it, have you experienced it?[49]

"It will be observed that this teaching on conversion has an essentially Augustinian structure: God in grace gives us the faith and love that he requires of us. John Wesley focused on this Augustinianism, with which he claimed to identify, when he declared, in his memorial sermon for Whitefield:

> His fundamental point was, 'Give God all the glory of whatever is good in man'; and, 'In the business of salvation, set Christ as high and man as low as possible'. With this point he and his friends at Oxford, the original Methodists, so called, set out. Their grand principle was, There is *no power* (by nature) and *no merit* in man. They insisted, all power to think, speak, or act aright, is in and from the Spirit of Christ.[50]

---

49   *Sermons on Important Subjects*, pp. 664–65.
50   *Works*, VI, p. 178.

"Working with this perspective, Whitefield followed the Puritans in presenting the conversion process in a two-sided way, as Augustinians typically do. When speaking psychologically and evangelistically, he depicted the realizing of one's sin and need, the praying and seeking to which this must lead, and the decision-making that faith and repentance involve, as a person's own acts, which we must ask for the Holy Spirit's help to perform. When speaking theologically and doxologically, however he interpreted the entire process as one which the Holy Spirit works from first to last, in which each of our steps Godward is taken only because the Holy Spirit is moving us forward by his secret action within us. God's irresistible prevenient grace (meaning, the Holy Spirit's work that dissolves resistance away) overcomes our natural inability, as slaves of sin, to turn ourselves to God: that is how we come to be born again and converted.

"This, then, was the theological frame within which Whitefield admonished: 'See that you receive the Holy Ghost, before you go hence [i.e. die]: for otherwise, how can you escape the damnation of hell?'[51] Without the Holy Spirit there is no transformation through new birth; without this there is no salvation for anyone; and, though God has his own sovereign ways of breaking into people's lives, only those who seek the Spirit's influence, and open themselves deliberately to it, can expect to undergo it in a converting way.

"The key principles of Whitefield's gospel message are now before us. On these themes his printed sermons ring endless changes, with remarkable rhetorical freshness and pungency, the impact of which, so we are told, was much intensified by his pulpit manner. 'The Lord gave him a manner of preaching, which was peculiarly his own', wrote John Newton.

> His familiar address, the power of his action, his marvellous talent in fixing the attention even of the most careless, I need not describe to those who have heard him, and to those who have not, the attempt would be in vain. Other ministers could, perhaps, preach the Gospel as clearly, and in general say the same things, but ... no man living could say them in his way.[52]

"All the evidence suggests that this was fair comment. Unmatched in his day for applying Reformed teaching about conversion and the converted life to the conscience, Whitefield was entirely free of doctrinal novelties. All he ever preached about, or desired to preach about, was personal salvation and godliness, and for that Puritan orthodoxy served him supremely well.

---

51 *Sermons on Important Subjects*, p. 489.
52 Dallimore, *George Whitefield*, II, p. 534.

IV

"Revivals—that is, animatings and deepenings of the awareness of God, of the sense of sin, of the knowledge of Christ, and of the evangelical responses of faith, repentance, righteousness, prayer and praise—have from time to time characterized the inner life of Protestant communities ever since the Reformation.[53] The revival pattern of fresh outpourings of the Holy Spirit to reverse spiritual decline has recurred many times. The human lightning-rods through whose ministrations the power of God strikes in revival are naturally called revivalists, and the ministrations themselves are denominated revivalism. The title of this essay speaks of Whitefield's 'Reformational Revivalism'. We are now in a position to scrutinize this phrase, to justify the description, and to form an opinion about Whitefield's place in the history of Christian springtimes down the centuries.

"But was Whitefield a revivalist? Here a distinction must be drawn, for the world 'revivalist' has a contemporary meaning that both dilutes the significance that it has when applied to Whitefield and distracts the attention from what Whitefield was actually doing—or perhaps we should say, was being used to do. Revivalism nowadays is a name for an American institutional development among conservative churches that directly reflects the populism, love of novelty and entertainment, fascination with technique, and consumerist orientation that have characterized America during the past two centuries. In terms of spiritual significance, this kind of revivalism has lost most of its link with revivals in the sense that Jonathan Edwards and George Whitefield and the Wesley brothers gave to that word. Revivalism in modern America means mounting what Charles Finney called 'protracted meetings', that is, a linked series of gatherings with a centrally evangelistic purpose, at which, in addition to forceful preaching that calls for decision and action, there is a programmed back-up of music (solos, choir items, and congregational songs, often with some twist of novelty), plus testimonies with an arresting human interest, plus ordinarily a modicum of hayseed humour from the emcee and the preacher, so that the entertainment dimension remains strong throughout. The purpose of the meetings is to renew Christian vision and commitment, and in particular to bring about on-the-spot entries into the reality of the new birth. By confronting people with one or two larger-than-life celebrities to admire and enjoy, and by grafting on to the vestigial remains of a church service something comparable

---

53 I have presented the morphology of revival in *Keep in Step with the Spirit* (Leicester: IVP, 1984), pp. 235–62, and in *God in our Midst* (Ann Arbor: Servant Books; Milton Keynes: Word Books, 1987).

to variety entertainment, these meetings are designed to stir up, warm up and open up the audience in the early stages so that they will be readier for decisive commitments later on. Such is modern revivalism, and today's revivalists are those who regularly minister within this kind of framework, whether in churches and meeting halls or on radio and television. Professor Stout sees Whitefield as their distinct but direct progenitor, and so tends to describe Whitefield's ministry in a way that assimilates it to the modern development. But the differences between what Whitefield did and what revivalists nowadays do are at least as important as the similarities, and we shall misconceive Whitefield if we do not see this.

"There is a watershed dividing the propagation of Christianity by Whitefield and his peers in the eighteenth-century awakening from the revivalism that has just been described. This parting of the ways is not always well plotted on our theological graphs. It does not concern the substance of our presentation of Jesus Christ as Saviour of sinners; nor does it relate to how we emphasize the importance of feeling and facing our need of him; nor does it touch the pietistic presupposition that our relationship with God is the most important issue for everyone; nor does it occur over the priority or otherwise of evangelism, for Whitefield went on record saying: 'God lets me see more and more, that I must evangelize';[54] nor does it have anything to do with the personal styles of different evangelists (Whitefield the dramatic actor, Wesley the paternalist martinet, Finney the prosecuting attorney, Billy Graham the giant-size man in the street, and so on). On all these matters the two sorts of revivalism see eye to eye at the level of principle, and are in full harmony with each other. The cleavage is over a single question: whether we approve of Whitefield and the other eighteenth-century leaders sending people away from the preaching to pray for a change of heart through new birth, and to keep praying and using the means of grace till they know they have been given what they sought, or whether with Finney and most moderns we opt for the so-called 'invitation method', 'drawing the net' by calling for an immediate full-scale cognitive and volitional commitment to Christ in faith and repentance. The assumption that immediate conversion is within everyone's present power has far-reaching implications (it is semi-Pelagian at least, perhaps Pelagian), and the effect of making it is inevitably manipulative, for it turns the applicatory part of the sermon into a tussle of wills between preacher and people and radically obscures the sovereignty of the Holy Spirit in the bestowing of spiritual

---

54 *Letters of George Whitefield*, 1734–42, p. 277.

life.[55] I spoke of Whitefield's revivalism as 'Reformational' to make clear that on this issue he was in solidarity with more than two centuries of Reformed thought—not to mention Luther's theology as it was before Lutherans adjusted it[56]—and that he could not have countenanced the pragmatic anthropocentrism sponsored by Finney. Finney and his modern revivalist followers require people to find God; Whitefield, and those who have stood in the Whitefieldian succession, as did Spurgeon and Lloyd-Jones, required them to seek God. There is a difference.

"Was Whitefield, then, in full accord with the Reformation and Puritan heritage to which he laid claim? In broad terms, the answer is yes; but on the surface, some differences appear.

"We must carefully grant that no one with an itinerant ministry on Whitefield's pattern, and no one with comparable powers of rhetoric and projection, had ornamented British Christianity during the previous two centuries. Reformers like John Bradford, and Puritans like Richard Baxter and John Bunyan, excelled in evangelistic applications of gospel truth, but none of them could hold a candle to the torrential outpourings of compassionate persuasion that flowed from Whitefield's lips and heart every time he preached.

"We must grant too that only in a culture where interest in playwriting, playgoing and playacting had blossomed, as it did in England in the early eighteenth century, could a sanctified barnstormer like Whitefield emerge. Whitefield like the Puritans before him, opposed actual theatres as centres of vice,[57] but whereas the Puritans had been negative about acting too, with a negativism ranging from mild to furious, Whitefield, as we have seen, was deploying his actor's expertise in the pulpit all the time, and his dramatic way of conceiving life and its relationships, including the Christian's faith-relationship with 'the dear Jesus', went beyond anything that had been known in earlier times.

"And finally, we should grant that by his regular preaching outside churchly contexts, Whitefield, though himself an Anglican clergyman who took his office seriously and who saw himself as serving all the churches all the time, did in fact unwittingly encourage an individualistic piety of what we would call a parachurch type, a piety that gave its prime loyalty to

55 See J.I. Packer, *Among God's Giants: The Puritan Vision of the Christian Life* (Eastbourne: Kingsway, 1991), ch. 18, 'Puritan Evangelism', pp. 383–407.
56 See M. Luther, *The Bondage of the Will* (trans. O.R. Johnston and J.I. Packer; London: James Clarke, 1957), pt. 7, pp. 273–318.
57 Stout, *The Divine Dramatist*, ch. 13, 'Dr. Squintum', pp. 234–48.

transdenominational endeavours, that became impatient and restless in face
of the relatively fixed forms of institutional church life, and that conceived
evangelism as typically an extra-ecclesiastical activity. To foment tension
between discipleship and churchmanship was the last thing Whitefield
wanted to do, but involuntarily he did it. By contrast, the Puritans both sides
of the Atlantic, and Protestants generally before Whitefield's time, were
consistently churchly in outlook, and were always careful to set personal
religion in a communal, ecclesiastical frame. Whitefield's own preaching
about the fellowship aspect of discipleship seems not to have gone further,
however, than to urge faithful participation in the life of the religious
societies.[58] Thus in effect, as Mark Noll observes, 'Whitefield helped shift
the theological emphasis on preaching. Up to the early 1700s, British
Prostestants preached on God's plan *for the church*. From the mid-1700s,
however, evangelicals emphasized God's plans *for the individual*'.[59] So it has
been among evangelicals ever since.

   "All these are significant moves beyond, or away from, the Puritan model,
and should not be played down.

   "Basically, however, the assertion that Whitefield's mind and method as a
revivalist were Reformational still stands. For, in the first place, the doctrinal
solidarity is real and obvious. Whitefield's evangelistic message centred, as
we saw, on what was central in the theology of the Reformers and Puritans,
namely human fallenness and inability for spiritual good; the sufficiency,
glory and accessibility of Jesus Christ; the law demonstrating the reality of
our sin to our consciences, and the gospel promises leading us out of all
forms of self-sufficiency and self-reliance to trust Christ alone for salvation;
and finally, the sovereignty of the Holy Spirit, and of God through the Holy
Spirit, in bringing sinners into newness of life. Regeneration, or new birth,
had not been a central focus of thought for the Reformers, but pastoral
Puritanism had developed the doctrine to the full dimensions that
Whitefield's preaching gave it, and here, supremely, solidarity is seen. Then,
in the second place, Puritanism in its pastoral aspect was essentially a
movement of revival, as I have tried to show elsewhere;[60] and Whitefield's
ministry was a true ministry of pastoral revival, blessed by God to the
quickening of saints and the conversion of sinners in a most outstanding
way. The Great Awakening of 1740, the Cambuslang revival of 1742 (the

58 *Sermons on Important Subjects*, no. 8, 'The Necessity and Benefits of Religious Society',
pp. 107–18. This was actually Whitefield's first sermon.
59 M. Noll, 'Father of Modern Evangelicals?', *Christian History* (Spring, 1993), p. 44.
60 *Among God's Giants*, ch. 3, pp. 41–63.

'Cam'slang Wark', as Scottish locals called it), the Cheltenham visitation of 1757,[61] and many other exalted episodes that were put on record, bear ample witness to this.

"The conclusions to which I believe this survey leads can be stated thus: (1) Whitefield was in essence very much a Reformational revivalist. (2) Though not everything he said and did was totally wise, and though there were weaknesses as well as strengths in his pattern of working, yet his pietistic priorities, according to which being alive to God is what most matters, were magnificently right. (3) The overall quality of his ministry as he sought to embody the compassion of Christ in pointing and directing lost souls to faith in Christ, was beyond praise. (4) A good dose of Whitefieldian revivalism should God raise up a preacher capable of imparting it, would do today's churches more good than anything I can imagine. 'I speak to sensible people; judge for yourselves what I say' (1 Cor. 10:15)."[62]

---

61 Dallimore, George Whitefield, II, pp. 392–93.

62 J.I. Packer, The Spirit With The Word The Reformational Revivalism Of George Whitefield, Article for 'Essays in Honour of James Atkinson' (Library of Princeton Theological Seminary, Sheffield: Sheffield Academic Press, 1995), pp. 167–189.

APPENDIX 5

CENTENNIAL COMMEMORATION

The following series of messages were preached at the Old South Church in Newburyport, MA, where George Whitefield lies buried beneath its pulpit. The sermons were given on the one hundred year anniversary of his death—Sept. 30th, 1870. On this memorable occasion many luminaries were in the audience including the President of Princeton, and Whitefield biographer, J.B. Wakely (who led in prayer). At the front of the church stood the chair in which he died as well as his bible, and the ring from his finger with which he wrote (with its single diamond) upon the rich man's window pane "One thing is needful". It was a special day; a holy day; God's presence was among His people on this solemn day. Three of the former pastors of the Old South were still living and present. Each of these men knew members of the congregation who had known Whitefield personally and recorded their recollections of him. In 1870 it was still a day of large things for the Church: D. L. Moody was still in his prime of life and bringing in a harvest of souls into the Kingdom; C. H. Spurgeon was at the Metropolitan Tablernacle in London reigning as the Prince of Preachers for his day. This was an epoch in the history of the Church whereby the pulpits of the land (both in America and Great Britain) still had an influence upon society. It was a time when preaching was still rich with the eloquence of the great doctrines of the bible and the Hand of God was still upon those faithful gospel-bearers in mighty Holy Spirit power. We weep today for the bankrupt Church and the sleeping Bride. Our hope is that hearts will be stirred by reading these pages and fresh work will be commenced honoring God and advancing His Kingdom.

We now present this rare and out-of-print document as a testimony both to the men who produced it and to the memory of George Whitefield whom they honored.

CENTENNIAL COMMEMORATION OF THE DEATH OF GEORGE WHITEFIELD IN THE OLD SOUTH CHURCH NEWBURYPORT, MASS., SEPT. 30, 1870

By Rev. J.F. Stearns, D.D. Formerly Pastor of that church

Newburyport, October 17, 1870

REV. J.F. STEARNS, D.D.,

Dear Sir:—The undersigned, Committee of Arrangements for the Centennial Commemoration of Whitefield's death, respectfully request of you a copy of your Commemorative Discourse for publication, feeling sure that the life of such a man, portrayed in so vivid a light, cannot fail to do great good.

We are, yours, very sincerely and respectfully,

> ISAAC H. BOARDMAN
> HENRY COOK
> J.B. CREASEY
> C.S. DURFEE
> EDWARD GRAVES
> WILLIAM GRAVES
> J.A. HORTON
> W.H. JOHNSON
> E.W. LUNT
> P.G. LUNT
> J.N. PIKE
> G.L. ROGERS
> T.C. SIMPSON

Newark, N. J., November 11, 1870

HON. I. H. BOARDMAN and others,

GENTLEMEN,—I cheerfully comply with the request with which you have honored me, to furnish for the press a copy of my discourse at the Centennial Anniversary of the death of the great English and American preacher, George Whitefield. It has cost me more labor than I anticipated, chiefly from the wealth of materials and the difficulty of selecting and condensing so as to present any thing like a just view of so remarkable a character within the limits of a single discourse. But it has been a labor of love, and with all its imperfections I place the result at your disposal.

Your honored names appended to the request revive in me the memory of scenes long past, of tender and most affecting interest. With my fervent prayers that Heaven's best blessings may ever rest on you and the beloved church and congregation which you represent, I beg leave to subscribe myself, with respect and esteem, your friend and former pastor,

J. F. STEARNS.

COMMEMORATIVE DISCOURSE

There are some movements which make a wild foam on the surface of the stream, and leave it the same. There are others which turn a current, and it flows on in a new channel over half a continent. There are sounds which stun the ear for a moment and then are silent. There are others which when once uttered echo on forever. The eloquent voice which more than a century ago spoke words of love and power to quivering thousands, is heard still in its effects, and by them, he that uttered it, "being dead yet speaketh."

On Sabbath morning, June 20, 1736, there knelt before the bishop of Gloucester, in the old cathedral town of Gloucester, Gloucestershire, England, to be ordained with others to the Christian ministry, according to the forms of the Church of England, a young Oxford student of thoughtful mien and remarkably prepossessing appearance. He was somewhat above the middle stature, well-proportioned, of a slender form, fair complexion, regular features, small, lively dark blue eyes, in one of which—the effect of measles—was observable a slight squint, not disfiguring, but rather adding to the general expressiveness of his face—and distinguished for the peculiar sweetness of his countenance and the native grace of his manners. His youth, for he was only twenty-one years of age and had not yet taken his first degree, served to increase the interest, always felt in serious and religious minds, for so sacred a transaction.

He was one of a small, despised but eminently devout and resolute band, who, marking the degeneracy of the times and determined to resist it, had begun, within a few years, to be known at Oxford as *Methodists*, because, as it was said, "they lived by rule and *method*" and were distinguished for their strict habits of life and religious observances—called also by some, by way of derision, "Sacramentarians," "Bible moths," "Bible bigots," the "Holy" or "Godly Club."

This young man, I need not say here to-day, was GEORGE WHITEFIELD. Although so young, he had gone through varied experiences. Left fatherless at a very tender age in the care of his mother, who since her husband's death had been struggling for a maintenance by carrying on the Bell Inn at Gloucester, which had been the support of the family during the father's life, he was exposed in childhood to many evil influences; and though sent to the grammar school in his native town, where for a time he made good proficiency, becoming restless and despairing of ever reaching the university, which had been his early ambition, he left the school, became an assistant in the public house and at length, to use his own expression, "put on his blue apron and snuffers, washed mops, cleaned rooms, and, in a word, became a common and professed drawer." Even then, however, as during his whole early life, he was not without better aspirations. Sinking at times deeply into sin, he was often roused to a keen sense of his guilt and folly, and often resolved, and for a while kept his resolutions, to endeavor after a better life. He was descended from a religious ancestry, his great grandfather and one of his great uncles having been ministers of the Church of England; and from his earliest years, the pulpit and the tavern seem to have mingled strangely and grotesquely in their influence on his forming character. At length a turn was reached unexpectedly, and he went back to school, completed his preparatory studies and entered Pembroke College, Oxford, where he supported himself, as did other poor students of his day, by acting in the capacity of a *servitor*, for which his experience at the inn afforded him some special qualifications.

Before taking this step, while he was yet in the grammar school of St. Mary de Crypt, his religious feelings had undergone a considerable change, and he reformed his own life, and made some reformations among his dissolute school-fellows. On coming to Oxford, and finding the general character of his fellow-students adverse to all his best aspirations, he withdrew himself, with alarm, from their society. "It was quickly solicited," he says, "to join in excess of riot with several who lay in the same room. But God gave me grace to withstand; and once in particular, it being cold, my limbs were so benumbed by sitting alone in my study, because I would not go out among them, that I could scarce sleep all night. But I soon found the benefit of not yielding; for when they perceived they could not prevail, they let me alone as a singular odd fellow."

It was in the midst of these conflicts, that his attention was turned to the despised Methodists. "They were then," he says, "much talked of at Oxford. I had heard of them and loved them before I came to the university. For above a twelve-month, my soul longed to be acquainted with them, and I was strongly inclined to follow their good example, when I saw them go through a ridiculing crowd to receive the holy Sacrament at St. Mary's." At length an opportunity occurred. He made the acquaintance of Charles Wesley, who by degrees introduced him to his brother John and the rest. He became one of them—imbibed their spirit, caught their evangelical fervor, adopted their rules of life, and being much younger than either of the Wesleys came largely under their influence.

At first his inexperience and defective knowledge led him into some serious mistakes. He became first a mystic, then an ascetic. He prayed much and long, lying prostrate on the ground, or kneeling in the cold night air under the trees. He practiced monkish austerities, used unsuitable food, fasted immoderately, neglected his person, dressed meanly, and altogether so lost the balance both of mind and body that he fell into a severe sickness which well nigh cost him his life. This last by the grace of God proved a salutary discipline. He had before caught what he regarded as a ray of divine light, showing him that true religion does not consist in a round of outward observances, but is "a union of the soul with God or Christ formed within us," from reading that excellent little treatise, Scougal's "Life of God in the soul of man." But now, he describes his case, "God was pleased to enable me to lay hold on his dear Son by a living *faith*; and by giving me the spirit of adoption to seal me, as I humbly hope, to the day of everlasting redemption. At first, my joys were like a spring-tide and overflowed the banks; go where I would, I could not avoid singing of psalms almost aloud. Afterwards, they became more settled, and blessed be God, saving a few casual intervals, have abode and increased in my soul ever since."

In coming, at so early an age, to receive holy orders, this young candidate had not rashly or thoughtlessly thrust himself forward. Friends, well acquainted with his character, had marked his ripe qualifications and commended him to the bishop. The bishop himself had observed his deportment both in the church and in the works of beneficence to the poor, the sick and the prisoners, and his care for the souls of those around him in which he spent his leisure hours; and sending for him, much to his surprise, and expressing pleasure at seeing him, said, on learning his age, "Notwithstanding I have declared I would not ordain any one under three and twenty, yet I shall think it my duty to ordain you whenever you come for holy orders." He had hitherto felt the deepest aversion to what seemed to him so premature a step. "That saying of the apostle" he said, "not a novice lest being puffed up with pride, he fall into the condemnation of the devil," and that first question of our excellent ordination office—-

"Do you trust that you are inwardly moved by the Holy Ghost to take upon you this office and administration; used even to make me tremble when I thought of entering the ministry." It was with him, as with the youthful Jeremiah, when he replied: Ah Lord God! Behold I cannot speak for I am a child!" Often, in an agony under a sense of his insufficiency, his prayer was "Lord, I am a youth of uncircumcised lips. Lord send me not into thy vineyard yet." He corresponded with his Oxford friends, hoping they would justify him in his views. But their answer was "pray ye therefore the Lord of the harvest that he would send thee and many more laborers into his harvest." Some suggested that, by thus holding out against what seemed to them so obvious a purpose of divine providence, he might even be found fighting against God. And he himself, especially after the interview with the bishop, began to feel that he could no longer resist.

It only remained now, that he prepare himself for the result. Having carefully examined the thirty-nine articles and satisfied himself of their scriptural soundness, he tested his qualifications by those required in St. Paul's epistle to Timothy, and by every question that he knew would be proposed to him in the ordination service, and "sealed his approval of them," as he says, "every Sunday, at the sacrament." He came to Gloucester a fortnight before hand, hoping for leisure to give himself up to prayer and the composition of sermons. But his mind was disturbed and he could not write. He read carefully the several missions of the prophets and apostles, wrestling with God to give him grace to follow their examples. He had an interview with the bishop and put into his hands an abstract of his private self-examinations. Saturday, the day before the ordination, was spent in fasting and prayer. That evening he went out alone to a hill near the town and prayed fervently for about two hours, for himself and his fellow candidates. On Sabbath morning, he rose early and prayed over St. Paul's epistle to Timothy; dwelling especially on the precept "Let no man despise thy youth." Is it strange if there was a peculiar glow of heavenly beauty in his face, as he knelt there to be set apart to his great office? He had been up into the mount communing with God many days. And like Moses, when he came down from Sinai, "the skin of his face shone" with the radiance which he had caught in that presence. Look thoughtfully upon him—that young apostle, receiving from the great Head of the church his high commission to become the herald of a new and most surprising dispensation of his Spirit—

"a chosen vessel" to "bear his name" and tell the story of his love to scoffing or adoring thousands. Do you ask, what thoughts were working in that bosom? God only knows. But we have a glimpse of them in his own simple and unaffected testimony. "When I went up to the altar, I could think of nothing but Samuel's standing a little child before the Lord with a linen ephod. When the bishop laid his hand upon my head, my heart melted down and I offered up my whole spirit, soul and body to the service of God's sanctuary." "I call heaven and earth to witness, that I gave myself up to be a martyr for him who hung upon the cross for me. Known unto him are all future events and contingencies. I have thrown myself blindfold, and I trust without reserve into his almighty hands. Only I would have you observe that till you hear of my dying *for* or *in* my work you will not be apprised of all the preferment that is expected by—-*George Whitefield*."

Look now to the condition of the field to the ploughing, sowing and reaping of which this young devotee of Christ was to be assigned. All the accounts agree in the assertion that the spirit of true piety, both in England and America, had fallen into a very low state. It was an age of heartlessness—of infidelity and skepticism in religion and most appalling corruption in morals—the age of Hume and Bolingbroke and Collins and Wollaston and Tindall—when such men as Dean Swift could occupy one of the high places of honor and influence in the church, and such a thoroughly rotten moralist as Lawrence Sterne sit undisturbed in his parsonage and be the "delight of the fashionable world—the delicious divine for whose sermons the whole polite world was subscribing"—when Frederic of Prussia was the greatest monarch in Europe and Voltaire the greatest philosopher, when England had a Robert Walpole for her prime minister; and the archbishop of Canterbury gave balls and routs in Lambeth palace. Whitefield's description of what he saw and encountered at the school of St. Mary's and the university at Oxford, seems but a trifle compared with the deliberate utterances of this popular writer. "I say, I am scared as I look around at this society, at this king, at these courtiers, at these politicians, at these bishops, at this flaunting vice and levity. Whereabouts in this court is the honest man! The air stifles one with its sickly perfumes!" Bishop Butler, Arch-bishop Secker, Dr. Watts and many others testify to the melancholy decay both of faith and piety. What made the case worse was, that there seemed to be no power left in the church to roll back or stay the tide of ungodliness. The brave old martyrs of the Reformation—the Latimers and Ridleys and Bradfords and Rogerses had passed into history; the sturdy and devout Puritans and Non-conformists, the Howes and the Bateses, the Henrys, the Baxters and the

Flavels were remembered, if at all, only by few; the sincerely pious and exemplary Dissenters, the Wattses and the Doddridges, pressed by the weight of an arrogant establishment, were confined to narrow room and had grown *judicious* even in their fervor. The great distinguishing doctrines of the gospel had come to be handled daintily, and too much zeal and ardor for the conversion of souls was dreaded as enthusiasm or fanaticism. No doubt there were true and earnest men, both in the establishment and out of it, serving God and endeavoring honestly to defend and preach the holy principles of the gospel; but, chilled by the unholy influences around them, they had settled into their nests and contented themselves with a very feeble proclamation of the truth. Many of them had grown timid or disheartened, and could exert little influence to reform a dissolute, or arouse a slumbering community. And what was true of England was true likewise, though not without important differences and abatements, of America. New England Puritanism was fast dying out and a new form of polite religion which disturbed no man's conscience and excited no man's sensibilities was taking its place. The biography and writings of President Edwards and other productions of the time make the fact painfully apparent, both in the coldness and emptiness of the piety, and the prevailing moral corruptions of the age. It was a feeling widely prevalent among the best men, that, unless God should grant to his church some special interposition of his grace, true religion must soon die out and the whole community sink down into infidelity and ungodliness.

But God did grant such an interposition. The Great Awakening, which in America commenced at Northampton under the ministry of Jonathan Edwards, and in England, almost simultaneously, showed its first faint pulsations at Oxford in the "Holy Club" of the two Wesley's, Kirkman and Morgan" a short time before Whitefield came to the University, was one of the most remarkable manifestations of Divine love interposing for the rescue of its own imperiled cause, the discumfiture of its foes, and advancement of its interests, which are to be found in the whole history of the church. The men immediately engaged in it knew but very little of its scope and purpose, and took only a step at a time following the track marked out for them, as best they could, by the light of their feeble lanterns. Their measures were the simplest possible, and were shaped by the circumstances,—preaching, praying, singing, exhorting, conversing, expounding the scriptures. In England, they and those who were in sympathy with them were organized into *societies*, bound together by a few simple rules to an earnest and constant pursuit of their great object. Such societies had been formed more than half a century before by the earnest-minded old Puritans, and some of them still remained, though fallen into neglect. These were revived and more organized, some larger and some smaller, all over the kingdom; which became the scene of some of Whitefield's most efficient labors and the source of some of his holiest impulses and consolations. Of machinery—*tactics* such as we have sometimes seen in modern revivals—these men had very little. But there was a power behind them impelling them forward, which, though unseen, neither they nor their bitterest foes were able to resist. It revolutionized the church, it saved the age, it opened a path which, if followed steadily and with resolute purpose, would lead us on to the millennial glory.

Having in view such an interposition, Divine Wisdom knew well how to provide for itself suitable instruments. Whitefield was not a man of great intellectual powers, nor a man of eminent learning; but he was a quick man, an ardent man, a man who conceived vividly and executed promptly, a man in whom prudence, though not wanting, was always subordinate to beneficent action, a man of vast endurance, and indomitable perseverance, an eloquent man carrying his heart always at his tongue's end, a man who sympathized warmly and deeply with all humanity, a man of God who verily believed Christ's Gospel which he had undertaken to preach, to be the best thing ever known in the world; on the whole a great man, for he is a great man who does great things, however you may analysze him, a man mighty to do just what the age for which he was raised up of God demanded of a man.

It is not likely that Whitefield had any adequate conception when he set out, either of what was in him or what he was appointed to do. His simple aim was to preach Christ crucified and save souls by bringing them to him. If he expected a great religious movement about to take place, it is probable he looked to John Wesley as the leading spirit and to himself only as one of many subordiante helpers. He had no scheme. He was not a schemer any way. He was no organizer such as Wesley was. He had "thrown himself," as he said, "blindfold into God's hands," and trusting in him he meant to proclaim, energetically and faithfully, wherever God should open to him an opportunity, the everlasting gospel of his Lord.

Whitefield entered upon his work with great self-distrust. Popularity took him by surprise. And it is much to his credit, young as he was, that it nevers seems to have disturbed seriously his humility. In looking forward to the ministry, he had intended, as became a prudent young student of divinity, to provide himself, in advance, with a good stock of sermons—at least a hundred. But his design was frustrated, and only one, prepared, not for the pulpit, but for "a small Christian society," one of those praying circles, probably to which reference has already been made, was now in his possession. He had sent it, when he was deprecating premature ordination, to a friend, a clergyman, in order to convince him how unprepared he was for the pulpit. But the needy parson, tempted by opportunity, kept it a whole fortnight, cut it in two and preached it morning and evening to his own congregation, and sent it back to its owner with a guinea for the loan.

His first pulpit effort was in Gloucester, in the Church of St. Mary de Crypt, where he was baptized and where he first received the Sacrament of the Lord's Supper. Curiosity brought together a large number of his townsmen, and at first, he says, he was "a little awed," but taking courage from the conviction of God's presence, and greatly helped by the practice he had had in public speaking, both at school and in his ministries among the poor and to the prisoners in Oxford jail, he soon rose above his youthful timidity, and the fire kindling as he went on, "was enabled to preach with some degree of Gospel authority." He used, no doubt, that *society sermon*, for his subject was: "The necessity and benefits of religious society"—-that is of social piety, or the intercourse of devout minds in prayer and for mutual edification. The effect was immediate. "Some mocked, but the most were deeply affected." The complaint was made to the bishop that he "drove fifteen mad by the first sermon." The good prelate replied, "I hope the madness will not be forgotten before the next Sunday." Whitefield's own remark was, as he recorded the incedient: "Before then, I hope that my sermon on 'He that is in Christ is a new creature' will be completed. Blessed be God, I now find freedom in writing. Glorious Jesus!"

> "Unloose my stammering tongue to tell
> Thy love immense, unsearchable."

In this last sermon and the doctrine it contained, he found the instrument of some of his first and chief triumphs. Marked tokens of the power that was with him soon began to be discernable—at Bishopgate church, at the Tower and other places in London, at Bath, and particularly at Bristol. "The word," he says, "through the mighty power of God, was sharper than a two edged sword; and the doctrine of the new birth and justification by faith in Jesus Christ made its way like lightning into the hearer's consciences." The tide rose when it was once started, with wonderful rapidity. In London, constables were placed at the church doors to control the crowd; "one might, as it were, walk upon the tops of people's heads," so densely were the churches packed. For three months there was no end to the people's flocking to hear the word of God." He preached generally nine times in a week. "The people were all attention and heard like people hearing for eternity." "On Sunday mornings long before day, you might see streets filled with people going to church with lanthorns in their hands, and hear them coversing about the things of God." At Bristol, at his second visit, multitudes came on foot and in carriages a mile out of town to meet him. He preached five times a week and the congregations grew larger and larger. "Some hung on the rails of the organ loft, others climbed on the leads of the church, and altogether made the church so hot with their breath that the steam would fall from the pillars like drops of rain." In the crowd were persons of all ranks and denominations; and during the last day of his stay there, he was occupied from seven in the morning till midnight, talking with and giving spiritual advice to awakened souls.

That we may know something of the hidden sources of his power during this period, let us take a glimpse of his *inner life*. He had some very sweet Christian experiences, communing with God, studying the holy scriptures on his knees, and praying for divine assistance. "Early in the morning, at noonday, evening and midnight, nay, all day long," he says, "did the blessed Jesus visit and refresh my heart." "Sometimes, as I have been walking, my soul would make such salies, that I thought it would go out of the body. At other times I was overpowered with a sense of God's infinite majesty that I would be constrained to throw myself prostrate on the ground and offer up my soul as a blank in his hand to write on it what he pleased." One incident strongly reminds one of a passage in the life of President Edwards. He had been expounding the Scriptures to a company of people when there came up a terrific thunder storm. Many were afraid to go home, so he went with them. The theme which the scene suggested was, "the Coming of the Son of Man." As he returned, the people along the way were rising from their beds in the greatest consternation "seeing the lightning run along upon the ground and flash from one part of the heavens to another." But instead of terror, his own thoughts were filled with joyful adoration. In company with "a poor but pious countryman," he was in the field praying, praising, and exulting in the glory of God—and "longing for that time when Jesus shall be revealed from heaven in a flame of fire." "Honest James and I," he says, "were out in the midst of the lightning, and were never more delighted in our lives. May we be as well pleased when the Son of God cometh to judgment." Thus was God fitting him for and inducting him into, the great and far-reaching work to which he had called him.

But it was not the design of infinite wisdom to confine the labors of this its chosen apostle to a single country or a single continent. On the opposite side of the great Atlantic, England had a narrow line of weak but growing colonies, where the seeds of a new Empire were beginning slowy to germinate. The two Wesleys, with one or two of their associates, had gone out under the patronage of Gen. Oglethorpe, the founder of the Colony of Georgia, to preach the Gospel to the natives and provide means of grace for the colonists. Their mission was a failure, except as John Wesley received there a new spiritual quickening, which he ever afterwards regarded as the beginning of his spiritual life. But their first reports fired Whitefield's emulation. They both invited him to join them; and after some delays the way was opened. Meanwhile his popularity at home was rising higher, and tempting preferment was offered him. But this did not swerve him from his purpose. A voice from within, which as yet he could but partially interpret, called him to America. And to America he went, heeding not the remonstrances of friends, and turning his back on a career of widening influence and popular admiration, which might easily have taken captive a less self-consecrated spirit. It proved a voice from the new world, like that heard by Paul when he was to pass from Asia into Europe: "Come over and help us." And without stopping to forecast the future, he followed it implicitly, as the voice of God. Delays were interposed, and the intervals were filled to the last moment with his zealous ministries. So was the passage. But, all the while, his face was set though he would go to America.

On his arrival in Georgia, finding himself alone, (for his friends the Wesleys had abandoned the enterprise, and leaving only a single assistant had gone back to England), he at once addressed himself to his work. One of his first projects was the founding of an orphan house to which he had been incited by the example of the celebrated Franke. It was a good object, though but partially successful; and he pursued it through life; but it was chiefly significant as furnishing the providential clue, by which his steps were to be guided through the yet unexplored labyrinth of his eventful itinerary. Most of his first preaching circuits were undertaken in its interest. It opened to him some of his best opportunities. It sent him hither, and it sent him thither—back to England that he might raise funds for it, and again to America that he might superintend its concerns. It drew forth some of his tenderest, humane affections. It served to develop parts of his nature which might otherwise have wanted an object. But, wherever he came and whatever his immediate errand, everything became subservient to the one great ultimate aim of his life, the salvation of souls and the quickening of the divine life in the hearts of Christians by the preaching of the Gospel of the Son of God.

Whitefield had now, mapped out as it were before him, the whole broad field of his life's labors. His parish or diocess if I may so denominate it, consisted of two grand districts—one a vast continent just beginning to be peopled, but destined to play a mighty part in the history of the world; the other a populous and powerful nation—the seat of empire and the head of Protestant Christendom. Both needed to be evangelized, awakened from spiritual slumber, quickened by the power of a divine life, made to throb in every fibre of their mighty frames with the pulsations of a living, active, energetic piety. The accomplishment of this great result, under God, constituted the life mission of GEORGE WHITEFIELD. He traversed these vast regions, up and down, backward and forward, for more than thirty years, with unflagging ardor. The fire of his burning soul kindled and flamed in every corner. Between the two, the ocean was his highway. He crossed the Atlantic thirteen times and that at a period when the passage was long and the discomforts many. From a comparison of dates, I judge that he was actually at sea two years and a quarter, and on board ship a considerably longer time, encountering storms, collisions, hunger, sea sickness, alarms of hostile attacks and the rough ways of the roughest of men. "This comes of your praying," said one with an oath when they had narrowly escaped the peril of immediate destruction. Of the remaining thirty-one or two years, somewhere about nine were spent in this country, in preaching and kindred labors in the populous towns, the sparsely settled country and among the aboriginal tribes—in what Whitefield himself used to call, "hunting for sinners in the wilds of America." The rest of the time, about two-thirds of the whole, was devoted to similar efforts in his native land.

It would be pleasant and profitable, could we follow him in his vast circuits, and trace step by step the exertions which he made, the difficulties and perils which he overcame, the traits of character he displayed, and the wonderful effects which accompanied or followed his ministry. A recent writer has said of him, during the period of thirty years constituting the great body of his public life, that "the facts of his ministry are of one complexion. One year is just like another, and to follow him would be going over the same ground." This is true, in the general, but not in the particular. For while the same great end is kept always in view, and the same measures employed with substantially the same results—there is scarcely a scene or record, where the details are preserved, which would not furnish, in the hands of a master, the subject for a distinct picture worthy a place in the great picture gallery of the Church's history.

Whitefield's first return from America was the introduction to a remarkable change in the methods of his preaching. He had been in this country only about four months when the wants of the orphan house and the necessity of securing priest's orders in order to the full discharge of his new duties seemed to require his return. It was altogether contrary to his original intention, and he had to tear himself away from his new parishioners, they exacting from him a solemn promise "before God" to return to them as soon as possible. Up to this time he had been a great stickler for order. All his sermons he had carefully written out, and the first extemporaneous prayer as well as the first extemporaneous sermon on which he ever ventured was deemed worthy of a special record. He preached only when and where he was invited by the regular clergymen, and though he exhorted and expounded with great freedom in private houses and elsewhere, would have been shocked at the thought of *preaching* anywhere but in a church. But the time had come for him to cast aside such close trammels. It was not a measure of his own seeking but a providential necessity. The incapacity of the churches to contain the multitudes had already suggested the experiment. But now on reaching London, to his great surprise, he found most of the pulpits closed against him. The Archbishop of Canterbury and the bishop of London received him kindly and approved his plans. But among the clergymen generally, dislikes, which had begun to show themselves before his departure, had, during his absence, ripened into concerted opposition. He took priest's orders but received no invitations. It was much the same in the country. The people were eager as ever to hear. But how to get access to them? This led to the adoption of *field preaching*, a measure first reported to by Whitefield himself and which, more perhaps than any other, characterized the great religious movement, in which he was the chief actor.

The first experiment was made at Kingswood, near Bristol. It was in a region of coal mines. The colliers were a rude and almost savage people. Few ventured to walk in their neighborhood and when roused they were the terror of Bristol. Before he went to America people had said to Whitefield, "Have we not Indians enough at home."? "If you have a mind to instruct Indians, there are colliers enough in Kingswood." Unwilling to be idle, he now resolved to see what could be done for them. He gathered around him a few hundreds and began to discourse to them. Presently he had, at the same and neighboring places, congregations of two, five, ten and even twenty thousand. He took his stand upon an elevated spot and made his clear, strong voice audible to the remotest listener. The trees and hedges were full of people. All was hushed the moment he began. The preacher's own soul, as he looked round amidst the deep silence of the multitude, was filled, he tells us, "with a holy admiration." As for the poor colliers, to whom such precious truths were new, "having no righteousness of their own to renounce, they were glad to hear of a Jesus who was a friend to publicans and sinners and came not to call the righteous but sinners to repentence." The first token of the deep feeling wrought in them, was discernable in the "white gutters cut by their tears," as they coursed plentifully down their black, coal-begrimed cheeks. "Hundreds and hundreds," we are told, "were brought under deep conviction, which, as the event proved, ended in a sound and thorough conversion." On one of these occasions, as we are informed by a contemporary periodical, the multitude of all classes that were drawn together, with the coaches and horsemen, covered three acres of ground.

A few weeks later the same experiment was repeated at London. The church at Islington had been offered him by the vicar, but the church warden objected, so he betook himself to the churchyard. Shortly after, on a Sunday morning, he appeared at Moorfields, since so noted for its close connection with his London movements. It was a large open space much frequented by the populace on Sundays and holidays. The crowd was great. Some warned him that he would never come out of that place alive. He went in between two friends, who were soon separated from him by the pressure of the rabble and compelled to leave him to their mercy. But instead of offering him the slightest indignity they "made a lane for him," passed him along through it to his place. On the evening of the same day, he preached again on Kennington Common, two miles from London, to an assemblage estimated at upwards of twenty thousand. Similar scenes wre repeated again and again at these two places during several successive weeks. Of one of them Whitefield himself says: "Such a sight I never saw before. Some supposed there were above thirty or forty thousand people and near fourscore coaches, besides great numbers of horses; and there was such an awful silence and the word of God came with such power!"

Meanwhile and afterward he made extensive tours through the country including an excursion into Wales, preaching in every considerable town in just such places as offered themselves, and everywhere with similar results. The deep interest awakened by his preaching, caused a rush to him in private, so that all his intervening hours were occupied in counseling and instructing awakened souls, or praying, exhorting and expounding the scriptures, in the religious societies. Of these he sometimes visited two or three in a day, and continued his efforts in them sometimes far into and even through the night. Even at private houses, whither he went for such purposes, people crowded round the door in such multitudes that he was obliged to ascend by a ladder to an upper window, or clamber over the tiles of the neighboring houses, in order to get access.

It is strange that, seeing among the people such a thirst for hearing the word, he should have grown less fastidious than formerly as to the ways by which the waters of life should be distributed? As a good Episcopalian, he still wore his gown and, where he could advantageously, used his prayer-book. But where a pulpit was not ready to his hand, a table, a tub, a horseblock, the steps of an inn, the stairs of a windmill, even the cudgel players' stage served an excellent purpose; and as for a church, his field and street preaching seemed no more than what his great Master had sanctioned, "who himself had a mountain for a pulpit and the heavens for a sounding board, and when the gospel was rejected by the Jews, sent his servants into the highways and hedges." "I hope," he says, "I shall learn more and more that no place is amiss for preaching the gospel."

Nor is it strange, that, amidst such scenes, he caught a new and grander conception of the great work of God of which he was chosen as the instrument. Now he begins to see evidences of some vast divine plan about to be executed. "I believe," he says, "God will work a great work in the earth. Whatever instruments he may make use of I care not. What am I, O Lord, that thou should'st honor me?" Now he begins, as never before, to be conscious of a special and peculiar mission. "The whole world," he says, "is my parish. Wherever my Master calls me, I am ready to go to preach His everlasting gospel."

It was in the full spirit of these new views that, having accomplished the specific objects of his voyage to England, he returned to America. And here the same wonderful career opened itself before him. I might well have occupied the whole time allotted me to-day in describing this portion of his work. The movement in England, surprising as it is, by no means surpasses in grandeur that which took place in this new country. Here as there, there had been a great decline of Evangelical piety. Here as there God had *already* begun to revive His work. The partial awakenings which attended and followed the great earthquakes of 1727, and especially the great revival which began at Northampton in 1734, were no doubt part and parcel of the same divine impulse which was now working such results on the other side of the water. Whitefield was not the first instrument of the work there or here. He was indeed himself one of its products and here lay one of the secrets of his power—he was a living organ which the divine life, already quickened, had itself developed for its own purposes.

He landed at Lewiston on Delaware Bay, and made his way through the forests on horseback, sixty miles, to Philadelphia. The churches could not contain the multitudes. From the steps of the Court House, he preached to congregations of from six to eight thousand. On board a shallop at the wharf four hundred feet distant, every word was heard distinctly and the whole intervening space was filled with people. Thence he went to Newport, preaching on his way in the towns and villages of New Jersey, and making the acquaintance of those ardent and congenial spirits, the Dutch pastor Frelinghuysen and the Tenants, Rowland and Blair. Back through Philadelphia, he journeyed south on horseback, occupying more than a month and preaching almost every day with surprising effect. Arriving in Georgia, his first warm welcome from his friends was accompanied by an outbreak of religious feeling from the children of the orphan house. His sense of the divine goodness almost overwhelmed him, and with his characteristic humility and holy joy he could only exclaim, "Why me? Lord, why me?"

It was during the autumn of the same year, the year 1740, that he made his first visit to New England. His friends were expecting him eagerly, and those of the opposite spirit had been warned publicly against him. The leading ministers of Boston, Coleman, Sewall, Prince, Foxcroft, Cooper, Webb and others gave him a warm welcome. He preached first in the churches, then from a scaffold outside of Mr. Byles' meeting-house, and finally on the common. The people thronged to hear, in the same countless multitudes. "O how did the word run," is his own exclamation. "I could scarcely refrain from crying out, 'this is none other than the house of God and the gate of heaven.'" Dr. Coleman said of one of his services, it was the most pleasant he ever enjoyed. Governor Belcher attended on the preaching and paid the preacher the most affectionate attentions. Mr. Secretary Willard did likewise. Good old Mr. Walton of Roxbury, the successor of Mr. Eliot, said of his doctrine, "it is Puritanism revived." he went out to Cambridge, and preached first in the Church and then in the College yard. The Faculty and a great number of ministers being present, he preached from St. Paul's words, "We are not as many who corrupt the word of God," and made a close application of his subject to tutors and students. Among the latter many genuine conversions and a general religious improvement was the result. Having visited and preached in most of the neighboring towns, he made an excursion to the eastward as far as Portsmouth and preached twice every day in going and coming. Then taking his leave of Boston, he journeyed westward in the same manner, went to Northampton and had a fraternal interview with President Edwards, who gave him kind advice and wept during the whole time of his preaching, paused a day at New Haven, dined with the President of the College, preached with great plainness on the necessity of true conversion to the character of a Gospel minister, met the Governor who with tears expressed his strong approval of his preaching, and passing on through Connecticut, New York, New Jersey and Pennsylvania, embarked for Charleston and so returned to Savannah. At the place of his embarkation he records: "It is now the seventy-fifth day since I arrived at Rhode Island. I was then weak in body, but God has renewed its strength. I have been enabled to preach, I think, one hundred and seventy times in public, besides exhorting frequently in private. I have traveled eight hundred miles and gotten above seven hundred pounds for the orphan house. Never did I perform the journey with so little fatigue or see such a continuance of the divine presence in the congregations to whom I have preached."

It was on this grand triumphal march of the gospel herald, that he came for the first time to old Newbury and blew here the first strong blast of that gospel trumpet whose echoes I seem to catch even now, as they linger round the walls of this consecrated edifice, and repeat themselves, from generation to generation, in the hearts of this community. Of this visit we find in his journal this quiet but significant record: "*Sept.* 30. Reached Newbury about *three.* Here again the power of God accompanied the word. The meeting-house was very large. Many ministers were present and the people were greatle affected." A memorable date, brethren, in your history—that of Sept. 30, 1740, hardly less than that of Sept. 30, 1770.

I have thus far only entered upon the *borders* of this wonderful history and given you only a few specimens of its surprising occurrences. Similar scenes filled the whole thirty years which ensued. Some of the most remarkable are among those to which I cannon even allude. Such were some of those which attended him in Scotland, where the circumstances were in many respects quite different from those in England and America. The amount of labor he performed was such as to exceed belief, were not the facts so well authenticated. The 18,000 sermons which he preached , some of them an hour and a half long, and averaging five hundred in a year, make but a fragment. In one single week he received more than a thousand letters from persons asking counsel about their souls. On the Sabbath he preached usually four times in a day, besides administering the Lord's Supper, and conducting all the devotional exercises, and was quite restive when, on account of sickness, his physicians limited him to the "short allowance of preaching but once a day and thrice on a Sunday." Labor indeed seemed to be his life. "A pulpit sweat," as he quaintly termed it, was his most efficacious restorative. "One physician," he says once, "has prescribed a perpetual blister; but I have found perpetual *preaching* a better remedy. When that grand catholicon fails it is all over with me." It was much the same with his travels. He visited Scotland fourteen times, went over to Ireland twice; "and as to England and Wales," as a biographer observes, "he traversed every county in them from the Isle of Wight to Berwick on Tweed, and from Land's End to North Foreland." "To ride hundreds of miles on horseback," says another, "from one end of the kingdom to the other, resting a day or two and then starting off on a new tour in another direction was an ordinary occurrence." Five times in the same way, he visited New England, preaching all the way at every considerable place. And everywhere, during the whole thirty years with substantially the same results. Where-ever he came the people surged together like the waves of the ocean. They hung upon his lips, they watched every movement of his person, they gave themselves up into his hands. He seemed to play upon their moral and emotional nature as the musician on the pipes of an organ. They were melted into tears, they cried out in alarm for their souls. Cool and unimpassioned men like Dr. Franklin emptied their pockets against their own purpose, at his appeals for the orphan. He moulded their thoughts; he revolutionized their permanent character; by the grace of God, he turned the worst of sinners into the most blessed and holy saints.

Whitefield's chief success was among the common people. He had a deep sympathy for them, and his style of thought and speaking was eminently suited to their wants. It has been noticed that he approved of slavery. He did so, in common with most persons of his times. But no man labored harder for the enslaved race, or was more endeared to them. "Master," said a poor negro woman, as she sat on the ground and looked earnestly in his face, when he was rising from supposed mortal illness: "Master, you first go to heaven's gate. But Jesus Christ say, get you down, you mustn't come here yet. Go first and call some more poor negroes." "I prayed the Lord," he says, "that if I were to live, this might be the event."

But Whitefield's ministry was by no means confined to the poor or ignorant. Men of the highest distinction for talents, learning and literary and social culture, here and in England, attended admiringly on his preaching. Multitudes of them yielded to its power. The accomplished Lady Huntington became, as it is well known, one of his most zealous and efficient supporters, and by her influence and wealth, numerous chapels all over England became the copious fountains of the same type of doctrine and piety. She drew around him also a large circle of the nobility and gentry of the land. Lord Bolingbroke, Horace Walpole, the historian Hume, Lord and Lady Chesterfield, several of the ladies of the Chesterfield family, Sir Charles Hotham, nephew of Lord Chesterfield, the Earl of Bath, Lord Dartmouth, and quite a number of the nobility of Scotland frequented his ministry, commended it for qualities which they could appreciate, and many of them became true and warm-hearted converts to the truth and piety he inculcated. The poor negress who looked up to him so piteously stands counterbalanced in the escutcheon of his ministry by a "king's daughter among" his "honorable women."

It is true he had his reverses. Such was that which in England followed his memorable breach with the Wesley's. That breach was to Whitefield one of the worst trials of his life. He wept over it and prayed against it; he begged his friends not to open a controversy but to agree to differ. Whitefield was a strong Calvinist, perhaps at that time an extreme one. Wesley became an Arminian and thought it his duty to come out in opposition. Among the adherents of both the dispute waxed warm. Whitefield returned from America after an absence of two years to find his ministry at first almost deserted. Many of his own spiritual children turned coldly upon him. "So prejudiced," he says, "by the dear Wesley's dressing up the doctrine of election in such horrible colors, that they would neither see, hear nor give any assistance." But this did not last long. Whitefield's popularity returned, the moment he was again fairly before the people, and was even increased. Both parties settled into their own proper positions. The breach of affection was healed. Both pursued separately the same general object. The great Methodist church, so fruitful in zealous and efficient labors here and in Europe, was the result on the one hand; and, on the other, good old Puritan Calvinism, which might otherwise have suffered deterioration by a diluting compromise, received a new and we trust a lasting lease of life, vigor and beneficence. Whitefield, being once asked by a zealous partizan "if he thought we should see John Wesley in heaven," replied promptly, "No sir, I fear not. He will be so near the throne and we at such a distance that we shall hardly get a sight of him."

Such likewise was the opposition which he encountered here in New England, on his second visit, after a four years' absence. During that time there had been a great change in the state of public opinion. The great religious impulse which first attended his preaching had encountered the forces of false zeal, disorder and fanaticism. Unsound or injudicious leaders had arisen. Parties had been formed and were lashed up into a high state of excitement. Old father Moody gave him a cordial welcome when he landed at York. But immediately there arose elsewhere a most violent opposition. Three of his old friends were drawn into it. Disorders with which he had nothing to do were charged to him as the culpable cause. All the forces of worldliness and declining piety, in the pulpit and out of it, were marshaled in fierce opposition. One association of ministers after another protested against his admission to the pulpits. Harvard College, piqued by some severe, perhaps too severe, strictures he had made on the state of religion in that institution, came out with one of the bitterest invectives. Some of the charges made against him were quite curious. He was an enthusiast. He was a priest of the Church of England, and yet Dr. Colman had allowed him to administer the Lord's Supper in a Congregational Church! He had expressed the opinon that a considerable number of the ministers of the day were unconverted men. He had "treated the great and good Archbishop Tillotson shamefully" by expressing such an opinion of him. His preaching to such crowds was a great waste of *money*, taking the people off from their work. The worthy tutor Flynt of Harvard gives an estimate, in his journal, of the time and other charges in people's attending upon his ministry at "one thousand pounds per diem." His allowing people to go singing psalms and hymns along the streets as they traveled from one place of meeting to another was a great impropriety. His extemporizing was a very *lazy* manner of preaching." His itinerating was bad. He had said in one of is journals: "God seems to show me that it is my duty to evangelize and not to fix in any particular place." They did not believe he had any such call: he had taken it up "of his own head." It had a tendency to make people discontented with their own ministers. Some of the clergy had got the notion that he had a plot to turn them all out of their comfortable berths and supply their places with a new set of men to be brought over from England or trained up by the Tennants at their "log College" at Neshaminy. Besides all the rest, the suspicion was quite rife that he was either an Arminian or an Antinomian, and some of them could not make up their minds which. So the storm raged; and for a time it seemed as if his day was over. But he acted prudently, explained some things and apologized for some things spoken too hastily, confessed that "Peter-like he had cut off too many ears," and going quietly on, was sustained by the great body of those who still adhered to the doctrines of the New England fathers, and still preached the same benign gospel with the same success to the same eager irrepressible multitudes as before. Much

the same was his experience among the Presbyterians of the Middle and
Southern States. New and old *sides* there were divided much as the new and
old *lights* in New England. But parties soon began to know their positions
and the lookers on learned to form their own judgments. Whitefield, in his
later days, had few opposes except the opposes of warm-hearted, evangelical
and aggressive piety.

These he always had and could expect no less. Men in high places, bishops
and ecclesiastics tried the force of their satire upon him and even loaded him
with obloquy. Foote, the comedian, ridiculed him on the stage and set the
benches in a roar with merciless caricatures. The baser sort threw stones at
him, pelted him with foul missiles and assailed him with vulgar abuse. Once
a ruffian ascended the pulpit stairs in order to attack him. Once, an assassin
made his way by false pretenses into his bed chamber and assaulted him
murderously in his bed. Once, on coming out of his pulpit in the crowd, he
felt a movement of his hat and wig, and turning met the point of a drawn
sword with which a man was attempting to stab him. He seems not to have
had a large share of physical courage. He used to call himself a coward; and
once, at sea during an expected attack, while Mrs. Whitefield was employed
making cartridges, "her husband," he says, "wanted to get into the hold of
the ship, hearing that that was the chaplain's usual place." But he had a large
share of *moral* courage, which, in any emergency affecting his ministry,
always stood him in stead. The way in which he braved the mob during the
Whitsuntide revelries at Moorefields, planting his pulpit in the very face of
the mountebanks and their men, and competing with them *successfully* for
the attention of the multitude seems to us little short of presumption. You
may guess, he says, "there was great noise among the craftsmen." "My soul
was indeed among lions." Yet, in spite of all sorts of hostile demonstrations,
seeing the audience gathered around him disposed to hear, he quietly gave
notice of a third service to be held at the same place at six o'clock in the
evening, which service he held and carried through, though the opposition
was more concerted and more fiend-like than before. On another occasion
the very leaders of a mob, bent on mischief, taunted him and called him a
coward because he had finished his sermon and was getting down from his
table-pulpit just as they got on the ground. He promised them "they should
hear some more presently," and soon after, taking his stand upon a flight of
stairs, began to preach. Pretty soon they began to grow riotous, whereupon,
feeling a sudden impulse, he leaped down from the stairs into the midst of
them, at which they all ran like a flock of frightened sheep. At Oxmantown
Green in Ireland, where the "Ormond and Liberty boys," used to have their

Sunday fights, he ran a terrible gauntlet nearly half a mile through a storm of stones from a popish mob, "taking," he says, " a fresh stone at every step" which "made him reel backwards and forwards till he was out of breath and all over a gore of blood." He thought he got more blows than Stephen and was in hopes, he says, "that like him he should go off in this bloody triumph to the immediate presence of his Master." His friends got him into a house, and a carpenter offered him his wig and coat that he might get off in disguise, and he put them on; but ashamed of himself for not trusting in his Master, he forthwith threw them off again with contempt.

Few men ever had more of this sort of abuse. The poet Cowper's well known lines, though perhaps too general, present this side of the world treatment of him with graphic truthfulness. But he lived it down. Of the most virulent of his oppose'rs multitudes became his converts, and some his pupils and assistants in the gospel ministry. Such was the man who said, "I came with stones in my pocket to break your head, but you have broken my heart."

Whitefield had a warm social nature and many attractive social qualities. He had really no *home* and very little that would be called domestic life. But he was a welcome guest among people of all ranks in society. Dr. Franklin who had a strong regard for him, once wrote him a polite note inviting him to share his house during his stay in Philadelphia. Whitefield's reply and Franklin's rejoinder are both characteristic. "If you make me this offer for Christ's sake," says Whitefield, "you will not miss your reward." Franklin rejoins, "do not let me be mistaken. It was not for Christ's sake but for your sake." Whitefield was married and had one son whose death in infancy was a deep sorrow to him. It has been intimated that his married life was not happy. It may be so; though his wife seems to have been a worthy woman, and he always speaks of her with respect and tenderness. His views of marriage seem however to have been quite too utilitarian. Two curious letters are extant, written at an earlier day, when he was soliciting the hand of another lady. One, written to the lady herself, sets forth in formidable array the privations and self denials to be encountered in being the wife of a man occupied as he is. The other addressed to her parents, though intended for her eyes, explains his reasons for wishing to marry, and respectfully and properly asks permission to address her. But it adds, quite emphatically, "You need not be afraid of sending me a refusal, for if I know my own heart, I am free from that foolish passion which the world calls love." This proposal, the young lady, it seems, did not accept; and Whitefield, when he had reflected on the matter, thought it best that she did not. Probably it was.

Indeed a man, who like him, was always on the wing, restive when obliged to be "in winter quarters" and longing like a caged bird to get into the fields, who was so devoted to one particular department of his Master's service as to find little or no place for anything else, ought not to have married. And, yet, as all the accounts testify, Whitefield had a nature "susceptible of the most generous and tender friendship." These are the words of John Wesley who adds, "I have frequently thought that this of all others, was the distinguishing point of his character. How few have we known of so kind a temper, of such large and flowing affection." It was this, he thinks, that attracted and knit to him so strangely the hearts of others. "Love shone in his very countenance and breathed in all his words, public and private. Was it not this that, quick as lightning, few from heart to heart, which gave life to his sermons, his conversations, his letters?" Particularly felicitous was his intercourse with women. His office brought him into intimate relations with not a few, and those of all ages and ranks. "But his whole behaviour" says the same indubitable authority, "was a practical comment on that advice of St. Paul to Timothy: "Entreat the elder women as mothers, the younger as sisters with all purity."

Indeed, I know not where is to be found such an assemblage of the most attractive human virtues as appeared combined in this man of God separated from the world, this devotee of Christ. Economical in his expenses, frugal in his diet, regular in all his habits, scrupulously neat in his person, a pattern of order and propriety, he united in an admirable degree the perfect gentleman with the devoted Christian. He handled a great deal of money, yet nobody was able to fix upon him the slightest taint of avarice or unfaithfulness. With a simplicity as guileless as a child's, a frankness as open as the day, a delicacy that would not wound the most sensitive nature, a liberality that never stood upon trifles where the main thing was secured, a charity that was slow to suspect evil, a generosity that never disparaged others, nor arrogated to himself the praise which belonged equally to them, a candor which took reproofs kindly and was ever ready to confess discovered errors and faults, a singular meekness in the endurance of injuries and insults, of which few men have ever met more, he united a boldness in the reproof of error and sin which never blenched before noble-man or rustic benefactor or opponent, and a firmness in maintaining essential truth which, when the case came to worst, would sooner sacrifice the dearest friendship than betray the trust which he believed to be committed to him of God. A reformer by profession, he was scrupulously conservative of all that was good. Called to act at a time when, to use his own words, "we must be either disorderly or useless," he took no liberties that were not manifestly necessary, and, amidst many provocations to the contrary, adhered to the last, to the church of his fathers. No man was ever freer from sectarianism. The cry, "I am a churchman," I am a dissenter," wearied and pained him. There was no moroseness in his nature; his cheerfulness is proverbial. No man wept more tenderly over the ruin of the sinner, and no man rejoiced more exultingly over his conversion. No man rolled the thunders of Sinai with greater awfulness. No man sang in sweeter, gentler strains the songs of Bethlehem. Few could have borne the flattery which he received without being spoiled, and few the ill treatment without being soured. But he wearied of his popularity; and as to the abuse, he said once to a friend: "Blessed be God, contempt and I are pretty intimate and have been for above twice seven years." His character, during life, was subjected to the severest tests. Certainly he had faults—the faults all of them of an ardent and impulsive nature—which disappeared as his character matured. Those who knew him best loved and honored him most; and most of the opposition which he encountered was got up in his absence, and most of the contempt and ridicule came from persons who knew very little personally of him. His sense of sin was keen, his humility unfeigned, his gratitude to God overflowing, his faith strong, his love ardent, his hope unwavering, his walk with God all his life long "quite in the verge of heaven." He loved his work and yet he longed to go home. Worn, wasted and sick with excess of labor, and the powers of life in him evidently getting low, he still worked on to the utmost of his bent, and one of his last characteristic sayings was "Lord, I am weary *in* thy work, but not weary *of* it."

But we must hasten on to the close of his career. He had taken a tearful leave of his friends in England, preaching his last field sermon where he did his first, to his old friends the colliers at Kingswood. He crossed the Atlantic in May and was warmly welcomed. The Governor, Council and Assembly of the State of Georgia paid him a visit and attended divine service at the Orphan House. He made several extensive tours and showed much of his former vigor. Still he was really a sick man and could not do as he once did. A ride of sixty miles on horseback or a pulpit sweat was no longer a sure restorative. But he turned his thoughts northward—to use his own words, employed on a former occasion, "Affection, intense affection cried out: Away to New England, to dear New England." He reached Boston about the first of August and spent several weeks preaching there and in the neighborhood. Thence he came to Newburyport and preached once, intending to go eastward. But his friend, Parsons, detained him. He preached three times in Rowley and was to have returned hither. But falling sick, he went back to Boston, and resting there a few days again turned his face eastward. The catalogue of his labors from the time of his arrival at Newport to that of his death, as given by Dr. Pemberton in his commemorative sermon, is, considering his feeble state, as wonderful as that of any part of his life. From August 4th to September 1st he preached every day except one. His sickness, which commenced at Rowley, took up three days. His journey from Boston to Portsmouth "pretty much indisposed," says my authority, caused an interval of two days more. On the 23d, 24th and 25th he preached each day at Portsmouth, on the 26th at Kittery, the 27th at Old York, the 28th at Portsmouth again, the 29th at EXETER. Mr. Parsons had met him at Portsmouth and engaged him to spend the Sabbath at Newburyport. He rode from Portsmouth to Exeter on horseback, fifteen miles, on Saturday morning. The concourse of people more than filled the church, and a sermon in the open air suggested. Mr. Parsons remonstrated: "as I really thought," he says, "it was throwing away his life." But the people were thronging to hear him and he was never the man to be sparing of himself. So they made a platform for him by throwing a board or two across tow casks; and there he stood, bolt upright, with nothing to lean against, in a damp hot atmosphere and preached, it is said for two hours on the duty of self examination, from St. Paul's words: "Examine yourselves whether ye be in the faith." It was his *last sermon*. In the course of it, he expressed either the wish or the belief, that so it would prove; for he longed for his dismission. He had longed for it often during thirty years and more, and was often "in a strait betwixt two." He rode that evening fifteen miles more to Newburyport, and, after tea, retired to his room. In the night he was seized with a severe fit of asthma, and on Sabbath morning, about six o'clock, Sept. 30th, just one hundred years ago to-day, breathed his faithful soul out into the hands of his Redeemer and now shines, as the promise is to "them that turn many to righteousness," "as the stars forever and ever."

It was according to his own express desire that he was buried in front of this pulpit. This church was peculiarly endeared to him. It grew directly out of the great religious movement of which he was so conspicuous an instrument, and as I have always heard, it was by his advice that it adopted the Presbyterian form of government, a favorite one with him, though he was not of its jurisdiction. Great efforts were made to remove the remains elsewhere. Gentlemen from Boston urged their removal thither, as Mr. Parsons thought, quite too pertinacious, and seemed hardly courteous in their presentation of arguments. "Newburyport," they said, "is but a small place, hardly known on the other side of the water." "It *shall* be known," answered Mr. Parsons decisively. They pushed their suit until his resolute nature was quite roused, and bringing down his strong fist upon the table he reiterated, "Shan't go! Shan't go!" and that settled the question.

On Sabbath morning a vast concourse of people from all the surrounding region gathered in and around this house of worship. But the eloquent voice to which they expected to listen was silent. Mr. Parsons came to the pulpit, and announcing the sorrowful event, preached to the disappointed and sorrowful multitude from the words: "For me to live is Christ and to die is gain." The elders and deacons of the church assumed, in the name of the congregation, the whole charge of the burial which took place during the week following, including the preparation of the vault; and the funeral procession, which was nearly a mile long, was joined by many thousands of people. The pulpit was hung with mourning emblems, the vessels in the harbor displayed their flags at half mast. The funeral sermon was preached by Mr. Jewet, of Rowley. Mr. Rogers, of Hampton, rising to lead in prayer was so overcome with his emotions that he broke out, "O, my father, my father!" then stopped and wept, the people weeping with him all over the house. After prayer the congregation led, by one of the deacons who gave out the hymn line by line, according to the old custom, sang, "Why do we mourn departing friends, or shake at death's alarm?" And, the body being laid in its place, and the congregation dismissed with the blessing, they "went weeping through the streets to their respective places of abode." So did "devout men carry him to his burial" and, all over England and America, hundreds of thousands "made great lamentation over him."

In England, in accordance with Whitefield's expressed wish, the venerable and beloved John Wesley, as soon as the news came, was designated to preach the commemorative sermon, which he did on the Lord's day, Nov. 15th, in the two chapels in London, of which Whitefield had had the charge—a sweet and sacred testimony from one who loved him well, though they had differed and separated, and alike honorable to the speaker and the lamented subject of his touching eulogy.

I may naturally be asked here, what was the secret of Whitefield's wonderful power, and I must detain you for a few words in reply, though the subject has been elsewhere so fully and ably discussed. He was, no doubt a very remarkable orator. His voice, strong as the blast of the clarion and melting as the softest notes of the flute, was at his perfect command and responded perfectly to all his emotions. Garrick said he could have made men weep though he had uttered nothing but the word *Mesopotamia*. Dr.

Franklin compared the pleasure derived from his oratory to "that received from an excellent piece of music." His style was simple, direct, almost homely sometimes, going straight to the common heart. He had a wonderful faculty of making men feel as if he were speaking individually to them. He told a story admirably and applied it as well. He had too an astonishing dramatic power. The anecdote of Lord Chesterfield, I believe, is not disputed. It is said, Whitefield was describing the perils of a poor blind beggar, groping his way on the edge of a precipice. Chesterfield had followed the preacher till he had brought the man out upon the giddy edgy, and there presented him just toppling over. "Good God" cried Chesterfield, starting from his seat as if to rescue him, "he is gone!" We have some specimens of his bursts of eloquence, which are quite unique and must have been thrilling. But all this and a great deal more in the same line, does not account for its effects. It would have exhausted itself by repetition in a few years at most, and grown stale.

If I am not mistaken, two elements are chiefly to be recognized. The first is in *himself*—in his own mental and religious character, especially the latter, in that absolute self-consecration which he made at his ordination and maintained through life, in that glowing piety and constant "walk with God" which was manifest in his daily deportment, and closely connected with that though greatly favored by his mental and emotional organization, in the force and vividness with which he conceived, felt, believed and communicated to others, the great, simple, heart-searching doctrines of which he was the herald. These last were to him present realities. The New Birth by the spirit of God, the justification of the sinner by the blood and righteousness of Christ, the utter ruin of apostate man by the guilt and corruption of sin, the sovereignty of grace, the eternal rewards of the believer and the unbeliever, God's holiness, the inexpressible love of Jesus (for these were the staple of his preaching—these and what belongs to them) were not doctrines merely but living facts, which he just as much believed as he saw the sun shining in the heavens. As he stood amidst the thronging thousands gathered to listen, his inward eye looked straight into their eternal future. He saw sinners standing upon the very verge of the "bottomless pit," and he wept bitter tears and uttered heartfelt cries in his efforts to save them. He saw Jesus, just as clearly, as Stephen saw him at his resurrection, "standing at the right hand of God" and beckoning them to himself; and he cried aloud, and with the tenderest pathos, begged and pleaded with them at once to go to him. He spoke not in his own name but in God's, whose messenger of love he fully believed and felt himself to be; and, so believing, he spoke with what he was accustomed to call "Gospel authority." His fine voice and perfect action answering to all his thoughts and emotions as the tones of a musical instrument, to the lip and finger of a skillful performer, no doubt, did wonders for him; but it was not these, but the thoughts and feelings they expressed, that produced the effect.

It was the "powers of the world to come," with which he lived constantly in loving and adoring intercourse, pervading his soul, seizing and appropriating to their use his remarkable physical and conceptive faculties and speaking out in every utterance of his voice and gesture of his body. Whitefield, with all his oratory, would have been nothing, comparatively, without his religion—nothing indeed in any other department than that of a preacher of that religion. To that he gave himself with a singleness of aim and energy of purpose hardly paralleled in the history of human action. It was the powerful lens which concentrated into one burning focus all his thoughts, passions and abilities.

The other element is to be found in what I may call the *specialty of his position*, or more specifically in his special mission from God as the apostle of a remarkable era. A man of his character would have mighty power in almost any circumstances. But that does not tell the whole story. We indulge here no superstitious fancies. In Whitefield there was nothing more supernatural than in any of the rest of us. Both he and the times in which he lived were subject to the same laws, natural and spiritual, which control all other persons and times. But there is one fact not to be disputed. The times in which he acted, were in a religious point of view, remarkable times. He was himself the product of them. All over England and America there was, before he came upon the stage and during the whole course of his action, upon it, an unusual waking up to the reality and binding obligations of the religion of Christ. That is a simple historical fact. Truths which, at other times, skim the surface of men's minds, now, in the hands of those who felt their power, took hold of the deepest springs of the heart. Men and women, old and young, high and low, cultivated and uncultivated bowed to their force as does the forest to the blast of a tempest. It is equally clear, as a matter of history, that of all the instruments of that remarkable movement, George Whitefield was endowed with qualities which most eminently fitted him for that service. It was as if he had been made and fashioned expressly for it.

Now, believing as I do, in common with most of my religious countrymen, that there is really a GOD, a living, personal God, thinking, feeling, willing, acting in the affairs of the world, I cannot but ascribe this most beneficent religious movement and the fitness of the man for it, in virtue of which he worked for the accomplishment of its ends with the same precision and certaintly of aim as the main spring works upon the cogs and wheels of a watch to effect the designs of its maker, to the providence and grace of this great Disposer of all things. And just in this divinely ordained fitness of the man to the work do I find one of the main secrets of the preacher's wonderful power. Talent is not merely subjective. As far as it is that alone, it falls dead. All the great men of the world owe their greatness to their adaptation to their time and place. And Whitefield's is to be found, not in his mental and emotional organization only, not by any means in his art, not indeed in his eminent Christian zeal, fervor and devotion independently considered, but in the fact that he was a chosen instrument fitted by the divine hand to perform just the work which the divine purpose of compassion for a degenerate and sinking age had undertaken to accomplish. Whitefield was not the only one of his class. Edwards, Tennent, Rowland, Parsons, in America; Wesley, Berridge, Rowlands, Howell Harris, Griffith Jones, in England and Wales, produced some of the same effects. But he was *facile princeps*—the chief of them all. And in proportion as he was so was his divine commission the more apparent. So his contemporaries seem to have judged. Parsons says: "I have often considered him as an angel flying through the midst of heaven with the everlasting gospel to preach to them that dwell on the earth. Wherever he flew, like a flame of fire his ministry gave alarm to all sorts of people." "In some such manner," says another, "have I been tempted to conceive of a seraph, where he sent down to preach among us and to tell us what he *had heard and seen above.*" "It is certain," says Henry Venn, "that his amazing popularity was only from his usefulness; for he no sooner opened his mouth as a speaker than God commanded an extraordinary blessing on his word." Whitefield, I repeat the opinion, would have been, with all his eloquence, comparatively a common man without his gospel, and the simple but stupendous truths to which he gave utterance in its name; and, even with these, he could never have attained to the same eminence except as the divinely chosen and fitted instrument of the all-conquering grace of God in the GREAT REVIVAL.

And now what has been the result? The lapse of a century has sufficed to remove from the world all the direct effects on the hearts of individuals. There were few here who had any distinct recollections of him when I came to Newburyport, thirty-five years ago [1835]. Mr. Bartlett remembered him, but had not much to tell. Mrs. Clarkson, whose husband was a step-son of Mr. Parsons, and who was often in the family, remembered him as "a cheery old gentlemen, a very cheery old gentlemen." She had heard him "joke mother Parsons about her old cap." Perhaps the cap did not quite come up to his very nice notions. A very old woman then living in the lower part of Lime street remembered seeing him spread out his hands and, beckoning to the children in the gallery, call to those "dear little birds" "to come and fly to the arms of their Saviour." Mrs. Sarah Eaton, a woman of rough speech and manners who had been bed-ridden for several years, had very clear recollections of the day of his death, and in the account she gave, represented, no doubt, the adverse side of popular opinion. "She was a gal then," she said, "and had no religion herself;" and when she met the people in the streets going away and they told her Whitefield was dead, she told them she was "glad on't;" for "it made me so *mad*," she said, " to see 'em all running a'ter him." The thousands and hundreds of thousands, that loved his ministry on the one hand or hated and reviled it on the other, have all gone to their account; "also their love, their hatred and their envy is now perished."

Still there are and must be vast results left on the church and the world. And what are they? The exact answer to this question God only can give; for he only can unravel the net-work of influences and assign to each their part in any great event in the world's history. The most we can say of any one man, in any case, is that he had a *great hand in it*. Plain it is, from what we have seen, that the crisis was one of the most momentous. Equally plain that the deliverance wrought by the divine hand was among the most signal. It saved the age.

If we should undertake to number the actual conversions, no doubt we must fail. The judgement day alone can furnish the materials. Henry Venn says of Whitefield: "The seals of his ministry, I am persuaded are more than could be credited could the number be fixed." John Newton says: "It seemed as if he never preached in vain. Perhaps there is hardly a place in all the extensive compass of his labors where some may not yet be found who thankfully acknowledge him as their spiritual father." John Wesley challenges contradiction. "Have we ever heard of any person who has been the blessed instrument of bringing so many sinners from darkness to light and from the power of Satan unto God." An able recent writer says of him and his associates: "No such harvest of souls is recorded to have been gathered by any body of contemporary men since the first century." Such results do not end with the life of the converts! Among these arose, even in Whitefield's time, not a few of the ablest and best ministers of the Gospel, beginning a true apostolic succession of the best sort, whose type, so far from being effaced, is multiplying itself from age to age in all our evangelical denominations. Several important institutions for this purpose owe their origin to this movement. Dartmouth College is one of them. So is Princeton. So are the two principal classical and theological colleges in Wales, those of Balla and Trevecca.

Whitefield organized no new denomination such as Wesley organized, but he was instrumental in infusing a new spirit into the existing ones. By his clear, earnest and faithful inculcation he restored and gave new life to the old puritan doctrines, when they were fast passing into neglect or becoming diluted. In the church of England the evangelical portion owes its existence unquestionably, to his influence. The elements of evangelical piety introduced by his ministry into the ranks of the nobility, both in England and Scotland, have produced and are still producing some of the most beautiful fruits of Christian culture and large-hearted benevolence. The great Methodist denomination, now so powerful and so efficient for good here and in England, was in the beginning made up largely of his converts, and owes to his ministry some of the best elements of its character, though it does not bear his name. The Baptist church felt the power of the same movement, and in this country certainly, gathered into itself, eventually, many of the churches formed during its progress. The Presbyterian church of Scotland was re-invigorated and received an element of spiritual life and practical beneficence greatly needed to modify and counterbalance its doctrinal stiffness. The Presbyterian church of Wales, otherwise called the Calvinist-Methodist church, now the strongest church in the Principality, was directly and confessedly the child of his ministry. Wales was in a most deplorable state. Whitefield's ministry shook it from end to end and pervaded it through and through with a new spirit. There the results took a distinct organization, which is at the present moment, strong, efficient, and growing. The Presbyterian church in this country owes a vast deal to the same movement. Not only Princeton College but Princeton Theological Seminary, and all the spreading fruits that have come forth from both may be fairly traced to it. And as for Congregationalism in New England—*orthodox* Congregationalism, now so strong, so energetic, so aggressive in all parts of the land, it may be justly said to have been saved almost from extinction, under God, by the great revival to which this "Burning and Shining Light" of his age contributed so much. Nor only saved. It too, as well as the other denominations, received from the movement a new energy.

We may trace, also, in a large degree, to this source the whole systems of aggressive movements on the ranks of sin and wretchedness throughout the world by which the modern evangelical church is distinguished. A recent writer has very justly remarked that "Whitefield was the very first

Englishman who seems to have thoroughly understood what Dr. Chalmers aptly called the aggressive system. He did not sit tamely at the fireside mourning over the wickedness of the land. He went forth to beard the devil in his high places. He dived into holes and corners after sinners." Mark his characteristic expression, borrowed, as I have somewhere heard, from Brainerd's Indians: "*hunting* for sinners." No doubt, the zeal which now characterizes the efforts of the church for home and foreign evangelization, as well as the introduction of the most approved measures now in use for the promotion of religion owes very much to the quickening influence of the great work of grace of which he was so conspicuous an instrument. The Protestant Reformation was to a great degree outward, among institutions, doctrines,forms and methods of worship. The churches thus emancipated, re-organized and indoctrinated by the Protestant movement, now needed another, which should put life and practical energy into their body. And this was accomplished, more than by any other means, by what we may call, with due qualification yet with manifest justice, the WHITEFIELDIAN REVIVAL.

It is thus, and by similar results of his great ministry, that today, after he has already sung in glory and his precious and sacred remains have reposed under this favored pulpit an entire century, this great "PRINCE OF PREACHERS," as he was justly called by the sainted Toplady, "being dead yet speaketh,"—speaketh in every corner of the land that gave him birth,—in England, Scotland, Wales, Ireland, and by an echo of the same, in India, Africa, China, Australia, and wherever the martial and commerical power of England has made its influence predominant; speaketh through all the borders of this then young and feeble but now vast, powerful and growing country; speaketh, not in one of the denominations only, of which none could claim to appropriate this large-souled catholic spirit, but in all who still love the truths he taught and the Saviour whom he served; speaketh in every mission established by English speaking men in every corner of the globe, speaks now and will speak louder and louder as the voice echoes on down the coming century and to the remote generations. He needs no costly pile to preserve his Memory. The beautiful monument that stands in the corner of this church, with its emblematic flame rising to heaven, is indeed a worthy tribute. We guard and will guard with care, in this our loved house of worship, his honored dust. You, my dear brethren of this ancient church, have a tender and sacred trust committed to you to protect these mortal remains of one so justly reverenced. But the chief honor we can do to his memory is to feel in our own hearts his burning love for Jesus and the souls of his fellow-men, and make the motto of our lives the same with his, who said "O that I had a thousand tongues—the ever-loving, ever-lovely Jesus should have them all."

The other exercises of the morning were a voluntary on the organ; a sentence from Beethoven; invocation and reading of the scriptures by the Res. F. W. Bakeman, of Newburyport; prayer by the Rev. Randolph Campbell, of the same city; singing by the choir, of the hymn beginning, "How rich thy bounty, King of Kings." The Commemorative Discourse followed, occupying nearly two hours in delivery. After the singing of an anthem—"Blessed are the people"—the Rev. Dr. Stearns pronounced the benediction.

AFTERNOON

Invitations to be present and take part in the services of the afternoon, had been extended to several of the eminent clergy of the land, sons of Newburyport and others. So far as possible it was desired to have all the denominations with which Whitefield especially labored, represented among the speakers.

The Rev. George W. Blagden, D.D. of the Old South Church, Boston, presided, and introduced the speakers to the audience. Prayer was offered by the Rev. J. B. Wakeley, D.D., of Newburgh, N.Y. Dr. Blagden then made a statement in regard to Whitefield's Orphan House in Georgia which is added as a note at the close of this pamphlet. He spoke also of the lessons of the day, gathering them all under the saying of the apostle, "Jesus Christ the same yesterday, and today, and forever." The duty of giving the heart to the Saviour for whom Whitefield labored, in order worthily to commemorate his death, was enforced upon the audience.

The pastor of the church, the Rev. Charles S. Durfee, then read letters received from several who had been invited to be present on the occasion, regretting their inability to do so; among them, Rev. John Stoughton, D. D. and Rev. Henry Allon, of London, Eng; President McCosh, of Princeton, N. J.; Rev. John Hall, D. D., of New York, and John G. Whittier, of Amesbury, Mass.

The Rev. Ashbel G. Vermilye, D. D., of Utica, N. Y., pastor of the First Presbyterian Church, Newburyport, from 1850 to 1863, was then introduced by the President.

Dr. Vermilye said: "A century and a quarter ago witnessed a strange sight in this venerable old town, then a place of about two thousand inhabitants.

An immense crowd is hurrying, at 5 or 6 o'clock in the morning, to the corner of High and Federal streets. And some of them, men and women too, young and old, have come, riding or afoot, even from Rowley. For what strange thing? Of all other strange things, to hear a sermon! But the preacher is George Whitefield. He gives out his text:—"Ye are the salt of the earth, but if," &c. And then his voice rolls over the assembly, as he begins: "and whom does the apostle *mean*, when he says, *ye* are? Why you, ye saints of Newbury; but I much fear me ye have lost your savor!" Then, after a warm and stirring address to Christians, he turns an appealing voice to sinners; and the audience is moved by his words, as human oratory has seldom moved men.

On the same spot a stone was thrown at him, which struck the little bible he held; when, in a powerful tone, he exclaimed: "I stand in the king's highway and hold in my hand the king's commission; and I must and will preach:" which he did without further interruption.

At a later period, he preached in this church, even before it was finished. "Didn't we have good times," said an old lady who died aged 105 years, "when we used to sit on the benches, and Mr. Whitefield preached." And it was with his usual power. You would have seen souls bowing, occasionally a smile, but more often a tear; and one, I know, the ancestor of a great and Christian posterity, was converted while clinging to the pulpit-rail to prevent being crushed away by the crowd. Such was the impression he made, that after eighty-two years, a bed-ridden old lady whom I knew, could not speak of him without excitement in her voice and manner. When 16 years of age, she had herself walked with her mother to Exeter (fourteen miles) to hear him. One hundred years have passed since he was buried, as other men are; not an echo of his voice lingers in any living ear; and yet there is eloquence to gather men, even in the name of Whitefield—as it has gathered us this day. What gave him his influence and power?

We have read of the prophets, what they said and did; and was not he, in his kind, a prophet? Look at him, and you see a plain man in gown and bands and wig, with a cast in his eye, a stern look, but alert and quick in his movements. In his preaching, he turns no gilded periods, as rhetoricians do; digs no mines of thought, nor scatters their treasures abroad in ingots of gold. His mental gifts and acquirements are not great. He wrote no book. He occupies today no niche in the minds of men anywhere near Edwards, as one of "the dead but sceptred souls that rule us from their urns." But in that man, physically weak, mentally not eminent, who lies there, perhaps, panting and exhausted by some field-preaching, you will find the very "spirit and power" of Elias; that which made *him* great, first of all his *spiritual* power.

First, Whitefield's mind was burning with great ideas. Not great as men are apt to estimate ideas. The fuel that made his furnace hot, came from none of the usual fields of thought. It was not by his grand handling of scientific or other truths of the kind, that he surprised cold critics like Chesterfield into a momentary sympathy and a reluctant homage. But, two thoughts from God's book had taken full possession of his soul—man a lost sinner, in danger of death; and redemption by Christ and the renewing of His Holy Spirit, the only remedy. Upon these two themes he rung the changes through eighteen thousand sermons, with a readiness of diction and a power of illustration that was amazing. He felt the truth he uttered, burned with it; and his audiences saw the flame, felt the heat, and themselves caught fire before the intense energy of the speaker.

Second, I think the state of the times and of his audiences must be considered. The gospel had long been withheld from them. They knew nothing of its great prime truths. No wonder, then, they staggered and reeled before the mighty vision of its verities thus newly presented to them: before *him,* as he grappled and shook and tugged at their consciences with tremendous zeal, till rooted prejudices gave way. "I came," said one, "with my pocket full of stones to break your head, but you have broken my heart." Peter the hermit was, no doubt, an orator; but he roused Europe to a congenial task. They followed him willingly in crowds, though only to perish by the way. Whitefield found his hearers dead, till he brought the unaccustomed gospel to bear upon them; then they arose and followed him by thousands to a new, a holier, an eternal life.

Third, His voice must be mentioned—without which he would not have been Whitefield, nor have produced such marvelous effects. You know the power of sound to thrill, charm or terrify; but nothing can move us like the human voice uttering great thoughts with passion and flame. And his was a wonderful voice, loud beyond the ordinary compass of good voices—they say it could be heard a mile; and yet it was not a storm of mere noises in the ear, but modulated to pass from the roll of the thunder to the zephyr's murmur as it gently shakes the leaves. With his voice, too, went the vivid illustration, the rapid transformation of style, the whole harmonious manner. It is not always *what* a man says, so much as *how* he says it. And Whitefield's loving, emotional nature, his imagination quick to breathe life into an incident, his dramatic power and fine voice, added to *what* he said the charm of a manner the most moving, winning, melting. Sometimes he touched the smiles, and then the tears; and he touched the smiles that he might afterwards draw the tears—for you know how near smiles and tears lie together. Sometimes his speech was like a cloud, dark, portentous, thundering; and as, with face and manner all ablaze, he exclaimed, "Oh! The wrath to come, the wrath to come," who could resist the contagion of such earnestness? They seemed to see the impending ruin, and felt the danger he described. Dr. Smalley, who heard him when a boy, says:—"I was altogether absorbed in the services of this bold preacher, his stern look, his great voice, his earnest words; and as I thought of my soul, and of Christ, and salvation, I was so carried away in my feelings, as not to know where I was. I could not keep my eyes off from him. I saw him in his prayer, his eyes wide open, looking on high; and I certainly thought that he saw that Great Being up there, with whom he was talking and pleading so earnestly." An old lady of 98 years told me the anecdote, usually attributed to Rowland Hill, but which I think must belong to Whitefield: that a lady, richly dressed, was sitting in the front pew, whose manner annoyed him greatly. Closing his Bible he exclaimed, "no more preaching here today—we are going to have an auction. An auction! Yes, a lady dressed in silk—who bids?" Then he portrayed vanity, the world, Satan, as bidders; till she was pale and purple with rage. But then, changing his voice and whole manner, he said:—"but hark! I hear another—it is the Saviour's voice—I'll give my life for her;" and the lady burst into tears.

Fourth, I can only add, that the Holy Spirit was with him. That rare oratory would have lacked its soul, without that which made his whole life peculiar,—"a man *full* of the Holy Ghost"; full, so full, as to keep his heart and eyes and speech overflowing continually with love to God and man. And so he went moving round the world; a comet, if you will; but one whose train was a cloud of stars, gathered from collieries, the most unlikely places and material of earth, to shine forever among the jewelry of heaven. And then he died; silent at length, who for 30 years had never been silent, on the great themes of Christ and human salvation: silent even when dying,—as he had once predicted; for, said he, "God has permitted me to testify so often for him, that he will need no dying testimony from me":—died, and was buried. There have, no doubt, been more stately funerals than his. England poured from her coffers a more elaborate and showy mourning when George 2nd died; and Warburton the bishop, who thought Whitefield "mad," went to his grave with more pomp of ceremony. But when Whitefield died, a genuine and unusual grief infected the whole community. As they had crowded to his preaching, as that of a flaming angel, so they now crowded weeping to his burial. But *is* Whitefield dead? True, there stands his cenotaph, and in the little vaulted chamber that holds his remains the bare skull, when you touch it, gives no echo of life. And yet—what means this gathering? No! to be dead is not to be remembered, to have done nothing that lasts. And, in this sense, Whitefield is not dead. During the rebellion they used to sing, "John Brown's soul is marching on." And *his* soul is marching on. He founded no sect; but he transfused his soul into every denomination and sect. And it is marching on, in England, Wales, America; as the storm of the tropics marches, in waves successive, that reach and resound on distant shores. Such men do not come often; they would not be such treasures if they did. But who, in our day, would not hail as an angel from God him who in the place of Whitefield's ashes, could re-kindle Whitefield's fires; whose single voice could revive religion as his did, and multiply converts by such thousands?

The next speaker was the Rev. George S. Hare, D. D., of Boston, who said he was here, as he understood, because he was a Methodist, representing an organization which included nearly one-half of Protestant Christendom, and in its congregations nearly one-fifth of the people of the nation. He spoke of Whitefield as a Methodist, sketching his early life, his connection with the Wesley's, who, he said, founded more churches than the apostles. He recited the vows of Whitefield when he entered the ministry, and dwelt at some length upon the marvels that attended the preaching of Whitefield and the Wesleys. The differences of opinion between them were dwelt upon, and yet their substantial unity was maintained and the opinion expressed that all differences were at an end with them in heaven. Whitefield stood forth as the founder of the Calvinistic Methodists, and Wesley of the Arminian Methodists. At Whitefield's death the Calvinistic Methodists became separated into three divisions: the Lady Huntington connection, who had about sixty chapels; the New Connection of Whitefield Brothers, who had been mainly absorbed in other sects; and the Welsh Calvinistic Methodists, who had a chapel in every village of Wales, which country was inscribed all over with the signatures of Whitefield's labors.

The President then announced Rev. Rufus W. Clark, D. D., of Albany, N. Y., who spoke as follows:—

Standing in this pulpit, brings vividly to my mind the services and scenes of the past. In this church I worshipped God in childhood, and learned to reverence the sanctuary and the institutions of religion. At this altar I received the holy rite of baptism, and within these walls my honored father served as an elder of the church for forty years. His familiar face, and the forms of most of those who occupied these pews, in my youth, have passed away from earth. They have ceased their worship here and joined the general assembly and church of the firstborn in heaven.

I am reminded of the able and faithful ministers who here unfolded divine truth; enforced with eloquent lives the duties of religion, and have passed to their reward in heaven. The venerable Dr. Dana appears before me, the embodiment of Christian sanctity, the able expounder of the doctrines of Christianity, and defender of a rigid orthodoxy at a period when errors were creeping into the churches.

Succeeding him came the Rev. Samuel P. Williams whose son bearing his name is with us today, and whose fervid eloquence and intellectual power, impressed not only his own congregation, but this entire community. I easily recall the earnestness with which I listened to his discourses, especially those which he delivered shortly before the close of his earthly labors. The accomplished and scholarly Dr. John Proudfit followed him, whose social qualities and personal attractions, as well as finished puplit efforts, won my affection and admiration. Recently, after valuable services rendered elsewhere, he has been called by the Master to his heavenly kingdom. The living successors of these eminent divines, whom the present pastor has welcomed here today, we rejoice to know, are occupying post of wide usefulness, in other parts of the Lord's vineyard.

But the occasion upon which we have assembled, calls us to commemorate the memory and achievements of the prince of preachers, whose dust rests beneath this pulpit. As his life and the incidents connected with his history have been so fully and ably presented by the gentlemen who have preceded me, it only remains for me to gather up a few of the lessons of the hour, in accordance with the suggestion of our presiding officer, that the value of past history lies in the benefits it confers upon the present time.

From the career of George Whitefield we learn first the power of individual effort in the service of Christ. The age in which we live is distinguished for organized action in associations and societies. This form of Christian labor is necessary, and is attended with great good. But as we study the history of the church and of the extension of the Redeemer's kingdom, we find that God's special blessings have rested upon individual consecration to him. The church has advanced under great leaders, inspired by a holy ardor; and giving their entire intellectual and moral forces to the service of God. Moses was more to the cause of truth and righteousness than thousands of the Israelites. When he was upon the mount receiving the law, and the people were rendering divine honors to a golden calf, the strength of the church seemed to abide in his soul. His individual faithfulness was the pillar that upheld the spiritual kingdom, amid the darkness of heathenism and the perils of apostasy.

When the gospel was to be established in the Gentile world, while several disciples were appointed to their work, one was divinely commissioned to prosecute it with signal vigor and success. St. Paul was the soul of the enterprise, and to him was given the power to overcome great difficulties and establish Christian churches amid Jewish bigotry and Pagan superstition.

The Reformation of the sixteenth century was, under God, wrought by individual rather than associated effort. In single minds the light of divine truth was first kindled; in single hearts the resolution was formed to smite the fabrics of error and oppression, that crushed the nations of Europe. Luther stands forth the spiritual power around which the friends of freedom and truth rallied, and from which they received their enthusiasm and hopes. Whitefield and Wesley, of whom we have heard so much of interest today, appear before us in the line of entire consecration to God, and hence of leadership. One was distinguished for his eloquence, and sway over the hearts of the multitudes who thronged to listen to him, and the other for his organizing power; while both were animated by the most intense religious fervor. Whitefield was probably the instrument of bringing more souls to Christ than any preacher since the time of the apostles. He fired with new zeal the hearts of his ministerial brethren. He aroused churches to a fresh activity, and widely developed the latent powers and resources of the people of God. He had faith in that union with Christ which imparts to the mind a superhuman energy, and gives the greatest success to Christian labors. His achievements reveal what is possible to any one who will make the service of God the supreme end of his being, and resolve to know nothing among men "save Jesus Christ and Him crucified."

Whitefield also expressed the unity and catholicity of the Christian church. While riding in the cars to this city today, I was accompanied by an old friend and townsman who is an Episcopal clergyman. He claimed Whitefield as an Episcopalian, because he was brought up in that church and retained through life, his connection with it. The Methodist brother who has just addressed us, has endeavored to prove that Whitefield was a Methodist, because of his connection with the Wesleys, and others, who established this great and influential denomination. As his remains lie under the pulpit of a Presbyterian church, the Presbyterians might, perhaps, present a claim to him based upon this fact. But the simple truth is: he was too large a man for any one denomination. He belonged to the universal church of our Lord Jesus Christ. He held the great doctrines common to all evangelical sects;

was ready to labor in cordial fellowship with all, and possessed a zeal for the honor of the divine head of the church, that today, would be a blessing and a power to the ministry, of every name throughout Christendom. We contemplate his catholic spirit with peculiar admiration at the present time, when so many earnest members of the various denominations are not only expressing their fellowship, but seeking to make the unity that prevails, a power for the advancement of Christ's kingdom. Let existing sects rise to the standard of consecration, and labor that he reached, and by a natural law they would move together, and feel the inspiration of one faith, and be guided by one Lord.

The career of Whitefield also reveals to us the secret of ministerial success. He was not a man of extraordinary intellectual abilities. His pulpit power did not consist in the depth of originality of his thoughts; nor in logical skill; nor in treasures drawn from the various departments of learning. His style was simple, and his printed discourses present few attractions to the reader. His voice was remarkably rich, sweet and powerful. His emotional nature was easily moved, and he possessed the gifts of a natural orator. But the power within him that gave life to every thought, force to every truth, impressiveness to his illustrations, and kindled in his soul the flames of intense feeling and made his eloquence irresistible, was the power of the Holy Spirit. What he had of talents, more or less; what he had of gifts, natural or acquired, he laid upon the altar of God, and God breathed into his body and soul His own Spirit. This enabled him to prosecute his work with strong faith and high expectations of success. This made his sermons penetrate the consciences, stir the feelings, sway the reason and mould the lives of his hearers. This made him a spiritual force in the church that has been felt to this hour, and will grow with the growing kingdom of God through all time.

Let us who are here, and the ministry of our day, obtain this Divine Spirit, and under the augmented power of the American pulpit, the church will awake and put on her strength; the truth will be mighty to the pulling down of the strong holds of sin, and we may discern in the horizon the dawn of the millennial glory.

Rev. Alexander King, of London, England, was presented to the audience as a representative of the land of Whitefield's birth.

He expressed his great gratification at being enabled to take part in this solemn and sacred celebration, and trusted that all present might carry away in their hearts the inspiration of the memories awakened here today. He regretted the absence of Dr. Stoughton, Mr. Bickersteth and Mr. Allon, who would have so worthily represented the evangelical communities of Great Britain; and as the only representative of the British Christians, thousands of whom were now in spirit present with that meeting, earnestly desiring to honor the memory of the great preacher, and to bless God for His labors in the gospel.

Mr. King mentioned that he had, himself, frequently come across the tracks of Whitefield's wonderful work, both in England and in Ireland. A few years ago he had preached in the noble church erected to the memory of Whitefield at Kingsdown by Bristol, and stood upon the scene of his marvelous work amongst the colliers in that region. In Bristol, in London, and in many other places throughout England, amongst Christians of various denominations, the sacred and loving memory of the name of the man of God is as fresh and fragrant today as though the present generation had heard his voice and felt the spell of his matchless eloquence.

In Ireland, many years ago, he had himself been led to open-air preaching, when even the old Methodist preachers—the heroic Evangelists of an earlier era—had abandoned it; and he thanked God he had had a glorious success and was permitted to preach the gospel in that way in every part of that country, to hundreds and thousands who would not otherwise have heard it. He was also glad to testify that he had never been stoned or maltreated by the poor Roman Catholic people, many of whom received the word with gladness; and he wished to record there that day that he had been sustained and animated in that effort by remembering the glorious work which God had enabled Whitefield to perform, in darker days and often at the peril of his life. He invited the audience to appreciate the sacredness and moral grandeur of this occasion.

We are not hero-worshippers! We do not canonize our departed saints. We do not put sentimentalism for piety. He doubted if we were sentimental enough. Yet we do homage to the memory of heroic Christian zeal. We remember it is written the righteous shall be in everlasting remembrance, and we bless God for the great grace bestowed upon His servant, and for the glorious results of his faithful and abundant labors. Mr. King urged special attention to the lesson of true catholicity and brotherly love to be learned by all the churches from this commemoration of the life and work of Whitefield. In conclusion he affectionately admonished all to catch fresh inspiration for the work of God from the touching solemnities of this day, and besought each Christian present to realize the power of a consecrated life!

The closing benediction was pronounced by the pastor. The exercises continued from two o'clock till nearly five. They were pleasantly varied by the singing of two appropriate hymns by the choir, whose "modest and excellent manner of performing their part" was much commended.

The only decorations were a wreath of laurel surrounding the cenotaph; a painting of the old church hung at the side of the pulpit; and in front of it a portrait of Whitefield, kindly loaned for the occasion by Mr. W.P. Johnson, of Chelsea. The chair in which Whitefield died, the property of the American Board of Commissioners for Foreign Missions; a ring worn by him, now in the possession of John Tappan, Esq., of Boston; and a medal struck at the time of his death, were on exhibition in front of the pulpit, together with Rev. Mr. Parsons' writing desk, given to the church for the use of its pastors. On it was placed the old Bible of the church, from which Whitefield had often read.

NOTE

The statement of Dr. Blagden, referred to in his opening address, is as follows: "Rev. George Whitefield came to the then infant colony of Georgia, about the year 1750, and at that time established a charity called, "The Union Society," so named because it was of all religious denominations, for the support and education of orphan boys." He had really begun the establishment of this Orphan House in 1738, during his first visit to Georgia, and it was first proposed to him, he says, by his dear friend Charles Wesley, who connected the scheme with Gen. Oglethorpe. He had heard and read what Professor Franck had done in Germany. This institution is still in existence, and last year celebrated its one hundred and twentieth anniversary. Joseph Story Fay, Esq., who now resides in Boston, whole resident in Savannah, was President, and did a great deal for it. Bethesda, Whitefield's ancient site for the House, had been abandoned. Through Mr. Gay's instrumentality it was repurchased and resuscitated. Edward Padelford, Esq., of Savannah, lately deceased, a native of Taunton, Mass., was a most generous benefactor while living, and in his will left it a legacy of $100,000. The venerable Lowell Mason was Secretary from 1824 to 1827. The society has commenced this year a new building of a substantial character. Whitefield was on a visit North to obtain some pecuniary aid for this society, when he sickened and died at Newburyport. Last year, the Union Society received a likeness of Whitefield and a volume of sermons preached in England on the occasion of his death, a present from the Rev. John Lockwood, Torley Bridge, Halifax, England. According to the original charter, it was to be granted as long as three members celebrated the anniversary, which is St. George's day, April 23. There were three gentlemen prisoners of war on board of a British mon-of-war, who craved permission from the commanding officer to go ashore and celebrate this anniversary under an oak tree, at Sunbury, Ga., which was granted. The three original members were of three denominations—Protestant, Catholic, and Israelite. [See Gillies' *Life of Whitefield,* pp. 188, 189, 202.]

The life of Lawrence Sterne and that of Whitefield covered nearly the same period. Whitefield was born December, 1714 and died September 30, 1770. Sterne was born November 24, 1713, and died March 18, 1768. Both were graduated the same year. Whitefield at Oxford and Sterne at Cambridge.

Frederic the Great was born January 24, 1712, and died August 17, 1786. Voltaire was born February 20, 1694, and died May 30, 1778.

When his youthful popularity at one time was rising very high, one of the London papers began to advertise him. Much annoyed he wrote to the printer "begging him not to put him into his paper any more." The printer flatly refused, saying, "he was paid for doing it and would not lose two shillings for anybody."

The words of one of the invitations deserve notice. John Wesley wrote thus: "Only Mr. Delamotte is with me till God shall stir up the hearts of some of his servants who, putting their lives in their hands, shall come and help us. What if thou art the man, Mr. Whitefield?" "Do you ask me what you shall have? Food to eat and raiment to put on;—a house to lay your head in such as your Lord had not, and a crown of glory that fadeth not away." "Upon reading this," Whitefield writes, "my heart leaped within me and as it were echoed to the call.'

It is worthy of note that he almost never records a success, whether in his journals or in his most familiar letters, without an expression of or a prayer for humility. "O, that I was humble, that I was thankful; help me, my dear friend, to entreat the Redeemer to make me a little, a very little child." It was one of his favorite expressions: "Nothing sets one so much out of the Devil's reach as humility."

Once in Scotland he speaks of preaching seven times in one day, viz: once in the church, twice in the girl's hospital, once in the old people's hospital and twice in a private house. "Notwithstanding which," he adds, "I am as fresh as when I rose in the morning," and all this with wonderful spiritual effects.

Dr. Franklin's testimony on this point is remarkable as coming from such a source. "It is wonderful," he says, "to see the change made in the manners of our inhabitants. From being thoughtless and indifferent about religion, it seemed as if all the world were growing religious; so that one could not walk through the town on an evening without hearing psalms in different families in every street."

Phillis Wheatley, a young negro slave of the age of seventeen, wrote a poem commemorative of him, in which occurred the following touching lines referring the earnestness with which he preached Christ crucified:—

"Take Him, my dear Americans, he said;
Be your complaints on his kind bosom laid;
Take Him, ye Africans, he longs for you,
Impartial Saviour is His title due.
If you will choose to walk in grace's road
Ye shall be sons and kings and priests of God."

Dr. Franklin's testimony on this point is very explicit. "I knew him intimately he says, "for upwards of thirty years; his integrity, disinterestedness and indefatigable zeal in *every good* work I have never seen equaled—I shall never see excelled." Dr. Franklin, it must be remembered, was not a convert of Whitefield, nor was he a man to waste words on anybody.

Whitefield was eminently a devout man as all his writings show. Yet he was not tied to set forms or rules. When he was too weary to pray he did not hesitate, as he himself intimates, to go silently to his bed. The Rev. Cornelius Winter, who was in the closet intimacy with him, speaking of his frame of mind on Sabbath mornings as more than ordinarily devotional, adds, "I say *more than ordinarily* because, though there was a vast vein of pleasantry usually in him, the intervals of conversation evidently appeared to be filled up with private ejaculations. His rest was much interrupted and his thoughts were much engaged with God through the night." He sometimes spent whole nights in prayer.

The Rev. Jonathan Parsons was the venerated and beloved first pastor of the First Presbyterian Church in Newburyport, a man of great energy and force of character, a thorough theologian, a warm-hearted preacher of the gospel and one of the most distinguished of the revivalists of his day. A very cordial attachment subsisted between him and Whitefield, of many years standing.

A leading motive with this church in departing from the Congregational order, was the desire to secure toleration for their separate existence as a church, which they could not do under the Congregational church as then by law established. Neither they nor Whitefield had any repugnance to Congregationalism *as such*. But he had a special predilection for Presbyterianism, Episcopalian as he was, and pronounced the Presbyterian

Church of Scotland "the best national church in the world." Hence his advice. The church organized itself at first provisionally, but became Presbyterian as soon as it took any denominational character. It was never Congregational.

The most authentic account of the death and funeral is probably that contained in a letter of Mr. Parsons to Dr. Gillies, Whitefield's biographer, a copy of which is now in the possession of Jacob Stone, Esq., of Newburyport, and was published with his consent, by Rev. Mr. Vinton, to whose kindness I am indebted for calling my attention to it in 1869, in the Congregational Review. Most of the facts stated above were derived from that source. The conversation with the Boston gentlemen was related to me by the late venerated Dr. Andrews of Newburyport. Mr. Parsons is not quite so circumstantial, but says, contrasting their interview with him with the very courteous one of the delegation from Portsmouth: "Several private gentlemen from Boston came to my house and in a manner that appeared pretty sovereign they made sort of *demand* of Mr. Whitefield's body to carry to Boston and bury there. I told them that I could not consent to their taking the body from us—that I meant to submit to the righteous providence of God and would not contend, but was not willing to have his body carried from the place *where he had desired it should be laid.*" Mr. P. says, in this letter, "I could give a long account of Mr. Whitefield's tours through New England for thirty years past, as I kept a journal of all the opportunities I had with him." He also intimates that, in respect to his last visit, death and funeral, "the public have been much imposed upon," and throws some discredit on the competency of Mr. Smith as a witness, from whom most of the current accounts are largely taken. He says of him: "His (W.'s) servant seemed like a man bereaved of his senses, and said many things that could not be to his honor to mention."

So is the Lady Huntingdon connection in England and another small body called, I think, the Whitefield Methodist.

The "*Societies*" of that day were the precursors of our evening prayer meetings.

Erected by the munificence of that large-hearted giver, William Bartlet, Esq.

It is to be regretted that no fuller report of Dr. Hare's address could be obtained.

APPENDIX 6

THOUGHTS ON THE WHEREABOUTS OF WHITEFIELDIAN MATERIAL

There is a Holy Grail in Whitefieldian material that is *missing*. The whereabouts of his personal papers and manuscripts have kept previous Whitefield biographers simply perplexed. To accept the notion that Whitefield ceased writing a Journal after the age of thirty (his last known Journal—published in the century after his death) goes against the philosophy of Whitefield's life. He was a "Methodist"; and being a Methodist he established ingrained habits early in his life from being a member of Wesley's Holy Club. He always maintained a daily account of his life. He kept meticulous records of his daily schedule not wanting a "fragment of time" to evaporate needlessly. On a recent visit to Dr. Williams Library in London we (Dr. Digby James and myself) examined a few pages from Whitefield's diary for 1735 (his complete diary for 1736 is located in the British Library in London). These pages from his 1735 diary were sent by a Whitefield biographer, Robert Philip, to a friend of his. These pages were subsequently donated to The Congregational Library (which is located at Dr. Williams's Library, Gordon Square, London). This is *extremely noteworthy* for it reveals to us that Philip had access to Whitefield's personal papers when he was writing his biography. Where did Philip get them? And, more importantly, where did he leave the cache of the rest of Whitefield's papers? Obviously John Gillies had them at one time. Perhaps John Erskine (another friend of Whitefield) had them as well. Luke Tyerman had access to them. Dallimore surmised that they have been lost. Others surmise that Whitefield ceased keeping a journal because he became "increasingly disinclined to publish accounts of his own work and personal experiences." It is too hard to accept the notion that the meticulous Whitefield ceased keeping a daily record of his life past the young age of thirty! To reinforce this argument, another "rare find" was located by Dr. James and myself in London. We visited the museum at John Wesley's Chapel in London. Behind a glass case was a page from Wesley's diary. What is remarkable about that is it looked *exactly* like the page from Whitefield's diary in the Congregational Library! The handwriting distinguished the two men but the format was *identical*. Obviously it was John Wesley who taught the young Whitefield how to be a Methodist and keep a detailed account of every day. Whitefield was a good student and copied this "method" of living for the rest of his life. Therefore, to accept the notion that Whitefield ceased keeping a daily record of his life after the age of thirty appears ludicrous. Why would he break old habits so young? The answer is *he didn't*—we maintain that he kept a daily account of his life up to the age of fifty five, when he died in 1770 at Jonathan Parson's manse in Newburyport, MA. Now accepting this hypothesis (and it is the only logical one) we must ask the question—Where are the Whitefield papers? Where are his Journals from the age of thirty to fifty five? Here are some suggestions:

1. *Bohemia Manor in Maryland—the Bayard home*. George Whitefield stayed often at Mrs. Bayard's home and kept his papers there when traveling. In fact, it was Dr. J.R. Bayard Rodgers (a descendant of Mrs. Bayard) who gave his last known Journal to Princeton in 1816. The "Whitefield Room" can still be visited today. There is a recorded incident where a new owner of the Bayard mansion found a barrel of papers in an attic and burnt them because they were infested with mice. If Whitefield's missing Journals were in that barrel then that was *a tragedy of historical proportions*. They could have been destroyed in that fire.

2. *Robert Philip:* since Philip had access to Whitefield's diary and letters he may have retained the lion's share of this cache personally. An investigation into whether he has any living relatives would prove beneficial; then contacting them to see if any of Philip's private belongings still exist.

3. *John Gillies:* Dr. John Gillies of Glasgow, Scotland was one of Whitefield's closest friends. He had full possession of Whitefield's papers when he wrote the "Memoirs". Is there a descendant of John Gillies who can help us? Please contact us if you have any clues as to the whereabouts of any missing Whitefield papers.

4. *John Ryland's Library:* in Manchester, England, is where the Methodist Archive is located. Perhaps there is an unmarked box there with Whitefield's Holy Grail.

5. *An Attic in Wales:* it has been surmised that the papers are in someone's attic in Wales (perhaps a relation to Elizabeth Whitefield?).

6. *George Whitefield's brother James:* an interesting connection is the following: The Georgia Historical Society came into possession of a rare family portrait of Whitefield in 1888. It was donated by Eliza Grigg who was a relation to Elizabeth Johnston who was James Whitefield's daughter. It is quite possible that some Whitefield relation could have the papers. If anyone knows the ancestry of James Whitefield please contact us. I personally would like to know if I am related to Elizabeth Johnston! (wishful thinking).

7. *Bethesda Orphan House:* the Orphan House in Savannah burned to the ground from a electrical storm. The new buildings are *not* on the same location as the original structure. There was a *basement* or cellar where Whitefield kept barrels of goods such as produce, rum, and quite possibly his Journals. The cellar is still there on the property! One has only to locate the exact boundary of the original house (which I can come very close to doing, having walked it out already) and then *dig.* We need permission to do this of course and *money.* I am hopeful that permission would be granted but raising the money to do this is quite another problem. There is also a missing graveyard at the Orphan House containing the remains of some twenty people. If we could find the original foundation and dig beneath it we would locate the cellar which is at least six to ten feet below the ground. There could be many historical objects there—hint to the Georgia Historical Society!

8. *Other theological institutions such as Princeton, Harvard, Drew, etc.:* the missing cache of Whitefieldian material could simply be in an "unmarked" box laying in a room unnoticed by time. Someone has to search these unmarked boxes. My friend Richard Owen Roberts, when doing his research in London for his mammoth *Whitefield In Print* told me there are *many* unmarked boxes in Libraries and academic institutions as he came across them himself. Perhaps an interested archivist could begin the search.

EXISTING WHITEFIELDIAN MATERIAL

There is *finally* a larger amount of Whitefield material available thanks to Quinta Press and Dr. Digby James. The publishing of the *George Whitefield Works* CD by Quinta Press has made available many heretofore unpublished works. In it are facsimile's and reset editions of much material concerning Whitefield. Also published by Quinta Press are additional letters of Whitefield taken from copies of the Journal of the Presbyterian Historical Society, the Evangelical Library, and letters taken from the Proceedings of the Wesley Historical Society. When Dr. James convinced me (cruelly) that I had to give a pint of blood to see the Whitefield material held in the

Congregational Library, London—I believed him! And was relieved to find I could see Whitefield's diary pages without a needle! Dr. James has also obtained additional letters of Whitefield from the "Christian Treasury, 1868". Hopefully, the publication of this new biography on Whitefield will spark some interest in more Whitefieldian material being made available!

As this volume was about to go to press I learned that there is a collaborative project to produce a critical edition of Whitefield's extent letters. This project is part of the IMEMS Centre and Periphery strand, and is being planned in conjunction with Dr. David Ceri Jones (University of Aberystwyth), Professor Bruce Hindmarsh (Regent College, Vancouver), and the Jonathan Edwards Centre at Yale University. To date they have abour 2,500 letters.

SIGNIFICANT PLACES CONNECTED WITH WHITEFIELD

There is much Whitefield information not previously published which is helpful to our understanding of his magnificent life. The following information concerns "places" where Whitefield preached. Here is a helpful list:

The *Whipple House in Ipswich, MA* has Whitefield's Geneva Bible and a portrait.

Next to the *Congregational Church in Ipswich, MA* there is a rock containing the so-called "Devil's footprint". Tradition has it that Whitefield preached with such power in the original church building here that the devil was "ousted", and where he landed he left his evil footprint in the rock! Of course, this is just fun but nevertheless the footprint is there!

In *Rowley, MA* (a place Whitefield often preached) there is the "Pulpit Rock" from which he often held court! This is a short distance from the Linebrook Church, whose origins are connected with Whitefield's ministry in the area. There is a sign describing Pulpit Rock that can be seen from the road nearby. The signwriter changed Whitefield to Whitehouse halfway through the text!

In *West Brookfield, MA* (in the middle of the state) there is a rock that has a plaque upon it stating that Whitefield preached there on 16 October 1740. Turn off route 9 up Foster Hill. At the top of the hill on the left is what looks like white gates leading into a field. The preaching rock is half-way across the field on the left hand edge.

The *Court House in Philadelphia* (opposite the Liberty Bell in Independence Square) is where Whitefield often preached from the steps and balcony landing. Later this building was where the early meetings of the Continental

Congress were held and the Declaration of Independence drafted. Visiting Market Street, on the other side of the square, will give one a good idea how large a place it was when Whitefield preached there.

The stature of Whitefield at the University of Pennsylvania is the only statue of Whitefield in the world. He made a contribution to the founding of this institution in 1740. Note: Permission in advance is required to visit the statue in the University quadrangle, at South 36th and Spruce.

The Orphan House Hospital Park (already mentioned) is in Edinburgh, Scotland. Dr. James and I researched this and found that it is indeed the scene of remarkable revival. The location is George Heriot's School, Lauriston Place, Edinburgh. One has to "sign in" and wear a name badge (as we did) to gain access to property.

Dunfirmline. North of Edinburgh across the Firth of Forth was the base of the Erskines and the Associate Presbytery. A memorial to Ralph Erskine stands outside the former presbyterian church building (Ebenezer Erskine is buired at Stirling). The building had become a café and was up for sale when I visited. It was here that these enthusiasts for presbyterian church government told Whitefield that he should only preach for them as they were the Lord's people. Whitefield declined to do so as those outside of the Associate Presbytery clearly needed to hear the gospel.

The High Kirk Church Yard in Glasgow, Scotland is the scene of revival as well. Whitefield would stand in the graveyard and preach from tombstones to thousands. The High Kirk is now known as Glasgow Cathedral.

Cambuslang, near Glasgow. The church building has William M'Culloch's gravestone embedded in the wall. Most of the text is unreadable due to erosion. Many of the gravestones have been vandalized, having been pushed over or had graffiti sprayed on them, or both. The Preaching Braes is a short distance away. Follow the metal fencing and you will find a gate with a plaque on it (probably covered with graffiti). This will take you down a path into the natural amphitheatre which, at the height of the revival, held 30,000 people. You are likely to find broken bottles and beer cans littering the site.

Moorfields, London: Whitefield's Moorfield's Tabernacle was rebuilt in 1868 and a plaque on the side of this building in Tabernacle Street shows that the original Tabernacle stood nearby. It is just up the road from Wesley's Chapel in City Road, which itself is opposite the Bunhill Fields Burial Ground where many famous Nonconformists are buried, including John Bunyan, Isaac Watts, John Owen and Daniel Defoe. This area was the scene of remarkable revival, where thousands would come up from London to the open air to hear Whitefield as he preached his heart out amidst Merry Andrews, bear-baiters, and puppet shows.

Kennington Common, London: this was the scene of remarkable revival. It is still a public park today and is a wide open green space where one can easily imagine Whitefield preaching beneath the hung prisoners in chains!

Tottenham Court Road, London: his original chapel is gone. The rebuilt chapel was destroyed by the last V2 strike of World War II in 1945. Elizabeth Whitefield was buried beneath the pulpit and her remains may still be there. The existing church is the Whitefield Memorial Church and is used by the American Church in London. It can be visited with permission. A portrait of Whitefield (see cover photo) hangs in the vestibule.

The Tower of London Chapel: can be visited today with a guided tour. Whitefield preached here early in his career. The Tower is a royal palace and the location of the British Crown Jewels. It also has the spot where several "traitors" (including some of Henry VIII's wives) were executed.

Dummer, Basingstoke: the ancient Anglo-Saxon chapel there is still in pristine condition, including the pulpit that Whitefield preached from. Whitefield preached here for several months, filling in for his good friend (and fellow Oxford Methodist) Charles Kinchin.

Stonehouse, St. Cyr: this chapel is famous for Whitefield's visits. His journal maintains that he preached from the church yard here, because the chapel was too small to contain the hearers!

Kingswood, Bristol: "Whitfield's Tabernacle" here is in ruins. The tombs in the graveyard are desecrated and one sepulchure even has its lid off! It badly needs repair. A charitable trust has been set up to try and raise funds for rennovation. Nearby is Hanham Mount where Whitefield first preached to the miners of Kingswood. The spot is marked with several plaques and a pulpit.

There is a town in New Hampshire called "Whitefield" named after him after his death.

The most remarkably preserved Whitefield site is in Rodborough. The church, *Rodborough Tabernacle* is the same as in George Whitefield's day. He used to preach from the grave yard, standing between two chestnut trees! The chair in the pulpit was Whitefield's and they also have his walking stick.

Minchinhampton Common, Whitfield's Tump: can be visited. This ancient burial mound was the spot where Whitefield would preach to twenty thousand in the open air with the wind at his back! It is beside one of the greens of the local golf course—watch out for stray golf balls!

BIBLIOGRAPHY

PRIMARY:

John Richard Andrews, *George Whitefield, A Light Rising in Obscurity* (London: Morgan and Scott, 1879).

George Whitefield's Journals (Edinburgh: Banner of Truth Trust, 1998).

Joseph Belcher, D. D., *George Whitefield: A Biography, with Special Reference to his Labors in America* (American Tract Society, 1860).

Albert D. Belden, D. D., *George Whitefield—The Awakener, A Modern Study of the Evangelical Revival* (New York: Macmillan Company, 1953).

Rev. John Berridge, A. M., *The Works of John Berridge* (Gospel Press, Montana).

J. Wesley Bready, *England Before and After Wesley* (London: Hodder & Stoughton, 1938).

Richard L. Bushman (ed.), *The Great Awakening* (Chapel Hill, NC: University of North Carolina Press, 1989).

Edward J. Cashin, *Beloved Bethesda, A History of George Whitefield's Home for Boys, 1740–2000* (Macon, GA: Mercer University Press, 2001).

Faith Cook, *Selina Countess of Huntingdon* (Edinburgh: Banner of Truth Trust, 2001).

Arnold Dallimore, *George Whitefield, The Life and Times of the Great Evangelist of the 18th Century Revival, Volumes One and Two* (Edinburgh: Banner of Truth Trust, 1970, 1980).

Sherman Day, *Historical Collections of the State of Pennsylvania* (Philadelphia, PA: George Gorton).

Jonathan Edwards, *Works*, Vol. 1 & 2 (Peabody, MA: Hendrickson Publishers, 2003).

Arthur Fawcett, *The Cambuslang Revival, The Scottish Evangelical Revival of the Eighteenth Century* (Edinburgh: Banner of Truth Trust, 1996).

John Gillies, D.D., *Memoirs of Rev. George Whitefield, Revised and Corrected with Large Additions and Improvements* (Hunt & Middletown: Noyes, 1838).

J.P. Gledstone, *George Whitefield Supreme Among Preachers* (Belfast: Ambassador Publications, 1998).

Edwin Noah Hardy, *George Whitefield: The Matchless Soul Winner* (New York: American Tract Society).

Michael A. G. Haykin, *The Revived Puritan* (Canada: Joshua Press, 2000)

Stuart C. Henry, *George Whitefield: Wayfaring Witness* (New York: Abingdon Press, 1967).

Helen C. Knight, *Lady Huntingdon & Her Friends* (Grand Rapids: Baker Book House).

William Jay, *Memoirs of the Life and Character of the Late Rev. Cornelius Winter* (New York: Samuel Whiting & Co., 1811).

D. M. Lloyd-Jones, *The Puritans, Their Origins And Successors* (Edinburgh: Banner of Truth Trust, 2002).

Curt Daniel, Ph.D., *The History and Theology of Calvinism* (Springfield: Good Books, 2003).

D. Macfarlan, D. D., *The Revivals Of The Eighteenth Century, Particularly At Cambuslang* (Wheaton, IL: Richard Owen Roberts Publishers, 1980).

Iain H. Murray, *Jonathan Edwards A New Biography* (Edinburgh: Banner of Truth Trust, 1987).

Iain H. Murray, *The Puritan Hope, A Study in Revival and the Interpretation of Prophecy* (Edinburgh: Banner of Truth Trust, 1971).

National Library of Wales Journal, Volume XXVI, Number 3, Summer 1990.

National Library of Wales Journal, Volume XXVI, Number 4, Winter 1990.

National Library of Wales Journal, Volume XXVII, Number 1, Summer 1991.

National Library of Wales Journal, Volume XXVII, Number 2, Winter 1991.

National Library of Wales Journal, Volume XXVII, Number 3, Summer 1992.

National Library of Wales Journal, Volume XXVII, Number 4, Winter 1992.

Edward S. Ninde, *George Whitefield: Prophet and Preacher* (New York: The Abingdon Press, 1924)

Robert Philip, *The Life and Times of the Reverend George Whitefield, M. A.* (1837).

John Pollock, *George Whitefield and the Great Awakening* (Tring: Lion Publishing, 1972).

Richard Owen Roberts, *An Annotated Bibliography of Revival Literature* (Wheaton, IL: Richard Owen Roberts Publishers, 1987).

Richard Owen Roberts, *Whitefield in Print* (Wheaton, IL: Richard Owen Roberts Publishers, 1988).

J.C. Ryle, D.D., R. Elliot, A.B., *Selected Sermons of George Whitefield with an Account of his Life and a Summary of his Doctrine* (London: Banner of Truth Trust).

J. F. Stearns, *Centennial Commemoration of the Death of George Whitefield,* 1870

Joseph Tracey, *The Great Awakening* (Edinburgh: Banner of Truth Trust, 1976).

Luke Tyerman, *The Life and Times of the Rev. John Wesley, M.A., Three Volumes* (London: Hodder and Stoughton, 1870).

Luke Tyerman, *The Life of the Rev. George Whitefield,* Vol 1 & 2, Hodder And Stoughton, London, reprint by Good Books, Springfield,.

George Whitefield Works on CD-ROM (Weston Rhyn: Quinta Press, 2000).

J.B. Wakeley, *A Portrait of Rev. George Whitefield, M.A.* (New York: Carlton & Lanahan, 1871).

The Journal of Charles Wesley, Vol. 1 & 2 (Stoke-on-Trent: Tentmaker Publications, 2002)

John Wesley, *The Works of John Wesley, Vol 1–8* (Grand Rapids: Baker Books, 2002).

George Whitefield, *The Works of the Reverend George Whitefield, M.A.* Vol 1–6 (Edinburgh: Edward and Charles Dilly, 1771).

George Whitefield, *A Journal of a Voyage from London to Savannah In Georgia, In Two Parts* (London: James Hutton, 1739).

George Whitefield, *Continuation of the Reverend Mr. Whitefield's Journal from his Arrival at London, to his Departure from Thence on his Way to Georgia* (London: James Hutton, 1739).

George Whitefield, *A Continuation of the Reverend Mr. Whitefield's Journal, from his Arrival at Savannah, to his Return at London* (London: James Hutton, 1739).

George Whitefield, *A Continuation of the Reverend Mr. Whitefield's Journal, During the Time he was Detained in England by the Embargo* (London: James Hutton, 1739).

George Whitefield, *A Continuation of the Reverend Mr. Whitefield's Journal, from a Few Days after his Return to Georgia to his Return at Falmouth* (London: 1741).

SECONDARY:

Archives of Old South First Presbyterian Church, Newburyport, MA.

Archives of Bethesda Home For Boys, Savannah, GA.

Articles from *Arminian Magazine,* London, 1782.

Articles from *Lloyd's Evening Post,* London, issues from April 1764– December 1767.

Articles from the *Pennsylvania Gazette,* issues 1739–1741.

Mack M. Caldwell, *George Whitefield Preacher to Millions* (Anderson, IN: The Warner Press, 1929).

Ray Comfort, *Whitefield Gold* (Gainesville, FL: Bridge-Logos Publishers, 2005).

Joseph M. M. Gray, *George Whitefield and his Master's Voice* (Whitefish, MT: Kessinger Publishing, 2005).

Gurney, *Whitefield's Eighteen Sermons* (London, 1771).

Hugh J. Hughes, *Life of Howell Harris* (London, 1892).

William Howland Kenney, *George Whitefield, Dissenter Priest of the Great Awakening* William and Mary Quarterly, 1969.

Frank Lambert, *Pedlar in Divinity: George Whitefield and the Transatlantic Revivals* (Princeton: Princeton University Press, 1994).

Stephen Mansfield, *Forgotten Founding Father* (Nashville, TN: Highland Books, 2001)

Susan Martins Miller, *George Whitefield Clergyman and Scholar* (Philadelphia, PA: Chelsea House, 2001).

J.I. Packer, *The Spirit with the Word: The Reformation Revivalism of George Whitefield,* article for "Essays in Honour of James Atkinson", Library of Princeton Theological Seminary (Sheffield: Sheffield Academic Press, 1995.

Ted S. Rendall Library, Olford Ministries International, Memphis, TN.

James Robe, *The Revival of Religion at Kilsyth, Cambuslang and Other Places in 1742* (Glasgow: William Collins Publisher, 1840).

Bishop J. C. Ryle, *Christian Leaders* (London: 1868).

Henry Scougal, *The Life of God in the Soul of Man* (reprint Fearn, Tain: Christian Focus Publications, 1996).

Aaron C. Seymour, *The Life And Times of Selina, Countess of Huntingdon* (London: Wesley Historical Society, 1906 reprinted Stoke-on-Trent: Tentmaker Publications).

Ruth Gordon Short, *George Whitefield Trumpet of the Lord* (Washington, DC: Review and Herald, 1979).

William Stephens, *Journal of the Proceedings in Georgia, 1742*.

Harry S. Stout, *The Divine Dramatist, George Whitefield and the Rise of Modern Evangelicalism* (Grand Rapids, MI: Eerdmans Publishing Company, 1991).

Luke Tyerman, *Life of Charles Wesley,* Vols 1 & 2 (London: Hodder and Stoughton, reprinted Stoke-on-Trent: Tentmaker Publications).

Bennet Tyler & Andrew Bonar, *Asahel Nettleton Life and Labours* (Edinburgh: Banner of Truth Trust, 1975).

John Wesley, *Journal of John Wesley* (London: Epworth Press, 1938).

George Whitefield, *A Collection of Hymns for Social Worship,* (London: Henry Cock, reprinted by Quinta Press, 2000).

William and Mary Quarterly, VII, No. 4, 3rd Series (Oct., 1950).

William and Mary Quarterly, XXVI, 3rd Series, (1969).

William and Mary Quarterly, XXXIII, No. 1 (Jan. 1976).

William and Mary Quarterly, XXIX, 3rd Series (1972).

INDEX

Bolingbroke, Lord, vol. 1: 162. vol. 2: 74, 75, 76, 159, 161, 544
Born Again, vol. 1: 64, 427
Boston, New England, vol. 1: 408, 409. vol. 2: 86, 112, 286, 379
Boston Common, vol. 1: 258, 404
Brainerd, David, vol. 1: 360
Bready, J. Wesley, vol. 1: 102
Bristol, England, vol. 2: 162, 221, 273, 298, 362, 424
Bryan, Jonathan, vol. 2: 38
Bunyan, John, vol. 1: 55, 151, 501. vol. 2: 401, 511
Burr, Aaron, vol. 2: 297

C

Calvin, John, vol. 1: 181, 454, 457, 495, 514. vol. 2: 159, 511
Calvinism, vol. 1: 181, 306, 435, 436, 495, 498, 513. vol. 2: 367
Calvinistic Methodists, vol. 2: 159
Cambuslang, Scotland, vol. 1: 466, 485. vol. 2: 19–39, 247, 575
Carr's Ferry, vol. 1: 7
Catholic Spirit, vol. 1: 437
Cennick, John, vol. 1: 154, 160, 433, 434, 454, 459. vol. 2: 28, 29, 62, 128, 129
Charles, Prince, vol. 2: 60
Charleston, SC, vol. 1: 319, 330, 332, 338, 419. vol. 2: 235, 236, 286, 385, 440
Chesterfield, Lord, vol. 2: 74, 251, 552, 560
Christ Church College, vol. 1: 24
Christian History, vol. 1: 262. vol. 2: 86
Church of England, vol. 1: 33, 97, 102, 129, 159, 161, 181, 221, 329, 465, 467, 471. vol. 2: 120, 298, 312, 359, 401, 403, 404
Church of Scotland, vol. 1: 467, 471. vol. 2: 17
Cole, Nathan, vol. 1: 402, 404, 413
Coleman, Benjamin, vol. 1: 277, 374. vol. 2: 86, 104, 106, 107, 112
Cooper, William, vol. 1: 275, 374. vol. 2: 105, 541
Cork, Ireland, vol. 2: 223, 323
Cotton, John, vol. 1: 367, 368
Courcy, Richard de, vol. 2: 167
Covenanters, vol. 1: 465, 470

Conventicle Act, vol. 1: 133
Cowper, William, vol. 1: 67. vol. 2: 547
Creek Indians, vol. 1: 31, 55, 79, 86, 229
Crocker, Rev. Josiah, vol. 1: 364, 365

D

Dallimore, Arnold, vol. 1: 6, 150, 151, 205, 451, 455. vol. 2: 54, 87, 141, 230, 282, 371, 501, 506, 571
Dalton House, Newburyport, MA, vol. 2: 499
Davenport, James, vol. 1: 373, 374, 413, 414, 417,
Davies, Samuel, vol. 1: 209, 497. vol. 2: 274, 279, 280
Deal, England, vol. 1: 61, 62, 64, 65. vol. 2: 131, 155, 158
Delamotte, Elizabeth, vol. 1: 205–208.
Delamotte, Thomas, vol. 1: 205
Dickinson, Jonathan, vol. 1: 266
Dickson, David, vol. 1: 49
Dissenters, vol. 1: 99, 182, 453. vol. 2: 174, 367
Dixon, Thomas, vol. 2: 437
Doctor Squintum, vol. 2: 194, 343–346, 356, 357
Doddridge, Phillip, vol. 1: 172. vol. 2: 69, 214, 237, 281
Downs, The, vol. 1: 60, 65
Drew University, vol. 2: 500
Drury Lane Theatre, vol. 2: 346
Dublin, Ireland, vol. 1: 94, 162. vol. 2: 223, 224, 317, 322, 323
Dunfermline, Scotland, vol. 1: 467, 472, 473, 478. vol. 2: 575

E

Earthquake, vol. 1: 370, 510. vol. 2: 174, 284, 540
Edinburgh, Scotland, vol. 1: 489, 491, 492. vol. 2: 19, 27, 39, 160, 269, 319, 320, 330, 356, 364
Edmonds, John, vol. 2: 131
Edwards, Jonathan, vol. 1: 154, 257, 261, 265, 267, 343, 360, 377, 379, 401, 410, 497. vol. 2: 20, 21, 280, 330, 491, 492, 503, 532

Edwards, Sarah, vol. 1: 381
Eells, Earnest, vol. 2: 89, 110
Election, doctrine of, vol. 1: 506, 508, 511
Enfield, Conn., vol. 1: 383–385
Erskine, Ebenezer, vol. 1: 465–469, 472, 474, 476, 477, 498
Erskine, John, vol. 2: 571
Erskine, Ralph, vol. 1: 323, 465, 467, 471–477, 498
Exeter, New Hampshire, America, vol. 1: 3, 4, 6, 198. vol. 2: 289, 450, 499, 504, 550
Exeter, England, vol. 2: 162, 171, 323

F

Fanning, Thomas, vol. 2: 500, 501
Fawcett, Arthur, vol. 2: 17, 21
Fawcett, John, vol. 2: 153
Federal Street, vol. 2: 289
Fetter Lane Society, vol. 1: 97, 172. vol. 2: 120
Finney, Charles, vol. 1: 365, 501. vol. 2: 520
Fletcher, John, vol. 1: 163. vol. 2: 78, 336, 393, 394, 415
Foote, Samuel, vol. 2: 341, 343, 344, 345, 347, 546
Foxcroft, Thomas, vol. 1: 275, 374. vol. 2: 104, 107, 541
Franck, Professor, vol. 1: 85, 251, 253
Franklin, Benjamin, vol. 1: 151, 255, 307, 309, 310. vol. 2: 165, 166, 244, 245, 411, 413, 414, 493, 512, 547, 569
Franklin's epitaph, vol. 1: 313
Frederica, Georgia, vol. 1: 82. vol. 2: 37
Frelinghuysen, Theodorus, vol. 1: 266, 267. vol. 2: 541

G

Garden, Alexander, vol. 1: 323, 327, 329, 332–338, 458
Garrick, David, vol. 1: 162. vol. 2: 346, 426, 551
Gee, Joshua, vol. 1: 374
Gentleman, The, vol. 2: 143, 220, 221
George II, King, vol. 1: 228. vol. 2: 280
Georgia Gazette, vol. 1: 239. vol. 2: 433, 436
Gibb, Adam (of Associate Presbytery), vol. 1: 474, 478. vol. 2: 23

Gibralter, vol. 1: 63, 68, 70
Gill, John, vol. 1: 514, 515
Gillies, John, vol. 1: 4, 9, 32, 484, 487, 491. vol. 2: 3, 83, 229, 246, 270, 290, 297, 320, 337, 352, 409, 448, 571, 572
Gladman, Capt. vol. 1: 258
Glasgow, Scotland, vol. 1: 482, 486, 487. vol. 2: 27, 161, 269, 297, 320, 338
Gledstone, J. P., vol. 1: 31, 174, 455. vol. 2: 3, 117, 376
Gloucester, England, vol. 1: 15, 16, 31, 32. vol. 2: 45, 52, 273, 327, 527
Graham, Billy, vol. 1: 152, 217. vol. 2: 335, 505
Grant, Capt. vol. 2: 236
Great Awakening, vol. 1: 197, 261, 267, 357, 379, 380, 401, 418, 497. vol. 2: 532
Gurnell, William, vol. 1: 501
Gurney, Joseph, vol. 2: 366

H

Habersham, James, vol. 1: 60, 61, 65, 221, 233, 235, 322, 455, 456, 473. vol. 2: 43, 48, 376, 377
Half-way Covenant, vol. 1: 379
Hampshire, England, vol. 1: 36
Hampton Common (Minchinhampton), vol. 2: 45, 46
Hancock, John, vol. 2: 499
Hankinson, Elizabeth, vol. 2: 137
Harris, Gabriel, vol. 1: 40. vol. 2: 54
Harris, Mrs. Gabriel, vol. 1: 51, 53
Harris, Howell, vol. 1: 109, 125, 134, 143, 149, 150, 154, 160, 267, 454, 459. vol. 2: 5, 21, 38, 43, 62, 70, 125, 163, 243, 512, 554
Harris, Robert, vol. 1: 501
Harris, Rev. Sampson, vol. 1: 43
Harvard College, vol. 2: 93–96, 379, 447, 545
Henry, Matthew, vol. 1: 15, 34, 35, 38, 40, 198. vol. 2: 183, 514
Henry, Phillip, vol. 2: 313
Henry, Stuart Clark, vol. 1: 105, 147, 357
Heriots, George, vol. 1: 492. vol. 2: 575
Hervey, James, vol. 1: 40, 41. vol. 2: 213, 215, 217, 299
Hill, Rowland, vol. 2: 315, 394